THE TREASURY AND WHITEHALL

THE TREASURY AND WHITEHALL

The Planning and Control of
Public Expenditure, 1976–1993

COLIN THAIN
and
MAURICE WRIGHT

CLARENDON PRESS · OXFORD
1995

Oxford University Press, Walton Street, Oxford OX2 6DP
Oxford New York
Athens Auckland Bangkok Bombay
Calcutta Cape Town Dar es Salaam Delhi
Florence Hong Kong Istanbul Karachi
Kuala Lumpur Madras Madrid Melbourne
Mexico City Nairobi Paris Singapore
Taipei Tokyo Toronto
and associated companies in
Berlin Ibadan

Oxford is a trade mark of Oxford University Press

Published in the United States
by Oxford University Press Inc., New York

British Library Cataloguing in Publication Data
Data available

Library of Congress Cataloging in Publication Data
Thain, Colin.
The Treasury and Whitehall: the planning and control of public
expenditure, 1796–1993 / Colin Thain and Maurice Wright.
Includes bibliographical references.
1. Expenditures, Public—Great Britain—History. 2. Great
Britain. Treasury. 3. Great Britain—Appropriations and
expenditures. I. Wright, Maurice, 1933– . II. Title.
HJ7764.T48 1995 336.3′9′0941—dc20 95-12126

ISBN 0–19–827784–9

1 3 5 7 9 10 8 6 4 2

Typeset by Best-set Typesetter Ltd., Hong Kong
Printed in Great Britain
on acid-free paper by
Biddles Ltd., Guildford and King's Lynn

PREFACE

This book is about the Treasury—Her Majesty's Treasury. It is an account of its role, and its relationships with the Whitehall departments, in performing the central function of government—deciding how much to spend and on what. It aims to provide a comprehensive account of the Treasury's control of public spending from 1976 up until the Budget of March 1993. It is based on research undertaken in the period 1988–92.

Most of the debts we have incurred while writing this book are irredeemable, although we hope its publication will be accepted by some of those who have contributed to it as part-payment. Our colleagues at Exeter and Manchester underwrote our research activities by their acceptance of the additional teaching and administration which our absence imposed upon them at various times in the last five years. Senior civil servants in the Whitehall departments in London, Edinburgh, Cardiff, and Belfast were generous with their time, correcting our errors and misunderstandings, and through endless hours of discussion and argument helping us to arrive at a more complete understanding of expenditure politics.

We owe a particular debt of gratitude to Sir John Anson, which we are happy that we can acknowledge publicly now that he has retired from the Treasury where he held the position of Second Permanent Secretary responsible for public expenditure. He risked letting us loose on his senior colleagues, encouraging them to talk with us freely and frankly. Senior civil servants in all departments work long hours under great pressure; those in the Treasury on the expenditure side more than most. Our enquiries, interviews, and requests for written comments on Working Papers and draft chapters were an additional burden. We were rarely made to feel it was an unwelcome one, or that we were interrupting more important or pressing business, despite mounting evidence to the contrary as from time to time during the course of an interview armfuls of files marked 'urgent' were dumped in overflowing in-trays. Some of those we interviewed later in our schedule even seemed pleased that we had at last got round to them. All of them, and those senior officials we interviewed in the Whitehall and territorial departments, were unfailingly generous with their time. Their frankness we have protected by letting them speak collectively or through their 'grades'. Only where individual civil servants are identified in the public record, such as the reports of Parliamentary Select Committees, do we attribute statements of fact or opinion to particular officials.

Drafts of Working Papers and chapters, and a draft of the whole manuscript, were read and commented upon by many of those whom we interviewed in the Treasury and the spending departments. We are grateful to them for their suggestions for the improvement of the analysis and the argument, and for pointing us to other material; while we have not always agreed with them or followed their advice, they have also saved us from the embarrassment of numerous errors of fact and interpretation. The responsibility for the book, its judgements, and conclusions is ours alone. The account we give is not an authorized version; still less is it a semi-official history, licensed by the Treasury. We were not asked for, nor would we have given, undertakings about what we would write.

Stephen Wilks read the whole manuscript, and made countless valuable suggestions for its improvement. Martin Burch read and commented on drafts of the chapters on Next Steps and the Cabinet. We are grateful to both of them, and to Kate Baker whose consummate skills with the word-processor ensured a constant flow of clean and legible drafts.

At various times in the lifetime of this project we have been helped financially by several organizations. It was conceived, designed, and launched during the tenure of Personal Research Fellowships awarded to us by the Nuffield Foundation. Thereafter the research and preparation of the book was supported by the Leverhulme Trust and the ESRC (R000231395). In 1988 Colin Thain was awarded one of the first three Lloyd's of London Fellowships endowed to mark the tercentenary of the insurance market. We are grateful to them all for their support.

C.T. and M.W.

Exeter and Manchester
November 1993

CONTENTS

PART V. THE OUTPUTS OF THE SYSTEM

PART VI. EFFECTS AND EFFECTIVENESS

LIST OF FIGURES

LIST OF TABLES

ABBREVIATIONS

AEF	Aggregate External Finance
ARCD	Appropriation and Resource Control Division
CAP	Common Agricultural Policy
CBI	Confederation of British Industry
CPRS	Central Policy Review Staff (the 'Think-Tank')
CSD	Civil Service Department
CSO	Central Statistical Office
CTC	City Technology College
DFE	Department for Education
DFP	Department of Finance and Personnel
DHSS	Department of Health and Social Security
D.o.E.	Department of the Environment
D.o.H.	Department of Health
D.o.I.	Department of Industry
D.o.T.	Department of Transport
DRC	Department Running Costs
DSS	Department of Social Security
DTI	Department of Trade and Industry
EDX	Expenditure Committee of the Cabinet
EFL	External Financing Limits of Nationalized Industries
EMU	European Monetary Union
ERM	Exchange Rate Mechanism of the European Community
EU	European Union
EYF	End-Year Flexibility
FCO	Foreign and Commonwealth Office
FDA	First Division Association
FIS	Financial Information System
FM	Financial Management
FMI	Financial Management Initiative
FMU	Financial Management Unit
GDP	Gross Domestic Product
GEP	General Expenditure Policy Group of HM Treasury
GGE	General Government Expenditure
IFS	Institute for Fiscal Studies
IMF	International Monetary Fund
IOD	Institute of Directors
LASFE	Local Authorities Self-Financed Expenditure

MAFF	Ministry of Agriculture, Fisheries, and Food
MINIS	Management Information System
M.o.D.	Ministry of Defence
MPO	Management and Personnel Office
MTFS	Medium-Term Financial Strategy
NAO	National Audit Office
NCT	New Control Total
NDPBs	Non-Departmental Public Bodies
NEDC	National Economic Development Council
NIESR	National Institute of Economic and Social Research
NIO	Northern Ireland Office
NPT	New Planning Total
ODA	Overseas Development Agency
OECD	Organization for Economic Co-operation and Development
OFTEL	Office of Telecommunications
OMB	Office of Management and Budget
OMCS	Office of the Minister for the Civil Service
OPCS	Office of Population, Censuses, and Surveys
OPSS	Office of Public Service and Science
PAC	Public Accounts Committee
PAR	Programme Analysis and Review
PEO	Principal Establishments Officer
PES	Public Expenditure Survey
PESC	Public Expenditure Survey Committee
PEWP	Public Expenditure White Paper
PFO	Principal Finance Officer
PPBS	Planning, Programming, and Budgeting System
PSA	Property Services Agency
PSBR	Public Sector Borrowing Requirement
PSDR	Public Sector Debt Repayment
RC	Running Costs
RPE	Relative Price Effect
RPI	Retail Price Index
RSG	Rate Support Grant
TUC	Trades Union Congress
ZBB	Zero-Based Budgeting

1

Introduction

Governments spend large and increasing amounts of their taxpayers' money. In good times and bad the pressures to respond to the demands of the producers and consumers of public programmes for health, education, income support, and the protection of the environment for example, and even defence despite the ending of the cold war, are proof against the good intentions of politicians and the best efforts of administrators to reduce the costs of government. Most governments spend more than they are able or willing to raise in taxes, financing the resulting deficits through government borrowing. In the UK after the general election of April 1992 public spending was projected to increase by 12 per cent over the three years to 1994–5, and the PSBR to rise to £50 billion or nearly 8 per cent of GDP by 1993–4. The newly elected Conservative Government of John Major sought to constrain a rapid rise in both public spending and borrowing, as had the Labour Government sixteen years earlier.

While attitudes towards public spending had changed radically in the intervening period, and inspired profound changes in the administrative culture of Whitehall, nevertheless the difficulties of managing and controlling public spending continued to plague Conservative Governments of the 1980s and 1990s as they had those of Harold Wilson and Jim Callaghan a decade earlier. 1976 was a turning-point in the politics of public spending. Since the end of the Second World War public expenditure had played a key role in economic policy-making. In the heyday of the Keynesian consensus, adjustments to the total of public spending and specific changes to key items within that total (for example public-sector investment) formed an integral part of an active fiscal policy. When the economy was depressed, the pump was primed; when the balance of payments or sterling gave policy-makers cause for concern, or when the economy was 'overheating', spending programmes were pared back. Similarly when governments became concerned about growth and the need to 'plan' the economy, public spending took the lead in encouraging the private sector to increase output. In political terms too, levels of spending became highly significant. Party competition in the 1950s and 1960s centred upon the issue of who could 'deliver' more in terms of welfare spending. The ability of the government to 'touch the accelerator' through public expenditure increases led to academic interest in the 'political-business' cycle as general elections coincided with higher real income.

From 1976 public expenditure totals were no longer predicated upon assumptions about the achievement of full employment in the medium term: containment actually became a goal of policy, despite rising levels of unemployment and falling output. The advent of the first Thatcher Government consolidated this change: public spending was seen as an economic evil, reductions in its level would lead to lower inflation and financial stability. The Medium-Term Financial Strategy unveiled in 1980 codified its new place in the order of things: medium-term reductions in total spending were deemed necessary for the achievement of a whole set of objectives, including reductions in monetary growth (Thain 1985). It was not that public expenditure ceased to be economically important, but that it was no longer to have the lead-part in macro-economic policy; rather it was to be in the supporting cast helping to achieve what were regarded then as more important monetarist goals. Paradoxically, the Thatcher years also show how extraordinarily difficult it was to cut the real level of spending—one of the themes which run through this book. We show that, despite political resolve, strong leadership, and seeming public support for action against the 'bureaucracy' of government, total spending has continued to rise in real terms. Of equal significance, the general elections of 1979, 1983, 1987, and 1992 showed that the level of public support for the NHS and other key aspects of the welfare state constrained the cost-cutting ambitions of a government of the radical right.

Policies both for growth and for restraint have been frustrated by the tendency for expenditure to rise faster than intended or anticipated: it appears to have a momentum independent of the declared aims of policy. In seeking the explanation for this phenomenon there are many diverse and complex elements. Besides the aims and constraints (and opportunities) provided by an international economic system, which since the early 1970s has brought the economies of the industrialized countries into a state of increasing interdependence; besides the familiar politics of expenditure opportunism and expediency, there emerged in the mid-1970s the less familiar politics of cuts and squeezes, elevated to ideology and doctrine in the 'new right' politics of the Conservative Governments after 1979. In turn, the supporters of these ideas were confronted and challenged by ingrained societal attitudes and expectations nurtured by more than two decades of growth-politics, and articulated through elected representative bodies and their bureaucracies, and organized groups representing special and general interests and clientele. The resultant compound of these multiple, diverse, changing, and conflicting elements—public expenditure politics—emerged from policy processes which themselves were subject to change, and which reflected profound changes in the administrative culture of Whitehall (and of course local government).

Why is it that modern British governments find it so difficult to control public spending? Any adequate answer to that question must include an assessment of the institutions and processes through which expenditure policy is made and carried out. At the centre of those processes is the most important institution of British government, the Treasury, Her Majesty's Treasury. Its structure, organization, and role in policy-making, its relationships with the Whitehall spending departments, and the processes through which decisions are made about how much to spend and on what are the central concerns of this book. It does not deal directly with taxation policy, which until December 1993 was made separately through distinct policy processes and at a different time of the year, although in our contextualization of expenditure policy, we explain how it shaped and influenced macro-economic policy. Nor does it deal with the central control of local government finance, although the determination centrally of the aggregate of local government finance and the level of revenue support grant are part of our agenda, as are the consequences for the control of the public expenditure total of their over- and underspending. As sponsors, spending departments bid on behalf of local authorities and other statutory bodies such as health authorities and public corporations which are not represented directly in the process of deciding allocations with the Treasury. The issue of the accountability of the Treasury and the spending departments to Parliament is dealt with only indirectly here. Parliament plays only a minor role in the determination of the annual spending total and its allocation among the spending programmes of Whitehall departments. Its committees, notably the PAC and the Select Committee on the Treasury and the Civil Service, have had some influence on the procedures of expenditure control, and we consider these and other determinants as appropriate. But Parliamentary control of expenditure policy occurs largely *ex post facto*, after the Autumn Statement/Budget has been presented as a *fait accompli*. Parliament's main contribution is made after the conclusion of the annual spending round.

More than twenty years ago Heclo and Wildavsky (1974, 1981) sought to illuminate the characteristic properties of British central government by focusing on the processes of planning and controlling public expenditure. Their elegant and thoroughly readable account has continued to enthral successive generations of scholars and students of British government. By an unfortunate accident of timing, it appeared just as the Treasury began a reappraisal of the efficacy of its control system; and, as we have explained, as attitudes towards the role of public spending had begun to change. Within a couple of years of publication, PESC was in deep crisis as inflation and the ambitions of Labour Government spending ministers combined to expose the inherent weaknesses of the principles and practice of the Treasury's control. Wildavsky's encomium that the British system was the best in the world had a hollow ring: 'Nowhere else in the world, to our knowledge, has the annual budget been replaced with an effective mechanism to control public spending several years into the future' (Wildavsky 1975: 143).

What Heclo and Wildavsky wrote about the practices of central administrators has proved more durable. Their critique of the weakness of collective decision-making, and of the quality of analysis and advice available to the Cabinet, has a contemporary echo in the debates over the role and capacity of the central departments which surrounded the abolition of the CPRS in 1983 and the Civil Service Department in 1981, the reconcentration of the responsibility for the management of the Civil Service in the Treasury, the expansion of the Prime Minister's Private Office, and the creation of the Efficiency Unit. Our own ambition is more modest. Our aim is not to expose the workings of the core executive, although our focus on the key department leads inescapably into a discussion of some of the broader issues, such as collective responsibility, with which Heclo and Wildavsky were concerned. Nor do we seek to test explicitly the validity of particular theories of budgeting, as more recently in Dunsire and Hood's careful but inconclusive study of the management of cut-back (1989). The work of public-choice, Marxist, corporatist, and other theorists examined there is mainly concerned with general explanations of the phenomenon of government growth. 'Why government grows' is not the central concern of this book, although we have something to say about the proximate causes of that growth in the particular circumstances of budgeting in the UK. We employ selected theoretical propositions and insights in the organization and analysis of our material.

Our broad theoretical stance on budgeting comes closest to that of Wildavsky in his last books and articles where he argued a cultural theory of government growth (Webber and Wildavsky 1986; Wildavsky 1988). The testing of that theory cross-nationally must await the successor to the present book, when we extend the analysis comparatively to the budgetary systems of the remaining G7 countries. Meanwhile, in the context of the study of a single budgeting system, we share his belief that the kind of institutions, the processes of decision-making in those institutions, and the norms of the budgetary behaviour of ministers and officials determine policy preferences and hence outputs.

The general theoretical perspective of the book is that which we have developed and employed in our previous work on the analysis of public policy (Thain 1987; Wilks and Wright 1987, 1991; Wright 1988*a*, 1988*b*, 1991). There we have argued that policy areas such as education or transport or health or a meta-policy area such as public spending can be analysed and compared within (and between) countries by adopting an approach which seeks to reveal the 'governance structure' by which the relationships of those who participate in the making and carrying out of policy are regulated. While such structures may take the form of policy networks, equally they may take other forms, the dominance of a government department or public body, or one or a few organized interests for example. The task of the analyst is to determine what the structure is, how it came about, how it operates, and who benefits.

The years covered in this book, 1976–93, are dominated by those of the Thatcher Governments, and it may be read as an historical record of their objectives and achievements in planning and controlling public spending, the burdens of which they declared at the outset 'were at the heart of Britain's decline'. We believe that in order to understand how public spending is planned and controlled it is necessary to adopt an explicitly historico-analytical approach. As we have argued above, 1976 was a turning-point in contemporary expenditure politics, and an obvious starting-point, although we have found it necessary to go back further still to explain some elements of the system. The conclusion in 1993 is prompted partly by pressure from our publishers to stop somewhere, but rather more by the fact that the general election in April 1992 brought the Thatcher era to a close. In the event we were persuaded that the changes made to the Treasury's control system in the summer of 1992 were important enough to justify a further extension of our analysis. Our account ends fittingly with the very last occasion of a Spring Budget, in March 1993. Since then the Unified Budget presented in November/December has combined both tax and spending decisions.

The central argument of the book is that the Treasury failed to achieve both the short-term and medium-term objectives for public spending set by successive governments through the years 1976–93. It failed also to achieve its historic mission to restrain the growth of public spending. We argue that the causes of that failure inhere in the constitutional and practical limitations to the exercise of Treasury control. In other than exceptional and temporary circumstances, such as acute economic or financial crisis, the Treasury cannot dictate to departments nor impose its will upon them. Their relationships are interdependent; their room for discretionary manœuvre mutually constrained. The paradigm of the politics of public spending at the heart of British central government is negotiated discretion.

Within the historical perspective we have adopted, the framework for the structure of the book and the organization of the analysis comprises five elements: context, institutions, actors in institutions, the interaction between actors, and the output of that interaction. We would argue that the study of the process of a particular policy sector requires the simultaneous contextualization provided by the macro-level analysis of the development of that sector, for example the historical role of the state through its institutions and agencies in that sector and their relationships with other key participants, and the macro-economic and political objectives of successive governments. In our contextualization of the processes of making and carrying out expenditure policy in Part I we look in Chapter 2 at the changing politico-economic context within which public expenditure policies were formulated and implemented, trace the evolution and development of macro-economic policy since the 1970s, and discuss the changing role of government and governmental attitudes towards public spending. At the conclusion of the chapter we provide a diagrammatic summary of the main trends in public spending through the whole period 1976–93, a reference point for readers as the argument unfolds in the rest of the book. In Chapter 3 we trace the development of the PESC/PES system of planning and controlling public expenditure from its origins in the 1950s, through the publication of the Plowden Report in 1961, down to the introduction of cash planning in 1982. We then examine in Chapters 4 and 5 the origins and evolution of three key components in the attempts of Conservative Governments in the 1980s and 1990s to change the Whitehall administrative and managerial context: the Financial Management Initiative, the creation of 'Next Steps' Executive Agencies, and the evolution of the 'Contract State' through the implementation of the principles of market-testing.

The other elements of our organizing framework—institutions, actors, interactions, and outputs—combine and integrate the approaches and insights of the 'neo-institutionalists' (e.g. March and Olsen 1984; Hall 1986; Krasner 1988) with those derived from our own work on policy communities and networks. Institutions have rules, procedures, and systems of authority. They allocate roles, impose obligations and duties, and they place expectations on the behaviour of their members. To understand the participation of individuals and of groups of individuals in the policy process, it is necessary to appreciate their institutional origins, loyalties, and motivations.

Institutions regulate the use of authority and power and provide actors with resources, legitimacy, standards of evaluation, perceptions, identities and a set of meanings. They provide a set of rules, compliance procedures, and moral and ethical behavioural norms which buffer environmental influence, modify individual motives, regulate self-interest behaviour and create order and meaning. (Olsen 1988)

In Part II we examine the structure and organization of the principal institutions: the Treasury and the spending departments. Chapters 6 to 8 employ the concepts of policy community and policy network to identify the principal participants, to explain their roles, and to characterize their interaction. In Chapter 9 we focus specifically on the norms of policy and behaviour which determine the regulation of their relations within a policy network. Chapter 10 explores the determinants of the paradigm of 'negotiated discretion', which we argue characterizes those relationships, and identifies some of the tensions and frustrations which arise consequentially.

This understanding of institutions, actors, and their interactions is then applied to the analysis of the interrelated processes of planning and control, which for analytical purposes are dealt with separately in Parts III and IV. Chapter 11 examines the means of determining the priorities of public spending: how the aggregate is decided, and the process of allocating it between competing functions. The centre-piece of that process is the Public Expenditure Survey which is dealt with in the next chapter. Both the determination of priorities and the Public Expenditure Survey processes are predicated upon the collective responsibility of the Cabinet for spending policies. The principle and practice of that responsibility are examined in Chapter 13, which looks also at the use of the Star Chamber and the Expenditure Committee (EDX) of the Cabinet. Separate and special arrangements are made for planning and controlling public spending in Scotland, Wales, and Northern Ireland, and we discuss this territorial dimension in Chapter 14.

Part IV explores the interaction between the principal participants in the control of public spending 'in-year'. Chapter 15 provides a broad overview of the control and monitoring processes, the main mechanisms of which—the Reserve, cash limits, running costs, and end-year flexibility schemes—are dealt with in detail in the next four chapters.

The outputs of the policy-making processes are dealt with in Part V. Chapter 20 charts the changing public-spending objectives of governments since 1976 and measures the extent to which they were achieved. This is followed in the next chapter by an analysis of which spending departments have 'won' or 'lost'. The four concluding chapters of Part VI bring together the analysis and arguments of the previous chapters in a wide-ranging assessment of the effects and effectiveness of the public-spending planning and control system. Chapter 22 examines the evolution of the PES system to 1993, and assesses its effectiveness as a means of organizing and regulating relationships between the Treasury and the spending departments, and for delivering government objectives, for evaluating programmes, and providing for the collective discussion of priorities by Cabinet. It concludes with an assessment of the major beneficiaries of the system. In Chapter 23 we analyse the effectiveness of the Treasury's control, specifically in delivering in November the Planning/Control Total targeted in the July Cabinet, and, more generally, in constraining the growth of public spending over the whole period 1976–93. This leads on to an exploration in the next chapter of the limits to Treasury control and an assessment of the extent to which the pressures for greater flexibility in the administration of that control released by the implementation of the Financial Management Initiative (FMI), 'Next Steps', and market-testing have sharpened the inherent tension between central control and departmental autonomy. In the last chapter we discuss how the processes of making and carrying out policy might be improved to enhance the effectiveness of the Treasury's control. We consider first the organizational effectiveness of the Treasury, and then the institutions and processes for achieving collective responsibility through the Cabinet. Finally, we speculate on the circumstances in which a paradigm shift in public-spending control might occur, substituting central prescription for negotiated discretion.

In the preparation of this book we began with the material available in the public domain: Parliamentary Papers, Government White Papers, Blue Books, and reports. These and secondary sources are surveyed in one of our early Working Papers: *Public Spending Planning and Control 1976–88: A Classified Bibliography* (Thain and Wright 1988b). Subsequently our main source has been the accumulation of data arising from interviews with senior officials in the Treasury and the Whitehall spending departments. In the Treasury we interviewed at levels from Senior Executive Officer to Permanent Secretary in all the Expenditure Divisions, and in the central divisions responsible for expenditure planning, financial management, and the pay and management of the Civil Service.

A different perspective on the Treasury's control and its relationships with Whitehall was provided by our interviews with Principal Finance

Officers and their senior staff in the Finance Divisions of the spending departments. It both provided a necessary corrective, and diminished the risk that we would become too closely identified with the perspectives of the Treasury's Expenditure Controllers. The Principal Finance Officers took a keen interest in our research, and read and commented on drafts of papers and chapters which we wrote on their organization and relationships with the Treasury. We are also grateful to those serving and former Permanent Secretaries in the Whitehall departments with whom we conducted a fruitful correspondence on the basis of some of our early Working Papers. At an early stage of the research, Sir John Bourn, the Comptroller and Auditor General, provided useful advice on how we might proceed. Throughout the book we have tried to protect the anonymity of all those we have interviewed.

At the outset we rejected the use of structured questionnaires, as inappropriate to the complexity of the issues we wished to research. We believed also that senior officials would be unable or unwilling to respond in detail. We considered but rejected tape-recording and transcribing our interviews. Apart from the admissibility of such methods, and the inhibiting effect of their use if permitted, we were concerned that transcription was both costly and immensely time-consuming. In the end we decided on open-ended interviews, conducted jointly after we had informed ourselves as fully as possible from the materials available in the public domain. Each interview was conducted as a continuous seminar discussion keyed to an agenda of identified issues. We each took responsibility for particular issues and contributed to the discussion as appropriate while the other made detailed and occasionally verbatim notes. In this way we were able to conduct a continuous, informal, progressive, and flexible dialogue lasting some one and a half to two hours, and obtain a detailed record of the discussion. Subsequently this was pulled together, structured, and organized around the themes and issues discussed at the interview. In this way we accumulated a rich source of material comprising documents of some 2,000–4,500 words in length which we drew upon in the preparation of further Working Papers. Interviewing a large number of Treasury Expenditure Controllers and senior staff in the Finance Divisions of the spending departments enabled us to construct, verify, and refine the analysis and interpretation of events and issues as the research progressed. Interviewees were then invited to comment on revised drafts of Working Papers, and later chapters of the book based upon them. In all we wrote and circulated twenty-five Working Papers in the Treasury and the spending departments. The references are provided in the bibliography.

Technical terms are explained where necessary at appropriate points in the narrative. Two used throughout the book require some brief explanation here. First, the Treasury's definition and classification of the total of public expenditure for planning and control purposes in the annual Survey changed several times during the years 1976–93. Until 1988 it was referred to as the Planning Total, thereafter as the New Planning Total until it was replaced by the New Control Total in July 1992. We use each specifically for the appropriate period of time, but when discussing the whole of the period 1976–93 or a part of it which includes the years 1992–3 we use the term Planning/Control Total. Secondly, we use the more familiar titles to describe the hierarchical status of civil servants. Thus, Permanent Secretary rather than G1, Deputy Secretary rather than G2, and so on. The titles and corresponding grades of those senior officials with whom we are mainly concerned are as follows: Permanent Secretary (G1), Second Permanent Secretary (G1A), Deputy Secretary (G2), Under Secretary (G3), Assistant Secretary (G5), Senior Principal (G6), Principal (G7), and Senior Executive Officer (G8).

PART I

The Context

2

The Politico-Economic Context

Public-spending decisions are taken within a context provided by the political and economic objectives of the government of the day, and the strategies and policies designed to achieve them. 'All governments need objectives for total spending which are consistent with a coherent macro-economic policy framework. The balance between a government's objectives for fiscal policy, the tax burden and public expenditure is a matter of economic as well as political significance' (Sir Terence Burns, Permanent Secretary, HM Treasury, in Burns 1993: 1). From the mid-1970s onwards, the objectives of public expenditure policy became more closely linked to the control of public borrowing and the money supply than had been the case hitherto. Macro-economic policy provided the specific framework for discussions of public expenditure in each PESC or PES round. In this chapter we look at the changes in the politico-economic context, and identify four interlocking themes. First, the period since the early 1970s is one of growing uncertainty in economic theory, and increasing ideological debate and disagreement about economic policy-making. Secondly, as a result of that uncertainty, and compounded by policy failure, confidence in the ability of policy-makers to influence the economy waned (Middleton 1989). Thirdly, as a consequence of both these factors, governments since the mid-1970s have been searching for rules and frameworks—such as the Medium-Term Financial Strategy and, until recently, membership of the Exchange Rate Mechanism (ERM) of the European Monetary System—upon which to anchor economic policy. Fourthly, policy-makers were also motivated during the period by a concern to reverse Britain's long-term relative economic decline. And here in particular, public expenditure was highlighted by the New Right as a major causal factor in stifling enterprise and initiative.

THE EVOLVING POLITICO-ECONOMIC CONTEXT, 1970–1979

By the early 1980s, the 'Keynesian Social Democratic' system which had dominated economic policy-making since the end of the Second

World War had been overturned. In general terms it is possible to
identify a 'moving consensus' (Rose 1984), which formed the basis of
economic policy from 1944 to the mid-1970s. This involved the acceptance that governments had a role in ensuring sufficient demand in
the economy to maintain full employment. This was buttressed by
the economic ideas of Keynes, that governments *could* achieve that
objective principally by managing demand through the use of public
spending and changes in taxation. Internationally, UK governments
were active in helping to establish the 'Bretton Woods' institutions, such
as the IMF, which were to ensure that domestic Keynesian policies
were not overturned by recession in the world economy (see
Cairncross 1985). A crucial part of the system was the fixed exchange
rate regime, which acted as a constraining framework for UK economic
policy, since higher inflation could not be accommodated through
periodic devaluation. A third element in the consensus was that key
'social actors' such as the TUC and CBI had a role with government
in managing the economy. The consensus moved in the late 1950s
and early 1960s to embrace a more active interventionist role for
government in the supply-side of the economy. There was increasing concern by policy-makers that economic growth was lagging behind that of France and West Germany: the UK's relative economic
decline joined the economic policy agenda. In an effort to emulate
the success of French economic policy, both Conservative and Labour
Governments of the 1960s experimented with indicative economic
planning.

One by one the pillars of this consensus crumbled. The decline of the
'Keynesian' system was gradual, presaged in the 1960s by problems with
inflation. A combination of changes in the international economy, the
long-term relative weakness of the UK economy, policy failure by UK
governments, and concern about the role of the trade unions led to the
crises of the 1970s. At first there was an attempt to shore up the consensus and adopt innovatory policy tools, but finally a 'monetarist' system
briefly supplanted the Keynesian system through the radicalism of the
early Thatcher years. By 1985 policy had shifted towards a more eclectic
approach, yet still with a rhetorical bias firmly rooted in 'New Right'
thinking (Bosanquet 1983).

Economic ideas become modified when they are employed by those
involved in the political process. What results is often an amalgam of
political ideology, pragmatic responses to social and political pressures,
and shades of various schools of economic thought. In much monetarist
writing there is a strong antithesis to the neo-Keynesian attachment to
public expenditure. Friedman clearly states the salience of cutting pub-

lic expenditure. The twin problems of economic policy, inflation and low growth, were:

both largely the common consequence of the same basic cause: too big and too intrusive a government. Higher government spending provokes taxpayer resistance. Taxpayer resistance encourages government to finance spending by monetary creation, thereby increasing monetary growth and hence inflation ... Government spending plus government intervention reduce output growth, thereby further raising inflation for any given rate of monetary growth. (Friedman 1980: 55–6)

This view emerged strongly in the first Public Expenditure White Paper of Mrs Thatcher's first government. Public spending, it was asserted, was at the 'heart of Britain's present economic difficulties', as over the years 'public spending has been increased on assumptions about economic growth which have not been achieved. The inevitable result has been a growing burden of taxes and borrowing' (Cmnd. 7746: 1).

It is important to note that coincident with the breakdown in the Keynesian system was the increased salience to policy-makers of the issue of the UK's long-term economic decline. Through the 1970s and 1980s the issue of tackling decline moved up the political agenda. The early approach in 1970–2 of the Heath Government involved an experiment with what Harold Wilson dubbed 'Selsdon Man' policies, a 'quiet revolution' in which the dynamism of the economy would be unleashed through tax cuts, less state intervention, and reform of industrial relations. Heath was not an advocate of social market economics, rather he was an advocate of the selective use of free market solutions if those promised to improve economic growth. The Labour Government's attempt in the period 1974–9 to reverse decline, against a mounting economic crisis, involved a much diluted and modified version of the Left's Alternative Economic Strategy, with nationalization, the creation of a National Enterprise Board and 'planning agreements', and a more traditional tripartite 'industrial strategy' bringing together the TUC and CBI in an effort to remove barriers to economic growth.

By far the most concerted and deliberate attempt to give priority to reversing decline was made in the early years of the Thatcher Government. The responsibility for decline was firmly placed with the governments of the post-war consensus. Chancellor Howe's first Budget speech in June 1979 set the tone when he argued that the UK's poor economic performance was due to intervention by governments which had stifled enterprise. He committed the Government to a strategy aimed at strengthening individual incentives through tax cuts, reducing the role of the state and liberating the private sector, and reducing

public spending and borrowing. Chancellor Lawson's policies (in particular from 1985 to 1988) attempted to accelerate economic growth
through tax cuts and supply-side reforms. Throughout the 1980s and
early 1990s the Conservative Governments of Thatcher and Major emphasized the way policies have created an 'enterprise culture' and
'popular capitalism', the fruits of which were said to be the creation of
a more competitive economy.

The crisis of the 1970s

Even allowing for the unprecedented shock administered to the world
economy by the 1973 oil price rise, Keynesian economic policies had
become progressively less successful. In each successive boom inflation
and unemployment were higher. The advent of 'stagflation'—simultaneously high inflation with low growth and high unemployment—was
something with which traditional Keynesian theory could not cope.
Policy-makers throughout the OECD countries therefore began a
search for techniques which would better deal with the phenomenon;
and the control of inflation was to dominate the policy agenda (OECD
1979).

In the UK, Healey as Chancellor presided over a major shift in the
emphasis of macro-economic policy, but one which fell short of an
outright repudiation of the post-war consensus. His approach was to use
whatever means were at hand to shore up that consensus while responding to the particular crises of the time (see Healey 1981, 1989). Under
his direction the Treasury began to attempt to deal with the inflationary
and deflationary consequences of the oil crisis by using traditional
Keynesian techniques. Wage inflation was to be moderated by the
'Social Contract' with the trade unions. This involved government commitments on a whole range of social policies, and reform of industrial-
relations legislation in return for 'restraint' on wage demands. The
Public Sector Borrowing Requirement (PSBR) was to be allowed to rise
as a proportion of GDP as output fell due to the recession. Internationally, Healey attempted to obtain a co-ordinated response by the
major industrial nations to avoid deflationary action in response to the
oil crisis exacerbating the world recession. The Treasury tried to obtain
an international agreement to support with loans those countries (including the UK) with major balance-of-payments problems; and, in
concert with the pro-Western members of OPEC, to introduce an active
policy to 'recycle' the surpluses being generated by the oil-exporting
countries.

Most of these policies were to prove untenable. The raft of international agreements Healey hoped for did not materialize. Yet the increasingly interdependent nature of the world economy was a constraint on domestic policies (Wass 1978). In 1975 the Treasury engineered a 'controlled depreciation' of sterling in an attempt to revitalize domestic production and ease the deficit on the balance of trade. But lack of confidence in UK policy by the financial markets turned the depreciation into a free fall. Market confidence in domestic policies was affected by the size of the Budget deficit and the failure of the 'Social Contract' to cope with the surge of inflation in 1974–5.

The sterling crisis in 1976 led to a request to the IMF for a loan. Following the subsequent negotiations, the Treasury agreed in December 1976 to adjustments in both the techniques and objectives of policy. Targets for domestic credit expansion were publicly announced; the PSBR was to be reduced; and public expenditure cut back. Earlier, in July 1976, the Treasury had introduced cash limits on public expenditure in response to the 'crisis of control'. Policy was in disarray. All the features of a classic UK economic policy crisis were abundantly evident—crisis Cabinet discussions, spending cuts, concern about the foreign exchange markets—together with a politically damaging and demoralizing submission to the IMF (see Burk and Cairncross 1992).

These changes in macro-economic policy, introduced in response to the exigencies of crisis, have been used as evidence for the proposition that the real change of direction in policy occurred under Chancellor Healey rather than under the Conservatives after 1979 (see, for example, Brittan 1983; Congdon 1989). This assertion deserves further scrutiny because it lies at the heart of the debate about economic policy since 1970. Our argument is that, although the Healey Chancellorship was marked by a radical shift in policy goals, the period after 1979 was much more significant.

In the years 1976–9 macro-economic policy was moved towards a monetarist system. The full employment objective was suspended. In his 1975 Budget speech, Healey noted that the Budget judgement would not be based on an 'estimation of the amount of demand which the government should put into the economy'. Later, in 1977, the Treasury dropped the Medium-Term Assessment (MTA) from the Public Expenditure Survey. Previously the MTA had been one of the cornerstones of spending plans and assumed that policies would ensure that full employment was maintained. There was an element here of the Government responding to the inevitable, since unemployment was rising against difficult circumstances of higher inflation and a poor balance of payments. But nevertheless the UK Government had joined other industrialized nations in giving priority to the control and reduction of inflation.

Policy actions during the mid-1970s show how the full employment objective became less sacrosanct. In the period from 1945 to 1973 governments of both major parties had usually reacted to rising unemployment with an active fiscal policy (increasing public expenditure or reducing taxation) and relaxing monetary policy. From 1975 an increase in unemployment produced a virtually neutral policy response. Not until the 1990s was the PSBR as a proportion of GDP as large as it was in 1974–5, despite the fact that unemployment rose to and remained at post-war historically high levels. In addition, during the Healey Chancellorship the PSBR was given a pivotal role in linking fiscal and monetary policy. In 1978 Healey took action to reduce the PSBR when the financial markets became concerned that fiscal policy was out of step with monetary policy as the large PSBR was adding to monetary growth.

The Bank of England began setting internal, unpublished monetary targets in 1973. This was followed during the rest of the 1970s by increasing emphasis on monetary policy in general and broad money aggregates in particular by the Bank and Treasury. This was a trend throughout the OECD as interest rates, the previous guide to monetary policy, became less reliable as an indicator because of high inflation. The degree to which monetary targets were taken seriously in the hierarchy of macro-economic policy tools was evidenced by the action of the Bank and Treasury in 1977. The authorities were faced at that time by an unusual set of circumstances for the period: foreign exchange markets had so regained confidence in UK policy in the afterglow of the IMF loan that, despite falling interest rates, sterling was appreciating. In its attempt to stem this rise by intervening on the exchange markets to sell sterling and buy other currencies, the Bank endangered the money-supply targets. The choice was therefore between stemming the rise in sterling to maintain the competitive position of UK exporting industries or maintaining the money-supply targets. The monetary targets were given priority and the Chancellor took the decision to 'unplug' sterling and allow it to float upwards (Congdon 1982). This tension between monetary policy and exchange-rate policy was also to be a feature of the implementation of the Medium-Term Financial Strategy (MTFS) after 1980.

Almost as significant was the less tangible change in the rhetoric of senior Labour Government Ministers and Treasury officials during the mid- and late 1970s, pointing to less confidence in the ability of governments to influence the economy. The most famous example was Prime Minister Callaghan's monetarist speech to the Labour Party Conference in September 1976, which was to be quoted approvingly by Conservative leaders and monetarist academics to support the view that the real change in policy occurred in 1976 and that the subsequent Conservative Government merely carried this forward.

However, there is contrary evidence to this view. While the Labour Government explicitly abandoned the full employment objective, macro-economic policy was not deliberately deflationary during the recession and was probably fairly neutral after 1975. The policy objective of full employment was frozen until the economic crisis abated and the task of the Government made easier. After the IMF loan was repaid, and in the run-up to the 1979 general election, Labour's Public Expenditure White Papers in 1978 and 1979 showed a renewed commitment to real spending growth. In addition, the Labour Government kept faith with the consensual element of the 1944 Employment White Paper by using an incomes policy as a means of cutting inflation without excessive reliance on deflationary monetary or fiscal policies.

It was clear that Chancellor Healey downgraded the role of fiscal policy: public expenditure decisions were no longer taken with an ultimate macro-economic goal in mind. Control of spending was elevated as a policy goal in its own right with the imposition of a cash-limits regime. But there is no evidence that policy was guided solely by the need to achieve money-supply targets. Monetary policy was always presented by Labour Treasury Ministers and their officials as supporting an anti-inflationary policy which included incomes policy and control of the PSBR. The Conservative leadership when in government was to repudiate the use of incomes policy and the 'corporatist' approach which underlay it and, more significantly, was to reject the notion that government *could*, except perhaps in the short term, actually influence employment and output through macro-economic policies (Treasury 1981*a*, 1981*b*).

Monetary policy was pursued in a way which supported the view that Labour Ministers were 'reluctant' or 'unbelieving' monetarists. In reality, policy was 'monetarily constrained Keynesianism' rather than monetarist (Fforde 1983; Smith 1987). While domestic credit expansion targets were set several years ahead, money-supply targets were announced on an annual basis rather than set in a medium-term context. There was concern that 'to pursue a determined and pre-determined de-escalation of the rate of monetary expansion would be to risk imposing serious costs on the economy' (Wass 1978: 100). Having set money-supply targets for sterling M3 Chancellor Healey ensured that monetary policy still took 'account of the fact that no one indicator can adequately describe all the monetary conditions in the economy' (Wass 1978: 100).

Under Healey, there was no medium-term nominal framework re-garded as a crucial part of the monetarist system (Burns 1988). He talked of a 'medium-term framework' in his letter of intent to the IMF, but this was no more than a grafting-on of some longer-term consider-ations to what were still short-term, *ad hoc* reactions of the Treasury to political and economic developments. No medium-term financial plan was agreed while Healey was Chancellor, although it was discussed as a possible option. While nominal aggregates, such as the PSBR and money supply, were brought into policy discussions, public expenditure was still planned in volume or real resource terms with annual cash limits tacked on.

Even rhetoric can be misleading. The statements of senior Labour Ministers have to be judged against the particular political and economic background of the time. Callaghan's famous 'monetarist' speech to the Labour Party Conference was a tactical political attempt to achieve multiple objectives: to appease the financial markets, to frighten the Labour Party into accepting the need for tough economic measures, and to make the right impression on the US Treasury Secre-tary whose support would be vital for the UK to obtain IMF support (Keegan 1984).

'BELIEVING MONETARISM': THE MTFS, ERM, AND AFTER, 1979–1993

In contrast, the approach of Margaret Thatcher and her economic team was motivated by a more wholehearted commitment to the monetarist system. The MTFS, which set economic policy-making in an explicit medium-term framework, replaced the short-term approach under Healey. It represented a far more 'rational' co-ordinated response than previous policies: limits to government action were incorporated into economic policy-making as a first principle. Changes and adjustments in policy there certainly were in the 1976–9 period, but we must look to the 1979–82 era for the real decisive break with the Keynesian system, and the change in those attitudes towards the use of public spending as a tool of economic management which had underpinned the Treasury's PESC system of planning and control from 1961 onwards.

Throughout the OECD countries in the late 1970s and 1980s policy-makers developed economic strategies based on medium-term financial and economic frameworks (Chouraqui and Price 1984; OECD 1987). It reflected their loss of confidence in the ability of Keynesian policies to reduce unemployment, the tendency to inflation, or low growth, and the difficulties of funding public-spending programmes. By contrast, in the UK from 1979, the framework adopted was the result of *ideological* commitment and sprang from a combination of political, economic, and intellectual factors.

The late 1960s saw the resurgence of interest in neo-classical economics, first in the USA and later in the UK. In the years of Opposition numerous advisers and policy think-tanks were influential in shaping the policy positions of Thatcher, Sir Keith Joseph, and their closest supporters. The network was drawn from the academic world, the City, journalism, and business (Keegan 1984; Smith 1987; Young 1989). Together they moved the Conservative Party towards a policy position which was an amalgam of various schools of monetarism and right-wing populism. But it was this in combination with the failures of the Labour Government's attempts at consensus politics which was to provide Thatcher and her supporters with the opportunity to win the policy debate. The creation of what has been called 'Mrs Thatcher's domestic statecraft' (Bulpitt 1986) was thus the product of a mixture of consequences of events, slowly changing ideas-in-good-currency fed by the contributions of intellectuals, accident, and opportunity.

The new Government in 1979 therefore had a mixture of policy advice and intellectual support for a change of direction in economic policy. Within the Treasury there was also a receptive climate, at least from the middle ranks of officials, including a future Permanent Secretary, (Sir) Peter Middleton. Even those senior officials who were sceptical of the full-blooded monetarist views of Nigel Lawson, the Financial Secretary, accepted the need for tighter control of public spending and borrowing, demoralized by the failure of the wages policy and industrial strategy of the departing Labour Government.

The MTFS

The Medium-Term Financial Strategy unveiled in 1980 was the clearest signal that the economic policy regime had changed (Buiter and Miller 1983). It represented an attempt to impose discipline on government policy-making by deliberately limiting the range of options open to the Treasury on monetary and fiscal policy. Money-supply targets were paramount and were supported by projections for the PSBR and an unprecedented set of plans to cut public spending in real terms. The MTFS was explicitly counter-inflationary: governments, it was stated, could only influence output over the medium term by supply-side (or micro-economic) reforms (Lawson 1984). Initially these reforms were limited, but nevertheless included the significant act of abolishing exchange controls in November 1979, the abolition of credit controls, some reduction in personal taxation, and a series of Acts reducing the power of trade unions. After 1983 the supply-side element of the strategy became more prominent, with large-scale privatization, the deregulation of financial markets, and tax-reforming measures.

The MTFS was intended to influence the expectations of a whole set of institutions and markets. For the first time the Treasury was deliberately reducing the scope for discretionary macro-economic policy. Financial markets were given a clear, public statement of the Treasury's policies over the medium term. Whitehall departments and agencies in the public sector were presented with a framework deliberately set to restrain resources available for public policies. Business leaders and trade union wage-bargainers were reminded that the Treasury would not act to reduce unemployment; inflationary wage demands would not be covered by money supply increases (Thain 1985).

Looking back over the evolution and development of economic policy in the UK since 1980 it is clear that most of the tenets of the monetarist revolution failed and were abandoned. Policy was not led by clear, transparent medium-term rules; stop-go policies were not replaced by a stable regime predicated on 'sound finance', consistent non-inflationary monetary policy, and by government limiting itself to what it could influence. There have been three episodes in macro-economic policy since the unveiling of the MTFS in 1980: first, the effective demise of that strategy in the mid-1980s; second, its replacement by an exchange rate policy rule, culminating in the UK joining the ERM in 1990; and the subsequent demise of that policy in September 1992 when sterling was 'suspended' from the system. Since the late 1980s there has been the emergence of a European dimension to policy with the Maastricht Treaty, the stuttering progress towards its ratification, and its aim of economic and monetary union. UK policy has been influenced intermittently by the economic convergence criteria which emerged as part of the EMU process. Throughout the period from 1980, UK economic performance has been on a roller-coaster of deep and sharp recession, followed by boom, followed by the longest recession since the 1930s. The one consistent element has been the importance, and latterly pre-eminence, of fiscal policy—the management of expenditure, revenue, and borrowing. But the 'crisis' of high and unsustainable levels of public borrowing which marked the mid-1970s has returned in the early 1990s to haunt and constrain the Treasury.

The demise of the MTFS

In the course of the thirteen years from 1980 the MTFS evolved and changed. The single target for broad money was later replaced by multiple targets for both broad and narrow aggregates, and finally it was abandoned altogether in favour of an objective for money GDP. It became less and less a rigorous medium-term framework, providing clear guidelines to financial markets and other economic actors, and increasingly an annually updated set of financial figures consistent with the broad thrust of the Government's policies. However, annual decisions continued to be taken against the background of an explicit medium-term framework, including goals for public expenditure. The MTFS has survived partly because of the political embarrassment its shelving would have created, partly because it proved to be a useful vehicle for changing the substance of policy actions whilst maintaining the aura of consistency, and partly because the annual exercise in setting out PSBR, public expenditure, and revenue figures provided the Treasury with a useful weapon in containing public-spending pressures.

Until 1991, it was on the fiscal side of the MTFS that the Treasury could claim the most success. As Figure 2.1 shows, the PSBR declined as a proportion of GDP from the crisis levels of the mid-1970s, and the generation of a budget surplus in the four financial years from 1987–8 to 1990–1 had last been achieved by Roy Jenkins in 1969–70. The economic growth which helped to generate these surpluses proved unsustainable. The recession which followed the Lawson boom has

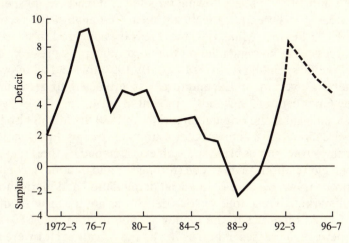

FIG. 2.1. The PSBR as a proportion of GDP, 1972–1997

Source: Based on Treasury 1993*b*

proved so long-lasting that the public-sector financial position has swung dramatically into deficit, with the public sector's finances moving from a budget surplus (PSDR) equivalent to 1 per cent of GDP in 1989–90 to a deficit (PSBR) of 3 per cent in 1991–2. The Treasury's forecast in March 1993 projected a PSBR of 8 per cent of GDP in 1993–4 and 6.5 per cent in the following year, falling to below 4 per cent by 1997–8 (Treasury 1993*b*). Outside the Treasury, using less optimistic scenarios for growth in the economy and higher forecasts of public-spending growth, analysts have predicted persistent annual public-sector deficits of the order of 7 to 10 per cent of GDP throughout the period up to 1997–8 (Martin 1992).

Just as the crisis of public expenditure control and economic turbulence in the mid-1970s produced a reassertion of Treasury control, so the looming fiscal crisis implied by the 1992–3 forecasts pushed the Treasury into instituting a 'new' top–down control on public spending and a medium-term review of spending priorities. In macro-economic terms, the level of public-sector borrowing led Chancellor Lamont to adjust one of the emergent orthodoxies of the 1980s—the achievement of an annual balanced budget—to the aspiration of achieving budget balance at the end of the economic cycle.

As we discuss in Chapter 20, although public spending was not reduced in line with 1980 objectives, it did fall as a proportion of GDP from 1982–3 to 1989–90. At that time it seemed as if the Treasury had squared the circle, entered a golden era when the trend rate of growth of public spending had been reduced compared with that prevailing in the 1960s and 1970s, whilst allowing targeted real increases in spending in key areas. By the end of the 1980s, measured against the record of other OECD Finance Ministries, the Treasury appeared to have been more successful in keeping a lid on the inexorable pressures for higher levels of public spending (OECD 1990). By 1993, this had a hollow ring as General Government Expenditure was projected to grow in real terms by 6 per cent in 1993 and 5 per cent in 1994.

Measured against the original intentions in 1980 the MTFS also failed as a precise monetary framework for four main reasons. First, economic relationships were not as clear and stable as assumed by the Treasury in 1980. The old relationship between sterling M3 and national income and prices broke down because of financial deregulation and innovations in financial markets. The public sector's deficit was not the most significant cause of rapid increases in the money supply. In both the 1980–2 and 1987–9 periods, increases in borrowing by the private sector were more significant. Indeed by the late 1980s, the public sector was actually in surplus. The interest rate weapon proved to be a blunt instrument for controlling private credit (Goodhart 1989) as companies and individuals increased borrowing despite high interest rates.

Second, there was an intellectual problem, brought sharply into focus as Conservative Governments attempted to implement the MTFS. What was the most appropriate measure of the money supply? What was the significance of the signals given by monitoring broad or narrow money? How did this relate to economic activity? The debate within the Treasury and No. 10 in 1980–1, created by the simultaneous appreciation of sterling, excess growth of the sterling M3, rising inflation, *and* recession and bankruptcy in the private sector, was a case-study in the sheer practical difficulty of trying to run policy using a narrow framework. In the end the Prime Minister's Policy Unit and her economic adviser, Sir Alan Walters, prevailed and monetary policy was eased (see Walters 1986; Burns 1988; Keegan 1989). Against the background of such intellectual uncertainty it is no surprise that fiscal policy—especially public expenditure and taxation—rose in prominence; these were at least less *uncontrollable* than the money supply. The aim of controlling spending and cutting direct taxation could be more easily packaged as examples of 'sound' and 'prudent' finance consistent with Conservative rhetoric. The problems over monetary aggregates also explain the desire of Chancellor Lawson to ground anti-inflation policy in a firmer framework, hence the increasing focus on the exchange rate and desire to enter the ERM (see Keegan 1989; Lawson 1990, 1992).

Third, conflicting policy objectives were not eliminated by the simple act of publicly announcing a clear economic policy agenda. Monetary policy was complicated by the abolition of exchange controls as sterling was prone to rapid inflows (and outflows) of capital. The deregulation of financial markets, and in particular the abolition of credit controls in 1980–2 and the lifting of restrictions on building societies and banks allowing customers to use 'equity withdrawal' as a means of adding to purchasing power, opened the way for a massive explosion of credit in the late 1980s (discussed by Congdon 1989 and Keegan 1989).

Fourth, the original 1980 MTFS largely ignored the exchange rate, which was said to be determined by market forces. But in 1981 the exchange rate was accepted as an indicator, and the Treasury acknowledged its importance in economic decision-making.

ERM membership

It was with Chancellor Lawson's conversion to the view that the exchange rate was the most appropriate guide to monetary policy in 1985 that the debate about joining the Exchange Rate Mechanism of the EMS was joined in earnest in Whitehall (see Walters 1990; Lawson 1992). Lawson became convinced of the need to supplement (and effectively replace) the MTFS with a clearer and more easily understood exchange rate rule through linking sterling to the Deutschmark. Indeed, the initial success of John Major, who succeeded him as Chancellor, in obtaining Prime Minister Thatcher's agreement to ERM membership looked as if it was going to be one of the most significant macro-economic policy decisions of the last two decades, and a decision supported by the British political, industrial, and commercial élites. If the MTFS had represented the high noon of a UK brand of monetarism, ERM membership appeared to represent the fuller integration of the UK into the European Community, and with it a commitment to long-term non-inflationary growth.

Within the ERM the overall goals of policy remained very similar to those of the 1980 MTFS document: the reduction of inflation and the introduction of supply-side reforms which would create the conditions for sustainable economic growth. Public expenditure played a key role in this. In terms of the mechanisms for achieving this, the official position was that macro-economic policy since 1990 was effectively based on two legs: maintaining sterling's position in the ERM, using interest rates if necessary; and fiscal policy set in order to achieve a balanced budget over the medium term. The latter represented a further change in the Government's formal public expenditure objectives. A balanced budget over the medium term is described as a 'clear and simple rule which ensures that a prudent fiscal policy supports monetary policy in the fight against inflation' (Treasury 1991*a*: 10).

In the event the 'experiment' of locking the UK into a D-Mark-dominated exchange-rate system proved even less long-lasting than the failed attempt to ground policy in a domestic monetary framework through the MTFS. ERM membership had contributed to a reduction in the underlying level of inflation from an annual rate of over 9 per cent in 1990 to under 4 per cent by the autumn of 1992. This was at the price of setting domestic monetary policy so tightly that the recession was elongated as output continued to fall and unemployment to rise.

The decision to suspend sterling's membership of the ERM in September 1992, effectively leaving the system for the indefinite future, was as significant a blow to the prestige and confidence of the UK's economic policy-making élite as the devaluation of sterling in 1967 and the recourse to an IMF loan in 1976. It was the result of a complex interplay of at least four factors (discussed in Treasury and Civil Service Committee 1992 and OECD 1993*a*). First, the foreign exchange markets were unsettled by the uncertainty about French ratification of Maastricht and the continuing problem of the Danish rejection of the Treaty. Second, sterling was particularly vulnerable to the subsequent pressures in the system because the UK domestic economy was in deep recession. Third, there remained an underlying lack of confidence in the markets that the UK authorities would defend sterling's position in the grid, confirmed by the decision not to follow the Bundesbank's raising of interest rates because of concerns about UK economic conditions. And finally, in the absence of any collective decision to realign currencies in the ERM, influenced in the main by the desire of one group led by France not to jeopardize the role of the ERM as a vehicle for monetary union, the system was ripe for speculative moves against weaker currencies by foreign exchange market leaders. Even the concerted action of Central Banks could not match the volume of private capital flowing in such an environment.

Policy post-ERM

After the suspension of ERM membership UK macro-economic policy moved almost exactly back to the eclectic position prevailing in the mid-1980s, with some changes in policy tools and presentation. Control of inflation remained the core aim of policy with, for the first time, an explicit 1–4 per cent target range set for the RPI (excluding mortgage interest payments). In order to achieve that target, and achieve inflation at the lower end of the range by 1996, monetary policy would be set after assessing a wide range of indicators: narrow money, M0, broad money, M4, the exchange rate, market interest rates, asset prices, and the state of the real economy. Implicitly, policy became more concerned with domestic output and employment within an overall anti-inflation constraint. Discretion had replaced policy rules.

Fiscal policy was set in a medium-term context with the aim of balancing the budget over the cycle but with no explicit policy to reduce the PSBR or reduce public debt as a proportion of GDP. The Treasury and Civil Service Committee was concerned at

the lack of a firm medium-term framework for fiscal policy, such as to add credibility to the Government's announced intention of bringing the budget back to balance. A strategy for deficit reduction in the medium-term is required under the terms of the Maastricht Treaty, whether or not the UK joins the ERM, and will be required for domestic policy reasons even if the UK does not ratify the Maastricht Treaty. (1992: p. xxxv)

Given the continued public commitment to reducing taxation in order to contain the pressures on public borrowing, the Treasury announced in July 1992 (predating the ERM crisis) a further modification to the public-spending control system. We discuss in later chapters the evolution and development of the public expenditure targets used by the Treasury. At this point it is important only to note that a 'New Control Total' was instituted along with a commitment to set top–down limits to this total; the NCT would only be allowed to grow in line with the potential growth rate of the economy; and discussions between the Treasury and departments would be about the division of this predetermined total. What this represented was a return to a policy of containing public spending within clearly published parameters, reminiscent of the MTFS in 1980.

In the aftermath of the ERM débâcle, the Treasury announced a number of potentially significant presentational changes. These changes were motivated by an awareness that the Treasury's credibility had been damaged by the ERM episode and by the failure to predict the scale of the boom and the length and depth of the recession. They also pre-empted demands for granting statutory monetary policy independence to the Bank of England; and, more prosaically, were an attempt to reassure financial markets that removing the ERM constraint and returning to a more judgement-based policy would not lead to a repeat of the mistakes made in the mid- and late 1980s. The first set of changes was termed greater 'openness'. The Treasury committed itself to publishing monthly monetary reports, following the regular meeting between the Governor of the Bank of England and the Chancellor. The Bank would be charged with producing a quarterly report on the progress towards the inflation target; after each interest rate change the Treasury would explain the detailed reasoning behind the policy change. The second change involved setting up a panel of seven independent economic advisers/forecasters (the 'seven wise men'). This group under the Chairmanship of the Chief Economic Adviser would produce quarterly reports on forecasts on the economy and provide policy advice (HM Treasury 1993*a*, 1993*c*).

A SUMMARY OF TRENDS IN PUBLIC EXPENDITURE

The main trends in public expenditure, together with an analysis of the objectives and achievements of successive governments, are discussed in detail in Chapters 20 and 21, when we look at the outputs of the system of planning and control. Here we summarize in Fig. 2.2 the trends in two key variables, General Government Expenditure (the broadest and most reliable measure of spending) in real terms, after allowing for

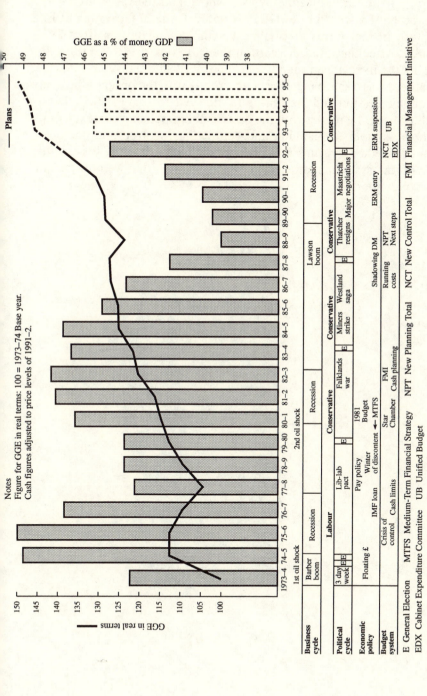

FIG. 2.2. Public spending, 1973–1996

Notes: Figure for GGE in real terms: 100 = 1973–4 base year. Cash figures adjusted to price levels of 1991–2. E = general election; EDX = Cabinet Expenditure Committee; FMI = Financial Management Initiative; MTFS = Medium-Term Financial Strategy; NCT = New Control Total; NPT = New Planning Total; UB = Unified Budget. *Source*: Based on data in Cm. 2219: 15.

general inflation in the economy as a whole, and the ratio of General Government Expenditure to GDP. Broadly, General Government Expenditure in real terms grew almost without interruption from 1977 onwards. After the rapid increase in the ratio of GGE to GDP in the early 1980s, its share gradually declined until the end of the decade when there was a sharp increase concurrently with the onset of the deep economic recession and the run-up to the 1992 general election. These trends provide the reader with the broad public-spending context within which the system of planning and control has evolved and has been operated by the Treasury and the spending departments. It is to the origin of that system, and its development to 1982, that we now turn in the next chapter.

3

The Origins and Development of the System of Planning and Control

THE PLOWDEN REPORT

The Plowden Report on the *Control of Public Expenditure* (Cmnd. 1432) published in June 1961 is conventionally seen as dividing off the old from the new; a watershed between the traditional annual control of Supply expenditure estimates, department by department, which had characterized the Treasury from the mid-nineteenth century onwards, and the new annual five-year published plans of functional programmes produced by the PESC system. This interpretation is both over-simplified and misleading.

PESC did not spring fully formed from the principles formulated in the Plowden Report—in some important respects it departed radically from them. There was in practice no sharp dividing line between the old and the new. There was rather a process of gradual transition in which the constituent elements of what came to be known as the PESC system of planning and control evolved pragmatically through the Treasury's experience of developing and implementing the novel concepts of aggregate public expenditure, appraisals of future resources and expenditure commitments, and annual allocations to functional programmes, in conditions of government growth willed by both Conservative and Labour Governments, and the constraints and opportunities of recurring financial crises.

This chapter traces the origins of the Plowden Report and describes the evolution and development of PESC up until the introduction of cash planning in 1982. It argues that the process was a gradual one, in which the principles of the new planning and control system were rooted in the official Treasury's response to changing government objectives in the 1950s; their effective implementation thereafter was constrained by political expediency as governments embraced economic planning for faster GDP growth, and by the exigencies of recurring financial crises.

A further over-simplification attributes to the Select Committee on Estimates, whose report in 1958 prompted the setting up of the Plowden

Committee, the prime responsibility for goading the Treasury into new ways of thinking about public expenditure and its control. While it played a part in that process, the ideas which were to surface in the Plowden Report were already being discussed within the Treasury before the Select Committee's inquiry began. They were inspired and initiated by senior officials, the culmination of a process of internal discussion and reflection on the need to adjust to the era of government growth begun by the Conservative Government in the mid-1950s. Without that discussion, it is unlikely that the Treasury would have been able or willing to respond so positively or so quickly to the committee's criticisms. In other words, what was said outside the Treasury was not altogether unwelcome or inconsistent with what was being said by some senior officials inside. The time was ripe, and the appointment of a committee of inquiry provided the opportunity.

On such a crucial and sensitive issue, it would have been surprising had the Treasury surrendered the initiative to an outside independent body, as recommended by the Select Committee. The Chancellor was persuaded by his senior officials of the need for an internal committee, whose members would be appointed by him and whose findings and recommendations would be reported confidentially to him. As so often in the past, the Treasury succeeded in regaining and retaining the initiative, which on this occasion had been temporarily seized by the Select Committee. Thereafter, it was able to dictate the direction, pace, and substance of changes to the traditional system of control, and to the consequential reorganization of the department in 1962. While the published version of the internal reports of the Plowden Committee provided a useful public demonstration of the Treasury's acceptance of the need of change, and even of a turning-point in the history of twentieth-century Treasury control, its real significance was that it signalled the Treasury's readiness and confidence to commit itself publicly to certain basic principles, firmly rooted in the internal rethinking begun earlier.

Senior officials in the Treasury's Public Sector Group had begun in the mid-1950s to discuss how to respond to the expected long-term growth in Supply expenditure; to the expansion of non-Supply expenditure generated by the investment programmes of the recently nationalized energy and transport industries; and to the expansion of social and environmental programmes. Discussion focused on the inappropriate and inadequate methods of controlling expenditure through piecemeal decisions on more than 2,000 line items in the annual Estimates. The concept of aggregate expenditure did not exist, and the Treasury made no judgement about the desirable total to aim for and its implications for taxation and borrowing. At that time 'there was very little work done and knowledge about the role and impact and composition and morphology even of Supply expenditure' (Clarke 1978: 4). Different kinds of expenditure were handled in different ways; confusion about 'above' and 'below the line' expenditure was not confined to outsiders.

A number of *ad hoc*, specific, and limited 'forward looks' were undertaken in the Treasury in the mid-1950s, for social services, defence, and the nationalized industries. At the same time, as background for public-investment decisions, an annual assessment of the development of the economy was begun in 1957. These 'long-term operations' did not evolve gradually into the broader concepts of public expenditure planning elaborated in the Plowden Report: that intellectual and administrative leap came about because of the need to move from the specific and limited long-term operations to the wider concepts of public expenditure as a whole. The first systematic attempt to do so occurred in 1958, when the Long-Term Economic Assessment for that year was converted into a long-term strategic paper based on an assumed annual growth rate of 2.5 per cent for GDP, with consideration of growth rates and implications for investment, defence and overseas expenditure, and consumption and civil expenditure. The exercise was a 'first run over the course' by a handful of very senior Treasury people. But 'it was a long hard road from these thoughts . . . to the creation of an apparatus on the resources side that would carry conviction to Ministers and departments, and an apparatus of expenditure control throughout the public sector which would be accepted and effective' (Clarke 1978: 22).

By the time the Plowden Committee reported publicly, some three years later, the Treasury was sufficiently confident about its ability to look ahead five years, both in surveying resources and in appraising the implications of expenditure policies. The substance of the Plowden Report reflected that confidence, and the principles enunciated incorporated the state-of-the-art within the Treasury at that time.

The Plowden Committee had begun work in October 1959 under Sir Edwin (later Lord) Plowden, who had been Chief of the Treasury's Planning Staff. Besides three outside members, six Permanent and Deputy Secretaries from the Treasury and other Whitehall departments were appointed as assessors, of whom one, (Sir) Richard Clarke, was appointed an assessor on taking over as Third (i.e. Deputy) Secretary in charge of public spending in January 1960. Clarke's ideas and influence on the Committee were decisive. It was 'an open secret that the principal ideas and analysis which made the Plowden Report so seminal a document came from the mind of Sir Richard Clarke . . . It was his imagination and insight that produced the first comprehensive picture of the public sector and laid down the main lines on which it should be measured and analyzed' (Goldman 1973: p. x). Clarke, rather than Plowden, is acknowledged as the prime mover and principal architect of the principles and later practice of PESC. His approach to administration was experimental (Clarke 1978) and this characteristic is evident in the translation of the Plowden principles into the PESC practice when he became Second (i.e. Permanent) Secretary in charge of the Treasury's Public Sector Group in November 1962, after the reorganization of the Department which followed the Plowden Report and the setting up of the NEDC.

The presence of the six assessors on the Plowden Committee provided for the formal participation of the Treasury and the opportunity for it to steer the committee along the lines already worked out, while representation from the Whitehall spending departments ensured that they were carried along with the new initiative. Besides the heavily edited published report,[1] a number of unpublished reports were made to the Chancellor.

The four major principles of expenditure control proposed in the report are familiar enough (see Pollitt 1977) and need only the briefest summary here: first, that regular surveys should be made of public expenditure as a whole, over a period of years ahead, and in relation to prospective resources; and that decisions involving substantial future expenditure should be taken in the light of them. Secondly, the committee emphasized the need for greater stability in decision-making; thirdly, the need to improve the tools of Treasury and departmental financial control; and, fourthly, the need to improve the collective decision-making of the Cabinet.

Ironically, while the committee attached most importance to the last point, to strengthen the position of the Chancellor of the Exchequer to control the anticipated growth in public expenditure over the next few years, it proved the most difficult to achieve in practice. In an unpublished interim report to the Chancellor, the committee recommended a Public Expenditure Committee of senior ministers to examine appraisals of spending and resources, and to consider large long-term expenditure proposals. Attempts to implement this proposal in 1961 and again in 1965 were unsuccessful. However, the creation of the post of Chief Secretary in 1961 did help to strengthen the Chancellor's position.

The committee's concern with long-term surveys or appraisals of public expenditure sprang from the need to 'get a background to discuss

[1] W. J. M. Mackenzie's 'translation' of the coded messages of a report written in an unknown tongue achieved a minor *succès d'estime* in the 1960s and was reprinted in Rose 1969.

five years ahead—a gradually developing frame of reference into which specific problems for discussion could be fitted as and when the decision had to be taken' (Clarke 1978: 29). The constituent element of these appraisals was to be provided by 'forward looks' for the big programmes, education, health, defence, public sector investment, which together comprised 85 per cent of public sector expenditure. The intention was that these programmes would be discussed between the Treasury and the departments in the period May to July, with the broad context provided by the expenditure and resources appraisals in the autumn. Amendments to the programmes would be made, if necessary, in the light of the appraisals.

At this stage, there was neither the intention nor the expectation that appraisals and forward looks would be used as methods of allocating resources or controlling spending. From the outset then, both the principles which guided Treasury thinking and informed the Committee's recommendations proceeded from the basis that individual expenditure decisions should be informed by knowledge of what resources would be available in the future and how much of these might be consumed by public expenditure. While public expenditure was increasing, and expected to continue to grow, it was not intended to limit that growth other than in relation to the likely resources available. Controlling public expenditure became an urgent issue in the late 1960s, and a critical one after the rapid growth initiated by the U-turn and 'Barber boom' of the Heath Government, and the rapid rise in public-sector costs and prices which took place in the inflationary conditions of the mid-1970s. The cause of the very acute difficulty in controlling expenditure experienced then can be partly traced to the early concern of the Treasury and the Plowden Committee with 'looking ahead', with what might happen in five years' time rather than what would happen year-by-year *through* a five-year period. That difficulty was exacerbated by the use of the constant price basis used to cost and revalue the planned allocations. Its adoption from the outset, and its use in the early PESC rounds, was a deliberate choice, justified partly on technical grounds, but mainly because it was feared that the Chancellor's independence in deciding tax policy would be weakened if the resources appraisal was conducted in terms of projections of future revenue. If it had been, the expenditure surveys would also have had to be measured in cash, in order to compare the two.

From the perspective of the 1990s, after more than a decade of cash control, the decision to plan and allocate public expenditure in volume terms through a five-year period measured in constant prices unique to each Survey appears an expensive mistake. But in the context of the

1950s and 1960s it was an entirely credible decision to have made and very much in line with Keynesian orthodoxy. Both Conservative and Labour Governments were converted to national indicative planning, and to the expansion of the public sector. A key concept in the various planning exercises was the alternative use of physical resources, between the private and public sectors and within the latter between competing programmes of public goods and services. It was assumed that planning and allocating resources in the public sector in volume terms enabled planners to identify real rates of growth or decline in each programme. What was obscured, and difficult to distinguish, was growth/decline due to changes in volume from that due to increases in prices and wages. Moreover, the emphasis was heavily on inputs; little attempt was made at that time to try to identify and measure outputs resulting from given volumes of inputs, or to measure productivity.

THE EMERGENCE OF PESC

Work on the technology of the new concepts of planning public expenditure aggregates and departmental programmes involved defining and classifying public expenditure by functional programmes. Attempts were made also to assess the economic impact of different kinds of expenditure. The time-period for expenditure surveys and programme forward looks was that used in the earlier exercises on defence, public investment, and education spending—five years. 'Hardly any thought was taken about what was the best practical period to take' (Clarke 1978: 47). By the time of the publication of the Plowden Report in July 1961, the Treasury had completed the first PESC Report covering the years 1960–1 to 1965–6. Following the report of a Ministerial Group to help the Chancellor review public expenditure, along the lines proposed by the Plowden Committee in one of its interim reports, Cabinet had instructed the Treasury to produce a public expenditure plan on the assumption that the ratio of public expenditure to GNP should remain at the current rate of 42.5 per cent.

The Treasury, having prompted the initiative, was ready to respond to the challenge. The preparation of the report involved the collaboration of twenty-four Whitehall departments in a new committee— the Public Expenditure Survey Committee, PESC, chaired by Clarke, by then Second Secretary to the Treasury responsible for public expenditure. The concern of the first PESC Report was to establish policies in twelve main policy areas, totalling some 80 per cent of public expenditure. Some were expressed in quantitative terms, as limits for the fifth year, in others there were merely qualitative assessments. Departments were not invited to bid; there was no allocation for each plan year.

The second PESC Report was completed in June 1962. While further technical development in the collection and collation of departmental programmes was made, and in the costings of aggregated departmental estimates compared with proposed target rates for public expenditure as a whole, the Treasury continued to search for a method of relating the analysis to ministerial decision-making. The earlier yardstick of the PE/GDP ratio was dropped because of changes in the definition of public expenditure. The most significant development occurred in an attempt to contain the risks of future expansion: serious attention was given to long-term allocation and control. For each of the largest (seven) programmes, the Treasury agreed with the department an approved annual rate of expansion for three or four years ahead. If a Minister wished to expand his programme beyond that rate he had to secure the approval of his colleagues, which involved discussion on the merit of the expansion and on its implications for the total of public expenditure.

This represented an important departure from the original intention of the Treasury, reflected in the Plowden Report, which was to agree long-term *policies* in each of the main areas which in aggregate would be compatible with the expected growth of resources. While this involved quantitative limits, it was the policies rather than the limits which were emphasized. Experience had shown (especially in defence) that, in order to keep within long-term financial limits, it was necessary to have compatible policies. Now by setting annual rates of expansion for each programme, it was hoped to contain the pressures from those policies, and enforce changes in them. 'The introduction of the "block allocation" was a first practical step towards long-term control' (Clarke 1978: 80). As yet, the figures for each block were not control figures but used for planning purposes. The allocations were limiting only in the sense that if a Minister wanted to do something new not provided for in the allocation, he had either to find room for its long-term cost, or seek Cabinet approval. While the permitted annual percentage increase in each block was revised each year in the light of ministerial decisions taken against the background of the PESC Report, the percentage increase was for five years ahead and remained unallocated through the five years.

A further step was taken in 1963 with the publication of the first Public Expenditure White Paper (PEWP). Apart from the political reasons for so doing at that time, it committed the Conservative

Government to the new public expenditure system, and made it more difficult for a future Labour Government to abandon it. The PESC Report was published for a second time in 1966. Responding to belated Parliamentary interest in the new system, the Treasury published a 'Green Paper' in 1969 which led to the publication of the Survey as an annual White Paper and to the setting up of the Select Committee on Expenditure in place of the Estimates Committee.

Increasingly through the remainder of the 1960s the Treasury turned its attention to the problem of making the emerging PESC system into an effective instrument of control. It grew increasingly anxious as the Plowden principle of relating expenditure to resources was turned on its head and exploited for political purposes by both Conservative and Labour Governments. A further difficulty was the tendency for departments to underestimate the future costs of maintaining existing policies. In order to persuade departments to be more realistic in their future costings, the Treasury had to accept increases in short-term estimates. The result was shortfall or underspending in year one programme expenditures, a characteristic of PESC (and PES) ever since. Allowance for the relative price effect (RPE—i.e. the tendency for costs to rise faster in the public sector than in the economy as a whole) appeared in the first published PEWP in 1963, but was not incorporated in the costing of programmes in that or the following year.

There were already signs that the Plowden concept of relating public expenditure to what resources were likely to be available would be difficult to maintain in the political circumstances of the 'dash for growth' in the early 1960s. The first PESC exercise had been premised on the assumption of the PE/GDP ratio being maintained at 42.5 per cent. This was followed in 1963 by more explicit targetry. Long-term expenditure plans were related not to the appraisal of prospective resources but to assumed or hoped-for increases in GDP. The phenomenon, which became familiar in the first half of the 1970s, of the repeated optimism of ministers about economic prospects first appeared in 1962 as the newly created NEDC examined the implications of a 4 per cent growth rate for the economy. While there were plausible political reasons to justify that decision at that time, it represented a repudiation of the Plowden principle. From the first PESC exercise, the Treasury's recurring dilemma had been between, on the one hand, following where the analysis seemed to lead, and on the other, giving greater weight to political factors which vitiated the logic of that analysis. Ministers often chose to ignore or relax objectives derived from the PE/GDP ratio.

The Labour Government elected in October 1964 inherited a system which was still evolving from the original concept of five-year appraisals of expenditure and resources, and forward looks for the big spending programmes. Responsibility for macro-economic policy was divided between the new Department of Economic Affairs and the Treasury, but the latter's responsibility for public expenditure was little affected.

The distinction between basic (or baseline) and additional spending which became a crucial part of the PES process in the 1980s had its origins in the Labour Government's decision to limit the growth of public expenditure to an annual rate of 4.25 per cent in the plan period 1964–5 to 1969–70. 'Basic' limits were laid down for the main civil programmes (a defence review had capped defence spending at £2 billion per annum at constant prices) which reflected decisions already taken in the previous PESC round. Departments were invited to submit bids for 'additional' programmes, reflecting the need to be seen to provide the opportunity for new ministers to argue the case for their manifesto policies. The aggregate of the bids inevitably exceeded what was thought affordable and had to be cut by two-thirds. This was done not through a series of bilateral meetings between the (new) Chief Secretary and the departmental Minister, as became the practice later. Instead, it was decided that a Cabinet Committee of the Chancellor, Secretary of State for Economic Affairs, and five non-spending ministers should conduct the allocation of the additional expenditure. Each of the ministers responsible for the main programmes was interrogated at a day-long meeting, and the committee allocated additional monies to particular programmes, according to the priority which it thought should be accorded each.

This method of allocation from determined priorities of public spending was novel, and on this occasion successful. But Clarke believed that the essential precondition for its success was the small number (eight) of programmes dealt with, which made it possible for the members to brief themselves on the detail of expenditure proposals, and to weigh a limited number of alternatives. His judgement was that this was impossible with more than twelve programmes. The 'politics of the expenditure process' dictated that this method of allocation was soon abandoned: there were too few non-spending ministers, and they had too little time or inclination to immerse themselves in the detail of programmes which spanned the whole of government activity. Spending ministers were also reluctant to risk alienating colleagues whose political support would be needed in Cabinet on future occasions, and wished to retain their right to argue their case in full Cabinet. The exercise in the collective determination of spending priorities was repeated on only one other occasion before 1992, in the circumstances of acute crisis in 1975, when Labour Ministers had to agree substantial cuts in public expenditure programmes to meet conditions prescribed by the IMF. But as Joel Barnett, the then Chief Secretary, makes clear (Barnett 1982) collective decision-making on that occasion was more a series of bilateral haggles over the Cabinet table than a collective discussion of priority.

The hesitant steps towards a system of allocation and control through the plan period, inherent in the blocking of expenditure by function and programme, proved inadequate in the conditions of the major economic and financial crises which occurred in 1966 and 1967. The need for *ad hoc*, speedy cost-cutting exercises vitiated the barely secure exercises for making allocations which the Treasury had begun in 1965. As happened in 1976, and again in 1982 and in 1992, the response to crisis signalled a major development in the system. The need to control the allocations through the five-year plan period by the imposition of limits became evident to ministers, Treasury officials, and departments. The new doctrine of control—'planning the path as well as the whole'—was officially proclaimed in the PEWP of January 1968. Quantitative limits on programme allocations were now attached to each of the five years. Planning the whole and ensuring the compatibility of expenditure policies had not been proof against the tendency for costs to increase year by year. For the first time, 'comprehensive control over public spending based on clearly defined objectives covering both the earlier and later years of the quinquennium was substituted for indicative planning five years ahead, and was buttressed by determined arrangements for monitoring expenditure against firmly based departmental programmes' (Goldman 1973: 10).

The 1967–8 exercise to cut public expenditure plans marked a turning-point in the development of the system of public expenditure control. 'The whole machinery of the public expenditure control system was thrown into action and employed for the first time at full stretch involving all departments and ministers and the inter-departmental instrument of PESC now much tried and tempered by experience over the years' (Goldman 1973: 10). More effort was now given to ensuring that the planned reductions were achieved, and that pressures for additional expenditure were contained. Here are to be found the beginnings of the use and management of the Contingency Reserve (see Chapter 16) as a control mechanism, while the origins of the sophisticated monitoring system of the Treasury's Financial Information System (FIS) is traceable from the introduction of the running tally system in 1966.

PESC emerged from its second major crisis, devaluation, with its procedures for controlling expenditure (apparently) strengthened. After 1967 ministers were more willing to accept the totals for public expenditure in the Survey as strict limits. One reason for their greater willingness was that those totals were made public, in a White Paper published in 1968 announcing details of the cuts to public spending agreed in Cabinet in the wake of devaluation. The lesson was not lost on the Treasury, which soon after committed itself to the publication of the PEWP on a regular basis.

Following the 1968 White Paper the Treasury conducted a general review of the planning and control system, and of the principles underlying it. Among other matters, this revealed the 'deficiencies in the techniques employed for collecting information about department programmes and in measuring these in constant terms' (Goldman 1973: 38). It also highlighted the inadequacy of many departments' methods of managing and controlling their spending programmes. 'To some degree at least the imposing array of tables in PESC reports, the White Paper and elsewhere which purport to be an account of departmental programmes suffer from serious deficiencies in underlying material' (p. 39). Such 'imperfections could lead to a failure of control', and risk 'embarrassing deviations between what is planned and forecast and actual performance'. Written in 1973, these comments by the former head of the Treasury's expenditure side proved prophetic. Within two years public expenditure was 'out of control', with a marked discrepancy between what was planned in volume terms at Survey prices and what was spent in cash terms.

The publication of an annual Expenditure White Paper and the appointment of the new Select Committee on Expenditure to monitor the Treasury's planning and control of spending were symptoms of the Treasury's growing confidence in the efficacy of PESC as it entered the 1970s. Within the department it was felt that there now existed a firm foundation from which the further development of the initial Plowden principles could be contemplated, and that this development would be aided by enlisting the support of Parliament and informed public opinion. Discussion centred upon three main issues: the need for an improved information system to monitor cash flow, especially at the local level; the desirability of more policy analysis, especially of the outputs and effectiveness of programmes; and the possibility of introducing programme budgeting to complement the input-emphasis of PESC.

Only the first of these led to a significant and enduring change in the 1970s. The construction of Treasury and departmental financial information systems, a prerequisite of effective cash control of expenditure, became urgent as the crisis of control in the mid-1970s provoked the initiation of cash limits. In the early 1970s, the introduction of programme analysis and review (PAR), which accompanied the attempts of the new Conservative Government to improve efficiency and effectiveness in the public sector, and experimentation with output budgeting, seemed more promising long-term logical developments of the steadily evolving PESC system. Both were overwhelmed, and eventually abandoned, by the more pressing need to restore control in 1976. Both reappeared in a different guise—as Rayner scrutinies and the concern with performance indicators, outputs, and value-for-money—in the 1980s, discussed in the next two chapters.

THE CRISIS OF CONTROL

In the space of three years the system for planning and controlling public expenditure moved into deep crisis. Whereas it was possible for Sir Samuel Goldman to claim in 1973 that the system had reached 'full maturity' and was 'probably superior to that found anywhere else in the world' (1973: 53), three years later it was difficult to resist the contention of a former senior economic adviser to the Treasury that public expenditure was neither planned nor controlled: 'We have not got a proper planning system, and we have not got a proper control system' (Godley 1975).

The breakdown of the machinery for planning and controlling public expenditure which occurred was precipitated by the decision of the Heath Government to increase public spending as part of the U-turn in economic and industrial policies provoked by the combination of rising unemployment and inflation. Whereas in its first two years of office the Conservative Government's spending had grown roughly in line with GDP, thereafter it was planned to grow very much more quickly; and actually resulted in higher levels still. The 1972 White Paper projected expenditure growth in real terms of 6.2 and 5.3 per cent for the first two years of the Survey. Thereafter, it was planned to decrease substantially. These plans proved woefully inaccurate as guides to what would happen, in both the short and medium term. The outturn of public spending for 1972–3 and 1973–4 was 6.9 and 8.5 per cent higher in real terms, the latter being more than double the growth of GDP.

The debate about the efficacy of PESC as a planning and controlling system focused on the plans and outturn for 1974–5. It was alleged that the actual spending for that year exceeded that planned in the Survey four years earlier by several billion pounds. The 'missing billions', as they became known, were the subject of critical comment of Treasury control in the newspapers, and debated in the House of Commons. They were seen by many commentators and MPs as proof that public expenditure was out of control. Wynne Godley, Special Adviser to the Select Committee on Expenditure and a former senior Treasury economist, alleged that of the 28 per cent increase in public expenditure between 1970–1 and 1974–5 only a half could be regarded as having been planned in the earlier White Paper or accounted for by subsequent announced policy changes. The remainder, totalling some £5 billion, equivalent to more than 10 per cent of total public expenditure for 1974–5, was thus largely unplanned. It had arisen 'by default'. Under hostile attack, the Treasury attempted to explain how the discrepancy had occurred; to refute the charge that public expenditure was 'out of control'; and to deny that PESC had proved inadequate as a system for planning and controlling aggregate spending. It argued that the cause of the overspend was due less to the inadequacy of its techniques of planning and control than to the operation of general economic and social factors—accelerating inflation, cyclical fluctuations, the oil crisis, and a change of government. It argued that policy changes initiated by government, and especially the incoming Labour Government of 1974, accounted for a substantial part of the discrepancy. Of the remainder, a large part was accounted for by volume changes beyond those originally planned and taken into account as those plans were revised each year. However, underestimating the relative price effect contributed £1.75 billion.

Far from disarming its critics, the Treasury's explanation invited the retort that accounting for every pound of the 'missing billions' was not the same as controlling them. Few were disposed to agree with the Treasury that excess of outturn over planned expenditure represented the inherent flexibility of PESC which provided both the opportunity and occasion for ministers to make and revise policies within the life of a four- or five-year survey. If that argument was accepted, it could be argued further that PESC was always vulnerable to rapid and successive policy changes, and the stability of decision-making at which it aimed had always proved illusory. The episode had merely served to emphasize the limitations of PESC as a control system.

The Select Committee on Expenditure was not convinced by the Treasury's explanations: 'The Treasury's present methods of controlling public expenditure are inadequate in the sense that money can be spent on a scale which was not contemplated when the relevant policies were decided upon' (1975). If the Treasury were to be criticized for failing to prevent ministers from approving increases of expenditure on existing programmes, it would be unfair unless it could be shown that the Treasury did not have information early enough to warn ministers of the consequences of continuing to finance programmes at the same or a greater level of provision—or that it had the information but failed to alert them to the full expenditure implications. The subsequent acceptance by the Treasury of the need for an early-warning device as an essential concomitant of cash-limits control is evidence enough that PESC did not provide that kind of control. Little progress had been made between 1970 and 1975 with the development of a comprehensive information system which, *inter alia*, would enable it to monitor the progress of expenditure (Butler and Aldred 1977). Apart from this, the episode revealed the difficulty of estimating costs accurately enough for the figures to be regarded and used as control figures. In the words of a former Treasury Principal: 'It effectively left to the spending departments . . . the reporting of their own misbehaviour. In the early 1970s the monthly returns came into the Treasury and were added up with virtually no enquiry into their authenticity' (Shapiro 1978). The running tally system introduced in 1968 was crude, and liable to abuse. The Treasury Officer of Accounts discovered that some departments were inventing figures for their monthly returns.

In particular, the Treasury emphasized the difficulty of forecasting the movement of public-sector prices and wages for the calculation of the RPE even twelve months ahead. In calculating an allowance for it, the Treasury adjusted upwards or downwards a trend derived from an extrapolation of past experience. As it admitted, this was scarcely better than an informed guess of what might happen in the following four or five years.

While the size of the increase in public expenditure which took place in 1974–5 was exceptional, partly reflecting the policy initiatives of the new Labour Government, the tendency for outturn to exceed planned expenditure was a more general phenomenon associated with the PESC system, first observed in the period of the 'dash for growth' in the early 1960s, and again under the Heath Government a decade later. The (then) Contingency Reserve was inadequate to provide for frequent policy changes between one Survey and the next, a shortcoming in the system which was not remedied until 1984 (see Chapter 16). There were also serious problems in providing reliable estimates of the costs of programmes, associated in particular with the relative price effect. But, crucially, the constant price basis used for measuring the volume of goods and services effectively indexed public-sector programmes against inflation. Once volumes were agreed, the monetary cost of providing those volumes was consequential. In a period of high and rising inflation, in which public-sector prices and wages tended to rise faster than in the private sector, this meant a very rapid increase of public spending.

PESC IN CRISIS

The failure to control public expenditure in the mid-1970s served to highlight weaknesses in the PESC system which had appeared in the early 1960s, but which had been obscured by the success with which control had been imposed, though not secured, following the 1966–7 financial crises. With the resumption of the more familiar public expenditure growth in 1972, these weaknesses reappeared. First, there was no reliable yardstick by which to determine the appropriate rate of growth to aim for. The Plowden principle of relating expenditure to prospective resources provided no guidance on the causal relationship. In any case, the 'rule of thumb' that public expenditure growth should be directly related to that of GDP was ignored when ministers wanted to increase public spending for political purposes, as in the national economic planning initiatives of both Conservative and Labour Governments in the 1960s. Again, in the 1970s, both parties responded to rising unemployment with policies for increased public expenditure predicated on rates of growth for GDP far in excess of historic trends. While governments were prepared to cut public spending for conjunctural-policy reasons, or as in 1976 at the behest of the IMF, such cuts were often cuts in future planned expenditure, and tended to be restored later as economic conditions improved or political expediency dictated. Except at times of acute crisis, there were rarely any clearly articulated and credible objectives for the aggregate of public expenditure.

The second difficulty was that five-year plans bore very little relation to what was actually spent. As predictions of what would happen through the plan period, and in the year of spending, the Surveys were seriously deficient (Else and Marshall 1981). Thirdly, the stability of expenditure decisions which Plowden hoped would replace the 'stop-go' of the 1950s proved largely illusory. Public-sector plans were not insulated in the 1960s and 1970s from the expedients of short-term economic and financial management. The Treasury's use of public expenditure as a tool of that management resulted in successive changes in the estimates of planned expenditure for particular Survey years. While agreeing in principle that the use of public expenditure for this purpose was undesirable, the Treasury was rarely able to withstand pressure from ministers at home or bankers and the IMF abroad for action to stimulate or depress the level of economic activity, or to reduce the burden of the PSBR. In the 1970s, Budgets and mini-Budgets of cuts and squeezes were commonplace. The planned expenditure for 1974–5 was revised upwards and downwards no fewer than seven times.

The fourth difficulty, that of controlling the rising monetary cost of programmes calculated in constant price terms, unique to each Survey, became increasingly obvious in the early 1970s and reached a crisis point in 1975 when the whole basis of PESC appeared to be undermined by the Treasury's loss of control described above. With hindsight it is obvious that there were weaknesses inherent in the PESC system as it had evolved from the Plowden principles which made it deficient as a financial controlling system: planning through the Survey emphasized the control of resources (measured in volume terms) at the expense of control in cash; and it lacked a comprehensive information and monitoring system capable of generating quickly and appropriately data on the commitment and consumption of resources by central and local authorities, and the flow of cash to finance those resources.

Most worryingly of all for the Treasury was its lack of control over local authority expenditure. In the 1970s the Treasury was never able to ensure through the PESC processes that the decisions to incur expenditure (when and how much) made by several hundred local authorities conformed with levels of planned expenditure. From the mid-1950s until 1974, central government's share of the total of public expenditure declined, while local authority expenditure as a proportion of the total rose from less than a quarter to a third. The increase reflected the responsibility of local authorities in expanding areas such as education, health, social services, housing, and environmental services. This decentralization of spending had taken place in the 1960s and early 1970s, a period of steady, if unspectacular, economic growth and relatively full employment, when the Treasury was developing the concept of real resource allocation through PESC. With its emphasis on real resource costs, PESC was not well suited to impose a strict financial discipline on decentralized spending authorities in the conditions of rapid inflation which followed the energy crisis of 1973. But in any case, local authorities were excluded from the centralized PESC negotiations. One result of this was that until 1975–6, the estimates of levels of relevant expenditure for calculating the rate support grant were not consistent with figures which appeared in previous Public Expenditure

White Papers. The White Papers were, therefore, inadequate as a means of control.

The Treasury's implicit acknowledgement that it could not control the monetary costs of expenditure programmes, later explicitly confirmed in a Budget speech by the Chancellor of the Exchequer, meant that PESC was near to collapse. Two alternatives were canvassed:

To go forward and make PESC work and to introduce a financial control system into it, and have a positive planning system . . . [or] to go back and have, as it were, control in the very crude sense of having a Treasury which tried to keep expenditure down and which does not commit itself to real resource use for years in advance. (Select Committee on Expenditure 1975: para. 11)

The implication of the latter alternative was the abandonment of the PESC principles, as conceived in the Plowden Report and implemented through the trial of experience in the succeeding decade, and a return to a 'solely cash system' not unlike that which Gladstone had helped establish in the second half of the nineteenth century. The former alternative, 'PESC-plus', meant more than simply adding cash control to PESC, although that alone would prove difficult enough. It meant a 'positive planning system' in which control of public expenditure included the wider and neglected concept of effectiveness, an attempt to measure outputs, and an attempt to measure and verify the use of resources to achieve stated policy objectives. The major difficulties in going forward in this sense were the need for a comprehensive information system and a means of measuring performance. The two were to come together as dominant themes of public expenditure planning and control in the 1980s under the aegis of the FMI, discussed in the next chapter.

THE INTRODUCTION OF CASH LIMITS

An explicit choice could be avoided for a time. In the grave economic and financial crisis of 1975–6 the immediate need was to restore financial control as quickly as possible. In retrospect the decision then made to introduce cash limits, and the determination of the official Treasury to avoid a recurrence of a situation in which it could be blamed for a 'loss of control', combined to move PESC towards a mainly cash-control system, although this was not to become apparent until the experience of a further cash crisis precipitated the abandonment of volume planning and the initiation of cash planning in 1982.

The modifications made to PESC reflected the urgent need to restore control and, with the onset of the financial crisis in 1976, to implement substantial cuts in planned expenditure for 1977–8 and 1978–9. An essential prerequisite of cash control was the development of a computerized information system which would permit the monitoring of the cash flow of individual programmes and the aggregate of public expenditure on an almost daily basis. Progress towards this began in 1974–5 when the Treasury, the Civil Service Department, departments, and management consultants reviewed departmental and Treasury procedures for collecting, collating, and updating financial information. From that review evolved the rudiments of FIS, a comprehensive financial information system. Until 1976–7 the Treasury's main sources of information were the quarterly departmental returns submitted within about five weeks of the end of each quarter. These were insufficient and came too late to alert the Treasury to where overspending was occurring or likely to occur. With the development of FIS, monthly figures became available within ten days, and showed for each of the new cash-limited blocks what had been spent, and what remained for the rest of the financial year. Monthly appreciations were supplemented by fuller analysis, five times a year, showing both volume and price changes which had taken place within each block, together with a revised estimate of the outturn for the year. With such information, the Treasury was better able to distinguish overspending caused by higher than expected prices from that caused by changes in policy. The monitoring of the cash flow on the new cash-limited blocks of departmental programmes was made against the background of newly constructed expenditure profiles for each, providing a detailed picture of the rate of cash flow and its characteristics.

Cash limits were introduced in April 1976 to cover the monetary costs of rising public expenditure and embraced some three-quarters of central government Vote expenditure, excluding social security payments and some other kinds of demand-led expenditure. About the same proportion of local authority current expenditure was cash-limited through the RSG and supplementary grants. Cash limits were prescribed for a year ahead and applied to the year one volume figures in the Survey. The volume of services and goods for that and the four succeeding years was still determined annually through the PESC process in real terms. Through the Survey, the Treasury continued as before to plan and allocate expenditure on a constant price basis in the light of the resources thought likely to be available. Each year the costs of those volumes were revalued on a new price basis which reflected the actual movement of pay and prices the previous year. The implementation of the principles of cash-limits control, and the operation of the new system by the Treasury is discussed in detail in Chapter 17.

CASH PLANNING

The decision to introduce cash planning arose from the conjunction of the particular circumstances of rising public expenditure in the period 1978–80 with the Conservative Government's commitment in 1979 to reduce the size of the public sector and to cut public expenditure in real terms as part of its economic strategy to reduce the level of inflation. The context was set by the debate on budgetary reform precipitated by the Armstrong Report (1980). Together these factors provided a reason and an opportunity for the Treasury to improve its control procedures and to reassert the primacy of cash control, to which it had rededicated itself in 1976.

After the unprecedented cut-back in public spending in 1976–8, following the introduction of cash limits, public expenditure rose again: in 1979–80 by 5.9 per cent in real terms, and a year later by 3.3 per cent. While this was due less to any loss of control by the Treasury, and rather more to the collapse of pay policy in the winter of 1978, and the pre-electoral boost to public expenditure in the Labour Government's 1979 Budget, nevertheless the Treasury was clearly anxious that the tight discipline of the early years was being steadily eroded. A further source of anxiety was the future effectiveness of a cash-limits regime in the absence of a formal incomes policy for the public sector, to which the Conservative Government had declared itself opposed.

The abolition of the Pay Research Unit was widely interpreted as a political decision, representing the firm intention of the Conservative Government, but particularly the Prime Minister, to control Civil Service pay in the wake of the large increases stemming from the work of the Clegg Comparability Commission. It was partly a reaction to the helplessness of the Government and the Treasury as the effects of those awards went through the system, contributing to the substantial over-shooting of the Survey expenditure plans for 1979–80 and 1980–1. The decision was also strongly influenced by the advice of the Prime Minister's Policy Unit, which had as one of its main tasks the oversight of the implementation of the central economic strategy (Burch 1983). It also persuaded the Chancellor of the Exchequer that volume planning, even with cash limits, effectively indexed the public sector against inflation. If the anti-inflationary strategy was to be achieved, plans had to be in cash.

A further major factor in the decision to introduce cash planning was the Treasury's experience since 1976 of the operation of the system of cash limits plus volume planning. Although expenditure plans for year one of each Survey were cash-limited, the continuance of volume planning in constant (Survey) prices for years two and three (and four, until 1980) enabled departments to argue from the basis of 'entrenched entitlements'. Once volumes had been agreed for future years, it was difficult for the Treasury to resist pressure from departments to revalue the costs of providing those agreed volumes in line with the general movement of pay and prices which had taken place the previous year. Moreover, any squeeze on volumes or costs in year one which resulted from tightly drawn cash limits, in which the Treasury's assumption about inflation underestimated the movement of pay and prices, was not automatically carried forward in the renegotiation of years two and three (and four). It was possible for departments to 'unwind' the effects of a squeeze. Any saving through greater efficiency, resulting from the provision of the same level of services and goods with a reduced cash allowance, was not necessarily carried forward. Conversely, where a squeeze produced no such savings but a reduction in the provision of services, departments argued in the renegotiation for a restoration of the old (higher) planned volume total. A further difficulty in volume planning was in distinguishing changes in volumes from changes in the prices of those volumes. It was not always easy to determine whether an increased allowance in real terms represented merely the increased costs of providing the same level of goods and services, or in effect allowed for enhanced services. This was compounded by the lack of reliable indicators of performance and output; measurement was almost wholly in input terms.

A further reason for the introduction of cash planning was the need to continue the improvement of the arrangements for monitoring cash flow begun with the installation of financial information systems in the mid-1970s. Under the constant price system it was difficult to trace what was happening to the flow of cash, from the point where decisions were taken to commit expenditure to the point where outturn expenditure figures were available (Mountfield 1983).

Thus the circumstances of rising public expenditure in the looser regime after 1978, the operation of volume planning which made it difficult for the Treasury to sustain cuts in costs obtained through efficiency-gains or reduced service provision, and the difficulty of monitoring cash flow, were all factors in the decision to introduce cash planning. Those factors interacted with the political and economic objectives of the Conservative Government, and its declared strategy and preferred policy instruments. Cause and effect is impossible to unravel precisely, but more significant than the lines of causation is the coincidence of declared aim with need and opportunity. The Conservative Government's prime economic aim was to reduce, and eventually eliminate, inflation. Crucial to the achievement of that aim was the reduction of public expenditure. Reducing the size of the public sector was also a major political objective in its own right.

The details of the economic strategy for dealing with inflation and its formal expression in the MTFS were examined in the previous chapter. More important for the present discussion is that the MTFS represented a repudiation of real resource planning. It could be argued that real resource planning had been abandoned in 1976 with the abandonment of full employment as an objective of economic policy, and the discontinuance of the Medium Term Assessment. However, the Public Expenditure Survey continued to represent real resource planning for the public sector. With the advent of the MTFS, plans for the money supply, PSBR, and revenue were cast in cash. It followed that plans for public expenditure would need to be made in cash rather than 'funny money'. This was made explicit in the Government's announced intention that finance should determine expenditure.

Thus medium-term financial planning for the economy as a whole required public expenditure plans to be expressed in cash. Indeed in the early years of the MTFS the intention appeared to be that the aggregate level of public expenditure would be determined residually, after decisions had been made about the desirable target rates for money supply, borrowing, and taxation. The assumption, which proved false in practice, was that public expenditure could be adjusted downwards to accommodate judgements about what were desirable target figures for those variables. Very quickly, of course, pressures for more public spending in the economic conditions of a recession produced a reversal of the dictum that finance determines expenditure.

By the time of the announcement of the decision to introduce cash planning in March 1981, the Conservative Government was already experiencing difficulty, if not failure, in cutting public expenditure in line with its plans. The Treasury had been unable to deliver cuts of some £2.5 billion (1979 Survey prices) declared essential to the strategy. The time was ripe for change: as so often in the past, crisis provided both a stimulus and an opportunity. How could the system for planning and controlling public expenditure be made more effective as an instrument of the Government's economic strategy? Was it possible to make changes to the Survey which reconciled the need for a system capable of delivering cuts, and keeping a tight lid on the aggregate of expenditure, with the need to be seen to adhere to the principles laid down by Plowden?

While a decision to abandon volume planning carried some risk that it would be represented by critics as the end of the attempt to plan public expenditure begun two decades earlier, it was acknowledged even outside the Treasury that the rapid rise in public expenditure in the mid-1970s had exposed the weaknesses of trying to plan and control public expenditure in those terms. The abandonment of volume planning was a defensible decision: the argument would turn on what would replace it. With hindsight, the decision to introduce cash planning has the appearance of a logical, evolutionary, development: an extension of the short-term cash control initiated in 1976, and some insiders have represented it as such (Pliatzky 1982). However, the choice of cash planning rather than cost planning was much less straightforward or obvious than such an interpretation suggests (see Thain and Wright 1989*b*). It was made against a background of debate about the need to reform the budgetary process.

For some time, there had been criticism of the continued separation of expenditure and taxation planning, and in particular of the steady refusal of the Treasury and successive governments to publish provisional proposals in advance of the Budget. The appointment of an independent committee under the chairmanship of Lord (William) Armstrong in 1978, to inquire into the need for reform of the budgetary system, brought the issue to a head and provided a focus for the rumbling discontent. It reported in July 1980 and recommended the reform of budgetary practice to produce a more unified and coherent system for the planning of public expenditure and taxation, and to provide through a 'Green Budget' the opportunity for the public and Parliament to discuss provisional proposals before final decisions were made and incorporated in the Budget.

In 1982 the Select Committee on the Treasury and Civil Service conducted its own review of budgetary practice based upon the recommendations made in the Armstrong Report (Treasury and Civil Service Committee 1982*d*). Together, the inquiries constituted the most thorough review of budgetary practice since the Plowden Committee inquiry in 1961.

The committee's own recommendations were a partial endorsement of those made in the Armstrong Report. Responding to Treasury objections that the introduction of a December Green Budget would require a wholesale reform of the ministerial, administrative, and Parliamentary timetables, and would add a substantial burden to the administrative work of the government, it proposed more modestly a 'Green Book', which would be published, or which could be made readily available. It would bring together information about expenditure plans, medium-term economic assumptions, projections of revenue yields, and specific proposals for changes in tax rates and allowances. With the exception of the latter, those recommendations were accepted by the Treasury and the Conservative Government, and implemented from autumn 1982 in the form of the new annual Autumn Statement. It was not, of course, a Green Budget in the sense urged by the Armstrong Committee; nor (until November 1993) did it bring together expenditure and taxation plans. It was rather the institutionalization of the less formal process which had begun with the requirements under the Industry Act of 1976 for twice-yearly short-term economic forecasts to be presented to Parliament. In practice, while responding to the considerable pressure on it to make changes in budgetary procedures, the Treasury conceded very little to its critics. Pressures for budgetary reform subsided. Nearly a decade later, unprompted, Chancellor Lamont initiated the move to a Unified Budget in November 1993.

Five main advantages were claimed for cash planning, and the Treasury emphasized that the change to the price basis of the Survey was consistent with the principles formulated by Plowden. First, under a cash planning system ministers would discuss the cash which would actually be spent, and therefore that which would have to be financed by taxation and borrowing. Secondly, cash planning ensured that 'finance can determine expenditure and not expenditure finance', as had happened with volume planning. Thirdly, cash planning incorporated consideration of public sector costs, in particular pay. The Government's stance on public sector pay could be explicitly provided for. Fourthly, cash planning provided an incentive throughout the plan period for programme managers to adapt expenditure in relation to increasing costs. Efficiency gains could be carried forward from one year to the next. Fifthly, planning in cash terms required no revaluation from one price basis to another. Decisions in the Survey could be translated directly into cash limits and Parliamentary Estimates. It was also claimed by the Treasury that cash planning could reinforce desirable trends in the management of public expenditure programmes. Managers would be required to think more about the level of service which could be provided for a given fixed sum of money. There would be thus greater pressure on them to reduce costs, and to search for improved value-for-money. Volumes would not automatically be protected against rising costs. Almost as an afterthought, the Treasury claimed that managers would also have the incentive to assess what was being achieved, and to search for satisfactory indicators of output.

The significance of the Treasury's exposition and subsequent defence of cash planning was what was left unsaid. Its real (as opposed to ostensible) aim was to improve its control. It was quite prepared to trade greater uncertainty in planning for greater certainty in control. Planning in cash terms provided it with a blunter but more effective instrument for holding down the rising costs of public expenditure. This was to stand Plowden on its head. Where Plowden had insisted that control was inherent in the planning process and procedures, the Treasury's choice implied both the need and superiority of short-term control.

Cash planning was a more appropriate price basis to use in the preparation and calculation of public expenditure plans designed to reduce the aggregate of expenditure in real terms as an integral part of the Conservative Government's anti-inflation strategy. It was also more consistent with the Government's general stance on public sector costs, and its mission to make the public sector more efficient and effective. Cash planning provided a means to exert continuous downward pressure on costs, especially pay and jobs. From 1982–3 all public expenditure decisions were taken solely in cash.

CONCLUSIONS

In the history of the Treasury's control of expenditure, radical reform and innovation have been less important than the gradual evolution and adaptation of existing practice. From time to time that process of gradual change has quickened in response to the exigencies of financial or economic crisis, or to the exceptional conditions of national emergency, as in times of war. Both characteristics are evident in the period from the mid-1950s to the introduction of cash limits in 1976. A former Treasury Under Secretary described the process as: 'an iterative exchange between the general direction of ideas about the apparatus of control and the seizing of occasions offered by events . . . It means that the machinery is firmly grounded in fact and experience, and, in turn, this gives it considerable robustness' (Vintner 1979: 54).

Set in a longer historical context, the Plowden Report can be seen as a stage in a process of gradual evolution and adaptation, rather than as a turning-point between old and new methods of control; its proposals less a declaration of radical reform based on novel 'doctrine' than the public articulation of ideas and practices steadily evolved from Treasury thinking and cautious experimentation in the 1950s. Later, response to the events of economic and financial crisis proved more significant in the development of the evolving control system, as principles were tested and refined. This was:

less obvious but equally important to the practical development of executive control; each step forward arose from the exigencies of crisis, when responsible Ministers and officials were able to seize time by the forelock and get the next development approved as part of the apparatus in a way which would have been neither clear nor acceptable at the beginning. (Vintner 1979: 53)

The Plowden principles were not imposed on a reluctant Treasury by independent outsiders responding to Parliamentary criticism of the inadequacy of traditional methods of control. The transition from old to new was accomplished gradually as the Treasury responded pragmatically and opportunistically in the 1950s to the expansion of the public sector. The transition represented by the publication of the Plowden Report was managed by the Treasury which, successfully resisting the call for an independent inquiry, controlled the proceedings of the Committee and steered it towards conclusions which incorporated ideas worked out in the department over the past decade.

PESC as it had evolved by the early 1970s departed substantially from those ideas. Attempts to provide for more collective decision-making were abandoned early on. What were originally intended to be appraisals and forward looks of departmental *policies*, five years ahead, had become annual *allocations* through a five-year planning period, with quantitative costs attributed to individual programmes. The Plowden Report, reflecting Treasury thinking, had very little to say about allocation or control through costing. More effective control was thought to inhere in planning, by the relation of individual spending decisions to the general policy context five years hence. Experience soon revealed the weakness of such a concept. The need in 1965, and again more urgently in 1966–7, to obtain cuts in expenditure demonstrated that the 'path' as well as the 'whole' had to be planned and quantitative limits attached to allocations. The success with which PESC was developed into a control system at this time engendered an optimism falsified by the conditions of rapid expansion of public expenditure which took place in the next decade.

Most of the acute and difficult problems of planning and controlling public expenditure were already evident in the late 1960s as principle was gradually translated into practice, and practice constrained by the needs of political expediency, and the imperative of recurring economic and financial crisis. The Conservative 'dash for growth' and Labour national planning both inverted the Plowden principle that prospective resources should determine expenditure, while the continuation of stop-go policies made the stabilizing of expenditure decisions an unachievable objective. Technical difficulties in defining, measuring, and verifying public expenditure emerged early on, while the decision to opt for volume planning using a constant price basis was ultimately to damage the Treasury's credibility and all but destroy PESC.

In 1961 there were few critics; a decade on, none of any substance. Sir Samuel Goldman's valedictory judgement on his retirement from the Treasury in 1973 was that PESC was 'a fully functional apparatus for planning, programming and monitoring the public sector . . . The system had reached full maturity, and shown a capacity in determined hands to deal with widely-varying situations' (1973: 12). A year later Heclo and Wildavsky enthusiastically endorsed that verdict. PESC was 'the most important innovation in its field in any western nation' (Heclo and Wildavsky 1974: p. xvii). Their discussion focused on how a good system could be improved by providing for more policy analysis at the centre of British Government; Clarke's bold scheme for the integration of PAR with PESC was the subject of a well-received Civil Service College lecture (Clarke 1971); the Select Committee on Expenditure urged the Treasury to broaden its input-budgeting system to take more account of outputs; while the Treasury itself initiated studies of output budgeting, and toyed with concepts of PPBS.

The gradualism which had marked the development of PESC thus far and seemed set to continue was brought to an abrupt halt in the mid-1970s. The need to cut expenditure and restore control coincided with the crumbling of Keynesian consensus. The overriding concern since the failure to cut public expenditure in the early years of the Thatcher Government was to design and maintain a system which provided for the tight control of monetary aggregates while bearing down simul-taneously on costs. The planning imperative which drove the Survey in its early years, and which survived the importation of cash limits, has all but disappeared. The Treasury's brief and (with hindsight) disastrous flirtation with planning volumes of public expenditure was abandoned with the prescription of cash planning in 1982. The planning phase of PESC was over; henceforward monitoring and cash control were to be the dominant and dominating characteristics, as the Treasury rededicated itself to its historic mission.

4

The Treasury and FMI

The planning and control of expenditure through the 1980s and 1990s
has been conducted within the context of major changes in the size,
structure, and organization of the Civil Service, in major services such as
health and education, and in the relationships between central and local
government. The thrust of these reforms is consistent with a wider
international trend of 'new public management' (Hood 1991), all the
elements of which are recognizable in the UK context from, at least,
1979 onwards: 'hands-on professional management' in the public sector;
explicit standards and measures of performance, such as the definition
of objectives and targets, and indicators of success, expressed quantitatively; emphasis on output controls; disaggregated units in the public
sector, for example cost and responsibility centres; greater competition
in the public sector; movement away from a public service ethic, with
greater emphasis on private sector styles of management practice;
greater discipline and parsimony in resource use. All of these were
designed to achieve better value-for-money in the provision of public
services by a greater concern with economy, efficiency, effectiveness,
and enterprise.

The intellectual origins of the ideas which informed the new public
management in the UK in the 1980s derived from the Conservative
Party's acceptance the previous decade, under its new leader, of the
critique of the performance of the public sector by a spectrum of new
right theorists who challenged the prevailing orthodoxies of welfare,
planning, Keynesian demand management, producer-dominance, and
offered an alternative menu of neo-liberal prescriptions based upon
market principles of competition, consumer-choice, quality, and price.
A programme to reduce the size and scope of the public sector and to
make the remaining services more efficient and effective by the importation of private sector practices and managerial techniques was an
important part of the Conservative Party's manifesto at the 1979 general
election. The translation of that programme in the next decade into a
series of pragmatic initiatives has been described adequately elsewhere.
Briefly, the Civil Service was reduced in size, and its organization transformed by a series of measures designed to introduce more flexibility

into pay, recruitment, tenure, career structure, conditions of work, and industrial relations (Dunsire and Hood 1989; Fry 1984, 1988). Secondly, large parts of the public sector were privatized by, *inter alia*, the sale of assets, contracting out services to the private sector, and charging for common services provided within the public sector on a consumer–contractor basis (see Marsh 1991). Thirdly, the elimination of waste and the achievement of greater efficiency in the provision of many services provided by Whitehall spending departments provided a focus for the work of the Efficiency Unit set up in 1979, and the conduct of efficiency scrutinies throughout Whitehall departments (Metcalfe and Richards 1987, 1990).

All three elements have profoundly influenced the context within which the Whitehall spending departments plan, allocate, manage, and control their resources. More significant still was the Financial Management Initiative launched in 1982, and the implementation of 'Next Steps' which led to the creation of Executive Agencies. The implementation of both has had, and will continue to have, profound effects upon the relations between the Treasury and the spending departments, and is the issue which runs through all the remaining chapters of this book: central control and departmental autonomy. This chapter looks at the involvement of the Treasury and other central departments in the design and implementation of FMI leading up to 'Next Steps', which is the subject of Chapter 5.

THE ORIGINS OF FMI

While the origins of the Efficiency Strategy can be traced back to the Fulton Report, to PAR, and other attempts in the early 1970s to introduce accountable management into Whitehall departments, the appointment in 1979 of Sir Derek Rayner as Mrs Thatcher's personal adviser on efficiency in the Civil Service marked the beginning of the contemporary concern with efficiency and effectiveness in the Civil Service. His small Efficiency Unit was located in the Prime Minister's Office, to ensure both physical and intellectual independence of the two central departments, the Treasury and the (then) Civil Service Department (CSD), and to indicate her personal support. It reflected the importance she attached to making the Civil Service more efficient, and her belief that this could be achieved only through the stimulus of a successful businessman from the private sector. She distrusted the Civil Service to achieve this unprompted.

The main thrust of the Efficiency Strategy under Rayner was the design and conduct of one-off efficiency scrutinies and multi-departmental reviews aimed to secure cost savings through a programme of *ad hoc* reviews of various departmental activities. The two central departments and the Efficiency Unit were necessarily brought together; Rayner's Chief of Staff was brought in from the CSD. That department was closely involved in the scrutiny programme from the start.

The position of the CSD was nevertheless anomalous: it had been set up after acceptance of the Fulton Report, with responsibility for improving efficiency through better management, and for pay, personnel, and industrial relations in the Civil Service. Its record throughout the 1970s was modest. It suffered from an 'unresolved identity crisis'; lacked the authority and political clout of the Treasury; and its progress in reforming the Civil Service had been 'too slow and the impetus insufficiently sustained' (Wilding 1982). Its future under a Thatcher Government with the Efficiency Unit up and running was always precarious. In January 1981 the Prime Minister decided against abolition, although the reprieve was to prove short-lived. Its reprieve was part of a reappraisal of the role and responsibility of the central departments for promoting efficiency and effectiveness throughout the Civil Service. This took place in the winter of 1980–1 against a backdrop of unplanned rising public expenditure.

The failure to achieve the cuts in public expenditure planned in the 1980 White Paper, crucial to the Government's macro-economic strategy, triggered a reappraisal of the role of the central departments *vis-à-vis* the spending departments, which was to lead directly to the launch of FMI in 1982. While the latter's origins are partly to be explained as an evolution of the Efficiency Strategy there was also the urgent need to control public expenditure more efficiently and effectively in the future. Volume planning in PESC was abandoned in March 1981, and cash planning introduced the following year.

Moving to cash planning required better information for all three years of the Survey about the costs of both programme and administrative expenditure than most departments could generate from their financial management systems at that time. Progress through various CSD initiatives to introduce and improve management accounting had been slow and patchy. The Treasury was concerned not only at the inadequacy of departmental systems, but that in devising and operating them departments had been too independent of the centre. The Treasury Second Permanent Secretary (Public Expenditure) admitted to the PAC in June 1981 that 'the pendulum has swung a very long way in recent years and I think the view is taken that the time has come for the Treasury and CSD to adopt a somewhat more prescriptive role than in recent years' (PAC 1981: qu. 2700).

This more prescriptive role was foreshadowed in the Prime Minister's reprieve of the CSD in January 1981, announced in a White Paper, *The Future of the Civil Service Department* (Cmnd. 8170), which contained in essence all the ideas which were to be incorporated into the FMI. The spending departments were given formal notice of the Treasury and CSD's intentions in May 1981 in a joint memo: *Control of Expenditure: Departmental Responsibilities* (Treasury and CSD 1981). This set out the responsibility of the two central departments in their respective fields for 'defining the essential elements of an adequate system to monitor and control the use of resources allocated to departments'. It was the duty of the Treasury and the CSD 'to verify that such systems are in operation both within the central departments and within spending departments' (para. 10). It included 'prescribing the basic elements of departmental systems which are needed to provide (*a*) reliable and compatible information for the purpose of central co-ordination and control; (*b*) where central prescription is needed, satisfactory arrangements for monitoring and control within the departments' (para. 11). Moreover, the two central departments could set standards of adequacy for such systems, check that they were working reliably, and generally ensure that departments had effective and adequate arrangements to promote efficiency. The Head of the Home Civil Service emphasized that both departments had adequate existing powers to take on these tasks, and that the initiative would take place within the existing framework of responsibilities (Bancroft 1981). Nevertheless to forestall, or possibly meet, criticism from the departments that the central departments lacked authority to determine their individual financial systems, the Treasury and the CSD deemed it prudent to circulate, a month after their joint memorandum on central control, memoranda summarizing the roles and responsibilities of departmental Principal Finance Officers and Principal Establishments Officers (Treasury 1981*d*; CSD 1981). In both it was emphasized that those responsibilities could be carried out only by close co-operation with the Treasury and the CSD. Attention was drawn to the need to provide the central departments with 'information they need for their tasks of allocating and control'. This meant, among other things, 'ensuring compliance with standards and methods of financial administration prescribed by the Treasury'.

The ground was now prepared for the more interventionist role that the two central departments proposed to play. The strategy was announced in a White Paper the following month, July 1981: *Efficiency in the Civil Service* (Cmnd. 8293). This was partly a progress report on achievements to date, and a summary of the new initiatives begun by the Government. Reiterating that the 'central departments must see that each department has a proper system for controlling resources and promoting efficiency, and that they are working well', the White Paper signalled two other new key initiatives which were to be incorporated subsequently into FMI: top management information systems and de-centralized departmental budgeting with more responsibility for line managers.

By now the Treasury and Civil Service Committee's (1982*a*) inquiry into *Efficiency and Effectiveness in the Civil Service* had begun to take evidence and examine witnesses. Sir Ian Bancroft, Permanent Secretary at the CSD and Head of the Home Civil Service, gave oral evidence in July 1981, and submitted a detailed memorandum in October reporting progress and outlining future developments (Bancroft 1981). The inten-tion was partly to demonstrate publicly (and no doubt to the Prime Minister) that the CSD was playing its new interventionist role in pro-moting efficiency and effectiveness vigorously and to good effect. The greater emphasis on the prescriptive role of the central departments was repeated; a start had been made, mainly by the Treasury, to measure the effectiveness of expenditure programmes—the third element of FMI was to be the concern with performance indicators; and, most signifi-cantly, it was 'one of the Government's major aims to strengthen financial management across the Service as a whole . . . The Treasury is in the lead here'. The work was directed and co-ordinated within the Treasury by a new Financial Management Co-ordinating Group (FMCG), with representatives from the Efficiency Unit, the CSD, and the Government Accountancy Service.

The work of the FMCG led directly to the FMI. In 1981 it was concerned with the more effective planning and control of the cash cost of public expenditure programmes; the better matching of financial information needed for PES and Estimates with that needed for management; and the strengthening of internal audit. Work was also being carried out on departmental running costs, integrated with other work on management information systems, in order to improve the breakdown of departmental costs and to associate it with measures of output.

The significance of the FMCG's concern with running costs is that controlling and cash-limiting them required better departmental man-agement information systems and, crucially, decentralized budgeting, with line managers responsible and accountable for the costs they in-curred. The Treasury's aim to get better control of administrative expenditure thus reinforced the pressures for improved management systems. An exercise to identify and measure departmental running costs in 1980, and the Joubert Study (1981) of running costs control in the D.o.E., had revealed deficiencies in departmental management systems. To isolate and control running costs it was necessary to set up local cost centres within departments, and to give their managers budgets to cover both staff and non-staff costs. This represented a major change from the centralized control of administrative expenditure found throughout the Service. The message was clear: if the Treasury wished to obtain better control of running costs, and the benefits of the anticipated savings, it would have to encourage departments to decentralize budgetary authority.

The capacity of the Treasury to play a more positive role in promoting efficiency and effectiveness was enhanced by the Prime Minister's decision to abolish the CSD in 1981 and distribute its functions between it and the newly created Management and Personnel Office (MPO) brought into the Cabinet Office. The MPO inherited the CSD's general responsibility for the promotion of efficiency and effectiveness in the Civil Service, and was given its personnel and industrial-relations functions as well. The Treasury, with its control of pay and manpower restored, could now more easily devise and implement strategies for manpower planning and for controlling the costs of both staff and non-staff administrative expenditure. Nevertheless, the responsibility for promoting efficiency and effectiveness was formally shared with the MPO.

The work begun by the FMCG on financial management systems, running costs, and decentralized budgeting continued throughout 1981. Major reviews of financial management were undertaken in MAFF, D.o.I., and M.o.D., and studies were made of a budgeting system for controlling running costs in the Social Security Offices of DHSS, extended in 1982 to six other major spending departments. These and other feasibility and pilot studies designed to test the basic ideas formulated earlier were encouraging enough for the Treasury to announce to departments in May 1982 that 'the time had come for a general and coordinated drive to improve financial management in government departments' (Treasury and MPO 1982: para. 1). Nineteen major spending departments (together with twelve subsidiary agencies and commissions) were invited to work up programmes of action building on the feasibility and pilot studies, and to discuss them with the Treasury and the MPO. All the essential ingredients of the FMI contained in the White Paper *Efficiency and Effectiveness in the Civil Service* (Cmnd. 8616), which followed in September 1982, are to be found here.

THE AIMS OF FMI

The aims, objectives, and principles of FMI have been exhaustively discussed elsewhere (for details see Metcalfe and Richards 1987 and 1990; Gray and Jenkins 1991). Two aspects call for comment here. First, the emphasis on prescription signalled by the Treasury and the CSD in earlier statements, and endorsed in the Select Committee's report, is absent from the White Paper. It was now for each department to work out its own best pattern of managerial responsibility, financial accounting, and control, bearing in mind the general principles which should inform all departmental systems. The earlier threat of prescription was perhaps a response to pressure from the PAC, rather than a warning to departments to take the ideas of financial management seriously, or risk imposition from the centre. General prescription or 'systematization' was ruled out early on. Lessons of the past, from the USA with PPBS and in the UK with PAR in the early 1970s, had demonstrated that universal systems imposed centrally from above fail. The Treasury and the CSD preferred a pragmatic approach, 'rooted firmly in the needs of the job and those who manage it on the ground'. Secondly, central departments had learnt from experience that those systems and procedures worked best which had the full support of the staff required to use them. Thirdly, the wide range and diversity of government business meant that systems had to reflect the needs of the different scale, volume, and type of business of diverse departments, agencies, and Non-Departmental Public Bodies (NDPBs).

These three precepts subsequently guided the implementation of FMI down to the launch of Next Steps. However, the emphasis on continuity and a pragmatic approach meant that the speed of that process in the next few years would inevitably be represented by the 'management reformers' as foot-dragging by an unenthusiastic Treasury. We return to this and other criticisms of FMI later on.

The second comment on the launch of FMI is that there was no reference to the need for increased delegation of financial control from the Treasury, the logical corollary of financial management systems providing for the delegation of budgetary responsibility and control within departments to line managers. This was to resurface later in the Ibbs Reports, both the unpublished and published Next Steps versions, and to force the Treasury to confront head-on the dilemma of reconciling effective central financial control with decentralized managerial autonomy. This and other issues raised in the reports are discussed in the next chapter.

By the time of the first progress report on the preparation of departmental plans and action programmes in September 1983 (Cmnd. 9058), there was an expectation that the dialogue between the Treasury and the spending departments in the annual PES round, and at the time of the submission of new expenditure proposals, would be 'much more fruitful by the improved information which the new departmental systems produce'. It was anticipated that both the Treasury and the MPO would be able to reduce the need for prior consultation over many more minor matters. With this in mind these central departments were reviewing the existing rules and limits of delegated authority. As departmental systems developed, this process was expected to continue, but 'subject to the maintenance where necessary of common rules and standards across the Civil Service' (para. 46). The implication was clearly spelt out: both central departments would be more concerned with the assessment of the effectiveness of departmental systems and their capacity to generate accurate information than with the detailed casework on minor matters. This appeared at the time to signal the prospect of a major shift in the traditional control conducted by the Treasury's Expenditure Divisions, and in the attitudes, skills, experience, and training of Expenditure Controllers. Indeed, in 1981 the Treasury had begun a review of how these staff 'should be equipped for this role in promoting effective systems of financial management' (Bancroft 1981: para. 52).

Following the launch of the FMI, a small central Financial Management Unit was set up jointly by the Treasury and the MPO to help departments to prepare plans for the introduction of new financial management systems (see Russell 1984). It took over the work of the Treasury's FMCG. The Unit provided general guidance for departments, helped individual departments with implementation, and focused attention on the development of top management information systems, delegated budgeting, and the management of programme expenditure. Work on the latter focused attention on the relations between departments and the NDPBs through which many of their programmes were delivered. This was to become a major theme of the Next Steps initiative.

In 1985 the FMU was replaced by a Joint Management Unit, smaller in size, and more closely linked with the operational Expenditure Divisions in the Treasury and the management and efficiency divisions in the MPO. This reflected the increasing integration of the developing departmental systems and the information they generated with the central departments' control systems, most importantly the negotiations in the PES process.

As public expenditure continued to rise in real terms in both 1981–2 and 1982–3, pressure on the Treasury to bring it under control and to achieve the expenditure objective set by Government continued undiminished. Its determination to do so was evident both in stern injunctions to spending departments and in the process of implementing FMI. The message of the Government's *The Next Ten Years: Public Expenditure and Taxation into the 1990s* (Cmnd. 9189), published in July 1984, that firm control of public expenditure was an essential condition of reducing the burden of taxation to tolerable levels, was repeated in the report on the progress on FMI published by the Treasury and CSD in September 1984 (Cmnd. 9297). The tenor of this report contrasts sharply with that of earlier public statements. There is little about efficiency and effectiveness. There is a heavy and undisguised emphasis on the need to control spending through PES, complemented and linked to the developing financial management systems in the spending departments. FMI was unambiguously about allocation and the management and control of resources. Obtaining value-for-money was dependent on the quality of financial management within departments, and required a greater sense of cost-consciousness in managers.

Progress on the implementation of FMI varied across Whitehall, but by the end of 1984 most spending departments had set up top management information systems, and were in the process of computerizing and decentralizing their financial budgeting and control systems. The Financial Management Unit reported and circulated material on its work with individual departments, and advised on 'best practice' (see FMU 1985a, 1985b, 1985c). For example, the DTI established its Activity and Resource Management System (ARM) in 1983 to provide information for top management to decide manpower allocations and PES bids, and to consider the objectives and targets for Policy Divisions prior to submission to ministers. In the next two years it was progressively developed, and integrated with the PES bidding procedures. Local cost centres were set up in some of the research establishments and out-stations, and responsibility centres in some headquarters policy divisions.

In parallel with work on FMI, the MPO reviewed personnel work in departments with a view to giving line managers more responsibility; the Efficiency Unit continued, with the support of MPO, to conduct departmental and, increasingly, multi-departmental scrutinies; and work continued on running costs. It was clear that decentralized budgetary control within departments would enable departments to plan, allocate, and monitor their running costs, and, crucially for the Treasury, to obtain a tighter grip on them. By May 1985 the Treasury was confident enough to launch the new running costs regime, discussed in Chapter 18.

Much slower progress was made with the application of the FMI principles to programme expenditure, estimated in 1986 to be about 87 per cent of central government expenditure. Work had begun on this in FMU. Initially, most top management systems concentrated on reviewing administrative activities and costs, as part of the Treasury/FMU strategy to get better control of running costs expenditure, and ultimately to cash-limit them. Prompted by the Treasury through FMU, from about 1984 departments began to use their systems to review their performance in policy areas and programmes, and to relate the information and analysis generated to their administrative expenditure. At the same time, departments were beginning to use the increasing flow of information on programme performance in their internal preparations for bidding in the PES round (FMU 1985*a*).

Nevertheless there was concern in the Treasury and MPO that the implementation of FMI was proceeding slowly and unevenly among departments. In a review of budgeting in spending departments in 1985, top managers were 'still insufficiently involved in the budgetary process', and failed to integrate their dual functions of both deciding policy and considering the resource implications of those decisions. Complaints about central controls directed at the Treasury were often the result of the reluctance of Finance and Establishments Divisions to come to terms with the changes in their traditional role required by the delegation of budget control to line managers (Treasury 1986*b*).

The slow progress in implementing FMI attracted criticism from outside, and concern within the Efficiency Unit that, steered by the Treasury, it was aimed more at securing tighter central control of expenditure through PES than achieving 'cultural change' through the promotion of efficiency and effectiveness broadly defined. The National Audit Office reported that 'real progress had been made in the development of suitable systems' (1986: 11), but had found anxiety among middle and junior managers to control the costs for which they were held responsible in their budgets. The large and constitutional issue implied here was the extent to which greater personal responsibility for line managers was compatible with the maintenance of traditional ministerial accountability, an issue taken up in Next Steps. The NAO report was also critical of the slow progress on the application of FMI to programme expenditures. Reviewing this evidence and its own inquiries on FMI, the PAC concluded that progress to 1987 had been slow in some departments, and emphasized the importance of maintaining 'the momentum of the major shift in management attitudes represented by the initiative' (1988).

FRUSTRATIONS AND TENSIONS AT THE CENTRE

The division of responsibility between the two central departments, and between them and the Prime Minister's Efficiency Unit, was becoming increasingly a source of frustration among the 'management reformers' of the latter, and of tension in the relations between all three. While the FMU provided an organizational mechanism for bringing the staff of each together, nevertheless their different aims, methods, and ministerial support made it difficult to discern a clear and coherent strategy at the centre. The aim of the Efficiency Unit under both Rayner and his successor, Sir Robin Ibbs, encouraged by the Prime Minister, was to create the conditions in Whitehall for 'cultural change' in which civil servants would become increasingly committed to management, value-for-money, and results. While the main instrument of the efficiency strategy was departmental scrutinies, the long-term objective was to try to change the attitudes of civil servants—in short, to make them behave more like private sector managers. This task was part of the *Unfinished Agenda* which Rayner proclaimed in his valedictory memorial lecture (Rayner 1984). The staff of the Efficiency Unit were committed to an ideology of management reform. The approach of the Treasury and MPO was pragmatic, grounded in the design and implementation of practical measures to achieve changes in budgetary systems. The strategies were sharply different. Where the Treasury was mainly concerned through FMI with achieving value-for-money, tighter control of public expenditure, and cost savings through the more efficient management of resources, the Efficiency Unit saw FMI as only one element of a grander strategy to promote effective as well as efficient government. The strength of the Efficiency Unit was that it had the support and enthusiastic backing of the Prime Minister; its weakness, that it lacked organizational power, such as that possessed by the Treasury through its constitutional responsibility for expenditure. That weakness had become apparent early on in the initiation, conduct, and, crucially, implementation of departmental scrutinies, where it had to rely on the active co-operation of the departments.

MPO's position was unenviable. It had neither the Treasury's power, nor the Prime Minister's enthusiastic support. It had general responsibility for the promotion of efficiency and effectiveness throughout the Service, but was denied even the limited leverage of pay and manpower controls possessed earlier by the CSD but ceded to the Treasury. Besides its work jointly with the Treasury on FMU/JMU, the MPO continued the work begun by the CSD on improving personnel management procedures, and introducing greater flexibility into conditions of work and pay (Treasury 1987*b*).

The tension underlying the conflicting aims and intentions of the Treasury, the MPO, and the Efficiency Unit erupted in a fierce debate and struggle to dictate and control the course of the managerial changes into the 1990s. Two internal documents provided the focus: 'The Better Management of Government' and 'Next Steps'. The origins, substance, and implementation of the latter are discussed in the next chapter. The former document, written by Sir Kenneth Stowe, formerly Permanent Secretary at the DHSS, was the result of an invitation by the Prime Minister and the Secretary to the Cabinet to inquire into the distribution of the central management functions (see Hennessy 1989). The outcome of the discussion of his report in the autumn of 1987 was the winding-up of the MPO and the transfer of its management responsibilities to the Treasury. The Treasury's position was now considerably strengthened. More radically and controversially, Stowe had proposed a Management Board for the Civil Service, exercising the central oversight and supervision shared between the Treasury and the Cabinet Office, but this was unacceptable to both the Treasury and No. 10.

CONCLUSIONS

The benefits to the Treasury of FMI have in the event proved double-edged. Its aim to improve departmental financial management to generate greater efficiency through cost savings and productivity gains, and better information to enable it to control the allocation and use of resources, has been partly achieved by the successful introduction of running costs control, and by obliging departments to produce annual efficiency gains of at least 1.5 per cent of them. However, the application of FMI to programme expenditure (87 per cent of the total of central government expenditure) has proved more difficult. The extent to which the quality and quantity of management data thrown up by the new systems have provided the Treasury with the means to control departmental expenditure more tightly is a broader issue taken up in other chapters.

The disadvantage of FMI for the Treasury was the expectation that it nourished in departments that it would give them more freedom. While the Treasury conceded that arrangements for delegated authority would be revised, and allowed the possibility that controls would be operated more flexibly in certain circumstances and subject to general rules, it is unlikely that without the Ibbs Report those expectations would have been fulfilled so quickly. FMI always carried within the concepts of decentralization the risk that more would be demanded than the Treasury thought it prudent to allow, consistent with its prime aim to maintain a tight control of the Planning Total.

The benefits to departments are both short- and longer-term. In the short term, the implementation of FMI has resulted in greater cost-consciousness at all levels of management, and significant cost savings in particular activities and services. With experience, top management systems have become integrated into departmental processes for setting objectives, deciding priorities, allocating resources, and controlling their use by line managers. FMI has provided the opportunity for more rational financial management. Arising from the development of management systems, departments can now generate more and improved financial information to support and strengthen claims for additional resources in the PES round. In the longer term, departments hoped to benefit still more from greater freedom from Treasury control, as decentralized budgeting gave their Executive Agencies and NDPBs more financial and managerial autonomy.

Changes in managerial structures, processes, and attitudes which have resulted from the implementation of FMI have contributed to greater cost-consciousness among financial managers and the pursuit of better value-for-money, and interacted with changes in the budgetary processes for allocating, managing, and controlling resources at the centre. Within spending departments the processes for bidding for resources have become integrated with developed top management systems and decentralized budgetary control systems, examined in later chapters.

FMI was intended less to promote the radical management change thought necessary by the Efficiency Unit and some others in the Government, and many outside Whitehall; rather it was designed for the more limited objective of promoting changes in departmental financial management systems to achieve better value-for-money, to improve financial discipline, and to enhance the Treasury's capacity to control expenditure.

While the FMI came to symbolize 'management change' in the period up to Next Steps, in practice this was a mistaken attribution. Criticism that FMI failed to deliver the radical 'holistic' management reforms desired by the ideologues and zealots of the 'new right' at the Efficiency Unit and elsewhere is misconceived; it was not designed to do so. The

Treasury's aim was always a limited *financial* management revolution, designed to enhance the capacity of departmental systems to improve financial discipline and control and to deliver better information, to enable the Treasury to control public expenditure more efficiently and more effectively, if at greater distance, through increased delegated authority and managerial flexibility.

5

The Advent and Impact of 'Next Steps'

The Next Steps initiative unveiled by Prime Minister Thatcher in 1988 is potentially one of the most far-reaching reforms of the Civil Service in the twentieth century. The creation of ninety separate Executive Agencies, employing nearly 350,000 people (June 1993), responsible to Ministers for the carrying out of policy, will transform the public expenditure planning and control system within departments as well as more widely in Whitehall as a whole. It will change relationships between the Treasury and the departments.

The Next Steps initiative is about improving the efficiency and the quality of service delivered by public agencies. For the most part Executive Agencies are not responsible for deciding what those services should be. For example, the Vehicle Inspectorate tests vehicles, but has only an advisory function on what the structure and tolerance limits of those tests should be. The wider objectives of appraising and analysing transport policy, road safety, and the links between vehicle testing, driver licensing, vehicle registration, motorway design, all continue to remain with the centre of the Department of Transport. Similarly, although the Benefits Agency costs nearly £2 billion to run and distributes more than £60 billion in benefits, the responsibility for deciding on the structure and levels of benefits, for appraising and evaluating how far the agency meets its objectives, and deciding, by regulation, the circumstances and conditions under which payments can be made remains the responsibility of the DSS. The agency is one adviser among many. From the point of view of the Treasury, in expenditure terms, the biggest tasks of management and control lie in the programmes themselves—social security, defence, health, education—not the delivery of those services through Next Steps Agencies.

Next Steps raises many fundamental constitutional issues (see RIPA 1991; Davies and Willman 1991), for example about the size, structure, and conditions of the Civil Service, and the doctrine of ministerial accountability to Parliament. This chapter is concerned less with such matters, more with the way in which the initiative created and continues to create a series of important administrative and financial issues to be faced by departmental Finance Divisions and the Treasury's central and

Expenditure Divisions. Our interest is with the potential impact of the reform on the Treasury's control of expenditure; with changes in Treasury rules on the amount of freedom and flexibility in the operation of public spending control given to agencies and departments; and, with the consequences for the slimmed-down core of spending departments. We begin with a discussion of the initiation, formulation, and implementation of Next Steps, as both the principle and practice of the initiative have progressively evolved.

BACKGROUND AND FORMULATION

As we discussed in the previous chapter, the FMI was seen by the Treasury, at least in part, as a means of containing the pressures on public expenditure by creating financial management systems in Whitehall departments conducive to efficiency and cost-cutting. The Treasury always saw Next Steps as a development of FMI.

A number of other important efficiency reports and measures followed in the train of FMI and the Rayner scrutinies. The first of these was the interdepartmental review of purchasing initiated in 1983, which recommended the setting up of a Central Unit of Purchasing within the Treasury and the development of a purchasing/procurement specialism within departments supported by procurement units. The second was the *Multi-Departmental Review of Budgeting* (Treasury 1986*b*, 1986*c*) which carried on the debate about the need for further delegation of responsibility from the Treasury to the departments and within departments. Indeed, the review which led to Next Steps mentioned specifically that the Prime Minister's Efficiency Unit had closely monitored the progress made on the 'implementation of the Wilson report on budgeting' (Efficiency Unit 1988: 35).

All these initiatives worked within the grain of the aim of both the Treasury and Cabinet Office/Efficiency Unit to seek further improvement in the efficiency of the Civil Service. As discussed in Chapter 4, there was a divergence, however, between (Sir) Robin Ibbs, Head of the Prime Minister's Efficiency Unit, and the Treasury over the future direction of reform. The Efficiency Unit was concerned that the Civil Service reforms initiated after 1979 had ground to a halt, and more emphasis had been given to the inputs of the system (public spending) rather than the outputs (quality of management and service). Sir Robin Ibbs in particular was frustrated at the slowness of progress on reform, and wished to give the process more impetus (Flynn, Gray, and Jenkins 1990: 162). However, the Treasury and the Efficiency Unit shared a common concern, also addressed in the Multi-departmental Review on Budgeting, that the departments were not delegating enough down-the-line.

As a first step, the Efficiency Unit conducted an evaluation or stock-taking of how reform had progressed and what was needed in the future. It was backed by the Prime Minister, and did not formally involve the Treasury. The review began on 3 November 1986 and took the form of a ninety-day scrutiny, concluding on 20 March 1987. It had four specific tasks: to assess the progress of management reform in the Civil Service; to show which measures had led to successful changes in the culture of the service; to 'identify the institutional, administrative, political and attitudinal obstacles to better management and efficiency that still remain' (Efficiency Unit 1988: 33); and to make recommendations to the Prime Minister.

The result of the review (the so-called first Ibbs Report) was presented to the Prime Minister by Sir Robin Ibbs in May 1987, just before the general election. It was said to be more radical in tone than the final version of the report published in 1988. In its original form, it recommended the transformation not only of the Civil Service but also of many constitutional conventions as well. In essence Ibbs was recommending change affecting 95 per cent of the Civil Service and 'a change in the British constitution, by law if necessary, to squash the fiction that Ministers can be genuinely responsible for everything done by officials in their name' (Hennessy 1989: 620). The report was shelved by the Prime Minister for nearly a year. There were several reasons for this. The imminence of the election was the first factor. A report which stressed how much more reform was needed to produce effective management in the Civil Service would not have been consistent with what Conservative Ministers were saying on the hustings about their success in this area (Hennessy 1989). The second reason was that the implications of the review were potentially so radical that vested interests within Whitehall were affected, pre-eminently the Treasury with its legitimate concern to maintain control of public expenditure. It only reluctantly accepted the decision to go ahead with the Next Steps programme.

The debate in Whitehall

As the proposals were leaked and then circulated and discussed at the centre, a 'lively debate' ensued, according to Sir Robin Butler, Secretary to the Cabinet (Treasury and Civil Service Committee 1988c: qu. 256). At stake here was the Treasury's responsibility for controlling pay and expenditure, the source of its authority in Whitehall. Next Steps threatened its discretion in the exercise of that authority. Hence it was no surprise that 'a battle royal ensued in the autumn of 1987 which raged for several months' (Hennessy 1989: 618).

The Treasury was concerned that the design of the initiative should meet both the objectives of obtaining value-for-money *and* maintaining effective expenditure control. There was a risk that the changes to PES instituted since 1976 aimed at tight short-term control of public expenditure could be weakened by Next Steps. In the climate prevailing after 1979, with the introduction of the MTFS, this was seen as an issue with broader implications. Sir Robin Butler stressed that the 'Treasury were very anxious—and in my view quite rightly so—that this approach to delegation should not weaken the overall controls of public expenditure which are necessary for macro-economic purposes' (Treasury and Civil Service Committee 1988c: qu. 256). The common ground between the Cabinet Secretary and the Treasury was that the reforms needed to be tailored to get both proper control of expenditure and better value-for-money. Sir Peter Middleton, the Treasury's Permanent Secretary, stressed that 'the fact remains that controlling public expenditure is important. It is important in macro-economic policy terms, and also in micro-economic terms' (qu. 331). Specifically, there was concern over the inflationary (and public-spending) consequences should the Treasury lose 'control over the pay bill' if agencies were given greater flexibility (qu. 256). Middleton stressed that a system had to be established 'that makes sure we do not get huge leapfrogging pay claims elsewhere' (qu. 338). But he also argued that Next Steps carried the delegation and accountability developments in FMI a stage further (qu. 326) and the decentralization and devolution implied by the initiative was within the grain of Treasury aims and policy (qu. 327).

The Treasury consistently argued that it was in favour of 'the maximum possible degree of delegation that is consistent with those central controls which remain essential', provided that it was properly conceived and so long as the maximization of output did not prevail at the expense of control of costs in the new regime (Treasury 1988d: 68). Middleton dealt at some length with the issue:

I think that devolution can work in two ways. It can work to support Government policy, and it can work in the opposite direction. The real problem is that the vast majority of the expenditure we are talking about is not priced. If it is not priced, supply can always exceed demand as a general proposition. People can have high cost options rather than low cost options, and they can have more rather than less . . . So I think one has to take great care to ensure the energies one is releasing from this . . . move in the direction of Government policy, which is concerned both with outputs and inputs. (Treasury and Civil Service Committee 1988*c*: qu. 329)

In a memorandum, the Treasury emphasized that 'delegations appropriate to individual agencies will need to be considered on a case by case basis according to the needs of that agency in improving its efficiency, the rigour of the policy and resource framework in place and the adequacy of the necessary internal control systems' (Treasury 1988*d*: 68). This has remained, broadly, the Treasury's general position since 1988.

THE POLICY ANNOUNCEMENT

In the event, the Treasury's anxieties about the Next Steps initiative did not stop the Prime Minister approving the concept, and Cabinet formally ratified the policy. The Next Steps report of the Efficiency Unit was published on 18 February 1988.

The report concluded that the sheer size, diversity, traditional structure, monolithic nature, and rule-bound traditions of the Civil Service made it difficult to implement a rigorous policy of delegated budgeting. The approach adopted in FMI had resulted in a very slow pace of change. In addition, top civil servants were inexperienced in the necessary managerial skills required to implement change. The focus of the present system, it was asserted, was the provision of political support for Ministers, not the management of departments. Both Ministers and their senior officials were overloaded because of the increased 'diversity and complexity of work in many departments, together with the demands from Parliament, the media and the public for more information' (Efficiency Unit 1988: 4). What pressure there was for change came in the form of requests to departments to reduce the inputs into programmes, not to enhance the outputs or results achieved with those inputs. The review also concluded that there was no sustained external pressure in favour of improved managerial performance, apart from the 'useful but occasional rather than continuous pressures' exerted by the Prime Minister and her efficiency advisers. It was recognized that both the Treasury and NAO had begun to address the issue of value-for-money but that there was no sustained or systemic programme.

Following from these criticisms—very much in a historical progression from the Fulton Report in 1968—the report suggested three main priorities if management in government was to be improved:

First: The work of each department must be organised in a way which focuses on the job to be done; the systems and structures must enhance the effective delivery of policies and services. Second: The management of each department must ensure that their staff have the relevant experience and skills needed to do the tasks that are essential to effective government. Third: There must be real and sustained pressure on and within each department for continuous improvement in the value for money obtained in the delivery of policies and services. (Efficiency Unit 1988: 7)

A number of subsequent recommendations flowed from these three priorities, the most important of which was that agencies should be set up with executive functions, within a policy and resource framework constructed by the sponsoring department. The report was deliberately vague about what would constitute such an agency, other than that it should refer to 'any executive unit that delivers a service for government'. The choice of candidates for Executive Agency status was to be left to Ministers and senior officials, although it was noted that in some cases virtually a whole department might be suitable, or the range of functions might dictate the creation of a number of smaller units (p. 9). Later in the report it was noted that the relationship between a department and agency would vary with the type of service delivered. Some agencies might become candidates for privatization as a result of the initiative but 'any decision of this kind should be taken pragmatically— the test must always be adopting the structure which best fits the job to be done' (p. 10).

It followed from the recommendation to create separate agencies that there was a division of responsibilities between the various actors in the process. It was for Ministers and permanent departmental heads to provide agencies with objectives and priorities. This strategic role was seen as performed most effectively through the creation of a clear and 'well defined framework', within which the agency would be expected by the department to operate. It would prescribe ground-rules for policy, budget, and targets, and 'it must also specify how politically sensitive issues are to be dealt with and the extent of the delegated authority of management' (p. 9). Once this was in place, agency management should be left with as much freedom as possible to deliver the service. If the agencies were to be effective this should include freedom over recruitment, pay, and grading structure.

The report portended significant changes in constitutional practice. The Head of Agency was to be held personally responsible for the activities and performance of his or her agency, and would in due course assume the status of Accounting Officer responsible to the Public Accounts Committee. It was accepted that there would be a dual function:

the departmental head would be accountable for the framework set up by the department, and the Head of the Agency for performance within that framework. In practice, ministerial responsibility to Parliament would be fundamentally altered, and it was the view of the report's authors that 'if management in the Civil Service is truly to be improved this aspect cannot be ignored' (p. 10). There were two main reasons for that judgement. First, the agencies would not be given realistic frameworks within which to operate if the Minister was still operationally accountable for the detail of implementation; and second, if the constitutional position remained unaltered, there would be a danger that Heads of Agencies would not accept responsibility if there was a 'ready-made excuse' for regular ministerial intervention (Efficiency Unit 1988: 17). However, it is important to note that Chief Executives would remain personally accountable to Ministers for the performance and management of their agency and that Ministers would still remain constitutionally accountable to Parliament.

The key tasks of departments would be to clarify policy, set out resource constraints, but not to prescribe operational functions. In setting the broad parameters within which agencies were to operate, departments would vary the framework so that it was 'tailored to the job to be done' (p. 11). There was a need to improve the ability of the central core of departments to monitor the progress of agencies, which would require the prescription of effective indicators of performance. The report emphasized the significance and sensitivity of the framework documents required, the successful construction of which would require 'a balanced expertise in policy, the political environment and service delivery which too few civil servants possess at present' (p. 11). It was for this reason that senior departmental managers were urged to ensure that their staff were given the necessary training to undertake service-delivery functions. Since the central core of departments needed to change to be able to design frameworks, monitor performance, and evaluate results, it followed that senior departmental managers required the same sorts of flexibilities over staffing and structure which was recommended for the agencies. The report accepted that it was essential that the department handled the 'inevitable' political crises well in order to safeguard the agency and the confidence and morale of its staff.

The report did not absolve the central departments—the Treasury and the Cabinet Office—from the need for change: together their role was that of the leading manager of the major cultural changes implied by Next Steps. It was accepted that the detailed controls of the past would not be relinquished unless there was 'confidence in the new pattern'. The centre would not in future exert detailed control but have four limited, though crucial, roles: allocating resources, keeping pressure on departments and agencies for better value-for-money, maintaining an overview of changes in the Civil Service, and preserving the rules of propriety in the public service. The centre needed to be 'authoritative, demonstrably efficient and low cost, and a helpful resource to the departments, not a handicap' (Efficiency Unit 1988: 12).

In order to ensure that the initiative was given the necessary impetus, the last key recommendation of the report was that a full Permanent Secretary should be given the task of 'Project Manager', backed by the authority of the Prime Minister and the Head of the Civil Service. His task would be to plan and supervise the reform; report progress to the Prime Minister; ensure departments were given enough flexibility to handle their tasks; and help remove obstacles to change. The appointment of a senior experienced official was seen as crucial: 'the slow rate of progress on so many changes since 1979, even with ministerial support and an abundance of small units, is ample evidence of this' (p. 13).

The Prime Minister announced in a statement to the House of Commons on 18 February 1988 that the Government had accepted four of the recommendations of the Efficiency Unit that:

to the greatest extent practicable the executive functions of Government, as distinct from policy advice, should be carried out by units clearly designated within departments . . . Responsibility for the day-to-day operations of each agency should be delegated to a chief executive. He would be responsible for management within a framework of policy objectives and resources set by the responsible Minister, in consultation with the Treasury; it recommends, second, that the Government should commit themselves to a progressive programme for attaining this objective; third, that staff should be properly trained and prepared for management of the delivery of services whether within or outside central Government; and fourth, that a 'project manager' at a senior level should ensure that the programme of change takes place. (Parliamentary Debates, HC, 18 Feb. 1988, col. 1149)

Peter Kemp was appointed the first Project Manager on the same day, with the rank of Second Permanent Secretary in the Office of the Minister for the Civil Service (OMCS). Although Kemp was described as a 'Treasury-lifer', he began his career in the Department of Transport, before moving to the Treasury, where he was promoted in 1978 to Under Secretary in charge of Social Security. After service as head of the Treasury's Central Unit, he was promoted to Deputy Secretary in 1983 with responsibility for pay and allowances. In 1987 he became Deputy Secretary (Public Services). Kemp was controversially replaced as Project Manager by Richard Mottram in September 1992. Mottram moved to the post of Second Permanent Secretary in the newly created Office of Public Service and Science from a Deputy Secretary position in the M.o.D.

The Efficiency Unit in its report on Next Steps stressed the importance of the initiative being led from the centre. In doing so it was recognizing the need for regular injections of political and organizational support at a high level to enable any major change to be carried out. Peter Kemp stressed that this involved:

co-ordination, there is stimulation and there is going to be a great deal of pressure to be kept up. This is not because departments and Ministers are against any part of this, it is simply because the Civil Service is a very busy organisation and its day-to-day work tends to be important and the immediate often takes precedent over the longer term . . . So there will be a good deal of making a nuisance of myself and my team making a nuisance of ourselves with departments to make sure that they keep up what they are doing and that the enthusiasms . . . are actually translated into action. (Treasury and Civil Service Committee 1988c: qu. 71)

While enjoying the Prime Minister's support, he was nevertheless caught between the power and prejudices of Ministers and their departments and the cautious scepticism of the Treasury. In organizational terms his team had 'positional power but its resource base is small and its dominant style must be negotiation' (Flynn, Gray, and Jenkins 1990: 165). Kemp recognized that he had the advantage that he knew enough 'about the way the machine works and the Treasury to be able to understand their very, very reasonable concerns' and about Vote accounting and Public Expenditure White Papers (Treasury and Civil Service Committee 1988c: qu. 69).

The press conference given by the Minister for the Civil Service and the official Head of the Civil Service, Sir Robin Butler, after the Prime Minister's statement, made it clear that no major constitutional change in the role of Ministers or dilution of Treasury control over budgets, pay, or manpower was envisaged.

IMPLEMENTATION AND EVOLUTION OF NEXT STEPS, 1988–1993

In large part the Treasury's cautious, incremental approach to the initiative was reflected in the policy announcement and in the early implementation of Next Steps. Initially there was also reluctance on the part of departments; the Treasury and the Cabinet Office had great difficulty in getting some departments to nominate candidates for agency status.

The twelve[1] nominated initially were selected mainly because they already had a degree of distinctness from mainstream departmental business and therefore less day-to-day ministerial involvement; they already had a great deal of managerial independence and autonomy, or the potential for such independence (Goldsworthy 1991). Only one, the Employment Service, could be seen as representing a substantial and important tranche of service delivery. Agency status was to be granted only after detailed discussion and negotiation, and on a case-by-case basis. The key problem was (and remains) constructing a sensible and workable set of 'rules' with which to do it. Whilst rejecting the view that the Treasury had a veto, Sir Peter Middleton noted that it would be involved in formulating the criteria which candidates for agency status would be expected to meet, and in the 'formative stage' of negotiation. 'The resource framework then has to be agreed by the Departmental Minister, and the Department will put them to the Treasury for the approval of our Ministers' (Treasury and Civil Service Committee 1988c: qu. 334). His first concern was to see that the existing flexibilities were being used in full; thereafter the Treasury was willing to consider and discuss increasing them.

The initial target set by Peter Kemp, endorsed as 'very reasonable' by the Head of the Home Civil Service, was for 70–5 per cent of civil servants to be in agencies by the end of a ten-year period, that is by 1998 (Treasury and Civil Service Committee 1988c: qu. 255). The momentum has built up gradually. In 1988 and 1989 only nine agencies were launched, but by December 1992 this number had risen to seventy-seven, employing over 300,000 staff, or 50 per cent of total Civil Service manpower. By the end of 1992, a further twenty-nine agency candidates had been identified, employing 85,000 staff (69,000 civil servants). Once these candidates achieved agency status in 1993 and 1994, nearly two-thirds of civil servants would be employed by agencies (Cm. 2111).

The launching of the Employment Service Agency in 1990, and more critically the Social Security Benefits Agency in 1991, posed the first real challenge to Next Steps. Simply by virtue of its size (twice as big as any other agency, with 63,000 staff) and political sensitivity, the Benefits Agency 'will test the model to its utmost' (Metcalfe and Richards 1990: 232). Should it be successful in improving its service, it will bring sharply into focus the tension between the Treasury's predominant concern

---

[1] The candidates were the Employment Service, DVLA, Vehicle Inspectorate, HMSO, Non-Nuclear Research Establishments, Meteorological Office, Royal Parks, Historic Royal Palaces, Queen Elizabeth II Conference Centre, Resettlement Units, Passport Dept., and Companies House.

for the control of public expenditure and the Efficiency Unit's aim to improve output.

A potential candidate for agency status is first identified in discussions between the department, the Office of Public Service and Science (OPSS, formerly the OMCS), and Treasury, the alternatives of abolition, privatization, or contracting out having been considered and rejected. A proposal for agency status is then submitted for the approval of the departmental minister, and OPSS and Treasury ministers. In consultation with the OPSS and Treasury, the department then prepares the framework document covering the aims and objectives of the agency, its internal management systems, resources to be employed, performance measures, pay and expenditure regime, and the respective responsibilities of the Minister, core department, and Chief Executive. The Treasury must be satisfied that the core department has clearly analysed the tasks to be assigned to the agency, and whether they can be delegated. If extra flexibility or delegation is given it must be justified by expected increases in efficiency and effectiveness. The Treasury also needs assurance that the agency's financial management and budgetary system is robust and accords with best practice in the public sector. The appointment of a Chief Executive follows, normally after open competition. Together the department and agency then prepare corporate and business plans, and agree strategic targets with the Minister. The framework document is submitted for the approval of the departmental minister and then by him to OPSS and Treasury ministers. Notice is then given to Parliament of the launch date and targets.

The two critical stages are the acceptance of a unit as ready for agency status, and the work in preparing the framework document. There is a distinction between identifying a possible area of activity to be transferred to the agency model and the granting of agency status: 'identification as a candidate does not automatically imply that agency status will follow . . . Neither is it an indication of when, if granted, agency status might be achieved' (OMCS 1988: 3).

Performance targets are the other side of the coin to delegation. Managerial freedom can be given to Chief Executives but only if the Treasury has the confidence that the agencies can meet the so-called 'key performance targets' which are set externally. These targets normally cover financial performance, quality of service, and efficiency. The Treasury has devoted considerable resources to their development and provides a guide to setting targets and measuring performance for use in departments. The framework documents agreed between the departments, agencies, Treasury, and OPSS are an important vehicle for setting them, although the detail varies.

The prior-options exercise which forms part of the process of select-ing an agency candidate does not end after an agency is launched. As part of the drive by the Conservative Government of John Major to continue the privatization policy begun under Thatcher, agencies are periodically reviewed to see whether they should continue to be located in the public sector. Early candidates for privatization included the Driver Vehicle Operators Information Technology agency, the National Engineering Laboratory, the Vehicle Inspectorate, and Companies House (Cm. 2101).

CONCLUSIONS

FMI and Next Steps together provide an important context within which many of the debates about the Treasury's control of public ex-penditure have been conducted since the mid-1980s. As officials often noted to the Treasury and Civil Service Committee, Next Steps has merely brought into stark relief many of the unresolved issues in White-hall; the initiative did not create the tensions between the Treasury's macro-economic-driven objective of controlling expenditure and the departments' desire to have greater freedom to pursue their goals. As we shall see in later chapters, many of the issues raised by Next Steps run like a thread through other aspects of the operation of the planning and control system. Some, like the pressure for greater end-year flexibility and virement have been given greater salience by the exist-ence of agencies. We shall see also the divergence between Treasury rhetoric and practice: there is greater flexibility in the system of plan-ning and controlling expenditure than is at first apparent. In Chapter 24 we return to some of the broad issues raised by Next Steps, and show how the implementation of its principles has obliged the Treasury to concede greater flexibility still.

Next Steps tells us something too about the reality of Treasury power. It was not able to stop the initiative; but it was able to insert a degree of caution about the need to balance value-for-money with the need for the continued control of expenditure. The Treasury has had to co-operate with other actors in Whitehall; it has had to adjust policy in the light of pressure from the OPSS, Efficiency Unit, departments, and agencies. Yet there is also some evidence that once Next Steps was under way and the Treasury was satisfied about the policy rules, it took the initiative on many of the subsequent developments. But Next Steps also tells us something about the pressures under which core spending departments, and particularly their Finance Divisions, have to operate in the colder climate of the 1990s.

PART II

The Whitehall Expenditure Community

6

The Structure and Organization of the Treasury

The Treasury's wide range of economic and financial functions is relatively recent. Only since 1947 has it been formally responsible for the co-ordination of economic policy. Its main functions until then were the raising of revenue, largely through the subordinate departments of Inland Revenue and Customs, and controlling public expenditure. It had, however, in practice exercised a substantial and growing responsibility for the management of the Civil Service. Today its main function is 'to assist Ministers in the formulation and implementation of the Government's economic policy' (Cm. 2217). Its main responsibilities include advising Ministers on the formulation and implementation of the Government's economic, fiscal, and monetary policies; advice on economic developments and prospects in the UK and other major countries; planning and controlling public expenditure; the promotion of the UK's economic and financial interests in the European Community and the G7. Its other roles include the pursuit and encouragement of policies to improve the working of markets and the supply performance of the economy, and with other institutions the promotion of the stability, integrity, and efficiency of the financial system. With the reorganization of the central departments in 1987, the Office of Management and Personnel located in the Cabinet Office was abolished, and the Treasury resumed responsibility for Civil Service pay, personnel management, and industrial relations, and the promotion of greater efficiency and effectiveness in them.

The formal definition of the Treasury's role in planning and controlling public expenditure, set out in its annual *Department Report*, is

to plan and control public expenditure and the method by which it is funded to achieve outcomes in line with Government objectives; and to provide throughout the public sector (including the nationalised industries and local authorities) a framework for the management of public finances which enables the requirements of accountability and propriety to be met and pressures for improved value for money to be maintained. (Cm. 2217: 8)

In playing that role, the Treasury has four strategic objectives; first, the maintenance of an effective system of public expenditure planning to enable the Government to achieve its public spending objectives; secondly, the maintenance of effective control systems to ensure that spending ministers deliver and do not exceed the expenditure plans agreed upon. The third strategic objective is to co-operate with spending departments to improve financial management and obtain better value-for-money in the provision of public services; and the fourth, to help spending departments to ensure that the principles of account-ability, propriety, and regularity are observed in the management of their financial business.

Neither the role nor the strategic objectives are new. In practice, they are the formal articulation (in the language of the new managerialism) of the Treasury's unchanging responsibilities throughout the period 1976–93. Of course, the ways in which the Treasury has interpreted its role, and pursued its objectives, changed over time, and in later chapters we explain how it operated the PES system, and assess its effectiveness in achieving its strategic objectives.

In this chapter we describe the structure and organization of the department, focusing upon the Expenditure Divisions and those officials who serve in them or who have senior managerial responsibility for their work. We explain how Expenditure Controllers are recruited and deployed, and the skills and expertise which they acquire through work in the expenditure 'trenches'. Their effectiveness, and that of the Expenditure Divisions, is discussed in a more broadly based assess-ment of the efficacy of the Treasury's control in Chapter 25. In Chapter 7 we discuss the roles and responsibilities of Treasury ministers and senior officials in the formulation and co-ordination of expenditure policies.

MINISTERIAL RESPONSIBILITIES

The head of the Treasury is the Chancellor of the Exchequer. Consti-tutionally he is but one of a board of seven Lords Commissioners, of whom the First Lord is the Prime Minister; the board plays no part in the work of the department. The Chancellor is responsible to Parlia-ment for all Treasury business, as well as that of the Inland Revenue and Customs and Excise and several smaller departments. The five Junior Lords hold appointments as Assistant Whips, and play no part in the day-to-day work of the department. The junior Treasury Secretaries (Financial, Economic, and Parliamentary) formally rank as Secretaries

TABLE 6.1. *Treasury ministers, 1976–1993*

	First Lord (PM)	Chancellor of the Exchequer	Chief Secretary
Labour			
1974	Harold Wilson	Denis Healey	Joel Barnett
1976–9	James Callaghan		
Conservative			
1979	Margaret Thatcher	Sir Geoffrey Howe	John Biffen
1981			Leon Brittan
1983		Nigel Lawson	Peter Rees
1985			John MacGregor
1987			John Major
1989		John Major	Norman Lamont
1990	John Major	Norman Lamont	David Mellor
1992–Mar. 1993			Michael Portillo

to the Board. The Parliamentary Secretary, formerly the Patronage Secretary in the mid-nineteenth-century Treasury, is the Government's Chief Whip, and has no connection with departmental business. The Chief Secretary, who ranks second to the Chancellor, is not a member of the board. In recent years, there have been one or two additional ministers appointed to take responsibility for a part of Treasury business. Table 6.1 lists those who held the senior Treasury posts in the period 1976–93.

The allocation of ministerial responsibilities is decided by the Chancellor of the Exchequer. The Chief Secretary is second-in-command, and his main responsibility is the planning and controlling of public expenditure. The Financial Secretary has a general responsibility for the Treasury's Parliamentary business, although the Chief Secretary now takes charge of the Finance Bill, and prepares and presents the Estimates to Parliament. The Financial Secretary is normally responsible for all Inland Revenue taxes and duties, apart from the North Sea Fiscal Regime, and the general administration of that department. In recent years he has also been responsible for privatization and EC business.

The number and titles of other Treasury ministers vary with the needs of the department and the Prime Minister's allocation of posts to party supporters in both Houses. In the last twenty years there have been one or two ministers in addition to the Chancellor, Chief Secretary, and Financial Secretary. For some years under both Labour and Conservative Governments there were two Ministers of State, one for each

House, but no Economic Secretary. More recently the latter post has been filled, together with a fifth ministerial post—either the Paymaster General or a Minister of State.

In 1992 the Economic Secretary's main responsibilities were monetary policy and the financial system, including banks, building societies, and other financial institutions. He was also responsible for international financial issues and institutions, the North Sea Fiscal Regime, official statistics, and a number of departments which report to the Chancellor, such as the Department of National Savings, the Central Office of Information, the Registry of Friendly Societies, and the National Loans Office. In 1991, a fifth Treasury minister, a Minister of State, had responsibility for Customs and Excise duties and the general business of that department, in addition to that of Civil Service pay and management as noted earlier.

THE STAFFING AND ORGANIZATION OF THE CENTRAL TREASURY

The official Treasury comprises a central core of staff concerned with policy work, and until 1992 three largely executive businesses: the Civil Service Catering Organization, the Central Computer and Telecommunications Agency, and the Chessington Computer Centre. Before the transfer of the latter two to the Office of Public Service and Science in 1992, the total staff on the Treasury Vote in 1992 was 2,251 at a total (net) running cost of £75.6 million. By comparison, the other central policy department, the Cabinet Office, had a staff of 1,500 and annual expenditure of £87 million. There are other Whitehall departments comparable in size and cost, such as the Welsh Office, but the principal spending departments are very much larger: the DSS has a staff of 86,000 and costs £2.5 billion to run.

We are concerned here only with the 1,301 Treasury officials who comprise the central core, those employed in the Whitehall building bounded by Parliament Street and Great George Street to the east and overlooking Horse Guard Avenue and St James's Park to the west. Directly opposite Parliament Square, it is separated from Downing Street by King Charles Street and the Foreign Office. Using data supplied by HM Treasury, *Staff in Post* (1 Dec. 1991) we can see the distribution of the staff by Civil Service Group. Administrators and professionals (these are combined in Civil Service grades) totalled 877 and there were 52 junior professionals, who comprise mainly assistant statisticians and economists. If we exclude support services (178 staff) and messengerial services (194), we can identify 929 Treasury officials who contribute directly to policy work. More than a half rank as senior or middle managers. There are 34 senior managers (Under Secretary–Permanent Secretary) and 462 middle managers (HEO–Assistant Secretary), including four G4 posts and nine Administration Trainees. The senior Treasury official is the Permanent Secretary (G1), who is responsible for the co-ordination of the policy work and the management of the department. Beneath him, the work is divided into four operational sectors (see Fig. 6.1).

Finance and public expenditure are each headed by a Second Permanent Secretary (G1A); economic forecasting and analysis is the responsibility of the Chief Economic Adviser (G1A), who is also Head of the Government's Economic Service; and management and pay is headed by a Deputy Secretary (G2), who reports directly to the Permanent Secretary. A fifth sector comprises the Treasury's own establishment, finance, and information divisions. The posts of Principal Finance Officer and Principal Establishments Officer are combined in an Under Secretary appointment, reporting directly to the Permanent Secretary. Accounting advice in the Treasury is the responsibility of the Chief Accountancy Adviser, who is also Head of the Government Accounting Service. The line of responsibility here also runs direct to the Permanent Secretary.

The distribution of the central core staff among the sectors is as follows: First Permanent Secretary and Ministers' Support (80), Treasury Finance and Establishments (426.1), Economic Analysis and Forecasting (82.5), Finance (188), Expenditure (264), Management and Pay (222.1), and Accountancy Advice (38). This is a total of 1,300.7 staff. If the Treasury's expenditure function is defined broadly as all those who plan, manage, and control, or who provide advisory and specialist services, about a third of the central core staff are engaged on expenditure work. The distribution is: Expenditure (264.5), part of Management and Pay (64), part of Economic Analysis and Forecasting (31), and Accountancy Advice (38), giving a total of 397.5.

The public expenditure sector is the centre of the arrangements for the planning and control of public expenditure throughout the public sector. Headed by a Second Permanent Secretary, it is divided into Industry and Public Services, each commanded by a Deputy Secretary. Each of these is in turn subdivided into functional groups of Expenditure Divisions managed by Under Secretaries (G3); exceptionally, the Under Secretary in charge of the Defence divisions reports directly to the Second Permanent Secretary, as does the Under Secretary in charge of General Expenditure Policy (GEP). Each division is headed by an

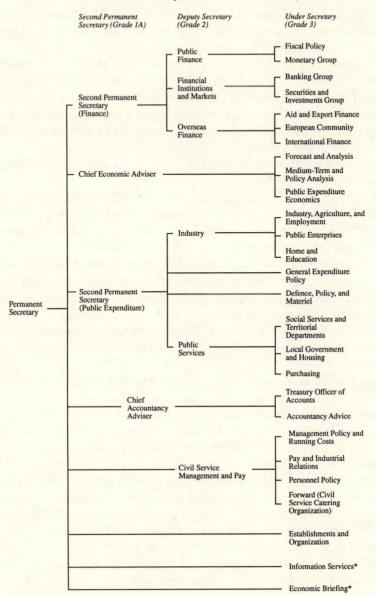

Fig. 6.1. Treasury operational sectors, 1992

* Assistant Secretary.

Source: Cm. 2217.

Assistant Secretary (G5), who is responsible for one or more sections headed normally by a Principal (G7) or somebody of equivalent rank. Outside the expenditure sector a few other divisions, under the command of the Second Secretary for Finance, have some expenditure functions.

In the management and pay sector, there are divisions dealing with financial management, running costs, pay, and pensions. Historically, the pay and management divisions have often been integrated with Supply in the Expenditure Divisions, but since their return in 1981 from the disbanded CSD have been functionally separated, reporting to their own Deputy Secretary. The running costs division is responsible for the general policy of the schemes introduced since 1986 to control manpower and administrative costs throughout the Service, and for market-testing. The financial management divisions are responsible generally for the introduction and implementation of FMI throughout the Service and for advising expenditure divisions on departmental management information systems, departmental management plans, the implementation of the review of departmental budgeting, policy evaluation, and Next Steps agencies.

Economic advice for the Expenditure Divisions is provided by one of the divisions commanded by the Deputy Chief Economic Adviser. Economists working on nationalized industries and on industry, agriculture, and employment are brigaded together. Issues of manpower planning and the provision of manpower data are also dealt with. Management accounting advice and expertise, and commercial and accounting advice, are available on a similar basis to each of the Expenditure Divisions from the Accountancy Advice Division, under the command of the Chief Accountancy Adviser. The Central Unit on Purchasing, under the command of the Deputy Secretary, Public Services, advises and helps departments to improve their purchasing practices, and monitors and reports on their achievements.

In the central divisions under the Second Permanent Secretary the General Expenditure Group (GEP) comprises three general co-ordinating divisions, responsible for the planning, monitoring, and control of aggregate public expenditure. The Under Secretary in charge reports directly to the Second Permanent Secretary. GEP also co-ordinates the maintenance and improvement of the Treasury's Financial Information System, which holds the data base for the whole of public expenditure. It is also responsible for the preparation and publication of the Autumn Statement (since November 1993, the spending side of the Unified Budget), the volumes of the departmental expenditure reports published in the spring, and for the preparation of annual and Supplementary Estimates to Parliament. One of its three divisions monitors expenditure against the annual planning totals in the Autumn Budget, and advises on the calculation of the Reserve and assesses departmental claims on it.

There are six groups of functional Expenditure Divisions organized on the 'port-hole' principle, in which each spending department is provided with a single point of entry to the Treasury. This structure is essentially that which emerged from the last major review in 1975 (discussed in Chapter 25). Since then only minor changes have been made, the most important of which occurred in August 1982. As a result of the integration of expenditure and manpower control, the Treasury's Expenditure Divisions were reorganized to ensure that responsibility for manpower control was given to that Expenditure Division which had responsibility for the rest of a department's expenditure. This resulted in the creation of a Territorial Division, which joined the Social Services Division to create the Social Services and Territorial Group. The Territorial Division took over the previous responsibilities of the Local Government Division in respect of Northern Ireland, Scotland, and Wales, and was additionally given the responsibility for manpower control and financial management in the three territorial departments. The Expenditure Groups (in 1993) were:

Industry, Agriculture, and Employment;
Public Enterprise;
Home, Transport, and Education;
Defence Policy, Manpower, and Materiel;
Social Services and Territorial;
Local Government.

Each group is subdivided functionally into two or three Expenditure Divisions, fourteen in all. Four other divisions have expenditure responsibilities, but are located elsewhere in the Treasury, in the command of the Second Permanent Secretary, Finance. The eighteen Expenditure Divisions are collectively responsible for the control of all departmental spending, both through the annual Survey and in-year. Each is managed by an Assistant Secretary (G5) and comprises two or three sections, each of which is managed by a Principal or Senior Principal or, sometimes, by a Senior Executive Officer. Fig. 6.2 shows the chain of command and responsibilities which link Expenditure Divisions to the groups and sections.

The Defence Policy, Manpower, and Materiel Group, which reports directly to the Second Permanent Secretary, has two divisions and six sections, three responsible for defence policy and materiel, the others

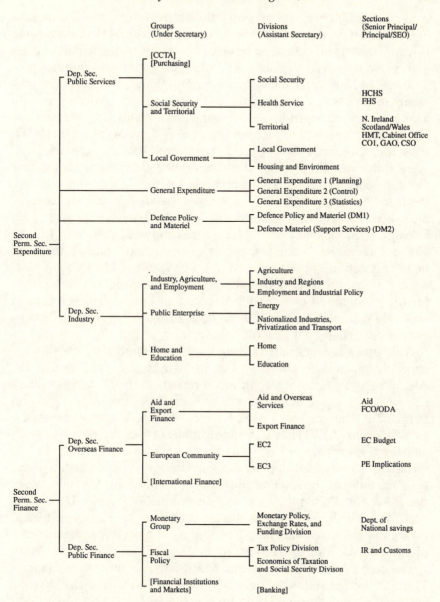

Fig. 6.2. The Treasury expenditure side: expenditure groups, divisions, and sectors, 1992–1993

Source: Civil Service Yearbooks; Treasury information.

dealing with defence support costs, the armed forces, manpower, pay, and works services. The Social Services and Territorial Group has three divisions and six branches responsible for social security benefits, health and personal social services, and the territorial expenditure programmes of Northern Ireland, Scotland, and Wales. The Local Government Group has two divisions and five sections, two of which deal with local government expenditure, the remainder with housing and environmental programmes, and some of the smaller departments like HMSO, PSA, the Ordnance Survey, and the Crown Estates. The Industry, Agriculture, and Employment Group is subdivided into three divisions and ten sections, separately responsible for the agriculture, fisheries, food, and forestry programmes, assistance to industry, and employment measures, and general industrial policy. The Home, Transport, and Education Group of divisions has four sections dealing with (*a*) the Home Office and Legal Departments, (*b*) schools and further and higher education, (*c*) science, and (*d*) broadcasting. The Public Enterprises Group of two divisions is subdivided into five sections responsible for (*a*) nationalized energy industries, oil and gas policy, (*b*) general policy on nationalized industries and privatization, (*c*) roads, (*d*) transport industries, and (*e*) post office industries.

Four other Expenditure Divisions with the same responsibility for expenditure must be added to this list. These are, first, part of the Aid and Export Finance Group which reports to the Deputy Secretary responsible for overseas finance and through him to the Second Permanent Secretary for Public Finance. The Aid and Overseas Services Division (AEF1) is responsible for the aid to developing countries, and for the expenditure of the Foreign and Commonwealth Office, including overseas development administration. Two of its three sections have the major responsibility for these functions. Second, part of the European Community Group, European Community Division 2, which deals with the forecasting and monitoring of EC payments and associated estimates and supply procedure, counts as an expenditure division. This Group also reports to the Deputy Secretary for Overseas Finance and to the Second Permanent Secretary for Public Finance. Third, in the Fiscal Policy Group, the Indirect and Direct Tax Division acts as the expenditure division for the Inland Revenue and Customs and Excise, reporting to the Second Permanent Secretary for Public Expenditure through the Deputy Secretary for Public Finance. Fourthly, the Monetary Policy Division of Monetary Group (MG1), with the same reporting lines, acts as the expenditure division for the Department for National Savings.

THE FUNCTIONS OF THE EXPENDITURE DIVISIONS

The main function of the Expenditure Divisions is to advise the Chief Secretary and the Chancellor on the allocation and control of financial and human resources throughout the public sector and on the promotion of the best value from those resources. More narrowly, they receive bids from departments for future expenditure in the conduct of the annual Survey, and advise the Chief Secretary in his discussions and negotiations with them and, since 1992, on the discussions in the EDX Committee of Cabinet. The Survey is the core element of the work of most Expenditure Divisions, and is dealt with in Chapter 12. Secondly, Expenditure Divisions exercise control of departmental expenditure programmes 'in-year', through the operation of cash limits, running costs controls, the need to approve programme expenditure above certain delegated limits, and the end-year flexibility and other similar schemes; they also consider claims for additional expenditure that draw down on the Reserve. In the exercise of that function, they monitor monthly and quarterly the cash flow of departmental programmes. Control and monitoring are dealt with in detail in Chapters 15–19. Thirdly, both in planning expenditure through the Survey round, and in exercising control 'in-year', Expenditure Divisions are concerned to obtain value-for-money through their encouragement and oversight of efficient and effective financial management systems and practices. Finally, they advise the Chief Secretary on the implications of new spending proposals which may arise outside the Survey round. The amount and importance of this and other extra-Survey work, apart from 'in-year' control, varies between Expenditure Divisions. While the Defence Divisions have a similar routine, there is a great deal of other activity, for example the continuous approval of contracts. The longer time-horizon—ten, even twenty, years is not uncommon for some defence projects—is a further factor which makes their routines and business different from other divisions. While the preparation of the investment and financial review of the nationalized industries is undertaken within the Survey structure, the timetable, structure, and content of the business of those divisions dealing with it also differ in some respects from those divisions dealing wholly with programme expenditure.

Proportionately, more business is handled at ministerial level than is the case in most other departments, and the relationship between an Expenditure Division and the Chief Secretary and his private office is particularly important. Even relatively junior Treasury expenditure officials have fairly regular contact with the Minister. A Principal is likely to be *the* expert on a matter under discussion between the Chief Secretary and a Secretary of State and is therefore expected to brief the Chief Secretary alone or with only one or two other officials present. During the hectic days of ministerial bilaterals, an official is likely to be in more frequent, even daily, contact with his ministerial boss.

Almost as important are the relationships which Expenditure Divisions have with the 'centre of the ring', which includes those Treasury divisions concerned with the public spending aggregates: GEP with the Survey totals, RC with the aggregate level of running costs. An Expenditure Division sees part of its mission to help them 'to make the macro-side of public spending hang together'. GEP is the key actor here. In a parallel way to an Expenditure Division's relations with its spending departments, the Under Secretary in charge of GEP will want to know whether an Expenditure Division can 'deliver' a given Survey outcome, and whether it provides a reliable estimate of the problems likely to be encountered. Thus assessments of 'openness' and 'reliability' enter into intra-Treasury relationships as well as between Expenditure Divisions and the Finance Divisions of the spending departments. Expenditure Divisions will be brought into initial discussions with GEP prior to the ministerial bilaterals, and then as the pace quickens be expected to keep GEP informed of the progress of discussions.

The degree to which Expenditure Divisions tap into the expertise available in the supporting Treasury divisions varies considerably. Some find the micro-economists, management accountants, operational research specialists, and the staff inspectorate valuable in supplementing their own expertise and providing another outlet for appraising departmental output and value-for-money data. A few Expenditure Divisions would prefer to have their own resources to be able to employ more specialist consultants. The view taken on the value of in-house support depends on the complexity of the material to be reviewed and the degree to which the spending department itself has access to better and more sophisticated sources of advice than the Treasury. A crucial factor here is the degree to which an Expenditure Division is concerned that its credibility will suffer with the department if the Treasury is seen to rely on internal advice which is too generalized and 'second-rate'. Where this is thought to be a risk, other private-sector sources can be drawn on *ad hoc*, or the spending department encouraged in specific circumstances to buy-in advice and appraisal and report back to the Expenditure Division.

The distribution of work in the Treasury's Expenditure Divisions is generally determined non-hierarchically. 'Who deals with the business, unlike in other departments is not necessarily or generally determined by hierarchy, but by who is appropriate, who is available and who has handled the issue before' (Assistant Secretary). Politically sensitive issues are often sent further 'up the line'. An Under Secretary may play a larger role in issues regarded as important because they transcend the responsibilities of divisions within the group, or involve significant policy developments, or relate to tactics on the conduct of the Survey. But as a general rule Principals are not just given 'dogsbody' tasks; there is a large amount of 'ebb and flow' of work between grades, and in a very busy period of crisis it is 'all hands to the pump'. A Principal is more likely to work closely with Deputy Secretaries than would be the case in most other departments. The division of work is partly the product of necessity, as there are relatively few Expenditure Controllers to shadow much larger numbers of officials in the spending departments, and partly the result of a departmental culture which emphasizes the flexibility of small numbers of officials in regular contact with each other.

The internal non-hierarchical distribution of tasks is reflected in the way business is conducted between the Treasury and the spending departments. Normal contact for a Treasury Expenditure Controller is with the grade above: a Principal will discuss issues with a departmental Assistant Secretary, an Assistant Secretary with an Under Secretary, and so on. This reflects the degree to which an Expenditure Controller in the Treasury has a wider span of control than his opposite number in a spending department. But it is not uncommon for a Principal to deal regularly with an Under Secretary and to attend meetings at which senior officials and Ministers are present. Conversely, an Expenditure Controller may go 'down the line' to an Executive Officer in a department to obtain information.

THE EXPENDITURE CONTROLLERS

The 124 officials in the Treasury (1991–2) with direct responsibility for the management and control of the expenditure of public-sector programmes at the section level or above, ranging in rank from Senior Executive Officer to Permanent Secretary, comprise the Expenditure Controllers. This definition excludes those who advise or provide specialized services identified earlier in the chapter.

The profile of a Treasury Expenditure Controller is constructed of recruitment, qualification, experience, and mobility. The Identikit picture of the entry of the best of the young arts graduates from Oxford and

Cambridge, trained on the job, moved frequently between jobs in different divisions, promoted to Assistant Secretary in their early thirties, and to Under Secretary a decade later, with the brightest going on to Deputy Secretary and Permanent Secretary—that picture was always a misrepresentation of what happened in practice. It is still less true today. Each year the Treasury recruits around half a dozen graduate Administrative Trainees through the Civil Service Commission. They provide one important source of future supply for the Principal posts in the Expenditure Divisions. Equally important is the supply of Principals and Assistant Secretaries from other Whitehall departments, and of direct entry Principals from the City, industry, and other professions. There is also now more movement within the Treasury between the specialist grades of economist and statistician and the administration group. Rachel Lomax, appointed Deputy Chief Economic Adviser in 1990, served previously as Under Secretary in charge of GEP. Recruited to the Treasury as an economist, she spent her first fifteen years as a specialist. Thereafter, she held administrative posts in both home and overseas finance, and spent a year as PPS to the Chancellor of the Exchequer. Nick Monck, appointed Second Permanent Secretary (Public Expenditure) in 1990, was employed as a professional economist on secondment from his former department, the Ministry of Power, to NEDO, the National Board for Prices and Incomes, and the Government of Tanzania.

Educational and professional qualifications include the classics and history traditionally associated with the dominance of an Oxbridge élite entry, but are now much more varied and representative of the main academic disciplines, and of other universities. Career prospects within the Expenditure Divisions, as with other parts of the central Treasury, are dependent not only upon performance but recognition as a 'fast stream' rather than 'mainstream' Principal. Even in the fast stream, only the very brightest can expect to move through to Assistant Secretary and management of a division by the mid-thirties (Treasury 1985c).

The professional controller

Expenditure Controllers are professional administrators, with skills and expertise acquired in a variety of posts prior to entering the Expenditure Divisions. They may also have obtained relevant experience extramurally in other public and private sector organizations, in addition to that obtained in other parts of the Treasury, and through formal training courses. Neither by qualification nor by training are they specialists comparable to (say) accountants or economists, although some Expenditure Controllers have been so trained. Nor are they specialists in terms of their knowledge and experience of particular subjects such as health, transport, or defence, although some will have had such backgrounds in Whitehall departments or in the private sector. Nor are Expenditure Controllers a race apart, distinguishable from other Treasury senior staff by recruitment, training, or career development. Successful careers in the Treasury are compounded of several different elements, but include movement between the Expenditure Divisions and other parts of the Treasury—finance, pay, and personnel management, and the central divisions. 'Versatility is an important quality for making a successful career in the Treasury' (Treasury 1988*a*: ch. 10). Expenditure Controllers need, and acquire with time and experience in the Expenditure Divisions, a great deal of specialized knowledge and experience of public expenditure, and the processes, rules, and conventions regulating it.

The Treasury's postings policy is designed to produce 'good all rounders' (Treasury 1985*c*: 11). Traditionally this has meant providing staff with the opportunity to broaden experience by working in a number of different areas, rather than by deepening knowledge as a result of long experience with work in the same area. In practice this has meant movement into and out of the expenditure side and, within it, between Expenditure Divisions. A consequence of the general policy of developing good all-rounders is a high turnover of staff. Providing a continuous supply of Expenditure Controllers from within the Treasury's own resources would require a much larger number of direct-entry graduates. Apart from the exacerbation of the difficulty in the last decade of obtaining an adequate supply of good graduates to the Civil Service as a whole, to do so would eliminate the claimed advantages of bringing into the Expenditure Divisions Principals and Assistant Secretaries from other departments, and from other public and private sector organizations. Those advantages were first articulated in the Warren Fisher doctrine in the 1920s which urged that 'the Treasury be staffed by a continual flow and circulation of principals with two to eight years training in other departments'. Not only did this ensure that the ablest and brightest of the young 'high-flyers' were brought into the Treasury, and to its attention, it provided the opportunity to retain the very best of them. It was also an important mechanism for the transmission of mutual understanding between the Treasury and departments and, through the creation and subsequent maintenance of working relationships, the formation of Treasury–departmental networks. It enabled those returning to their departments after Treasury experience of the Expenditure Divisions to better read the signals, and understand the Treasury mission and perspective. Conversely, the injection into the

Expenditure Divisions of administrators with experience and under-standing of different departmental perspectives granted a means to balance that of the Treasury. At the same time, furnishing a steady stream of recruits from the departments allowed a corrective to any tendency towards the inbreeding of a 'Treasury mandarinate'. In Chapter 25 we question the assumptions underlying the general policy of developing good all-rounders, and providing for the supply partly from postings from other parts of the Treasury, and partly from outside.

Skills and qualifications

There is no simple answer to the question what makes an effective Expenditure Controller. Their formal educational qualifications are no different from those of other Treasury officials, or indeed civil servants in other departments. While they have some special training for the job, no particular professional experience is thought more suitable and ap-propriate. Principals and Assistant Secretaries can be pitched in at the deep end without previous experience of work in the Expenditure Div-isions, or in some cases of the Treasury itself. While appointments at these levels are made from within the Expenditure Divisions, where newly promoted Principals or Assistant Secretaries may have spent some time previously at lower grades, recruitment to both also occurs from other parts of the Treasury, from other Whitehall departments, and from secondments from the City, business, and industry.

If, by definition, most Expenditure Controllers are potential high-flyers, then intellectual ability is both a prerequisite, marking out the official for preferment, and a *sine qua non*. In this respect there is little to distinguish them from their colleagues in almost all other parts of the Treasury. The skills which they come to possess are those which are developed or acquired with experience in the job (Principal). In what follows we depart from the method followed by Heclo and Wildavsky (1974) to construct a profile of the 'good expenditure controller' in the early 1970s. They relied mainly on what former Treasury officials *said* were the requisite skills; we prefer a more deductive approach based on interviews with serving controllers in all the Expenditure Divisions. We are not arguing that their account was inaccurate; indeed, the qualities they identified of political sensitivity, judgement, toughness tempered by suppleness, analytic ability, drafting skills—all of these are inherent in what follows. But unlike them we have tried to distil from discussions with practising controllers, about what they do and how they do it, some of the common qualities of mind and attitude which they evince. The picture we present is a general and not a universal one. There are of course important differences of subject-matter between divisions, most obviously the case with the Defence divisions, which require a different mix of the skills we describe, or indeed skills particular to that business. While that is an important qualification, nevertheless there is sufficient commonality between them to justify the approach taken here.

It is true of all large organizations, and certainly of most Whitehall departments, that effective management depends to a large extent upon the skill with which a line manager copes with the volume, variety, and complexity of the business with which he deals, within the limitations of human and physical resources and the constraints of time. In this respect the pressures on the Expenditure Controller may not appear to be so very different from those experienced by counterparts in the City or in business. However, the newcomer to the Expenditure Divisions from such occupations and from other parts of Whitehall is struck by the long hours of work, the sheer volume of paper, and the relentless and unending pace of activity. Pressures on Expenditure Controllers are more intensive and relentless than in comparable jobs in the spending departments. 'Quiet periods' are rare. Coping skills are essential. They require not only a capacity for hard and sustained work, but the ability and confidence to discriminate between what is important or sensitive and requires more time and energy devoted to it, and that which can be dealt with quickly or cursorily, or taken on trust.

Such skills can be developed and honed with time and experience in the job, but are predicated upon self-confidence and independence. From the outset an Expenditure Controller has to be quick on his feet, selective in what he chooses to look into, and not averse to 'flying by the seat of his pants' while learning the job. A newly appointed Expenditure Controller (Principal) was 'unprepared for the way one is supposed to "hop around" between issues'. His initial reaction was: 'get under the desk—this can't be real, let me do one thing at a time'. Another confessed that at first he had to read everything which came from the spending department three or four times merely to understand it.

As he or she acquires experience of the work and the people dealt with in the Finance and Policy Divisions of the spending departments, the Expenditure Controller becomes skilful in the recognition of an issue which is worth pursuing, and how far it can be taken. An Under Secretary expects his officials to find soft targets in their areas, and having identified them 'to be able to know how far they can reasonably go in going for them with some chance of success'. Knowing where and what to probe, how to do it, and critically assessing the chances of success are important skills learnt on the job. The development of 'good judgement' is predicated on an insatiable intellectual curiosity and inquisitiveness, and an unwillingness to accept unquestioningly the arguments and evidence urged on him by the spending department. It requires a mixture of intellectual arrogance, acuity, and toughness. 'Part of the *modus operandi* of being at the top of the pyramid is that you should know what questions to ask' (Assistant Secretary). Part of the skill in asking the right questions is the ability to do so without acrimony or rancour, conveying to the spending department the reasonableness and propriety of the requests for more information or further consideration—the acceptance that the Treasury is merely doing its job. 'Standing on rights' all the time would not be conducive to the smooth flow of business. A skilled Expenditure Controller, tending and cultivating his relationships with the Finance and Policy Divisions of a spending department, does not need to be constantly asserting the Treasury's right to be interested in an issue and to ask tough questions. Nevertheless there is a thin dividing line between reasonable requests for information and challenging the professional judgement of the department's policy specialists. There is little to guide the Expenditure Controller, other than experience in the job and his relationships with the department. The good Expenditure Controller learns that the Treasury is always on the strongest ground when questions are asked of departmental officials which those officials should have been aware of anyway. The sensitive issue of demarcation is avoided if the Expenditure Controller probes by saying 'You have no doubt in formulating this proposal considered issue *x*. Can I please have the figures?' (Principal). Here the professional judgement and appraisal is left with the department, but the Treasury is checking to see whether such assessment has been made or whether the department is geared up to undertake the task.

Expenditure Controllers are necessarily more numerate than they were twenty years ago. The volume of quantitative data has grown as value-for-money has assumed a more central place in the management of public money. Nevertheless, reliance on or, worse still, obsession with the 'numbers' risks missing what is going on behind them. They must of course 'add up', but the Expenditure Controller has to probe for inconsistencies and develop a nose for what they conceal or obfuscate. 'He must not be afraid to look a fool, and must avoid volunteering that he knows when he doesn't just to avoid looking ignorant. He must not be put off by glib explanations, but scratch away until he understands' (Principal).

Expenditure Controllers cannot function effectively without an awareness of what issues are or may become politically sensitive. This textbook cliché nevertheless points to a necessary skill which is acquired and developed through experience in the job, and exposure to ministerial business, often through service as a trainee administrator in the private office of the Chancellor, the Chief Secretary, or other Treasury ministers. The Expenditure Controller's 'antennae' are tuned to the different frequencies of the Chief Secretary, and to the departmental ministers with whom he deals. His reception of the 'signal' from the latter will inevitably be weaker and less important to him than that of his own Minister, but he cannot ignore it. With many issues that arise the degree of sensitivity is obvious enough from the substance or context or the way it is being handled. With other issues it is not certain whether they are or will become sensitive; there may be little by way of guidance to be gleaned from past practice or decisions. Although he can consult with others, and refer up the hierarchy, there are constraints of time and pressure of work, besides which the Expenditure Controller is expected to become quickly self-reliant and confident in his own judgement. What to take to Ministers and what to settle within the division often requires the exercise of a nice judgement for which there are no hard and fast rules. On the one hand, the Chief Secretary needs to be alerted early enough to issues which may create difficulties for him with his colleagues, and to be adequately briefed on the progress of expenditure issues and Survey bids. At the same time, divisions have to be careful not to submerge him in a welter of detail. 'Trying to identify what it is in a departmental argument that makes a difference' and needs to be brought to his attention is part of the Expenditure Controller's repertoire of skills (Principal).

The plea of 'political sensitivity' is often employed by departments in support of their arguments, and may be justified by the salience of the issue in a previous Cabinet discussion or in the Government's public posture. It can, however, be invoked to bolster a weak case. 'Doctors often "shroud wave", and the Department of Health can carry this on in discussions with the Treasury' (Principal). The skill of the Expenditure Controller is to detect when a department does have a problem which is genuinely sensitive politically, and to distinguish it from those issues where the degree of sensitivity has been exaggerated.

Negotiating skills are essential. Few issues are determined by a straight 'yes' or 'no'; most require a negotiated settlement in which conditions or 'strings' are offered or required, trade-offs between expenditures explored and agreed. The Expenditure Controller needs to be able to identify issues and opportunities where it is possible to treat with the department and strike a deal, and those where there is going to be an argument, and assess how serious it is likely to be. The Expenditure Controller must not only be able to propose the terms of a settlement, or be able to agree that proposed to him, he must also be able to deliver it. His future credibility with the department (and within the Treasury), their trust in his judgement, will depend on his negotiating skill in getting the equation of promise = delivery just right. The parameters of the negotiation are set by a variety of factors, the calculation of which involves some of the skills referred to above; but the conduct of the negotiation itself is an important skill and one which distinguishes the outstanding Expenditure Controller. A skilled negotiator, close to his spending department, will have a keen appreciation of the broad strategies of both it and his Chief Secretary, and of the room for tactical manœuvre between them. He will know in which areas and on which issues he can push. 'At times you need to be stubborn and push your luck' (Principal). But if the Expenditure Controller is going to be difficult and dig in his heels, he must 'flag up' his intention to the spending department and to his Treasury colleagues. Unlike in real trench warfare, the element of surprise is not a tactical weapon which the Expenditure Controller can draw from his arsenal. Departments, however, are less inhibited, and see the occasional use of the 'bounce' as a legitimate tactical weapon. Procedural rules of the game on prior-notification and the involvement of ministers make it uncommon. But 'trying it on' to see 'if the Treasury spots it' is part of the game, and serves to keep Expenditure Controllers alert and on their toes (Principal Finance Officer, Spending Department). A PFO has nevertheless to consider his credibility with the Treasury and not indulge too frequently in such 'try-ons'. The experienced Expenditure Controller is aware that the PFO may be responding to his own constituency in the Policy Divisions and may hope that the Treasury will reject the case being made. Expenditure Controllers do not always respond as the PFO hopes.

An advantage which the Treasury possesses over other departments is that of perspective. From its central position, and the centrality of the expenditure function, the Treasury is uniquely placed to see the 'bigger picture'. A skilled Expenditure Controller can perceive and make connections between policy issues and expenditure items which have arisen separately in different programmes. He can help to improve the effectiveness of expenditure by confronting programmes across a wide range of public expenditure. The process is iterative, but there is both a 'top–down' and 'bottom–up' perspective. The Chief Secretary and the Chancellor have a unique view of the totality of public expenditure, and through Cabinet and its committees, the opportunity to help shape and transmit down through the Treasury the general priorities in government spending. That context, progressively mediated by the perspectives of the Second Permanent Secretary and the relevant Deputy

Secretary, will in turn help to shape both Treasury and departmental attitudes towards individual programmes. 'Bottom–up', the Expenditure Controllers bring to their work with individual departments that 'bigger picture'. At the same time, Heads of Group are aware of what is going on across a wide range of programmes dealt with in their group of Expenditure Divisions. In a two-way process, the transaction of business between an Expenditure Division and a department will influence and be influenced by appreciation of what is happening elsewhere, and of course the context of the 'expenditure judgement' and the Chief Secretary's priorities. Treasury Expenditure Controllers emphasize that nowhere else in government can a 'rounded picture' be obtained. It is partly institutionalized because some Expenditure Divisions cut across departmental boundaries, programmes dealt with in two separate branches come together at the divisional level, and divisions are co-ordinated by Heads of Group at the Under Secretary level, and higher still. For example, the vocational and educational elements of training programmes devised and implemented by the Departments of Employment and Education come together at the Deputy Secretary level. More humbly, the connections between expenditure on broadcasting on the one hand, and arts and libraries on the other, come together in the hands of the Assistant Secretary in charge of the division. In the divisions handling the investment plans of the nationalized industries, there is an immediate opportunity for comparison and cross-connection because they are looked at in groups—transport and energy. As well, Expenditure Controllers have the broader context of the related programme expenditure, for example the British Rail External Finance Requirement is looked at in the context of the transport programmes and bids. As a result, Expenditure Controllers have a better, more rounded picture than any individual industry. Playing this card effectively without offending an industry and risking damage to relationships requires adroitness. Even so, there can be 'awkwardness'. The skilful controller appreciates not only the broader context within which any individual item of expenditure has to be assessed, but will understand the necessarily more limited perspective of the spending department. For his opposite number, the item may be of overriding and paramount importance: for him it may be but one of many such related items.

It would be surprising if the Expenditure Controller's range of skills and acquired expertise had changed greatly in the last twenty years. Control of public expenditure has become more not less important during that period, and the climate within which he/she has operated more stringent. Changes in the system of planning and controlling expenditure since 1976 have confirmed traditional Treasury attitudes towards spending, and the need to keep a strict and constant control of it. These have reinforced existing policy and behavioural norms rather than challenged or changed them. For example, the numbers engaged in expenditure control remain small, and controllers mobile and non-specialist. Basic beliefs about the qualifications, experience, and skills needed to do the job remain largely what they were. There are some important changes of emphasis, however. First, the extent of delegated authority to departments has increased. Secondly, there is more emphasis on the monitoring and assessment of the effectiveness of a department's financial management system. 'System-control' is partly a response to FMI which was formally launched in 1982, but mainly the result of the greater emphasis upon achieving value-for-money inaugurated by the Conservative Government in 1979. It can be argued that the Treasury's concern with 'systems' is an extension of the traditional surveillance of departmental Finance Divisions by Expenditure Controllers. We take up the argument about the effectiveness of the Treasury's Expenditure Divisions and the Expenditure Controllers who staff them in Chapter 25.

7

Making and Co-ordinating Expenditure Policy

The work of the Treasury's Expenditure Divisions, and in particular the activities undertaken in a particular Survey round described in later chapters, is carried on in a wider context. No individual Expenditure Controller approaches the task of shadowing Whitehall departments without being aware of the significance of a range of both broad and narrow factors which comprise the environment within which the politics of planning and controlling expenditure is conducted. The broad macro-economic strategy of the government of the day and the particular assessments made about the outlook for the economy provide the strategic context within which the work of the Expenditure Divisions is situated. Specific medium- and short-term public-spending objectives derive from and contribute to that overall economic strategy and provide the background to an individual PES round. In this chapter we describe the roles and responsibilities of Treasury ministers and senior officials as they contribute to the formulation of macro-economic strategy, the setting of spending objectives, and the making and co-ordinating of expenditure policies. The process is continuous and iterative. Expenditure Controllers in the divisions not only implement the policies decided upon by Treasury ministers and their senior officials: they help to define and determine them through their interaction with the Finance Divisions of the spending departments. We look at the latter in the next chapter, and in Chapters 9 and 10 examine their interaction.

We begin by considering the roles and responsibilities of the Chief Secretary and his most senior adviser, the Second Permanent Secretary; then we consider the Deputy Secretaries with command responsibilities and their Under Secretaries at the head of Groups of Expenditure Divisions; and, finally, we describe the organization and work of the General Expenditure Policy Division (GEP), whose Under Secretary acts in a 'staff' capacity to the Chief Secretary and the Second Permanent Secretary.

THE CHIEF SECRETARY

The Chancellor of the Exchequer is responsible to Parliament for all Treasury business, including the planning and control of public expenditure. In practice that part of his responsibility is discharged by the Chief Secretary, normally but not invariably a member of the Cabinet. With the Chancellor, he recommends the Control (previously Planning) Total to the July Cabinet who give him a remit for the conduct of the autumnal bilaterals, where he negotiates with his colleagues in order to achieve the Control Total limit. He is at the apex of that part of the Treasury whose officials' lives are regulated by the annual Public Expenditure Survey processes. His responsibilities also include in-year monitoring and control of both cash-limited and non-cash-limited expenditures, the approval or rejection of all claims for additional money which arise outside the Survey, and ensuring that the taxpayer obtains value-for-money. In carrying out these tasks he works closely with the Chancellor, and with the Second Permanent Secretary (Public Expenditure).

The origins of the office of Chief Secretary can be traced directly to the internal Treasury committee of inquiry chaired by Sir Edwin Plowden in 1959–61, and which culminated in the publication of the report: *Control of Public Expenditure* (Cmnd. 1432). As we explained in Chapter 3, the committee was concerned about the weakness of collective responsibility for public expenditure. In the traditional system, the Chancellor had the sole responsibility for decisions made piecemeal without Cabinet discussion or review, but it was feared that the growth of public expenditure inaugurated in the late 1950s would be difficult to contain within the limits of prospective resources unless he had the support of his Cabinet colleagues. In an attempt to provide for more collective judgement to be brought to bear in the discussion of expenditure issues, the committee proposed a Public Expenditure Committee of senior ministers to examine proposed annual appraisals of spending and resources. Two attempts were made to set up such a committee, first in 1960 and then again four years later, but neither survived.

The post of Chief Secretary was created in October 1961. Henry Brooke was appointed and given a seat in the Cabinet. The announcement emphasized the increased and growing burden on the Chancellor arising from his post-war responsibilities for national and international economic and financial policy, to which was now to be added the new responsibility of the longer-term planning of public expenditure. To relieve him of some of this pressure and to provide support in Cabinet, the Chief Secretary was made responsible for all the Treasury business concerned with the control of expenditure, Civil Service pay, and management, leaving the Chancellor free to concentrate on economic policy (Bridges 1964).

Jack (later Lord) Diamond was appointed Chief Secretary in the Labour Government which took office in 1964 and he served until 1970. For the first four years he did so outside the Cabinet. Nevertheless, he attended all Cabinet meetings when expenditure business was discussed, and presented and argued the Treasury case in Cabinet committees. From the creation of the post, it was decided that departmental ministers could not appeal to the Chancellor against a decision of the Chief Secretary. In the early years this helped to establish and maintain his authority, although departmental ministers continued occasionally to exploit personal relationships with particular Chancellors in attempts to circumvent his position on particular expenditure items. Diamond's (1975) account of his tenure emphasizes the subordination of the Chief Secretary to the Chancellor, besides the obvious need for decisions taken by the former to be consistent with the Chancellor's general policy. With the establishment of the PESC procedures and the annual routine of the Survey and publication of the Expenditure White Paper, the Chief Secretary became more obviously identified as the Minister responsible for public spending.

Joel Barnett served as Chief Secretary throughout the period of the Labour Government 1974–9, for the last three years as a full member of the Cabinet. An accountant by training, like Diamond, he had made his name as a back-bench MP by specializing in taxation matters, and this experience and expertise ensured that he rather than the Paymaster General (Edmund Dell) led for the Treasury. From this time onwards the Chief Secretary has assumed direct responsibility for the presentation of all financial business to Parliament. Although not initially a member of Cabinet, Barnett spent a great deal of time in Cabinet and Cabinet committees during the years 1974–7, presenting the Treasury arguments for expenditure cuts and negotiating with his ministerial colleagues. Unlike the Survey processes of the 1980s and 1990s, there was much more detailed discussion of expenditure decisions in full Cabinet (Barnett 1982). The July Cabinet meeting to decide the aggregate was regarded by both Treasury and departmental ministers as a 'key battle ground', at which departmental spending ministers would take the opportunity to remind their colleagues of the priority of their programmes. In the 1980s and until 1992 the Treasury proposal for the Planning Total was normally approved without much discussion, and without ministers arguing their individual cases. While it is true that the July total was that which the Treasury ministers and officials aimed to deliver, spending ministers knew from the experience of the past decade that that total could be increased by Cabinet decision at the November meeting as a result of the bilateral agreements in the autumn. Until 1992 the July total was normally less firm than Labour Prime Ministers tried to make it in the 1970s, when there was greater reluctance to reopen the decisions at the November Cabinet meeting.

Another important difference in the work of the Chief Secretary in the 1970s was the consequence of the need to obtain cuts in public expenditure outside as well as within the routine of the Survey processes. In November 1975 and twice in the following year the Labour Government, faced with a rapidly deteriorating economic situation, was obliged to make substantial cuts quickly. There were endless Cabinet meetings at which the Chief Secretary bargained bilaterally across the table with his colleagues. This practice was not repeated, nor was it necessary in the following decade, where failure to agree in bilateral negotiations was resolved by the newly created Star Chamber. Bilateral haggling in Cabinet was not conducted within an agreed order of priorities, and Barnett's dissatisfaction with the *ad hoc* and piecemeal procedures for taking expenditure decisions led him to propose a small committee of senior non-spending ministers to sift through all major programmes, discuss major as well as marginal changes in the allocation of expenditure, and put proposals to the Cabinet. This was similar to the experiments of 1960 and 1964. The Prime Minister agreed, but the committee chaired by the Chancellor met only once before the 1979 general election.

The preparation of the annual Expenditure White Paper through the Survey processes, together with the series of Budgets, mini-Budgets, and expenditure packages, meant that the Chief Secretary was more heavily burdened than in the past, or than his successors in the 1980s. From the very beginning Barnett was under considerable pressure. In the autumn of 1974 the new Government presented a Budget and a Finance Bill to Parliament, whilst simultaneously preparing a revised Public Expenditure White Paper:

While the Finance Bill was wending its tiresome way through Committee, my main responsibilities continued to lie in the area of public expenditure. I had to find time to read the papers in between reading my briefs to reply to amendments on the Bill, then leave from time to time, when John Gilbert [the Treasury Minister of State] was replying, to attend Cabinet Committees and bilateral meetings with spending Ministers. (Barnett 1982: 57)

There were eight Chief Secretaries between 1979 and the general election of 1992. Until the appointment of Norman Lamont to replace

John Major in 1989, each served about two years, roughly two PES rounds. Norman Lamont served for just over a year, but because he was appointed in July conducted two rounds of bilaterals. His successor, David Mellor, served from November 1990 until his appointment as the first Heritage Secretary after the general election in 1992. The frequency of these changes contrasts with the practice of Labour Prime Ministers of the 1960s and 1970s where Jack Diamond and Joel Barnett each served the full term of each administration. Another difference was that none of the Conservative Chief Secretaries was professionally qualified as an accountant, as both Labour Ministers had been. The higher turn-over under Conservative Governments is partly explained by the greater frequency of Cabinet reshuffles under the leadership of Mrs Thatcher, who enjoyed larger majorities in the House of Commons than all the Labour Governments of the 1960s and 1970s.

More importantly, under Mrs Thatcher the post became a proving-ground for young ministers, an opportunity to establish a claim for further ministerial advancement. Thus Leon Brittan (1981–3), John MacGregor (1985–7), John Major (1987–9), Norman Lamont (1989–90), and David Mellor (1990–2) were appointed as rising young men from junior ministerial posts. All were promoted subsequently to head their own departments. John Biffen (1979–81) was promoted sideways to Leader of the House, but was dropped from the Cabinet subse-quently in 1987 as a 'semi-detached' consolidator. Of the six appoint-ments made by Mrs Thatcher, Peter Rees (1983–5) was the least successful, judged in career terms, and after two years in the post was dropped from the Cabinet.

By the beginning of the Thatcher Governments the main function of the Chief Secretary had become firmly established as that of planning and controlling public expenditure, and securing cost-effectiveness. With the launch of FMI in the early 1980s he also became responsible for achieving value-for-money throughout the Civil Service. Both func-tions brought him into closer contact with the Treasury junior minister (either Minister of State or Paymaster General) responsible for Civil Service pay and management since their restoration to the Treasury in 1987.

The distribution of other Treasury business among Treasury minis-ters is a matter for the judgement of the Chancellor of the Exchequer. Given the burden of the expenditure business, the Chief Secretary is not normally given any other major responsibility, but in practice, since Joel Barnett's time, the Chief Secretary has piloted the Finance Bill through its Parliamentary stages, leading for the Treasury at most of the import-ant, long and exhausting, committee stages. He also prepares and presents the annual Estimates to Parliament, the winter and spring Supplementaries, and the cash limits and the in-year changes made to them.

The relationship between the Chancellor and the Chief Secretary is necessarily close and mutually supportive, although the warmth of their personal relationships varies with the personality and temperament of the two ministers. They are brought together a great deal, on formal and informal occasions in Treasury and Cabinet meetings, and on other occasions when policy options are reviewed, as in the run-up to the Budget when Treasury ministers and officials review their strategy and options at the weekend retreat at Chevening or Dorneywood. The centrality of public expenditure control to the achievement of the Conservative Government's main policy aim throughout the 1980s and 1990s of controlling inflation through the money supply, together with the aim of reducing and then restraining public expenditure growth, has meant that the Chief Secretary has inevitably been closely integrated into the development and the implementation of the Chancellor's macro-economic policy. A key element in that has been the setting of targets for the annual Planning/Control Totals.

The Chief Secretary's closest relationships are with the Second Permanent Secretary (Public Expenditure) and the Under Secretary in charge of General Expenditure Policy (GEP), the Group with responsibility for general strategic issues of both planning and control (see below). These half-dozen senior officials comprise his general staff; officials in the Expenditure Divisions are his line managers, through whom the expenditure strategy is implemented, programme by programme. The role and functions of the Second Permanent Secretary are to a considerable extent a reflection of those of the Chief Secretary, and are discussed in detail below.

In his own right as the Treasury minister responsible for public expenditure the Chief Secretary sits on numerous Cabinet committees. In May 1992 he was a member of seven of the sixteen standing committees and of one subcommittee (only the Prime Minister and Chancellor, on nine standing committees each, sat on more). Within the context of the Chancellor's macro-economic policy, he ensures that the Treasury's policy aims for expenditure are taken fully into account right from the start of any new policy initiative or review. At the appropriate stage, he will approve or reject proposals made by his colleagues which entail new or additional spending outside the Survey processes, or reserve the Treasury's position for a later stage. He may consult the Chancellor, or keep him informed of the expenditure implications of a particular proposal, but the final decision is his. The authority and position of the

Chief Secretary has been strengthened since 1976 by the adoption of the rule that Treasury ministers cannot be overruled in Cabinet committees on financial issues. If the Chief Secretary says no, his Cabinet colleague(s) must take the matter to Cabinet if they wish to seek to reverse his judgement. Until this change, the onus was on the Treasury minister to raise an issue to Cabinet level if his judgement in a committee had been overruled by his colleagues.

The Chief Secretary's main responsibility is with planning and allocating public expenditure. His aims for public spending, shaped in consultation with the Chancellor in the context of the evolving macroeconomic strategy, provide the starting-point for the Public Expenditure Survey each year. Some broad indication of their orientation may be evident in the Treasury's Survey *Guidelines* circulated to departments in March, or earlier still in the meeting of departmental Principal Finance Officers convened at the Treasury. From then until the meeting of the Cabinet in July, the Chief Secretary will be considering how far and in what way he can achieve his aim of balancing competing pressures in order to achieve a satisfactory outcome within the top–down Control Total.

Once the Cabinet has approved the Chief Secretary's recommendations for the Control Total, he begins on the preparation for the upcoming bilateral negotiations with his colleagues in the autumn. He agrees with his officials the Agenda (Letters) for each department. Here he might get involved in the detail of the preparation, meeting with Group Heads to discuss the line to be taken in each. Later he discusses the general strategy and the tactics to be employed in each meeting with the Second Permanent Secretary and the Deputy Secretaries, together with the Under Secretary from GEP, and the Group Under Secretaries for each programme.

One Chief Secretary described bilaterals as straight negotiations with his colleagues, and likened them to those with EC agricultural ministers over CAP, although the latter were longer and more exhausting. He occasionally overruled Treasury officials' advice on the grounds of political infeasibility, because what was suggested 'wouldn't run' or was politically inept, but this happened infrequently because senior Treasury officials were acutely aware of the politics and what was feasible. Normally, the line the Chief Secretary wants to take is well understood and reflected in the briefing material prepared in the Expenditure Divisions and by the Group Heads, often influenced by the Permanent and Deputy Secretaries. Occasionally, though, the Chief Secretary may ask for additional briefing to support the case he wants to argue.

The conduct of the bilaterals is described in Chapter 12, and here we note only that the initial meetings are formal with a very large attendance, with the Chief Secretary and the departmental minister making formal opening statements. Thereafter the negotiation proceeds in a smaller group, with discussion more sharply focused on the issues presented in the Agenda Letters. The period of the bilaterals is one of intense and constant activity for the Chief Secretary. While the pressure is most intense during the climax to the PES round, it continues throughout the year. Policy reviews initiated by a department or jointly with the Treasury involve the Chief Secretary, particularly when they are brought forward to Cabinet committee. Not only is a great deal of time taken up with the discussion of the expenditure implications of all new policies, the Chief Secretary is provided with the unique perspective of the 'broad picture' of the initiation and development of most new policies. Through his participation in Cabinet Committee discussions, he not only represents the Treasury view of the need, desirability, and affordability of any additional public spending, he is able to influence the emerging priorities of government spending. While the broad thrust of any policy initiative requires the support of Cabinet and its agreement to make sufficient new money available, the Chief Secretary has 'very considerable power' (in the words of one former incumbent) to determine priorities at the margin.

This is particularly the case at the time of the bilaterals. Here he operates under three sorts of often conflicting pressures: first, and pre-eminently, the pressure to deliver the Control Total which, inevitably 'oversubscribed', means that he must bear down on all his colleagues when he negotiates with each separately. Secondly, he must respond to the pressure from each of his departmental colleagues to provide sufficient resources to enable them to provide both the goods and services required by the statutory obligations imposed upon them and any additional resources which colleagues collectively in Cabinet may have agreed to in their approval of a new or revised policy. Thirdly, in resolving or trading off these two pressures he must try to ensure that the consequences of the series of bilateral negotiations are acceptable collectively to his Cabinet colleagues. While the priorities of spending may not be determined specifically after interprogramme comparisons of value-for-money, nevertheless the effect of the bilaterals is to adjust marginally the priority between one programme and another. If Cabinet is to approve the final settlement in November, the Chief Secretary must 'get it about right'. One former Chief Secretary held the view that it was easier to achieve a collectively acceptable settlement by proceeding through bilateral discussions with his colleagues, than through multilateral discussions in Cabinet as happened with the Labour Governments of the late 1970s. Paradoxically, until 1992 there was less formal opportunity for collective Cabinet discussion of the priorities of public expenditure under Conservative Governments, yet there was, it is argued, greater collective responsibility because the Chief Secretary's task is to 'inject collective responsibility into the separate discussions leading to settlement'. Conversely, under Labour the continual need to cut public expenditure *ad hoc* as recurring crises dictated meant that there was more collective discussion and responsibility for the schedule of cuts, but, as Barnett admits, little attempt to inject any order of priority.

Outside the Survey processes, the Chief Secretary often has to decide an issue of spending without reference to his colleagues. He may consult the Chancellor, and of course he has the advice of his officials. His judgement will be influenced by a variety of factors, but not least by his understanding and political feel for what his colleagues would find appropriate, prudent, and necessary in the particular circumstances. As with the decisions at the margins in his bilateral negotiations, these represent a judgement about the priority to be accorded to a particular expenditure need, and what will prove acceptable to his colleagues collectively.

The Chief Secretary's responsibility for the control as well as the planning of public expenditure means that, with the help of his Treasury officials, he must try to ensure that the outturn of expenditure is consistent with that of the final Planning/Control Total. In-year control of the flow of cash is regulated by each spending department subject to constant surveillance and review by Treasury officials. The two main instruments of regulation are the annual cash limits and the Reserve. Any changes to cash limits are subject to the Chief Secretary's approval and are announced by him to Parliament. In practice (see Chapter 17), cash limits are changed frequently throughout the year, reflecting unanticipated pressures on departments for increased or new spending. The Treasury will normally oblige the department to find offsetting savings in other cash-limited subheadings.

All new or additional spending which occurs in-year, and which cannot be financed through offsetting savings, is a potential call on the Reserve. All claims on the Reserve made by spending departments to their Treasury Expenditure Divisions or by ministers to the Chief Secretary are conveyed to GEP, which provides an assessment for the Chief Secretary, who has to decide to allow or deny them. He does so against the background of the current balance sheet of credits and anticipated debits. Since the revision of the rules in 1984 (see Chapter

16) the Treasury has secured a much tighter control of in-year demands on expenditure. The size of the Reserve is a matter for the judgement of the Chancellor and the Chief Secretary, advised by their GEP officials. Since 1984 it has increased as a proportion of the Planning/Control Total to provide for all additional spending however derived. (Following the introduction of the New Planning Total in 1988, the position became more complicated. The Reserve did not formally cover local authority self-financed expenditure or debt interest. In the new Control Total introduced in 1992 the Reserve again reverted to covering local authority self-financed expenditure, but neither Social Security spending nor debt interest.) The top–down pressures dictated by the macro-economic strategy interact with those coming up from below for more spending. Treasury officials try to estimate in a rough way what contingencies and unforeseen expenditure may arise in-year.

As the Cabinet minister with formal responsibility for planning and controlling public expenditure, the Chief Secretary has to account to Parliament for his performance. Until 1990 the principal formal occasion was provided by the debate on the Public Expenditure White Paper which took place shortly after its publication in the spring. With the conflation of volume one of that White Paper with the Autumn Statement this occasion was moved from the early spring to November, and debate on the public expenditure issues subsumed within that on the government's macro-economic strategy. The Departmental Expenditure Reports were then published in the spring and provided the occasion for a further general debate on public expenditure. Debates on the PEWP were poorly attended, and the Chief Secretary's expenditure policy as set out in it was rarely subjected to detailed and close examination. All Treasury Parliamentary Questions are formally addressed to the Chancellor. The Chief Secretary answers on expenditure matters, and with the Chancellor shares responsibility for Treasury answers on broader macro-economic issues. With the institution of the Unified Budget in 1993, public-spending matters are now firmly embedded in discussion about general economic policy, revenue-raising, and overall fiscal policy.

Less public, but more searching, was the annual review of the Government's expenditure and taxation plans by, first, the House of Commons Expenditure Committee and, then, from 1979 its successor, the Select Committee on the Treasury and Civil Service. In the December following the publication of the Budget the Chancellor and the Chief Secretary, accompanied by their senior officials, were called in and examined on the Government's published economic objectives and policies and its plans for public expenditure. On both, the committee had the written and published evidence of several specialist advisers, and so armed was able on most occasions to conduct a rigorous, often hostile, public examination of Treasury ministers and officials. Over the years the dialogue between the committee and the Treasury provided the main public forum for the discussion of the whole range of expenditure business which falls within the Chief Secretary's responsibility. It focused on some of the most sensitive and contentious issues in the planning and control of public expenditure: the price basis used for costing programmes; the determination of the priorities of public spending; value-for-money and performance indicators; the effect of the new planning total; and, latterly, the New Control Total. Many of the recommendations and suggestions for improvement in the processes of decision-making were accepted by the Treasury.

THE SECOND PERMANENT SECRETARY

The Second Permanent Secretary (Public Expenditure) is the senior Treasury official on the expenditure side of the department, responsible to the Chief Secretary and through him to the Chancellor for the management of the system for planning, monitoring, and controlling public expenditure, and for obtaining value-for-money. Until 1961 the (then) expenditure Second Secretary reported to the Chancellor of the Exchequer through the Permanent Secretary. With the creation of the post of Chief Secretary, with Cabinet rank, in practice he reported directly to the latter. But he remained an adviser to the Chancellor, and the Permanent Secretary remained in overall charge of the department. The Second Permanent Secretary is a 'notch below full Permanent Secretaries in pay but is treated equally with them in some respects, including eligibility for a place in the honours list' (Pliatzky 1989: 158). In practice he is on an equal footing with departmental Permanent Secretaries and attends their informal weekly meetings.

Appointments to the post are normally made from within the Treasury's own ranks, from among Deputy Secretaries who have spent time and had senior experience in expenditure and other Treasury business, but usually with time also spent outside the Treasury. Between 1972 and 1992 there were seven incumbents, either 'born and bred' by the Treasury or raised and nurtured by it. While continuity is a necessary factor, the exigencies of career planning and promotion at the top of the Treasury and in the Civil Service more generally, together with 'the grinding repetitiveness of some parts of the work' (former Second Permanent Secretary), mean that in practice few incumbents hold office longer than two or three years. Although Rawlinson's term included the consolidation of the cash-limits regime devised under Henley in 1974–6, the arrival of the Conservative Government, the unplanned rise of public expenditure in 1980–2, and the introduction of cash planning, there is no evidence that any of these events prompted his longer than usual stay.

The post of Second Secretary may be held by those near the end of their official career, as with Anson, Rawlinson, and Pliatzky. For those promoted at a younger age, it is a staging-post to further Whitehall advancement. It has not in practice been a stepping-stone to the Treasury's most senior post: the Permanent Secretary has in recent years been promoted from Treasury officials high up on the finance or economy sides. While experience of expenditure business in early or mid-career is not necessarily a bar to the top job, the evidence suggests that thereafter, at the levels of Under Secretary, Deputy Secretary, and Second Permanent Secretary, experience of home or overseas finance and/or the domestic economy is a prerequisite. Middleton (1983–91), Wass (1974–83), and (William) Armstrong (1962–74) were all appointed after such service and experience. Armstrong was promoted in the major Treasury reorganization of 1962 from the then position of Third (i.e. Deputy) Secretary, ahead of more obvious candidates who included Sir Thomas Padmore (then Second Permanent Secretary with responsibility for public expenditure). Sir Terence Burns's appointment in 1991 from the post of Chief Economic Adviser appears unusual, but like his predecessors he had had long service and experience in advising the

TABLE 7.1. *Treasury Second Permanent Secretaries (Expenditure), 1972–1992*

Name	Dates of tenure	Subsequent post
Nicholas Monck	1990–2	Perm. Sec., Dept. of Employment
Sir John Anson	1987–90	Retired
Sir Robin Butler	1985–7	Secretary to the Cabinet and Head of the Home Civil Service
Sir Alan Bailey	1983–5	Perm. Sec., Dept. of Transport
Sir Anthony Rawlinson	1977–83	Perm. Sec., Dept. of Trade; Joint Perm. Sec. DTI
Sir Leo Pliatzky	1976–7	Perm. Sec., Dept. of Trade
Sir Douglas Henley	1972–6	Comptroller and Auditor General

Chancellor on economic and financial policies, and his appointment reflected both that and his personal qualities.

Routes to the top

The career patterns of the two last incumbents of the post of Second Permanent Secretary are not untypical of high-flyers who reach the top of the expenditure side. Anson, the younger son of a baronet, was educated at Winchester and Magdalene College, Cambridge, where he took a First in Mathematics. He entered the Treasury at the age of 24. After various postings in the divisions, he was seconded for two years to the British Embassy in Paris as Financial Counsellor. This extramural experience was broadened by a four-year stint at the Cabinet Office, where he was promoted Under Secretary at the age of 42, and had responsibility for economic and industrial matters. Returning to the Treasury he had charge of GEP. Promoted Deputy Secretary at the age of 47, he headed in turn the General Expenditure, Industry, and Public Services Groups, before becoming Second Permanent Secretary at the age of 57. During that period he also served three years at the British Embassy in Washington as Economics Minister, holding simultaneously the post of UK Executive Director at the IMF and World Bank. He was made Companion of the Order of the Bath in 1981 and knighted shortly before his retirement.

Monck succeeded Anson in 1990, after six years as Deputy Secretary in charge of Industry/Public Enterprise. He was educated at Eton, King's College, Cambridge, the LSE (part-time), and the University of Pennsylvania. He joined the Treasury in 1969 after beginning his Civil Service career in the Ministry of Power in 1959. During the 1960s he worked in NEDO and the National Board for Prices and Incomes. Two and a half years were spent on secondment as an economist to the Ministry of Agriculture in the Government of Tanzania. At the age of 36 he was promoted to Assistant Secretary in the Treasury and spent two years as Principal Private Secretary to Chancellor Healey. The next move up the Treasury ladder was in 1977 when at 42 he was promoted to Under Secretary on the industry side, in charge of the Energy, Transport Industries, and Nationalized Industry Policy Divisions, where his responsibilities included a number of non-expenditure matters such as competition, employment, business taxation, profit-related pay, and privatization. He was a member of the British Steel Corporation Board. Of his time, 20–30 per cent was spent on such 'supply-side' issues. In 1980 he was moved to head the Home Finance Group, responsible for monetary policy and financial institutions.

Functions of the Second Permanent Secretary

The Second Permanent Secretary is the head of the Treasury's public expenditure command. Like a military commander he oversees campaigns proceeding on a large number of fronts, waged by his regiments in the field, the Expenditure Divisions, supported by a general staff provided mainly by the central divisions of GEP and RC. Whereas the Expenditure Divisions deal with the particular programmes of spending departments, the latter are concerned with the aggregates of expenditure and general policy. The distribution between the different but complementary roles played by the Expenditure Divisions and the central divisions is a crucial one to an understanding of the Second Permanent Secretary's responsibilities and how he operates. Of the general staff divisions, GEP's role is both central and crucial to the work of the Second Permanent Secretary, providing central intelligence, strategic advice, and the tactical co-ordination of both line and other staff elements. We discuss it further below.

The Second Permanent Secretary has four main roles, closely interrelated. First, he is in day-to-day charge of a large staff, operating a complex system geared to the annual delivery under Treasury ministers of a concrete objective—the expenditure Planning/Control Total—guided by the overall control of public expenditure, the economic and efficient use of public money, the promotion of financial discipline and control, and the securing of value-for-money. Secondly, he is the Chief Secretary's principal adviser in securing those objectives. Thirdly, as the principal co-ordinator of the disparate strands of expenditure policy represented by the individual contributions of eighteen Expenditure Divisions and GEP, and as the principal liaison and bridgehead between the expenditure sector and the economic and financial sectors of the rest of the Treasury, he helps to ensure the integration of expenditure and macro-economic policy. His fourth role is to represent the Treasury to the rest of Whitehall in all public expenditure matters and to secure and maintain good and effective working relationships in its control through his contact with opposite numbers in the spending departments. He is also the Treasury's Accounting Officer for the Contingencies Fund. These roles can be represented diagrammatically as a cruciform (see Fig. 7.1).

Management and leadership. The Survey and its regular rhythmic cycles of processes, punctuated by the two main Cabinet meetings in July and November, dominate the life of Expenditure Divisions' officials and their seniors. The leadership and day-to-day management of the staff

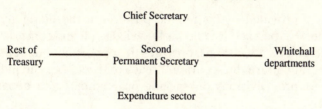

FIG. 7.1. The roles of the Second Permanent Secretary

who contribute to the Survey, and the process through which their contributions are made, are together the prime responsibility of the Second Permanent Secretary, more important even than his role as policy-adviser. This is only partly a reflection of the greater emphasis given to the managerial function throughout Whitehall in the last decade. Since the introduction of the Survey in 1961 the Second Permanent Secretary has had a system to operate with clear objectives and dedicated methods and staff. Even when 'management' was regarded by many top officials as something done by people lower down the hierarchy, and policy advice was the distinguishing hallmark of a Permanent Secretary, the Second Permanent Secretary was a manager concerned 'to keep the process going', and to deliver plans and essential controls. Although the Survey and its processes are now more elaborate and refined, the basic management task is recognizably that of the 1970s. In a way peculiar to the job of Second Permanent Secretary, 'management' issues also provide a link between the 'mechanics' of Survey control and the broader policy questions raised throughout the Survey. It is even less possible in his job to make a hard-and-fast distinction between 'policy' and 'management'.

The Second Permanent Secretary has a staff in the central Treasury of 228 (December 1991), of whom 124 are middle or senior managers directly engaged in expenditure control. While the Permanent Secretary is in charge of all Treasury personnel matters, they are handled in a collegiate way. The Second Permanent Secretary is thus heavily involved, and in practice is able to exercise a strong influence over appointments made to posts under his command, particularly appointments to the pivotal positions of Deputy Secretary and Under Secretary.

Providing direction and coherence through the Survey process is an important managerial task, and one which overlaps with his co-ordinative function. As the business flows upwards from the divisions he has an oversight of the information and judgement offered to the Chief Secretary, and the opportunity to contribute from the broader perspective provided by his unique position in the hierarchy. At the same time, that perspective and his knowledge of, and concern with, the Chief Secretary's policy aims, provides the opportunity to pull together in a coherent pattern the separate threads of the advice and judgements of Expenditure Divisions on specific programmes and departmental spending.

Specific mechanisms for achieving coherence and co-ordination obviously include arrangements for regular meetings with the staff. Since Rawlinson's tenure it has been standard practice for the Second Permanent Secretary to meet weekly with his Deputy Secretaries, all the Heads of Groups (G3), the heads of central control groups such as GEP, FM, RC, together with the Chief Accountancy Adviser, and a representative from the Pay side. The purpose of the Committee on Government Public Expenditure Control (COGPEC) is partly to review progress and to take stock. It is also an opportunity for the Second Permanent Secretary to provide background briefing on the development of policy at ministerial level, and to outline thinking on issues of concern to the expenditure side which are under consideration in other parts of the Treasury. For example, at the earlier strategy stage of the Survey he might give the Groups a 'feel' for how tough the next Survey is going to be. His aim will be to give the assurance that no one Expenditure Division is being 'picked off' to deliver higher cuts than another, but rather that the Treasury is going to be equally tough across the board. In addition, the Second Permanent Secretary will, along with GEP, give the Groups something of the 'colour' of Cabinet discussions, as conveyed by the Chief Secretary or the Chancellor. Such occasions also provide the opportunity for his colleagues to raise with him issues of common concern or particular difficulty in the Expenditure Divisions, and to talk them through. The Second Permanent Secretary also meets weekly in the Public Expenditure Group (PEX) with a smaller group of those centrally concerned with expenditure policy, including particularly the Deputy Secretaries and the GEP divisions, to ensure that all the strands of the Survey are started in good time and kept to schedule, and to discuss any issues of substance or procedure connected with the mechanics of the Survey. In addition to the formal and regular meetings of COGPEC and PEX, the Second Permanent Secretary will from time to time meet with Heads of Groups at a particular stage in the Survey cycle. For example, after bids have been received in the Expenditure Divisions he may meet with a 'limited cast' drawn from the Survey Heads of Group, to have a more focused discussion on the implications of the bids for the Chief Secretary's general strategy. The advantages of the relatively small number of Treasury people involved

in public spending control mean that, in response to the latest development or crisis, he 'can gather round *his* table the Deputy Secretaries and
Under Secretaries (Grades 2 and 3, in the new nomenclature) who deal
with every spending programme' (Pliatzky 1989: 157).

Through these and other more informal meetings, he is able to provide leadership and constant encouragement to Expenditure Controllers to try to ensure that they achieve a satisfactory outcome for the
programmes of their departments, while exercising constant vigilance in
delivering to the Chief Secretary the emerging Planning/Control Total.
The Treasury has an interest in ensuring that the outcome for a department's programme is not unrealistic and hence liable to store up future
trouble. Caught between the top–down pressures from Treasury ministers for greater economy, and the bottom–up demands of their departments, the job of Expenditure Controllers can be both lonely and
stressful. One Second Permanent Secretary emphasized the importance
of ensuring that they understood how their particular programmes fitted
into the 'bigger' picture of the Chief Secretary's expenditure policy,
received appropriate guidance in the balancing of conflicting pressures,
and were exhorted to exercise taut control and promote value-for-
money.

Policy advice and co-ordination. The second major function of the
Second Permanent Secretary is to provide advice on policy issues for
the Chief Secretary. In practice this overlaps with and is often indistinguishable from his third, co-ordinative, function. Advice on policy
and the presentation of options normally flow directly from the processes of co-ordinating and achieving an integration of the contributions
of the line managers in the Expenditure Groups and Divisions, the
general staff in the central divisions, the specialist advisers in other parts
of the Treasury, and those with responsibilities for macro-economic
policy-making.

The relationship between the Chief Secretary and the Second Permanent Secretary is similar to that of any Permanent Secretary and Secretary of State, particularly when, since 1976, the Chief Secretary has
been in the Cabinet. The Second Permanent Secretary is the senior
adviser and available to give advice on any issue that the Chief Secretary
is interested in. But the relationship is more specifically focused because
the interest is always directed to the aim of controlling public expenditure, whereas the interests of a departmental Minister and Permanent
Secretary are more disparate and their objectives less well-defined.

The two major strategic issues which the Chief Secretary must decide
are, first, the Planning/Control Total for the coming year and the remit

to be proposed to his colleagues at the July Cabinet, and secondly, the priorities to be given to particular departmental programmes within this 'envelope'. The Second Permanent Secretary has important inputs to both, which embrace his third function of co-ordination. The first of these decisions is taken within the context of the government's longer-term objectives for public expenditure, themselves closely related to financial and economic policy. Since 1979 these objectives have changed, from the aim of reducing public expenditure in real terms, to one of a reduction in the GGE/GDP ratio, to a reduction in the ratio over time. We explain the origins and development of the objectives in Chapter 20; here we are concerned only to explain the Second Permanent Secretary's contribution. As the objectives are expressed in quantitative terms, the assessment of historic trends and future prospects and their public presentation are essential ingredients in the discussion of the probable outcomes of different sets of assumptions. This work is carried out mainly by GEP (whose Under Secretary reports directly to the Second Permanent Secretary) and the economists, and brought together by the Second Permanent Secretary, who also takes account of the assessments of the Expenditure Divisions about the realistic objectives for each programme.

Judgements about both the short- and longer-term objectives for public expenditure are taken within the wider context of the prospects for the economy, and the government's macro-economic strategy. Here the Second Permanent Secretary (and GEP in parallel) acts as 'a key link between the public expenditure command and the rest of the department in the formulation of policy' (former Second Permanent Secretary). He has a bridging role between the Permanent Secretary and the macro-economic side of the Treasury on the one hand, liaising with them and injecting into their discussions the expenditure side's input, and the expenditure side of the Treasury on the other. Lower down, GEP in its 'staff' capacity has a similar bridging role. His (and their) interaction with the economic side is constant, as both respond to changes in the politico-economic environment, and the pressures, the context, and the evolving strategy for public expenditure. These Treasury-wide discussions include consideration of the fiscal adjustment and the PSBR, and their interaction with different levels of public expenditure and its financing. The Second Permanent Secretary is able to feed in information and inform others in the Treasury about the pressures on the expenditure side, as the Survey gets under way.

One venue for these discussions until 1992 was the weekly meeting of the Treasury's Policy Co-ordination Committee (PCC) chaired by the Permanent Secretary. Both Second Permanent Secretaries attended, together with the Chief Economic Adviser, the Accountancy Adviser, the Deputy Chief Economic Adviser, the five Deputy Secretaries (two from expenditure), the Chancellor's PPS, and the Head of the Information Division. From October 1992 this was replaced by a Management Board comprising the Treasury's top ten officials. The creation of the Board was a result of recommendations in a report on the Treasury's management structure, commissioned by Sir Terry Burns (Permanent Secretary) and presented by Howard Davies, the Director-General of the CBI.

The Second Permanent Secretary also attended the Chancellor's annual weekend seminar to discuss the Budget strategy, held at Chevening or Dorneywood. The three months leading up to the Budget and the publication of the Financial Statement and Budget Report, and the MTFS were a period of intense activity for the Second Permanent Secretary, providing both the context and the starting-point for the next Survey. In the discussions on the Budget he represented the expenditure side. At their conclusion he was in a better position to update his staff on the macro-economic outlook for the Budget and specific matters of concern to the upcoming Survey, such as the likely pressures on the PSBR target, and new forecasts on unemployment and inflation. He provided for them and the Chief Secretary an appreciation of 'where expenditure policy is going' as a result. This appreciation was constantly updated throughout the progress of the Survey, and communicated to his staff. Priority was given by him to ensuring that the Expenditure Divisions regarded the economic pressures on total spending very seriously in their relationships with departments. It was important therefore for the Second Permanent Secretary to keep them up to date with the development of economic policy.

At the beginning of the Survey, Treasury Heads of Group (G3) provided an assessment of the prospects for the programmes covered by their Expenditure Divisions in the light of economic and demographic factors, drawing on the advice of GEP and the macro-economists. They considered the probable impact on their programmes of different political options, both governmental priorities and commitments, and the demands of organized groups. These were put to the Chief Secretary, who provided guidance on which options he wished them to take account of. Their assessments were discussed in some detail with the Chief Secretary, the Second Permanent Secretary, and the relevant Deputy Secretary. GEP then pulled all this together in a wide-ranging assessment of the prospects for the Survey that incorporated the views of the Second Permanent Secretary. This brought together the three main elements: the Chief Secretary's aims for public spending in the context of the government's broad political strategy; the Second Permanent Secretary's appreciation of the prospects for the main expenditure aggregates in relation to current economic and fiscal policy; and the assessments of the trends, pressures, and prospects for the individual programmes fed through GEP from the Expenditure Divisions.

These three elements provided the basic material for the expenditure strategy to be proposed in the Chief Secretary's memorandum to the Cabinet on the allocation of resources within the Control Total. Each element and the assessment as a whole was updated as the departments supplied information about the demands on their programmes from late May onwards, and in the light of the Expenditure Divisions' best estimates of the consequent likely outcome on their programmes. By then, the Chief Secretary would also have received letters (formerly bids) from his spending colleagues. The balance struck at this stage was a matter for the judgement of the Chief Secretary advised by the Second Permanent Secretary (and GEP), who gave his views on the overall situation as he saw it, and offered advice on the kind of ministerial discussion to aim for. He ensured that the Chief Secretary had all the information he needed to make a 'practicable proposal' to his colleagues, one which he thought the Chief Secretary, with the help of the Expenditure Divisions, could deliver from them at the conclusion of the Survey.

During this period the Chief Secretary and the Second Permanent Secretary gave constant attention not only to the planned outcome of the total spending strategy, but to its distribution between programmes. The process was iterative, and the interaction between the total and its distribution constant. From 1992 the top–down pressure to hold the Control Total was paramount. Within that total, judgement about the relative weight and hence priority to be accorded the separate bids was compounded of several elements. While the information coming up from Expenditure Divisions about programme bids incorporated assessments of value-for-money, only some of this was quantifiable, more useful for within-programme, than interprogramme and cross-departmental comparisons. As we discuss in Chapter 11 comparisons across programmes and departments are more a matter of political judgement, reflecting the commitments of the government expressed in manifesto and party documents endorsed and particularized in Cabinet agreements; the needs of departments argued in their submissions; and the priorities they themselves attached directly or tacitly to different programmes. The Chief Secretary had his own views of the relative merits of his colleagues' bids, and in forming a judgement on each programme had the advice of the Second Permanent Secretary, GEP, one of the

Deputy Secretaries, and the Expenditure Division concerned. Informally the Second Permanent Secretary might advise on what seems to him to be a reasonable outcome in the light of the official advice tendered.

The Second Permanent Secretary sees everything submitted to the Chief Secretary, whether from the Expenditure Divisions and senior staff, or from the departments. At some times of the year he can spend up to two hours a day on average reading copies of such submissions and papers prepared by his staff. All but the most important submissions go direct from the Expenditure Divisions to the Chief Secretary, and the Second Permanent Secretary only intervenes if he feels the need to. In doing so he ensures that the Chief Secretary is properly serviced with good-quality briefings, adding to them where necessary, and informs himself of the efficient progress and dispatch of business. It also provides him with the opportunity to assess the performance of his staff. The contribution of the Expenditure Divisions' Assistant Secretaries and their Principals is crucial, and particular attention is given to the quality of their submissions and briefings. The Second Permanent Secretary himself contributes selectively to submissions on individual programmes, for example where papers omit reference to a related policy issue currently in play, or require a change of emphasis to reflect recent developments in ministerial thinking. He makes a much greater contribution to papers on general expenditure policy, either discussing them extensively in draft with GEP, or submitting them himself.

He also advises on specific cases where large sums of money or particular difficulties are involved, as they arise in the bidding process during the Survey, or outside it where departments are working up a new proposal or conducting a review of policy. He may himself stimulate such reviews in consultation with his senior staff where he considers it necessary. As well, he advises on issues which cause particular difficulty or political sensitivity. After the drafting of the Agenda Letters for the Public Expenditure Survey discussions to which he might contribute, the Second Permanent Secretary advises the Chief Secretary on the conduct of the bilaterals and on the preparation for the Cabinet Expenditure Committee (EDX). These and other Survey issues are discussed in Chapter 13.

New initiatives. The Second Permanent Secretary is concerned not only with the care and maintenance of the system of public expenditure planning and control, with 'keeping the process going': a crucial part of his managerial, co-ordinating, and advisory functions is his responsibility for major changes to the system. Thus Henley presided over the design and introduction of cash limits. In the 1980s Second Permanent Secretaries played a central role in a host of similar initiatives, such as the introduction of cash planning, the shift from manpower ceilings to running costs controls, the provision of end-year flexibility for capital programmes, the redefinition and change in the use of the Reserve, the definition of the (1988) New Planning Total, the new Departmental Expenditure Reports, the (1992) New Control Total. As well, at any one time there are a number of major expenditure issues affecting more than one Expenditure Division and its spending department, such as local government finance and the control of nationalized industries finance. These and major system changes have political and sometimes macro-economic implications and will normally involve the Chancellor as well as the Chief Secretary. Supported by GEP, the Second Permanent Secretary plays a central role in advising them on such changes and in supervising their effective and timely introduction. He also advises when and how to engage in dialogue with the Public Accounts Committee and the Treasury and Civil Service Select Committee.

Relations with departments. The Second Permanent Secretary's fourth function is to ensure that relations with spending departments are maintained in good working order, to facilitate the effective conduct of public expenditure business. This task is mainly managerial and supervisory, and his influence is expressed and transmitted indirectly through his senior staff and the Expenditure Divisions. Directly, he is available at all times for consultation by Permanent Secretaries on expenditure business, and on the discharge of their responsibilities as Accounting Officers. He receives a steady stream of callers during the year, to discuss some details of a bid, or resolve some 'failure of communication'. Occasionally a Secretary of State will ask his Permanent Secretary to enquire 'whether the Treasury was really being serious in taking a particular line in the Survey', but this is often merely a pretext to reiterate the department's position. Where the department believed that the Chief Secretary had not fully understood its position, a Permanent Secretary might call on the Second Permanent Secretary to suggest that the Chief Secretary might have been inadequately briefed by the Expenditure Division because the latter had not understood the issues. In most cases the Expenditure Division had understood and briefed the Chief Secretary appropriately, and the Permanent Secretary's visit was again an occasion to re-emphasize the case made by the department. Sometimes, where discussions between a spending department's Finance Division and its Expenditure Division have stalled lower down, a Permanent Secretary might go to see the Second Permanent Secretary to try to resolve the deadlock. The Second Permanent Secretary is sometimes consulted by his opposite number at an early stage of a policy review or initiative where the sums of money involved are large. Likewise, a Permanent Secretary might try to elicit his support for the creation or retention of a senior post.

There is no formal mechanism for bringing Permanent Secretaries together to discuss Survey issues or expenditure business more generally, but they are discussed from time to time at informal gatherings of Permanent Secretaries and *ad hoc* meetings are occasionally concerned with particular issues. The main interdepartmental meetings are held at Principal Finance Officer level, convened by the Deputy Secretary charged with the co-ordination of expenditure business in the Whitehall spending departments, and at Principal Establishment Officer level, convened by the Deputy Secretary in charge of Civil Service management and pay (discussed below).

In addition to the four main functions described above, the Second Permanent Secretary has a number of other responsibilities. The most important of these involves approving on the Chief Secretary's behalf some of the Supply Estimates, claims on the Reserve, and changes in cash or running costs limits. Here he exercises prescribed delegated authority to decide without reference to the Chief Secretary. The translation of the agreed Survey bids into Estimates does involve some bargaining between Expenditure Divisions and departmental Finance Divisions over the precise allocation to subheadings of items of agreed expenditure, but this is normally settled lower down without reference to the Chief Secretary. If an Expenditure Division anticipates future expenditure arising from a proposed allocation in the Estimates it will be referred to the Chief Secretary with advice from the Second Permanent Secretary on how it should be determined. All requests for Supplementary Estimates go first to the Second Permanent Secretary, who has discretion to weed out those 'which would waste the Chief Secretary's time' because they simply embody policy decisions which the Chief Secretary has already agreed. He also maintains a close watch on the Reserve, with the assistance of GEP, who provide both him and the Chief Secretary with a monthly report on the balance and forecasted claims and outgoings. He sees all the claims submitted through the Expenditure Divisions, and advises the Chief Secretary on those which are large or contentious. On the others, he may give guidance to his

Expenditure Divisions on the submission to be made to the Chief Secretary.

The Second Permanent Secretary is the Treasury Accounting Officer for the Contingencies Fund, and has to approve or reject claims from departments where provision has not yet been made in the Estimates or presented as a Supplementary Estimate. The categories of eligible expenditures are strictly defined in *Government Accounting*, and reflect previous understandings between the Treasury and Parliament. Whether to allow or deny a claim can involve delicate discussions with other Permanent Secretaries. Until 1992 the Central Unit on Purchasing was also part of the Second Permanent Secretary's responsibilities. After that date it became the responsibility of the Deputy Secretary (Public Services), as part of a Purchasing Group.

THE DEPUTY SECRETARIES

Most of the eighteen Expenditure Divisions fall within the commands of the two Deputy Secretaries responsible for Public Services and for Industry, who report directly to the Second Permanent Secretary. The remaining divisions are the responsibility of the Deputy Secretaries whose work is mainly concerned with public and overseas finance. The Deputy Secretary for Civil Service Management and Pay has some divisions within his command—pay and financial management, for example, which are central to the making and co-ordinating of expenditure policy. He reports directly to the Permanent Secretary, but has many close links to the Second Permanent Secretary. In the period 1976–91 there were thirteen appointments to the two Deputy Secretary posts on the expenditure side, and four to the Deputy Secretary post with responsibility for Civil Service Management and Pay after the transfer of some of the Civil Service Department's functions in 1981. Only two of these appointments were made from outside the department. The career patterns of both officials are similar: service as private secretaries to ministers, secondment to the Cabinet Office—the hallmarks of potential high-flyers. Hayden Phillips was Deputy Secretary, Public Services, 1988–90, and moved to Management and Pay, 1990–2. He was appointed at the age of 45 from the Cabinet Office, where he had been Deputy Secretary in charge of MPO, on secondment from the Home Office. There he had served as Roy Jenkins's Principal Private Secretary in 1974–6, following him to Brussels a year later as Chef de Cabinet. On return to the Home Office he served as Assistant Secretary and Under Secretary until secondment to the Cabinet Office in 1986.

(After the 1992 general election he became Permanent Secretary of the newly created National Heritage Department.)

Richard Wilson was brought into the Treasury to head the Industry command in 1990 at the age of 48. He too came from the Cabinet Office, where he had been promoted Deputy Secretary and appointed head of the Economic Secretariat in September 1987, having served previously as an Under Secretary in MPO. Prior to secondment, he had served four years as Principal Establishments and Finance Officer in the Department of Energy, following earlier service there as both Principal and Assistant Secretary. His first department was the Board of Trade, which he joined as an Assistant Principal in 1966, moving to the Department of Energy after his first secondment to the Cabinet Office in 1971–3. (After the 1992 general election he became the Permanent Secretary of the Department of the Environment.)

The appointment of these two officials from outside the department partly reflected the relevance of their recent experience in the Cabinet Office to the two Treasury posts, left vacant by the unusual rapid turnover of senior staff in the late 1980s. With these two exceptions, all those who have held one of the three Deputy Secretary posts since 1976 have had experience as Heads of Group (Under Secretary) on the expenditure side, besides experience as well on the finance side of the department. The career pattern of Andrew Edwards, appointed Deputy Secretary (Public Services) in 1990, is not untypical. He was previously Under Secretary with responsibility for the Local Government Group of Expenditure Divisions, and earlier had been Head of Group with responsibility for the European Community. As an Assistant Secretary he had served in the latter and in the General Expenditure Policy Division.

Since at least 1976 no Treasury Deputy Secretary on the expenditure or management and pay sides has failed to advance further to Permanent Secretary or its equivalent, after an average of two years in post. Five have been promoted Second Permanent Secretary in the Treasury, three to take charge of the expenditure side; and eight have been appointed to head other Whitehall departments. Some Treasury Under Secretaries advance no further before retirement from the Service; a few are appointed to senior posts outside Whitehall, in the National Savings Bank or the Charity Commission for example. Promotion to Deputy Secretary, however, carries the very strong presumption of a further advance within a short period of time. It is a stepping-stone to the top of the Civil Service.

The two Deputy Secretaries on the expenditure side have four main functions: first, to supervise the handling of a few major issues within their respective commands. It is not necessarily the case that the most important issues are dealt with at the Deputy Secretary or Under Secretary levels; they are often dealt with in the Expenditure Divisions by Principals or Assistant Secretaries, sometimes directly with the Chief Secretary or other Treasury ministers. What is a politically sensitive issue for a department or the Treasury may not be important in the conventional sense, and it is such issues which tend to rise to the Deputy Secretary level, and beyond to Ministers.

Coping with the sheer volume of paper which crosses the Deputy Secretary's desk is a major task. One estimate in 1992 was 140–50 papers per day at peak periods. This is a reflection less of bureaucratic 'paper-chasing' than that the Treasury is in constant dialogue with itself, and the writing and copying of papers are an important medium for conducting the arguments and counter-arguments at all levels. Officials recruited from other departments are impressed with the ease of formal and informal communication, through the copying of papers on a need-to-know basis (rather than being motivated by self-protection, as tends to happen in large organizations with more formal hierarchies).

The Deputy Secretary for Public Services is involved in some of the big expenditure projects which arise from the social security, health, and local government programmes. More broadly, each Deputy Secretary becomes the senior specialist—the 'Treasury's man'—with a special interest and responsibility in a few of the most important of the subject areas covered by his command. The Deputy Secretary in charge of Public Services cannot avoid some specialization in Local Government finance; the Deputy Secretary of Industry takes a similar broad responsibility for the main work on privatization. Treasury Deputy Secretaries have considerable discretion in how they define and carry out their jobs. While the subject-matter of the command will dictate the range of issues, what they choose to spend time on reflects not only the degree of ministerial interest but also their own previous experience and particular current interests.

The second function, co-ordinating expenditure policy, has several dimensions: within the command, across the Treasury, and across Whitehall. Achieving coherent and consistent expenditure policy within the command is more a matter for each Head of Group, but during the course of the Survey round the Deputy Secretary meets regularly with all of them to discuss progress, and at the end to discuss what issues to take up in the next round and the appropriate defensive and attacking strategies to be adopted. Normally the Deputy Secretary does not get involved in the detail of the Expenditure Divisions' responses to departmental bids, but takes a close interest in those programmes where there are real problems. One Deputy Secretary likened this stage of the Survey to a series of simultaneous chess-games: looking across all the boards, some games were straightforward and predictable, in others it was already apparent that the moves would be complex and the end-game difficult and drawn out. It was those 'games' he kept an eye on. Deputy Secretaries see the drafts of the proposed replies for the Chief Secretary's Agenda Letters, and may contribute points of substance or suggest improvements to drafting, for example by suggesting 'Don't show so much of our hand'. One important concern at this stage is to ensure that the Chief Secretary is getting the standard of service he needs, and that the Groups are getting specialist advice and support from the Treasury's central divisions, Public Expenditure Economics, Operations Research, Accountancy, and Financial Management for example. The Deputy Secretary is, however, more heavily involved at the ministerial bilateral stage, discussing the general strategy with the Chief Secretary, the Second Permanent Secretary, and the Under Secretary at GEP, and offering advice on tactics, and how to handle specific issues as they arise in the bilaterals. At this time of the year he might see the Chief Secretary once or twice a day. When the Local Government settlement is determined in May–July, the Deputy Secretary for Public Services sees the Chief Secretary as frequently. Outside the period of the Survey, there is less contact.

Two other roles which the Deputy Secretary plays as part of his responsibility for the work of the Groups within his command are: first, 'patrolling the boundaries' between the Treasury and the departments, keeping an eye on the progress of relationships between his Groups and the departments they shadow, to try to ensure that they are workable, effective, and in good repair; and, secondly, 'trouble-shooting', helping Groups to 'get it right' in their submissions to Ministers, spotting difficulties, and dealing with problem areas in the relationships with departments.

At the next level up, Deputy Secretaries have a responsibility for achieving coherence and consistency in expenditure policy across the Treasury. They 'span the divide between the various bits of the Treasury' (Second Permanent Secretary). This arises partly from their positional power as senior officials at the top of the department, partly from the nature of the business they supervise, and partly from their personal involvement with specific issues which are linked directly or indirectly with other parts of the Treasury. For example, local government finance touches the work of several other parts of the Treasury and the Deputy Secretary (Public Services) through his command responsibility and personal specialization is in a position to co-ordinate the Treasury's response on any interlinked issues which arise. More directly, local government finance affects many Expenditure Divisions within his and other commands across the department, and he is responsible for co-ordinating their interests and efforts. The interaction between the community charge/council tax and the benefits system required the co-ordination of the policy-interests of the social security, local government, and territorial divisions within his own command; at the same time the RPI implications of the level of community charge/ council tax required the co-ordination of the economists in the Chief Economic Adviser's divisions. Similarly, negotiations over the Local Government settlement in May–July involve the co-ordination of many different interests represented across several Treasury divisions. The Deputy Secretary takes the lead here, and in the bilaterals with the D.o.E. The Deputy Secretary (Industry) led for the Treasury on the Citizen's Charter, which in 1991–2 was a high-profile trans-Treasury issue, requiring a senior official to pull together the strands of different departmental interests. As a public sector policy concerned with issues of privatization, contracting-out, and so on, the Industry command was an obvious place to locate that responsibility.

The different interests represented within the expenditure, finance, management, and economic analysis sides of the Treasury sometimes require a more organized co-ordination, where for example a policy review is contemplated or under way in Cabinet. A Deputy Secretary may take the initiative and put together an *ad hoc* team from among those across the Treasury with relevant expertise or knowledge, or who have responsibility in the divisions, to analyse and report on the issues from a broad spending perspective. The aim is to provide Treasury ministers with the appropriate analytical support, while avoiding the impression that the Treasury is taking the lead in a policy review, trespassing on departmental turf. The small size of the department, its non-hierarchical and collegial methods of work, and its organizational flexibility make it relatively easy to set up a small team quickly and informally.

All three Deputy Secretaries are members of the Treasury's main formal co-ordinating committee, the Management Board, and formerly the Policy Co-ordination Committee chaired by the Permanent Secretary, and contribute from their different expenditure perspectives to the co-ordination of grand strategy. At the same time they ensure that the work of their commands reflects and is consistent with that strategy as it evolves. They are also members of COGPEC and PEX, more narrowly concerned with Treasury expenditure policy, discussed above.

The Deputy Secretary for Public Services has a particular responsibility for the co-ordination of the public expenditure business across the whole of the Treasury's expenditure side. The formal expression of this is his chairmanship of the Treasury Public Expenditure Committee (TPEC), to which representatives of all the Expenditure Divisions are invited, at whatever level they choose, from Under Secretary to Principal. Meetings provide a formal opportunity to initiate new proposals or procedures relating to the Survey and its conduct, or to revise and change them. It also provides an opportunity for individual Expenditure Divisions to raise issues relating to the Survey or the in-year control of expenditure. Proposals for changes to the Survey and its guidelines would normally be initiated and brought to the Committee by GEP or the appropriate central division—Pay, RC, FM. Through the Committee, Expenditure Divisions would be briefed on how to implement the new *Survey Guidelines*, for example on the application of end-year flexibility systems. Advice and guidance to the Expenditure Divisions on the interpretation of the *Guidelines* and the conduct of the Survey would fill out that provided by the Treasury to departmental PFOs in pre-Survey meetings and through the PESC circulation list. 'What we say to the troops on the ground will go beyond what we say to the "enemy"' (Chairman of TPEC). Specific major items of Survey business, such as the New Planning Total or the New Control Total, are normally discussed in specially convened TPEC committees.

A further level of co-ordination of expenditure policy—across Whitehall—is also the responsibility of the Deputy Secretary, Public Services. The main formal mechanism for this purpose is the circulation list of PFOs (or PESC), which provides the medium for transmitting formal communications about the conduct of the Survey. Through it the spending departments are given their 'Survey marching orders'. Six or seven times a year the Deputy Secretary chairs Treasury meetings of the twenty-five to thirty PFOs of the main spending departments. They provide an opportunity for discussion of general Survey issues: what the general ground-rules will be, how the Survey will be handled, and new Survey items included in the upcoming *Guidelines*, for example the adoption of a new approach to running costs control or end-year flexibility. Treasury papers for such meetings are prepared by GEP for general Survey issues, and by other divisions across the Treasury with appropriate responsibility and expertise, Pay or FM, for example.

Other than at meetings of the Cabinet's EDX Committee, the co-ordination of policies across Whitehall departments is more a Cabinet

Office than Treasury function, but the need arises occasionally on specific expenditure issues, and the Treasury tries to make use of relevant experience of the Deputy Secretaries. An example of this is the need to co-ordinate expenditure on departmental science and technology programmes, to try to ensure the best value-for-money. One Deputy Secretary who had moved from the Cabinet Office kept in touch with the Chief Scientific Adviser there, whose advice was helpful in the assessment of departmental bids.

The Deputy Secretary in charge of Civil Service Management and Pay reports directly to the Permanent Secretary and not the Second Permanent Secretary (Public Expenditure). While the command is not therefore formally a part of the expenditure side of the Treasury, working relationships between its divisions and those of the commands of the two other expenditure Deputy Secretaries are very close. This is particularly the case in those areas of responsibility—pay, running costs, financial management, and Next Steps—which are central to the work of all the Expenditure Divisions. The Deputy Secretary's sphere of responsibility cross-cuts other Treasury sides as well as expenditure. Civil Service pay negotiations and settlements and responsibility for advice on Pay Review Body recommendations and other public service pay and superannuation policies are of significance not only to the Expenditure Divisions, but to those in finance, and economic analysis and forecasting. Because of these links with other parts of the Treasury, the Deputy Secretary has more contact with a wider array of Treasury ministers than the two expenditure Deputy Secretaries. On pay, and especially costly or politically sensitive pay decisions, he sees a lot of the Chancellor, and is brought into frequent contact with the Treasury minister other than the Chancellor who has general oversight of the work of the Civil Service aspects of his command. Through work on public sector pay, the nationalized industries, Next Steps, running costs, and FMI, he reports to the Chief Secretary, and sees the Financial Secretary on Inland Revenue management issues. At lower levels his staff consult, liaise, and co-ordinate their work with divisions throughout the Treasury on all these issues—and directly with other departments, for example the OPSS (on Next Steps, Market Testing, and Civil Service management) and the leading spending departments on pay, for example health, education, and defence. The Deputy Secretary has responsibility for the network of Principal Establishment Officers (the principal officials in Whitehall concerned with personnel management) who are also often PFOs. He chairs the regular meetings of this group, as does the Deputy Secretary (Public Services) the meetings of PFOs.

HEADS OF GROUP

Immediately below the Deputy Secretaries are the Heads of Group. They occupy a 'pivotal' position in the making and co-ordinating of expenditure policy, responsible for the overall management and the general direction and co-ordination of the work of groups of Treasury divisions. Promotion to Under Secretary normally occurs in the early forties from within the department, although occasionally an appointment is made from elsewhere in Whitehall. Those promoted or moved sideways to manage the Expenditure Divisions will usually have had some previous experience of working there at an earlier part of their career.

The post of Head of Group provides the opportunity to broaden experience still further, and to hone those managerial skills and display that balance and judgement which will be needed for further progress to the Treasury's top posts. Each Expenditure Group comprises a number of divisions dealing with the programmes and issues of a range of departments. At this level, Heads of Group eschew the tactical considerations of dealing with the detailed expenditure business of a single department or programme, which they leave to their divisional heads, and concentrate on the broader sweep of a concerted strategy for handling several programmes and a number of departments. The determination of what is feasible and desirable within parts of the Group has to be constantly tested and refined by reference to the evolving grand strategy of the Treasury ministers. Heads of Group are detached, but not insulated, from the pressures from above and below. Their concern is to achieve a coherent and consistent response to a group of spending departments which is both sensitive to the aims and strategies of their ministers and practicable in terms of the Chief Secretary's overall expenditure objectives. At the same time they contribute a distinctive Group perspective to the formulation of the grand strategy for achieving those objectives. Through their formal participation in co-ordinating committees such as COGPEC and TPEC, and informally in meetings and consultations with GEP, the Chief Secretary, the Second Permanent Secretary, the Deputy Secretary, and the heads of their own Expenditure Divisions, Heads of Groups play a key role in the progressive alignment of the strategies of the expenditure side as a whole and those of its component groups.

While concern with strategy and co-ordination is their main function, Heads of Group also take responsibility for particular issues which arise in the work of their Expenditure Divisions, where for example there is overlap between divisions or a need to co-ordinate Group interests with other parts of the Treasury. The Under Secretary may also assume a personal responsibility for an issue, where the Chief Secretary or Chancellor has shown particular interest. He may also take a personal responsibility for some issue of intrinsic importance, or those where he has relevant previous experience. In circumstances where he rather than an Assistant Secretary or Principal in the Expenditure Division is freer to do so, he may sometimes take charge of an urgent piece of business.

GENERAL EXPENDITURE POLICY GROUP (GEP)

The nerve-centre of the expenditure side of the Treasury is the General Expenditure Policy Group (GEP), positioned between the operational Expenditure Groups and Divisions on the one hand and the Chief Secretary and the Second Permanent Secretary on the other. Its three divisions comprise a central intelligence unit for the whole of the expenditure side. The General Expenditure Planning Division (GEP1) is responsible for general policy on public expenditure planning, the co-ordination of the Survey, the preparation of the expenditure side of the Unified Budget (previously Autumn Statement), and the Departmental Expenditure Reports published in February. It is also concerned with issues of long-term expenditure and the co-ordination of policy reviews. The General Expenditure Control Division (GEP2) is responsible for general policy on Parliamentary Supply matters, Estimates, and Contingencies Fund. It is also responsible for the in-year control of expenditure, including running costs, cash limits, and the Reserve. The General Expenditure Statistics Division (GEP3) monitors the Control Total through the year, and monitors and forecasts Supply Expenditure. It provides analyses and data on all types of public expenditure, and is responsible for developing information systems and new data.

At the heart of the Survey process, the main functions of GEP are to co-ordinate and focus the energies and efforts of the eighteen Expenditure Divisions and their Heads of Group to ensure the delivery of the Planning/Control Total targeted by the Chief Secretary and the Chancellor and its allocation between competing programmes, and to try to ensure that that total is not exceeded in-year. Through its many stages, from the drafting of the *Guidelines* to the publication of the Budget and the subsequent post-mortem evaluation, the progress of the Survey is supervised, managed, and steered by the Under Secretary and the staff of the three divisions. From a perspective above the many battles waged in the trenches of the Expenditure Divisions in the months leading up to the autumnal bilaterals, GEP sees and monitors the progress of the war;

advises the Chief Secretary where tactically, and with what weapons, an advance might be made; warns where ground may have to be conceded; and provides successive forecasts of probable outcomes as the Survey proceeds. In Chapter 12 we explain in more detail how these tasks are performed in the course of the Survey round.

The Under Secretary at the head of the Group occupies a pivotal position on the expenditure side. It is one of the Treasury's key posts, and appointments to it are made from among the department's rising stars. For most it is a staging-post to the department's top jobs. Both Alex Allan (1990–2) and Rachel Lomax (1988–90) had served previously as the Chancellor of the Exchequer's Principal Private Secretary, normally the mark of a high-flyer. Rachel Lomax was promoted out of GEP to Deputy Chief Economic Adviser. Andrew Turnbull (1985–8) moved directly from the Under Secretary post to the Prime Minister's office as Principal Private Secretary, a route followed by (Sir) Robin Butler (1977–80), who returned from No. 10 to head the expenditure side as Second Permanent Secretary before appointment as Secretary to the Cabinet. After the 1992 general election, Alex Allan moved from GEP to No. 10 as Mr Major's Principal Private Secretary; Andrew Turnbull returned to the Treasury and succeeded Nick Monck as Second Permanent Secretary. (Sir) John Anson after service as GEP Under Secretary was promoted to Deputy Secretary on the expenditure side, and finished his career as Second Permanent Secretary.

The Under Secretary acts in a 'staff' capacity to both the Second Permanent Secretary and the Chief Secretary, as described earlier. At the very heart of the expenditure process, it is the most demanding job on the expenditure side, and one of the most demanding in the Treasury as a whole. It provides an opportunity for the incumbent to display qualities of judgement, tactical awareness and acumen, powers of analysis, negotiating and presentational skills, and a keen appreciation of the politics of grand strategy and ministerial sensitivities. Just as an Under Secretary in charge of a Group of Expenditure Divisions has a broader expenditure perspective than any single head of a division, so the GEP Under Secretary sees a broader picture still across all Groups, and brings to that picture the detachment of an 'outsider'. Through contact with both the Chief Secretary and the Second Permanent Secretary, the Under Secretary has greater familiarity with the changing politico-economic context which provides the frame of reference for evolving expenditure strategy as the Survey progresses. While an understanding and appreciation of that context is necessary for Heads of Groups, the Under Secretary at GEP is involved in the shaping of that context through the transmission upwards of advice and intelligence on the 'bottom–up' pressures mediated through the Expenditure Divisions, and is at the same time one of the main channels through which the Chief Secretary's thinking about general strategy and his instructions about particular priorities and programmes are conveyed. As the central co-ordinator, the Under Secretary is a key member of those Treasury committees mentioned earlier in the chapter, COGPEC concerned with the co-ordination of expenditure business across the whole of the Treasury, PEX and TPEC within the expenditure side, and PESC outside the department across the Whitehall spending departments.

8

The Whitehall Spending Departments

There is no official definition of Whitehall spending departments. Here and throughout the book we use the term to describe those departments, ministries, or offices directly supervised by a Minister, which negotiate separately with the Chief Secretary in the autumnal bilaterals,[1] and whose officials deal directly with the Treasury Expenditure Divisions. (For a discussion of the definitional problems see Pollitt 1984; Rose 1987; Dunleavy 1989a.) In 1992–3 there were nineteen spending departments, all of whom (with the exception of Overseas Development) had Cabinet Ministers. These comprise the 'main spending departments' identified in Table 8.1. This table shows the main departments which constitute the core of Whitehall. Each department's subordinate 'departments' are shown where these are classified as such by the Treasury in public expenditure documents. There are a number of other organizations classified as 'units' for the purpose of the public expenditure and Supply Estimates process, for example Executive Agencies and Non-Departmental Public Bodies, most of whom deal with the Treasury only indirectly through a main sponsor department.

We show the level of expenditure in 1992–3 planned for each main spending department. Three measures are used: spending counted as part of the New Control Total, central government's own spending, and gross running costs. Table 8.1 also shows the total staff employed by those central government departments. We have chosen these measures to highlight the varying amount of resources used by departments, according to the degree to which responsibility for expenditure moves from the core of Whitehall departments to satellite agencies and insti-

[1] Until 1992 the arrangements for the minor departments varied from year to year, but there were annual bilaterals for all the major departments. The Chairmen of the Inland Revenue and Customs and Excise had bilaterals too, with the responsible junior Treasury minister. The other departments of the Chancellor of the Exchequer, the small legal departments, and the Cabinet Office were normally handled at official level, subject in all cases to the approval of the Chief Secretary. Following the changes in 1992, the procedures have only changed marginally. Bilaterals form part of a process involving EDX, although the Chief Secretary continues to have discussions with Ministers in charge of the major departments. Arrangements for the smaller departments remain much the same.

TABLE 8.1. *The main spending departments, 1993*

Main department (with subordinate 'departments')[a]	Expenditure in 1992–3 (£bn)[b]			Central government manpower
	New Control Total	Central government expenditure	Gross running costs	
Ministry of Defence	23.8	23.8	6.2	138,000[c]
Foreign and Commonwealth Off. (Overseas Development Administration)	1.4 (2.2)	1.4 (2.2)	0.5 (0.7)	8,200 (1,700)
Ministry of Agriculture, Fisheries, and Food (Intervention Board)	2.2	2.4	0.4	11,200
Dept. of Trade and Industry[d] (Exports Credits Guarantee Dept., Off. of Fair Trading, Off. of Telecommunications, Off. of Electricity Regulation, Off. of Gas Supply)	1.7	1.6	0.5	11,500
Dept. of Employment Group (ACAS, Health and Safety Commission)	3.5	3.2	1.5	58,400
Dept. of Transport	6.8	2.6	0.5	11,500
Dept. of Environment (Off. of Water Services, Ordnance Survey, Property Holdings and Central Support Services, PSA Services)	41.0	4.2	0.9	20,400
Home Off. (Charity Commission)	6.0	2.5	1.6	51,600

Department				
Lord Chancellor's and Law Officers' Depts. (Crown Off., Scotland, Crown Prosecution Service, Northern Ireland Court Service, Land Registry, Public Record Off., Serious Fraud Off., Treasury Solicitor's Dept.)	2.4	2.1	0.9	29,500
Dept. for Education (Off. for Standards in Education—Ofsted)	7.2	3.8	0.1	2,700
Dept. of National Heritage[e]	1.0	0.9	0.03	800
Dept. of Health (Off. of Population Censuses and Surveys)	28.2	27.8	0.4	6,900[f]
Dept. of Social Security	61.5	69.1	2.7	82,600
Scottish Off.[g] (Agriculture and Fisheries Dept., Industry Dept., Education Dept., Environment Dept., Home and Health; Forestry Commission,[h] General Register Office (Scotland), Scottish Courts Administration, Scottish Records Off.)	12.7	5.9	0.4	13,400
Welsh Off.	6.0	2.9	0.1	2,400
Northern Ireland Off.:[i] Dept. of Finance and Personnel, Dept. of Health and Social Services, Dept. of the Environment for NI, Dept. of Education for NI, Dept. of Economic Development, Dept. of Agriculture for NI	6.6	6.7	0.7	142,900[j]

TABLE 8.1 (cont.)

Main department (with subordinate 'departments')[a]	Expenditure in 1992–3 (£bn)[b]			Central government manpower
	New Control Total	Central government expenditure	Gross running costs	
HM Treasury and the Chancellor of Exchequer's Depts. (HM Customs and Excise, Inland Revenue, Crown Estate Office, Dept. of National Savings, Government Actuary's Dept., National Investment and Loans Office, Paymaster General's Office, Registry of Friendly Societies, Royal Mint, Central Statistical Off.)	3.6	3.6	3.0[k]	105,100
Cabinet Off. and Off. of Public Service and Science[l] (HMSO, Central Office of Information, Chessington Computer Centre, Central Computer and Telecommunications Agency, Parliamentary Commissioner and Health Service Commissioners)	1.5	1.5	0.1	2,400

[a] Primarily based on the Treasury's Groupings and ordering of departments for the purposes of the Public Expenditure and Parliamentary Estimates documents. They are broadly based on ministerial responsibilities. Included are changes announced after the 1992 general election.

[b] Figures are for the main and subordinate departments combined, unless otherwise stated.

c If armed forces manpower (covered by programme expenditure) were included the total would be 403,000.

d Following the 1992 general election the DTI took over most of the responsibilities of the Dept. of Energy, with the exception of responsibility for energy efficiency, which was transferred to the D.o.E. The new Secretary of State revived the title of President of the Board of Trade.

e Created after the Apr. 1992 general election and headed by a Cabinet Minister. It is the product of a merging of the Office of Arts and Libraries (from the Lord Chancellor's Dept.), responsibilities for broadcasting (from the Home Office), sport (from the DFE), tourism (from Employment), heritage (from Environment), and film and export licensing of antiques (from the DTI).

f If total NHS staffing (covered under programme expenditure) were included the total figure would be 879,000.

g The Scottish Off. is unusual in that it is based around separate policy depts., discussed in Ch. 14.

h The Forestry Commission is unusual constitutionally as it has the legal status and functions of a government dept., since 1992–3 reports directly to the Secretary of State for Scotland but is also responsible to the Minister of Agriculture and the Welsh Secretary, and has a statutorily appointed Chairman and Board of Commissioners with specific duties and powers.

i The NIO is treated as any other UK dept. in terms of public expenditure planning and control, the NI depts. are not; although both the NIO and the depts. are accountable to the Secretary of State for NI. Discussed in Ch. 14.

j The running costs and manpower figures include the NIO and the NI depts. Strictly speaking central government manpower here should be 200, i.e. only for the NIO as this is treated as a UK dept., but in practice the Treasury agrees a global running costs and associated manpower limit for the government of Northern Ireland, only a part of which (that for the NIO) is monitored and controlled by the Treasury.

k Of this figure the departmental Treasury accounts for running costs of £97m.

l Created on 29 May 1992. It is within the Cabinet Off. and reports to the Chancellor of the Duchy of Lancaster and Minister of Public Service and Science. It combines the responsibilities of the former Off. of the Minister for the Civil Service (with its Next Steps Agency Team, Units on the Citizen's Charter, Efficiency, and Market Testing) with the Off. of Science and Technology (created out of the Chief Scientific Adviser's Off. and science responsibilities transferred from the DFE). The dept. is also responsible for the policy on open government. It is highly integrated into the Cabinet Office.

Sources: Based on: Cabinet Office 1992; Cm. 2219; and FCO 1992.

tutions. The level of expenditure also varies according to the definitions used by the Treasury for the purposes of presenting public expenditure planning and control goals.

The New Control Total definition includes spending by central government departments on their own programmes and support channelled through those departments to local government and nationalized industries. It is spending so categorized for which each Secretary of State or Minister negotiates with the Treasury in the annual PES round. Central government spending is narrower and involves only those programmes directly controlled and carried out by central government departments. Running costs are narrower still, involving only the administrative spending by central government and the costs of wages and salaries of officials employed by Whitehall departments. From 1986 the Treasury introduced a separate control regime for running costs, delineating such spending from wider programmes involving goods and services and capital expenditure aimed at achieving the policy goals of a department (discussed in Chapter 18).

Several examples from the table illustrate the point about variations in spending levels. In the case of the Ministry of Defence all New Control spending is made up of spending by central government as there are no transfers or grants to other agencies. In contrast the Department of the Environment is nominally responsible for £41 billion of public expenditure, yet only about a tenth of this is directly spent by the department on its own central government programmes. A similar, if less extreme, pattern emerges for example with the spending profiles of the Home Office, Department of Transport, and the Department for Education, all of which dispense grants and support to local authorities and have relatively small central government budgets. It is also clear from a close examination of the running costs figures used in the table which departments are particularly labour-intensive. The three largest running costs budgets are for the Ministry of Defence, Department of Social Security, and the Treasury (to support the Chancellor of the Exchequer's other departments). Together they spend nearly £11 billion (or more than 50 per cent of total running costs) to support more than 325,000 civil servants. But in terms of the relative importance to the whole expenditure of a central government department, though large, the running costs allocations to Defence and Social Security represent only 26 per cent and 4 per cent of their total central government spending respectively. In contrast the Treasury's total running costs allocation represents 80 per cent, the Home Office's 64 per cent, and the Lord Chancellor's and Law Officers' 42 per cent of their total central government spending.

It has been argued that the level and type of budget has important implications for the politics of resource allocation. Dunleavy (1989*a* and 1989*b*) argues that bureaucrats will protect their core (essentially their running costs) budget at the expense of bureau budget (core plus direct payments to the private sector), programme budget (roughly, central government spending in our table), and super-programme budget (the New Control Total here). Rather like peeling an onion, it is asserted that the 'rational' bureaucrat will allow cuts in the super-programme budget first, followed by the programme, and then the bureau budget, protecting the core. A number of points can be raised in objection to this model.

However elegant the theorizing, it is flawed because it does not allow for the complexity of the public expenditure planning and control system. First, bureaucrats cannot protect their 'core' (that is running costs) because since 1986 these have been ring-fenced by the Treasury and subject to ever-more rigorous controls. For example, running costs allocations are made on the assumption of at least 1.5 per cent efficiency gains. Second, whatever the bureaucrat's view (and there is a great deal of concern among departmental officials about running costs), ministers are less concerned about the levels of spending on core budgets, rather more exercised by the bureau, programme, and, contrary to Dunleavy's views, the super-programme budgets, because they form the means by which policy goals are achieved. Third, while it is true to assert that spending by agencies outside Whitehall has traditionally been the source of the first and easiest pickings for cuts by central government departments when the spending climate has been tough, this has had more to do with the type of spending involved (capital rather than current) than its perceived relationship with a wider super-programme budget. It is also not true to say that total spending by local authorities or regional Health authorities or Police authorities has been cut in order to protect budgets closer to the core of Whitehall; the evidence points to the reverse being true. Spending in real terms on total Department of Health programmes (using the NCT definition) rose 31 per cent between 1987 and 1992, whereas the central government element of that spending rose by only 22 per cent, total Home Office spending grew by 42.5 per cent, and its central government spending by only 33.3 per cent.

In the rest of this chapter we provide a brief survey of the main changes which have affected the spending departments since the late 1970s. We then analyse their functions. This is followed by more detailed analysis of the structure, role, and functions of departmental Finance Divisions and of Principal Finance Officers.

THE CHANGING CONTEXT

Since 1976 there have been many changes in the 'geography of administration' (Hennessy 1989). The most important of these was the abolition of seven departments in the period up to 1992, including the Civil Service Department in 1981, the Departments of Trade and Industry in 1983, the DHSS in 1988, and the Department of Energy in 1992. Six new departments were created, including Transport separated from the D.o.E. in 1976, the re-creation of the DTI in 1983, the establishment of the D.o.H. and DSS in 1988, and the creation of the Department of National Heritage after the 1992 general election.

There have been frequent classification changes, and transfer of programmes and parts of programmes between departments, with consequential organizational adjustments. Among these are the loss of functions resulting from the privatization programme of nationalized industries and public corporations, previously sponsored by departments. Some of this loss has been balanced by new responsibilities for regulatory agencies, such as OFTEL (under the DTI's wing), created to oversee the newly privatized corporations. Policy innovations are also responsible for changes in the administrative geography. Law reforms, for example, have led to the creation of the Serious Fraud Office and Crown Prosecution Service.

The biggest single impetus to organizational change in Whitehall is the Next Steps Executive Agency initiative, discussed in Chapter 5. By the summer of 1993 there were ninety Executive Agencies or Defence Support Agencies under the aegis of Whitehall and Northern Ireland departments. Whilst Ministers remain responsible for the work of agencies, and each Minister's core departmental staff continues to have oversight for many financial and policy questions, nevertheless the structure and mode of operation of Whitehall departments have been radically changed. As we shall see, this has not only entailed running down a large part of the headquarters finance function, but it has also affected the relationships between officials both within and between departments, and led to the creation of a triangular network of department–agency–Treasury.

The structure and organization of all departments have also been affected by a range of financial initiatives since 1979: the impact of FMI, the running costs regime, relocation out of London, the winding down of the central services provided by the PSA, market-testing, and, to a lesser extent, by discrete developments such as the purchasing initiative. As many of these developments are at a relatively early stage of implementation, our classification of the spending departments, their functions, and their Finance Divisions provides a snapshot in time, *circa* 1992.

The structure and organization of central government in the three territories of Scotland, Wales, and Northern Ireland is different from the other spending departments, reflecting their different constitutional, historical, and social settings. These differences combine to produce very different processes for allocating and controlling their expenditure, meriting separate treatment later in the book (Chapter 14). Even after direct rule in 1972, Northern Ireland has remained the most distinctive of the three territories in terms of its public administration and public spending. The Northern Ireland Office (NIO) is a Department of State and treated by the Treasury like any other spending department. The six Northern Ireland departments are not treated in the same way. They are not Departments of State, and are not responsible to the NIO but report directly to the Secretary of State, who takes on the monitoring and control functions previously exercised by the Stormont Parliament. They are effectively responsible for everything except 'reserved or exceptional matters', mainly security and constitutional matters which are the responsibility of the NIO. Because of the unusually circumscribed powers of local councils, and despite the existence of statutory authorities (responsible for services such as education, housing, health, and personal social services), the Northern Ireland departments are responsible for many 'parish pump' issues not normally associated with the policy divisions of other spending departments.

DEPARTMENTAL FINANCE DIVISIONS

The expenditure business of each Whitehall spending department is conducted mainly but not exclusively through its Finance Division. Structure and organization varies with the size, function, and historical evolution of each department, and with the size of spend. The larger departments, such as D.o.H., DSS, D.o.E., and the territories tend to have a separate dedicated Finance Division (or Branch or Group); the smaller departments, for example Cabinet Office/Office of Public Service and Science and DTI, combine the finance function with establishments or more widely manpower and personnel functions. The M.o.D. alone has an Office of Management and Budget (OMB).

The head of the Finance Division is the Principal Finance Officer, a key departmental appointment normally filled at the Under Secretary level, although in some departments, when the finance function is combined with establishments or manpower, the appointment is at Deputy

Secretary level. Uniquely the M.o.D.'s OMB is headed by a Second Permanent Secretary, reflecting the size and complexity of the department's current and capital programme budget and the largest running costs of any Whitehall department.

There is greater variation still within Finance Divisions. The M.o.D.'s OMB has sixty-one branches and sections performing financial functions; most other departments have between six and twenty. The number is partly related to the range of functions, and the complexity of the making and delivering of policy. Despite these differences, four financial functions are common to most Finance Divisions: the Survey, running costs, internal audit, and accounts (see Thain and Wright 1992*e* for further details).

In the Scottish Office the finance function is the responsibility of 'central services', which since the mid-1970s has operated like most finance and establishments divisions in other spending departments. The PFO has responsibility for the finance of all five Scottish departments. Beneath him one Grade 5 deals with PES, running costs, the management plan, and the departmental plan for the whole of the Scottish Office, while three others work like mini-PFOs in the Scottish Office departments responsible for propriety, accountancy advice, and monitoring. The Welsh Office also has a central services division. Within it the PFO's command is slightly unusual. He has responsibility for a Policy Division on local government finance. Its inclusion in the Finance Group creates tension in the department as it bids for resources like all other Policy Divisions yet it is not distanced from finance in the same way. Part of the justification is the need for the PFO to have directly under his command a division dealing with the highly significant and fast-moving area of local government finance and local government organization, and because support for local government represents about half the total spending under the responsibility of the Secretary of State for Wales, and the Finance Group has responsibility for negotiating this with the Treasury. The PFO and PEO roles are separated in the Welsh Office and their functions are unusual in that the purchasing function comes under the PEO, together with a number of other 'efficiency' tasks (staff inspection, market-testing). The departmental management plan is also his responsibility as the manager of the Welsh Office's Administration Vote.

While in constitutional theory the NIO is the most important 'department' in Northern Ireland, in practice this is the Department of Finance and Personnel (DFP), responsible for the allocation, control, and efficient use of the spending of the six Northern Ireland departments. It has a similar status to that of HM Treasury on the mainland. It leads on discussions with the Treasury on the Public Expenditure Survey and is regarded as the 'manager' of the Northern Ireland expenditure block, including the expenditure of the NIO even though this is subject to separate discussions between the Treasury and NIO. The core of the DFP is divided into two groups: Resources Group and Personnel and Management Services. The Resources Group is in effect a 'mini-Treasury'. Within the Group there are divisions responsible for supply of finance and manpower to the departments and NIO which mirror the work of the Treasury's Expenditure Divisions in respect of the mainland departments. The appropriation and resource control division (ARCD) deals with the bulk of the liaison work with the Treasury on public expenditure. It has responsibility for the Estimates, cash limits, and running costs, and pulls together the advice to the Secretary of State on how the bids from the Northern Ireland departments and NIO for a share of the block should be handled. The Personnel and Management Group is responsible for personnel policy throughout the Northern Ireland Civil Service (but not the NIO, which has to negotiate separately with the Treasury on staffing and grading because its Estimates are handled directly by the Treasury).

The spending of the NIO is treated in the same way as that of any other UK spending department; it is subject to the same relationship with the Treasury, and to the same accounting arrangements as other mainland departments. It is treated by the Treasury as a UK department and is subject to Treasury scrutiny for expenditure which is carried on a UK Parliamentary Vote,[2] that is, mainly NIO administration and spending on law and order. Thus although the NIO's public expenditure provision is derived from the overall block for which the Secretary of State is responsible, its Estimates are presented by the Treasury to Parliament and its expenditure is scrutinized by it rather than the DFP. The NIO is subject to double-scrutiny as the Treasury wishes to be satisfied that its expenditure is justified and cost-effective and the DFP wants to be sure that the NIO is not pre-empting too large a share of the total Northern Ireland block. The DFP tries to avoid conducting the same detailed type of scrutiny as the Treasury, and in fact the Treasury will be more familiar with the minutiae of NIO spending than its Northern Irish counterpart.

The Treasury historically granted the DFP and its predecessor department the right to determine delegated authorities for the spending

---

[2] The Chief Secretary presents to Parliament only two Estimates on Northern Ireland along with other Supply Estimates: one Vote for NIO administration and law and order expenditure; and a Vote transferring over £1bn to the Northern Ireland Consolidated Fund.

of public money, but this dispensation does not apply to NIO spending. The unusual arrangement over the NIO does, however, allow for some Treasury meddling in the Northern Ireland block, albeit constructively. This is partly the product of timing. The GB Supply Estimates (including those for the NIO) are presented to Parliament by the Treasury in March, whereas in a unique arrangement Northern Ireland Supply Estimates are presented by the Secretary of State in May. Thus the Treasury might increase an NIO Estimate in the light of increased spending on law and order, thus pre-empting a larger share of the Northern Ireland block; and since the expenditure tends to be of an 'inescapable' kind (spending on counter-terrorism) there is little the DFP can do. This can work both ways, as the Treasury might scale down the NIO Estimate providing the DFP with a windfall gain for the block.

The number of staff employed wholly or partly on financial functions in the Finance Divisions of the nineteen spending departments is impossible to calculate reliably, and staffing levels are being continually affected under the impetus of Next Steps and market-testing. In 1993 something of the order of between 1 and 7 per cent of all civil servants performed some financial function. About 400 officials in the headquarters of the DSS were employed in 'resource management'; 600 officials or just over 7 per cent of D.o.E. staff were employed on 'financial and central administration'; and about 5 per cent or just under fifty officials in the newly created Department of National Heritage were employed in the finance division. Across Whitehall as a whole, just under 200 'senior staff'—from Permanent Secretary to Assistant Secretary—were employed in Finance Divisions.

Few of these senior staff have professional qualifications; nor is it thought necessary that they should have. Their qualifications, skills, and previous Civil Service experience are similar to those of top civil servants in any division of any department. Familiarity with the technical rules and procedures of government accounting, the Survey, and Estimates is acquired with time and experience in the Finance Division. Skill and judgement are needed to manage simultaneously relationships with the Treasury's Expenditure Divisions and their own Policy Divisions and agencies. Unlike their colleagues in the latter, they have 'to act as a surrogate for both the Treasury and Secretary of State' (PFO, major department), balancing their responsibility as the department's guardians of propriety and financial discipline with that of representing the department to the Treasury, and reflecting the latter back to the Policy Divisions and agencies. Judgement about what issues to take to the Treasury, when, and in what form, is crucial and is acquired with experience. Equally, experience teaches when to resist and when to support the arguments of colleagues.

There has been a noticeable improvement in recent years in the quality of staff recruited to Finance Divisions, largely the result of the increased prestige of the divisions themselves. Where there was once a 'feeling that with rare exceptions time in finance was wasted; it was a backwater', 'participation in finance and management work is being encouraged among staff'. Finance Divisions are now 'leavened with good quality people from Policy Divisions'. This has mutual benefits as it 'encourages understanding with Policy Divisions more aware of the Finance Division function, pressures, perspective and vice versa' (Assistant Secretary, medium-sized department). This applies equally in those departments with a small finance function. 'In career terms it is invaluable to see the failings of other bits of the department through the finance issue . . . you see how the department works, you see programmes "in the round"' (Assistant Secretary, small department). There has been a similar improvement in the status of the PFO. PFOs are now less likely to be appointed on the basis of length of service in the Finance Division. Two or three years in the Finance Division is seen as an important stage in the career development of those marked out for the top posts.

There are several reasons why the finance function has become more important. First, the increased emphasis on financial management via FMI has increased the salience of Finance Divisions internally. In most departments Finance Divisions have taken the lead in devising delegated budget systems. This has led to a commensurate need to ensure that they are staffed by good-quality people and that a representative sample of Policy Divisions is brought into them. In addition, the Treasury now expects more detail from departments on output, value-for-money, and financial management, and this has further emphasized the importance of having a sound Finance Division as the 'window on the Treasury'.

The tighter public expenditure regime since 1976, and increasingly since 1979, has put a premium on a department's ability to present its case well to the Treasury. In the days of volume planning, the finance function was more mechanical, less nuanced, than it is in a cash-based regime. The Finance Division is pivotal in bringing together bids for programmes and running costs and in ensuring that Survey deadlines are met and requisite information is provided. The formalization of the autumnal bilateral system in the 1980s and the creation of the EDX committee in 1992 has also meant that PFOs and senior staff are more central as key advisers to Ministers as they prepare to meet the Chief Secretary than they were in the 1960s and 1970s.

The number of changes in accounting practices and organizational systems since 1979—from privatization to Next Steps, Departmental Running Costs, and market-testing—has tended to push the tasks of Finance Divisions to the forefront of departmental politics. In negotiations with the Treasury over financial arrangments for a proposed Executive Agency, Finance Division officials have high-level involvement with the Cabinet Office/OPSS Next Steps team. Most Finance Divisions are responsible for putting together the departmental management plan, which often brings with it an adjudicatory role between different parts of the department with incompatible objectives. Dividing the running costs 'pot' at the beginning of the financial year usually involves the PFO or his senior staff in advising the Senior Management Board on issues of the utmost sensitivity to all divisions and agencies.

Permanent Secretaries have been obliged, through FMI, Next Steps, market-testing, and other initiatives, to take a closer interest in finance matters, and to provide their Finance Divisions with the necessary support where changes are made to financial management systems. It is also a reflection of the greater importance of the managerial role of Permanent Secretaries in the changed 'culture' of the Civil Service in the 1980s.

Since 1979 the structure, organization, and work of the Finance Divisions of the Whitehall spending departments have undergone a process of continuous and profound change. The privatization programme and the creation of new regulatory bodies have had an impact on departments' policy responsibilities, and thus indirectly on the workload of Finance Divisions. Some departments have been particularly affected by the loss of sponsored nationalized industries: the DTI, Department of Transport, and the former Department of Energy, for example. This has affected relationships with the Treasury, as the management of departmental decline often creates as much (or more) tension as bidding for resources to fund departmental growth.

Finance Divisions have been affected by the Next Steps Executive Agencies initiative almost as much as their departmental Policy Divisions. The process is cyclical. Finance Divisions have first to respond to the granting of agency candidate status for a particular aspect of departmental work and this has entailed reorganization and co-ordination to ensure that the department's case can be well presented in discussions with the Treasury and the Next Steps Cabinet Office/OPSS team. The second stage is the launching of an agency when (usually) a separate branch is created to deal with it and the Finance Division. At this stage the hiving off of some central finance functions is completed. The Fraser Report was critical of what it saw as lack of 'fundamental reassessment of the size of the centre of the department', following the setting up of Next Steps Agencies (Efficiency Unit 1991: 19).

A further factor is a consequence of Whitehall-wide changes in public spending planning, control, and monitoring systems. This began in 1976 with the introduction of cash limits. Since 1979 there have been numerous changes which have had an impact on Finance Division structure and work. The most significant have been the FMI, with the impetus to delegated budgeting which has incrementally seeped down into most areas of departmental work and has also meant the gradual acceptance of a 'value-for-money culture'; running costs control and management plans, which have led to organizational change and acted as a further spur to delegation and greater awareness of financial management; and the recent and potentially far-reaching Whitehall policy of dispersing Civil Service jobs out of London through relocation. In addition, there has been a raft of less wide-ranging, but nevertheless significant, initiatives, such as on purchasing and procurement, and on accommodation (as a product of the breakup of the functions of the PSA), all of which have entailed organizational adjustments and changes in the 'mission' of PFOs and their staff.

Two developments with potentially far-reaching implications for the role, structure, and organization of Whitehall departments launched in 1991 have gradually gathered pace: the Citizen's Charter and market-testing. The most highly publicized initiative was the Citizen's Charter unveiled by John Major. Its aim was to encourage increased efficiency and value-for-money: by setting, publishing, and monitoring standards for public services; ensuring an increased flow of information to the citizen about services available; consultation with the public on changes and improvements; ensuring courtesy by public servants; and setting out remedies, including in some cases refunds, when services have not been delivered to standard. By the end of 1992, twenty-eight charters had been published, covering all public services such as schools, hospitals, police, council housing, postal services, tax and benefit offices, and job centres. What is not clear as yet is the degree to which improved performance by departments and agencies as measured by 'Chartermarks' (awards for good service) feeds through into discussions about public spending. All departmental public expenditure annual reports now include an assessment of the number of charters in operation, together with an appraisal of success in achieving high standards of service.

In November 1991 the Government committed itself to seeking further ways of improving the efficiency of the delivery of public services through the operation of competition (Cm. 1730). All departments and agencies were required to assess the degree to which their services could be tested in open competition with the private sector. In some cases market-testing would lead to services being supplied by a private sector agency replacing civil servants, in others the service would continue to be provided in-house. As incentives to encourage departments, the Treasury agreed to allow full VAT recovery on all new service contracts from April 1993, and departments and agencies were allowed to plough back any savings resulting from market-testing into other programme expenditure. Market-testing procedures were also streamlined by the Treasury in March 1992, placing the emphasis on output and performance in service contracts and allowing potential suppliers greater flexibility. In 1992 market-testing targets agreed between the departments and OPSS (to be tested by 30 September 1993) covered activities involving £1.5 billion in expenditure and employing more than 44,000 civil servants (Cm. 2101). Services covered in the exercise include accommodation and office services, estate management and security, training and recruitment, internal audit, and information technology. We discuss the possible ramifications of market-testing in Chapter 24.

A final factor is the result of specific policy changes. It is important to bear in mind that the relationship between the Treasury and Departments is not just expenditure-driven. There is a broader policy context. A Minister and his finance officials have contact with the Treasury and discuss specific departmental policy proposals as well as general government policies. It is not uncommon for Treasury Expenditure Divisions to be invited to join departmental or interdepartmental working parties looking at possible future changes in some specific aspect of policy. Inviting the Treasury 'made sense' to the department even if the Treasury qualified its attendance with the proviso that this was without prejudice to future expenditure demands, as the Treasury would be more aware of the context in which the departments operate.

Since 1976 there have been many policy initiatives and developments which have led to structural and organizational changes in most Whitehall departments affecting Finance Divisions. Most of these changes have resulted, in part, from an ideological commitment to centralize, deregulate, privatize, or introduce market-based programmes into the public sector. Thus the D.o.E. Finance Division has had to respond to a major shake-up in local government finance; the DFE to new forms of state educational provision such as opted-out schools and CTCs; the

D.o.H. to the process of health service reform and then the implementation of Trust hospitals and delegated GP budgets; and the DTI to a
scaling-down of its interventionist role to that of a regulatory and advisory 'enterprise department' and then the return to a more activist role
under the President of the Board of Trade after 1992; the Ministry of
Agriculture has evolved from a department concerned primarily with
producer interests to greater concern with environmental issues, and
increasingly away from concentration on animal health issues to that of
the quality of food for human health.

THE FUNCTIONS OF PFOS AND THEIR FINANCE DIVISIONS

The primary responsibility of a spending department is to conduct its
Minister's policy and statutory functions as efficiently and effectively as
possible within the financial and manpower limits determined by the
government as a whole. The key roles are played by the Permanent
Head of the department, the Principal Finance Officer (PFO), and the
Principal Establishments Officer (PEO). The Permanent Secretary is
responsible to the Minister 'for the economical, efficient and effective
management of public funds and other resources entrusted to the department in pursuit of the Government's objectives and for maintaining
high standards of administration throughout the department' (Treasury
1989*b*: annex 6.2, para. 2). He is the Accounting Officer, signs the
appropriation accounts, and appears before the Public Accounts Committee to answer questions arising from the accounts about the financial
propriety and regularity of spending, and the prudent, economical, and
effective administration of the department. Both the PFO and the PEO
are given responsibilities by the Permanent Secretary to aid him in
achieving these aims. They report directly to him, and are the department's chief advisers on all financial matters and on the management of
people working in the department.

The role of the Principal Finance Officer

The principal duties of a PFO are planning the use of resources given to
the department; seeking better value-for-money each year for those
resources; controlling and reporting expenditure and programme performance; ensuring financial propriety; and co-operating with the
Treasury and other departments on financial issues. In addition, the
Permanent Head expects the PFO to ensure that line managers are

made aware of their responsibilities for the management of resources, and that this should be achieved less by detailed control and more by providing an appropriately robust framework. PFOs are also charged with advising the Permanent Secretary, and other senior staff, prior to appearances before the PAC to answer questions about financial propriety, regularity, and value-for-money arising from the appropriation accounts.

All proposals from Policy Divisions or sponsored bodies which have expenditure implications are submitted to the PFO for appraisal and costing prior to submission to the Treasury. Increasing emphasis is now placed on the PFO's traditional role of ensuring value-for-money in public expenditure. This involves relating inputs of cash and other resources to outputs achieved; consideration of the full costs of activities (including depreciation and costs incurred by other departments as a result of departmental expenditure); ensuring that line managers have relevant information from control systems to be able to review performance and achieve value-for-money; and specifically through linking the PES process, scrutinies, and performance reviews so that guidance can be issued to line managers and so that all proposed expenditure has been appraised for performance before submission to the Treasury. The PFO and PEO share responsibility for the detailed control of financial, manpower, and other resources. The PFO has derived responsibility for Vote control and control of cash limits throughout the department and procedures for delegating financial authority to line managers.

One of the PFO's central responsibilities is the control and monitoring of budgets within the department, as the key mechanism by which objectives and allocations of resources are recorded, expenditure is controlled within the overall limits on departmental resources, and performance is ultimately reviewed. Specifically, the PFO is expected by the Permanent Secretary to ensure that the budgeting system has a timetable consistent with PES and Supply Estimates procedures; that the Permanent Secretary and Senior Management Board is advised which budgets should be challenged and reviewed; that budgets are in line with overall targets and priorities; and that line managers improve their budgeting arrangements through setting objectives, establishing output and performance measures. More generally, the PFO is responsible for ensuring that all the department's financial systems conform to the Treasury's five principles and five characteristics and that departmental rules and procedures are consistent with *Government Accounting* (Treasury 1989*b*).

Clear guidance is issued to the PFO relating to PES and the Estimates, and on co-operation with the Treasury and OPSS. The PFO is expected to ensure that the department's procedures meet the demands of the annual PES and Supply Estimates. This involves co-ordinating the review of spending priorities in accordance with Treasury guidelines and advising ministers and senior managers on reallocation of resources, possible savings, and the need for additional resources. The PFO has to make certain that all relevant information, statistical returns as well as data to support PES returns, reaches the Treasury on time and in the form required. He has also to ensure that his colleagues consult with other departments which may be affected by proposed programmes. The PFO is responsible for the smooth operation of the Estimates preparation procedure, and their consistency with PES allocations. The PFO co-operates closely with the Treasury and Cabinet Office to ensure that expenditure is kept within allocation, and that the central departments are given adequate information on the department's methods and financial management. The PFO represents his department in formal Survey meetings at the Treasury and in other discussions with it on expenditure matters. The terms of the 1989 PFO Memorandum stress two further requirements:

The Treasury will look to you as the department's PFO for information. Where correspondence is conducted direct between line managers and the Treasury it will be copied to you. You should consult the Treasury in advance on any new proposals outside the categories of delegated authority . . .

You will make managers aware of Cabinet Office instructions on the preparation of papers for Cabinet and Cabinet Committees, and advise on the requirement to consult the Treasury and Cabinet Office as appropriate on expenditure and manpower implications; and on what is to be achieved, by when and at what cost, and how this achievement is to be measured where proposals have value for money implications. (Treasury 1989*b*: ch. 6, annex 6.2, paras. 38–9)

The PFO is responsible for ensuring that the department has clear procedures consistent with Treasury and Cabinet Office guidelines on management accounting, programme appraisal, evaluation, cash management, running costs, Vote and other controls, internal audit, and contingent liabilities. Where a department sponsors a nationalized industry or has responsibility for NDPBs, the PFO is charged with advising the Permanent Head on the financial memoranda appropriate for the paying of grants and delegation of authority. PFOs are also responsible for advising him on the capability of the financial control systems in place to meet the responsibilities to the PAC and to Parliament.

While all PFOs accept that part of their task is to guide and help their Policy Divisions and agencies to obtain, retain, and allocate resources, their 'mission' includes as well a responsibility for designing and imple-

menting financial management and information systems to give effect to
the principles of FMI. At one level, this means trying to ensure that the
department has clearly defined policy aims, set in terms of priorities
or tasks, and that these feed through to the information system and
financial planning; at another, some PFOs exploit the potential of computerized financial information to involve Policy Divisions and agencies
more closely in decisions about the internal allocation of resources.

Departmental PFOs and PEOs and their Finance and Establishments
Divisions have key roles in their departments' relationships with the
Treasury's expenditure divisions and central divisions (Pay, Management, FM, Next Steps). Co-operation with the Treasury was formally
prescribed as a duty of the PFO, PEO, and their divisions in 1981. (The
background to this was explained in Chapter 4.) It had of course been
provided for since the middle of the nineteenth century, both in statute
and in agreed 'rules of the game'. As we noted above, the memorandum
constructed by the Treasury and Cabinet Office for issuing by the Permanent Secretaries to their PFOs has clear instructions about the requirement to co-operate with the central departments. The rules of
co-operation are long-standing and include the need to agree with the
Treasury such items as delegated authorities, as well as bringing in the
Treasury at a formative stage in any policy discussions which could have
financial or manpower implications.

The practice of channelling *all* departmental communications with
the Treasury through the PFO and the Finance Division was also
reaffirmed in 1981. Where Policy Divisions wished to deal directly with
the Treasury they could do so only with the authority of the PFO.
The implementation and consequences of this rule are discussed in
Chapter 9.

PFOs claim that their Finance Divisions are able to take an overview
of departmental activities, mirroring the role of the Treasury Expenditure Divisions in relation to the spending departments. The 'best operators in the Policy Divisions realise that we can help them make a better
case. We have a wider range and are able to take a strategic view'
(Assistant Secretary, medium-sized department). Such expertise, it is
argued, derives from having an overview of the department's work and
having to deal regularly with the Treasury. This applies equally to small
as to large departments. 'There was a need for the department and the
Treasury to have someone who has the whole picture' (Assistant Secretary, small department). The relations of PFOs with the Treasury, the
confidences and mutual trust which are the hallmark of effective relations between the Finance Division and Expenditure Division, are
discussed in detail in Chapters 9 and 10.

Finance Divisions

The Finance Divisions, which support the PFO and enable him to fulfil his key roles, have both traditional financial functions and a contemporary concern with the design and implementation of financial management systems. They have a 'legalistic', almost constitutional, role of helping to ensure the proper use of public funds by their colleagues. The function of ensuring standards of regularity and propriety, and in particular protecting the Accounting Officer, is regarded as of equal importance to the tasks of obtaining and allocating resources and modernizing departmental financial management procedures. It would be misleading to regard this as being entirely based on relations with the Treasury, although these relationships are important. Many Finance Divisions spend as much time on matters to do with the internal organization and efficient and economical running of their departments, as we discussed earlier. But through the PES process, the agreement of Estimates and in-year additions to budgets, Finance Divisions are the focal point for the practical business of dealing with the Treasury to obtain and retain resources. Essentially it is the task of a Finance Division to try and ensure that its Minister obtains enough resources to be able to achieve his or her policy goals. This involves getting as much out of the Treasury as possible, and ensuring that the resources obtained are distributed as effectively as possible. To do this it has to act partly as a 'mini-Treasury' in relation to its own Policy Divisions, weeding out poorly argued cases, trying to ensure that those which most need resources get them. The Finance Division has to ensure that bids to the Treasury are presented credibly, with the necessary supporting data, and that they reflect the stated objectives of the department.

Finance Divisions perform three internal and three external functions. Although the internal functions divide into three categories, there is considerable overlap between them: ministerial support; top management; and liaison with Policy Divisions and agencies.

Ministerial support. PFOs are often 'called in' by ministers to discuss ongoing financial matters across the range of departmental activities, for example to discuss preparation for the PES, the autumnal bilaterals, in-year requests for resources, and financial management issues. The degree to which a PFO is involved in ministerial briefing varies with the style and personality of ministers. Some ministers prefer to get very involved in the detail of a PES bid, and want to feel able to defend every item. Others take a more relaxed view and are happy to 'allow it all to go in and see what comes out at the other end of the bilaterals' (PFO, medium-sized department). Invariably PFOs will discuss major financial issues with ministers—from irregularities to prospective overspends. There is also a sense in which the PFO and his staff act as a filter between the department and the Minister. One PFO was keenly aware of the pressure on his Secretary of State's time and of the importance of maintaining the Minister's credit with the Chief Secretary by not 'firing off on all issues of concern to people in the department'.

Top management function. Here the Finance Division often provides the secretariat or support services to the department's top or senior management board or group on PES and PES-related public expenditure issues. The precise organizational setting and approach varies with the department. In most spending departments PES issues are dealt with by some form of Senior Management Group (consisting of Permanent Secretary, Deputy Secretaries, Finance and Establishment Under Secretaries, and senior staff from Executive Agencies) prior to submission to the Minister. The degree and sophistication of the involvement of a Finance Division varies with the size of department, complexity of tasks undertaken, and departmental history and 'culture'. It is also partly a function of personality. Much depends on the degree of interest taken in the 'nuts and bolts' of expenditure policy by the Permanent Secretary. Finance Division may be involved at an earlier stage in specific PES co-ordinating groups to ensure that all parts of the department, including agencies, have the opportunity to submit detailed bids, and to standardize and collate them in a manageable package before submission to senior management. Increasingly, this PES co-ordination function is being married to delegated budgeting systems on departmental running costs (DRC) and, in some cases, programme expenditure as well.

Liaison with Policy Divisions and agencies. Much time and effort in a Finance Division is taken up in getting Treasury approval for programmes outside the PES and Estimates procedures. In addition, Finance Divisions are usually involved in approving and checking submissions to the Treasury made by Policy Divisions or agencies for extra resources in-year, or for claims for end-year flexibility on capital expenditure or running costs. Some have traditionally exerted strong central control over these processes, whereas others have for various reasons (including lack of specialized finance resources) kept a looser rein. In those departments which have individual programme committees, the Finance Division is represented and PFOs and their senior officials expect to have a large input into any discussion of projects coming before such formal or informal groups, probe Policy Divisions to make sure that they have thought through the rationale and objectives of their proposals, and press to ensure that the outputs projected are proportionate to the expenditure envisaged. Most PFOs expect to have some form of veto over whether an in-year bid is made or not, although in practice all Finance Divisions are constrained by the internal politics of their departments. PFOs and their staff have to balance the desire to keep control of the finance function against the pressures within the department not to let finance determine policy. For this reason, PFOs try to ensure that representatives from Policy Divisions and agencies are included in any review of departmental finance arrangements.

Increasingly, Finance Divisions have to show that they too represent value-for-money for their departments. The pressures of market-testing ensure that this will continue. In the 'mission statements' provided by Finance Divisions in Departmental Public Expenditure Annual Reports, the emphasis is placed on the advisory and specialist support services made available to other parts of the department. The Home Office's Finance and Manpower Department 'encourages and assists management to increase the use of quantified indicators in forecasting future requirements' (Cm. 2208: 86); and in MAFF the Finance Group 'provides advice to policy groups on post-project evaluations' (Cm. 2203: 49).

Finance Divisions have three specific external functions: liaison with the Treasury; liaison with the PAC and NAO in ensuring propriety and regularity in the use of public money; and liaison with House of Commons Select Committees.

Liaison with the Treasury. Predominant among the tasks of Finance Divisions is the co-ordination of their department's relationship with the Treasury. In most departments it is responsible for compiling and co-ordinating PES bids, or at least acting as a contact point for their preparation. As well, it supervises the preparation of management plans, prepares the case for Supplementary Estimates, and co-ordinates with the Treasury the production of the annual Departmental Public Expenditure Reports. It remains the case that in most departments the Finance Division is regarded as the 'window' on the Treasury, in the same way as the Treasury Expenditure Division is the sole window on a department. Practice varies as to the degree to which this is a formal rather than an active function. In smaller departments lacking the resources to support a large Finance Division, the practical necessities dictate that the Policy Divisions take on a large amount of the work in liaising with the Treasury. Even in those departments with significant staff resources in their Finance Division, there may be a tradition or a developing trend to allow and even encourage Policy Divisions to deal directly with the Treasury. We discuss the conduct of relations with the Treasury in more detail in Chapter 10.

It would be misleading to characterize all the links between the Finance Divisions and the Treasury as being Treasury-led or imposed. Not all internal control functions and reforms in financial administration and procedure are carried out because the Treasury is 'looking over the shoulder' of the Finance Divisions. In many Whitehall departments the Finance Division has a history and culture of actively seeking ways of ensuring economical administration and, in the period since 1979, many have taken their lead from ministers determined that their departments should be in the forefront of the drive to introduce market mechanisms into public administration. As a result of this, many departments—such as MAFF on public purchasing or the DTI on 'hard charging' for internal services—take the lead in introducing financial innovations and these have been taken up by the Treasury as models for other departments to emulate.

Ensuring propriety and regularity in the use of public money: liaison with the Public Accounts Committee and National Audit Office. The bedrock of the external activity of the PFO and Finance Division relates to the Parliamentary requirement to account for the use of public money. This stems from the historic role of Permanent Secretaries as Accounting Officers for most or all of the Supply Votes assigned to departments. Through accident of history some, though not all, discrete agencies or NDPBs under the wing of departments have their own Accounting Officers, although the advent of Next Steps Agencies has led to questioning of the viability of Permanent Secretaries acting as Accounting Officers for agencies whose Chief Executives are meant to be held accountable for their activities (see Efficiency Unit 1991: 8).

Accounting Officers are called to account for the spending of money to the Public Accounts Committee of the House of Commons and the Committee's agent, the Comptroller and Auditor General (whose role since 1983 has been strengthened by the National Audit Office). Under terms defined by *Government Accounting* (Treasury 1989*b*), Permanent Secretaries issue memoranda to PFOs/PEOs outlining how they and their staff are to assist them in the accounting function. This is an important corrective to the tendency to view financial arrangements as only Treasury–department-based. As one senior Finance Officer commented, the 'responsibility for departmental management systems was the department's not the Treasury's. The PFO and staff were responsible to the Permanent Secretary (as Accounting Officer) for the good conduct of the system not to the Treasury.'

Liaison with Select Committees. Another important function of the Finance Divisions is to provide support for senior staff appearing before Select Committees. This also often involves the preparation of memoranda requested by the committee. Increasingly the sixteen functional committees conduct inquiries into public expenditure questions relating to the departments they shadow, in addition to the regular general reports of the Treasury and Civil Service Committee.

9

The Whitehall Expenditure Policy Network

Previous chapters described the structure and organization of the Treasury and the principal spending departments; examined the broad context within which the work of the Expenditure Divisions and the departmental Finance Divisions is conducted; and analysed the skills, professional expertise, and behaviour of the Expenditure Controllers and the PFOs and their staff in the Finance Divisions. In this chapter we explore the dynamics of the relationships between the Treasury and the spending departments, using the concepts of policy community and policy network (Wright 1988*a*, 1988*b*, 1991) to identify and characterize the principal players and their roles, and to identify and explain the behavioural and policy 'rules of the game' by which their relationships are regulated.

THE PUBLIC EXPENDITURE POLICY COMMUNITY

The membership of the public expenditure policy community is drawn from a wide variety of domestic and international statutory and non-statutory organizations and groups. We can, however, distinguish broadly two types of membership, according to the concentration of key resources of authority and information, and the regularity of interaction between members. Those (parts of) organizations, and individuals within them, which interact on a regular and routine basis in the processes of making and carrying out of policy have 'insider' status. 'Outsiders' have some contact irregularly with other members of the policy community, over some expenditure policy issues or problems, but their interactions tend to be *ad hoc* and non-routinized. Of course, the significance of their interaction and its impact on the policy process may be considerable when it occurs, for example a critical report on waste or inefficiency in a spending department by the Comptroller and Auditor General.

Insider groups are of two types: (1) central departments with responsibility for expenditure policy (such as the Treasury, the Cabinet

Office and Office of Public Service and Science (OPSS), and (formerly CSD and CPRS), the Prime Minister and Prime Minister's Office, and Cabinet and its committees; (2) those parts of the nineteen main spending departments which were identified in the previous chapter. There are four categories of outsider groups, distinguished by their statutory status, financial basis, and their roles in the policy processes. First, those statutory groups can be identified which are financed wholly or partly out of public sector funds and which contribute regularly to the policy processes but do so mainly through the intermediation of 'insider groups'. Such statutory sponsored or client groups include most Policy Divisions of most spending departments, Executive Agencies, and NDPBs within Whitehall; and local authorities, public corporations, health authorities, trust hospitals, opted-out schools, and consumer organizations outside it. Secondly, other statutory publicly financed groups can be distinguished by their roles in the policy processes as legitimizers or regulators and supervisors. Thirdly, non-statutory groups, self- or other-financed, include most organized interest groups, together with political parties and their policy-making organizations, and back-bench committees of MPs; groups which advise and provide commentary on expenditure policy; and consumers and clients of public services. Finally, there are some external 'outsider' groups drawn from the EC, IMF, and G7. The membership of the expenditure policy community is shown in Fig. 9.1.

The 'insiders' identified here share a common interest in the issues and problems which arise in the making and carrying out of policy for the planning and controlling of public expenditure. Their common purpose is to achieve what each may separately perceive as a satisfactory outcome. While each aims to maximize its particular values—controlling expenditure, building roads, protecting the environment, providing health care, and so on—their interdependent relationships constrain the maximization of any one set of values. The exercise of discretion in the use of resources which each possesses in different combinations and amounts is mutually constrained.

The outcome on any particular policy issue or problem depends on the management of relationships with other organizations in the policy processes, as policy-makers seek to exploit the potential for the exercise of power which they and their organization possess by virtue of resources of authority, finance, information, expertise, and organization. The amount and the mix of these resources vary among organizations, and with the particularity of the policy issue or problem. The management of those relationships is the policy-maker's function, partly 'balancing' and partly 'optimizing': 'He must maintain those relationships

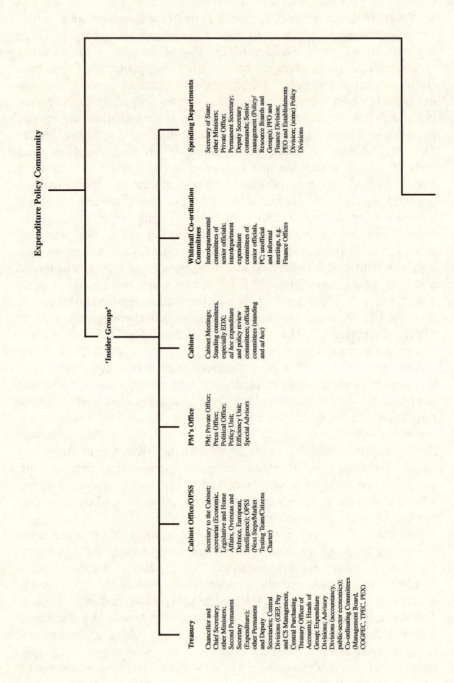

Expenditure Policy Community

'Insider Groups'

Treasury

Chancellor and Chief Secretary; other Ministers; Second Permanent Secretary (Expenditure); other Permanent and Deputy Secretaries; Central Divisions (GEP, Pay and CS Management, Central Purchasing, Treasury Officer of Accounts); Heads of Group; Expenditure Divisions; Advisory Divisions (accountancy, public-sector economics); Co-ordinating Committees (Management Board, COGPEC, TPEC, PEX)

Cabinet Office/OPSS

Secretary to the Cabinet; secretariat (Economic, Legislative and Home Affairs, Overseas and Defence, European, Intelligence); OPSS (Next Steps/Market Testing Team/Citizens Charter)

PM's Office

PM; Private Office; Press Office; Political Office; Policy Unit; Efficiency Unit; Special Advisors

Cabinet

Cabinet Meetings; Standing committees, especially EDX; *ad hoc* expenditure and policy review committees; official committees (standing and *ad hoc*)

Whitehall Co-ordination Committees

Interdepartmental committees of senior officials; interdepartment expenditure committees of senior officials, PC; unofficial and informal meetings, e.g. Finance Offices

Spending Departments

Secretary of State; other Ministers; Private Office; Permanent Secretary; Deputy Secretary commands; Senior management (Policy/ Resource Boards and Groups); PFO and Finance Division; PFO and Establishments Division; (some) Policy Divisions

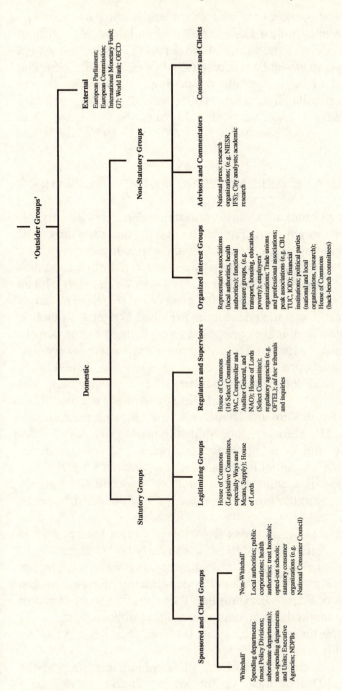

Fɪɢ. 9.1. The expenditure policy community, 1992–1993

between inflow and outflow of resources on which every dynamic system depends; he must adjust the controllable variables, internal and external, so as to optimise the values of the resulting relations, as valued by him, or by those to whom he is accountable' (Vickers 1965: 195). The priority accorded to balancing and optimizing, as resources are exchanged in the particular circumstances of an issue or problem, will vary with the policy-maker's judgements of reality and value—his 'appreciative system'.

THE WHITEHALL EXPENDITURE POLICY NETWORK

Within the policy community, those interdependent 'insider' organizations and groups which participate in the making and carrying out of policy for the planning and control of public expenditure comprise a 'governance structure', which exhibits the characteristics of a permanent, stable, closed policy network in a steady state (Wright 1991). It has a limited, clearly defined membership, prescribed by the Treasury's circulation list of PFOs; it includes all the principal Whitehall spending departments. There is an inner core of members defined by the density of their relationships with the Treasury, which itself occupies a nodal position in the network. It comprises the Treasury Expenditure Divisions, GEP, and the central divisions of the management and pay side, together with the PFOs and PEOs and their senior staff in the Finance and Establishments Divisions of the nineteen main spending departments. Ministerial membership (other than Treasury) is defined by bidding and negotiating for resources and routine direct participation in the autumnal bilaterals and the Cabinet's EDX Committee, and *ad hoc* by membership of ministerial and official Cabinet committees engaged in the formulation or review of policy with spending implications.

This expenditure policy network has evolved over a long period of time. It predates the setting up of PESC in the early 1960s, which served mainly to institutionalize the traditional interdependent relationships between the Treasury and the spending departments, focused on the annual allocation of Supply Expenditure. Its origins are to be found in the reform of the methods of Treasury control of public expenditure in the first half of the nineteenth century. The core membership has remained remarkably stable.

Criticism of the exclusiveness of the PESC planning system in the 1960s and early 1970s by local authorities led to the creation of a Consultative Council, drawn from their representative associations, to negotiate with the Treasury over the settlement of the then Rate

Support Grant, but it was never accorded 'insider' status, and was abolished in the 1980s. Attempts to involve Parliament more directly in the formulation of expenditure policy, through the implementation of the Armstrong proposals for the reform of budgetary practice for example, were strongly resisted by the Treasury in the early 1980s. The Treasury has similarly preferred to deal with public corporations, nationalized industries, NDPBs, and more recently Next Steps Agencies, indirectly through the intermediation of their sponsor spending departments.

The dominant coalition of those engaged in the formulation and carrying out of spending policies within the Treasury and each spending department has a particular perception of policy problems and issues: how it identifies, defines, and thinks about expenditure policy—its 'perceptual schema' or 'appreciative system'. This comprises perceptions or appreciations both of 'facts' and of values relevant to particular policy issues. While their appreciative systems are dissimilar, they share a mutual interest in optimizing their individually perceived values within mutually constrained interdependent relationships. That interest is predicated upon agreement on a transcendental value. Thus while the Treasury and each spending department has a hierarchy of self-interested organizational values to which different weights are attached, there is a sufficient consensus on a collective core value or values integral to their relationships and the exchange of resources. Two such core values bring the members of the network together and keep them together: first, the agreement on the need for the orderly, annual regulation of public spending policies within the accepted context of collective government; and secondly, agreement on the maintenance of the network itself—a preference for the regulation of relationships through the network rather than an alternative form of 'governance structure', such as prescription by the Chancellor.

The policy agenda of a network *ipso facto* reflects and reinforces its core values. The issues which get on to it are consistent with those values; those which threaten them will be avoided or kept off, either by tacit agreement, or by the control and manipulation of the agenda by its inner-core members—here the Treasury and the PFOs. Issues perceived by some or all members as incompatible with core values may be redefined and reformulated to make them acceptable and manageable.

The rules of the game

The behaviour of members of a policy network in their relations with each other is regulated by two kinds of interconnected 'rules of the game'—policy rules and behavioural norms. Policy rules relate to the substance of expenditure planning and control, and regulate or guide the conduct of such business in the policy processes. They define and prescribe how policy is perceived collectively, what that policy is, and how it is to be applied in practice. Some of these rules are statute-based: for example the Exchequer and Audit Acts which prescribe the form of accounts, the Appropriation Acts which provide authority to spend money for purposes voted by Parliament. They include also rules which relate to the propriety and regularity of spending codified in *Government Accounting*, and to the authority delegated to departments to decide some types of expenditure within limits approved by the Treasury. Other policy rules or guidelines, equally binding on members, have no such basis in statute: the requirement to seek Treasury prior-approval; permission to vire expenditure within subheadings and cash limits; the prescription of cash limits, which requires Parliamentary approval but not statutory authority; the Survey *Guidelines* which prescribe a code of practice to be followed for each new Survey. Formal policy rules regulate the discussions between Expenditure Divisions and spending departments over the operation of the schemes for running costs, end-year flexibility, cash limits, and the Reserve. Policy rules such as these can be changed explicitly as a result of affirmative action by the Treasury after consultation, even negotiation, with departments.

The policy rules which define the general limits for the exercise of delegated authority without seeking prior Treasury approval, and those which apply to particular types of spending within different spending departments, are reviewed annually by each Expenditure Division, discussed with the Finance Division and, where appropriate, renegotiated with it and the relevant Policy Division. The Ryrie Rules, named after Sir William Ryrie, formerly Second Permanent Secretary in charge of public finance at the Treasury, provide a good example of non-statutory policy rules of the game, regulating the conduct of an important aspect of expenditure business. Devised in the early 1980s, the rules defined the conditions under which private sector money could be used to finance public sector projects. As the Government could borrow at the lowest rates, a spending department arguing for raising funds directly from the money-markets had to demonstrate an advantage to offset the higher cost. Private finance was allowed under the rules only if it could be shown that this would result in improved efficiency. Very little private financing took place under the rules in the 1980s, but in 1992 the conditions were modified to provide greater opportunity for the introduction of private sector money.

Policy rules or guidelines are not necessarily codified or written down. A code of policy or practice may be inferred from the conduct of the members of a network. Tacit and informal policy rules may be no less binding on its members, between a Treasury Expenditure Division and a departmental Finance Division, for example. Self-evidently, policy rules reflect the core values of a network; they may also serve to embed and reinforce them. In the analysis of relationships below we identify some of those rules.

In the interpretation and application of formal policy rules to concrete issues which arise in dealing with a department's expenditure, and in considering issues which arise in the negotiation over bids in the Survey, and in the exercise of 'in-year' control, there is both the opportunity and need for the Treasury's Expenditure Controllers to exercise discretionary authority. While an informal 'policy rule of thumb' might be invoked by an Expenditure Division, how and why that 'rule' has emerged and is operated is influenced by the norms which guide the behaviour of Expenditure Controllers. For example, if an item of expenditure appears to an Expenditure Controller to be 'novel or contentious' or to raise some issue of financial principle, an Expenditure Division may 'call it in', regardless of the size of the expenditure or any agreed policy rules of delegated authority. Similarly, an Expenditure Division might 'ring-fence' an item of expenditure in the Survey negotiations. The policy rules evolved in the end-year flexibility schemes (see Chapter 19) to permit carry-forward of certain items of capital expenditure are not invoked by the nationalized industries and Expenditure Controllers in the Public Enterprises Divisions; both find it mutually more convenient to achieve carry-forward by changing the External Financing Requirement.

Behavioural norms are those rules of the game which guide or regulate the behaviour of the members of a policy network, or set limits to the exercise of independent discretionary authority by them. When Daubeney (Disraeli) attacked Mildmay (Russell), 'his answers were poisoned and his lance was barbed and his shot was heated red-hot because such things are allowed. He did not poison his enemies' wells or use Greek Fire, because those things are not allowed. He knew exactly the rules of the combat' (Trollope 1949: p. viii). In a similar manner, Expenditure Controllers and their opposite numbers in the spending departments know exactly the rules of their combat. Just as policy rules and guidelines reflect and reinforce the core values of the network, so the norms of behaviour will influence and help determine those rules. Policy and behaviour are inextricably linked and may become difficult to distinguish in the operation of a network: the way the network behaves may be the policy. Norms can be distinguished by what members say or write or believe them to be, or inferred from their conduct to each other in network relationships. In Chapter 6 we identified and explained some of the behavioural norms of the Treasury's Expenditure Controllers, and in what follows (and in the next chapter) we provide further evidence of their influence in the interactions with other members of the network.

The behaviour of individual members in a network is determined not only by behavioural norms and policy rules, but by the strategy adopted by the dominant coalition within each organization. While we can observe or infer from their behaviour the broad outlines of members' general strategies, we are unable to describe the origins and details of the strategy adopted in the circumstances of a particular policy issue or problem. The anterior politics of the decision-making processes within the Treasury and the spending departments requires a much deeper level of inquiry than is possible here. However, one important general factor which is a function of network membership is the constraint on discretionary room for manœuvre imposed by the strategies of other members and the consequent deployment of their resources. Any strategy is thus partly, sometimes mainly, a reflexive anticipation of other strategies: a balancing of individual aims and values with those of others in the context of interdependence and acceptance of the network's rules of the game. Satisfactory outcomes for individual members depend on the devising and implementation of a strategy by each to manage its relationships with the others. As we have said, this is partly a balancing and partly an optimizing function.

The behavioural norms of Treasury Expenditure Controllers

What influences the behaviour of an Expenditure Controller in the network? First, there are general bureaucratic norms of behaviour which distinguish civil servants from, say, City businessmen or the middle managers of large firms and corporations. Some of these are formal and codified; others are conventional or customary modes of behaviour, accepted ways of doing things. Secondly, there are departmental norms of behaviour which distinguish the behaviour of Treasury civil servants from those in other departments (for a comparison see those of the D.o.E. in Wilks 1987). These derive partly from the functions of the department—its 'mission'. They are partly institutionalized, in the formal and informal structures of the department, and partly socio-cultural. Thirdly, within the Treasury, and within the general contours described by the other two, there are the specific norms of behaviour of Treasury civil servants in the Expenditure Divisions, compared with their colleagues in, say, overseas finance, fiscal policy, or economic forecasting. Again, they will derive from formal and informal institutional structures (for example, the Expenditure Divisions and their relationships to other parts of the Treasury); from the expenditure control function and how it is defined, and revised over time; and from the socio-culture of life in the divisions. The Treasury itself acknowledges that the latter is distinguishable from other parts of the department, when it notes in its official guide to the department that work in the public expenditure sector 'is sometimes referred to colloquially as service in the trenches' (Treasury 1988*a*: ch. 3).

Using Heclo and Wildavsky's (1974) account of the behavioural norms of Treasury controllers as a reference point, we can examine to what extent norms have remained the same, have changed in emphasis, or have been supplemented by others. Before doing so we need to remind ourselves that their account was based on interviews conducted in the late 1960s and early 1970s, before the rapid growth of public expenditure in the middle of the latter decade, the crisis of control which ensued, and the introduction of cash limits in 1976. That was a period of confidence in the planning and control system—the high noon of PESC. Secondly, we need also to allow for the historical and unchanging mission of the Treasury as the department with responsibility for controlling the spending of other departments. The nature of the mission, the formal and informal institutional structures created and evolved to perform it over more than a hundred years, and the culture reflected, reinforced, and transmitted by those structures, have together determined enduring patterns of behaviour. For example, the antecedents of present Expenditure Divisions divided by departmental function can be traced directly to the Supply Divisions created in the reorganized mid-Victorian Treasury (Wright 1969). The Gladstonian watchwords of economy and efficiency resonate with the tenets of the new managerialism associated with FMI.

Expenditure Controllers remain today what they have always been, essentially reactive. It is for departments to propose expenditure. The Treasury's task is to save money, not to encourage departments to spend it. While this remains true generally of the attitude towards spending of all controllers, as a generalization it requires some qualification in the climate of the 1980s and 1990s, where more attention is paid to the effectiveness of spending. It is recognized in the Treasury that there is a tension between the traditional desire to save money and the more recent concern for value-for-money. For the Expenditure Controllers the priority is to deliver to the Chief Secretary the best they can in terms of the cash figure for their programme(s) during the Survey discussions. It is for senior Treasury officials, at Deputy Secretary and

Second Permanent Secretary level in particular, to inject caution into the discussion and ensure that the value-for-money case for additional spending is fully aired. In any event, during the course of discussions between a spending department and the Treasury, an Expenditure Division might suggest options for reduction to help finance an item of expenditure with a higher priority. It sometimes suggests to a department alternative ways of financing a project or programme where there is agreement on policy. However, attempts to be constructive can be misinterpreted or viewed with suspicion by a department, a nationalized industry, or an Executive Agency. From the vantage of a central viewpoint, Expenditure Controllers 'sometimes spot things which they miss, and you can try to persuade them that it is worthwhile to devote time and energy to doing something' (Principal, Expenditure Division). But suspicion of Treasury motives is deeply rooted and departments tend to mistrust what on the face of it appears to be a positive, constructive initiative. The Treasury is 'typecast', and it is difficult to play against the role expected of it. There is also acceptance of the need and desirability in certain circumstances of allowing expenditure now to make a saving in the future. 'Spend to save' is a precept which Expenditure Controllers try to follow.

Three key norms of behaviour are scepticism, detachment, and informed criticism. The latter describes the classic behaviour pattern of Expenditure Controllers over the last hundred years: the questioning, the probing of the weak points of an argument, 'getting behind the figures', 'poking around behind the numbers' asking for more information, the use of tactical delay, and demurring to new, novel, or contentious items of expenditure.

The Expenditure Controller has neither time nor the depth of specialist knowledge, nor the resources, to 'redo' the work of the department. Nor would he want to do so, were there more time and resources. Historically, the Expenditure Divisions, and the Supply Divisions which preceded them, have never sought to match the specialist knowledge and expertise of the spending departments nor to challenge their professional and technical competence. The control-function is defined as one of critical inquiry, requiring skills, expertise, and professional judgement which complement those of the department. That judgement may be different from that of the department, but it is not technically superior nor can it be a substitute for it. To reach it the Expenditure Controller must be informed enough to probe and pick away at the case put up to him. He must know enough to ask the 'right questions', and to ask for relevant kinds of information. He is, of course, dependent upon the department for information, but not wholly reliant. Part of his skill is the acquisition of other kinds of information from within the Treasury and extra-departmentally, to increase the store of his independent knowledge and understanding, and to develop a distinctive and perhaps alternative point of view. Obvious sources outside the department include the 'trade press', the reports of the NAO, PAC, and Parliamentary Select Committees, ministerial statements, and the results of academic research and private consultancies.

The Expenditure Divisions are now better served by the supporting advice and services of other, specialized Treasury divisions. There is now an Accountancy Adviser with three divisions providing a range of specialist advice. The Deputy Chief Economic Adviser specializes in public expenditure economics, and has staff working on manpower, public enterprises, and Operations Research. None of this support and service was available in the early 1970s. The effect is that Treasury controllers now have the opportunity to be better primed and briefed with material to question the methods of analysis, the accuracy of the conclusions drawn from it, and the expenditure implied by them. Some Expenditure Divisions claim that their economic advice is superior to that available to the departments with which they deal.

Less obvious but more important sources of opinion and advice are the formal and informal networks within the Treasury and with other members of the Whitehall expenditure policy network, for example the Cabinet Office, the PM's Private Office and Policy Unit, and ministerial private offices; as well as the network of interdepartmental committees of officials which shadow ministerial Cabinet committees. Effective Expenditure Controllers are by definition well connected, and exploit the policy network to keep abreast of current issues and problems. Background information helps to 'contextualize' specific expenditure issues and Survey bids which come before them. Information obtained informally through the network may supplement what is known already, or broaden the context. It may also be useful directly in a negotiation with a department. Where it has been obtained informally from sources within that department, the Expenditure Controller may have to balance the short-term advantage which such knowledge gives him against the risk to his relationships in the longer term.

It is not suggested here that better-informed Expenditure Divisions now provide alternative analyses, forecasts, or arguments in support of departmental bids for additional expenditure; rather that they are better placed to play the traditional adversarial role. Moreover, the range of relevant questions has increased with the greater concern to obtain value-for-money through improved efficiency and effectiveness in the use of resources to achieve particular outputs. Some feared that FMI

would make the Treasury's task in controlling expenditure more difficult, as expenditure proposals supported by unit-cost calculations and
output data appeared less challengeable. There is little evidence of that.
If anything, it has provided controllers with the means to ask more
searching questions rooted in a better database.

Scepticism and detachment, two norms with which the behaviour of
Expenditure Controllers is commonly identified, are inherent in the
mission to control spending. While it is difficult to demonstrate that as
a result of the loss of control in the mid-1970s they are more sceptical,
more than a decade of Conservative governments committed to the
reduction of public expenditure has served to reinforce and sanctify
traditional Treasury attitudes. It is perhaps less true than when Heclo
and Wildavsky wrote that Expenditure Controllers are sceptical of most
quantitative analysis. The production of value-for-money data in prescribed forms at different stages of the Survey process, or as part of in-
year monitoring, is now customary. While Expenditure Controllers
retain a properly sceptical outlook on what such data is claimed to
demonstrate, it is not rejected out of hand as inferior to an 'informed
hunch', as may once have been the case. A much greater degree of
numeracy is required or has to be acquired than was the case twenty
years ago. But Expenditure Controllers emphasize the importance of
not becoming obsessed by the numbers, and the need 'to poke about
behind them'.

Detachment is institutionalized in the structures of the Treasury as
well as in its culture. It is difficult for a controller to be 'captured' by a
spending department, to 'go native', or even to become committed to its
aims. Belief in breadth of experience rather than depth of knowledge
ensures that frequent movement between posts is a fact and a way of
life. On average Expenditure Controllers spend no more than two to
two and a half years in an Expenditure Division before being moved,
barely time to learn the job and to identify targets to attack, and less
than the three years minimum recommended by the Treasury itself.
Culturally, 'enthusiasms' are difficult to generate and sustain, given the
essentially hostile climate within which Expenditure Controllers work,
and the unremitting process of restraining the enthusiasms, commitment, and special pleading of departmental Finance and Policy Divisions and their clientele.

It is true now, as it has been historically, that Expenditure Controllers
are not expert in the subject-matter of their divisions' responsibilities
but nor are they the laymen or gifted amateurs derided in some earlier
accounts. They are professional controllers who acquire a distinctive set
of skills, and who have access to a range of other relevant skills and

professional advice; their unique claim is the opportunity and the expertise to see expenditure in a broader context and from a wider perspective than those with whom they deal. The 'bigger, rounded' picture which the unique perspective of the Expenditure Controller provides is made up of any or all of several elements. The coming together of programmes at the Head of Group level in the Treasury provides the possibility to detect common themes and trends which, viewed from the middle, in the round, may suggest the need for a general response to a number of disparate items of expenditure. Below them, controllers in the divisions are well placed to see connections between the parts of different programmes, as well as to detect gaps. If it is rarely the case that the Treasury is able to achieve a more effective integration of related programmes, it can occasionally point to the need for better co-ordination. Perhaps the most obvious advantage is that a controller can look across the range of a department's programmes with a detached eye. What to a departmental Finance or Policy Division is an issue of overwhelming importance, to a controller will be only one of several such issues. He may think it important, but his assessment is less 'short-sighted', his perspective wider. The significance of the 'bigger picture' in more effective control of spending is difficult to assess. Certainly the opportunity exists for it to influence the behaviour of controllers in their divisions, through the co-ordination of different kinds of expenditure business, and higher still through the broader perspectives of Heads of Group and Deputy Secretaries.

One advantage which is difficult to measure is the trade-off at the margin. With programme expenditures coming increasingly together as the sphere of responsibility increases up the hierarchy, the possibility exists for controllers to confront and compare expenditure bids at the margin and to assess priorities. There is no formal mechanism for this. Although meetings at the group level, the co-ordination of bids by GEP, discussions with the Chief Secretary, will all help to identify relative strengths and weaknesses of parts of bids, the Treasury's order of priorities will be concerned with attacking weak parts rather than attempting to compare at the margin the costs and benefits of one item of expenditure against another. To some extent those priorities are shaped by political judgements made in Cabinet and Cabinet committees through the course of the year. We discuss these and related issues in Chapter 11.

Behavioural norms are partly institutionalized in the structures of the Treasury (small divisions; a handful of controllers; a flexible, adaptable, and highly responsive command structure; small, well-integrated central divisions), and in the socio-culture which emphasizes the importance of good communication networks between divisions, with extension into the spending departments themselves. The smallness of the Treasury, the ease and informality of relationships, is emphasized by all, and contrasted favourably with many of the larger, less flexible departmental command structures, with their more formal and slower lines of communication. Written and verbal information can be circulated, absorbed, and processed quickly, transcending formal hierarchical structures and relationships. Small teams can be organized quickly, cutting across responsibilities and hierarchies. The Treasury can and does respond quickly where necessary, and there is advantage in doing so. 'The fastest mover of any department in Whitehall', in the judgement of one Treasury Deputy Secretary with long career experience in another major Whitehall department. Issues blow up quickly and the Treasury has to take a view. Departments only get in touch with the Treasury when it is necessary, urgent, or critical for them to do so. They want a prompt and authoritative reaction. The Treasury has to respond in days rather than weeks.

The extent and ease of consultation and co-ordination, particularly the copying of papers, impresses those brought in on transfer or secondment from other departments. There is also more opportunity for informal communication than there is in other departments, and than once there was in the Treasury. One Under Secretary had noticed a change in the Treasury culture over the last twenty years: 'it now operates as though it were an open-plan office; with more open-doors, and people dropping-in'. Professional informality among Expenditure Controllers provides an important medium for the circulation and exchange of assessments of the strengths and weaknesses of officials in the Finance and Policy Divisions of the spending departments, and the financial management systems they operate.

The influence on the behaviour of Expenditure Controllers of the concern since 1979 with cutting costs, obtaining better value-for-money, and improving the management of public expenditure programmes, is more difficult to assess. It represents the most obvious difference, if one rather of emphasis and degree and of 'managerial style', than of kind, between the late 1980s and the early 1970s. The Treasury has always been identified with principles of economical and efficient expenditure. Allied to effectiveness, the three have acquired a political salience under Conservative governments which distinguishes the present Treasury from its immediate predecessors. What was always inherent and implicit in the Treasury's function has been articulated in the formal rhetoric of Raynerism, FMI, and Next Steps. But the extent to which that 'new managerialism' has influenced the behaviour of Expenditure

Controllers is difficult to assess. (For a preliminary assessment of its effect on the Civil Service generally, see Metcalfe and Richards 1990.) Much energy in recent years has been expended by senior Treasury officials in encouraging Expenditure Controllers to see their tasks in the context of the drive for efficiency, value-for-money, and improved financial management.

There is confidence in the Treasury that spending departments are now better able to quantify the output of their programmes. Even though this might mean that departments' bids are less easily rebutted as a consequence, senior Treasury officials regard this as a bonus for the Treasury too, as Expenditure Controllers have a better basis on which to discuss departmental requests. In the end the Treasury can still fall back on the defence that, although the case is well supported, it cannot be accommodated within the envelope of available resources. Here again, behaviour is affected by the institutionalization of norms in organizational structures, and by the prevailing socio-culture. New formal structures include Treasury divisions such as FM and RC, and account-ancy advice, whose *raison d'être* is managerial efficiency and effective-ness, and which provide support and advice for Expenditure Divisions (and departments) on financial management systems.

Other kinds of structural changes are to be found in some of the new policy rules, for example the Survey *Guidelines*, which incorporate the new emphasis on the collection of various kinds of data on performance and output. These and other structural changes both reflect and re-inforce the prevailing socio-cultural climate in which Expenditure Controllers operate—in a general way, they give more time and attach greater importance to obtaining better value for each item of pro-gramme expenditure. First, there is more emphasis on outputs, and less on inputs. This has a long history, going back at least to the programme studies instituted by Sir Richard Clarke in the 1960s (discussed in Chapter 3), and later concerns with PPBS and PAR. There has been a bigger drive since 1983 with the introduction of cash planning. This was partly a response to the concerns of the Government with efficiency and effectiveness, but also because, once volume planning was removed, the Treasury and departments had to look at output issues separately. Under the volume planning regime, volume figures were used as a proxy for output. Secondly, departments are now required to provide more data on intermediate and final outputs. Thirdly, departments have financial management systems and financial manage-ment plans, both of which are monitored and evaluated by Expenditure Controllers and the Treasury's FM Division. One Expenditure Division estimated that it spent up to a third of its time in ensuring that its spending department had a good system and that it was working properly.

Conducting relations within the network:
the channels of communication

What is communicated between members of the expenditure network, the mode of communication, and the level at which it takes place, is regulated by behavioural rules of the game. While most of these are common to most members, there are some important differences reflecting different traditions and culture. The most important rule is that the relationships between the Treasury and the spending departments are normally conducted bilaterally. For both, the Expenditure Division and the Finance Division normally, but not invariably (the Territorial Departments are an important exception, discussed later), provide the focal point or window of access. The Expenditure Division is the window to its spending department for the rest of the Treasury. Similarly, the Finance Division provides the window to the Treasury for its Policy Divisions, agencies, and NDPBs.

Most departments have internal rules which ensure that any business with the Treasury which has financial or resources implications has to be cleared with Finance Divisions. These are also responsible for the preparation of the PES bid and the Estimates which follow the settlement, and bring together the contributions of Policy Divisions and agencies to both. In most departments the Finance Division acts routinely as a 'postbox' for communication with the Treasury. More importantly, in larger departments it contributes to the development and presentation of policy.

There are mutual benefits in conducting relationships mainly through the ED–FD nexus. First, each side is better able to achieve coherence and consistency, speaking with 'one voice' rather than several. It also helps to ensure that the policy rules of government accounting, for example the authorization of spending and its regularity and propriety, are observed. Secondly, where the department is large enough to justify specialist Finance Divisions there will be accumulated experience and expertise in dealing with the Treasury available to its Policy Divisions. This service function has become more important with the need to justify and support demands for additional money with value-for-money data. The Finance Divisions can help Policy Divisions to present their arguments in the most advantageous manner, advise on the kind and quality of supporting data which will be necessary, warn what the Treasury is unlikely to accept, and use their negotiating skills on their behalf.

Thirdly, the Finance Division can act as a 'Treasury across the water', filtering and weeding out poorly presented, ill-considered, or irregular expenditure proposals, acting inquisitorially in much the way that the Expenditure Division does, but with the crucial difference that its aim is to help the department obtain sufficient resources to do its job. As one PFO put it: the Finance Division tries to 'maximise the opportunities. If we missed a trick the Treasury wouldn't tell us. The difference is that the Finance Division tries to ensure that Policy Divisions don't miss a trick.' Finance Divisions will probe and ask hard questions because some proposals from Policy Divisions and agencies are poorly presented and 'wouldn't get past the Treasury'. Sometimes they will allow something to go to Treasury in order for it to be turned down. One PFO thought that allowing an agency or Policy Division to 'get their fingers burnt' was sometimes helpful in establishing the Finance Division's credentials with other Policy Divisions and agencies. It can happen, however, that something it would like the Expenditure Division to turn down gets through; the Expenditure Division may be too busy to give it sufficient attention. With a mutual interest in the improvement of financial discipline and control, and where relationships between an Expenditure Division and Finance Division are good, the PFO and Treasury Assistant Secretary (G5) may even discuss informally who should take the lead and 'do the work'. As one PFO explained: 'When the Treasury are busy I will sometimes ring [the Grade 5] and ask him if he or I should do the work on this one.' If relationships are good, and interests are shared on an issue, then either can play the role.

A Finance Division's credibility with its Expenditure Division partly depends upon it being able to demonstrate a continuing concern with financial regularity, discipline, and control. However, if it appears to be too close to the Expenditure Division it risks criticism from its own Policy Divisions and agencies that it is doing the Treasury's work for it, and is insufficiently sensitive to the aims and needs of departmental ministers reflected in their expenditure proposals. Staying close to the Expenditure Division, establishing relationships of trust and reliability, may be the best strategy for a Finance Division promoting and protecting the interests of the department as a whole. But many Policy Divisions and agencies remain unconvinced, arguing for a more formal, distant relationship; or, preferably, dealing directly with the Expenditure Division themselves.

The advantages to a spending department of a single window to the Treasury are obvious enough. The Finance Division can maintain an oversight of the department's financial business, provide consistency and coherence in its dealings with the Treasury, and, where appropriate, control the flow of information to the Treasury. By providing a departmental focus for access to the Treasury, it can prevent the possibility and risk of different and possibly uncoordinated approaches to the Treasury from several different parts of the department. The advantages to the Treasury are not immediately self-evident. Allowed unrestricted access to the Policy Divisions and agencies, it could pursue tactics calculated to secure maximum benefits by playing one division off against another. But in practice it has more to lose by such tactics; and more to gain through the maintenance of good, close, and workable relationships with a Finance Division.

Most departments have an unwritten behavioural rule, and agreement with their Expenditure Division, that the Treasury does not approach a Policy Division or agency without informing the Finance Division. Similarly, there is an expectation that Policy Divisions and agencies will not communicate directly with the Treasury, unless cleared first with the Finance Division. On routine matters, for example where an Expenditure Division needs to check a figure or clarify a point in a submission, the Treasury will deal directly with a Policy Division, and the rule is not rigidly applied. As one PFO explained: 'The FD would not object to the Treasury going to the Policy Division for narrow factual information but we would get annoyed if this went further than just routine probing.' Where a Policy Division has approval to talk to the Treasury on a minor technical matter, it can happen that the discussion 'escalates' to a substantive issue. But both sides tend to play by the rules for their mutual long-term benefit. Attempts by Policy Divisions to 'cut corners' and go direct to the Treasury are soon 'pulled up short' by the Finance Division. Similarly, any major transgression by the Treasury would produce a sharp reminder from the PFO to an Expenditure Division's Under Secretary about compliance with the rules. While Finance Divisions are not absolutely rigid about departmental observance of the rules they 'try to keep the strings in their own hands'. And for the most part, Policy Divisions are content to allow their Finance Division to manage the interface with the Treasury.

Executive Agencies tend to be less happy at communicating with the Treasury through the intermediation of the Finance Division. Many would prefer more direct contact, in the belief that their case would be better and more convincingly argued. Some doubt that their Finance Division is sufficiently familiar with the business of the agency to get the 'right tone of voice'. In some spending departments, there is a belief among Policy Divisions that the Finance Division's credibility with the Treasury depends to some extent on its being seen to get tough with its own Policy Divisions and agencies. One Executive Agency Under Secretary (G3) in charge of resources and planning represented this as part of the Treasury–departmental game: Finance Divisions 'try to second guess us to arm themselves with something to give the Treasury'. In those departments where agencies formerly had separate and direct relationships with the Treasury as grant-aided bodies, the change of regime has produced some tension. They may remain unconvinced of the benefits of a 'single window' on the Treasury. Where the department does not obtain all the agency requires, the result can be represented as a Finance Division failure.

The intermediary status of the Finance Division can cause difficulties with both Policy Divisions and agencies. One source of frustration is that they lack understanding of the accounting rules and conventions:

They tend to get worked up about issues which are perfectly clear in accounting terms where the Treasury and Finance Division both know that nothing can be done. For example, a Policy Division Grade 5 wants to raise an issue with the Treasury on retention of receipts. We point out that it is clearly a non-starter, but he insists in arguing that it is merely a case of 'getting it to the right level and we'll get it sorted out'. It can mean burning our fingers as well as theirs, if we take things sometimes. If we continually take such issues to the Treasury Expenditure Division we would strain relationships with the Treasury. (PFO, main spending department)

Where there are good, easy relationships between the Finance Division and the Expenditure Division, the Assistant Secretary (G5) might phone the Treasury and say: 'I don't think you'll agree but I have to send it.' An alternative course of action is for the PFO to take the matter to his departmental Deputy Secretary and explain why Finance Division did not want to take it to the Treasury. It might then be decided not to send a case from a Policy Division or agency unless more work was done on it—on costs or outputs for example. The Policy Division is told that it would not stand a chance without such further work. Often this is sufficient, and the issue is dropped.

In some departments, on some issues, there is direct communication between a Policy Division and the Treasury. For example, the DFE Science Branch deals directly with the Treasury Expenditure Division on the grant-aided research councils. Smaller departments, such as the (former) Department of Energy and the DTI, tend to be less rigid about communication with the Treasury. In both there is a tradition of Policy Divisions dealing directly, partly because of the specialist nature of the subject-matter, and partly because of the small size of the Finance Division, which lacks the specialist divisions and the economies of scale of larger ones. But even here the Finance Division is involved in the preparation of bids and proposals which have resource implications. As with other departments, it deals with the Expenditure Division on the PES bid and Estimates.

In much the same way that the Finance Division provides the window on the Treasury for departmental Policy Divisions and agencies, so the Treasury tends to conduct its relationships with the spending department through the Expenditure Division. Thus an Expenditure Division relays, directly and indirectly, 'messages' about policy on pay, running costs, and financial management from its central divisions, who have little direct contact with Finance Divisions. They are regarded by PFOs as a 'brooding presence' behind many of the initiatives which are transmitted by Expenditure Divisions, sometimes with an unconcealed lack of enthusiasm. There is a widespread belief among departments that Expenditure Divisions often act under direction from Treasury central divisions, or are constrained in their room for manœuvre in discussions or negotiations with departments by pressure from them. Care has to be taken not to read too much into this. Just as the Finance Division may use the Expenditure Division as a 'whipping boy' in its dealings with its own Policy Divisions and agencies, so the Expenditure Division may invoke directly or implicitly in its communications with Finance Division the spectre of the Treasury central divisions. In meetings between the Expenditure Division and Finance Division, central divisions are often represented, but their people tend to remain in the background and say little.

The lines of communication between the Treasury and the Scottish and Welsh Offices are more complex than is the case with other spending departments. There is no single window out of the Treasury, nor out of the spending department. While most financial business is dealt with between their Finance Divisions/Groups and the Treasury's Territorial Expenditure Division, on such matters as the management plan, running costs, and financial management generally, the Scottish and Welsh Office Policy Divisions deal directly with the relevant functional Treasury Expenditure Division on issues relating to specific programmes, health or education for example. The Scottish Office has contact with no fewer than eleven of the Treasury's eighteen Expenditure Divisions, and the Welsh Office, with nine. Managing multifaceted relationships within the network is more complex than is the case with the relationships between the Treasury and the English functional departments. However, because of the block arrangement (discussed in Chapter 14), fewer issues go to the Treasury, there is 'less traffic'.

The Territorial Expenditure Division does deal with all the Northern Ireland business, however, although the Northern Ireland Department of Finance and Personnel (DFP) exchanges information from time to time with the Treasury's other Expenditure Divisions. It acts as a mini-Treasury in relation to the Northern Ireland departments, besides its role as a Finance Division in its contact with the Treasury's Territorial Division. It is regarded by the Northern Ireland departments in the same way as the English spending departments' Policy Divisions regard the Treasury: DFP challenges the departments on their individual programmes, probing to find out why their spending per capita is higher than in the UK and whether it is justified. There is a constructive tension in the relationships, but on the whole the Northern Ireland departments prefer to deal with the DFP and have it as a buffer between them and the Treasury. The Northern Ireland Office (NIO) has a particularly sensitive balancing act to perform since its programmes are scrutinized by the Treasury yet its expenditure comes out of the block managed by DFP. In the past NIO was tempted to go to the Treasury first and then, in effect, pre-empt resources from the block. Now there is a conscious effort to approach both central departments simultaneously. The DFP operates under similar rules of government accounting to those which govern relationships between the Treasury and Finance and Policy Divisions in mainland departments: Northern Ireland departments are not expected to deal directly with the Treasury and where they do it is only with the knowledge and agreement of DFP; similarly, the Treasury is expected to deal with the DFP alone, although the NIO is an exception to this rule.

Levels of communication

The level of communication varies with the nature of the expenditure business, its significance and urgency, and the personal relationships established between individual members of the network. Whom Finance Divisions deal with in the Treasury is determined mainly by the organization of the Expenditure Divisions and the way in which the business is dealt with in each of them. In Chapter 6 we noted the collegial rather than hierarchical distribution of the business within Expenditure Divisions. Levels of communication between Finance Divisions and Expenditure Divisions reflect also departmental traditions, while on any particular issue personality and expediency may play an important part. There are no hard-and-fast rules regulating the levels of communication. The so-called convention that spending departments are obliged to deal with the Treasury at one level or grade down is more a reflection of the organization of the Expenditure Divisions, in which Treasury Principals (G7) have the immediate day-to-day responsibility for the expenditure of a department. It is to them that the heads of departmental Finance Divisions (G5) dealing with PES, Estimates, in-year control, and so on, look for their day-to-day contact. Principal (G7) tends to be the working level. 'Even when an Estimates Clerk writes £2m off your expenditure at Estimates time, it wouldn't go above Grade 7' (Assistant Secretary, medium-sized department). Treasury expenditure officials of Assistant Secretary (G5) rank tend to have a broader responsibility for a number of departments, and deal with the broader policy issues, sometimes with the Assistant Secretaries of Finance Divisions, but more commonly with the PFOs (at Under Secretary or Deputy Secretary level). The latter have some contact with Treasury Under Secretaries, but less regularly. Among Finance Divisions there is a common complaint of the remoteness of Treasury Under Secretaries, that they tend to 'remain in the background', and get involved only if an issue rises towards ministerial level. Policy Divisions and agencies also complain that Finance Divisions deal at 'too low a level' with the Treasury. This is partly a reflection of the wider frustration with the intermediary role of the Finance Divisions noted earlier, and the belief that their arguments for additional expenditure, or authority to spend, would convince more senior Treasury officials.

Convenience, availability, and who is handling the business in the Treasury frequently determine at what level and with whom the Finance Division communicates on a particular issue, although often there is no alternative as a particular Treasury official is the only contact. Personal contact by telephone or meeting may take place several times a week, and during the Survey cycle several times a day. In the DES (now DFE) the Finance Division Assistant Secretary met the Treasury Assistant Secretary three or four times a week, and was in daily contact with the Expenditure Division's Principals and other officials. Most Whitehall departments are within easy walking distance of the Treasury, and *ad hoc* meetings are easy to arrange. Because of their location the territorial departments are 'somewhat outside the Whitehall village' (Thomas 1987: 15), although all three retain offices in Whitehall with small ministerial-support teams. There is less opportunity to 'drop in' on the Treasury, and 'face to face' meetings are more difficult to arrange. Business between Finance Divisions and the Treasury Expenditure Divisions tends to be conducted more formally, with a greater risk of misunderstanding.

PFOs, and some Assistant Secretaries, tend to have informal arrangements with Treasury Assistant Secretaries to exchange verbal notes and brief each other on the background to current business, irrespective of what else is happening. One PFO had a regular 'Tuesday-call' with the

Treasury Under Secretary, whether or not they had business to conduct, just to keep in touch and find out what pressures each had. The origin of this informal arrangement was partly because the Treasury Under Secretary was involved in the detail of departmental running costs, partly because of friendly relations between them, and partly because the Treasury Under Secretary was 'someone you could do business with'.

As the levels of communication are not regulated by hard-and-fast rules, a Finance Division has some room for manœuvre to try to work through those Treasury officials who have shown themselves more sympathetic and supportive of the department's policies, and conversely to avoid those who have proved awkward or difficult. There are obvious limits to this, given the small number of people involved, and the concept of the single window. As one PFO explained: 'We steer towards those who are most helpful and away from those least helpful. We can also deal up and down the hierarchy. We try to go to whom we think can deliver.' This is true also of Treasury Expenditure Controllers.

The involvement of ministers is likewise governed by behavioural norms. A decision by a minister on either side to involve himself directly and formally, or a decision by officials to raise an issue to ministerial level, automatically prompts a like response from the other side. There is a strong behavioural presumption in the network against the personal involvement of ministers. That is not to say that the issues are determined by officials on both sides without ministerial aims, thoughts, and interests being taken fully into account: conducting business on behalf of the ministers takes place simultaneously at many different levels in the hierarchy. But business which is conducted personally by the Minister, through a ministerial letter to his opposite number, or a formal or informal meeting with him with officials present on both sides, is a different mode of communication. Dealing up the official hierarchy slows down the progress and settlement of an issue between the two sides. It adds further levels of complexity, and may introduce 'status as well as argument' into the discussions between the two sides. Communication at the ministerial level introduces a further, formal dimension which may make it more difficult and time-consuming still to reach a settlement. At certain times, as in the autumnal bilaterals, and on certain big issues—a policy review for example—the personal involvement of ministers is both expected and necessary, and both sides work towards that culmination. At other times, each side may threaten implicitly or even directly that it will have to take an issue to its minister. Knowing when and how to play the 'ministerial card' is part of the tactics employed by both.

The mode of communication

Behavioural norms prescribe the appropriate mode of communication: formal or informal, written or spoken. Some of these are prescribed generally for conducting business within and between Whitehall departments: the use of official and semi-official letters; the 'copying' and circulation of letters and reports to those who 'need to know'; informal soundings and approaches; off-the-record conversations; and the rules and conventions regulating the setting-up, work, and minutes of official interdepartmental committees and working parties, the status and 'locus' of *ad hoc* meetings and discussions. These general bureaucratic norms are supplemented by others which apply specifically to the conduct of particular kinds of expenditure business—the preparation and submission of Agenda Letters in the Survey for example, and by local ground rules established in relations between an Expenditure Division and a Finance Division over a period of time, for example telephone 'consultations', the exchange of verbal background information or briefing, informal prior-warning notices.

Communication between a departmental Finance Division and Treasury Expenditure Controllers is a mixture of the formal and informal, the impersonal and personal. Guidelines, rules, and conventions provide for the preparation and timetable of such formal submissions to the Treasury as the PES returns, the bid letters, Estimates and Supplementaries, authority to spend. The Treasury responds formally by letter to those submissions, and to a variety of in-year requests for authority to commit expenditure where approval is necessary, permission to vire, calls on the Reserve, and so on. As well, the Expenditure Division itself initiates business, for example on running costs and management plans which may require a formal response from the Finance Division. Exchanges of letters, submissions, and returns between the Expenditure Division and the Finance Division represent the formal statement of what each is requesting, arguing, committing, approving, or refusing, at different times and stages in the process from proposal to decision. At the end of the process, the formal statement of what has been decided provides the authority for the department to act in a particular way, or not. It is important that both sides should agree on what has been decided, and that the details of the decisions should represent accurately what was agreed. In arriving at that decision the formal exchanges of letters represent the official positions of each side at a particular time and stage in the process. As the issue is batted back and forth between the two, those positions may incorporate the substance of or responses to any informal communications between them.

These exchanges, at various levels and in different modes, are helpful to the mutual understanding of the 'line' adopted by each side, and the objectives which they are pursuing. At the same time they provide the means to explore the room for manœuvre in the formal discussion of the arguments deployed on each side, where agreement is not possible straight off. The formal exchange of letters is complemented by a constant exchange of information, views, and ideas, relayed informally. Informal relationships between a Finance Division and its Expenditure Division provide opportunities for both sides to explore, test, and sound out each other's arguments and evidence, and the degree of commitment; and provide a mechanism to convey signals of admonition, advice, and encouragement.

Informal exchanges can help to move the business forward in a mutually agreeable direction, or indicate that no such agreement is possible. Where good relationships exist, 'you can say to the Treasury: I think this can be delivered subject to my Minister agreeing, and I think I can persuade him' (Assistant Secretary, Finance Division, main spending department). An Expenditure Division official might confide to his opposite number after receipt of a formal letter: 'I'm under pressure from my colleagues, so don't press this line again in future' (Principal). A supportive and sympathetic Expenditure Controller might indicate informally to a Finance Division the kind of argument which might be employed in a formal submission to convince the Treasury. He might hint in a phone call that 'if you had said this we might have been persuaded', providing encouragement for the Finance Division to respond formally with a supplementary note explaining that it had forgotten or overlooked the point in the earlier submission.

The positions taken up formally in submissions can be explored in informal communications and sometimes an understanding or accommodation can be reached. Equally, there may be very little room for flexibility on one or both sides, and such communication may serve mainly to underline or reinforce the formal position set out in letters. Such information is useful in gauging the strength of commitment to the line being run formally, and in influencing the tactics adopted subsequently. For example, whether to elevate an issue to ministerial level is partly dependent upon a judgement of the likely response of the other side and the prospect of success or failure. Informal communication also provides a quick and easy mechanism to convey requests for more information, clarification, or explanation, without recourse to a formal request.

Most informal communication is by telephone. *Ad hoc* meetings between officials at different levels serve the same purpose. Because of the geographic proximity of most departments to the Treasury a chat between opposite numbers, or even larger gatherings of Expenditure Division, Finance Division, and Policy Division officials can be convened at short notice. For example, at the time of the bilaterals there is 'furious work' between officials. Between the ministerial meetings consultations can be intense. Where a minister or his officials have promised further information during a previous bilateral, officials will discuss informally with Expenditure Division what is required and how it should be presented. Parts of the bid may need to be recalculated—'supposing we did it this way?' The key here, as at other times in the year on other issues, is 'reading the signals', as well as responding formally to the official positions taken up by each side. 'With experience you learn to pick up signals of what might be acceptable, what might be the best way to present a case' (Assistant Secretary, medium-sized department).

Contact between the Treasury Expenditure Division and its department also takes place at the time of discussion of a new policy initiative. Departments commonly invite Expenditure Division officials to take part in working parties or policy reviews. As there are invariably expenditure implications, the Treasury has a legitimate interest, but invariably reserves its position. Such occasions provide the opportunity for the Treasury to meet and listen to officials from Policy Divisions. For example, the Treasury was represented on the DES working groups which led to the White Paper on *Qualified People*, and in departmental discussions of science expenditure performance indicators and student loans policy. The Department of Transport tries to involve the Treasury 'constructively and co-operatively' in the main issues facing the department. There was a joint-study on the roads programme, in which the Treasury Under Secretary participated on the basis that the Treasury reserved its position on the 'affordability' of any policies which emerged from it. The Treasury was also involved in the discussions on the Channel rail-link. The Treasury nearly always accepts invitations to take part in such discussion groups and working parties, its motives a mixture of curiosity and the need to be informed at an early stage of the potential expenditure implications, in order to be able to brief the Chief Secretary in advance of any policy announcement.

There are opportunities for an exchange of views at 'annual get-togethers'. Many Finance Divisions have a 'round-up' financial management meeting with the Expenditure Division to review past performance and future prospects. The relevant Treasury Under Secretary may take the chair. Besides Expenditure Division officials, representatives from the Treasury's central divisions normally attend. One

PFO described such meetings as 'not very exciting', their purpose being to enable the Treasury to satisfy itself about the department's management systems, management plans, and performance measures. In recent years the agenda of such meetings has included the problems of defining and applying output measures, and candidates for Next Steps Agency status.

One important mode of informal communication between the Finance Division and the Expenditure Division is the reciprocal use of contacts as 'sounding boards'. Their use is very much dependent on good, informal relationships of trust and confidence. Finance Division can 'sound out' its Expenditure Division on a probable official reaction to a proposal it might make, test the acceptability of a proposed course of action, obtain 'early warning' of a Treasury line which may have policy implications for the department. Conversely, the Expenditure Division can 'sound out' the likely departmental reaction to a Treasury line. In general PFOs and Finance Division officials try to keep the Treasury informed of what is about to happen, and to avoid a *fait accompli* or professional embarrassment to the Expenditure Division— for example by the Treasury learning of a major departmental policy issue from reading the newspapers. 'We wouldn't want the Chief Secretary to read something and ask for a briefing from the Expenditure Division and for them not to know anything about it' (PFO, major spending department). When to sound out is a matter of tactical judgement. One PFO explained that his department would not sound out the Treasury's reaction to a putative departmental initiative too early in the process. 'As it gets near to Ministers, then we would sound them out. To do so before is to risk wasting time.' There are other risks too: 'If we were thinking of introducing a borrowing regime for [x], it would be unwise to talk to the Treasury too early, and risk a reduction in grant.'

Using the Expenditure Division as a sounding board is not without difficulty for the Finance Division, if informal communications give the impression to its constituents in the Policy Divisions and agencies that it is getting too close to the Treasury. The Finance Division has to walk a 'tightrope between the Treasury on the one hand and the rest of the department on the other. They have to be careful not to appear to be on anyone's side other than that of the department as a whole' (PFO, main spending department). One Finance Division described the tension in the relationship between it and the Expenditure Division because there 'really was no moratorium on using the information acquired by their Expenditure Division'. But if the Expenditure Division used information obtained through the informal channels to 'rubbish proposals' rather than to 'evaluate them sensibly' there was the real risk of the supply being cut off, or the flow of useful information being reduced.

Information and understanding can also be obtained by visits to institutions, organizations, and establishments connected with a spending department. Most Finance Divisions encourage their opposite numbers in Expenditure Divisions to 'get out and about', to see for themselves what is happening in schools, social security offices, research establishments, naval dockyards, nationalized industries, and agencies. The belief is that such exposure will help Expenditure Divisions to see behind and beyond the figures. While an Expenditure Controller can use his eyes and ears to good effect, the symbolic effect of site-visits is probably more important: the perceived willingness of the Expenditure Controller to get out from behind his desk, see for himself, and to talk to people on the ground. The effect on the spending department may be disproportionate to the actual knowledge and understanding acquired from such a visit. It may inspire greater confidence subsequently that the Treasury understands a problem or the need for a particular item of expenditure. The Expenditure Controller's judgement may now seem more authoritative, when backed up by reference to knowledge acquired at first hand. Conversely, it may also have given him greater confidence in the position he decides to take up. At the same time site-visits provide an opportunity to explain to people on the ground the Treasury's concerns and its distinctive perspective. This can be useful, as many line managers and specialists in Policy Divisions in departments, and those in public corporations, regional bodies, and quangos, deal with the Treasury only indirectly through the Finance Divisions, and as a result often associate the Treasury unfairly with uncompromising negativeness. At the same time there is advantage for the Finance Division that its Policy Divisions and agencies may better appreciate the need to maintain close relations with the Treasury, after policy people have had contact with Treasury officials 'on-site'. A further advantage is that the Expenditure Controller may be able to add to his contacts and extend his information network. Not all have time to make site-visits routinely, and compared with the practice in other Whitehall departments there is less contact with outside interests. 'When you ring someone up at the Treasury they are more often than not at their desks' (Assistant Secretary, major spending department).

Acquiring and using information in the network

Through such channels of communication, the Treasury and the spending departments principally, but other members of the network too, exchange information and other resources of authority, money, and expertise. To present and argue the case for money, spending departments need information from the Treasury (and other members of the network) of various kinds, both formal and informal, for example formal guidance on the preparation of the Survey, hints on the line to take in an official letter. Conversely, to plan and allocate expenditure for the public sector, and to ensure that the general values of efficiency, economy, and effectiveness are achieved together with the ministerial target for the annual Planning/Control Total, the Treasury is reliant on the spending departments for information and expertise. While spending departments are not the only source, they are the main one. This reliance derives from the basic behavioural norms of Expenditure Controllers to which we referred above—they do not seek to match the specialist knowledge or expertise of the spending departments, nor to 're-do' their expenditure proposals.

There are three main categories of information which the Treasury seeks in its transactions with the spending departments: first, basic data about expenditure business, across the range of issues covered—whether this is about bids for more resources in the Survey discussions or details of a policy change requiring in-year funding from the Reserve; secondly, information which enables controllers to gauge the quality of a department's financial management system, both as part of the routine of Survey discussions when output and value-for-money data are required and more generally during in-year control discussions or policy reviews when the Expenditure Divisions are probing to find out how well a department is 'delivering'; and thirdly, information about the quality, reliability, and trustworthiness of the people in the departments and agencies.

Acquiring this range of information easily and in the quantity and quality needed, at minimal cost in terms of time spent, is a pivotal skill of an Expenditure Controller. Ease of acquisition is also a benchmark of how 'workable' relationships are between the Expenditure Divisions and spending departments, for at every stage of the business information is vital to achieve the different purposes of expenditure monitoring and control. The combination of pressure of business and the short tours of duty of most Expenditure Controllers makes Expenditure Divisions particularly reliant on departments supplying information on current issues and, often, even on how the Treasury handled an issue in the past. 'We take a lot on trust, since we haven't got the time to deal with all aspects of a department's work, so we are dependent on them for information' (Assistant Secretary, Expenditure Division). This dependence is most marked in dealings involving basic factual data; less so when it comes to the interpretation of that data. Expenditure Controllers will sometimes question the data provided by departments; occasionally an Expenditure Division will work up alternative sets of figures in order to provoke a department into justifying or improving its presentation of data. The Treasury may ask a department to improve its sources of data. For example, the Treasury ran two simplified economic models on housing benefits and on social security benefits which were especially useful in assessing the economic impact of changes in benefit levels. Nevertheless, the Expenditure Divisions in those policy areas would still go initially to the departments for their calculations. Then, using the simplified Treasury models, it would run the figures and gain a feel for whether the department's data was 'about right' or not. If there were obvious problems the Expenditure Division would go back to the department and say 'Is there any reason why we should not take these figures to the Chief Secretary?'—thus often provoking the relevant Finance Divisions and Policy Divisions to look again at their submission.

Information is needed to conduct a dialogue about the need for additional expenditure or about the value-for-money of a particular project. The period of 'shadow-boxing' during the Survey cycle (see Chapter 12) is primarily about 'information-seeking sallies'. When issues become in-year matters, Expenditure Controllers rarely say 'no' straight away to a request by a department; they will ask for further information and follow this up with later contact. Increasingly, the information required is based on output and value-for-money data. A department stands a better chance of getting a proposal considered further if it is presented with supporting information which stresses the benefit to be gained in terms of departmental efficiency, and shows how the proposal fits within a rigorous framework of departmental objectives.

Expenditure Controllers use the exchange of information as a means of establishing relationships of mutual trust. Encouraging departments to talk about potential problems at an early stage—using the Expenditure Division as a 'sounding board'—is important. But fine judgement may be required to ensure that the department does not feel that knowledge so acquired will be used against it later in Survey discussions. An experienced controller learns to differentiate between casual 'chats' with his opposite number in the department about developments which may be being considered, and more substantive information. Treasury officials are aware of the importance of departmental ministers being able to ask their officials to do 'think-piece work' without prejudice or commitment. Should an Expenditure Controller have been told about this and mention it in bilateral briefing papers, the Chief Secretary may have to tread carefully to avoid divulging his source and possibly souring relations between officials. In such cases the Chief Secretary may say to his ministerial colleague 'Have you thought of handling this issue in this way?' A good Expenditure Controller will be able to make a judgement about the information being supplied and ask: 'Is this background or contextual?' He may have to say to his opposite number 'I would rather you didn't tell me about this as I would be embarrassed if I couldn't discuss this with the Chief Secretary.' But the Treasury official is after all employed to monitor and control expenditure and has a duty to perform that role thoroughly; he is entitled to make use of most of the information he gathers, whatever the source. A departmental official will accordingly have to make clear upon what basis the information is being given and the Treasury official make a judgement about whether an 'off the record' briefing is consistent with his responsibilities to the Chief Secretary. A deliberate breach of a clearly understood trust would obviously harm relations between officials. Once an Expenditure Controller breaks this trust it becomes more difficult to obtain early warning of problems in future dealings. The establishment of such relationships requires delicate handling and the controller must try to be aware of and sensitive to the 'other person's context'.

The exchange of information is one of the most important ways of determining the robustness of a department's financial management system and, equally important, the reliability and quality of the people who run it. An individual Expenditure Controller will use both 'accumulated wisdom' within the Expenditure Division—'watch out for x'—and direct knowledge to build up a picture of reliability. If the quality of information proves to be high—if for example a Finance Division has 'done some of its own work' of screening and filtering expenditure proposals before forwarding a request from a Policy Division—then positive conclusions may be drawn about the people and the system. Since much of the information received is taken on trust, if a department's management system in a particular policy area is regarded as good, the Expenditure Division is more likely to accept a line being offered by the department. This is invariably supplemented with personal assessments. The way in which information is presented can be as important as the quality of the data. If, for example, an opposite number in a Finance Division has summed up a case, weighing the pros and cons judiciously, rather than merely presenting a case as self-evidently correct, this will carry more weight and further strengthen that official's reliability in the eyes of the Expenditure Controller.

Information is also a means of establishing credibility. This is a two-way process: Expenditure Controllers must be able 'to deliver on a proposal' when this has been promised; but equally the departmental Finance Division or Policy Division must also be reliable. If an Expenditure Division probes for information and there is a 'stunned silence' at the other end of a telephone line, the reaction may prompt questions about the reliability of the person involved. If this happens frequently, or if a contact in the department has constantly to refer matters to others, then an Expenditure Controller will seek more authoritative and reliable sources of information. A good departmental contact 'knows what is going on', and an Expenditure Controller soon learns with whom to keep in touch and whom to cut out.

In the next chapter we examine how relationships are managed and maintained within the network, compare the benefits of good relationships, and consider the causes and effects of the tensions and frustrations which may arise.

10

Managing the Relationships: Negotiated Discretion

THE DETERMINANTS OF THE RELATIONSHIPS

Relationships between the Treasury's Expenditure Divisions and the Financial and Policy Divisions of spending departments cannot be characterized as either inquisitorial or co-operative or collaborative or adversarial. They may be any or all of these simultaneously, depending upon the nature of the issue and its priority, the kind of contact, and the experience and mutual understanding of the parties and their preferred strategies. On occasion they may also be confrontational or conflictual. Relationships will vary over time, and be influenced by the broader contextual factors to which we have referred in earlier chapters. While an inquisitorial mode is appropriate to the early probing of the Treasury in the Survey shadow-boxing, an Expenditure Division may be engaged simultaneously on other issues of in-year control, such as the implications of new legislation, and here relations with the department may be more accurately characterized as co-operative or even collaborative. This disposition to seek agreement, through mutual accommodation in negotiations, may characterize the early discussions between an Expenditure Division and a Finance Division on most parts of a bid. But relationships may become more or wholly adversarial on one or two contested issues, as the parties begin to bargain in the bilaterals or provide support for their Ministers in Cabinet and its committees.

However they may be characterized on any particular issue at any particular time, in general both the Expenditure Division and the spending department (and its agencies) have the incentive of mutual self-interest to make those relationships 'workable' and 'effective'. But they are never comfortable or 'cosy'; there is always a 'slight edge' in the dealings between the Treasury's Expenditure Divisions and the departments. This is partly the product of differing values and interests— crudely, an Expenditure Division wants (normally) to keep spending down and a department wants to increase it. It may also reflect a temporary dislocation of normal working relationships, perhaps promoted by departmental attitudes towards the Treasury's 'right' to interfere; or by evidence, at least in the Treasury's view, of incompetence by the department. Frustrations, tensions, and frictions in the relationship may arise anywhere across the whole range of expenditure business. There are, however, some kinds of issues which regularly disturb or temporarily dislocate it. A particular area of tension involves the Treasury's control of running costs and the departmental management and use of resources. We deal with these issues in Chapter 18.

What determines whether relationships between an Expenditure Division and a Finance Division are good or bad? First, as we have explained, different kinds of relationships can coexist, depending upon the type of issue, time of year, and, to some extent, the compatibility of the officials concerned. Simultaneously, the Finance Division can be conducting its relationship with the Expenditure Division in the 'business-mode' on one issue, negotiating adversarially on another, briefing its Minister for a confrontation in a bilateral on a third, and having a 'flaming row' on a fourth. While the relationship between them is conducted formally and sometimes simultaneously in these different modes—adversarially, confrontationally, conflictually, and, on some issues where there is an identity of interests, collaboratively— each side needs the other. Their discretionary behaviour is mutually constrained.

There are three main elements to their interdependence, the first of which is the constitutional and cultural context in which expenditure business is conducted in Whitehall. The collective nature of central government, the federation of equal 'states', reinforces the disposition to seek agreement and to avoid conflict. Secondly, discussions about the allocation of resources cannot be made by a central strategic authority such as the Treasury, informed by considerations of political and economic rationality, without the co-operation of the supplicants. While in times of crisis resources can be allocated almost by fiat—for example, a Treasury decision to cut all departmental budgets by 10 per cent, or to freeze allocations—even that kind of decision requires the political support of the Chancellor's ministerial colleagues, and its implementation the co-operation of departmental and Treasury officials. Above all, neither the Treasury nor departments can perform their respective functions satisfactorily, achieve their policy aims, and try to optimize their values, without exchanging the resources of authority, finance, information, and expertise which each possesses in different amounts and combinations. Discretionary authority to act is negotiated between them.

The key to the relationships between Expenditure Divisions and Finance Divisions is information. For both it is the prime resource, and the substance and mode of its exchange determine the nature of their interdependent relationships. While Finance Divisions are obliged to provide the Treasury with certain kinds of information in prescribed forms at particular times of the year, for example baseline calculations in the Survey round, how much argument and supporting evidence is presented, in bids for new money or authority to commit money already allocated, is to a certain extent at the discretion of the department. Because Expenditure Divisions do not attempt to match the knowledge and expertise of the departments, they have no independent authoritative source to draw upon comparable to that of the department. Their strength derives from their authority to probe the cases presented by the Finance Divisions, to ask questions, to request information, and to demur; and from the threat of the exercise of that authority. Interdependence is reflected in the importance all PFOs and their officials attach to good, long-term working relationships. The key is mutual self-help: a mutual interest and understanding of their different aims, pressures, and difficulties, and a willingness to try to accommodate them.

Mutuality is not formally prescribed, except in the broadest context of the collective nature of British central government; nor can it be assumed. It inheres in relationships of trust, confidence, openness, and honesty, determined by the intellectual and behavioural skills of the Expenditure Division (and Finance Division) officials. Respect for the intellectual ability of Treasury Expenditure Division officials is a necessary ingredient; a Finance Division needs to have confidence that 'they know what they are doing'. Most Policy Divisions and their Finance Division colleagues believe that the best of the Expenditure Division officials are extremely capable, although there are significant exceptions. Criticism is less of their intellectual ability than the breadth of their experience. But given a basic level of capability, the establishment of good working relationships is determined more by personal qualities and behaviour. Informality is essential in good working relationships, and not all Expenditure Division officials are congenitally able or have the confidence to operate in such a mode. It is evident that all spending departments have experienced at some time Treasury officials with whom it was difficult or impossible to develop a relationship of trust and confidence. As we have explained in the previous chapter, in such instances the Finance Division deals up and down the hierarchy (although often there is no alternative but to deal with a difficult Treasury Expenditure Controller), avoiding those who are 'awkward'. Of course 'awkwardness' is a matter of judgement and perspective. There may be good reasons for Treasury 'awkwardness', and Finance Division has an obvious interest in searching out those whom it believes to be more sympathetic and supportive of its objectives. Nevertheless, all PFOs and their senior officials emphasize the importance of informality, and that personality is a factor, both positively and negatively. We may conclude that not all Expenditure Division officials are endowed with the personal qualities which enable them to contribute to the establishment of good working relations. In fairness to the Treasury we quote here a positive rather than negative example of good working relationships, and paraphrase the words of a PFO.

The Expenditure Division Principal who dealt with the programme expenditure of a large department knew a lot about the department and 'understands our operations better than some of us'. He was encouraged and made regular site-visits to inform himself of day-to-day operations. He had the advantage of being able to take an overview of the work of several specialized Policy Divisions, who themselves were not in a position to see how programmes came together. It was also a matter of his personality and attributes. 'He is impressive; he knows his stuff. He gets about, talks to people, listens, and is bright and interested.' He was also 'Treasury born and bred, so he doesn't need to learn about the Treasury's culture or ways of doing things. He can get straight into learning and absorbing the business of [the department]' (PFO, major spending department).

A trusting and confident relationship between an Expenditure Division and a Finance Division calls for honesty, openness, and frankness in their dealings with each other. This does not mean that each side reveals its 'hand' to the other at the outset: the relationship is occasionally collaborative on some issues, but it is not collusive. In preliminary skirmishing at the official level, a Finance Division may hold back some information, and present other material selectively. But in response to probing from the Expenditure Division, it will normally accept that the Treasury has a right to such information, if it thinks the Expenditure Division is acting reasonably. Where relationships are good, an Expenditure Division and a Finance Division are honest and open with each other. As one departmental Assistant Secretary admitted: 'Policy Divisions will cut corners enough without Finance Division doing it as well.' Candour is reciprocal. A Finance Division may signal informally to its Expenditure Division that it is obliged to put up a case which it thinks inadequately or poorly supported by the evidence; and, as we explained in the previous chapter, may invite the Expenditure Division to 'do the work on it'. Similarly, on some issues, currently running costs and management plans, it is apparent to many PFOs that their Expenditure Division is not always wholly committed to the Treasury line they are obliged to follow in their formal communications. Interpreting the signals, the Finance Division can see that their Expenditure Division is 'going through the motions' or 'their heart isn't in the letters they are obliged to write'. After a formal request for revisions to a department's management plan, one Expenditure Division Principal told his opposite number informally: 'I had to send that letter, it was drafted for me by Running Costs Division. I should have told you about it before it arrived.'

Relationships of trust and confidence permit both the Expenditure Division and the Finance Division to warn each other when limits have been reached, where there is a danger of overstepping the mark. We deal below with the issue of legitimate areas of Treasury interest and involvement, but note here that a Finance Division with good lines of communication can be frank with its Expenditure Division and warn it that what it was doing or proposing to do was 'not on'. One PFO who enjoyed close and friendly relations with a Treasury Under Secretary was able when necessary to express frankly and pithily down the phone that the Treasury's behaviour was unacceptable. This would be done without prejudice to the relationship; indeed, it was a sign of the robustness and usefulness of the relationship that there was a channel for conveying such a message informally, without the need to take up official positions on either side and spend time exploring and resolving differences through formal communications, perhaps involving ministers. Of course, on some issues it is both necessary and appropriate for one or both to proceed in that way.

Both Expenditure Divisions and Finance Divisions dislike being surprised by the action of the other. While they may disagree, each likes as much forewarning as possible of what is about to happen. Predictability provides reassurance. If they are close to each other and there is mutual trust and confidence between individuals, then the element of surprise or being caught unawares is reduced. When both sides are acting 'reasonably' then their reactions to each other are more predictable. But when the Expenditure Division is being difficult, a Finance Division can usually understand the reason for it. The Expenditure Division may itself be responding to the pressures of the Chief Secretary, or to lines being taken by the Treasury's central divisions.

Trusting relationships mean that an Expenditure Division and a Finance Division can rely on what each communicates informally. They have confidence in each other's judgement and reliability. Where there is a promise of action in a particular way, or delivering an outcome, there can be a legitimate expectation of fulfilment. Agreements reached informally at meetings, or on the phone, are honoured. Confidence in the judgement and sensitivity of Expenditure Division officials is vital. A Finance Division needs to feel that the Expenditure Division understands the department's aims, policy, and problems, and that Treasury officials are informed and 'know what they are doing'. As we saw above, it was accepted in one department that the Treasury's Principal was in a good position to see how the department's programmes came together, an overview denied to each of the department's specialized Policy Divisions, but also that his personality, knowledge, and skill were as important in earning the respect of the department.

Trust and confidence in people is probably more important than the financial management systems they operate, but it is not easy to separate the two. The Treasury takes a particular interest in the financial management systems through one of its central divisions, and some of its concerns are transmitted through the Expenditure Divisions. But most PFOs rejected the notion that Expenditure Divisions assessed their systems directly, although of course indirectly Treasury officials could scarcely avoid forming a judgement about their effectiveness from day-to-day contact. Management systems and issues arising from them are discussed informally at annual get-togethers between the Finance Division and its Expenditure Divisions, as we explained in the previous chapter.

ADVANTAGES AND BENEFITS OF GOOD RELATIONSHIPS

Why should an Expenditure Division and a Finance Division try to establish and maintain effective working relationships? Why are those relationships essentially co-operative? Here we separate those benefits which are mutually enjoyed, from the benefits enjoyed by one or other. In practice there is considerable overlap.

Mutual benefits

Mutual understanding of each other's aims and difficulties, and a willingness to do business in the context of that appreciation is potentially of benefit to both. The perception that the game played between them is positive-sum, rather than zero-sum, means that they 'have a vested interest in each other's success'. The key is 'negotiations of a proper kind and a mutual understanding of what matters'. Those negotiations should be 'win/win and not win/lose' (PFO, major spending department). While one side might on any issue achieve more than the other, the distribution of benefits between them varies, and over a period longer than that of a single PES round, each records both gains and losses. If a Finance Division felt that it consistently lost out to its Expenditure Division over a period of years, and, more importantly, thought that its case was not being represented fairly to the Chief Secretary, it would have little incentive to continue to conduct its relationships co-operatively. The reciprocal benefits are illustrated in this exchange of informal information between a Finance Division Principal and his opposite number in the early stages of a PES round. He tried to give the Expenditure Division Principal 'a good idea of what the departmental bids will be, to help them understand and to provide them with a better focus for their appraisal'. In return, the Expenditure Division sketched out the likely parameters of its official response, and indicated what kind of trade-offs might be required, and quid pro quos offered. Such information was helpful to the Finance Division not only in preparing its bidding strategy, but in advising its Policy Divisions of the likely Treasury response to their bids. This served to enhance the credibility of the Finance Division's relations with the Treasury in the eyes of its departmental constituents. Advance notice of the nature and context of the department's bids not only helped the Expenditure Division in the ways suggested, but conveyed to its constituents— the Chief Secretary's office, GEP, RC—that it was close to its Finance Division.

While both an Expenditure Division and a Finance Division stand to gain something from an effective working relationship, the conventions dictate that neither would claim to have won, even though both had obtained some satisfaction. Rather, as one PFO explained, 'relations are better when both have purported to have lost'. In other words, each can imply to the other that it had conceded or lost to the other. Thus the Expenditure Division is helped in maintaining its credibility within the Treasury because of the department's admission; and the Finance Division can use the Treasury's claim of failure to represent to its constituents within the department that its strategy and tactics have been effective.

The relationships are long-term. Finance Division has to deal with its Expenditure Division constantly on a variety of recurring and *ad hoc* issues, year in, year out. It cannot allow relations to break down over an issue to the point where it affects relationships in the future. Their continuance depends upon both sides being prepared to lose a battle to the other, but in the knowledge that both will be in good shape to continue to fight the longer war. An illustration of this is the readiness of a Finance Division and an Expenditure Division to accept the PES settlement after final Cabinet agreement, not to prolong the arguments about the bids, but to work hard together to translate them into agreed Estimates.

There is mutual benefit in good working relationships, in that both can manage their business more expeditiously. The timetables for annual recurring business such as PES, Estimates, Supplementaries impose strict deadlines, while the management of *ad hoc* crisis issues may be more demanding still in the use of scarce time. Helping each other to manage the business is a benefit which PFOs and their Finance Divisions emphasize. While there is a strong element of professional pride in complying with deadlines for the submission of financial returns, in answering queries, or in dealing with requests for information, at busy times of the year they may find it difficult to satisfy all the demands. A Finance Division can help an Expenditure Division manage its business if relations are good, or make it more difficult if they are bad. Informal communications can help establish what is urgent and important. For example, a Finance Division may be unable to provide information in the form required and at the time scheduled in the Survey guidelines. If relations are good, a Finance Division official can 'ring up the Treasury Expenditure Division and ask what their priorities are, and we can come to a sensible working arrangement. We can concentrate our efforts to maximum effect; scrub some issues and get down to key ones' (PFO, major spending department). If relations are difficult the department might get things in on time but not complete, or not quite in the form the Expenditure Division would like. One Finance Division Principal found his opposite number unhelpful and negative: 'Everything was taken at the same level of importance—there was no prioritization. Therefore there was no sharing of information about what was vital and what was less vital.'

There are other benefits to the Finance Division, some immediate:

If you present your case well and get it in on time this helps. If it is half-baked and you don't give them enough time to look properly at it they give you more hassle. But if the case is well thought through and in on time, they are more reticent about pressing you and there is generally less probing. (Assistant Secretary, Finance Division, major spending department)

Meeting deadlines and providing information in a form helpful to the Expenditure Division can bring longer-term benefits. One Finance Division changed its forms and procedures for making returns to the Treasury, which made it easier for the Expenditure Division and GEP to deal more quickly with the business. The Expenditure Division wrote and thanked the Finance Division, and complimented it on having a good financial system. The goodwill generated as a result encouraged GEP to give them more time on some tasks connected with the preparation of the management plan.

If a Finance Division and an Expenditure Division lack confidence in each other, if there is little trust between them, issues which could be settled at the official level by Principals, Assistant Secretaries, and the PFO tend to go higher up the hierarchy. This takes more time on both sides, and adds a further dimension of organizational complexity. More importantly, the higher the level to which an issue rises the less time there is for the Treasury and the department to discuss options. Crucially, there is less room for manœuvre: 'you have eminence as well as argument in the equation when Under Secretaries and above are involved. You get more win/win situations if matters are dealt with at a lower level' (Assistant Secretary, major spending department). This is still more true if issues which can be resolved much lower down rise to ministerial level. Relationships may become very formal, confrontational, even conflictual. One PFO distinguished two modes of conducting relationships—the 'business-mode', where relationships of trust and confidence meant that the Treasury and the department could cooperate to their mutual benefit; and the 'negotiation-mode', where relationships will be conducted more formally, hierarchically, and perhaps involve ministers. However, some business which by convention or statute must be taken at ministerial level is handled co-operatively through the 'business-mode'.

An example where trust is needed occurs when a department requests to move money round between activities. This can be raised to a high level, and it may be appropriate that the negotiation-mode should be employed at that level. But a Finance Division and an Expenditure Division would normally expect to be able to establish informally beforehand the parameters within which an agreement might be reached. 'If you keep your distance, this becomes harder. Trust is involved here and is essential.' There is a clear distinction in the type of business. Getting new money out of the Treasury is more difficult than getting additional money for an established activity. Relationships become more 'antagonistic' as they move from the 'business' to the 'negotiating-mode', as they do when seeking new money. One Finance Division Assistant Secretary explained the difference:

The higher you go in [the department] though, the more difficulty there is with the Treasury. At Under Secretary and Deputy Secretary level people are keen on policy and they need money to fund their ideas and they go to Treasury expecting it and can't see why they can't have the resources they want. Further down the hierarchy they are keeping the 'ship afloat'. Therefore they need to satisfy Treasury's requirements. They need to establish a modus vivendi.

Issues of programme rather than administrative expenditure are more likely to rise up the hierarchy and involve ministers. A very sharp distinction in the way the business is handled was apparent in one large department, where the size and potential sensitivity of its programmes meant that ministers were 'actually and formally' involved from the start, and the mode was 'negotiation'. By contrast, the administrative expenditure, although large, was generally dealt with at the official level through the 'business-mode'. But again unusually, the level was higher than normal on the Treasury side, where the Under Secretary was involved in the discussions between the two departments. This reflected the size of the bid, the scope for realizable cuts, and the personality of those involved. The settlement of the bid was usually made at the Under Secretary level, subject to the approval of Ministers. 'It would be unusual for our recommendation to be changed by Ministers, although sometimes they ask for something to be looked at again' (PFO, major spending department).

Advantages for Finance Division

Apart from the considerable mutual benefits which both a Finance Division and an Expenditure Division can derive from close, effective working relationships, there is the further advantage for the spending department that through the 'business-mode' it may be able to build up and profit from the support and sympathy of the Expenditure Division for its aims and policies. PFOs emphasize the need to ensure that the Expenditure Division understands the department's problems and difficulties. If the Expenditure Division is to 'win' more resources for the department in the internal Treasury competition (always allowing for the wider politico-economic context in which a department may or may not have a high political priority) it has to be persuaded of the merit and value of the department's policies, and assured that they represent value-for-money. If the Expenditure Division is supportive, then a Finance Division will want to ensure that it is provided with the arguments and evidence to convince GEP, and the Chief Secretary and his senior advisers. Most of this evidence will be formal and committed to writing, but the informal relationships are important in establishing what kinds of evidence are needed, in communicating difficulties, and in off-the-record briefings. Over a period longer than that of a single PES round,

Finance Division would hope through its relationships to impress upon the Expenditure Division that it had an efficient and effective financial management system; and exercised tight control over requests for new money, as well as in the commitment of that already approved. The aim is to secure the commitment of the Expenditure Division to the department's aims and policies. The strength of that commitment is a factor in the Expenditure Division's briefing of the Chief Secretary, and hence in the decisions taken at the margins to allocate resources to one department rather than another.

Sympathy, support, and a willingness to argue on behalf of the department are products of the longer-term relationships which both sides have mutual interest in keeping in a state of good repair. Achieving mutual understanding through informal relationships takes time. From the departmental perspective, it is often irritating that just as they had 'won someone over', they tended to be moved on. From the Treasury's perspective, rotation is partly justified and necessary to avoid the possibility of 'capture', or Expenditure Division officials 'going native'.

A further advantage to the department from good relationships with the Expenditure Division is that the latter are more willing to 'move things quickly' when the occasion demands. For example, if a Secretary of State intends making a speech in which some of the issues raised have expenditure implications, a Finance Division can informally brief the Expenditure Division in advance of the time-scale of the proposed expenditure and any anticipated problems or difficulties. This can be done in a 'civilized way' without antagonism, and Expenditure Division will respond in a similar way. There is a benefit to the Treasury too. It gets to hear of something about to happen before it is made public. On the basis of its informal soundings the Expenditure Division is in a position to brief the Chief Secretary, or to respond when the matter becomes public.

Treasury advantages

The Treasury benefits too, other than in the ways already described as mutual to both an Expenditure Division and a Finance Division. The Expenditure Division cannot do its job without information. While the department cannot refuse to supply it when requests are made officially, it can provide it late or in a form which makes the Expenditure Division's task of scrutiny more difficult. The closer the Expenditure Division is to the department the more and better the information it can obtain. Crucially, if the relationship is at arm's length, a Finance Division may control the flow to exclude all but that which it is obliged to supply. Background knowledge, informal briefings on problems and difficulties, advance notice, and so on, may be withheld. If the Expenditure Division is to be able to make informed and sensible judgements, and brief the Chief Secretary about the merit of departmental proposals, it has need of such information. Expenditure Division officials need to 'get behind the figures', to be able to read between the lines of the official submissions. As we explained in the previous chapter, they are not wholly dependent upon the Finance Division to do that, but it is helpful to have access through the relationships.

The Treasury collectively benefits from good working relationships between Expenditure Divisions and Finance Divisions because normally it is concerned with making an informed and sensible distribution of resources between departments. In all but the very exceptional circumstances of acute crisis, such as 1976, it will not want to exercise control in a blunt, negative way. An uncompromising approach by an Expenditure Division might be enjoined upon it by the Chief Secretary's strategy. If he signals that a department's spending plans have low priority, Expenditure Division has little option but to reflect that priority in its stance. Where there are good relationships it might signal to the Finance Division that it was obliged to take such a position. (We discuss below the case of an Expenditure Division pursuing a tough line without direct political support.)

Besides the collective interest, good relationships are of great potential benefit to the individual Expenditure Controller. In the ways described above, an Expenditure Division with good close working relationships will be better able to advise the GEP Under Secretary about what can be 'delivered' from the department in the PES round. It will be in a better position to judge Finance Division's response to a particular proposal—what it might accept on certain conditions, and what it would reject—all of which helps the Chief Secretary to judge the mood of negotiation. In the formulation of an expenditure strategy, judgements have to be made about what is negotiable and with whom, what can be delivered, and how hard a proposal can be pressed and with what expectation of success.

Trusting relationships of the kind described are not cosy or necessarily comfortable. The opposed values of the two organizations mean that there is always an edge to the relationships. While an Expenditure Division and a Finance Division may co-operate to help each manage its business more effectively, only rarely will their interests on a particular issue be sufficiently similar for them to collaborate. The friendly, personal relationships which may exist between particular officials in each department, and which are characteristic of effective informal communication, coexist with institutional adversarialism. 'It is true most of the time that they can work together because of trust, but it should be true all of the time. But there are patches when relations are bad and adversarial' (PFO, major spending department). Relationships vary with issue and season.

In the autumn, we will be helping the Treasury to write the Autumn Statement. Simultaneously, the Treasury is making a virtue out of large increases in [our departmental] spending, having said a few weeks earlier that we can't have additional monies. There are times of boom, slump and tension. But generally relations follow the rhythm of the Survey. The Survey dominates everything. (PFO, major spending department)

Relations on particular issues can also be confrontational. 'Rows' can be ritualistic, part of the adversarial procedure for testing the commitment and degree of firmness of each side on an issue. They can also be symptomatic of a deterioration in relationships, or a sign of failure to establish the case in informal communication between particular officials. But PFOs and their officials emphasize that they cannot afford to let relationships break down to the point where they are conducted mainly or wholly formally. 'We have to get on with each other; we spend a lot of time in each other's company' (PFO, major spending department). As we have explained, the potential benefits are considerable. The Treasury too has much to lose, but a tough, uncompromising line which, if pushed far enough, might endanger the relationships may be enjoined on the Expenditure Division, or be the result of Expenditure Division officials who lack the self-confidence or personality to get closer to the department. Relations may become strained where the Treasury lacks confidence in the organizational strength of a departmental Finance Division, or where it perceives it to be incompetent, for example an inability to provide information requested by an Expenditure Division.

TENSIONS AND FRUSTRATIONS

Frustration or irritation with an Expenditure Division's behaviour is not uncommon. Tension is inherent in a relationship premised upon the observance of the norm of 'reasonable behaviour' by both sides. Finance Divisions understand and show some sympathy with the Treasury's role: 'They have a job to do', and there is little resentment at their trying to do it.

On the whole, there are fewer disagreements about the right of the Treasury to ask for information when this involves departmental

Finance Divisions. 'It is in both our interests to have good working relationships, even when we disagree' (PFO, medium-sized spending department). On the other hand, departmental policy divisions can be 'very abrasive' at what they regard as unwarranted Treasury interference, characterizing the Expenditure Divisions as 'forces of darkness'. Finance Divisions expect the Treasury to be 'difficult'. Provided the cause of the difficulty is predictable or a Finance Division able to understand the reasons for the Treasury's behaviour, no lasting damage is likely to be done to the relationship. Even a 'flaming row' on an issue is not necessarily a symptom of poor relations, but in context seen on both sides as part of the process of testing out. Normal 'business-mode' relations may be resumed after the issue has been determined, or more likely conducted on other issues simultaneously with the flaming row. Neither side wants to raise too much to a higher, more formal (perhaps ministerial) level, and restrict the room for manœuvre by officials.

The signs of tension and frustration in good working relationships, or that relationships are bad, are unmistakable. It may be confined to a single issue, or be more generally symptomatic of a general change. The clearest signal is the escalation of an issue. The involvement of more senior officials in the Treasury may signal an unwillingness or inability to achieve a settlement through the business-mode lower down. The PFO gets involved earlier and more frequently in issues which would not normally come to him; a Deputy Secretary at the Treasury may get brought in. The escalation of cases to ministers which normally would have been settled at the official level is another sign. Escalation may be accompanied by an exchange of 'tart and silly letters'. 'You don't get silly letters unless there are misunderstandings' (PFO, major spending department).

Expenditure Controllers learn to detect clear signs of when issues have become more sensitive and when friction is likely to emerge. The most obvious sign is disruption to normal patterns of contact. Where an official in a department would normally provide some early warning of a potential problem, this may not happen in a particular case. Requests for information may take longer to be processed. Departments may start to 'stand on rights' and challenge the Treasury to justify the constitutional or administrative basis of its request for data. Officials may not offer prior warning when a ministerial letter has been sent to the Chief Secretary. Sometimes a departmental minister may ask his officials to deal with certain issues and not tell the Treasury. Where this happens it becomes more difficult to do the 'ground-clearing' for the bilaterals. The Chief Secretary may ask for his officials to be involved in a major policy review. The Treasury has no constitutional right to join such a review or to obtain data produced for it. The experienced Expenditure Controller will not attempt to use the constitutional approach but rather will take the line: 'it would be helpful if you gave us the data, there will be less demands made on Ministers if we agree on the basis of the discussion and it would save time if we worked on one set of data rather than two' (Assistant Secretary).

It is difficult in practice to distinguish a temporary disruption to normally business-like working relationships from deliberate 'dirty tricks' or 'bounces', where a department is trying to gain some advantage. Indeed, frequent 'bounces' may be a sign of some significant breakdown in relationships between a department and an Expenditure Division, which may be brought to the attention of ministers. Occasional 'try-ons' by departments, on the other hand, are regarded as part of the expenditure 'game', understood as such by both sides. Some Expenditure Controllers expect one or two 'nibbles' each year; a few complain of 'trench warfare'. Departments may be testing alertness by trying to get a poorly constructed case past an Expenditure Division. Similarly, not all examples of a department trying to push the Treasury into making a quick decision result from malicious intent but may reflect the problems faced by a Finance Division in getting decisions out of their Policy Divisions. More often than not, 'bounces' or 'dirty tricks' are nothing more than the result of departmental ministers taking too long to decide on their approach and their officials having to rush business to the Treasury at the last minute. When such cases arise, Expenditure Divisions will try to be accommodating. They will 'take umbrage', however, if it happens too often and Expenditure Controllers may be 'sticky' about an issue and brief the Chief Secretary to take a similar line. This may involve ministers being asked not to make a statement until the expenditure implications have been fully analysed. It may not be only the Treasury which takes issue with a department wishing to rush through a decision because a Minister has prevaricated. Often policy matters involve the territorial departments and they may wish to consider the possibly profound impact of a policy initiative on their programmes. Most Treasury officials emphasize the existence of a generally high degree of co-operation between officials, and a shared commitment to making collective government work.

Even so, Expenditure Divisions do have clear views about what constitutes a divergence from acceptable behaviour by a department or agency. The most frequently mentioned form of this is 'being surprised'. Stability and predictability are the watchwords of a good Treasury–department relationship. If a department does not send a message saying that its Minister will be in touch with the Chief Secretary, if an Expenditure Division is 'surprised' by a major element in a Survey bidding letter, or if no early warning is given of a looming political crisis which will affect expenditure decisions (for example, the salmonella-in-eggs scare), these are regarded as examples of unacceptable behaviour which damage relationships.

For a departmental PFO and his staff, 'more sharply pointed questions' from the Expenditure Division, or where 'they knock off bits at the margin to see what happens' are warning signs of possible deterioration, or a change of attitude on the part of the Treasury. Equally, a failure to respond quickly to an urgent Finance Division request, or lack of prior warning through the usual channels, are symptoms. More formality in conducting the relationships, with a consequent reduction in the information volunteered by the department, may signal incompatibility between a Finance Division and a particular Expenditure Division official.

From the perspective of a Finance Division, frustrations can be caused in several ways. Some may be serious enough to provoke deterioration or change, but no Finance Division can afford to neglect to keep its relationships with the Expenditure Division in good repair over a period longer than that of a discrete issue or an annual round of PES. There are four main ways in which relationships are affected adversely by the behaviour of the Expenditure Division (we leave aside the behaviour of the Finance Division): when the Finance Division considers it to be acting 'unreasonably'; when the legitimacy of the Treasury's intervention on an issue or in an area is questionable; when the 'rules' of accounting procedures are applied unnecessarily; when other Treasury divisions are involved. The last three of these can all result in 'unreasonable' behaviour, but it is useful to distinguish this analytically as a separate category.

Unreasonable behaviour

What is 'unreasonable' in the circumstances of a particular issue, its political salience, and the internal pressures on an Expenditure Division, is a matter of subjective interpretation. There are no objective criteria by which to measure whether it is acting unreasonably. There are, however, unarticulated but recognized norms of behaviour. 'All men of good will know what is a reasonable approach—the Treasury sometimes oversteps this' (PFO, major spending department). Reasonable behaviour is acting with 'good cause', having regard to the facts and the argument. Understanding of an Expenditure Division's tasks and roles means that a Finance Department can sympathize with a view and stance taken up by it, provided that it is grounded in argument. A willingness to listen to a Finance Division's pleading and to consider the arguments, being prepared to be persuaded, is reasonable behaviour; conversely, an unwillingness, the application of blunt 'brute force' is unreasonable. 'Heavy-handed obstruction', and an unconstructive, negative attitude is justified in the eyes of a Finance Division only in the exceptional circumstances of an IMF-type crisis. One Assistant Secretary explained that Finance Division got particularly annoyed when the Treasury based its decisions on 'irrationality', or 'despite the facts' imposed a decision. On occasions there was a tendency for the Treasury to assume that 'if they don't have the best arguments, something's wrong'. They assume that they 'don't get their facts wrong'; and sometimes 'use a sledgehammer to crack a nut'. The same official quoted this example of such annoyance with Treasury behaviour. An NDPB was brought back into the department as a Next Steps Agency, and the arrangements for superannuation were changed in consequence. The number of staff transferring back was wrongly estimated, and the department had surrendered more money than was necessary. The department expected the Treasury to repay the extra sum, but instead the Treasury kept it as a 'windfall'. The use of 'brute force' in this way causes ill-feeling in a Finance Division, and particularly in agencies. It makes the Finance Division's job more difficult, because the suspicion and hostility of Policy Divisions towards the Treasury is apparently vindicated.

A source of irritation and frustration, which can spill over to more serious friction between a Finance Division and its Expenditure Division, is an 'unreasonable' request for information. All Whitehall PFOs and their officials report an over-zealousness on the part of some Expenditure Division officials, or all Expenditure Divisions at certain periods of the year. There is a widespread feeling that the Treasury asks for too much information, and scepticism that all of it is necessary, useful, or indeed used at all. One cause of this is the increased emphasis on obtaining value-for-money, and the Treasury's demands for data on output, measurement of performance, and efficiency savings on running costs. PFOs believe that many of these requests originate from the Treasury central divisions, which are considered remote from the real world of the Finance Division and Expenditure Division, and unaware or uncaring of the impact of continual requests for more and more information. They argue that the Treasury does not always understand or sympathize with the amount of work involved in preparing and presenting data in the form requested. The purpose of the request for information is not always apparent. They believe that frequently Expenditure Divisions merely transmit requests, and are often therefore just 'going through the motions'. There is also the suspicion that sometimes Expenditure Divisions ask for information which they think the Finance Division ought to have, as a reassurance for the Treasury that it is doing its job internally, or in attempts to 'second-guess' the Policy Divisions or agencies. Requests for more and more information from an Expenditure Division make life more difficult for a Finance Division, first by increasing its own workload and, secondly, by making its position worse *vis-à-vis* its Policy Divisions and agencies. These lack the Finance Division perspective and so, when requests are relayed to them, resent Treasury interference, harbour suspicions that such information will be used against them, and fail to see benefits in more resources as a result.

Reactions can vary, from the explicitly cynical: 'The Treasury love information. We try to keep them happy by sending as much as we can. They can't turn you down straight away if they have to look at your submission' (Assistant Secretary, major spending department). Others, critical of the general increase in the amount of information requested by the Treasury, 'wonder why the Treasury don't come and see them and have a look at whatever it was they wanted to know about, rather than this constant request for more information'.

'Brute force' behaviour by the Treasury on an issue is sustainable if the Expenditure Division has support up the hierarchy, all the way to the Chief Secretary. If the department, or one or other of its programmes, has been earmarked or signalled for tough treatment, then a Finance Department may wish to involve its own Minister. If it suspects that the Expenditure Division is being obstructive, or an individual official being over-zealous, without the explicit and direct support of the Chief Secretary, it will try to get an agreement at the Under Secretary level. But the Treasury normally avoids a reaction which polarizes an issue starkly as yes/no, win/lose. 'It is normally more a question of emphasis' (PFO, major spending department).

'Unreasonable' behaviour by an individual Expenditure Division official can cause problems for a Finance Division, unless it is able to work through a more sympathetic official in the same division—at the same level, or a higher grade. Here we need to distinguish 'unreasonableness' due to personality rather than the mode of operation of the Expenditure Division. Departments get irritated when they feel that the personal view of an Expenditure Division official has intruded and influenced a decision 'against the facts'. In its extreme form, acting without 'good cause' is found in a few Expenditure Division officials whose attitude appears negative, unhelpful, or obstructive. One PFO described the experience of his Finance Division with the 'abominable no-man'. Such officials tend to ask 'dozens and dozens of questions effectively putting the brakes on' the process of agreeing a mutually acceptable settlement. This can be self-defeating for the Treasury. One official asked for more and more information. As the data piled up, the more obscure and distant became the substantive issue: 'he can't see the wood for the trees, so he's asked for more bundles of twigs' (Assistant Secretary, Finance Division, major spending department). If the official cannot be avoided, a Finance Division may react by controlling the flow of information. 'We feed him with less information than before; wait for him to ask rather than offering. This is difficult when the instinct is to provide a good flow of information, but when it is used to obstruct you have to act in this way' (PFO, major spending department).

If acting 'unreasonably' is likely to prove counter-productive in all but those situations of major crisis, or a large issue where there is political support right up to the Chief Secretary, why do some Expenditure Division officials operate in this way? The explanation from the perspective of the PFOs and their Finance Division is, first, personality. Some Treasury (and Finance Division) officials are congenitally incapable of operating informally, and informality is considered essential in good working relationships. 'You have to be able to have a comfortable discussion.' Secondly, it can be due to a lack of experience or self-confidence. It is 'easier to say no. The safest thing to do is to say no.' To say 'yes', or more likely 'we have a problem here, let's try and sort something out', requires confidence (PFO, medium-sized spending department). To try to discuss and agree the parameters of a possible arrangement is much harder. Thirdly, there is the suspicion that some Expenditure Division officials who behave in this way are overly influenced by informal expenditure 'targets' set for the departments they shadow in discussions between Expenditure Divisions and GEP in the early stages of the PES round. There is the belief among Finance Divisions that Expenditure Division officials' effectiveness is partly measured by their success in delivering expenditure totals to the Chief Secretary and that there is pressure on them to demonstrate that they are 'earning their salary'. Whether this induces a degree of over-zealousness in some officials is arguable. A fourth reason, not volunteered by departments, is that such behaviour is provoked by that of their own Finance Divisions. Not all Finance Division officials are congenitally capable of establishing informal working relationships; nor do they always act 'reasonably' with good cause. They admit that they sometimes 'try it on'.

Legitimacy of Treasury interest and involvement

The Treasury can overstep the limits of a 'reasonable approach' if a Finance Division feels that its interest in an area or issue is inappropriate. The behavioural rules of engagement are unwritten, and the boundaries ill-defined. One such rule is that the Treasury does not attempt to substitute its judgement for that of the department on a policy issue. As policy and expenditure are closely bound together, the line between a judgement on the substantive policy and its cost and effectiveness can be a fine one. Where the effect of a Treasury decision is to change the policy substantially, a Finance Division would 'scream and protest'. If the Treasury pushes too hard, and squeezes resources too tightly then a statutory duty or function might be sufficiently jeopardized in the department's judgement for the matter to rise to ministerial level. The Treasury cannot ignore the policy implications of its decisions, and their consideration is part of the context within which it operates, constraining certain options, and inducing it to consider backing off when the legitimacy of its interest is questioned. Finance Divisions get irritated when the Treasury disputes the legal inevitability of some kind of spending. Where there is a statutory obligation to pay benefit, grants, or compensation, the Treasury will sometimes push a Finance Division to test if the general principle is applicable in a particular case, or question the sums to be paid. Where the issue has become one of public and Parliamentary concern, argument about entitlement can quickly escalate to ministerial level and draw in the Treasury Solicitor, even the Attorney General. On one such issue a department was clear on the legal position over compensation, but its estimate of the costs of doing so was disputed by the Treasury. The PFO thought the Treasury's behaviour was 'short-sighted but not untypical'; the Treasury suspected that the lack of advance warning of the expenditure implications was an attempted 'bounce'. In some departments there is a 'grey area', where interpretation of statutory entitlement leaves it unclear what the expenditure implications are. One area where any Treasury encroachment is resented is the internal management of the department, particularly running costs expenditure and management plans.

Encroachment of the Treasury into areas where it has no or dubious 'legitimacy' is part of the game of testing those limits, to see if the department would notice it and accept the extension of the boundaries. 'There are conventions about things they have a legitimate interest in and areas which are to do with the internal management of the department' (PFO, major spending department). It is accepted that the

Treasury can change those conventions, but the attempt to do so has to be articulated and 'we have to force them to bring changes on to the table'. An example of the Treasury trying to redraw the boundaries, and change the rules, occurred with the reassignment to departments of the expenditure of the Property Services Agency on its abolition. The Treasury assumed a mode of action as correct which was disputed by departments, as contrary to the way such issues had been handled in the past. The Treasury responded by saying those are the 'rules'. Departments argued that the rules had been redrawn without consultation, and asked for them to be written down and debated with them.

The setting up of Next Steps Agencies has meant that some departments have been obliged to give the Treasury more information on the internal management of the department than before. Departments acquiesced because they accepted that sensible arrangements had to be made in a new and developing area. But Treasury too had to be reminded formally (by at least one large department), on several occasions, that it had been given information because of the special circumstances and not because the department accepted the Treasury's right to it as a general rule.

Another area where the Treasury tries to extend its boundaries of legitimate interest is the Survey. If an issue can be defined as 'Survey' it is subject to its procedures, timetable, and rules, from which there is no appeal. PFOs complain that sometimes the Expenditure Divisions try to graft on to the Survey expenditure business which should properly be dealt with outside it. Their own interest, of course, is to try to get the Treasury to give approval for new money outside the Survey, thus ensuring its inclusion subsequently as baseline expenditure.

Tension and frustration in the relationship can arise from the accounting procedures and rules which prescribe the formal and legal conditions determining the propriety of spending, and the levels of delegated authority. Expenditure Divisions as well as Finance Divisions have to work within them, and both are subject to rules administered by the Treasury Officer of Accounts. This official 'holds the rule book for the Expenditure Divisions' and frequently a sympathetic and supportive Expenditure Division is obliged to say 'no' to a Finance Division because of his ruling. Other potential sources of irritation are the increasing number of special Treasury 'exercises', for example on the sale of surplus land and buildings, which entail additional work for Finance Divisions and, through them, the Policy Divisions, to produce information for the Treasury which it is claimed is often not used.

There is some irritation, too, over the levels at which decisions are made in the Expenditure Divisions. As we explained in the previous chapter, communication is mainly at Principal and Assistant Secretary level in the Expenditure Divisions. Treasury Under Secretaries are rarely involved. Some departments claim that the failure to involve senior Treasury officials is a major cause of the Treasury's neglect of long-term thinking and strategy. Their perception, whether accurate or not, stands in marked contrast to that of Treasury officials, who emphasize the capacity of a small, highly integrated expenditure side to achieve coherence and a broad perspective at the Under Secretary and Deputy Secretary levels. One PFO believed that the Treasury had made no contribution to the development of long-term thinking about a policy area in his department in the last twenty years: 'They seemed concerned with devising schemes of their own to restrain the department and with asking for more and more information.' While this may be an exaggeration, and the Treasury able to provide contrary examples, nevertheless the sentiment is widely shared among spending departments.

One effect of the lack of involvement of senior Treasury officials is to increase the tension between a Finance Division and its Policy Divisions. As we explained in the previous chapter, a frequent complaint of the latter is that the Finance Division deals at too low a level in the Treasury, especially when the decision is unfavourable to them. Requests to Policy Divisions for information to argue with Treasury Assistant Secretaries and Principals, sometimes Higher Executive Officers, are a source of resentment, especially when the Finance Division appears to lose the argument. It is not easy for a Finance Division to convince its constituents that establishing good working relationships at these levels is more productive over a period of time than attempts to circumvent them on a particular issue.

Relationships are not affected in the longer term by success or failure in obtaining resources in the PES round, or on any item of expenditure outside it. There is no positive correlation between good relations and success. PFOs emphasize that, whether departments win or lose short-term battles over particular issues, they have to continue to do business with the Expenditure Division and trusting and confident relationships are essential for that purpose. Where relationships lack those qualities, because of personal incompatibilities, a Finance Division's task (and that of an Expenditure Division too) may be more time-consuming, but the outcome is not normally very different. It may take longer to achieve, involve more senior officials, even ministers, but an unhelpful, negative Expenditure Division official would not succeed if a Finance Division held firm, unless he had support for his stance right up to the Chief Secretary. The latter would need to convince and carry his Cabinet colleagues for a broadly based 'get tough' policy. In most years, the

PES round is 'tight'—how tight is explored in the interactions between an Expenditure Division and a Finance Division.

Whether a department is more or less successful in obtaining resources is affected more by the general policy context in which the relationships are conducted: the commitments of the government, the priorities established by the Cabinet, and the salience and political sensitivity of particular issues at the time decisions are made. For example, the Department of Transport obtained more resources in the period 1988–90 because the priority given to the expansion of transport systems changed. Relationships between the Finance Division and its Expenditure Division were not easier or better as a result. The arguments were about larger increments than in the early 1980s, when the department operated a 'care and maintenance' regime. It is true, of course, that the Chief Secretary and the Treasury had to juggle with the departmental packages to keep them within the 'envelope' of the Planning Total before 1992. The Cabinet provided no explicit rank order of priorities, although it confirmed or amended that proposed to it at the end of the PES round in November. Both before and after the changes of 1992 the Chief Secretary had discretion and flexibility, apart from his general policy stance, to influence attitudes of particular Expenditure Divisions in their dealings with Finance Divisions, and in turn to be influenced by the arguments of particular Expenditure Divisions advanced in support of proposals from the latter. How determinedly and effectively an Expenditure Division is prepared to argue the case for a particular item of expenditure can be affected by its relationship with a Finance Division.

The size of department can make a difference to the quality and effectiveness of relationships. Where a department has few programmes, a small staff, and modest expenditure, relative to other departments, there is more time and opportunity for an Expenditure Division to scrutinize details of expenditure. This is partly a function of Treasury organization, where the responsibility of an Expenditure Division's Principals varies, from the large expenditure programmes of defence, health, or social security, to the much smaller programmes of energy conservation or agriculture. What might be a major item of expenditure for discussion between an Expenditure Division and the Finance Division of a smaller department can be subsumed in the 'rounding up' of numbers in a larger one, where the Principal has neither the time nor the resources to scrutinize details which, for another colleague, may be the main focus of his attention. PFOs in smaller departments find this irritating, complain that the Treasury's 'standard policy' approach is insufficiently sensitive to differences in scale and size of spend, and hint that relationships with Expenditure Divisions can be affected.

There is little evidence that the loss of function through transfer, hiving off, or privatization affects the relationship. Although, again, the rate of the reduction of staff where programmes are being run down is as much an issue for dispute between the Expenditure Division and the Finance Division, as proposals for increases.

Surprisingly, the movement of Expenditure Division officials does not appear to have a serious adverse effect on the relationships. Despite the turnover of Principals and Assistant Secretaries at much higher rates than those thought desirable by the Treasury itself, there is little evidence that relationships are affected other than in the short term. Finance Divisions find it 'mildly irritating' when Expenditure Division officials are moved on, mainly because they have to begin again on 'house-training'. 'A newcomer may want less detailed information because he wants to take time to learn the job and only wants key details. But in time things settle down. Much depends on the personality of the person involved' (PFO, major spending department). Newcomers may lack experience, and for a short while appear unduly cautious, but good working relationships can be established quickly if he or she possesses the personal and intellectual qualities discussed earlier. Inexperience in the Expenditure Division is less important than unfamiliarity with Treasury culture, how things are done. 'Born and bred' Treasury officials have an advantage over those brought in from elsewhere, especially from the City, industry, and other parts of the public sector. Among these, caution (bred of inexperience and lack of confidence) may be compounded by lack of knowledge and understanding of how things are done in the Treasury. Gaining the support of such an Expenditure Division official may be less beneficial materially if he/she is unable to argue and present cases *ex parte* within the Treasury. Mobility is part of Civil Service culture. 'We are now used to the situation where they all move around frequently; this is as true in the departments as in the Treasury' (PFO, major spending department). Some Finance Divisions find the movement into and out of their own Policy Divisions more of a problem. The turnover of PFOs is more rapid still. The criticism that mobility inhibits continuity, disrupts relationships, and puts Treasury at a disadvantage is much exaggerated. The 'collective memory' of past processes, procedures, and precedents is less important than sometimes alleged. One PFO, an ex-Expenditure Division official, described his former colleagues as 'free and independent spirits', less bound by the approaches or decisions of their predecessors than commonly supposed. There is also the potential benefit to the Finance

Division that frequent movement ensures that a Treasury 'no-man', or an Expenditure Division official with whom there is little rapport, will soon move on.

The issues which are productive of most tensions and frustrations in the relationships between the Treasury and the spending departments are running costs and management plans. In 1986, after consultation with spending departments, the Treasury introduced new policy rules regulating administrative or running costs, separating them from programme expenditure in the bidding and allocating processes, and in the prescription of cash limits. Most, but not all, departments were also obliged to prepare and submit three-year rolling management plans. The Treasury emphasized the greater autonomy and managerial flexibility which the new rules provided, enabling departments to vary expenditure within running costs provision between the numbers and grades of staff, their pay, accommodation, and allowances. The departments' perception was quite different. They saw the new rules as limiting the scope for their discretionary behaviour. They could no longer switch expenditure between programme and administration, and were obliged to produce plans relating to the management and use of those resources allocated to departmental administration and management, matters of internal managerial autonomy. These contrasting perceptions of the intention and effect of the new policy rules reflected very different organizational appreciations, of both fact and value, on issues of particular sensitivity to departmental officials. The result has been frustration and irritation with the rules and with their application, and the emergence of a 'painful and high conflict area' for both Expenditure Divisions and the spending departments. We examine the source of this tension and analyse the operation of running costs control in Chapter 18.

PART III

Planning Public Expenditure

11

Determining the Priorities of Public Spending

Each year the government has to decide how much public expenditure to finance from its prospective resources for three years ahead. It has to decide what priority to give to public expenditure, compared with the claims for the alternative use of those resources. In the last decade this issue has attracted more critical attention, partly because of the Conservative Government's claim to decide the priority of public expenditure within the formal planning framework of the MTFS, and the long-term strategy for public expenditure outlined in a Green Paper of 1984; partly because of its aim to reverse the ratchet of rising public expenditure which characterized the governments of the previous two decades, professing instead to be guided by the criterion that 'revenue determines expenditure'.

The government has to decide not only how much in total it wishes to spend in the public sector: it has simultaneously to decide how to allocate that total between the competing claims from spending authorities to finance their expenditure programmes. As those claims are greater in aggregate than any total for public expenditure which a government may consider affordable or wish to target, it follows that the process of allocating resources will accord deliberately or implicitly relative weights to different programmes of expenditure.

In this chapter we explain how and by whom the priority of total public expenditure was determined in the period from 1976 until the introduction of the New Control Total in 1992. We argue that it was not determined residually after calculation of prospective revenue, as claimed initially by Conservative Governments, but partly as a result of 'top–down' considerations concerned with broad macro-economic strategy, and partly 'bottom–up' as a result of the pressures from spending ministers for additional resources during the Survey. The process of deciding was continuous and iterative, and the final total represented a trade-off between the two. The processes for determining the total of expenditure were changed in 1992 with the introduction of the New Control Total, and were intended to impose a 'top–down' limit on the aggregate available for each public spending round. We discuss the nature and effects of this change later in the chapter, and take up the issue of the collective responsibility of the Cabinet for determining the total in the new Cabinet Committee procedures in Chapter 13.

In this chapter we compare the processes and their effects, from 1976 to the introduction of the New Control Total in 1992, and then discuss the effect of the determinants of the relative priority of programmes now competing for a predetermined quantum of expenditure prescribed in the New Control Total. The argument here is that, before 1992, neither in the Survey process nor in Cabinet were explicit cross-departmental comparisons made. We conclude that the determination of the priority of the Planning Total and its distribution was politically rational, a necessary but not sufficient condition of an effective system. We begin with a brief discussion of the importance of priority in government, and distinguish between types of priority and the levels at which such issues may be considered.

Priority is about choice. Choice can be deliberate and the consequential allocation of resources intended; or inferred from such action or inaction with consequences for allocations which may be unforeseen and perhaps unintended. It can result from the application of some rational criterion, or from irrational or arbitrary behaviour. However rationality is defined (and we return to this in Chapter 22), rational activity will include some element of deliberate choice between alternatives, and an explicit or implicit ranking of preferences or priorities. As we saw in Chapter 3, the process of making decisions about public expenditure is claimed to be a more rational one since the implementation of the Plowden Report in the mid-1960s. This is most obviously the case in the attempt to *plan* public expenditure over a number of years.

Within Whitehall, the opportunities to choose and order priorities of public expenditure occur at three interrelated and overlapping levels. At the top is the total of public expenditure, relative to alternative and competing claims for those same resources, against the background of the government's broad macro-economic strategy and in the light of its medium-term objectives for public spending. The decision of how much public spending should be in total

is not just a straightforward choice between higher or lower aggregate figures. Any government is likely to have a number of different reasons for wanting to control total inputs. One may be concern about the implications for the aggregate level of general taxation and borrowing . . . concern with the level of public sector borrowing is generally not an end in itself, but a means to other objectives: [in 1985] those for the rate of monetary expansion, for the growth of nominal incomes and ultimately for inflation. And the composition of every given level of PSBR—and in turn of public expenditure—can substantially influence these monetary effects both in the short and longer term . . .

All this means there cannot be complete divorce between questions about total spending inputs and their allocations. Some aspects of composition may have implications for the appropriate totals; and both the total and the distribution of spending have implications affecting both macro-economic and micro-economic policies. Eventual decisions about planned levels of input are bound to involve trade-offs between the different aims. (Sir Peter Middleton, Permanent Secretary, Treasury, in Middleton 1985: paras. 24–9)

At the next level down, there is an ordering of priority between expenditure programmes—defence, health, education, and so on. Thirdly, within those programmes, spending authorities decide how much they want to spend on particular services and activities. Choice at each level is affected, and may be constrained, by what is decided or being decided at the other levels in a continuous and iterative process. Priorities within a departmental programme may be affected directly by the priority accorded the whole of public expenditure in a particular year, or years. Conversely, the aggregation of approved bids from spending departments may lead to a reassessment of priorities, with some way being found to finance a larger total. Equally, the response to events and crises, and the availability of revised data about economic growth, revenue, borrowing, and the PSBR may lead to a reallocation of expenditure, and hence priorities, at any or all levels.

DETERMINING THE PRIORITY OF THE PUBLIC EXPENDITURE PLANNING TOTAL, 1976–1992

Governments have to decide annually what priority should be accorded public expenditure, given other competing claims for those resources. The choice is constrained in several ways, but most obviously by the pressures to continue 'inertial' public expenditure at existing 'real' levels, as well as by pressures to finance additional public expenditure. While from its inception PESC was intended to provide a better means of comparing different kinds of expenditure, by considering all claims at the same time and for a period of years ahead, the Plowden Report said little about how the overall priority for the total of public expenditure was to be determined. Early on, comparison of expenditure plans with 'prospective resources' led to an explicit link between the total of public expenditure and an estimated or targeted rate of growth of GDP. Thus, in the 1960s, the total of public expenditure was often derived from the calculation of past expenditure, plus a percentage increase roughly corresponding to GDP plans for growth. A later 'rule of thumb' was that public expenditure could be allowed to grow at the same rate as the estimated growth of the 'productive potential' of the economy. In the 1970s this 'rule' was displaced by a more explicit link between expenditure growth and hypothetical estimates of the growth of GDP, on the assumption of full employment. The priority of public expenditure compared with other claims was thus often predetermined, and only rarely decided after consideration of how it should or could be financed, through taxation or borrowing, or the priority of other claims on resources. In practice, the priority given to public expenditure proved greater still, especially in the early 1970s, as the total of cash expanded in order to finance planned volumes, almost regardless of their cost or the implications for other claims on those resources.

Since 1979 two issues have dominated the discussion of how government decides how much to spend in the public sector. The first is the extent to which the Planning/Control Total has been determined by the Conservative Governments' objective of reducing the growth of public expenditure, either in real terms or as a share of GDP; the second is the extent to which the principle that revenue determines expenditure provides a practical criterion for determining that total. The two are interrelated, both in theory and in practice. From the formulation of the principles of the MTFS in 1980, Conservative Governments produced an annual framework within which macro-economic decisions which affected the total of public expenditure were made. The framework provided for the coming year, and two further years, projections of the growth of money, PSBR (PSDR), revenue, expenditure, and estimates of inflation and economic growth. In most years, the Conservative Government's major macro-economic priority was the control of inflation. To that end, it attempted through the MTFS to provide a broad framework to guide its own macro-economic policies, and the expenditure and behaviour of decision-makers in the public and private sectors.

The link between rising public expenditure and (often) hypothetical and unrealistic expectations of rising economic growth, which characterized much of the 1970s, was broken. Public expenditure was to be determined residually, after consideration of the projection of revenue and borrowing over the medium-term period. This borrowing, through the prescription of targets related to the control of the money supply, was an important component of the strategy for dealing with inflation.

Targeted reductions of the PSBR, derived partly from the revenue projections, bore down on planned expenditure totals. Combined with the objective of reducing the size of the public sector, this produced the early planned attempts of the Conservative Government to cut public expenditure. In the broad sense, of taxation *and* borrowing, revenue helped to determine the total of public expenditure, at least in principle.

Plans for public expenditure were to be determined by the strategy adopted in the annual MTFS. The planned real-terms cuts in the early 1980s reflected the grand macro-economic strategy of controlling inflation through a progressive reduction of the money supply and PSBR. Revenue appeared to determine public expenditure. It soon became apparent that according public expenditure a low (and historically lower) priority through the MTFS was insufficient to ensure that the planned totals in the Survey were achieved. In practice, for a variety of reasons (discussed in Chapter 22), those totals were not achieved. As we have seen, for nearly a decade public expenditure grew in real terms by about 2 per cent per annum.

As targets for the money supply and the PSBR proved increasingly elusive, and the MTFS less significant in the Conservative Government's macro-economic strategy, with the coincidence of falling inflation and expanding money supply, doubts were expressed about the extent to which the totals of public expenditure in the Survey were determined residually. As we explain in Chapter 20, the initial objective of cutting public expenditure in real terms through the plan periods became progressively less ambitious, succeeded by the aim of maintaining public expenditure constant in real terms, and then, more modestly, reducing the GGE/GDP ratio in the medium term. Doubt grew about the extent to which the Government's objective determined or influenced the totals prescribed in the annual Surveys.

In a continuing dialogue with the Treasury and Civil Service Committee throughout the 1980s, the Chancellor, Chief Secretary, and Treasury officials insisted that the determination of the then Planning Total was guided by two criteria: that public expenditure should be linked to GDP; and that revenue should determine expenditure. The committee was consistently sceptical of the Treasury's contention that the PE/GDP ratio could provide any meaningful guide to the setting of public expenditure totals in the short term, while agreeing that it was a valid and useful medium-term objective. They concluded after discussion with the Chief Secretary that it 'played hardly any role during the planning process in determining the annual expenditure total' (Treasury and Civil Service Committee 1988*a*: para. 25). By December 1988, the Chief

Secretary was prepared to concede that the ratio was not a criterion used in setting the public expenditure totals. 'The ratio is really there to indicate a trend' (Treasury and Civil Service Committee 1988*b*: qu. 113). 'We certainly wish [public expenditure] to reduce as a proportion of national income . . . But we do not necessarily see the public sector as absorbing a particular and consistent proportion of national income.'[1] His reply was in response to the suggestion that perhaps the Government had a more precise objective, 'a point or plateau', which was regarded as an optimal level of public expenditure in terms of national income. The implication was that, year by year, the Government set a target level which moved it towards such a point or plateau. The Chief Secretary rejected the suggestion: 'We do not have an end in view' (qu. 125). He was more explicit still in his evidence, when he told the committee that the public expenditure totals were determined 'not on some mechanistic formula, but as a result of the aggregation of a whole series of individual decisions with the spending departments' (qu. 116). Whether or not the Planning Totals are an aggregation of accepted and 'affordable' bids will be discussed a little later on. We have first to examine the other argument, that expenditure was determined by revenue. This is turn raises prior questions about the role and status of the MTFS.

The Treasury's view of the significance of the MTFS in determining the public expenditure totals was summarized in 1985 by M. C. Scholar, then the Treasury's General Expenditure Policy (GEP) Under Secretary with responsibility for the preparation of the Survey:

Each year in the Budget when the MTFS is revised and reviewed the Government makes its dispositions about public expenditure on the widest of definitions . . . From that framework in the MTFS the planning totals are derived and the Government or the Cabinet makes its own decision about the appropriate level of public expenditure planning totals against the background of the MTFS document for that year. (Treasury and Civil Service Committee 1985*a*: qu. 32)

---

[1] The ratio is inherently flawed, as the committee and others have pointed out. The measurement of GDP, a year or more ahead, is a difficult and hazardous exercise. Deriving a fixed total of public expenditure from such estimates would be liable to error, both currently and in the future as more accurate data on GDP became available. Retrospectively, GDP might be shown to have differed considerably from the estimate upon which a planning total was determined. A large and growing element of public expenditure is accounted for by transfer payments. Demographic trends affect the level of GGE and will cause the ratio to rise unless GDP grows correspondingly. Conversely, unforeseen changes in the take-up of services or benefits in the course of a year will cause the ratio to decline. The weight of these criticisms was eventually acknowledged by the Treasury in 1992, when public expenditure policy was refocused to constrain the growth of GGE to 2% p.a. in line with the trend rate of growth in the economy.

His successor, Andrew Turnbull (Mrs Thatcher's and then John Major's No. 10 Principal Private Secretary), confirmed that interpretation, albeit in language which appeared to contradict his Chief Secretary's assertions that the planning total was built up by aggregating the agreed claims of the spending departments: 'instead of building up plans from below and then subsequently finding the revenue to finance them the aim was to set a framework for expenditure, taxation and borrowing so that it was not simply taxation that was the residual from this process' (Treasury and Civil Service Committee 1987c: qu. 3).

Within the broad framework of the annual MTFS, projections of revenue and estimates of borrowing (or surplus) were made for the year ahead. The totals for public expenditure were derived from the summary statement which accompanied the Departmental Reports (which replaced the Spring PEWP) published a month or so earlier. The total for the year ahead was that agreed at the end of the last Survey, published in the Autumn Statement in the previous November, revised to incorporate any subsequent policy changes. The revenue and borrowing estimates in the MTFS referred to the Planning Totals for the year after next, that is, some twelve or thirteen months ahead. The planned total of public expenditure for the same period was year two of the Survey. There are two major issues: first, the extent to which the year two total when revised during the Survey was determined by or within the MTFS framework, on the basis of projections of taxation and borrowing; secondly, the extent to which those projections were revised during the course of the Survey. To deal with the latter first. The concern here is that the total for the coming financial year (year one of the Survey) was determined finally in November on the basis of projections of taxation and borrowing derived from an MTFS and Budget six months earlier. By the time the year one Survey total was about to be implemented, in the financial year beginning in April, those projections were more than a year old. If they were not revised during the Survey, they might prove inaccurate. This has always been a difficulty with the PSBR, described memorably by one Treasury official as the difference between two very large numbers. Throughout the year the estimates of the borrowing (or surplus) requirement were continuously revised, influenced by the level of economic activity and the cash control of capital and current expenditure programmes. However, it was not normal practice for the Treasury to revise its estimates of revenue during the course of the Survey and to adjust the Planning Total accordingly. 'We would only revise the revenue estimates for the medium term once a year, and that would be done at the time the MTFS was published with the Budget', the Chief Secretary told the Treasury and Civil Service Committee (1988a: qu. 6).

Although short-term forecasts of revenue were revised during the year, parallel with those for the PSBR, expenditure plans were not altered to reflect them. While the opportunity existed to revise the expenditure Planning Total at the time of the Budget, a month or so before the beginning of the financial year, it was rarely used. To do so would have been 'imprudent' in the Chief Secretary's judgement. The result, he admitted, was that 'expenditure provisions tend to follow on a little behind the revenue projections'; but he defended the lag on the grounds that it was more prudent to provide for a regular and consistent flow of public expenditure than have a 'jerky pattern, which does no good either for individuals or for programme expenditure plans' (Treasury and Civil Service Committee 1987*c*: qu. 107).

The Treasury and Civil Service Committee remained unconvinced by his argument and concluded, consistent with its scepticism voiced over the previous five years, that the revenue criterion for determining the total of public expenditure was not followed in practice. On an earlier occasion it had dismissed as 'threadbare' the Chancellor's argument that the revenue implications of the expenditure profiles contained in the 1984 Green Paper (Cmnd. 9189) on long term expenditure had been translated into successive MTFSs, and hence that the Government had taken full account of revenue in its expenditure plans. The committee pointed out that, in practice, public expenditure had frequently exceeded the MTFS assumptions and that, as a result, borrowing, asset sales, and taxation had had to be adjusted. 'In the past, expenditure has evidently determined finance despite the MTFS' (Treasury and Civil Service Committee 1986*a*: para. 13). That conclusion was confirmed by later events of a different kind. The revenues for 1987–8 and 1988–9 were substantially greater than originally forecast at the time of the 1987 Budget. If revenue determined expenditure, then expenditure could have been increased, the Committee argued. 'Instead, there seems to be a presumption that if revenues turn out to be greater than expenditure, then lower taxes or lower government borrowing should balance the equation rather than increased expenditure' (para. 29). The unforeseen buoyancy of revenue in 1988–9, due to much greater levels of economic activity than forecast and the very considerable consumer spending, produced substantially revised estimates of the surplus at the time of the Autumn Statement and again in the last quarter of the 1988–9 financial year. The total of public expenditure was not adjusted to accommodate some of that additional surplus.

Revenue might still have determined expenditure in the way insisted upon by the Government, without every additional surplus pound being allocated to public expenditure either during the preparation of the

Survey or in the course of year one spending. Provided that the alternative uses of the additional revenue were compared, it would be consistent with that criterion if those resources were allocated to lowering taxation or borrowing, or increasing the PSDR. It is not clear that such comparisons were made and the relative priorities of expenditure, taxation, and borrowing/debt repayment decided upon in that way. To make them, the Treasury and Government would require up-to-date estimates of revenue and to feed them into the medium-term planning of the Survey. The Chancellor always resisted calls for the publication of revised revenue estimates in the Autumn Statement, on the grounds that the process of deciding about revenue had not yet begun and that he did not want to pre-empt options, as well as to avoid the possibility of private sector decision-makers profiting by such knowledge. But, unless expenditure and taxation were considered together, the priority of public expenditure claims could not be said to have been determined directly by revenue. Moreover, it was difficult without updated revenue projections to assess the rationale of the Planning Totals in the Autumn Statement.

The Chancellor and his officials were plainly opposed to any such change throughout the 1980s. Indeed, as we explained in Chapter 3, the publication of the first formal Autumn Statement in 1982 represented a concession to the criticisms voiced in the Armstrong Report on Budgetary Reform and by the Treasury and Civil Service Committee over the years, but fell short of the radical reform proposed for a 'Green Budget' bringing together revenue and expenditure. In some years, 1985 and 1986 for example, there were no revenue projections at all. It was only in 1992, on the initiative of Chancellor Lamont, that the Treasury accepted the need for a unified Budget, bringing together revenue and expenditure decisions.

Indirectly, revenue did help to determine expenditure before 1992, in the sense that it was determined by the level of economic activity. If GDP is growing, and inflation is constant or increasing, then revenue will increase if tax rates and thresholds are not adjusted. If public expenditure is allowed to grow in real terms, while declining as a proportion of GDP, then to that extent more expenditure can be financed. This was the Conservative Government's declared position in 1988–9, acknowledging at the same time that a slow-down in GDP might lead to a reduction in the affordable growth of public expenditure.

We now return to the issue of the extent to which the MTFS provided the framework for deciding the Planning Total in the Survey. The MTFS incorporated the Planning Totals from the updated Autumn Statement of the previous November. In July the Chancellor indicated to the

Cabinet the prospects for the economy, while the Chief Secretary provided a similar prospectus for total public expenditure. 'At that stage we either decide that we will reaffirm the planning total that was agreed in previous years, which has often been the case, or perhaps we decide something different as was the case [in 1988]' (Treasury and Civil Service Committee 1988*a*: qu. 103). That 'something different' might of course be a decision to increase public expenditure as happened in the 1986 Autumn Statement, in the run-up to the 1987 general election, and again in 1991. When it was 'something different', it was assumed that the Chancellor and/or the Chief Secretary proposed a new 'affordable' total for consideration by colleagues. Where the decision reaffirmed the Planning Total for the old Survey incorporated into the MTFS, the relationship with revenue appeared still more tenuous—the revenue projection influencing or determining that total having been made nearly eighteen months previously.

How were the totals agreed at the July Cabinet before 1992? On what basis did the Chief Secretary recommend a total to his colleagues? There are two not wholly consistent possibilities to consider: first, the argument that the total of public expenditure was mainly determined 'top–down', within the framework of the MTFS, in the light of the medium-term revenue and borrowing/surplus projections, and the broad objective of reducing or stabilizing the GGE/GDP ratio; secondly, the bottom-up aggregation of bids from departments. We have discussed the revenue criterion above, concluding that the evidence does not support the contention that revenue determined expenditure and that there was no 'mechanistic formula' for determining expenditure's share of GDP.

Before the July Cabinet the Chief Secretary and Chancellor discussed in general terms the size of the 'envelope' for the public expenditure Planning Total within which they hoped and expected to fit the results of the negotiations with spending departments in the bilaterals, and the Cabinet and/or the Star Chamber, as it then was. The lower limit was the Treasury target total recommended to the July Cabinet and announced publicly subsequently. The upper limit of what was acceptable and consistent with the strategy was not revealed. For obvious reasons the Chief Secretary would not wish to reveal his negotiating margin in advance of the bilaterals. Some indication of what it was could be deduced from the deliberate leaks and press briefings by both the Treasury and spending departments. In some public spending rounds the band was very narrow, and the upper limit very close to or even identical with the lower one.

Throughout the PES round GEP provided the Chief Secretary with

updated information on the upper limit consistent with the achievement
of the broad policy aim for public expenditure growth represented by
the PE/GDP ratio, and the judgement of the Chancellor and the Chief
Secretary of the progress which should be made towards it in any one
year. Revisions to the MTFS estimate of GDP affected the upper limit.
More could be afforded (without adversely affecting the ratio) if, by the
autumn, GDP was expected to grow faster than had been expected six
months earlier. Conversely, if that early estimate was later perceived as
too optimistic, the upper limit was scaled down, if the Chief Secretary
and Chancellor decided that the adverse effect on the PE/GDP ratio
was not politically acceptable. They decided, as in the past, that the
objective represented by the ratio could be relaxed to accommodate
those increases in public expenditure that were felt desirable, necessary,
or unavoidable; or that progress towards it could be made more slowly.
They had to trade-off the pressures for increased spending, for whatever
reason, against the maintenance of, or progress towards, the objective
for public spending growth as a whole. The elasticity of the upper limit
varied with both the economic and electoral cycles.

It is impossible to say authoritatively what the upper limit was in most
years of the period 1976–92, and hence whether the final Planning Total
came close to it, or fell comfortably below it. As part of its general
negotiating stance the Treasury encouraged or even fuelled speculation
about the size of the envelope, as appeared to be the case in 1990 and in
1991. Thus it was widely reported in the press that the former round was
much tougher than usual, that the Treasury would have difficulty in
delivering a total less than £8 billion greater than the July target. In
practice, the Treasury's upper limit was probably somewhat higher than
that which it achieved. The Star Chamber was threatened but not
seriously contemplated. In an exceptionally tough round, the Treasury
would not have allowed a half of all bids, however compelling, or
declined to trigger the Star Chamber. Allowing the total to rise by £7.7
billion in a pre-election year, and one of recession, was not an altogether
unwelcome outcome. At the same time, the Chief Secretary emerged
from the round with a reputation for toughness—the increase allowed
was a 'success'.

Throughout the period 1976–92 the Treasury refused to publish details of the size and distribution of the bids for additional resources; nor
would it provide official confirmation of those that were accepted after
negotiation, and those that went to the bilaterals. However, both it and
the spending departments provided tactical off-the-record briefings for
the media, from which some of the data in Table 11.1 have been constructed. This table shows the effects of the spending departments' bids

TABLE 11.1. *Bidding for additional resources* (£bn cash)

	Treasury target (July)	Bids over target	Excess bids accepted after negotiation	Bids outstanding	Star Chamber yes/no	Reserve	Final Planning Total (Nov.)	Accuracy of target
1992	244.5[a]	14	—	—	EDX	−4.0	243.8[b]	−0.7
1991	221.0	16	—	8–9	no	−3.0	226.6	+5.6
1990	192.3	16	—	6–8	no	−2.5	200.0	+7.7
1989	179.4	10	3–4	6–7	no	−4.0	179.0	−0.4
1988	167.1	9	—	3	no	−3.5	167.1	0
1987	154.2	6	—	3	yes	−2.0	156.8	+2.6
1986	143.9	7	3	4	yes	−2.8	148.6	+4.7
1985	136.7	5–6	—	2–3	yes	−0.5	139.1	+2.4
1984	132.0	6	2	2.5	yes	−0.75	132.1	+0.1
1983	126.4	6	2	1	yes	−0.25	126.4	0
1982	121.0	5	3.5	1	no	−2.5	119.6	−1.4
1981	110.0	7	3–4	3.5	yes	—	115.2	+5.2

[a] This was set after the reform of PES which included the New Control Total and the use of the Expenditure Committee of the Cabinet (EDX).

[b] A misleading figure since classification and other changes brought the old Planning Total figure down from £244.5bn to £242.5bn. On an adjusted basis the Nov. figure was £243.8bn, the same as targeted in July.

Sources: The Times, Financial Times, Public Expenditure White Papers, Autumn Statements.

for additional resources on the Planning Totals for the spending rounds from 1981 to 1992. The 'Treasury target' is the lower limit of the 'envelope', the Planning Totals derived from the previous plans. The next three columns are rough approximations of the size of the excess bids. A later column shows the effect of using the Reserve to offset the impact of bids in excess of the Treasury's lower limit. For example, in 1989 the Treasury was able to accommodate £3–4 billion excess bids *and* reduce the Planning Total by reducing the Reserve by £4 billion. In the 1990 Survey, the Planning Total would have been £2.5 billion higher if the Reserve had not been reduced. The final Planning Total agreed by Cabinet in November was published in the Autumn Statement, and the final column in Table 11.1 shows the extent to which this was greater or less than the lower limit. In seven of the twelve years the outcome of the PES round exceeded the original lower limit. While this was only publicly acknowledged by the Treasury in briefings to the press (*The Times*, 23 July 1992), it was undoubtedly a factor in the decision to introduce the New Control Total in 1992. We discuss this a little later on in the chapter.

A 'top–down' interpretation of the determination of the Planning Totals in the period before that change emphasizes the greater significance of the Chief Secretary's predetermined 'big numbers', whether or not influenced by the MTFS framework, and assigns a lesser role to the pressures building up from the departments for additional spending. Or, more accurately, that interpretation assumes that some of those pressures had to be accommodated (how much was affected by the Chancellor's economic judgement and strategy, and the political desirability of more expenditure, as in 1986–7, in 1991–2, and 1992–3), and were already discounted in the 'envelope'. This is inconsistent with a 'bottom–up' interpretation of the Planning Total in its purest form. On such an argument, the Planning Total was determined mainly by aggregating the departmental bids; there was no upper limit or constraint. In practice an aggregated total was constrained by taxation and borrowing levels, estimated GDP, and projected sales of assets, and the Government's objective for public expenditure. There were, therefore, constraints or 'limits', which were determined 'top–down', even before the introduction of the New Control Total in 1992.

Up until that time, the Chief Secretary tended to emphasize more the significance of the bottom–up aggregating process in determining the final total. Asked by the Treasury and Civil Service Committee in 1988 why the Planning Total for 1988–9 had been fixed at £156.8 billion, he replied that it represented the outcome of his negotiations with the spending departments. While seeking to keep tight control of public expenditure, he admitted that the Government do not seek to keep it so tight and clear cut as to aim particularly at one percentage point within £1bn. The final planning total figure is, of course, the outcome of a whole series of different bilateral, in some cases trilateral, and in a few cases quadrilateral discussions between the Chief Secretary of the day and the individual spending departments, and the reason you get what looks superficially as a rather odd total is the aggregate of those individual decisions. We do not specifically aim at £156.8bn; that is the aggregate that is built up from the outcome of a whole series of individual discussions. (Treasury and Civil Service Committee 1988*a*: qu. 99)

More explicitly still, the Chief Secretary in a subsequent examination by the Treasury and Civil Service Committee affirmed that 'public expenditure must be judged on its merits and its necessity', and reiterated the significance of aggregation: 'In so far as the following year is concerned, we have set the totals of expenditure, not on some mechanistic formula, but as a result of the aggregation of a whole series of individual discussions with the spending departments' (Treasury and Civil Service Committee 1988*b*: qu. 116). The Chief Secretary's concern to emphasize that the public expenditure total was decided pragmatically, 'on its merits', and that the total was determined by an aggregation of necessary and 'affordable' bids, did not convince the committee, who were 'inclined to believe that the overall quantity of public expenditure was determined from the top down' (para. 25). Part of the Chief Secretary's insistence on the 'bottom–up' approach was the result of attempts to rebut the repeated criticisms by the Treasury and Civil Service Committee that insufficient consideration was given by the Government to the determination of priorities in public expenditure. Thus the Chief Secretary's evidence reflected an attempt to demonstrate that he and his officials compared bids and judged their relative merits, and to resist the criticism that the total was imposed from above. It does not, however, entirely explain the repeated insistence on pragmatism and aggregation.

Let us assume that the Chief Secretary and his officials did proceed in that way. How then were relative priorities between bids established? How was it decided which bids to accept, revise, or reject? A strict, pragmatic, 'on its merits' approach could produce an unsupportable expenditure total, a total which required greater revenue, borrowing, economic growth than estimated or thought desirable. Clearly there were constraints and perhaps 'limits', whatever may have been the practice in the mid-1970s. This is implied by the balance between 'affordability' and 'necessity', between the merits of the spending departments' 'needs' and how much the Government believed it could 'afford' or wanted to afford, given its other macro-economic objectives.

Neither the 'top–down' nor the 'bottom–up' focus is independently an adequate explanation of the determination of the Planning Totals in the period 1976–92. In practice, the pressures for more public spending from below, however merited and irresistible individually, were confronted inevitably by the 'bigger picture' composed of the Government's broad expenditure objectives and its macro-economic strategy, as well as by the need to adjust both at certain times in order to respond flexibly to the pressures of immediate events, and to react adequately to the intermittent crises to which public services are prone. The drawing of the line, the trade-off between the two, was determined finally in the November Cabinet, after the conclusion of the Autumn bilaterals and any reference of outstanding claims to the Star Chamber and/or Cabinet. How was that line drawn? It seems probable that the Chief Secretary and Chancellor, advised by their officials, agreed the totals at which desirably they would wish to settle—the 'envelope' within which a settlement would prove acceptable. It is probable, but not assured, that the Chief Secretary was able to conclude his bilaterals (and any Star Chamber negotiations) within that 'envelope', as happened in 1988, 1989, 1990, and 1991. On other occasions he was obliged by the continuing pressure from spending ministers to settle outside it. In any case, his judgement of what the 'envelope' should be was often revised between July and September in the light of new economic and financial data, or by events at home or abroad, or by a calculation of the probable date of an impending general election.

The New Control Total introduced in 1992 has profoundly changed the processes for determining the aggregate. The top–down/bottom–up interaction described above has been replaced by the imposition of top–down limits for each of the three Survey years. Those proposed in 1992 represented a squeeze on existing plans and a commitment that over the medium term the NCT would grow by no more than 1.5 per cent in real terms year on year. The NCT was presented as a more 'precise, transparent and quantifiable objective' (Treasury 1992*d*: 12) than the GGE/GDP ratio or the (now discredited and abandoned) New Planning Total.

In determining the New Control Totals the Treasury reverted to a policy norm of the 1960s and 1970s that spending should grow in line with the productive potential of the economy as a whole. From an assessment of the latter, the Treasury derived a reasonable operational target for the NCT, allowing for future trends in cyclical social security payments and debt interest. The result of this was the imposition of an annual limit of 2 per cent real growth for GGE (in line with the estimated growth of the economy), and 1.5 per cent real growth for the

NCT. While the latter represented a maximum, the limit might be lowered, and control further tightened, if GDP growth proved less than estimated; if the overall fiscal position deteriorated; if the Treasury found it difficult to constrain the growth of some programmes; or if items outside the NCT, such as interest payments, were rising faster than the trend. If it was found that many of the latter grew by more than 5 per cent in real terms, then the NCT limit would have to be reviewed in order to keep the growth rate for GGE within the 2 per cent target.

DETERMINING PRIORITY BETWEEN PROGRAMMES

If in most years between 1976 and 1992 the aggregate of the bids for additional spending exceeded the limits within the 'sealed' Treasury envelope, how was the line drawn by the Chief Secretary and the Cabinet? The answer to that question requires some explanation of how the Chief Secretary and his officials decided between the relative priority of the bids in the Survey process, and whether the introduction of the New Control Total and new Cabinet Committee procedures in 1992 have made any difference. How the Cabinet decides on those claims unresolved or irresolvable between the Chief Secretary and the spending minister after the conclusion of the bilaterals is dealt with in Chapter 13.

The Treasury subscribes unambiguously to the principle of prescribing priority in public expenditure planning: 'A constant theme running through the public expenditure process is better planning and management to increase value for money year by year. That means starting with a clear view of what could be achieved, deciding the priority objectives, and then pursuing them in the most efficient way' (Treasury 1988c: para. 71). More narrowly, John MacGregor, when Chief Secretary, stated publicly that value-for-money could not be pursued without explicit consideration and ordering of priorities (Treasury 1986a). At various times since 1976, Treasury ministers and officials have affirmed their support for that view. With the accession of the Conservative Government in 1979 committed to reducing the size of the public sector, and public expenditure, and obtaining better value-for-money, the issue became more salient. The work of the Efficiency Unit, the Rayner Scrutinies, and FMI became the main instruments for the achievement of those objectives within individual departments. Through the setting of objectives and targets, and the measurement of performance, departments were increasingly obliged to consider and order the priorities of their own expenditure programmes, and to indicate in their bids what they were.

How then did the Chief Secretary and his Treasury officials analyse and compare bids for additional resources and provide an assessment which enabled the Cabinet to consider and finally determine the priorities between programmes? While the preparation of the Survey, bringing together all programmes, provides the main focus for a consideration of relative priorities, it is claimed that this process is continuous throughout the year. We examine first the occasions for comparison provided by the Survey.

Both Treasury ministers and officials repeatedly emphasized the difficulty of determining the priorities of expenditure by comparing the relative merits of different departmental programmes. When Chancellor of the Exchequer, Nigel Lawson told the House of Commons:

In government there is no utilitarian calculus that permits numerical comparison of the respective benefits of, say, the extra military aircraft as against more disaster relief, or more equipment for research councils . . . Whatever the group of Ministers or Departments involved and whatever the forum or setting, there can be no magic mechanism for setting priorities within and between programmes. However detailed the factual basis provided by the officials and however sophisticated the analyses of outputs and performance for the programme concerned, in the end there has to be a political judgement and a political decision. (Parliamentary Debates, HC, 6 Dec. 1984, col. 624)

This denial was reiterated by Andrew Turnbull, then Under Secretary in charge of the Treasury's General Expenditure Policy Group:

In any organisation one can choose the level at which one decides to conduct a debate about priorities . . . So one has to provide successive tiers of decision-making. [Nurses' pay] comes up in the discussion about the health programme. In the course of a Survey, the health programme is in effect bidding against all other programmes, with the forces coming from higher pay for people who work in the Health Service being one of the main pressures that the Secretary of State for Social Services has got to take account of . . . There is no mechanism in which a particular factor of that kind can be related to something very specific in say the transport programme. (Treasury and Civil Service Committee 1987c: qu. 33)

Nevertheless, Treasury ministers and officials claimed that consideration was given to the relative priority of departmental programmes of expenditure in the Survey process.

At the beginning of the Survey, Treasury Heads of Group (Under Secretary) provide an assessment of the prospects for their programmes in the light of economic and demographic factors, drawing on the advice of GEP and the macro-economists. They consider the probable impact on them of different political options, both governmental priorities and commitments, and the demands of organized groups. These are put to the Chief Secretary, who will provide guidance on which options he wishes them to take account of. Their assessments are discussed in some detail with the Chief Secretary, the Second Permanent Secretary, and the relevant Deputy Secretary. The Second Permanent Secretary, with GEP's help, then pulls all this together in a wide-ranging assessment of the prospects for the Survey.

The Chief Secretary and the Second Permanent Secretary give constant attention not only to the planned outcome of the total spending strategy, but to its distribution between programmes. The process is iterative, and the interaction between the total and its distribution constant. In addition to the top–down pressure to maintain the agreed Planning Total, judgement about the relative weight and hence priority to be accorded the separate bids is compounded of several elements. In the assessment of individual bids for additional resources, Expenditure Divisions are sensitive to the priorities of the Ministers of the departments they shadow. They also take account of the efficiency and value-for-money of those programmes. But little attempt is made to compare performance and cost-effectiveness between programmes at this level or between departments at the higher, Group level. This is not only inherently a technically difficult exercise: there is doubt whether the present development of performance indicators and measurements of output, efficiency, and effectiveness are capable of generating data on a common basis which would enable this to be done cross-departmentally. Such data as are available are used to determine the strength of an individual bid, *ad hoc* and on its own merits. Andrew Turnbull, Under Secretary in charge of the Treasury's General Expenditure Policy Group, admitted to the Treasury and Civil Service Committee that:

Ultimately the Treasury's job is to make sure that bids for different resources compete against other resources and we are trying to maintain some kind of envelope to ensure that the policy on public expenditure generally which has been endorsed is adhered to. *But ultimately it comes down to the strength of the case that is made.* (Treasury and Civil Service Committee 1987c: qu. 37; emphasis added)

Expenditure Divisions are programme- and department-specific. Cross-departmental comparisons could occur only at a higher level, that of the Group, where an Under Secretary has responsibility for a group of Expenditure Divisions and hence departmental programmes. No attempt is made here to compare and weigh the relative merits of departmental bids. The Under Secretary's task is not to try to impose an order of priority across those departmental programmes for which he has responsibility, which could be recommended to the Chief Secretary as consistent with his expenditure strategy, the policy aims of individual ministers, and the strengths of the individual bids. The Survey strategy for each Group is concerned much less with determining priorities than how each bid should be dealt with separately to deliver a total expenditure package for the Group's programmes which will help the Chief Secretary achieve his targeted Planning Total (interview, Treasury Under Secretary).

Nor from its unique central position, and its 'staff' rather than line functions, does GEP attempt any cross-departmental comparison to establish the relative priority of all the bids (interview, GEP Under Secretary). Its principal strategic, co-ordinating function is to assist and advise the Chief Secretary how best to achieve his policies for public expenditure. It sees all the bids, and pulls together the separate responses to them of the Expenditure Divisions, mediated through Heads of Groups. GEP advises the Chief Secretary on the broad implications for his expenditure target, and together with the Expenditures Divisions and Group Heads helps him in the choice of the appropriate tactics to be used in each of the bilateral negotiations to secure an outcome consistent with his target. The Chief Secretary is sensitive to political priorities and has his own views on the relative merits of his colleagues' bids, and in forming a judgement about them has the advice of the Second Permanent Secretary helped by the Deputy Secretaries and GEP.

The normal practice when a Minister proposes additional expenditure to the Treasury is for 'the Chief Secretary to ask whether there is some other proposal on which that Minister can find economies' (Treasury and Civil Service Committee 1986*a*: qu. 3). His resolve and purposefulness in seeking additional expenditure is tested by the extent to which he is prepared to rank a bid for new or increased expenditure against existing expenditures. In practice, the department's claim for additional resources should be partly or wholly offset by savings found from other parts of its programmes. A previous Chief Secretary, John MacGregor, admitted to the Treasury and Civil Service Committee that 'Where there are heavy pressures from one department for extra expenditure one does ask that department to rank its own priorities and see whether it could be making offsetting savings' (Treasury and Civil Service Committee 1986*a*: qu. 141). This practice led the Chairman of the committee, Terence Higgins, to suggest that the bilaterals were in effect 'bi-verticals' (qu. 140):

There is comparatively little discussion about whether one's overall programme should be cut as against another's. The way in which the discussion takes place tends to segregate the thing between departments and there is too little discussion as to whether this or that department should gain or lose and also it is an argument which depends on the particular influence of the Minister concerned.

His attempt to obtain assurance from the Chief Secretary that the Treasury was not excessive in asking departments to find offsetting savings, and that there might be a case for reordering expenditure between programmes of departments, elicited only the response that it was difficult to find the perfect machine for allocating priorities. Comprehensive zero-based budgeting was not practicable, a point he had made earlier to the House of Commons.

However, the Treasury conceded that there was no general presumption about funding an increase from within the same departmental programmes, with the exception of the Ministry of Defence and the Scottish Office which had block budgets. If compensating savings could not be found 'the additional bid may be allowed and the economy found elsewhere'. It was also possible that the bid might be permitted to queue for an allocation from the Reserve during the course of the year.

The Treasury's practice of looking for offsetting savings within a department's programme seemed to the committee to reinforce departmental boundaries 'rather than to encourage a broad look across the whole spectrum of government expenditure'. To support that conclusion they cited the example of the allocation of more money to the inner cities programme in 1986. Despite the higher political priority given to that programme by the Government, the Chief Secretary admitted that no assessment had been made of whether offsetting savings could be found from programmes in other departments.

The method of making changes to public expenditure programmes 'in-year', after the conclusion of the Survey, provides further evidence of the difficulty of making interdepartmental comparisons. When a department bids for additional resources, other than at the time of the preparation of the Survey, the normal practice is for the Treasury to seek offsetting savings within that department's programmes.

In an 'ideal-type' system, the priority of such 'in-year' bids would be compared with the established order of priorities of programme expenditure in all spending authorities, to establish whether they had a better claim than those expenditures already allocated, assuming no additional resources were available. Of course, changing existing allocations 'in-year' would be costly, but that cost would be entered in the comparative calculation; it might be outweighed by the benefit (however determined) of the new bid. The practical difficulties of making such comparisons are very great, exacerbated by a lack of comparative data on input-output ratios, and by utilitarian criteria for determining comparative benefit. There is little evidence, however, that such comparisons are even attempted. Whether at the time of the Survey bilaterals, or when 'in-year' changes are contemplated, the Treasury puts the onus on the department to reorder its own programme priorities to make room for additional spending. The advantage in this, from the perspective of the Treasury, is that it maintains pressure on departmental costs and efficiency and, if successful, avoids a call on the Reserve. It also avoids a multilateral negotiation: it is easier to deal with one department than several simultaneously in an attempt to fund an addition in one from savings in others. Any such reallocation which demonstrably benefited one minister at the expense of another's programme would be insupportable politically, except in time of acute crisis when collective will could, for a limited period of time, prevail over the separate interests of individual ministers.

If a department is unable to fund the whole or a part of the additional expenditure from offsetting savings within its own programme, the Treasury may allow a claim on the Reserve (see Chapter 16). As such claims arise at different times of the year, and each is dealt with *ad hoc* and on its own merits, it follows that any comparison between competing claims on the Reserve is partial and limited. The Chief Secretary responded to the suggestion that the Treasury should be more concerned to look for cross-departmental savings when 'in-year' changes in expenditure are considered, by emphasizing the additional problems that it would create:

If we were to seek cross-departmental savings, it would destroy one thing that seems to me generally to be rather important for each individual programme in the Government's budget, and that is the consistency in-year for managers of knowing what resources are available to them so that they are able to plan satisfactorily within those resources. If therefore in-year, because I had to find extra resources for one programme, I were to seek a reduction in a different programme, it might not be a cost-effective reduction in terms of the effect that it would have on the performance of that particular programme. (Treasury and Civil Service Committee 1988*a*: qu. 115)

As the committee pointed out in reply, that same consideration applied equally to a department permitted to make an in-year change in priority as a result of finding its own offsetting savings.

Any doubt that there might be about the principle or practice of interdepartmental comparisons was removed by Turnbull's explicit response to criticisms that increases were funded by offsetting savings within the same programme or department:

> You appear to be assuming a system in which there are very direct comparisons between programmes and Ministers are being asked to transfer money from one programme to another quite explicitly. It does not happen normally in quite that explicit fashion. There is an envelope which has been set by the planning total and within that individual Ministers are seeking to make additional bids. Sometimes they are successful; sometimes they will make economies themselves and sometimes those economies will be felt elsewhere. But it is rarely of the kind where one Minister's additional bid is directly financed by a transfer from another programme. (Treasury and Civil Service Committee 1986a: qu. 4)

He went on to challenge the committee's assumption that an increase in one programme should be matched directly against a decrease in another, 'as opposed to the generality of programmes'. In other words, the Treasury was more concerned with the size of the Planning Total than attempting to measure and compare relative priorities within it. The object was to keep the total 'in line'. To do that the Survey process was concerned not with interdepartmental comparisons of marginal increases or reductions, but with balancing increases against decreases in the 'generality of programmes'. This involved juggling increases and decreases to keep within the envelope, but not comparisons between programmes. It is difficult to resist the conclusion that the purpose of the Survey is less to determine priority than, in Andrew Turnbull's words, 'to try to balance the bids and savings and effectively juggle with them until it produces a new package but staying within the envelope' (Treasury and Civil Service Committee 1986a: qu. 7).

The Treasury has two main counter-arguments to criticism that it does not attempt interdepartmental comparisons in the preparation of the Survey. The first argument is that priorities are determined continuously throughout the year and not confined to the bidding processes of the Survey. Secondly, that priorities are mainly matters for the political judgement of ministers acting collectively. We deal with the latter argument in Chapter 13 when we discuss the implications of the changes made in 1992 for securing collective responsibility of the Cabinet.

John MacGregor, when Chief Secretary, claimed that there were consultations between officials, ministers, and groups of ministers at all times during the Survey, 'thereby enabling a rigorous formulation of priorities to emerge'. How they emerge is not clear:

All through the year I am very conscious that when one is looking at new policy initiatives and the impact of outside events on public expenditure, one is frequently having to take decisions about priorities. There are considerable outside pressures and views expressed about priorities which often affect the decisions, not least in fact the debates that take place in this House. So, there are a whole series of points during the year when the whole question of priorities comes into one's mind. It is very difficult to describe precisely where they all occur. (Treasury and Civil Service Committee 1986a: qu. 139)

The Treasury and Civil Service Committee was not impressed with this argument and pronounced itself unable to discover how the Chief Secretary decided to take a tough or lenient line in the bilaterals, or how overall priorities were fixed.

John Major's claim, when Chief Secretary, that the bilateral negotiations 'involve testing departments' bids as rigorously as possible against all the other competing bids so that from this process a new pattern of priorities can emerge', is difficult to reconcile with his evidence, and that of other Chief Secretaries and senior Treasury officials, to the Treasury and Civil Service Committee (Major 1988: para. 19). As we have seen, on several occasions they denied that such comparative tests could be made between departmental programmes. However, the priority of each claim for more resources was assessed against the 'envelope' of the total planned expenditure agreed by Cabinet in July, and which Treasury negotiators aimed to deliver in November. The Treasury also looked for evidence of departmental prioritization, and its Expenditure Controllers made their own evaluation of whether a department's programmes delivered value-for-money. Andrew Turnbull, Under Secretary in charge of GEP, told the Treasury and Civil Service Committee that: 'If we detect, for example, that a programme is not producing good results, is not effective, we will brief the Chief Secretary to raise that and that would be one of the arguments to deploy' (Treasury and Civil Service Committee 1988a: qu. 67).

The Cabinet is involved not only at the end of the Survey process in November, but at the July meeting and, since 1992, at meetings of the Cabinet's Expenditure Committee (EDX) and 'frequently' at Cabinet and Cabinet Committee meetings throughout the year. Thus it is claimed that the Chief Secretary's public expenditure assessment to his colleagues at the July Cabinet 'provides an opportunity for Cabinet to discuss both the overall total of public expenditure for the next three years and priorities between and within programmes' (Treasury 1988c: para. 33). At such times, it is claimed, priorities emerge as new and revised policies are discussed and agreed, the result of manifesto commitments, political reaction to current issues, events, and crises, and as a result of policy reviews. It is difficult to see how the claims of new and revised policies which arise from the latter can be brought together and compared with the claims of existing programmes. Policy reviews, however and by whomever initiated and conducted, may take place continuously, but they are not conducted simultaneously throughout all spending authorities, as for example in comprehensive zero-based budgeting. Any priority given or withdrawn from a programme or service as a result of an *ad hoc* policy review is not compared explicitly with an existing order of priorities. While more attention may now be given to the principle of zero-based budgeting (MacGregor, Parliamentary Debates, HC, 26 Feb. 1986, col. 507), its application is piecemeal. Fundamental policy reviews of regional development, industrial policy, social security, the NHS, higher education, defence, and transport have taken place within recent years, and have had the effect of changing the relative priorities of different expenditure programmes. But the results of such reviews and their implications for the priority of expenditure have been considered *seriatim*, and not compared with each other or existing programmes cross-departmentally. This is meant less as a criticism than an observation; still less is it meant as a recommendation. The point being made is that the insistence of Treasury ministers and officials that the activity of determining the priorities of public expenditure programmes is a continuous one, and not simply something that is decided at a specific point in the Survey process, has the clear implication that interdepartmental comparisons are not provided for systematically, nor conducted comprehensively.

There is little evidence of the Cabinet's concern for broad reviews of priority as such in the period 1976–92 (Castle 1980; Barnett 1982; Pym 1984). Nevertheless, substantial shifts between programmes can and do occur over time, and they represent changes in the relative priority of those programmes. For example, the balance between programme expenditure on defence, housing, education, law and order, and industry, was substantially changed over the period 1979–92. Some of those changes were the consequence of an act of deliberate political will, to give a higher or lower priority to a particular programme— defence, for example, as a result of the NATO commitment to increase real spending by 3 per cent per annum. Although the decision may be made without a comparison of the relative merits and priority of all programmes, it nevertheless represents the intention to adjust those priorities. The decisions of the Conservative Government in 1979 to spend more on law and order and much less on industrial programmes have had effects on the relative priorities of other expenditure programmes.

Large changes may result equally from the cumulative effect of small incremental steps. Since the mid-1970s, both Labour and Conservative Governments have frequently resorted to cutting capital spending, particularly that undertaken by local authorities and public corporations. Spending on total public sector asset creation (the broadest measure of capital spending) in real terms declined between 1982–3 and 1988–9 from just over £30 billion to £27.5 billion (1990–1 prices), rose to stand at over £32.5 billion in 1989–90, but fell sharply to about £27 billion in 1992–3. Within this total central government spending grew slightly over the period, whereas that of local authorities fell by 40 per cent from £12.5 billion in 1989–90 to £7.5 billion in 1991–2 (see Treasury 1992*b*).

It cannot be objected that governments determine the priority of certain kinds of spending ideologically; or that the rationale for adjusting an existing order of priority is mainly political. The objection is that other kinds of relevant information and modes of analysis may be given too little weight in that political judgement, and that the mechanisms for determining relative priority through Cabinet and Cabinet Committee are inadequate. While the changes introduced in 1992 apparently gave the Cabinet the opportunity to play that role, the Treasury's control of the agenda will ensure that it retains the initiative. Ministers collectively have no alternative source of information about spending bids. They are dependent upon the Treasury's advice and recommendations. But in any case, on the evidence of the period 1976–92, ministers evince little interest or political will to engage in detailed and complex cross-departmental comparisons, except in moments of acute crisis such as occurred in 1976 and 1992. Even were they to be willing, had the time and energy to play that role, and the Treasury allowed them to do so, there are cognitive limits on the capacity of ministers collectively to read, absorb, and grasp the details of each spending programme to enable them to exercise a judgement independently of the advice and recommendations offered by the Treasury. In the 1960s, when PESC programmes were fewer in number, less detailed, and unencumbered by performance indicators and value-for-money assessments, Sir Richard Clarke, then in charge of the Treasury's expenditure side, was sceptical that ministers could handle the business of more than eight or nine programmes and make informed judgements about relative priority.

Whatever criteria and modes of analysis are used in determining the priority of different kinds of expenditure, the process of ordering and reordering is constrained in practice by factors over which governments often have little direct and immediate control—witness the debate on structural and cyclical factors in the growth of spending in 1992–3. The Treasury emphasizes the preponderance of demand-led programmes, expenditure in which is determined, for example, by demography, changes in the structure of social groups and household formations, and the level of economic activity. Such constraints, like financial contributions to the EU, may be more determinate of relative priority than deliberate choice.

The Treasury claimed that the 'Survey procedure is designed to give Ministers the fullest information on which to make their judgement within and across departments' (Treasury 1986*d*). The evidence examined above for the period from 1976 to 1992 suggests either that such information was not made available in a form which would enable ministers to make comparisons; or, that that information was provided but largely disregarded. Treasury ministers and officials admit that cross-departmental comparisons were not made systematically to determine relative priority in the Survey process, or when 'in-year' changes were made. It is difficult to see how the results of a series of bilateral negotiations could provide, *faute de mieux*, the basis for ministers to make their own comparisons. At best, they will be presented with a set of *ad hominem* arguments and evidence about the merits of individual bids.

Whether or not they had the means to 'make their judgement', it could only be a partial and limited one. Not all bids were considered and compared at the same time collectively by the Cabinet and its committees. Those settled at the bilateral stage, or earlier still, were not reopened and compared with those unresolved. It is by no means certain that the priority afforded a claim settled in the bilateral, or at an earlier stage of the process, was superior to a claim unresolved in that process and taken to Cabinet or Cabinet Committee. Finally, there is little evidence that ministers had the opportunity or the political will to engage in such an exercise, even if the means to make cross-departmental comparisons were available to them. Cabinet spent little time at its July meeting on expenditure matters, while the purpose of the November Cabinet meeting and Star Chamber was more to resolve disputes than to determine priority in the way suggested.

A strength of the system up until 1992 was that the Planning Total and its component parts represented a politically rational outcome, one that normally all ministers were prepared to accept, however reluctantly, and which each Minister believed defensible to his department's constituents. The extent to which the Planning Total achieved in the Autumn Statement was broadly consistent with the overall politico-economic strategy, collectively determined upon earlier by the Government, also represented a rational outcome. But as we have emphasized, the system operated interdependently by the Treasury and spending departments could not guarantee to deliver a planned outcome. The achievement of a politically rational outcome was a necessary but not sufficient condition of an effective system before 1992, and was its most important justification. As the financing of a continuously growing aggregate became more difficult with the deep recession into which the economy plunged at the beginning of the 1990s, and the PSBR rose sharply, the need to establish a more effective control of that aggregate became paramount. Consequently, the issue of determining the relative priority within the top–down limits of the New Control Totals became critical as those totals squeezed the resources available to finance the ineluctable future growth of some of the largest spending programmes, particularly social security. The implications of the changes made in 1992 on the Survey processes for determining priorities, and the role played by the new Cabinet Committee, EDX, are discussed in Chapter 13 in the broader context of the Cabinet's collective responsibility for public spending.

12

The Public Expenditure Survey

It is now thirty years since Plowden reported that 'decisions involving substantial future expenditure should always be taken in the light of surveys of public expenditure as a whole, over a period of years, and in relation to prospective resources'. There has been an annual Survey of public expenditure every year since. In Chapter 3 we traced the origins of the Treasury's system of planning and controlling public expenditure and showed that its development has been for the most part gradual and progressive, the result of practical experience and opportunism. We saw also that that evolutionary process had been punctuated by periods in which the system responded to external shocks and crises, such as devaluation in 1967, and the crisis of control in the mid-1970s, and to changed political and economic objectives.

While the introduction of cash limits in 1976 represented a departure from previous practice, and reasserted the need to control monetary aggregates, the system remained recognizably that which had evolved over the previous decade, designed to produce medium-term resource-based plans. That system proved incapable of delivering the Conservative Government's changed political objective of cutting public expenditure in real terms. There were, of course, other reasons why the Government was unsuccessful in the period 1980–2, but the indexing of inflation in the public sector through the use of constant price measurement and the relative price effect was held to be an important contributory factor. The abandonment of volume planning and the introduction of cash planning in 1982 was a turning-point in the development of the Survey.

These and other changes, such as the introduction of the annual Medium Term Financial Strategy, the abolition of centrally determined pay factors, the separation of programme and running costs expenditure, and the changes made in response to the fiscal crisis in 1992, mean that the processes for planning and controlling public expenditure through the Survey are now very different from those of the 1970s. This chapter describes and explains those processes as they had evolved by the late 1980s and early 1990s—up to the decision in 1992 to introduce the Unified Budget and the New Control Total. It remains to be seen whether those changes will have a lasting, significant effect on the PES process of decision-making. But in any case such an assessment requires an understanding of the system's evolution up to that point, and that is what we provide in the first part of the chapter. In the concluding section we assess the state of the Survey in the 1990s and discuss the immediate and obvious effects of the 1992 changes.

THE POLITICO-ECONOMIC CONTEXT OF THE ANNUAL SURVEY

The broad macro-economic strategy of the government of the day and the particular assessments made about the outlook for the economy as a whole provide the strategic context within which the work of Treasury ministers, their officials in the Expenditure Divisions, and spending ministers and their officials in Finance Divisions is situated. As explained in Chapter 2, since 1980 this context has been provided by the MTFS, which has drawn together the monetary and fiscal policies of government.

The operation of the fiscal side of the MTFS in tandem with the PES round is complex and iterative. Economic policy-making goes on all the year round. There are key points of 'stock-taking' in the Budget and (formerly) the Autumn Statement. The economic background to the Survey is formed of several factors. There is the reaffirmation or adjustment to the medium-term goals set out in the Budget Red Book, for example on the PSBR and tax objectives. In the short run, there are always particular economic circumstances in any financial year, such as concerns about the economy overheating or failing to come out of recession. The Treasury's economic forecasts have an important role to play; so, too, do the particular political as well as economic concerns of the Chancellor. Fiscal policy-making revolves around projections for GDP (as background to the PSBR and public spending objectives), inflation, and unemployment. These projections have knock-on effects on public spending (for example, increases in social security, training programmes) and taxation (falling or rising revenues). There are also demographic factors which need to be taken into account. Together these factors provide the core of the macro-economic context for each public spending round of policy-making.

Each Survey has its own 'character', determined not only by that macro-economic context but by a mix of short-term economic, political, and social factors as well. Part of the work of each Treasury Head of Group is to ensure that the Expenditure Divisions understand and appreciate the significance of these factors and, more widely still, the politico-economic context. The government collectively may have an attitude towards spending: generally favourable in the period of the last Labour Government; antagonistic in the early years of the Conservative Governments of the 1980s, becoming selectively positive in later years, up to 1992. Some programmes may be given higher priority than others. Within the overall objectives set for the aggregate spending totals, specific medium-term objectives have been fashioned for specific programmes and these feed into the Survey discussions. For example, defence spending in the period from 1978 to 1985 was given special preference recognized in the commitment to NATO of 3 per cent per annum real growth. The commitment itself created a substantially altered balance of advantage in favour of the M.o.D. in spending negotiations (the M.o.D. 'got what they wanted without asking') and affected the morale of the relevant Treasury Expenditure Controllers. This was, however, followed by a period after 1985 when the NATO growth commitment was abandoned and the M.o.D.–Treasury relationship was changed substantially. The Labour Government gave a high priority to spending on industrial and employment policy programmes in the last years of the 1970s. Spending on law and order was afforded special status, even within the generally unfavourable spending climate, following the election of the Conservatives in 1979.

There are short-term changes of emphasis too. Government collectively responds to the political timetable: in the run-up to general elections spending deemed important in securing re-election, such as on social programmes, is given higher priority. Crises provoke changes in prioritization, for example during the Falklands War and the miners' strike in 1984–5; and more subtle changes in the perceived political mood (green issues, congestion on roads, educational standards) can often result in the reversal of spending trends. This constant ordering and reordering of priorities is not always explicitly articulated but is discussed ceaselessly in-house in the Expenditure Divisions. Changes in climate occur and a good Expenditure Controller has to be able to make sharp intuitive assessments of the state of the political game, the effect this has on the mind of his or her Minister, and to analyse the relative strength of the case made by the department he or she shadows.

With this broad politico-economic context, up until 1992 decisions about the size of planned public sector spending were made partly as a result of what was considered economically justified or rational, and/or politically desirable or necessary; and partly as a response to continuous pressures for more or less public spending. To over-simplify: while the political and economic strategy of the government collectively might dictate less public spending, and the Treasury acted as a restraining force on the upward progression of spending, the strategies of departmental ministers representing a variety of different pressures normally dictated additional public spending. Up to 1992 the Survey was the public expression of the resultant of the tensions and collisions of the macro-politico-economic strategies of the government of the day, represented by the Chancellor's judgement, and the meso-politico-economic strategies of individual ministers in Whitehall spending departments.

THE SURVEY PROCESSES, 1976–1992

The Public Expenditure Survey

is a marathon exercise. It is not simply the period of negotiation in September and October, though that feels long and gruelling enough. In truth the Survey process is almost a continuous one. As one ends, the next is being planned. Frequently, one set of negotiations will end with an understanding to review a particular area of policy. (John Major, then Chief Secretary to the Treasury, in Major 1988: 6)

The Survey Guidelines

The Survey was conducted each year according to agreed *Guidelines* which provided the policy and procedural rules of the game within which substantive issues could be discussed and negotiated between the Treasury and spending departments. Drafted in the Treasury's General Expenditure Policy (GEP) Division, they were cleared first with the Expenditure Divisions, and then circulated for comment to the Principal Finance Officers of all the spending departments. The agreed *Guidelines* were given Cabinet 'clearance', usually by correspondence prior to the March Cabinet meeting. Not only were they not discussed at Cabinet, they might not appear as an item on the Cabinet agenda. Dispute at that stage was rare, Ministers having been briefed by their Principal Financial Officers at the draft stage, when any problems could be discussed and sorted out with Treasury officials.

The *Guidelines* included rules about the technical preparation of the Survey—for example, the procedures for updating baseline expenditures. In addition, they specified the form in which departmental returns had to be framed, and the timetable for the conduct of the various stages of the Survey. Guidance might also be given on the information required to accompany the Minister's bid for resources. He might be required to review his programme(s); to indicate new priorities, and to explain how and why he had reordered old ones. He might also be required to provide value-for-money and output data in support of the bid, and advised how this should be done. The *Guidelines* might make reference to the procedures to be adopted for dealing with pay in the bids, but with the introduction in 1986 of a separate control regime on the running costs there was no guidance on a central pay assumption.

These early Treasury–departmental exchanges were regarded as essential if the Survey was to proceed smoothly through all its stages. The Treasury aimed to minimize the possibility of problems arising later due to a misunderstanding of what was required, when, and in what form. For example, the 1989 *Guidelines* recorded previous agreements about how local authority elements were to be treated in the new Survey following the introduction of the then new Planning Total.

PESC

In drafting and discussing the *Guidelines* with the departments, the Treasury no longer made use of the Public Expenditure Survey Committee, whose acronym had come to symbolize the whole of the process of planning and controlling public expenditure. As an interdepartmental committee of Principal Finance Officers chaired by a senior Treasury official, PESC had long ceased to play a central and crucial role in the planning of expenditure, as it did in the 1960s following the implementation of the Plowden Report. Nor for some time had it played the role described by Heclo and Wildavsky (1974, 1981) of agreeing a report on the projection of the costs of existing policies. As a committee, it continued to meet under the chairmanship of a Treasury Deputy Secretary until the early 1980s, with the task of overseeing the Survey and discussing the PESC report, comprising baselines plus bids prepared by the Treasury. The report was, however, discontinued in the mid-1980s as a 'waste of time'. In effect it had become a preview of the Survey material, but couched in language bland enough to make it sufficiently acceptable to all the departmental PFOs to ensure an agreed report. Agreement on substantive issues was unlikely as departments preferred to reserve their positions until later in the (then) PESC round. References to PESC disappeared from Treasury descriptions of the planning process (Treasury 1986*d*, 1988*c*); and 'the Survey' replaced 'PESC' as the insider's shorthand for the system of planning and controlling public expenditure as a whole.

PESC no longer meets as a collective. With some 200 names, including the PFOs of all the main departments, 'it is no more than a circulation list' for Treasury instructions and advice on the conduct of the

Survey. As we explained in Chapter 7, some two dozen PFOs of the main spending departments meet informally on an *ad hoc* basis, perhaps four or five times a year. These meetings are convened by the Treasury Deputy Secretary (Public Services), as the occasion warrants, mainly to discuss issues of common concern connected with the conduct of the Survey.

The baseline

The decision on 'what can be afforded' in any future year was derived from immediate past decisions—'what was afforded last year' (and currently being spent)—and what was planned to be spent in the two years ahead. The baseline for the latter two financial years, years one and two of the new Survey, was the total planned expenditures shown in the last Autumn Statement. The government then had to decide by what amount the projected total for the new year three should be increased to take some (but in practice not the full) account of the likely movement in pay and prices. Following the introduction of cash planning in 1982–3, there was no automatic revaluation of planned totals to reflect the actual movement of pay and prices in the previous financial year; nor any attempt to predict and provide in the future for the actual movement in those items. The practice was to revalue on the basis of the GDP deflator used in the MTFS (itself a political statement, since the government wished to underestimate inflation) minus an assumed 'efficiency' gain of about 0.5 per cent. The government did not necessarily follow such a course. Raising the year three baseline by the full amount of inflation created a bias against the Treasury. If it wished to avoid the real growth of expenditure overall, the Treasury had to negotiate money away from low-priority departments in order to give more to those with a higher priority.

Not providing fully for inflation in the general uplifting for year three allowed for reallocations between programmes and the possibility for some programmes to grow faster than inflation. Not all departments needed to be given full allowance for inflation; some needed more. Such factors were then the stuff of the subsequent negotiations when the bids were made. On demand-led programmes like social security separate forecasts were made of what was likely to be spent. But the year three baseline for each was established in the same way by applying the 'uplift-factor'. The difference between the baseline figure and the forecast was treated as a bid in the Survey. The calculation of the baseline therefore affected how the Treasury subsequently looked at departmental bids. In a cash-based public-spending regime there was no presumption that a department would be automatically compensated for inflation.

The baseline totals for three years ahead were the old plans rolled forward. Any policy changes made since the publication of the Autumn Statement and the MTFS were not included in the baselines but incorporated as an agreed part of the appropriate departmental bids for additional resources in the new Survey round. The resulting totals might be 'unaffordable', in the sense that they were inconsistent with assumptions made about the PSBR or tax levels, or with the government's general policy stance on public expenditure. The Chancellor might then advise that less should be 'afforded' than those totals suggested. This was a common reaction of the Conservative Governments throughout the 1980s, with the totals for future planned expenditure set lower than those for present and past spending, without much indication of how the historic trend of rising expenditure was to be halted or reversed.

Establishing the baseline for the three years of the Survey was from the outset an automatic, computer-based exercise, recording the updating of planned expenditures in the previous Survey and the new year three. But even baseline expenditure had to be justified; there were no absolutely inescapable commitments. The *Guidelines* instructed departments to provide data on the baseline calculations by April so that the Treasury computer could be updated. GEP also agreed with Expenditure Divisions what general output data on baseline expenditure departments were expected to provide. As well, individual Expenditure Divisions relayed special requests to their own departments. This output data provided the means to check whether departments had met the expenditure targets agreed with their Expenditure Divisions in earlier Surveys. Departments were required to explain how the agreements struck last year had begun to feed through into output. They had to indicate what they expected this baseline expenditure to produce in the way of outputs. This information was used subsequently by the Treasury to evaluate bids for additional resources and claims of value-for-money. The baseline output data became the 'baseline of output measures' for the bids. Expenditure Divisions sometimes used the data instrumentally to have a go at the baseline if they thought that baseline expenditure 'on the ground' had been less effective than expected. Sometimes, departments offered reductions on their baseline expenditure to offset bids for additional resources.

The Budget, normally presented in March, provided further updated information about prices, revenue, growth, unemployment, and interest rates but did not lead to recalculation of the baseline. It might, however, affect departmental bids for additional resources above the baseline later on, and the attitude of the Treasury towards them in the bilaterals.

BIDDING FOR ADDITIONAL RESOURCES

Once the baseline had been established, departments were notified by the Treasury of the agreed figures for the 'nine-year spread' (five past years, the current year, and three forward years). They then bid for additional resources for the coming year, as well as for the two succeeding years. Most of these bids were the subject of continuing discussions between the departmental Finance Divisions and Treasury Expenditure Divisions throughout the year. Agreement might have been reached some time before the baseline had been established. The nature of the bids reflected a variety of different pressures. First, additional resources might be required to finance a new policy already agreed by government (through Cabinet or Cabinet Committee); secondly, to finance the extension of an existing programme, the costs of which were the subject of continuing negotiation between the Treasury and the department concerned; or, thirdly, to maintain an existing level of service. Here the argument might turn on the ability of the department to improve efficiency sufficiently to compensate for, say, higher than allowed for costs of non-pay items. Fourthly, additional resources might be requested to provide for a larger clientele or increased demand for a service, greater than that estimated in baseline calculations. Fifthly, occasionally a request might be made for resources for a new programme. Although in practice such requests fell early in the subsequent negotiating process, they could provide a department with a useful bargaining device.

Preparations in the spending departments

For the departments a new Survey round began before the completion of the old. The Finance Division discussions with its Expenditure Division on the translation of the settlement published in the Autumn Statement in November into Votes and Estimates in the New Year provided some early indication of the 'flavour of the next round', and how the Treasury was thinking and moving. The handling of in-year control issues provided further evidence.

In November/December Finance Division circulated departmental guidelines to its Policy Divisions and agencies with guidance on strategic issues, for example the department's priorities in the new round, and major policy issues such as the handling of running costs and the reopening of a management plan. There was also guidance on the technical details of the conduct of the departmental bidding process. The policy focus reflected in the *Guidelines* was decided by the Secretary of State on the advice of the department's Senior Management Group, which normally included the Permanent Secretary, Deputy Secretaries, and other heads of directorates and the Chief Executives of agencies. In January Finance Division issued a 'commissioning minute' to all Policy Divisions and agencies inviting bids, briefly surveying the prospective Treasury Survey *Guidelines*, and containing a few paragraphs on particular policy points, for example on whom to consult before making a bid. In the spring, PFOs attended meetings convened by the Treasury Deputy Secretary (Public Services) to discuss major issues arising in the upcoming round, and to comment on drafts of the Treasury's Survey *Guidelines*. Until March, when the latter were circulated, departments were uncertain about the GDP uplift factor to be used in calculating baseline expenditure for third-year totals.

Bids from Policy Divisions and agencies collated by Finance Division were discussed by a PES Group, whose function was to determine the broad strategy for the department's bid and its main priorities, and to advise the Senior Management Group. The membership of the two groups normally overlapped, to ensure that the latter's responsibility for the development of policy and management fed into and informed the deliberations of the PE Group. The membership of the latter varied between departments, but was normally composed at the level of Deputy Secretary and Agency Chief Executive, with secretarial service from Finance Division. Practice varied between departments; much depended on the interest and enthusiasm of the Permanent Secretary for the PES exercise and communication with the Deputy Secretaries.

The bidding process in agencies began earlier and took longer than in Policy Divisions. Where the agency had an Executive and a Commission, its Management Board proposed a strategy to them for discussion in the context of the agreed plan. When this, or an alternative, had been agreed by the Executive and the Commission, it went forward with other bids to the Secretary of State.

Preparations in the Treasury

The Chief Secretary's aims for public spending, shaped in consultation with the Chancellor in the context of the evolving macro-economic strategy, provided the starting-point for the Public Expenditure Survey each year. Some broad indication of their orientation might be evident in the Survey *Guidelines* or in the earlier PFOs' meeting at the Treasury. From then until the meeting of the Cabinet in July, the Chief Secretary considered how far and in what way he could achieve his aims through the setting of the Planning Total.

Between the circulation of the Survey *Guidelines* in March and the receipt of the bids in May/June, the Expenditure Divisions prepared for the forthcoming round. Advice and guidance on the interpretation and application of the *Guidelines* was provided for the Expenditure Divisions through the Treasury Public Expenditure Committee (TPEC), chaired by the Deputy Secretary (Public Services). As explained in Chapter 7, this briefing was different from that provided for the departmental PFOs through PESC, which he also chaired. The latter was concerned more with explaining the rules; the former with how they were to be applied in the coming round. At the same time, Heads of Group were briefed and updated on the development of macroeconomic policy both prior to and following the Budget and the MTFS by the Second Permanent Secretary, formally through COGPEC and PEX, and informally through meetings with him and with their Deputy Secretaries. This information was conveyed by Heads of Groups to their Expenditure Divisions, as preliminary to group discussions of prospects and tactics for the coming round in each Expenditure Division. Each Group talked over the approach to be adopted, considered whether and how to tackle problems left over from the last Survey, and made predictions of the substance and size of the bids expected from their departments.

At about the same time, the Head of GEP met with each Group to take 'stock' of what had happened since the conclusion of the last Survey. The agenda included discussions of the implications of formal and informal policy reviews for particular programmes, and of any problems 'flagged-up' in the last Survey. The implications of decisions on spending proposals or programmes made in-year, outside the Survey, were also discussed. GEP provided a general appreciation of what kind of Survey it was likely to be, in the light of the government's objectives for public spending, and the Chief Secretary's current thinking about strategy. It tried to 'refresh the seasonal message of gloom and doom', to avoid Expenditure Divisions discounting the annual repetition of the need to be tough.

Heads of Group then provided a general assessment of the prospects for the programmes covered by their Expenditure Divisions in the light of economic and demographic factors, in which they considered the probable impact of different political options, both governmental priorities and commitments, and the demands of organized groups. Their assessments were then discussed in some detail with the Chief Secretary, the Second Permanent Secretary, and the relevant Deputy Secretary. The latter might indicate which areas or programmes were vulnerable, and those which were not providing good value-for-money, or where productivity might be raised by moving resources. The discussion involved both technical and policy/political issues. The Chief Secretary indicated which options he wished each Group to take account of.

GEP then helped the Second Permanent Secretary to pull all the assessments together in a wide-ranging review of the prospects for the Survey, bringing together the three main elements: the Chief Secretary's aims for public spending in the context of the government's broad politico-economic strategy; the Second Permanent Secretary's appreciation of the prospects for the main expenditure aggregates in relation to current economic and fiscal policy; and the assessment of trends, pressures, and prospects for each programme fed through GEP from the Expenditure Divisions. These three elements, updated as the Survey progressed, provided the basic material for the expenditure strategy to be proposed by the Chief Secretary to the July Cabinet when Ministers had to decide the Planning Total for the coming year.

The bids

The formal bid letters from the Secretaries of State arrived in the Treasury towards the end of May, each Minister bidding separately to the Chief Secretary. The main purpose was to outline the 'big numbers' of the bid, and to provide the Secretary of State with the opportunity to state and explain the political reasons for the priorities of his proposed spending. Normally most of the issues raised in the letter were predictable and no surprise to the Expenditure Division, related to subjects which were 'very much in play'. Any new issue or emphasis in the letter would normally have been signalled elsewhere, in an earlier communication with the Expenditure Division, or for example in ministerial speeches or statements. Particular kinds of information prescribed in the *Guidelines* might be included in the bid letter, or more probably provided by the department's Financial Division in the more detailed letters to the Treasury which accompanied it.

Some departments preferred to keep the bidding letter short, a 'few paragraphs', and to send some of the supporting detail in accompanying letters. One department sent off twenty such letters within a week of its official submission. Other departments with a spread of disparate activities might send a longer letter. In response to the Expenditure

Division's request some departments might be asked to bid on a 'net basis', providing a 'packaged' or 'bundled' bid in which programme increases and reductions were netted off. But the practice varied, and some Expenditure Divisions requested more detailed bids, disaggregated to show how the bid had been compiled. There were tactical advantages in showing 'offsets' in the bid, but this risked the Treasury responding that they should be greater.

There was no formal contact with Expenditure Division during the preparation of the bid in May, although in some departments there was informal exchange and some advance notice of what the bid contained, and even some hint of the Treasury's probable reaction to parts of it. But generally there was little contact, since the tight time constraint meant that Finance Division was preoccupied with ensuring that the 'pages are in the right order' and that 'the figures add up'.

Copies of all the bids and the accompanying letters were received by GEP, which maintained a 'scorecard', updated weekly as the bids were examined by Expenditure Divisions before and during the ministerial bilaterals. After all the bids were in, 'everybody wants instant reactions and answers: how big are they, how can they be beaten down?' (GEP, Under Secretary). GEP tried to give the Expenditure Divisions a couple of days, to 'crawl all over the letters in detail', before providing any general assessment for the Chief Secretary and the Second Permanent Secretary. This preliminary scrutiny was vital because some of the technical annexes to the bid letters might be disguised requests for more money. As one GEP Under Secretary emphasized: 'We have to see what these are, Secretaries of State are very clever at not saying "I want an extra £5bn" but carefully wording their submission to justify extra money and hiding the figures. We have to get behind the chat and the figures.'

Normally the bids contained few surprises, and conformed closely to the predictions of the Groups made in earlier discussions with GEP. Where those proved inaccurate and the Treasury was 'surprised', GEP tried to establish the reasons for failure. Judgement of the quality and reliability of Expenditure Divisions' assessments, and more particularly that of those making them, was crucial as successive appreciations of the probable outcome of the negotiations over the bids were made, and hence the likely success or failure of the Chief Secretary's strategy. Judgements of why an Expenditure Division was wrong were tested against a background of GEP's own intelligence: what it knew about each Expenditure Division, its track record in previous Surveys, its closeness or distance from its departments, the quality and flow of its information, and its ability to read and interpret signals sent by those departments. GEP's own intelligence also included knowledge of those departments which were difficult, and those Expenditure Divisions with difficult relationships with particular Finance Divisions. GEP also assessed the style in which each Expenditure Controller conveyed resolution and toughness to the spending departments. With those who were 'soft' on their departments, or who had a tendency 'to go native', the Head of GEP would 'probably blow a fuse and lay it on thick that things were very difficult this year'. But both GEP and Expenditure Divisions recognized that it was 'a bit of a game' (GEP Under Secretary).

GEP's aim at this stage was to get a 'first fix'. It pressed Expenditure Divisions to provide 'guesstimates' of the likely outcome to negotiations over their bids. Each Group of Expenditure Divisions was then asked for an assessment of (*a*) the lowest possible outcome; (*b*) what the Treasury might be able to get away with. A Group might respond by offering a 'band' of probable outcomes. GEP might then ask for the implications of delivering at the lower end, where the Group had indicated a higher level. GEP's task was to challenge the Expenditure Divisions. This was necessary, expected, and not resented. The Group's assessment included indications of 'soft bits' of the bid, hard areas, and those parts which would prove difficult to resist. Expenditure Divisions were also pressed to establish what additional information was likely to be required on particular programmes to enable a full assessment of the bids to be made. This provided the agenda for action for each Expenditure Division prior to the July Cabinet.

At the same time as the meetings with each Group and individual Expenditure Divisions, GEP began to work up a general appreciation of the overall picture and to develop ideas to put to the Chief Secretary for the formulation of his grand strategy for achieving the targeted Planning Total. The implications of all the early reactions and guesses on the probable outcomes were brought together and set against the top–down assessment made earlier by the Second Permanent Secretary. At this preliminary stage, GEP assessed whether the overall assessments by the Expenditure Divisions were pitched too high or too low to deliver the targeted Planning Total. The aim was to

get some number which is achievable bottom–up, but which is consistent with the top–down number. There are tensions. Something has to give: either you have to be tough and brutal in the negotiations, or revise fiscal or borrowing strategy. Finding out where the limits are in both directions is part of GEP's task in the Survey. (GEP Under Secretary)

The initial aim was to achieve the target for the Planning Total without any contingent changes in the targets for the Reserve and the proceeds from privatization. Here the GEP Under Secretary had to try to avoid giving Group Heads and their Expenditure Divisions any encouragement that there was room for manœuvre on either. The pressure on them to deliver had to be maintained to the end of the process. However, at that time, but not sooner, in good years but not bad, 'a rabbit can usually be brought out of the hat', whether this was a bit more on privatization proceeds or a reduction in the Reserve, where negotiations in the bilaterals had failed to produce the aimed-for reductions in bids (GEP Under Secretary).

GEP was well placed to form a view about what was happening across all eighteen Expenditure Divisions, and to detect common themes and threads running through the aggregate of the bids. At the same time, it was able to provide Expenditure Divisions with an indication of the Chief Secretary's general stance, and the development of his thinking in reaction to the moving 'scorecard', progress in the Expenditure Divisions, and GEP's own commentaries and assessments. GEP prepared for the Chief Secretary an assessment of inescapable bids, an outline of bids agreed already, for example as a result of policy commitments since the last Autumn Statement, advised what room for further flexibility remained, and how all this fitted in with the overall targets for public expenditure. PEX or COGPEC also met to look at the 'big picture'. If the predicted outcome in GEP's assessment was too out of line with the global figures in the Chief Secretary's strategy, Heads of Groups were asked to go away and look again at their targeted outcomes.

The Chief Secretary thus had an overall picture from the outset of what might happen. As the process of discussion between Expenditure Divisions and departmental Finance Divisions gathered pace in the run-up to the July Cabinet and the subsequent bilaterals, there was continuous communication between GEP and Expenditure Divisions to enable the former to keep abreast of 'the state of play' on each bid and to brief the Chief Secretary accordingly. From the receipt of the bid letters onwards, he was very much involved in the development of the strategy for achieving his expenditure objectives. After GEP had provided an initial assessment of bids and probable outcomes, the Chief Secretary might give instructions for a tougher stance. Groups would be told to be more ambitious in their assessments of what they could deliver by way of cuts. Occasionally, he might indicate that an Expenditure Division was being too tough on a particular programme. The Head of GEP discussed the implications of such instructions with the Groups concerned, and reported back to the Chief Secretary what might be needed in order to deliver more cuts in particular programmes, and advised and warned on the likely political fallout. In turn, the Chief Secretary provided further guidance on his expenditure priorities, and his readiness to deal with those Cabinet colleagues whose programmes might be adversely affected.

'Shadow-boxing'

Bids were rarely settled at the official level as a result of early discussions between the departments. A period of shadow-boxing between each Expenditure Division and the departmental Finance Division continued until Cabinet met in July to decide the expenditure totals for the next three years. The purpose of this process was to enable both sides to brief their respective Ministers for the bilateral negotiations, the formal expression of which was the preparation of an agreed 'Agenda Letter', which the Treasury dispatched to each Secretary of State by the end of August. The aim of the discussions at the official level was to clear as much of the 'undergrowth' as possible in order that the Ministers had a clear, agreed agenda: to expose the issues, to agree the implications of the expenditure figures contained in the bid, to make sure that the Treasury had all the relevant information, or to confirm that that information was not available to the department. From the Treasury's point of view, it was essential that both sides agreed on the salient figures, and the main points of difference between them, so that the ministerial bilateral was a meaningful exercise. Treasury officials probed for weak points in the department's case so that they could produce a comprehensive brief for the Chief Secretary, and help him compose the Treasury's formal response to the bid in the 'Agenda Letter'. The intention of the sparring in the 'official bilaterals' was not to resolve the outstanding issues, but rather to separate the significant from the peripheral.

'Clearing' might begin with the Expenditure Division firing off an 'examination paper' of questions to the Finance Division about the bid, asking for more detail, explanation, or information. These might relate to the information provided by the department in compliance with the *Guidelines*, for example about pay, output data, and value-for-money assessments. The Expenditure Division might earlier have identified 'soft bits of the baseline' and now run some of these in its response to the bid letters. If agreed with the department, such offsets might release savings which could help to finance increases elsewhere in the bid. Sometimes the intention was, as one department alleged, to provide the Chief Secretary 'with easy routes' to reductions, for example by probing for more cuts in declining programmes than were offered in the bid.

In one department, the Expenditure Division selected a half-dozen of the main bids. 'The Grade 5 and Grade 7 [Assistant Secretary and Principal] came over and cross-examined four or five Finance Division people face-to-face. As a result a better understanding was achieved on both sides.' In another case a meeting resulted in a revision to the bid: the Expenditure Division officials indicated that the department had no need to bid for additional resources on one item because it ran on from baseline expenditure. Expenditure Division also suggested how to bid on an item of new expenditure arising from an additional statutory commitment. The informal meeting was held on the basis that it did not prejudice further formal negotiations between the Expenditure Division and the department, but in official correspondence between them there were references to the discussions, and these helped to move towards agreement.

The Expenditure Division might also ask the department to cost various options for reduction, although it might not intend to run all or any of them later in the ministerial bilaterals. The purpose was to feel out the department, and to assess whether any of them were worth running as full-blown options later on. For example, an Expenditure Division might ask the Finance Division to cost a reduced level of activity in a particular part of a programme, and try to get it to establish a linear input/output relationship so that in the later bilateral negotiations the Treasury could read off the savings in inputs from a particular reduction in output. The Finance Division might counter with the argument that the relationship was non-linear. The number of potential options varied, from a handful of bits and pieces to a fairly full shopping list. Costing them required the co-operation of Policy Divisions and agencies, who were often reluctant to provide what they saw as ammunition to be used against them by the Treasury later on in the bilaterals. One Secretary of State with experience of ten spending rounds got 'tetchy' and almost refused to comply. His Finance Division had 'to show him the rules'.

Probing and responding, pushing and pulling, were essential ingredients in the process of seeking more information which might be useful to both sides in the subsequent negotiations. It also enabled the Treasury to explore weak parts of an argument, and to test the department's commitment. Both sides were anxious to avoid the possibility of dispute later in the bilaterals on issues which could be clarified at an earlier stage. Communication between an Expenditure Division and the Finance Division, by letter, phone, and meeting, was continuous. On occasion they might exchange strongly worded letters, but would normally alert each other of their impending arrival.

The three elements of the expenditure strategy—the Chief Secretary's expenditure aims in the context of the government's broad politico-economic strategy, the prospects for the main expenditure aggregates in relation to current economic and fiscal policy, and the assessments of the trends, pressures, and prospects for the individual programmes—all were constantly updated as the bids came in from late May onwards. The balance struck at that stage was a matter for the judgement of the Chief Secretary, advised by the Second Permanent Secretary, who gave his views on the overall situation as he saw it, and offered advice on the kind of ministerial discussion to aim for. He ensured that the Chief Secretary had all the information he needed to make a 'practicable proposal' to his colleagues at the July Cabinet, one which he thought the Chief Secretary, with the help of the Expenditure Divisions, could deliver from them at the conclusion of the Survey.

During this period the Chief Secretary and the Second Permanent Secretary gave constant attention not only to the planned outcome of the total spending strategy, but to its distribution between programmes. The process was iterative, and the interaction between the total and its distribution constant. In addition to the top–down pressure to maintain the agreed Planning Total, judgement about the relative weight and hence priority to be accorded the separate bids was compounded of several elements. First, while the information coming up from Expenditure Divisions about programme-bids incorporated assessments of value-for-money, only some of this was quantifiable, more useful for within-programme than interprogramme and cross-departmental comparisons. As we discussed in the previous chapter, comparisons across programmes and departments were more a matter of political judgement, reflecting the commitments of the government expressed in manifesto and party documents endorsed and particularized in Cabinet agreements; the needs of departments argued in their submissions; and the priorities the departments themselves attached directly or tacitly to different programmes. The Chief Secretary had his own views of the relative merits of his colleagues' bids, and in forming a judgement had the advice of the Second Permanent Secretary helped by the Deputy Secretaries and GEP. Informally the Second Permanent Secretary might advise on what seemed to him to be a reasonable outcome in the light of the official advice tendered.

In preparation for the July Cabinet GEP prepared two papers for the Chief Secretary. The first summarized the bids for additional resources. It incorporated inputs from each Expenditure Division relating to specific bids, in which the form of words used to describe the bid was cleared and agreed with the department. The purpose was to provide

Cabinet with a neutral description of each bid, in uncomplicated language, based on items of programme expenditure. There might be some discussion or even argument with the department about how a bid should be described, but this related to emphasis and nuance rather than substance. Nevertheless the acceptance of an agreed form of words was necessary if some progress was to be made towards a final settlement. The second paper to Cabinet, the Chief Secretary's Memorandum, was drafted by GEP in liaison with the Second Permanent Secretary (Public Expenditure). In it the Chief Secretary commented on the bids, drawing upon material from the Expenditure Divisions, outlined his position on the totality of the bids, and asked the Cabinet to agree to his proposed remit for the rest of the Survey, often in a formula of words to the effect of getting as 'close as possible to the previously agreed Planning Total'. Briefing for the July Cabinet was provided by GEP, but how much and on what depended upon the personality of the Chief Secretary.

The general context for Cabinet's discussion of the implications of the aggregate and the bids for the total of expenditure was provided by a paper on the general economic outlook presented by the Chancellor. Together with the Chief Secretary he advised Cabinet on the appropriate limits for public spending in the next three years. The framework of the MTFS and the Planning Totals from the previous PEWP provided the basis of their advice. John Major, when Chief Secretary, told the Treasury and Civil Service Committee that 'at that stage we either decide that we will reaffirm the planning total that was agreed in previous years, which has often been the case, or perhaps we decide something different' (Treasury and Civil Service Committee 1988*a*: qu. 103). In 1987, 1988, 1990, and 1992 the government did reaffirm Planning Totals. However, the Chancellor's economic strategy might dictate 'something different', as might consideration of what would be politically desirable, as happened in the 1986 Survey in the run-up to the 1987 general election. A leaked exchange of letters between the Chief Secretary, David Mellor, and Michael Howard the Employment Secretary in the 1991 Survey round showed the difficulty of maintaining this stance in a recessionary pre-election period. The Chief Secretary reminded his colleague that Cabinet had agreed at a meeting in May 1991 that 'if we are to preserve our distinctive reputation for financial discipline and avoid the prospect of significant increases in tax rates or borrowing next year, we must keep any increases in amending [*sic*] from current plans to the absolute minimum' (*The Times*, 24 Sept. 1991).

The limit set was usually but not invariably less than the aggregation of the baseline and the additional bids. It was not immovable. Rather it was taken to represent the desirable total towards which the Treasury hoped to move the departments. In the end the Cabinet had to decide how close an approximation was acceptable. In practice, even where the Cabinet agreed to maintain the 'bottom-line' planning total, the sum total of all excess bids after the hectic activity of the autumn frequently breached this figure. The Treasury nevertheless hoped to gain Cabinet agreement anyway to maintain (or even reduce) the Planning Total figure as a symbolic first victory in its attempts to restrain the growth of expenditure.

The bilaterals

The Cabinet having agreed the aggregate Planning Total for the year ahead, the Chief Secretary and his Treasury advisers had then to try to deliver to it that total. At the same time the Treasury discussed with departments provisional figures for years two and three.

At the end of July, the Chief Secretary put into effect the Cabinet's commission to him to get as close as possible to the affirmed Planning Total by writing to each department in response to its bid—the 'Agenda Letters'. He also suggested where savings and offsetting reductions might be made to accommodate bids for additional resources. In the 1991 Survey the Chief Secretary was particularly tough, asking his colleagues to 'look hard not only at their bids, but their base-lines as a whole, in order to eliminate net bids on discretionary programmes'. The leaked exchange of letters in September 1991 showed that the Employment Department had bid for an extra £700 million, whilst the Chief Secretary in his Agenda Letter had proposed savings of £345 million. There was no attempt to compare and offset increases and reductions in different departments in the flurry of letters between the Chief Secretary and his Cabinet colleagues.

GEP's Under Secretary tried to ensure that there was internal consistency of tone and direction across the whole range of Agenda Letters, allocating them and the programmes to which they referred among himself, the Head of GEP1, and his deputy. Together they monitored the progress of the Expenditure Division discussions and ministerial bilaterals through to their conclusion in November.

The Agenda Letters were drafted by the heads of the Expenditure Divisions—Assistant Secretaries and Principals. Heads of Group saw all the drafts and tried to ensure that the detailed response was placed in a wider, appropriate context. The 'feel for the context' was important. Uninvolved in the detailed scrutiny of the bids, Under Secretaries were more detached and had broader experience. What a head of an Expenditure Division thought important might not be the most effective way for the Chief Secretary to conduct his argument. The Head of Group ensured that the latter was able to understand what was being said to him; that the line being taken was convincing; and that the arguments were in a form which he could use in the bilaterals. As Head of the Group, the Under Secretary also looked across several departments and saw what was happening on several fronts: 'Whether a good wheeze here can be applied elsewhere'. The Agenda Letters filtered through the Deputy Secretary to the Chief Secretary. The former might occasionally add a point of substance, but normally would not expect to do so unless he had experience of a particular programme. The drafts were then agreed with the Chief Secretary; sometimes he got involved at an earlier stage in their preparation, meeting with Heads of Group to discuss the line he wanted to take.

Some Expenditure Divisions showed the Finance Division informally a draft of the proposed Agenda Letter, with heads but no numbers. Even where it was not alerted informally, it was possible for the Finance Division to predict what the Treasury would 'run' in the letter. The proposed areas and items for reduction normally caused no surprise, if it had read the signals from the earlier exchanges with the Treasury. The Agenda Letter was normally considered by a department's Senior Management Group, with the Finance Division producing notes to help explain the significance of the Chief Secretary's proposals. The general lines of the response agreed, the Finance Division compiled a briefing pack for the bilaterals, and collated reactions to it from policy divisions and agencies. These were then fed through into the Senior Management Group, which agreed the advice tendered to the Secretary of State.

Before the bilaterals began, a Finance Division tried to agree the 'numbers', so that both sides started from the same base-calculations. An Expenditure Division's aim was to get its case for the bilateral solidly grounded in the data. There might be 'tweaking at the edges', and second or third drafts of the Agenda Letter incorporating fairly minor adjustments. Both sides aimed to avoid wasting time in the bilaterals in discussion of the numbers rather than their respective interpretations of them. Even at this late stage, the options exercise might not be completed, as an Expenditure Division might have asked for further information to enable it to be as clear as possible about an option it proposed the Chief Secretary should run in the bilaterals. The aim was to be able to defend to him, and in the bilaterals, the consequences of, say, a given reduction in output for a given cut in resources. While an Expenditure Division could not be sure how the department would respond in the bilaterals, it wanted to have a clear picture of the data needed to pursue a particular line. It wanted to avoid the embarrassment there to the Chief Secretary if the department produced data which the Expenditure Divisions could have obtained earlier through the options exercise and the 'shadow-boxing'.

Bilateral negotiations began in September, their aim to resolve those differences which remained outstanding from the earlier discussions of the bids between Treasury officials in the Expenditure Divisions and those in the Finance and Policy Divisions of the spending departments. Not all departments were involved; some bids were settled without ministerial intervention, and, on occasion, a late compromise by a Minister in accepting offsetting reductions or withdrawing a bid altogether removed the need for further discussions. Those bilaterals which took place were conducted between the Chief Secretary on the one hand and a departmental Minister or Ministers on the other. The Chancellor was very rarely brought into the discussions. From 1976 appeal over the head of the Chief Secretary to the Chancellor was formally inadmissible, but in practice relationships were not regulated as rigidly as that implies. While there was a strong presumption that the Chief Secretary's decision would not be overturned, the Chancellor might see a spending minister and discuss it informally with him (Lawson 1992: 720).

The period of the bilaterals was one of intense and constant activity for the Chief Secretary, requiring a combination of intellectual skills to master complex and detailed subject-matter, physical stamina, and determination. He needed to be able to master simultaneously anything up to a couple of dozen very detailed briefs, and to conduct a ceaseless round of meetings with his colleagues, some of which often lasted four or five hours. While he had the support, advice, and briefing of his officials, he alone conducted the negotiation with his ministerial colleague.

The Chief Secretary operated under three sorts of often conflicting pressures: first, and pre-eminently, the pressure to deliver the Planning Total which, inevitably 'oversubscribed', meant that he had to bear down on all his colleagues when he negotiated with each separately. Secondly, he had to respond to the pressure from each of his departmental colleagues to provide sufficient resources to enable them to provide both the goods and services required by the statutory obligations imposed upon them, and any additional resources which colleagues collectively in Cabinet might have agreed to in their approval of a new or revised policy. Thirdly, in resolving or trading off these two pressures he had to try to ensure that the consequences of the series of bilateral negotiations were acceptable collectively to his Cabinet colleagues. While the priorities of spending were not determined specifically after interprogramme comparisons of value-for-money, nevertheless the effect of the bilaterals was to adjust marginally the priority between one programme and another. If Cabinet was to approve the final settlement in November, the Chief Secretary had to 'get it about right'. One former Chief Secretary held the view that it was easier to achieve a collectively acceptable settlement by proceeding through bilateral discussions with his colleagues, than through multilateral discussions in Cabinet, as happened with the Labour Governments of the late 1970s. Paradoxically, while until 1992 there was less formal opportunity for collective Cabinet discussion of the priorities of public expenditure under Conservative Governments, there was, it is argued, greater collective responsibility because the Chief Secretary's task was to 'inject collective responsibility into the separate discussions leading to settlement' (former Chief Secretary). Conversely, under Labour the continual need to cut public expenditure *ad hoc* as recurring crises dictated meant that there was more collective discussion and responsibility for the schedule of cuts, but as Barnett (1982) admits, little attempt to inject any order of priority.

One former Chief Secretary described bilaterals as straight negotiations with his colleagues, and likened them to those with EC agricultural ministers over CAP, although the latter were longer and more exhausting. He occasionally overruled Treasury officials' advice on the grounds of political infeasibility because what was suggested 'wouldn't run' or was politically inept, but this happened infrequently because senior Treasury officials were acutely aware of the politics and what was feasible. Normally the line the Chief Secretary wanted to take was well understood and reflected in the briefing material prepared in detail in the Expenditure Divisions; Group Heads provided briefing on wider issues and on tactics. Neither the Permanent nor Deputy Secretaries were involved in the detailed briefing, but all the material was filtered through them, and they also advised on tactics. A Deputy Secretary might also provide the opening and closing speaking notes for the Chief Secretary; the Chief Secretary sometimes asked for additional briefing to support the case he wanted to argue.

In the late 1980s and early 1990s, the Second Permanent Secretary divided the spending programmes between himself and his Deputy Secretaries on the basis of their day-to-day responsibilities, knowledge, and experience. A recent incumbent took most of the larger programmes, such as defence (both because of its size, and because the Under Secretary reported directly to him), social security, and education. He also took responsibility for those programmes handled outside the expenditure command, such as the overseas programmes and the revenue departments. The Deputy Secretary (Public Services) took responsibility for the D.o.E., health, and territorial programmes, and the Deputy Secretary (Industry) took industry, employment, and agriculture. The Second Permanent Secretary attended the initial meeting on each programme with the Chief Secretary to consider the general strategy for that programme, but attendance at the bilaterals thereafter was split between him and the Deputy Secretaries who covered the programmes on which they were leading. Thereafter, the Second Permanent Secretary advised the Chief Secretary on the appropriate tactics on the few programmes where parts of a bid remained unresolved, whether to 'have another go', perhaps tête-à-tête with the departmental Minister, or to consider invoking the Star Chamber. Where the latter was instituted, the Second Permanent Secretary advised on the overall strategy and the individual tactics with regard to each bid, but could not himself attend, as the Star Chamber was a Cabinet subcommittee. However, GEP provided part of the secretariat, which established a useful link.

The Head of GEP was involved in private discussions with both the Chief Secretary and the Second Permanent Secretary on the formulation and progressive development of the overall strategy. As explained, briefing on the details and tactics for each separate bilateral was provided mainly by the Expenditure Division concerned and its Head of Group. GEP's contribution was concerned mainly with the overall picture, which it was uniquely placed to provide, and to ask hard questions from its detached, above-the-battle perspective. It might press for more progress on a particular bilateral because of the need to get nearer the global target for the Planning Total, and in the knowledge that cuts elsewhere were more difficult to obtain. The Head of GEP also tried to ensure that all the angles were covered, in case the Chief Secretary was pressed hard on a particular issue.

The first meeting of a Treasury–departmental bilateral was normally very formal, with a large attendance. The Treasury's representatives, besides the Chief Secretary, included normally the Second Permanent Secretary, as well as the Deputy Secretary with responsibility for the programmes concerned. Treasury Under Secretaries with responsibility for an expenditure group—social services, or home, transport, and education, for example—attended as appropriate, together with those Heads of Division (Assistant Secretaries) and their Principals who together had responsibility for particular programmes within a group. In addition, a representative from GEP attended, together with those from the Treasury territorial expenditure divisions. On the other side, the departmental representatives included the Secretary of State, the

Minister of State concerned with the programme(s) under discussion, the Permanent Secretary, and senior officials from the Finance Division. Representatives from the territorial departments often attended, and at the Permanent Secretary level.

At this first formal meeting the Secretary of State outlined his bids, and the Chief Secretary made formal comments in reply. Some discussion and haggling might take place, but the real negotiations began at the second and subsequent smaller bilaterals, with discussion more sharply focused on the issues presented in the Agenda Letters. Nothing was given away by either side at the first bilateral. Subsequently, there might be several meetings between the Chief Secretary and the Minister before an agreement (or impasse) was reached. Few meetings were shorter than three hours; in 1988 several went on for longer than five. The most protracted 'involved six separate meetings of an average of three hours each' (Treasury and Civil Service Committee 1987*c*: qu. 149). The attendance and format varied. Sometimes it comprised small groups of officials on both sides; on other occasions the Chief Secretary and an official might talk to the Secretary of State and his official, sometimes for an hour or more; or the two Ministers might have a tête-à-tête, with officials from both sides sent away to discuss and report back. Where only one or two officials were present, then normally the Head of the Expenditure Division (Assistant Secretary) would attend to cover the detail, and the Head of Group, to advise on tactics, for example by passing notes to the Chief Secretary suggesting 'if we give up £40m on this we can get £50m off that'.

At the second bilateral, some things might be given away. Between bilaterals, consultations between officials on both sides was intense, following up points where further information had been promised. There might be recalculations: 'supposing we did it this way . . .'. The key, one Deputy PFO explained, was to read the 'signals' as well as to respond to the formal positions taken up by the Chief Secretary, his advisers, and the Expenditure Divisions. 'With experience you learn to pick up signals of what might be acceptable, what might be the best way to present a case.' It was an advantage to have in the departmental team people with experience of the bilaterals. Each successive bilateral with a Secretary of State began from a new base, as he reduced his bids. One estimate from a Deputy PFO was that normally 'you get about a third of what you have bid'. For each bid 'you need to know where the bottom line is'. The negotiations were not quid pro quo: for agreed reductions, the Treasury offered nothing in return.

The notes of such bilaterals and the agreements reached were often long, complex, and themselves the subject of further discussion between the Treasury and a department. After agreement at the bilaterals (or in Cabinet), Finance Division had to agree the 'fine print' of the settlement. The months from October to December were taken up with the translation of the agreed bids into Estimates, and, in departments, with a 'share-out' of those parts of the bid which were settled on a group basis, such as running costs, or where the Survey settlement did not specify a particular division of resources.

What kinds of arguments were deployed in those negotiations? How were they conducted? In the process of continuous discussions throughout the year with departmental Finance Divisions, the Treasury Expenditure Divisions built up a picture of what the department was trying to do and how well it was doing. Its programmes were subjected to scrutiny, analysis, and evaluation in a continuous process. As one Survey ends, 'the next is being planned'. There might have been an 'understanding to review a particular area of policy', and this would be put into operation. 'By the time the Survey negotiations begin, a great deal of material will have been assembled on how policies are working and on the options for change' (Major 1988: 6). Since there were relatively few Treasury officials in the Expenditure Divisions to cover the range of spending, and a proportionately greater number of officials responsible for spending, the Treasury had to be selective in the areas of expenditure to be scrutinized in this way.

The department's bid was calculated in cash. It comprised requests for additional resources for some of its programmes; for others it offered reductions where it estimated a lower level of provision was required, or where the service was being cut back or scaled down in accordance with a policy decision. It might volunteer savings on some programmes which were thought to be less cost-effective. The Treasury Expenditure Controllers also pressed for cuts in the 'soft' part of the baseline in order to make room for a bid for extra resources. Over the past few years, the Treasury had obliged departments to achieve annual gains in productivity; for running costs this was set at a minimum of 1.5 per cent, although the Treasury pressed for greater gains where feasible. The amount requested varied from department to department. In bidding, departments were expected to provide evidence of such efficiency gains. In its scrutiny the Treasury encouraged them to set more ambitious targets. Signs of poor departmental efficiency or inadequate programme performance appraisal made it easy for an Expenditure Controller to find a weakness in a bid and brief the Chief Secretary accordingly.

The Chief Secretary sometimes asked the department for 'non-specific reductions'. The Finance Division might then, without disclosure to the Treasury, run a few options of those areas where cuts could be made, and give its Policy Divisions an opportunity to examine them. A departmental Deputy Secretary and his divisions might react by objecting to a proposed 'pecking order', and propose alternative priorities for cuts, or slicing the cuts differently between them. Alternatively Finance Division might say to each of its Deputy Secretaries 'We think these are the soft parts of your bid and we have put you down for x cuts'. But before submission to the Secretary of State, they had the opportunity to object, argue, and propose alternatives. One departmental Finance Division had to take the initiative because inviting Policy Divisions to identify cuts was fruitless: they 'never offer up cuts "cold"' (PFO, major spending department). This had the advantage for a Policy Division that it was not seen to be volunteering cuts, but responding to pressure from the Finance Division. It was then in a better position to sell the idea to its constituents. In one large department, a more 'democratic' approach had proved possible in recent years, and the Finance Division had been able to involve its Policy Divisions more closely in hard choices. Instead of imposing decisions upon them, there was a more negotiative process, aided by computerization. Previously, the Finance Division had to make decisions often without consultation because in a non-computerized form it could not handle the enormous amounts of data required for a wide-ranging exercise of alternative options, or respond quickly enough in the fast-moving bilateral negotiations. After the change, it could get information from the Policy Divisions, rework it according to changed assumptions, and send it back quickly. As a result, the burden of choice moved much more towards them, with the advantage for the Finance Division that it was blamed less for imposing decisions. It was better able to play its proper role of facilitating decisions. Without an objective method of prioritizing cuts which commanded the confidence of the Policy Divisions, the guided democratic approach was felt to be a more effective way of combining flexibility and movement with some degree of consensus.

The distribution of the settlement agreed with the Treasury was an exercise in intra-departmental politics. Finance Division normally knew which bids had been 'stuffed', as Policy Divisions and agencies were required to give the Secretary of State the bottom line for each bid to enable him to negotiate with the Chief Secretary. During the course of bilaterals, a Finance Division did not normally consult Policy Divisions and agencies, but Deputy Secretaries were involved where there were changes to bids or tactics. The bids and the priorities between them were the Secretary of State's, and in the course of a negotiation he might change the rank order, or even drop a bid entirely. The allocation of the running costs settlement was the most sensitive part of the share-out, and often the most contentious where Policy Divisions and agencies felt aggrieved at the Finance Division's apportionment of reduced shares following an unsuccessful departmental bid.

The relative price effect

In the discussion of departmental bids, both before and at the time of the bilaterals, departments often supported their bids for additional resources by providing evidence of the effects of differential price increases on their programmes. Since 1981, the Treasury's aim had been to switch attention and emphasis in the planning of expenditure from inputs to outputs. One important consequence of that change was the abandonment of the principle of the relative price effect (RPE) and attempts to measure and provide for it in the allocations to departmental programmes. Time and again, Treasury ministers and officials insisted that the RPE was flawed methodologically, and inappropriate in practice to a cash-planning regime: attempts to measure the differential effects of inflation on departmental programmes failed to take account of gains in productivity, efficiency, and the quality of a service, it was argued. If the effects of inflation were compensated in full, there was less incentive for programme managers to produce the same output with fewer resources. As many departments were in a monopsonist position, they could dictate or influence the prices they paid for goods and services, rather than passively accept the levels set by suppliers.

From the abandonment of volume planning in 1982, it was suspected but difficult to prove that departments continued to collect data about the movement of the prices they paid for the supply of goods and services for individual programmes, and used such data to construct price indices for their programmes. This was never admitted publicly, but it was suspected that 'volumes had gone underground' (Pliatzky 1983). The Treasury conceded only that some departments might make 'own-cost' calculations for their internal use. It denied that they were used in discussions or bilaterals between the Treasury and the spending departments.

In practice, the position was not quite so clear-cut. First, it was admitted that a number of departments construct 'programme specific price indices, or figures for expenditure deflated by such indices' (Treasury and Civil Service Committee 1988*a*: app. 3). These were of three kinds: commodity-input price effects, programme-wide input price effects, and output unit costs. The Treasury encouraged departments to collect information on commodity prices and their effects in order to monitor the efficiency of their purchasing arrangements. It also encouraged them to collect data on unit costs. It was, however, sceptical about the validity and value of programme-wide input price data. Such data on programme-wide relative price effects was held to be worthless. The Treasury argued that programme-wide input-price data was disparate, mixing the very different price effects of several different kinds of expenditure. Input-data was useful only if the commodity stayed the same over time. For example, lumping together YTS payments, dock labour payments, and computer prices in a Department of Employment programme-wide input-price index was unhelpful. Moreover the collection and collation of data on that basis was time-consuming. But as one Chief Secretary acknowledged, 'if you ever conduct a public expenditure discussion it is pretty impossible to stop your colleagues discussing what may best suit their argument'. They argued that 'there are relative price effects that involve extra expenditure for their budgets' (Major in Treasury and Civil Service Committee 1988*d*: qus. 132 and 166). He confirmed that data on commodity-input prices and output unit costs might in certain circumstances be admissible in negotiations.

In the course of the survey discussions departments will bring forward evidence of the position they face . . . whether it is on pay, procurement or whatever. That is taken into account in the settlement that is reached. It is not taken to the point of calculating formal indices, but in a number of cases pay or rents, for example, were brought in as evidence of a need for additional provision. (Major, qu. 25)

On some occasions (as here) the arguments marshalled and deployed by departments relating to the relative price effect and departmental price differentials 'are compelling for one reason or another and the cash settlement tends to reflect that' (Major, qu. 166).

   Not only was the Treasury prepared on some occasions to adjust cash allocations to particular programmes to accommodate relative price effects, it was also prepared to compensate departments retrospectively for the adverse effects of such price movements.

We do not generally admit the principle of retrospective additions to programmes as a result of past historic relative price effects that were malign to the programme. It would be an exceptional programme but we would not rule it out of discussion and we did not [in 1988] in terms of the transport programme. (Major, qu. 171)

Negotiations with the Department of Transport over the road-building programme resulted in a planned increase of 20 per cent between 1988–9 and 1989–90. The Secretary of State had argued that civil-engineering costs had risen after remaining static for many previous years. While the Treasury did not relate that precisely to the relative price effect . . . it was a factor the Secretary of State drew our attention to and which we discussed during the public expenditure round. So, in essence, on this occasion, and in view of the importance of the road programme, we accepted that there were genuine problems facing the road building programme. That was the basis of the very significant increases in resources for road building programmes, for maintenance programmes and indeed the increased bridge strengthening programme that is necessary over the next five to ten years. (Major, qu. 168)

The Chief Secretary, asked by the Treasury and Civil Service Committee what his response would be to a Minister who argued that he had been unable to carry through a particular programme agreed between himself and the Treasury because the inflation assumption provided in his cash allocation had proved incorrect, replied:

Sympathetic to the extent that I would be prepared to admit that as an argument during our discussion and would not regard it as wholly offside, but not to the extent that I would automatically cede up the loss the Secretary of State felt he had suffered in the previous year. I would regard that as a legitimate matter for the Secretary of State to raise with me, but I would not automatically accept it as a claim I would have to necessarily meet in the public expenditure negotiations. That would depend on the resources available to meet it, the relative priority and importance of the programme and in particular the relative priority of that programme set against other priorities it was apparent had to be met during the public expenditure round. (Major, qu. 169)

The Treasury could be persuaded; and it was prepared to administer flexibly the rule that departments are required to live within cash allocations which do not provide for the full effects of inflation. There was a real incentive, if any was needed, for departments in negotiations with the Treasury to construct and present time-series data showing the differential effects of inflation on their programme. Where this related to specific commodity input-price effects or output unit costs they had some expectation of success. The Treasury was willing even to protect some departments from the effects of above-average increases in pay. In recent years, the D.o.H. had been uniquely protected from the relative price effect of wage increases in the NHS (Major, qu. 167). Besides the allowance for pay provided in the cash plans agreed in the negotiation, the awards to nurses, doctors, and other groups made by review bodies and agreed to by the government were 'met in full or nearly in full'.

In discussion of claims for additional resources grounded in arguments about the RPE and historic price differentials, the Treasury looked for evidence that the department was trying to meet rising costs by offering savings within the programme: 'the extent to which the programme is trying, itself, to consume the difficulties it faces as a result of particular price increases' (Major, qu. 172). It also sought explanation of why prices had gone against a department, and encouraged it to consider changing the mix of inputs within a programme in order to reduce costs. As well, it encouraged all departments with purchasing-power to 'make rather than take prices'.

The conduct of the bilateral negotiations

'People imagine that the negotiations are simply a process of political horse-trading. I wish it were that simple. Reality is both more mundane and more complex, and certainly more exhausting' (Major 1988: 7). The bilaterals were confidential. Evidence of how the negotiations were conducted is not easy to obtain, other than from the occasional leaks to newspapers and the anecdotal memoirs of Ministers and civil servants. Such revelations have tended to reinforce the claims of those who characterize the process as 'horse-trading' or bargaining, with the strong implication that decisions made thus lack 'rationality'. What is usually meant by this implied criticism is that decisions made about the financing of public expenditure programmes should be taken in some more 'objective' way, in which the merits of individual cases are assessed according to some agreed economic or financial or other criterion, compared, and ranked. The lack of any such acceptable criteria, and the difficulty of making valid comparisons given the lack of comparative data on performance and output, was discussed in the previous chapter. In their absence, the exploration through informal argument and counter-argument of the nature and extent of differences, and the attempt to negotiate and bargain the terms upon which those differences might be settled, is a rational procedure. Often those who argue for a 'rational' system are trying to remove politics from what is the most political of activities—fighting for resources. It is of course easy to characterize the process, as some have done, as 'mere haggling' or 'horse-trading', with overtones of the disreputable or dishonest behaviour popularly associated with those who deal in horses, in which the qualities of the horse may be misrepresented, and the purchaser misled by inaccurate or false information.

Both horse-traders and Ministers in bilaterals are engaged in a negotiation, seeking to establish the terms on which they can agree a settlement, and perhaps strike the bargain. We can characterize their conduct as, first, a transaction between parties who exchange information and signal intentions. Secondly, that transaction is adversarial rather than inquisitorial or adjudicatory. The parties seek to persuade each other through argument of the merits of the case. Thirdly, at this stage there is no arbiter, nor any appeal to objective, independent valuations. These characteristics determine a fourth: the process and settlement are 'satisficing' rather than optimal. While each party aims to maximize its values and satisfaction, it is also prepared at least to contemplate accepting something less; there is a willingness to seek compromise which accommodates conflicting interests.

A negotiation need not entail bargaining. A discussion may lead to a mutually acceptable agreement. In bilaterals, however, it was inherently unlikely. By definition, the bilateral was necessary because previous discussions had failed to produce an agreement, or to settle differences. Ministers had to negotiate the terms of a possible settlement in which both parties were obliged to 'give and take'; they had to bargain.

How then were the bargains struck? Bilaterals in the 1980s and 1990s under Conservative Governments were conducted in a different political and economic context to that of the late 1970s. Until 1992 there was no atmosphere of crisis or impending crisis as there was then, and government attitudes towards public spending had changed. A more concerted attempt was made to measure and assess performance, aided by improvements in departments' management information systems, spurred on by FMI and associated efficiency initiatives. But while the opportunity existed for both sides in the bilateral to play the game with improved and new 'counters', the rules of the game do not appear to have changed all that much, on the evidence of contemporary participants (Rees 1984; Bruce-Gardyne 1986; Lawson 1992).

In the spending round concluded in the autumn of 1990, the leak of a draft letter exposing the negotiating tactics of the Secretary of State for Health in his bilaterals with the Chief Secretary provided an insight into how that game was played (Thain and Wright 1990*g*). Kenneth Clarke had bid for £2.7 billion new money. The Treasury demurred and sought reductions. Kenneth Clarke responded with an opening offer to reduce his bid by £172 million, which the Treasury considered inadequate. Department of Health officials then learnt from officials in the Treasury's Expenditure Division that if they offered up a reduction of the order of £500–600 million it would be regarded as 'constructive'. On the advice of his officials, the Secretary of State then offered reductions totalling £431 million. At this point, the draft of a letter to the Treasury was leaked. It revealed both the Department of Health's 'negotiating margin', and its 'bottom line'. The latter was about £1.8 billion, and hence the negotiating margin was some £800–900 million. The final settlement, at £2.2 billion, was some way above the bottom line.

The 1990 bilaterals were unusual in another respect: Prime Minister Thatcher chose to intervene publicly. Before the Conservative Party

Conference, Mrs Thatcher wrote to those Ministers who had not yet settled to remind them of the need for restraint, and threatening that an appeal to the Star Chamber would result in their securing less than was on offer in discussion with the Chief Secretary. While Prime Ministerial exhortations to parsimony in the bidding process were common enough at the time of the July Cabinet, and even in the run-up to the bilaterals, a calculatedly public reminder to colleagues locked in discussions with the Chief Secretary was unusual. Nor was it Mrs Thatcher's only intervention. Her intercession on child benefit was decisive: she overruled the Treasury's insistence on a fourth successive freezing of Child Benefit, after the Minister for Social Security had apparently already conceded the principle to the Chief Secretary. The grounds on which she did so were dictated by political expediency, following the disastrous Conservative result at the Eastbourne by-election, and divisions among her back-benchers over the principle and payment of Child Benefit. It is less clear how much pressure was brought to bear on Mr MacGregor when summoned to No. 10 to discuss his position on education vouchers and his difference with the Chief Secretary. Shortly after, he settled and the Star Chamber was stood down.

The effect of the former Prime Minister's public intervention on her other colleagues is difficult to gauge. It is true that, shortly after, those Ministers who had equally publicly let it be known that they were contemplating an appeal to the Star Chamber settled their differences with the Chief Secretary. Public statements were of course part of the tactics employed by both sides to pressurize each other. It is possible that the four or five Ministers who were holding out settled a little sooner, and for a little less, than they would have done without the Prime Minister's intervention. More likely, those Ministers were less deterred by the Prime Minister's threat than their belief that they had got almost as much as they had expected, if less than they had hoped for, from the bilaterals. Most won between a third and a half of what they bid for, an average amount. As with Kenneth Clarke, they had obtained a settlement above their bottom lines. Little more was to be gained by appealing over the Chief Secretary's head in defiance of the Prime Minister's public admonition.

If the bilateral was brought to an agreed conclusion the parties had to agree what it was they had decided. Notes of the agreement were prepared by the Treasury, cleared with all those involved on the Treasury side, and then sent to the department. Further negotiation and amendment might take place on both sides, to try to 'shade' the points made in argument in the bilateral in an attempt to secure further advantage.

A number of general observations may be made about the conduct of the bilaterals. First, Treasury officials and their opposite numbers tried to define (and perhaps narrow) the areas and size of potential disagreement before the ministerial bilaterals began. In that process, the Treasury learnt something of the negotiable limits: what the department might be prepared to offer for 'openers' and what it might be prepared to settle for in a 'next-best' strategy; which items were non-negotiable; and a feel for the 'bottom line'. Conversely, by the autumn, the department had a pretty good idea and feel for the general 'tone' of the Survey round, and of the Treasury's attitude to its bid. The strategy adopted by each was influenced by consideration of 'anticipated reactions'.

Secondly, the conduct of the negotiations was influenced by the degree of priority attached to the department's programme(s). The Minister's negotiating position was strengthened if his programme had an established political priority from an earlier manifesto commitment, or a party or government pledge, or because it had acquired an enhanced priority as a result of some political development or a recent policy review. Thirdly, the personality, ability, determination, and status of the Minister and the Chief Secretary were factors which affected the outcome of the negotiation. 'Political clout' was a more important ingredient, especially where a department had an acknowledged priority, such as DHSS in 1988. Fourthly, there is little evidence from the 1970s onwards that Treasury ministers and officials attempted to use the bilaterals as a vehicle for explicit interdepartmental comparisons in order to rank bids in an order of priority. Each bid was considered on its merits.

Finally, the kinds of evidence and arguments deployed in the bilaterals suggest that there was more flexibility in the planning of public expenditure than was apparent from the formal position adopted by the Treasury. In practice, it was responsive to the arguments made *ad hominem* by each department; each case was decided on its merits. However, if greater priority was accorded a particular programme as a result of the 'compelling' evidence of the effects of relative prices within a programme, or output unit costs, that decision was made without consideration of the relative priority of other programmes where comparable evidence was not provided or was unobtainable, or was ruled inadmissible. Without the submission of such evidence from all departments, for all programmes, interdepartmental and interprogramme comparisons were partial and incomplete. The admissibility of such data was accepted only in cases defined by the Treasury as exceptional. If it was accepted that all departments could legitimately argue from such premisses, the discipline of cash allocations bearing down on costs would have been at risk, a short step to volume planning and the resumption of 'entrenched entitlements'.

Where no agreement had proved possible on a bid, or parts of it, the Minister or the Chief Secretary might appeal to the Star Chamber. Both sides wanted to settle as much as they could in the bilateral, not least because the absence of officials on both sides increased the unpredictability of Star Chamber judgements. It was in the interests of both to keep as much in their own hands and control as possible. The composition, convening, and work of the Star Chamber is discussed more fully in Chapter 13.

Following meetings of the Star Chamber, where it was necessary to convene it, the Cabinet met in November to approve the agreements reached in the Survey round, and to resolve any outstanding differences which the Star Chamber might have been unable to settle. Here the Cabinet decided (or ratified) where the final line was to be drawn, which was often higher than that set at its earlier meeting in July, as in 1990 when the Planning Total was set some £8 billion higher than that agreed earlier. The publication of the agreed totals for the next three years in the Autumn Statement followed shortly after, and completed the bidding and allocating processes of the Survey. It remained to convert the Survey figures into Parliamentary Estimates and fill in the details of the broad agreements in Departmental Reports which were published early in the New Year.

The post-mortem

An internal Treasury post-mortem and evaluation of the whole PES round was conducted at the conclusion of the Survey processes in November. A written report was prepared on the Treasury's performance in the Survey, with lessons to be learnt for the future, and recommendations on how to do better next time. It provided an opportunity to 'fund experience'. Its preparation was the particular responsibility of the Treasury's Second Permanent Secretary (Public Expenditure) and his 'chief of staff' in charge of GEP. In practice it was co-ordinated by the Assistant Secretary in charge of GEP1, who invited contributions from all the Expenditure Divisions, Heads of Group, and Deputy Secretaries, and himself prepared the initial draft of what was in effect the 'official history' of the Survey. After discussion with Deputy Secretaries and the Second Permanent Secretary, it went to COGPEC. It provided a factual account of what happened at each stage in the process, and details of the bids and how they were settled. The series of reports comprise the Treasury's collective memory of what occurred and why, year by year, to be drawn upon by GEP as an *aide-mémoire* in the preparation of future Surveys. From it, it was possible to track departments' bidding records, strategies, and successes; to identify those which bid high or low; and to spot changes in approach and tactics. It provided as well a written record of the accuracy of Treasury predictions and 'guesstimates' of the outcomes, division by division, and overall. As well as reporting on what happened, it contained recommendations for action. It consolidated reactions and suggestions made during the Survey, as experience showed the effectiveness or otherwise of certain tactics or courses of action. Procedural changes were also noted: how particular kinds of data should be handled by the Expenditure Divisions, or the procedure for conducting a bilateral with a particular department. It also highlighted those areas and parts of programmes to which special attention should be given in future Surveys—'soft bits' where the potential for more cuts looked promising. Reflecting upon the experience of the past twelve months, the review could lead to major system changes such as the redefinition of the Planning Total in 1988, or to changes in the rules of the game to be discussed with PFOs and included in the next Survey *Guidelines*. At the same time, there was an assessment of the strengths and weaknesses of the preferred expenditure strategy, and of the effectiveness of the tactics employed by each Expenditure Division.

CONCLUSIONS: THE SURVEY IN THE 1990s

The Survey is methodologically almost unrecognizable from that eulogized by Heclo and Wildavsky in the 1970s. The overriding concern since the failure to cut public expenditure in the early years of the Thatcher Government has been to provide and maintain a system which provided for tight control of nominal expenditure while bearing down simultaneously on costs. The planning imperative which drove the Survey in its early years, and which survived the importation of cash limits, has all but disappeared. The Treasury's brief and (with hindsight) disastrous flirtation with planning volumes of public expenditure was abandoned with the prescription of cash planning. It remained vestigially in the prescription of Planning Total aggregates for three years ahead, but the programme allocations which comprised them became little more than stylized projections after 1984 when the size of the annual Reserve was increased and its use changed as an explicit device to control all changes to planned expenditure, both in-Survey and in-year. These planning projections became control totals after the introduction of the New Control Total in 1992. In effect the Survey has become a more elaborate and technically sophisticated successor to the annual estimating process of the *status quo ante* Plowden.

The process by which those decisions are made, legitimated, and made public has changed much less. What takes place, and when, in the stages of the annual Survey cycle is similar to the situation a decade or more ago. Of course procedures have become more elaborate, and with time, experience, and repetition many have become institutionalized. They also reflect the changes in methodology described above, as well as the increasing emphasis on obtaining value-for-money. Some informal structures for dealing with expenditure business have become more formal, as in the set-piece Cabinet rituals in October and November. The *ad hoc* arrangements which were sometimes made in the 1970s for the collective resolution of conflict in the Survey negotiations between the Treasury and spending ministers were formalized in the 1980s with, first, the institution of the Star Chamber, and then after 1992 by EDX. Other processes of negotiation and agreement have become more formally structured by the codification of practices relating to both policy and behaviour. The Survey *Guidelines*, the 'rules' governing the form, content, submission, and handling of 'bidding' letters, the consolidation of baselines, and 'shadow-boxing', are all examples of both.

What the Survey deals with has changed too. The continual redefining of public spending has served to manage the presentation of public-spending plans and, by removing and then returning some categories of expenditure from the Survey—such as local authority self-financed spending, which was included in the Planning Total until 1989, removed from the New Planning Total, only then reinstated in the New Control Total in 1992—has been part of the Treasury's continual political battle to constrain public-sector agencies. How the Survey business is dealt with has also changed. Through the 1980s the bidding process became more formalized and its scope narrowed. Baseline expenditures were the totals agreed in the last Survey, and were revalued automatically, without negotiation. As a result, the negotiations between the Treasury and the spending departments became more sharply focused on bids for new or additional spending and, since 1992, on how one department's bid can be justified against that of others.

Public sector pay is also treated differently within the Survey. The use of cash limits as a surrogate public-sector pay policy was abandoned with the accession of the Conservative Government in 1979. Pay factors which were introduced in the early 1980s were abandoned in 1986, when running costs control was introduced, only to be reintroduced as a response to the fiscal crisis in 1992. The separation of programme and running costs expenditure, and the absorption of pay into the latter, has removed one of the most contentious and sensitive issues from the main Survey bidding process, and sidelined running costs into separate, parallel discussions. In practice this makes it easier for the Treasury to squeeze administrative costs and consequently harder for departments to submerge the costs of pay into wider programme bids.

The process of deciding about allocations and about the total has become both formalized and incorporated within the Survey cycle. The latter represents an important break with the practice of the 1970s. Since 1979 almost all decisions about public expenditure are taken within the Survey, or in relation to it. The mini-Budgets and expenditure packages which characterized the previous decade are a thing of the past. Cuts and squeezes are negotiated within the Survey process. The Unified Budget introduced in 1993 has further consolidated the link and trade-offs between expenditure, revenue, and borrowing first promised in the MTFS in 1980.

The medium of exchange in the bidding processes has been little affected by the formalization of the Survey procedures. Most decisions about the total and its allocation between programmes continue to be made as the result of mutually acceptable agreements negotiated between the Treasury and the spending departments; a few become the subject of bargaining conducted by Ministers face-to-face in bilaterals or before the EDX Committee of Cabinet. 'Arbitration' where differences proved irreconcilable became more common in the early 1980s, as appeals were made to the institutionalized Star Chamber. This procedure was further formalized in 1992 when the Star Chamber was replaced by EDX, which became an integral part of PES. There, or at the full Cabinet, some decisions were imposed upon contending parties, but in general imposition has become increasingly rare. Even the optimal size of the Planning Total 'decided' by the Chancellor and the Chief Secretary and recommended to the July Cabinet in the period to 1992 was negotiable, tacitly acknowledged in the exercise of the autumnal bilaterals which frequently produced a substantial overshoot, as in 1990 and 1991. Even the New Control Total in 1992, with its implied tightening of the top–down constraint on spending levels, was formally approved by Cabinet in the atmosphere surrounding the emergence of fiscal crisis.

Consequences for PES of the Unified Budget and NCT

The decisions in 1992 to unify taxation and spending decisions in a single Budget, and to introduce a 'top–down' Control Total for the aggregate of public expenditure for each of the three Survey years, marked a further stage in the evolution of the PES system. How far they will affect the processes of bidding, negotiating, and arbitrating described earlier in this chapter, other than temporarily in the crisis conditions of 1992–4, is as yet unclear. The evidence of one, interim, spending round, infused by the inevitable and necessary Treasury rhetoric of change and reform, is insufficient for judgement. The test of the new 'top–down' arrangements for determining the Control Total will come after the changes in the rules regulating the process have been absorbed and, crucially, subjected to the pressures of electoral politics in the run-up to a general election, which in 1982–3, 1986–7, and 1991–2 forced a relaxation of fiscal policy.

In the immediate aftermath of the 1992 fiscal crisis, changes in the behavioural rules of the game which underpin the PES processes reflected the urgent need to move the balance between departmental autonomy and Treasury control towards the Treasury, to secure tighter control of the expenditure aggregates, as the introduction of cash limits in 1976 and the abandonment of volume planning in 1982 had done previously. Neither signalled the displacement of the paradigm of negotiated discretion which has governed the relationships between the Treasury and the spending departments. Nor was there a permanent and irrevocable shift in the balance between them. Indeed, as the crisis which provoked each receded, and the changes to the rules 'beddeddown', spending departments began to seek ways of regaining discretionary room for manœuvre, ceded to the Treasury in the immediate aftermath of crisis, by exploiting loopholes and by pressurizing the Treasury to provide more flexibility in the administration of the new rules of the game.

The 1992 changes are comparable, representing less a system-change than changes to an evolving system. The rebalancing of Treasury control and departmental autonomy which has occurred represents a pragmatic response to the conditions of acute crisis, a further evolution of the PES system rather than its transformation. Any long-term shift in the balance between the Treasury and the spending departments which permanently disadvantaged the latter would be contrary to the general thrust of the reforms initiated by FMI and Next Steps, designed to decentralize managerial financial authority, and the Treasury's drive to introduce more flexibility into the determination of pay and conditions of work. However, the changes provide a further illustration of the persistent inherent tension between central control and departmental autonomy, a recurring theme of this and earlier chapters which we take up more broadly in the concluding chapters.

The Unified Budget and the NCT have three immediate consequences for the conduct and processes of the Public Expenditure Survey. First, the formation of the 'expenditure judgement' at the start of the PES round is now more explicitly derived from considerations of broader macro-economic policy. The Chancellor, Chief Secretary, and their officials now consider the impact of likely trends in spending alongside taxation and borrowing at the same time of year. The implications of this for the Cabinet's collective responsibility for economic policy and specifically for the aggregate of public expenditure are discussed in the next chapter.

Secondly, the new rules provide an incentive for spending departments to try to incorporate consideration of tax-expenditures into discussions about spending. For example, the £6.1 billion (in 1991–2) cost of mortgage tax relief could be set alongside the D.o.E.'s bid for housing expenditure. Conversely, the Treasury can argue the advantages of tax incentives, rather than expenditure, financing the delivery of a particular policy urged by a department.

The third consequence of the Unified Budget is that it will increase the pressure and workload on both the Treasury and departments. The latter will have less time to convert their spending allocations agreed in PES into Parliamentary Estimates. This is a particular problem for the territorial departments, as they require time to allocate their public spending 'blocks' generated by the application of the formula. The Unified Budget also adds to the pressure of work on the Chancellor of the Exchequer, reversing the trend since 1961 of the Chief Secretary assuming a greater share of responsibility for the Treasury's spending business. The Chancellor chairs EDX and is also involved in the preparation of a longer and more detailed single Financial Statement and Budget Report, incorporating the whole range of fiscal and monetary policies.

The Chief Secretary's role and responsibility have changed too. Bilateral meetings with spending ministers are still necessary to establish an agreed factual basis, to 'get all the figures to fit', and to discuss with them their requests for additional resources within the top–down constraints before EDX is convened; but 'you do not have to reach agreement with Secretaries of State, you simply set out the field so that you can inform EDX at the end of the discussion period' (Treasury and Civil Service Committee 1992: qu. 369). After the initial bilaterals the Chief Secretary's role is that of an agent and co-ordinator for the Cabinet Committee EDX. Throughout the period when EDX meets, and it met ten times in its first PES round in 1992, the Chief Secretary is involved in informing EDX about the options before it, 'keeping a score card and making sure that there is good communications between the committee and the Secretaries of State so that informed decisions can be taken' (qu. 369). If the Chief Secretary is now less involved in determining the allocation of the expenditure total between departmental programmes, sharing that responsibility with Cabinet, nevertheless he occupies a pivotal, influential position between individual Ministers in the bilateral discussions and the collective deliberations of EDX.

13

Collective Responsibility: The Cabinet, 'Star Chamber', and EDX

In the 1980s and early 1990s the Cabinet was formally involved collectively in discussions about public spending at least three times a year, in May/June, July, and November. Although *Guidelines* for the Survey were formally tabled for the Cabinet meeting in March they were not discussed. The May or June meeting normally involved a general discussion about the objectives to be set for the upcoming PES round.

A more substantial discussion of public spending policy took place at the July Cabinet. As we discussed in Chapter 12, the Cabinet had before it three papers: two from the Chief Secretary and one from the Chancellor. The Chief Secretary presented his colleagues with a neutral description of the bids he had received from his colleagues. He then provided a detailed analysis of his views on those bids, in total and on specific bids. The Chancellor provided a contextual paper showing the likely macro-economic background to the PES round. Cabinet then discussed these papers and had to decide whether to support the Chancellor and Chief Secretary's recommendation on the global target to be set for the aggregate of spending. The July Cabinet meeting would also agree to 'roll forward' the total planned for the new year three and again the strong presumption would be that this would be in line with the previously agreed formula of a 1.5 per cent rise in real terms above the old year three figure. Prior to 1992, the two Treasury ministers did not always recommend that the previous Planning Total be reaffirmed but might instead suggest that the Cabinet should ask the Chief Secretary to 'aim to get as close as possible to that total' and/or that the total should reflect the general goal of the government to keep spending at an ever lower proportion of GDP.

After the 1992 changes to PES, the role of Cabinet remained very much the same, apart from the very strong presumption that previously agreed New Control Total (NCT) targets for the following financial year should be maintained. The November meeting of Cabinet now hears a report from the Chancellor as Chairman of EDX on what allocation between departments within the overall ceiling is being proposed. This is followed by further, and in 1992 extensive, Cabinet debate and discussion. Ministers then have an opportunity to argue against the recommendation of EDX for their particular programme before the full Cabinet. Only after this are the programme allocations agreed and endorsed. Before the creation of EDX, a report was given by the Chief Secretary and, if it had been necessary to use the Star Chamber, from the Chairman of the Star Chamber as well, on the conduct of the PES round at its outcome. Cabinet then affirmed the Autumn Statement totals.

The above provides no more than an outline of the tasks before Cabinet, not of the degree or scope of the debate. Prior to 1992, the July Cabinet was mainly concerned with the balance of macro-economic policy, and very little with the priority of the total or composition of public expenditure. The Cabinets of Thatcher and Major did not spend as long on the details of public spending—whether a programme should receive an increase or not—as the Wilson and Callaghan Governments (Barnett 1982; Dell 1991). This can partly be explained by the different ideological commitments of the respective parties: whatever the crisis measures taken in the 1970s, Labour Ministers were more committed to the principle of public spending than most of the Ministers under Thatcher or Major (Ridley 1991). The other explanation is that of different Prime Ministerial styles and methods of operating. It is too soon to tell whether the creation of EDX will fundamentally alter this. Several clear conclusions can be drawn, however. First, EDX represents a move back towards general Cabinet discussion about public-spending policy as a whole. Second, in conjunction with the Unified Budget from November 1993, there is greater potential for Cabinet involvement in general economic policy discussions which were previously the almost exclusive preserve of the Treasury, its Chief Secretary, Chancellor, and First Lord. In the remainder of the chapter we look at the origins, purpose, and operation of two Cabinet Committees, and assess the degree to which the Cabinet acts collectively in decision-making on public expenditure. In particular we assess the rationale and role of the so-called 'Star Chamber'—an *ad hoc* committee of the Cabinet (MISC 62) set up formally by Prime Minister Thatcher in 1981 to adjudicate on bids for increased expenditure unresolved through the bilateral process. It was dubbed the 'Star Chamber' by Whitehall insiders after the Tudor institution of that name, in order to convey that same sense of trial by a small inquisitorial jury. Its successor, 'EDX', was set up as part of the further evolution of PES in July 1992.

THE STAR CHAMBER, 1981–1991

There is nothing new in governments seeking to create a forum for the adjudication of disputes between spending ministers and the Treasury. Throughout the period from the Plowden Report onwards Prime Ministers and their Chancellors and Chief Secretaries tried to create some form of subcommittee to strengthen the hand of the Treasury in the PESC process. A committee of non-spending ministers was created in 1965 to help Chancellor Callaghan to 'sit in judgement . . . on the claims of the major spending departments, and to report their suggested priorities, allocations and cuts in departmental programmes' (Wilson 1976: 70). This faltered because of the combination of the increased complexity of programmes to be assessed, personality clashes, and the preference of the Chancellor to conduct bilateral battles alone (see Wilson 1976; Barnett 1982; Pliatzky 1982). In 1978 a small and senior 'committee of non-spending Ministers' was created to 'sift through all major programmes, and then put proposals to Cabinet' (Barnett 1982: 154–5), but it met only once before the Government fell in 1979. As we shall see later in this chapter, EDX is closer in design and purpose to both these short-lived initiatives.

Margaret Thatcher was the least interested of modern Prime Ministers in 'organizational' responses to public policy problems. Since 1979 there have been fewer machinery-of-government changes than instituted by previous Administrations. Her policy-making style favoured small committees and 'even smaller, less formal groups of Treasury and economic department Ministers centred on the Treasury and Number 10' (Burch 1983: 411; see also Burch 1990).

The Star Chamber was a specific response to particular difficulties. It was created because of three interrelated factors. First, the 1979 and 1980 Survey rounds had been particularly difficult for the Treasury, set against the background of rising public sector pay, deepening recession, and ambitious targets to reduce the real level of public spending over the four-year period to 1984. There was therefore an incentive to strengthen the Treasury's hand in tackling the demands of the spending departments. Secondly, a response to this had been the appointment of Leon Brittan as the Chief Secretary 'who knew that his future depended on making the 1981 PESC round tough and making it stick' (Jenkins 1985: 115). His tough stance in the bilaterals with his colleagues produced a large number of appeals to Cabinet. Thirdly, and consequently, the Prime Minister set up MISC 62 to ease the pressure on Cabinet and, through the choice of a natural conciliator, William Whitelaw, as its Chairman, to assuage Ministers already concerned at the tightening of economic policy in the 1981 Budget. Whilst it can be argued that its creation was as much a reflection of Mrs Thatcher's style of leadership as of specific limitations in the PES procedures, it was remarkably similar in structure and composition (but not in scope) to Harold Wilson's committee in the 1960s and Barnett's short-lived scheme in 1978–9. It reflects an inherent and enduring problem of collective decision-making in British central government.

Personnel, organization, and procedures

The Star Chamber was activated on the decision of the Prime Minister in consultation with the Treasury and senior Cabinet colleagues when the bilaterals had left unresolved differences between the Treasury and one or more spending departments. The Cabinet formally approved its institution. In its early years the Treasury regarded it as too much of a conciliating institution which merely prolonged the PES process. However, at least one Chief Secretary in the 1980s regarded it as a useful vehicle to make clear statements of principle to his colleagues about the need for restraint. If the Survey had been a particularly difficult one and there were clear signs that the bilaterals would not resolve enough of the 'excess' bids, the Cabinet often decided early in the round to use the Star Chamber. In 1985 it was decided that it should be 'called into play' as early as June (*The Times*, 22 June 1985). In other years the Cabinet gave its approval at one of its meetings in October, after the conclusion of the bilaterals (*The Times*, 3 Oct. 1985).

Lord Whitelaw chaired the Star Chamber from 1981 to 1987. On his retirement Cecil Parkinson was appointed by Prime Minister Thatcher in 1988 to chair it, but the Star Chamber did not meet. John Major appointed John Wakeham as Chairman in 1990, but the Star Chamber was not needed in that year either or in the next, its last. Other members of the committee were appointed on an *ad hoc* basis by the Prime Minister in consultation with the Chancellor. Lord Whitelaw was regarded by officials and ministers alike as an excellent conciliator, and his approach to the task reflected that judgement. One of his colleagues, an erstwhile member of the Star Chamber, described him as 'so subtle a master of his craft that really to appreciate his skill one has to be in his confidence and know in advance his objectives and tactics' (Tebbit 1988: 213). There were usually three or four other senior Ministers in addition to the Chairman, the Chief Secretary, and the Chief Whip. Three principles governed their selection. First, a Minister must have settled any outstanding differences with the Treasury at the bilaterals stage or before. Tebbit comments on the 1983 Survey round: 'Cecil [Parkinson] had all but settled the Department's 1984/5 expenditure with the chief Secretary to the Treasury and I soon finalised the deal. That left me clear to become a member of the "Star Chamber"' (1988: 213). Secondly, the Ministers chosen were usually of senior rank, heading departments with small budgets and largely political rather than policy-making functions. Thirdly, the composition of the committee was usually representative of the balance of groupings in the Cabinet. Lawson described this as ideally consisting of 'three public spending hawks and one public spending dove' (Lawson 1992: 290). In 1983 the Star Chamber was made up of Whitelaw, Norman Tebbit (Trade and Industry Secretary), John Biffen (Leader of the Commons), and George Younger (Scottish Secretary). Its composition in the following year was only slightly altered, with Leon Brittan (Home Secretary) replacing Tebbit. In 1985, it included, in addition to Whitelaw, Biffen, Tebbit (then Chancellor of the Duchy of Lancaster and Party Chairman), Brittan (Trade and Industry Secretary), and Nicholas Edwards (Welsh Secretary) (*The Times*, 4 Oct. 1985).

The Deputy Secretary in charge of the Economic Secretariat of the Cabinet Office normally acted as secretary, with other civil servants from his Group providing administrative support. They liaised with the Treasury's Under Secretary in charge of the General Expenditure Policy Division (GEP) because of the highly complex nature of some of the material with which the Star Chamber had to deal, such as price and cost indices, level of client-demand, and so on. The 'E' Committee officials were normally the only civil servants present at the Star Chamber's deliberations; the official Treasury was not represented.

The procedure was 'spartan': the Committee would be faced by the Chief Secretary alone on one side and the spending minister on the other. The 1984 round of meetings was particularly intensive, 'virtually every morning for a full three weeks at the end of October' (Jenkins 1985: 116). Spending ministers were often required to attend more than one session. In 1984, for example, the Star Chamber had an initial meeting with the Defence Secretary, Michael Heseltine, and then 'had further sessions' when differences between the Treasury and Ministry of Defence had not been resolved (*The Times*, 3 Nov. 1984). On occasion, the Cabinet asked the Star Chamber to 'try again' to resolve outstanding problems before the final Cabinet meeting at which the Survey process was expected to be concluded ready for the Autumn Statement.

Inspired leaks over the years gave the impression that it was an ordeal for a Minister to present his case to it, especially if the Chief Secretary was regarded as having a good grasp of the issues. Ministers were not necessarily specialists on the financial and expenditure side of their department's work, and crucially lacked the support of their officials who accompanied them to the bilaterals. A confident and well-briefed Chief Secretary often knew as much, or more, about the background to a department's expenditure as the Minister.

In every public spending round from 1981 until its demise in 1991 the Star Chamber was set up in readiness. In the period between 1981 and 1987 it was used on six occasions. It was not needed in 1982, mainly because the quicker than expected fall in inflation meant that the cash allocation given to most departments would purchase a larger volume of goods and services than planned in the previous PEWP. As a result there was more slack in the system. The Treasury was able to reduce the Reserve by £2.5 billion, yet also reduce the Planning Total by £400 million on that planned a year earlier. In 1988, the Chief Secretary, Major, was able to settle the outstanding differences with the departments at the bilateral stage. He was aided in this by larger than forecast net receipts (counted as negative expenditure) on privatization and on the sale of housing by local authorities, and by lower expenditure on unemployment benefits as a result of a fall in the jobless total which was sharper than expected (Treasury and Civil Service Committee 1988*d*: p. vi). As a result of the combination of these factors the Planning Total was maintained and the Reserve was reduced by £3.5 billion over that planned in the 1988 PEWP.

There are several important points to make about the work of the Star Chamber. First, the Treasury conceded a fairly large proportion of the excess bids at the start of the bilateral–Star Chamber process. Such concessions did not necessarily mean that the pressure on spending departments was relaxed; it was more likely that if the Treasury wished to stick to the original Planning Total figure, and maintain the Reserve more or less intact, then other programmes had to be cut below the previously planned level. It was this ingredient which seems to have made the Star Chamber's task difficult in several of the Survey years.

Second, the Cabinet did not always confirm the Planning Total figure at its July meeting. The Cabinet's remit to the Chief Secretary did not always prescribe a figure to be achieved. Moreover, in 1981, 1985, and 1987 a figure higher than the previously agreed Planning Total was set. This was not always against the advice of the Treasury. In the Survey round of 1987, 'in a departure from past practice', the Treasury signalled that it 'may not be able to hold to the Treasury's target' and would 'try to get as close as possible' to it (*The Times*, 24 July 1987). Even when the Treasury did obtain Cabinet approval for the original Planning Total to be maintained this did not necessarily result in the figure being delivered. In 1986, all the leaks pointed to the Treasury wanting to accommodate pressure for more spending within the Planning Total agreed in the previous White Paper (*The Times*, 14 July 1986). The Cabinet decided to confirm the Planning total at £144 billion (*The Times*, 18 July 1986). The final total announced in the PEWP in the following January was over £4.6 billion higher.

Third, the use of and status of the Reserve was an important background factor. The Treasury's aim in most years was to maintain this as close as possible to the figure 'pencilled in' in the previous Autumn Statement. Departments frequently argued that excess bids could be covered by reducing the Reserve. The Star Chamber also sometimes recommended dipping into the Reserve as a way of resolving outstanding disputes which came before it.

The degree to which the Treasury had to reduce the Reserve at the end of the Survey period was one indication of how 'successful' the negotiations between the Chief Secretary and the departments had been. It was also a measure of the value of the Star Chamber from the point of view of both the Treasury and the departments: a lower cut in the Reserve than the Treasury realistically expected would indicate that the Star Chamber had been useful to it; a significant dent in the Reserve as a result of the Star Chamber's deliberations indicated that the departments had fared well out of the process. Using this as a rough-and-ready yardstick, in the years when the Star Chamber was in operation, the Reserve was maintained more or less intact in 1981 and 1983; it was reduced by more than £750 million in 1984, 1986, and 1987. Although these adjustments represented only a relatively small proportion of the Planning Total (between 0.4 and 2 per cent), they were often politically significant as evidence of the resolve on the part of the Treasury to squeeze spending, and on the part of the departments to force the Treasury to take a more relaxed attitude.

The Star Chamber was very much a product of the Thatcher style of governance and reflected her initial weakness in Cabinet in the early 1980s. It was seen by Ministers as a means of appealing over the head of the Chief Secretary to wider interests in Cabinet, yet its existence kept public spending haggling away from formal Cabinet, in line with the Thatcher approach. In the mid-1980s Chief Secretaries used it to draw out points of principle in the Treasury's continual battle with departments over the need for restraint. Thus until the late 1980s both the Chief Secretary and some of his colleagues regarded recourse to Star Chamber as a potentially useful tactic *in extremis*. These factors ceased to be so relevant after 1987. Mrs Thatcher had succeeded in composing a more amenable Cabinet, and arguably the ideological debate ceased to be so relevant after three election victories. The economic boom of the late 1980s also made it possible for the Treasury to concede public spending increases whilst reducing spending as a proportion of GDP. The fact that the Star Chamber was not required in 1990 or 1991 reflected the weakness of the Treasury's hand in not being able to resist demands for increased spending due to the effects of the recession and the imminence of the general election. Ministers had achieved enough of their goals not to press the case further; and both Prime Ministers Thatcher and Major intervened to overrule the Chief Secretary, over Child Benefit in 1990 and health spending in 1991.

The role of the Star Chamber

Whether the Star Chamber was brought into play in a Survey round and, if it was, how difficult its task would be, was determined by a combination of four factors, the most significant of which was the pressure on the Treasury to maintain its line on public spending. If the inflation rate was slowing, much of the pressure on spending plans was removed, as happened in 1982. On the other hand, a rising inflation rate added to the excess bids which the Treasury faced, as in the 1989 Survey round. Buoyant revenues reduced the pressure on the Chief Secretary to seek compensating cost to cover 'unavoidable' excess bids; faster than expected economic growth allowed the Treasury to concede a higher Planning Total in cash terms, while still producing a falling public spending/GDP ratio. It was claimed that the Star Chamber was set up early in 1984 'because the Government is afraid of a last-minute battle over expenditure disturbing financial markets' prior to privatization issues (*The Times*, 6 Oct. 1984). The Treasury felt constrained, because of financial and exchange market sentiment, to press for a tough Survey round which might result in the use of the Star Chamber.

The departments also challenged the Treasury's stance on public spending as a result of pressures they faced from client-groups, or because they felt their relative position in the Whitehall pecking order had been eroded. Such factors contributed to the appeals to the Star Chamber by the Minister of Defence and the Housing Minister in the 1984 round. The Social Services Secretary was said to have successfully resisted cuts in his bid both at Star Chamber and Cabinet, on the grounds that they might prejudice the wide-ranging review of social security under way in 1985.

The third factor was the political timetable. The Treasury was pressured in 1985 into relaxing its spending stance after the Government's defeat in a by-election at Brecon and Radnor. The imminence of a general election could also lead to a looser spending round, as departments pressed more forcefully political arguments in favour of their bids before a more relaxed and amenable Star Chamber. The relaxation of the Planning Total in 1986 was seen as a response to opinion poll evidence that the Government was vulnerable on health and education issues (*The Times*, 7 Nov. 1986). The aftermath of general elections could also add to the amount of 'unavoidable' bids which the Chief Secretary had had to concede. After the 1987 election this 'cost' was put at £1 billion (*The Times*, 15 June 1987).

The fourth factor was the role of personality and judgement: ingredients difficult to quantify in the decision to trigger the Star Chamber mechanism. They operated at several levels. A Chief Secretary who was regarded as a successful negotiator, on good terms with his colleagues, might be able to settle outstanding differences with the departments at the bilateral stage. John Major was credited with having performed well in the 1988 Survey, and the Star Chamber was not used. On the other hand, determined Ministers may press for an issue to be settled outside the bilaterals because of ideological differences with the Treasury line (Peter Walker) or for reasons of personality (Heseltine). An even harder element to quantify is the balance of personalities at the official level between Treasury Expenditure Controllers and departmental Finance Officers. An over-ambitious target set at the beginning of the cycle by Treasury ministers, or unrealistic bids by Ministers, could also shape the outcome of the later stages of the Survey.

In combination, these factors influenced the way a Survey round was conducted, and helped to determine whether the Star Chamber was used. One thing is certain: 'a decision by a Minister to appeal to the Prime Minister or full Cabinet depended on a complicated, purely political calculus. This was not necessarily related to the rights and wrongs of the Star Chamber settlement, let alone of any collective judgement by Ministers on spending priorities' (Jenkins 1985: 117). Equally, the personal qualities of a Chief Secretary alone, or a group of Ministers in concert, could not outweigh the pressures created by the need to keep macro-economic strategy on course, or defend what were regarded as vital services.

How successful was the Star Chamber in discharging its functions? Much depends on what the 'real' goals of the various actors in the game were at any one time in the Survey. From the Prime Minister's perspective, the Star Chamber was successful if it confronted issues with which he or she felt the Cabinet was ill-equipped to deal. It could be said to have performed a useful role, if it reduced the need for Prime Ministerial mediation between the Treasury and departments. On at least two occasions, in 1984 and 1990, there was a further stage in the process when an outstanding issue had not been settled in the bilaterals or in Star Chamber, and required a 'tri-lateral' negotiation between the Minister, Chief Secretary, and the Prime Minister.

It is harder to judge whether the Star Chamber was successful from the Treasury's perspective. In one sense, its very existence represented a failure to resolve disagreements at the bilateral stage or, if necessary, at Cabinet. From the same perspective, it could be argued that the Star Chamber was a time-consuming and inefficient way of dispatching Survey business, encouraging Ministers not to settle differences at the official level and in bilaterals, or even at the initial Cabinet meeting, but to defer until the further opportunity provided by the later stage. On the other hand, the implicit threat of the Star Chamber and its use was exploited by the Treasury as a deterrent in its 'games' with departments.

From the perspective of the spending minister and his department the Star Chamber's success could be measured by the extent to which they felt it provided them with an independent arbitration of an irreconcilable dispute with the Treasury, a court of last appeal against an unfavourable verdict. A spending minister who felt very strongly about a spending programme on an issue of principle could put his case to his colleagues and try to convince them. Ministers could, and did sometimes, win, even if the result tended to be marginal, given Lord Whitelaw's predilection for 'splitting the difference'.

The Star Chamber's role in the Survey process was essentially one of fire-fighting, providing *ad hoc* adjudication on disputes between contending parties. The fiscal crisis which erupted in 1992 called for a more permanent, broadly based institution, capable of taking a wider look at spending allocations. The Star Chamber had not developed, nor was it intended that it should, into a vehicle for deciding the optimal allocation of resources between competing programmes. Its role was a limited political one: a conciliation service for settling disputes between Ministers and the Treasury. It did not aspire to the grander role of helping in the determination of priorities implied by the Wilson and Callaghan experiments in the 1960s and 1970s, in large part because the Treasury throughout most of the period insisted that the Survey processes provided the battleground for the reconciliation of top–down and bottom–up pressures. It was only because of the stark reality of spending rising far faster than the growth of the economy, and a PSBR higher than at any time since the 1970s, that the Treasury accepted the criticisms of outsiders that PES, even with the Star Chamber, was unable to deliver outturn close to objectives, but led instead to Planning Totals ratcheted upwards throughout the three years of the planning cycle.

EDX, FROM 1992

The creation of EDX was essentially a quid pro quo for the Cabinet agreeing to the New Control Total, which not only threatened to squeeze the budgets of spending ministers but challenged the prevailing paradigm of negotiated discretion in their relations with the Treasury. In exchange for exerting more central control on the aggregates the Treasury proposed loosening its control over the conduct of discussions about how that total should be distributed. The Star Chamber was replaced by a standing committee of Cabinet which became a permanent, and not occasional and ancillary, part of the PES cycle.

Personnel, organization, and procedure

EDX shares some characteristics with the Star Chamber. Its membership also includes senior ministers with a sprinkling of more 'neutral' non-departmental ministers such as the Lord President of the Council, Lord Privy Seal, and the Chancellor of the Duchy of Lancaster. There are, however, some clear differences. First, EDX is not chaired by a 'neutral' figure, such as Whitelaw, but by the Chancellor of the Exchequer. And for the first time the Chief Secretary is a full member rather than one of the protagonists, as in the days of the Star Chamber. Portillo described himself as 'the handmaiden of and at other times the rapporteur for the Cabinet Committee EDX' (Treasury and Civil Service Committee 1992: qu. 369). Second, EDX is larger, with seven members against the three or four of the Star Chamber. Third, it is more avowedly heavyweight. In 1992 and 1993 it included three of the top five ministers in government. The inclusion of the President of the Board of Trade (Heseltine) and the Home Secretary (Clarke) in the first EDX Committee in the 1992 PES round was a politically astute means of locking two of the Cabinet's more interventionist pro-spending ministers into an institution charged with inaugurating a tougher spending regime in Whitehall. The other members, in addition to the Chancellor and Chief Secretary, were John Wakeham (Leader of the Lords), Tony Newton (Leader of the Commons), and William Waldegrave (Chancellor of the Duchy of Lancaster and Minister for Public Service and Science) (*The Times*, 11 Aug. 1992).

The committee's remit is also wider. Rather than adjudicating between the Treasury and one or two departments whose Ministers had not reached agreement with the Chief Secretary in bilaterals, EDX is expected to present to the Cabinet a package of decisions on spending allocations within the overall limit of the NCT. The Chief Secretary and his officials continue as before to tease out of departments information about their programmes—priorities, value-for-money—and attempt to limit their demands for resources in addition to those in their baseline. But now the Chief Secretary does not 'have to reach agreement with Secretaries of State . . . simply set out the field so that [he] can inform EDX at the end of the discussion period'. Portillo stressed that 'the Chief Secretary at the beginning and end has a similar role to the old one. In between he is informing EDX of the options that are before it, keeping the scorecard and making sure there is good communication between the Committee and the Secretaries of State' (Treasury and Civil Service Committee 1992: qu. 369).

The EDX Committee can also recommend the reduction of a department's previously agreed bid or its baseline, in order to arrive at an overall settlement within the total. It can also make recommendations which affect spending across the board, such as the 1.5 per cent pay ceiling for the public sector in 1992. It has the potential power to assume a broader more intrusive role still, closer to that recommended for the Cabinet Committee of senior ministers in the 1960s during the Wilson Government. In 1992 EDX faced the task of reducing £14 billion in excess bids, an estimated £5 billion of which were 'unstoppable', such as demand-led social security (*The Times*, 11 Aug. 1992).

How far EDX represents a radical departure from previous practice and presages a far more Cabinet-collectivist approach to spending decisions will depend partly upon how it chooses to interpret its remit, but also on the attitude and expectations of the Treasury and the Prime Minister. What has not changed needs to be emphasized. First, the Treasury remains in control of the agenda. The Chief Secretary's advice and suggested options form the core of the analytical advice to the Committee, with GEP continuing as the hub of the information network in the PES process. There is no Cabinet Office Secretariat (or CPRS) providing an independent financial and economic input, but Ministers can submit papers in support of their case. And Treasury officials are in no doubt that over time the 'bidding mentality' and the copious documentation which goes hand in hand with it is likely to return, threatening to overwhelm the capacity of EDX to deal with the business. As it was, EDX met ten times during its first PES round in 1992.

Second, the role of EDX falls far short of deciding relative priorities across the whole range of public spending—for example, whether Employment's training programmes rather than Education's further education spending would deliver best value-for-money. EDX's function will be to whittle down bids, and to agree an (albeit tougher) set of political compromises which will stick. Nor is it, or ever likely to be, an agent for opening up fiscal policy debates. Notwithstanding the Unified Budget the Treasury has put out of bounds discussion of the interplay between tax expenditures, tax measures, and public spending.

14

The Territorial Dimension

It is a 'paradox of territorially defined public expenditure . . . that it is *not* territorially determined: it is first and foremost functionally determined' (Rose 1982: 138). The territorial departments are different. There are unique constitutional, political, organizational, and structural features about the Scottish and Welsh Offices, and the Northern Ireland Office and departments. That distinctiveness is even more apparent in the way in which public expenditure is allocated and distributed in the territories. This chapter focuses on both the planning and allocative mechanisms of public expenditure in the territories. First, it devotes more attention to the territories than is normally the case in studies of UK government; secondly, it provides further support for our theme that the Treasury's systems exhibit both control *and* flexibility; and thirdly, the operation of the block and formula system provides an example of a non-statutory policy rule based on a mutual understanding between parties within the policy network, the implementation of which is subject to both sides observing behavioural 'rules of the game'.

The chapter begins by providing a brief historical overview of the methods of allocating resources territorially and the subsequent introduction of the 'Barnett formula' in the late 1970s. We discuss the current arrangements for allocating resources, stressing the importance of the formula and block. We then look at the way in which the territorial departments organize the internal process of bidding for resources. The use of discretion in the allocation of resources by the Secretaries of State is the subject of the next section. We conclude by posing the question, who benefits from the current system?

HISTORIC ARRANGEMENTS

Public spending was allocated to Scotland on the basis of the Goschen formula until the period immediately following the Second World War, although it remained the basis for allocating resources to Scottish education until 1958 (Keating and Midwinter 1983). The formula dates from 1891 and was named after George Goschen, who was appointed as

Chancellor of the Exchequer in Lord Salisbury's 1886–92 Adminis-tration. It gave Scotland 11/80ths of British spending on individual comparable programmes. It began as a means of calculating the grant for Scottish education but was extended to cover public expenditure as a whole and was based on objective population calculations made in 1891 (Heald 1980*a*). It survived long after the 1891 population shares ceased to be relevant and, as population declined in Scotland relative to that of England, the 'Goschen effect' enabled Scotland to receive a better than proportional allocation of resources (Heald 1980*b*).

Likewise, the allocation of resources to Northern Ireland was not made on the basis of the normal pattern of bidding to the Treasury alongside the other spending departments. In the 1920–38 period allo-cation was based on bilateral discussions between the Treasury and the Northern Ireland Ministry of Finance. By 1938, agreement had been reached between the two institutions that there should be 'parity of service provision for citizens of Northern Ireland with those in the rest of the United Kingdom' (Connolly 1990). In 1942 it was accepted that, on this basis, the province required extra resources, and by 1950 an allocative arrangement based on local needs had been agreed. This arrangement was accepted by the Treasury because it was satisfied that its bilateral partner, the Ministry of Finance, operated in a similar way to HM Treasury, and that the spending of monies allocated would then be subject to proper scrutiny (Connolly 1990).

During the 1960s and 1970s, formula-based systems of allocation lapsed but the principle of using the allocations agreed for English departments remained the bench-mark for discussions between the Treasury and the three territorial departments, the Welsh Office having been established in 1964. 'The basis of discussion almost always tended to be based on what was happening in England' (Assistant Secretary, Expenditure Division). In addition, the Secretaries of States' discretion had grown incrementally over the years. There was an apparent 'systematized position', with block arrangements *de facto* in place.

The collective decision, co-ordinated by the Treasury, to codify a formula-based approach to the allocation of resources to the territorial departments emerged from the debates on the devolution of legislative and executive power to Scotland and Wales during the mid-1970s. The Treasury led an interdepartmental review to determine the 'objective' public expenditure needs of each part of the UK (Treasury 1979*a*). The resulting Needs Assessment Study provided a statistical background of what each part of the UK received in terms of identifiable spending, and what each needed objectively in order to receive 'broadly the same level of public services' and ensure that 'the expenditure on them should be allocated according to their relative needs' (Treasury 1979*a*: 4). The report was heavily qualified with assertions that it was very difficult to measure needs 'objectively' and that it was difficult to weight 'subjective' factors. It was, however, the first detailed study of how resources were and should be distributed, and had as its guiding principle that the aim of any system should be to apply 'English policies to Scotland and Wales' (Heald 1980*a*: 11).

It was also to become a minor part of the political battle over whether spending was fairly distributed between the territories. The Welsh Office was keen on the report being published, whereas the Scottish Office was not (Heald 1980*b*). This was because it concluded that, using an array of objective measures of needs, in 1976–7 Scotland *should* receive per capita spending of 116, Wales 109, and Northern Ireland 131, on the basis of spending in England of 100; actual spending was 7 *higher* in Scotland and 5 *higher* in Northern Ireland, but 8 *lower* in Wales.

The then Chief Secretary, Joel Barnett, introduced in 1978 a formula based on the population balance between England, Scotland, and Wales, set at 85, 10, and 5 respectively. By this means, the territories would receive increments based on the spending increases or decreases obtained by comparable English functional programmes. It was therefore based on marginal changes in resources, not their overall levels. The other main policy rules of the formula and block system were that once a block of expenditure was created, the respective Secretaries of State would have a very great deal of discretion to switch between different programmes (in the case of Northern Ireland this flexibility did not extend to the spending of the NIO, which remained within the control of the Treasury), but that Secretaries of State should not, other than in exceptional circumstances, bid for extra resources for programmes already covered by the operation of the formula.

The introduction of the formula indicated that the Treasury accepted that the current balance of spending between the UK and the territories identified in the review was sufficient to justify entrenching it through introducing a population formula rather than some other kind. The Welsh Office had been unable to resist what would be a means of ensuring that it received less than its objective needs, as identified by the Treasury review. Of greater long-term significance were the strange dynamic properties of the formula: 'if applied over a reasonably lengthy period in which there was a substantial public expenditure growth, its operation would result in the convergence of expenditure shares towards population shares' (Heald 1980*a*: 13). This would produce relative benefits for England and Wales and a fall in share of public expenditure for Scotland. Yet if the assumptions were reversed, and expenditure was cut on comparable English functional programmes over an extended period (as the Conservatives intended in 1979 and 1980), then the formula would produce a relative increase in share of public expenditure to Scotland and a relative fall in England and Wales. The Scottish Office was aware of these properties of the formula.

The Barnett formula was introduced at a time of planned increases in public expenditure and a commitment by the Labour Government to devolution. It survived the advent of the Conservative Government in 1979 committed to neither. Separate functional programmes were set up within the PESC process for Scotland and Wales, from the 1980 Public Expenditure Survey onwards. The 1981 Public Expenditure White Paper was the first to include separate headings for spending in Scotland and Wales, and the White Paper itemized programmes both within and outside the block. Previously, spending which was nominally the responsibility of the two Secretaries of State was carried under separate programmes by the relevant functional department. The Northern Ireland Office and departments had had a separate programme since the imposition of direct rule in 1972. Having identified definitive Scottish and Welsh programmes and separated them out from the functional programmes of other Whitehall departments, it was then easier to allocate additional monies through a formula. The creation of separate Scottish and Welsh programmes was a means of formalizing what had become an accepted practice of treating spending under the control of the Scottish Secretary as a 'block', with some additional flexibilities granted to the minister to allocate to his own priorities (Heald 1980*b*).

Formula arrangements were agreed for Northern Ireland at the same time, although they varied slightly from those applied under the Barnett formula. The Northern Ireland formula was expressed in percentage terms (2.75) and was a population formula based on Northern Ireland's share of total *United Kingdom* population, rather than that of *Great Britain* as was the case with Scotland and Wales. Northern Ireland ministers and officials accepted the arrangement, assuming that the population-based figure would be periodically revised and that public expenditure would go down in the future, as a result of the changed climate in public expenditure management and control, and therefore minimizing the cuts faced by the Province relative to those faced by English/UK functional departments. In retrospect they made the same mistake of judgement as Scottish Office officials: the formula was not revised until 1993–4 and public expenditure has continued to grow in real terms inexorably since 1979, thus over time bringing spending in all three territories into line with that in England.

CURRENT ARRANGEMENTS

Under the block arrangements the Treasury allows each Secretary of State in the three territorial departments to allocate a given annual sum of money at his discretion after the PES settlement in the autumn. In theory, this allows territorial departments to allocate a larger proportion of their total public expenditure, say, to health rather than roads than would be the case from simply following the pattern of expenditure in England. Later in the chapter we discuss the practical limitations to the use of this discretion.

In practice it is the intention that the blocks define those programmes for which provision is determined by the operation of the formulae. There are three types of expenditure: for most functional programmes, allocation is made according to a fixed formula; second, for Scotland and Wales only, the provision of Aggregate External Finance for local authorities is at present formula-driven on the basis of the D.o.E.'s local government settlement, although this is the source of debate between the territorial departments and the Treasury; third, departmental running costs are partly derived from the operation of a formula but placed within an overall three-year settlement which involves the departments bidding for running costs on the basis of their management plans and subject to Treasury agreement (discussed in Chapter 18). Non-block expenditure is determined by the allocation of resources following bids made jointly with other departments (such as for national agriculture programmes) and, for some programmes, as the result of separate bids made by each territorial department, and subject to the same rules of the game as bids made by any other spending departments, discussed in earlier chapters.

In 1992–3 the block covered more than 90 per cent of expenditure under the responsibility of each of the three Secretaries of State. The Northern Ireland Secretary has in theory the greatest amount of discretion, since the block covers nearly 99 per cent of the New Control Total (or 91 per cent of all spending under the aegis of the Secretary of State), but this figure somewhat overstates his real discretion. Social security is included within his responsibilities because of the constitutional arrangements which followed the imposition of direct rule; all policy areas previously handled by the Stormont Government remained the responsibility of the Northern Ireland departments. In practice, social security is 'ring-fenced'; it is only nominally within the block and the Secretary of State has no real discretion to move money in or out of the programme. The Department of Finance and Personnel refers to the 'managed block', that is all block programmes minus Social Security.

The spending of the NIO is included in the block but is subject to the 'second-guessing' of the Treasury, which is responsible for the plans and Estimates of the NIO. At first sight, the inclusion of law and order spending as a 'comparable' programme seems anomalous given the particularly difficult security situation in the Province. The position is explicable because the baseline of law and order spending when the formula system was introduced in 1978–9 was already substantially higher per head than in the rest of the UK, reflecting ten years of 'the troubles'. Increments produced by the operation of the formula since that time based on English law and order spending have enabled the NIO to maintain this relatively favourable balance of funding. Indeed, given that the spending of the Home Office and Lord Chancellor's Department has seen the most dramatic real increases since 1979 of any Whitehall departments, Northern Ireland has in some years been relatively better resourced in this area than 'needs' would have warranted.

Other expenditure excluded from the block reflects the different mix of spending in each of the territories. In Scotland and Wales, national and local expenditure on agriculture, fisheries, and food is excluded, since this is the subject of joint bids with MAFF. Industry, energy, and employment programmes are also excluded because they are either the subject of separate individual bids by the two departments or are part of Great Britain-wide programmes led and administered by another spending department. In Northern Ireland, local agricultural programmes, and all industry, energy, and employment programmes, are within the block.

The central government formula

The formulae for the allocation of resources to the territories were revised in the 1992 Autumn Statement, in the light of population changes evident in the returns on the 1991 Census, having been unaltered since 1978. From 1993–4 the Scottish Office received 10.66 per cent of the increment (up or down) agreed and allocated to them on 'comparable' programmes in England and Wales (10.06 per cent of programmes which were wholly comparable with England alone); the Welsh Office was allocated 6.02 per cent of comparable English programmes; and the Northern Ireland Office and departments, allocated resources according to a 2.87 per cent UK-based population formula applied to comparable programmes in Great Britain.

The revised formula is far more significant as a means of allocating resources to the Scottish and Welsh Offices, covering over 92 per cent of total expenditure under the responsibility of each Secretary of State, than to Northern Ireland, where it represents only 68 per cent of expenditure after the deduction of the social security programme (see Thain and Wright 1992*f*: tables 3 and 4). Law and order programmes are derived from the formula consequentials of increases in specific grants, including police grants, given to English local authorities. More generally, services provided by local authorities elsewhere in the UK are funded in the Province on the basis of comparable provision. In other respects Northern Ireland has more programmes covered by formula arrangements than the other two territories.

The formula on Aggregate External Finance for local authorities

The Treasury's view is that AEF falls within the remit of the formula procedure. In discussions with the Scottish and Welsh Offices it has applied 10.06 and 6.02 per cent respectively to the uplifting for the D.o.E.'s local authorities' settlement in England. The Scottish Office is on record as wanting to remove the formula from the process. Both it and the Welsh Office object to the formula being applied to local authorities, for three main reasons. First, on principle they regard the two sorts of expenditure as separate. Previously under the old Planning Total, local government expenditure was included in the block arrangements and derived using the formula, but the aggregate exchequer grant was negotiated separately. This was something of a 'fiction' because the departments could not influence local authority spending patterns. The new Planning Total introduced in 1988 was intended to separate out what was controllable and what was not. Second, whether AEF spending programmes in the territories and the English regions are comparable is arguable. Third, both departments argue that the AEF is higher per head in Scotland and Wales for historical reasons than in England, and the formula uplift does not give the same percentage rise for their authorities as in England. The system thus puts pressure on both ministers to 'top up' the AEF allocation from the rest of the block, although this involves earmarking resources before block negotiations have begun within the territorial departments.

The Treasury's counter-argument is that any settlement ultimately requires agreement between the relevant Secretary of State and the Chief Secretary, and therefore it is open for a territorial Minister to challenge the use of the formula. By implication, in recent years, since the introduction of the New Planning Total, no Secretary of State has regarded the issue as important enough to press a point of principle. The Treasury's second argument is that the NPT (and subsequently the New Control Total) was introduced precisely to be a tighter instrument of control: AEF is the central-government-determined element of local authority spending, eminently controllable and therefore a good candidate for the automaticity of the formula-based approach. The issue remains a point of tension between the mainland territorial departments and the Treasury.

Running costs allocations

Running costs for the territorial departments are calculated in a slightly different way from those of other spending departments (discussed in Chapter 18). The territorial departments agree (usually at official level), at the same time as the latter, a global limit for DRCs on the basis of their three-year management plans. As with other departments, limits are agreed for a three-year period. For year one the respective blocks benefit from formula consequentials of what comparable English departments settle on their running costs. In practice they receive a global package of comparable increments, with running costs and programme allocations rolled together. The resources for departmental running costs are then taken out of the block as a priority allocation. It is the earlier agreed DRC limits which are the focus of attention in the territories rather than the increments received from particular comparable English/UK departments.

BIDDING FOR RESOURCES

The internal process

The existence of the block and the relative freedom this gives the Secretary of State to move resources around is an important factor in creating a different internal process in the territorial departments than in most other spending departments.

Searching for comparability. The PFOs in Scotland and Wales and senior staff in the Northern Ireland DFP routinely ask their colleagues in Policy Divisions/departments to suggest areas of English/UK spending which could be considered comparable to territorial spending and which had not previously been included in the arrangement. Both the Treasury and the territorial departments' Finance Staff regard this as 'joint searching after truth' in an annual co-operative exercise, rather than as a source of confrontation. Indeed, the Treasury initiates the process by providing a computer list, based on Supply Votes, of all the programmes and sub-programmes carried out in Whitehall and itemizing those which were thought to apply to each of the three territorial departments. They are then asked to comment and suggest omissions or unnecessary items. Here the aim is to get it right. In any event, from the department's point of view it is a 'vineyard well tilled' over the past decade and few new areas are identified. As a result, most of the debate about comparability is at a fairly low level, mainly about structural change in a Whitehall programme.

Mirroring the Survey internally. The territorial Finance Divisions in Scotland and Wales begin the PES process internally by inviting 'bids' from Policy Divisions in March. These internal bids are then brought together, and the Secretary of State advised at the time of his May bidding letter (on non-block spending) what pressures there are on his current resources. Although speculative at this first stage, it is a 'good first sighting shot', in ignorance of the bids made by the other spending departments. During the summer the internal bids are revised and refined as the Finance Division obtains signals about the conduct of the Survey in Whitehall, and gets to know what the other spending departments are bidding. In July, August, and September officials from the Finance Division have a series of bilaterals with their Policy Groups, pressing them on their bids in a similar way to a Treasury Expenditure Division: scrutinizing, interrogating, and testing for value-for-money, priorities, and so on. As a result of these 'bilaterals', changes will then be made to the Policy Groups' internal bids. The process is an open one within the department, with the opportunity for Policy Groups' bids to be challenged, and for both to question the assessments of Finance Division. These bids become a major determinant of the later internal allocation of resources after the Treasury has given the respective Secretaries of State the global block figure.

The position in Northern Ireland is slightly different. At the beginning of the Survey the DFP asks the Northern Ireland departments and the NIO to provide information about how their expenditure compares with per capita spending on the mainland, and to justify this on the basis of evidence of needs and demands. It asks them to surrender efficiency and other programme savings, which are placed in a 'pot' to be added to increments provided through the formula system. The Policy Co-ordinating Committee (PCC), made up of the Permanent Secretaries of the Northern Ireland departments and the NIO, together with DFP, advise the Secretary of State on bidding tactics in negotiations with the Treasury and on the ordering of ministerial programme priorities. In the end, as the DFP is regarded as the 'manager of the block', its views about what guidance should be given to ministers would normally prevail. Both at this early stage and after the Autumn Budget Survey results are known, Northern Ireland mirrors the Whitehall Survey processes far more closely than the other two territorial departments, in large part because of the preservation of a structure of separate and sovereign departments.

The block and formula system

As we discussed earlier, the formula-based approach is the predominant means by which resources are allocated to the territories, although less significant in the case of Northern Ireland than the other two departments. The Treasury allows each of the Secretaries of State to have discretion, within a recognized 'block' of spending, to distribute resources according to departmental priorities. Both the formula and the block are examples of a non-statutory arrangement based on an understanding or agreement between the Treasury and the respective Secretaries of State. Only in the case of Northern Ireland are the rules of the game covering the block and formula written down in an authoritative document, *Northern Ireland Block Budget: Ground Rules*. This was produced in 1979 by Treasury and Northern Ireland officials, with subsequent technical amendments over time. It even records different interpretations of the lines of accountability between the NIO, the Treasury, and DFP, where these have been the subject of contention and debate. No similar document exists for the other two territories and there the ground rules are based on ministerial correspondence, understandings, and practice based on precedent. Across all the territories the implementation of this non-statutory arrangement is subject to observance by both sides of behavioural rules of the game. The most significant of these is the willingness on both sides to 'take the rough with the smooth'. The phrase is used in discussion within the territorial departments and the Treasury, and conveys acknowledgement that settlements will be satisficing, not optimal; that gains will be offset by some losses.

Where those losses are substantial, or exceptional, then either side will try and negotiate a more beneficial settlement. Where comparable English/UK programmes used in the application of the formula comprise items not applicable to one or more of the territorial departments, the department concerned will be a net beneficiary, for it gains an increment of resources for which the need is less compelling or even absent in the territory compared with that in England or elsewhere in the UK. On the other hand, in certain circumstances the territorial department may be a net loser from the application of the formula in circumstances where the spending department's programme is declining and attracts less resources. If the comparable programme in the territory is declining less quickly, or increasing, then the application of the formula will result in 'consequential' expenditure allocated to the block which the territory might think inadequate to local conditions. Differences in local government structure, and different priorities in each of the three territories, may mean that the application of the formula delivers too few resources, at least from the perspective of the territorial department.

The Treasury accepts that in the comparability exercise it is impossible to ensure a precise fit between comparable expenditure in England and in the territories and that there will inevitably be gains and losses on both sides. But the annual co-operative exercise in spotting potential comparable programmes is intended to minimize legitimate grievances. Where there are genuinely different local conditions and local priorities and resources are moved at the discretion of the Secretary of State to meet them, the Treasury regards such cases as inherent features of the block arrangement and would not accept that the formula is delivering too few (or too many) resources.

Where the territorial department believes that the application of the formula has worked against it, the basic behavioural rule of the game, as we have explained, is that it must be prepared to take the rough with the smooth. Both the Treasury and the department will, however, test the limits of the rule, where they think they can obtain further advantage or minimize perceived losses. For the departments, this means bidding 'outside the block', or seeking 'add-ons' to that obtained through comparability: that is, bidding separately for additional resources to supplement the provision for one or more of the programmes covered by the block allocation. The presumption in the Treasury is that departments will not 'bid against the block', emphasizing that the agreed ground rules prohibit separate bids for additional resources for programmes included within the block and covered by the formula arrangement, other than in exceptional circumstances. The use of language here reveals the different emphasis and interpretation given by each side to the breach of the rule of the game: the territories refer to the process as 'outside' or 'add-ons' to the block; the Treasury 'against' the block.

The territories do not see the process of allocating through the formula as unchanging. Rather it is regarded as a 'bench-mark' against which to judge whether the department has been treated adequately and fairly in the Survey. Nevertheless, bidding outside the block carries an element of risk. To do so may invite the Treasury to open up the whole block and subject all the 'consequential' expenditures to close scrutiny; and, in the case of the Northern Ireland departments, open up discussion of their baselines—historically protected from Treasury scrutiny. Moreover, the Treasury would reiterate the need to take 'the rough with the smooth', and remind the department of those elements of comparable programmes where it had been a net beneficiary. A greater risk still is to prompt the Treasury to question the continued viability of the block and formula system.

With due regard to such risks, a territorial department might nevertheless decide to test the limits of what was acceptable within the rules of the game without seeking to change them. It might seek to present an issue as technical rather than one of substance, and invite the Treasury to consider the arguments on their own merits without reference to the principles of block allocation. If the expenditure is relatively small, the Treasury may counter with the argument that there were ample margins elsewhere in the block to cover the expenditure. Testing out the limits of the rules of the game works both ways. The Treasury might raise cases with the territorial department where it had benefited with windfall 'consequentials' from the application of the formula.

Where a territorial department feels strongly aggrieved at the unfairness or inequality of the application of the formula, in circumstances which are unusual or could not be foreseen, then it will bid separately for additional resources outside the block. For example, on one occasion the block did not provide consequential expenditure to provide for a programme undertaken in a territory, but initiated by another Whitehall spending department. The annual costs of the programme for the territory rose from £200,000 to £18 million. It bid outside the block on the grounds that there was no comparable programme within the English/UK departments' spending.

Every third or fourth year there is an issue which cannot be easily dealt with within the block, and a territorial department will mount a case on the basis that the expenditure is exceptional. When the Treasury agrees to the request, or acquiesces in the bending of the rules, it allows comparability to be supplemented by the occasional 'add-on'. But, on the whole, comparability provides the bedrock of territorial expenditure. Nevertheless, it is the degree to which the system allows for some 'windfalls', and Treasury agreement to the occasional special case, which will form part of a territorial department's 'feel' for whether it benefits from the formula and block system. Strategically, it is in the interests of the Treasury to allow the 'rules' to be bent on occasion. Likewise, it is in the interest of the Finance Divisions in Scotland and Wales and of the Department of Finance and Personnel in Northern

Ireland not always to press a case beyond perceived acceptable limits. Policy Divisions and departments within the territories may feel frustrated but ultimately have to accept that Finance/DFP officials see the broader picture and are able to judge the longer-term benefits and costs of pushing an issue so far and no further.

The formula-driven nature of the AEF settlement poses particular problems for the mainland territorial departments. The debate about how to handle the AEF is a 'genuine debate'. The Secretary of State has to decide whether to take the consequence of the AEF settlement, or whether it would form part of his bid outside the block, or whether other priorities dictate a different strategy. In any event it is part of the bilateral process and open to the Secretary of State to raise these sorts of issues. In arriving at an AEF settlement there are separate discussions between the Chief Secretary and the Secretaries of State for the Environment, Scotland and Wales, in the course of which each will argue the case for their 'territory'. Should a territorial Secretary of State want to bid for additional resources to cover an AEF settlement, the Chief Secretary would ask for the usual value-for-money, political, and intellectual justification for the case, and may still use the 'affordability argument' to turn it down.

THE USE OF DISCRETION: ALLOCATING RESOURCES INTERNALLY

The Secretaries of State have discretion within their blocks to move resources around according to their priorities, subject to the policy rule of the game that such allocations are not 'unusual or repercussive', that is, likely to run counter to overall government policy. The Secretary of State for Scotland had a block amounting, for example, in 1993–4 to £12.4 billion, out of total expenditure of £13.5 billion in his sphere of responsibility; the Welsh Secretary had £5.7 billion out of total spending of £6.3 billion; and the Northern Ireland Secretary had real discretion (that is, after excluding the Social Security programme) over £5.7 billion out of a total of £7.5 billion.

The Secretaries of States' discretion

The Treasury's granting of discretion to the Secretaries of State to vary spending within the block allocation is another policy rule, a concession limited by three factors: the Treasury retains the ultimate power to rescind it in exceptional circumstances (for example, Chief Secretary

Portillo floated the possibility of abolishing it in the 1992 spending round, as part of measures to deal with the fiscal crisis); the use of discretion is limited by the real world constraints on the territorial departments; and the concession effectively applies only to the period between the Budget and the publication of Departmental Public Expenditure Reports in January/February, and the publication of the Supply Estimates in March, or May in the case of Northern Ireland. The Treasury still retains a range of in-year controls over the spending of the Scottish, Welsh, and Northern Ireland Offices (although not the Northern Ireland departments, which are subject to scrutiny by the DFP), as with any other Whitehall department, once the financial year begins. Nevertheless, it is yet another example of greater flexibility in the operation of the public spending planning and control regime than the rhetoric of the Treasury suggests.

Within the block rules, the Secretary of State has 'absolute discretion'. At the time of the Estimates scrutiny, the Treasury will examine the effect of any discretionary allocation within the block, but the concern is primarily with consistency between allocation in the Survey and the Votes and with the regularity and propriety of the allocated spending, as would be the case with any Whitehall department. Of course, the Treasury Territorial Expenditure Division might question the exercise of the Secretary of State's discretion, and brief the Chief Secretary to raise the matter with his Cabinet colleague. But major battles over allocation within the block are rare. Where there is more than a minor shift of resources between programmes, the Treasury would remind the territory concerned that the additional resources to fund a programme at a higher rate would have to continue to be provided within the block in future years.

The real issue is whether a Secretary of State has the powers in statute to initiate a policy which departs from previous practice. The relevance of the policy rule of 'unusual and repercussive' arises when a Whitehall spending department may worry more than the Treasury about the repercussive nature of any policy development in a territory. Where the powers exist, the Secretary of State can take his own policy initiatives, but he would have to inform the spending departments. If they are unhappy the process becomes a consultation. In reality, the problem tends to arise the other way round: a UK spending minister has a 'bright idea', say on reform of education, and the territorial department has to follow suit and bear the costs within the block, whether it can be afforded or not.

But the discretion of each Secretary of State is not unfettered or open-ended. There are practical limits to his freedom of manœuvre.

First, there are the problems of feasibility and practicality when faced with the 'real world'. Each Minister is constrained by the extent of the commitments in existing programmes: 'It is not possible to stop the NHS in its tracks.' There is not much opportunity to move a great deal of resources around, unless ministers want to take a really bold initiative. To do so would normally mean cuts in other areas. There is a basic quantum restraint: 'the head-room is relatively small'. The territorial departments calculate their real headroom after allowing for the now 2 per cent (previously 2.5 per cent) uplift factor between year two and the new year three in any Survey, and after taking out any Supplementary Estimates agreed in-year which do not count as part of the block and formula system. Then the AEF settlement (in the case of Scotland and Wales), pay costs, and differential inflation are deducted to produce a realistic figure of the amount of resources available to the Secretary of State. The residuum is of the order of about 0.5 to 1 per cent of the total of each territorial block; for example, in the case of Northern Ireland a sum of about £30 million in 1992.

Second, most policies are UK (or certainly GB) based and this there-fore limits a Minister's real discretion. Pay, for example, is a large element of costs and these are determined for GB as a whole. The cross-border comparison is also a powerful limiting factor. If the English Transport department has an extra £200 million to spend, the Welsh Secretary is going to have to think hard about a decision not to spend £12 million, or the Scottish Secretary not to allocate £20 million, or the Northern Ireland Secretary not to spend £5.8 million. The territorial Secretary of State is in the same government as the Chief Secretary, and has to abide by the general goals agreed collectively. Normally he has to pursue resource allocation policies consistent with them.

There are also three specifically agreed limitations to the discretion of the Secretaries of State, in addition to the constitutional and practical factors mentioned above. First, a Secretary of State's proposed spending may have wider implications for the rest of the UK and his discretion may therefore be tempered if there are potentially repercussive effects from his actions. Second, the territorial departments are not immune from the general pressure exerted by the Treasury to obtain value-for-money as this is applied through the normal process of project appraisal and discussions on specific projects. And, finally, the Secretaries of States' discretion is constrained by overall government policies in re-lation to the size and scope of the public sector, and here the Treasury has a very specific role, for example over the control of running costs.

The aim of each Finance Division/DFP is to try and maintain for its Secretary of State what little room for manœuvre there is. Here the

Treasury has a means to ensure that the department has a vested interest in watching its costs and efficiency. The block does not give the territorial departments an easy life; they are not immune from the pressures prevailing in the 1980s and 1990s. The system in any event provides an inbuilt incentive for Finance Divisions/DFP to identify areas where greater efficiency and value-for-money can be produced as the Minister does not gain from waste in the use of resources, rather he loses the possibility to move resources elsewhere. Nevertheless, Ministers are able to move some resources at the margins. Successive Welsh Secretaries have diverted resources into health over the years as consequentials have been siphoned off into that programme. The reasons are partly historical: differential morbidity, different population structure, and independent Welsh initiatives, for example on mental health.

The share-out in the departments

After the Budget results are known, the territories have to allocate the resources to their Policy Divisions and departments within a period of six to ten weeks before the publication of the Department Expenditure Reports. Once the block quantum is known, the Policy Division or department indicates what kind of outputs, effectiveness, value-for-money are expected from a programme; the Finance Division responds, and provides an overall assessment from its wider perspective. Both the Policy Groups' bids and the Finance Division assessment are submitted first to the Management Group before going on to the Secretary of State. Thereafter it becomes a 'horse-trade' or a 'corporate decision' (depending on the territorial department in question), but ministers do have choices and options laid before them, however limited the headroom.

One of the key decisions required to be taken by ministers in Scotland and Wales is whether or not to 'top up' the AEF settlement of the previous July. This is a difficult and sensitive issue for both officials and ministers. Any decision to use the Secretary of State's limited headroom to give extra resources to local authorities may be resisted by those of his ministers who have no local authority spending in their policy area, and urged by those who have large elements of local spending and hence 'client' groups to satisfy.

Allocating money from the block to make up the difference between the running costs consequentials and the global departmental running costs total is a priority call on resources. No extra resources can be put into running costs above the ceiling agreed with the Treasury. Given that running costs allocations are tight, the distribution to budget-holders can be very sensitive. In one of the territories an Assistant Secretary spent six weeks in January/February trying to fit the department's allocation to budget-holders' needs. The DRC settlement was so tight that the Finance Division gave budget-holders 95 per cent of what they had got in the previous year and then asked them to 'bid back' for more. This was regarded as a 'painful' exercise, with the Permanent Secretary involved in agreeing the final allocation.

In Northern Ireland the process is similar to that in Whitehall spending departments. Once the Budget results are announced, DFP adds the global sum of increments obtained to the 'pot' of 'savings' gleaned from the internal process at the beginning of the Survey, the total of which is then available to be distributed between the Northern Ireland departments. Two priority claims have to be met: that of the expenditure of the NIO (negotiated and agreed separately with the Treasury) and the total, although not the precise division of, departmental running costs. Each Northern Ireland department then bids for its programme and running costs expenditure. The Policy Co-ordinating Committee advises the DFP on allocation, but the DFP has the final say in its submission to its minister. There then follows a series of bilaterals between the DFP Minister, acting as a Northern Ireland quasi-Chief Secretary, and his ministerial colleagues in charge of the other departments and the NIO. The Secretary of State acts as a referee, taking on the role of part-Prime Minister, part-Star Chamber on the mainland, in the event of an impasse in negotiations.

WHO BENEFITS FROM THE SYSTEM?

The formula and block confer benefits, as well as some disadvantages, to the Treasury and each territorial department. Some of these are inherent in the system, others result from its operation. It is very difficult to assess the empirical evidence about the operation of the formula because of the secretive nature of the decision-making process and because there have been three break-points in the operation of the system: the introduction of cash planning in 1982; the introduction of the new Planning Total in 1990; and the simultaneous revision of the formula and institution of the New Control Total in 1992.

Systemic factors

We noted earlier Heald's view that the formula arrangement has peculiar dynamic properties. The formulae prescribed for Scotland and

Wales were based on their share of Great Britain's population in 1978–9; that for Northern Ireland based on its share of UK population. If public expenditure as a whole rose in real terms, the application of the formulae would over time tend to bring expenditure in the territories into line with that prevailing in England. This would be to the advantage of Wales, which has historically been relatively poorly resourced compared with England and the other territories; and to the disadvantage of Scotland and Northern Ireland with historically high levels of funding. If expenditure fell in real terms the effects would be reversed.

There is a further factor which should theoretically accelerate these effects: the abandonment of volume planning in 1982 meant that the territorial departments could no longer protect their baselines through the effective indexing of their programmes against the impact of inflation. From 1983 to 1991, baselines between year two and the new year three of the Survey were uplifted by only 2.5 per cent, reduced to 2 per cent from 1992. This had the effect of speeding up the convergence of programme baselines in the territories with those in England, and made the level of inflation as important a factor in determining the degree to which spending trends in the territories converged with those in England as the application of the formula itself (Heald 1992).

The picture is, however, complicated by the fact that the formula was unchanged between 1978–9 and 1993–4. Since 1978 the population of Wales has grown relative to that of England; Northern Ireland's population has grown relative to that of Great Britain; and Scotland's population has declined relative to that of England. These changes have added a further dimension to the calculation of the benefits derived by the respective territories from the current system. The formula was amended in 1992, ostensibly to reflect the results of the 1991 Census, but of equal importance in the decision to revise it was the Chief Secretary's attempt to keep total spending in line with published targets. The change has benefited Wales and Northern Ireland at the expense of Scotland.

The data on identifiable public spending per head provides no conclusive proof about the impact of the formula on territorial spending. As Heald (1992) notes, the Treasury changed the measure in 1990 to General Government Expenditure per head, rather than basing statistics on the Planning Total. The result is yet further discontinuities in the time-series of financial data. Moreover, the formula has not been the only determinant of expenditure allocation: the uplift factor in year three is based on nominal inflation and the territories gain resources outside the formula as discussed earlier. What conclusions that can be drawn suggest spending per head in Scotland was maintained because the effects of the dynamic properties of the formula which should have worked to its disadvantage have been mitigated by the relative decline of its population. Conversely, Wales fared less well throughout the 1980s than would have been expected from the effects of the formula's properties because of its relative increase in population. The reduction in Northern Ireland's identifiable spending per head is explained similarly by the relative increase in population since the late 1970s.

There is some evidence that the territorial resource allocation system as a whole worked in favour of the interests of Scotland and Northern Ireland. This is in large measure because the formula and block system has been operated flexibly by the non-revision (until recently) of the formula on the basis of population shifts (to the benefit of Scotland) and the occasional additional allocation of resources above comparability (to the benefit of Northern Ireland). But Wales has continued to be disadvantaged by the system. The Principality has seen its relatively poor resourcing position before the introduction of the Barnett formula in the late 1970s deteriorate, predominantly because of the decision not to revise the formula in the light of population movements. This can be interpreted as further evidence of the lack of political clout by successive Welsh Secretaries of State, relative to that wielded by their Scottish and Northern Irish colleagues. What is shown by the Treasury's most recent data on spending per head for 1990–1 and 1991–2 is that the public spending regime as it applies to the territories is gradually achieving the Treasury's longer-term aim. Spending per head is converging with that in England.

The operation of the system in practice

Heald (1992) has identified four factors which he has labelled 'formula-bypass', the effects of which have meant that the territorial allocation system has never been operated on a purely mechanistic basis. First, the territories have regularly benefited from in-year supplements for public-sector pay awards, for example; secondly, the outturns of local authority expenditure in the territories have been different from that in England and higher spending has not necessarily been recouped in later years; thirdly, some items of spending in the territories have had no clear comparator in England and the expenditure implications have been covered by allocations outside the formula, for example when the privatization of water in England removed the comparative basis for consequentials for Scotland; and fourthly, the mathematical basis of the Barnett formula proved in practice an over-simplification. It was only a rough approximation of population levels in 1978, while the uplift factor for the baseline in year three was until recently based on an allowance for inflation, allocated uniformly to all departments, irrespective of whether a formula system was in place or not.

The perceptions of territorial officials and ministers of the costs and benefits conferred by the current arrangements go beyond the structural questions addressed above. There are, in addition, two perceived politico-administrative benefits to the territories. First, they avoid the detailed Treasury scrutiny of their programmes which occurs in PES processes with other spending departments. Their allocations are decided automatically by the application of agreed rules. This not only simplifies the procedure, freeing time and administrative resources, and avoiding detailed negotiations over relatively small amounts of money: it means also that there is less opportunity for the territories to be picked off by the Treasury on the basis of its knowledge of the comparable bidding strategy of other spending departments (and indeed the other territories) on similar programmes. It would be very difficult for the territories to be able to justify additional resources for every programme on the basis of additional needs and demands. The block arrangement is, on balance, advantageous to the territorial departments, while the Treasury gains from the arrangement because of the predictability and certainty of the allocative mechanism, and also saves time and administrative resources. Once negotiations are concluded with the spending departments and, presumably, settled in a way that gives some assurance that programmes have been scrutinized to eliminate waste and 'soft bits', then the territories are allocated resources consequentially. In so doing the Treasury ensures that over time the bench-mark for spending allocation throughout the UK will be that established for programmes in England.

Second, the territories are given some discretion and flexibility to allocate resources at the margins to reflect local conditions and priorities. Over time a territory can design its own strategies in priority areas—such as the *Making Belfast Work* initiative in Northern Ireland—rather than following an English policy model. While the amount of resources which can be moved in this way is very small (about 0.5 to 1 per cent of total block spending), within a block of more than £10 billion in Scotland and over £4 billion each in Wales and Northern Ireland there is opportunity to build up a distinct programme over a number of years. Granting this degree of discretion, with the proviso that such territorial programmes should not be 'unusual or repercussive', is an acceptance by the Treasury of the tradition of relative autonomy for the territorial Secretaries of State, which in turn reflects the sensitive electoral politics of the territories. It is also a means of ensuring that each Secretary of State has a vested interest in improving efficiency and value-for-money to release resources to be reallocated according to emerging priorities.

PART IV

Control and Flexibility

15

In-Year Control

Within each Treasury Expenditure Group, the flow and context of the business of an Expenditure Division is to a large extent structured and determined by the annual cycle of the preparation of the Survey. At the same time, much other business is only partly or remotely connected with that work. The separate categories of Survey and In-year Control, while recognizably those used in the Treasury, do not adequately convey the links and cross-walks between the two; for example, that an issue of in-year control may have consequences for the current or future Surveys; or, that issues which arise in the course of Survey discussions with departments may have implications for the development of policy which will be followed up later on 'in-year'. Nevertheless, the distinction between the two main types of work is helpful in the analysis and explanation of what Expenditure Divisions do, although we recognize that it is not as clear-cut in practice.

The quality and effectiveness of the Treasury's in-year control of departmental expenditure is determined mainly by its success in delivering the intended outputs of the Planning/Control Total: first, to ensure that resources are used only for those purposes voted by Parliament, consistently with prescribed standards of propriety and regularity in the use of public money; and, secondly, to deliver an outturn consistent with the Planning/Control Total. During the year, pressures for additional spending arise from changes in macro-economic strategy, revised or new political priorities, and events and issues which were unprovided for at the time of the Survey negotiations. Tight cash control has to be tempered with the means and willingness to respond flexibly where additional spending can be justified. In the next four chapters we deal in turn with the main mechanisms through which the Treasury provides for control and flexibility: the Reserve, cash limits, running costs controls, and end-year flexibility schemes. This chapter provides a broad overview of the in-year control and monitoring processes, looks at the principles and use by the Treasury of delegated authority, and concludes with a discussion of the use of formal and informal reviews of policy as an aid to controlling levels of future expenditure.

There have been major changes in the control environment in specific parts of the public sector. Central–local financial relationships have been the subject of frequent change since 1976. From 1979 the pace of change quickened, culminating in the introduction and subsequent abandonment of the community charge, centrally administered uniform business rating, and a planning regime under the new Planning Total which excluded locally raised expenditure from the headline public-spending planning total, and the New Control Total which readmitted it. Nationalized industries have been subject to a tighter financial regime since 1976. This has been mediated through several mechanisms: External Financing Limits (EFL) have been used as a cash limit and a means of ensuring that nationalized industries' finances were 'turned round' to ease the expenditure burden on the Treasury; specific financial targets have been set for break-even or return against capital; performance targets have been set for reductions in unit costs; and increasingly corporate plans have been used to determine the Treasury's response to the industries' request for financial support. There has been a whole new set of rules governing industries which have been or are being prepared for privatization. Taken together, such systemic factors can so affect the operating environment of the nationalized industries in particular that they are far more important in determining the outcome of any one annual Survey than the short-term discussions between the Expenditure Divisions and the departments and industries they shadow. 'In any one year taken separately, the Treasury's influence is very marginal. Over the long-term the effect of the creation of an operating environment can be substantial' (Second Permanent Secretary, HM Treasury).

Once a Survey round has been completed and the Chancellor has announced the results to Parliament in the Autumn Statement or, from 1993, in the Unified Budget (also presented in documentary form), the Expenditure Divisions are concerned with ensuring that the 'envelope' of cash provided for their department(s) is not exceeded in the financial year. This involves monitoring cash-flow and dealing with control issues in-year. In practice, such in-year monitoring and control begins from the Autumn Statement, even though this is made some four months before the start of the financial year. There is some tidying-up to do following the conclusion of the Survey, prior to the publication of (formerly) the Public Expenditure White Paper and (now) the individual Departmental Expenditure Reports in the following February. There may be classification changes or changes in economic category or in economic forecasts which affect the previously agreed Survey total. And the allocation of money agreed in the Survey discussions has to be converted into Parliamentary Supply Votes and Cash Limits.

Once the Survey outcome becomes an in-year issue, the principle guiding Expenditure Controllers is that they must be guardians of the Survey outcome. The Expenditure Divisions work 'within clear parameters: the public expenditure plans provide the discipline'. In-year discussions are most often about whether 'X or Y can be done or not within those figures' (Assistant Secretary). Individual Expenditure Controllers have limited discretion over this basic issue; items of spending are 'either in the package or outside'. Where they do have discretion is in judging whether a department has a good case now for a claim on the Reserve (see next chapter), or for delay until later in the year when the pressure on a department may become clearer.

The range of in-year monitoring and control tasks carried out by Expenditure Divisions varies considerably according to the type of department being shadowed. This variation in workload is reflective of whether the department itself is directly responsible for spending the money allocated to it (such as the FCO) or some of the department's functions are carried out by Executive Agencies, whether financed through normal arrangements or as trading funds; or whether it acts as a paymaster for other agencies within the orbit of central government (e.g. the Department of Employment and the training agencies); or, less directly still, hands on resources to a different tier of government (e.g. the DFE and Local Education Authorities); or has only a co-ordinating or sponsoring role in regard to agencies which raise most of their resources from the market-place (e.g. the Department of Transport and British Rail).

In practice, it is very difficult to separate public-spending monitoring from control. The Treasury's Expenditure Divisions have to check a department's cash-spend partly in order to provide early warning of possible in-year control problems. We divide the two components of in-year work for purposes of analysis, while recognizing that, from the point of view of an Expenditure Controller, the distinction between monitoring and control is artificial.

MONITORING

Expenditure Divisions' monitoring work has become increasingly routinized since the introduction and subsequent development of the Treasury's Financial Information System (FIS). 'Profiles are set for departments' spending at the beginning of each financial year. Those profiles set out the expected pattern of spending over the year ahead. During the year they are compared with the actual pattern of spending so that action can be taken to correct any substantial divergence'

(Treasury 1989*b*: para. 53). There are similar systems which monitor local authority spending, and the financial position of nationalized industries, where officials will meet representatives of the industry on a monthly or quarterly basis. The Expenditure Divisions will meet regularly and formally, Controllers often monthly, with their departments to discuss these returns. The Expenditure Division would give its interpretation of the profile of spending outlined in the accounts. The departmental (or nationalized industries) Finance Division officials might disagree with the assessment, and a discussion would ensue. The Expenditure Division would not often query the arithmetic, but rather the possible interpretation of it. The meeting would conclude, if potential spending problems were emerging, with the Expenditure Division asking the department what actions they intended to take to rectify them.

Depending on the sort of information being discussed and the degree to which a department, agency, or nationalized industry is subject to market uncertainty, an Expenditure Division may have to spend longer trying to 'get behind the figures'. Whilst the collection of data on cash-flow may be 'mechanical', it may be difficult to get the department or industry to present it on time. And having managed to do that, it requires further resolution on the part of the Expenditure Division not to be overwhelmed by the figures but to find out what they imply for the development of a programme or policy. For example, a Treasury Expenditure Controller has to be aware that 'undue optimism' may have resulted in unchanged nationalized industry forecasts over successive months in-year which, if not challenged, may result in a sudden financing crisis later in the year.

Some assessments of data may be genuinely difficult for departments to get right. Much of the so-called 'routine' presentation of information is in fact highly charged and contentious. Examples of this abound in agriculture. There may be changes in estimates or world-price movements, the quality of the harvest, or the moisture content in cereals, all of which impact on the degree to which the Survey settlement can be held to without recourse to the Reserve. Expenditure Divisions are constantly engaged with their departments to produce realistic forecasts, which bear some relationship with past experience.

RECURRENT IN-YEAR CONTROL ISSUES

There are many types of problems which occur in-year which the Expenditure Divisions have to tackle. To an Expenditure Controller these represent just another part of the relentless flow of 'business' which must be dealt with. Here we distinguish for analytical purposes between two kinds of in-year control issues: routine items which fall into categories of spending deemed eligible for treatment under a number of special schemes, provided the department adheres to the scheme's rules previously circulated; and extemporary items which cannot be so accommodated but for which there may be a case for additional monies being provided. In practice some cases fall between the two, and there may still be room for judgement by an Expenditure Controller even when an item falls into the category of routine and systematized expenditure.

The Expenditure Divisions handle a large number of schemes which allow departments to carry forward under-spending between financial years. We deal with the various cash-limits capital end-year flexibility schemes (EYF), and the analogous EYF scheme for running costs in more detail in Chapters 18 and 19. Most of the in-year cash limits casework undertaken by an Expenditure Division is routine, and involves changes to a limit due to transfer of function between or within departments (see Chapter 17). The arrangements for this are time-consuming but are mainly 'technical'. Virement takes place between Votes, with one Vote going up and another down. As functions change so the running costs, for example, will have to be moved to meet this. Cash limits can also be adjusted because of a pay award made in-year. Often such changes will have been 'flagged-up' in prior government announcements, so in a technical sense they may not even be the result of a department formally asking for a cash limit revision. The Treasury still subjects such requests to 'rigorous scrutiny'. Whatever the reason for a request, the Expenditure Division will still ask for offsetting savings to be made. As a general rule, a request made for movement within the Survey envelope (moves within subheadings or if a new agency is being set up, unforeseen at the time of the Survey discussions) is flexibly treated; requests which do not fit into this category are subject to tougher Treasury scrutiny.

During any financial year issues arise which cannot be accommodated within the Survey total agreed in the previous spending round or for which no special scheme applies. Expenditure Controllers involved in expanding policy areas can expect to come across many such issues. A departmental request for additional spending in-year, if supported by the Expenditure Division, has to go to the Chief Secretary, whose approval implies agreement to 'draw' on the Reserve, discussed in the next chapter. Any such agreement is without prejudice to the following Survey discussions. Public-sector pay settlements which result from the recommendations of pay review bodies have become regular items on the agenda (such as those for nurses and the armed forces). Expenditure to fund these is approved subject to the ministerial response to the review body recommendation. If ministerial approval is given, there follows a delicate process in which the Treasury decides whether to allow full or partial funding from the Reserve, or asks the department to find the resources from within its existing budget. Even when full or partial Treasury funding is given, the department is expected to make a bid in the following Survey for money to continue supporting the pay settlement; there is no rolling forward of the Treasury funding.

A different set of problems is posed for the Expenditure Divisions which shadow nationalized industries. An Expenditure Controller has to judge whether an industry request for a revised EFL is justified and whether an agreed revision should be delayed until later in the financial year when a clearer picture emerges. Because the EFL is a function of trade and market conditions, not discretionary spending by departments, it can sometimes be less a case of whether an EFL needs to be revised than by 'how much' and when. Procedurally, a request has to be sent to the Chief Secretary, as a revision is a call on the Reserve. Most often, a request for an EFL revision is accepted because both sides agree that 'something needs to be done which is justified and is not provided for in the existing EFL' (Assistant Secretary, Expenditure Division). A request would be refused if the Expenditure Division thought the sponsoring department or industry was acting in an unjustifiable way.

DELEGATED AUTHORITY

In statute the Treasury is the accounting department responsible for the Consolidated Fund, the National Loans Fund, the Contingencies Fund, and the Exchange Equalisation Account, funds which are at the heart of the system of government finance. A cardinal principle of public finance is that expenditure requiring Treasury authority may not be charged to a Parliamentary Supply Vote unless the Treasury gives its authority. Functions imposed on the Treasury by statute cannot be delegated to another department unless the legislation itself provides for this. Subject to this proviso, the Treasury, in consultation with departments, agrees the level and categories of delegated authority, outside of which the Treasury has to be specifically consulted. The Exchequer and Audit Departments Acts of 1866 and 1921, and the National Audit Act of 1983, together with numerous Acts dealing with the financial arrangements for nationalized industries, recognize the Treasury's traditional role of ensuring that there is proper accountability to Parliament for the use of public money. Treasury ministers are responsible for the presentation of Supply Estimates to Parliament. Treasury authorization is required for the virement of money between subheadings of spending, and for some items of spending Treasury consent is a statutory requirement.

The implementation of the principles which underlie both FMI and Next Steps marks a significant strategic shift in the Treasury's exercise of control, towards increased delegation of authority to spending departments and executive agencies. The origins of this shift were explained in Chapter 4. As a result, line managers are now given more discretion to decide and commit expenditure, while the Chief Executives of newly created Executive Agencies have secured substantial financial autonomy through the framework agreements negotiated with their departments and the Treasury. Within the broad strategic context provided by the two initiatives, specific arrangements are made for granting or renewing delegated authority.

For some categories of spending, the Treasury delegates authority to individual spending departments to commit expenditure up to a set level without the need to seek Treasury approval. The Treasury can determine both the level and the categories of authority so delegated, outside of which it has to be specifically consulted. The Expenditure Divisions have a major role in determining these limits. Changing the levels of delegated authority can be used as a 'carrot' to encourage a department to improve its financial management, or can be a deterrent to dissuade a department from acting in ways not approved by the Treasury. As such, delegation is an important focal issue in the relationship between departments and the Expenditure Divisions.

The Expenditure Divisions have a great deal of discretion to grant levels of delegated authority. The general approach rests on finding the right balance between the Treasury's need for control in order to fulfil its responsibilities for public expenditure, and the department's freedom to manage within its overall allocations and limits. The levels and categories of delegated authority vary across departments, reflecting such considerations as the nature and size of a department's expenditure; the control systems in place within the department, and the Expenditure Division's degree of confidence in the quality of those systems and the way they are operated and managed; and the number and nature of cases that the Expenditure Division needs to see in order to satisfy itself that departmental systems continue to be operated satisfactorily. For example, during much of the 1980s the general delegated limits were £10 million for health programmes and £25 million for defence. An Expenditure Division will also seek, in accordance with FMI principles, to encourage departments to pass on delegations down the line wherever suitable, rather than holding them at the centre. Delegation does not extend to expenditure proposals which are 'novel or contentious'. Although these words are difficult to define precisely, their feel is generally well understood in both Expenditure Divisions and departments. They are intended to cover proposals of which the department or indeed the Expenditure Division has no past experience; or which could provoke a row. Expenditure Divisions are required to consider each year whether delegated authorities need review: this provides an opportunity for Expenditure Divisions to review the degree to which a department has improved its financial management and project appraisal techniques to warrant further delegation.

POLICY REVIEWS

It is often difficult to say who initiates a policy review. Detailed discussions about a programme may spring from problems spotted by the Expenditure Division during the Survey round which, after initial probing, are taken up later. Reviews may begin as part of the regular discussions between the Treasury and a department and then feed into wider policy reviews which result from a programme gaining higher political salience in a changed political climate. An Expenditure Division may be part of a working party set up as the result of ministerial, Prime Ministerial, or Cabinet decision. The NHS Review in 1988–9 and Education Review in 1986–7 are good substantive examples. Once a review is under way, formal and informal communication between the Treasury and the department is continual.

In reality, all the work undertaken by the Expenditure Divisions has a high policy content. Here we distinguish between formal reviews of government policy, which because of their expenditure implications will involve the Treasury's Expenditure Divisions, and the less formal, *ad hoc* policy reviews which occur in-year as the result of crises or political developments. In practice there is considerable blurring at the edges.

Formal policy reviews

Expenditure Controllers are frequently involved in the preparatory work for policy reviews covering aspects of the business of the department which they shadow, which often lead to Green or White Papers.

Recent examples in the late 1980s include student loans and the NHS Review. In addition, there are a number of semi-permanent features of expenditure control which produce an increased workload for Expenditure Divisions. The most obvious example of this is the annual pay reviews. The Treasury Expenditure Controllers are involved in overseeing the documentation prepared by the departments for the Review Boards and, in the case of some aspects of the review of armed forces pay, may actually co-write submissions or have the right to submit additional information. In any event, the Expenditure Divisions will have to be prepared to brief their Chief Secretary on the expenditure implications of an award.

A related type of formal review involves the working out in practice of a large meta-level government initiative such as FMI or Next Steps. As part of the annual cycle of work, the Expenditure Divisions pursue with departments their progress on introducing changes in departmental practice prescribed in government policy statements. The Defence Expenditure Group has been discussing with the M.o.D. for several years the introduction of a new management strategy incorporating FMI-style financial management information systems, performance targets, and indicators.

Informal policy reviews

There are many sorts of informal *ad hoc* policy work which involve the Expenditure Divisions. Some may begin at the official level, with the Treasury suggesting that an issue raised during Survey discussions should be given further consideration. A Treasury–department working group will continue at the official level until sufficient progress has been made for a report to be presented to the respective ministers.

Almost all Expenditure Divisions will have particular in-year projects which involve examination of an aspect of a department's financial management. The Defence Expenditure Group, for example, in the early 1990s concentrated on the M.o.D.'s management of engineering and repair services across the three Services. Studies resulting from particular problems thrown up in Survey discussions, or as in-year issues, usually involve linkages between various aspects of a department's activities so that Treasury probing elicits more general information about the quality of a department's management. Given the small numbers in the Expenditure Divisions, such specific and focused work is the most cost-effective way of 'sampling' the activities of the departments they shadow. Prompts on where best to probe can arise from consultants' reports, the work of the National Audit Office, or the Audit

Commission, as well as from Expenditure Controllers following their own hunches. Expenditure Divisions may encourage a department to review its bid in order to substantiate its case to the Treasury, for example on running costs allocations. This can be misunderstood by the department, and treated as a stratagem to squeeze the department further. It is, in any event, a delicate process, since whether a department gains from reworking its submission depends on how well bilateral negotiations proceed, the pressure on resources from other departments, and political prioritization.

Occasionally an Expenditure Division and its spending department have a shared interest in working together on a particular in-year policy problem. For example, responding to new circumstances, the government issues a general statement of intent to take a policy initiative. The Expenditure Division and department concerned then try to find a way of funding it. The issue may not be large enough to merit inclusion in later Survey discussions, or to prompt a reordering of departmental priorities. The Treasury–departmental discussions then focus on procedure, how to handle the issue, whether the expenditure envisaged can be absorbed or whether it is necessary to reopen previous agreements. Similarly, Treasury Expenditure Controllers may be part of a working party trying to remove a long-standing problem facing a department, such as the increasing costs of medical insurance borne by consultants. Here the Expenditure Division's role is less that of saving 'candle-ends', more that of collaborator in a joint endeavour 'to get something done'.

16

The Reserve

The Reserve is a sum of unallocated money provided for each financial year of the Survey to enable the Treasury to finance increases to public expenditure without revising the Planning/Control Total. It is an important element of the Survey, a mechanism which enables the Treasury to plan and control public expenditure more effectively and flexibly. Its definition, purpose, and use have changed over time, as the Treasury has sought to improve its control in response to the aims of successive governments to contain and reduce the growth of public expenditure. This chapter explains what the Reserve is and how and why it has been used by the Treasury since 1976. We begin by tracing its origins, examine how it is calculated, and then describe the changes made in the rules governing its use, the most recent and significant of which occurred in 1984. Before that date it was called first the Contingency Allowance and then the Contingency Reserve, and occasionally confused with the Contingencies Fund. The Fund has been used since 1862 to finance those expenditures urgently needed before additional Supply is voted by Parliament. It is separate and distinct from the Reserve.

THE CONTINGENCY ALLOWANCE, 1963–1976

There has been provision for contingencies in the planning of public expenditure since the introduction of PESC in the early 1960s, and the first published Survey in 1963–4. It was formalized in 1968. Thereafter it became standard practice to allocate a sum for this purpose for each of the Survey years. In so doing, the Cabinet had to decide how much planned and allocated expenditure it was prepared to forgo, in order to provide for unanticipated expenditure. Lord Diamond, Chief Secretary to the Treasury from 1964 to 1970, claims that that difficult choice had prevented an agreement on the procedure of providing an allocated allowance for each Survey year before 1968 (Diamond 1975).

Until 1976 the Contingency Allowance provided a margin between the estimates of total expenditure planned in the Survey and the estimates of what would actually be spent. From the earliest experience of the Survey, the Treasury observed that, in attempting to look three or four years ahead, outturn expenditure tended to be greater than anticipated after the third year. This was due to inadequate knowledge about the factors determining that expenditure, which were of two main kinds: unforeseen expenditure; and expenditures which arose from the development or revision of an existing policy, or from new policy initiatives. At the same time the Treasury acknowledged the need and the utility of providing for an element of flexibility in the planning and controlling of public expenditure. As (Sir) Peter Baldwin, the Treasury Under Secretary in charge of the General Expenditure Division, explained to the House of Commons Select Committee on Expenditure in 1971, the Contingency Allowance provided 'a workable system for accommodating changes which a government may want to make from time to time in their policies without their having to review the entire system of priorities as set out in their policies at that time' (Select Committee on Expenditure 1971: qu. 390).

In the period until 1976, the operation of the Contingency Reserve (as it came to be called) enabled departmental ministers to make claims on it during the course of the year not only for expenditure which was unforeseen, or to finance a policy development, but also to finance proposals which had been brought forward at the time of the Survey and which had not been wholly or partly approved by the Treasury. The Reserve provided

a little more room for manœuvre and it enables a disappointed departmental Minister to console himself with the hope that circumstances may permit some increase beyond planned expenditure in which case his temporarily rejected proposals may be accepted and financed out of the contingency reserve. Indeed he may have withdrawn his proposals on that very condition. (Diamond 1975: 83)

How extensive this practice was is not known. It may be inferred from the decision made in 1976 to use the Reserve as a control figure that the categories of additional spending financed through it before that date were not well defined, and the rules governing its use operated flexibly.

The 'crisis of control' and the introduction of cash limits which followed in its wake in 1976 led to a tightening of the rules governing the use of the Contingency Reserve, and a new determination to enforce them strictly. It was formally announced that it would henceforth be used as a control device, to contain additional expenditures. Cabinet now decided those claims brought to it by spending ministers which caused difficulty with the Treasury, against the background of a progress report on the state of the Reserve. At the same time the Treasury's position *vis-à-vis* the spending departments was also strengthened by a new rule of Cabinet procedure introduced by the Prime Minister. In effect, the Treasury ministers could no longer be overruled on financial matters in Cabinet Committee. The onus of appeal to full Cabinet was placed upon spending ministers—a reversal of the previous situation (Pliatzky 1982).

The general purpose for which the Reserve was intended originally, to meet unforeseen expenditure and to finance new policy initiatives, remained unchanged. However, the tightening of the rules meant that more emphasis was given after 1976 to the desirability of funding additional spending through savings on other programmes. The Reserve became a fund of last resort. Moreover, the Treasury began to distinguish between different types of additional spending. Expenditure which resulted from 'fresh ministerial decisions' was a legitimate charge upon the Reserve, provided no offsetting savings were possible. Expenditure which was demand-determined, and not directly under ministerial control once rates had been set, was not charged to it. 'Offsetting savings are always sought for them wherever possible' (Treasury 1982*b*).

The principle of the Contingency Reserve and rules governing its operation before 1984 provided an important advantage: they imposed a tight discipline on changes to public spending proposed by ministers 'in-year', that is after the allocations had been decided on in the Survey and published in the Expenditure White Paper. Such rules applied only to those rules which ministers could allow or disallow as claims on the Reserve, at their discretion. Set at a low level of some £1.5 billion, the Reserve imposed a tight control on claims for such additional 'discretionary' expenditure. When it was exhausted, any additional claims were unsuccessful. This advantage was offset by disadvantages which became more important as the Treasury tried to deliver to the Conservative Government a closer match between the total aggregate of planned and outturn expenditure in the difficult early years of the first Thatcher Government. While the Reserve was a tight control mechanism on discretionary additional expenditure, it provided no guide to the aggregate outturn of expenditure, because claims for non-discretionary expenditure, for example unemployment and social security benefits, were made and approved outside the mechanism of the Reserve. It had been decided to omit such 'uncertain expenditures' from the control system rather than to include them and risk the possibility of gross inaccuracies. With the introduction of the MTFS, and its prescription of the aggregates for public spending, revenue, and the money supply, economic management refocused attention on the control of the aggregate of public expenditure. However, as non-discretionary expenditures remained outside the discipline of the Reserve, such additions had to be funded at whatever level, except in the rare circumstances where it was possible to direct a minister to cut other programmes to accommodate them. The effect was that there was no overall in-year control figure. It was possible to overspend the Planning Total because of the amount of non-discretionary expenditure claims approved by ministers, while the Reserve remained underspent because of the rules allowing only those discretionary expenditures to count against it.

THE CHANGES OF 1984

In 1984 the purpose and operation of the Contingency Reserve was overhauled, its name changed, and new rules governing its use introduced. The main reason was the need to control the Planning Total aggregates more effectively, as part of the Conservative Government's macro-economic strategy set out in the MTFS. In 1980–1 and 1981–2 the Treasury had been unable to deliver the planned aggregate of public expenditure. Public expenditure grew in real terms by 5 per cent between 1979–80 and 1982–3. As unemployment grew in the recession of the early 1980s, there were large increases in unplanned expenditure on unemployment and social security payments, too large to be covered by offsetting savings in other programmes. At the same time there was substantial overspending by local authorities on (RSG) grant-aided services.

The new rules provide tighter control of additional expenditure both 'in-year' and at the time of the Survey negotiations. All additions to expenditure in each of the three years of the Survey are now treated as claims on the Reserve. This requires a much larger Reserve, which in turn means that a larger proportion of the Planning/Control Total is left unallocated. The implications of this are discussed below. In practice, the amount available to finance in-year changes to programme expenditure is greater than the Reserve in circumstances where the proceeds from the sale of assets under the privatization programme exceed the figure provided in the Planning/Control Total, set initially at £5 billion and then raised to £5.5 billion. Conversely, there is greater pressure on the Reserve where those proceeds are less than estimated. In 1988 the Reserve was underspent by £3.5 billion (its nominal size), because programme allocations were underspent and there were heavier than anticipated receipts from privatization. The previous year the Reserve had balanced, following an overspend of £1 billion in 1986.

The calculation of the Reserve

Until 1984, the calculation of the (Contingency) Reserve was made on the basis of the Treasury's accumulated experience of the regularity of claims for additional expenditure, which resulted from new policy developments during the year and unforeseen events. Both the incidence of that expenditure and its size as a proportion of total planned expenditure were difficult to predict. 'Getting it right was as much an accident as anything else', commented a senior Treasury official. The Reserve was calculated at about 1 to 2 per cent of total planned expenditure each year. The uncertainty of estimating through the Survey period meant that the Reserve for years two, three, and (until 1980) four, tended to be set at the higher end.

In the Public Expenditure White Paper of March 1982 the Reserve was substantially increased both for the immediate financial year and the two following years. This was a consequence of the overshoot of total planned expenditure which occurred in 1981–2. Provision for 1982–3 was doubled from £2 billion to £4 billion, and tripled for the year after, from £2 billion to £6 billion. The effect of these much greater allocations to the Reserve was that less public expenditure as a proportion of the Planning Total was allocated to departmental programmes than had been the case in previous years; in total nearly 3.5 per cent in 1982–3 and more than 4.5 per cent in 1983–4 was left unallocated. In the event, the Reserve was overfunded. In the following PEWP (Feb. 1983), the provision was reduced for all three Survey years.

The change in the rules governing the use of the Reserve in 1984 to provide a single fund for all changes in expenditure from wherever derived, implied a larger Reserve both in total and as a proportion of planned expenditure. Provision for the immediate financial year was more than 2 per cent of total planned expenditure in every year until the introduction of the new Control Total in 1993–4. In the same period the amount unallocated in years two and three increased sharply, amounting to nearly 6 per cent of the Planning Total in some Survey years.

Leaving larger amounts of total expenditure unallocated enabled the Treasury to adjust spending with less risk of breaching the Planning Total. In particular, this enabled it to provide for the expected overspend by local authorities on their grant-aided programmes, and on demand-determined programmes such as social security. Overshoots on local authorities' own expenditure were included as a call on the

Reserve until the introduction of the New Planning Total in 1989. LASFE was readmitted as a political call on the Reserve under the New Control Total introduced in 1992 and effective from 1993–4.

The purpose of the Reserve after 1984 was to cover any unforeseen eventualities, and was 'central to the process of monitoring and control of spending as the year proceeds' (Treasury and Civil Service Committee 1986a: app. 4). Claims on the Reserve, and the 'available margin', were regularly assessed. As the plans were rolled forward, part of the planned Reserve was allocated to departmental programmes 'to allow for any increased estimates in demand-led areas and discretionary policy additions'. At the end of that rolling forward process 'considerable uncertainties' remained in the estimated additional expenditure required in future years, and the revised totals for those years reflected that greater uncertainty.

The Treasury refuted criticism that the Reserve was calculated by aggregating an identified and quantified set of contingencies. 'If the probabilities could be viewed with this sort of precision, they would be added to departmental provision in the first place and a Reserve is not a matter of precise arithmetic or science, it involves broad judgements of likely needs and trends drawing on past experience' (app. 4).

The Treasury has no mechanism for determining the optimal size of the Reserve. It is a matter for the judgement of the Chancellor and his Chief Secretary, advised by the Treasury's General Expenditure Policy Group (GEP). They take into account the medium-term policy for public expenditure in the context of the macro-economic policy set by the MTFS. Such 'top–down' factors and pressures interact with those arising from below. Thus the Treasury will try to estimate in a rough way what contingencies and 'unforeseen' expenditures may arise in-year, as well as those which may arise during the course of the Survey negotiations, and draw upon the Reserve. The estimation of the 'unforeseen' is not much better than an informed guess of such possibilities as the trend of local authority spending, carry-forward under the end-year flexibility scheme, the pay claims of particular groups of public-sector workers. A convenient 'rule of thumb' employed by Nigel Lawson when Chancellor of the Exchequer was a ratio of Reserve to Planning Total of 1:2:3 for the three years of the Survey. With a figure of roughly 2 per cent for year one, this meant Reserve totals of 2, 4, and 6 per cent, which, translated into cash, provided totals of £3.5 billion, £7 billion, £10.5 billion in the Surveys from 1988 to 1990. In 1991, these sums were rebased to reflect nominal growth in the Planning Total. Reserves of £4 billion, £8 billion, £12 billion, were allocated for the PES cycle from 1992–3. With the introduction of the New Control Total in 1992 there was a further modification. A Reserve of £4 billion was set for 1993–4 in order to avoid the charge that NCT was based on an accounting sleight of hand, and to give the new control regime flexibility to allow for contingencies in its first operational year. For years two and three, it was set at £7 billion and £10 billion, lower levels than the previous years. This reflected the removal of cyclical social security from the NCT.

The Reserve is intended to signal to the spending departments, and the world at large, first that it is a realistic figure for meeting in-year claims; secondly, that it is a credible control figure for achieving the aggregate Planning/Control Total; and, thirdly, that it is set at such a level as to enforce discipline on departments and discourage them from pressing too hard for additional public spending. While the calculation reflects all three, the message may be distorted subsequently by what happens to receipts from privatization, as explained above.

MONITORING AND CONTROL

In-year control of claims on the Reserve is a matter for the Chief Secretary's judgement, advised by GEP. The latter keeps a balance sheet of credits against which any particular claim is assessed. For example, in 1991–2 the opening balance was £4 billion, to which may be added during the course of the year the proceeds of privatization where these exceed the planned allowance of £5.5 billion in the Planning Total for asset sales other than council houses; conversely, where the proceeds are less than that sum, the £4 billion balance is reduced accordingly. Underspending on allocations to departmental programmes will also inflate the Reserve balance. It follows that claims for additional spending can be financed out of that balance, or by the reallocation of expenditure which is 'saved' as a result of reductions which arise in-year. Balancing claims which may arise erratically and unpredictably throughout the year against a moving balance of ±£4 billion is an exercise calling for fine judgement. Andrew Turnbull, then Under Secretary in charge of GEP, explained to the Treasury and Civil Service Committee (1985c: qu. 205):

Departments notify divisions in the Treasury and they in turn notify the General Expenditure Division of what they think the claims will be which will arise during the course of the year. We keep a record of those and that helps us to produce our forecast of what is likely to happen by the end of the year. During the course of the year a number of decisions are taken. For example, an EFL of a nationalised industry may be changed. That will be announced. Those are the changes which are positively committed and decided, but at this stage of the year the largest part represents not changes that have been formally announced but changes that we think will arise by the end of the year.

All such claims, and those which arise unpredictably, are conveyed by the Expenditure Divisions to GEP, which provides an assessment for the Chief Secretary, who has to decide to allow or deny them. With the adoption of the year one Reserve as a control total, the Treasury is better able to resist claims on it. Year one allocations are agreed in the Survey, and additions to them thereafter are allowable only if the expenditure is of a non-discretionary kind. 'Year one figures are final and not the semi-final' (Assistant Secretary, GEP). Claims for discretionary expenditure should be the stuff of the Survey rather than eligible for Reserve monies, the Treasury argues. However, if the Reserve is increased by greater than anticipated proceeds from privatization, the Treasury's ability to resist such claims may be weaker. What may be definitionally 'discretionary' (ministers could say no) may become inevitable as a result of the pressure of events, and indistinguishable from eligible non-discretionary claims. For example, no provision was made in the 1989 Survey to increase war-widows' pensions. Ministers could and did refuse at first to make additions 'in-year'. However, the pressure to increase them eventually became irresistible as a significant number of Conservative back-benchers added their support to an all-party campaign. The Treasury agreed to make the additional money available, but not until April 1990.

MORE CONTROL, LESS PLANNING

The changes made to the Reserve since 1984 raise a number of questions about the effects of its use in the planning and control of public expenditure. First, the changes were necessary because the Treasury needed to improve its control. As the estimating of non-discretionary expenditure became a more uncertain exercise in the mid-1980s, it became more difficult to predict what the outturn of total planned expenditure would be, and to ensure that outturn matched plans. The Treasury needed to provide for uncertainty in order to make the Planning Totals more 'realistic'. If a larger proportion of total expenditure is left unallocated within a planned total, and the unallocated amount is substantial in size, it is easier to control total outturn within a predetermined Planning Total, provided the margin is ample enough. Increasing the size of the Reserve for forward years was one of several steps 'to make public expenditure planning totals more realistic' (Treasury and Civil Service Committee 1985*a*: qu. 147).

The provision of a larger Reserve, and more realistic Planning Totals, raises questions of the costs of the improved control thereby obtained. The most obvious cost might be an increase in the size of the total planned expenditure. If the government's aim is to reduce that total in real terms, or as a percentage of GDP, opting for a larger Reserve might be a high-risk strategy if the total of planned expenditure 'rises' to accommodate it. A smaller Reserve has the advantage that the planned total will be lower, but with the risk that it might be exceeded. A larger Reserve is disadvantageous only if it is additional to the Planning/Control Total, as used to be the case. If, however, it is used to finance a larger proportion of the Planning/Control Total, then the latter may not 'rise' significantly, and the larger Reserve ensures less likelihood of overspend.

A further cost of improved control through an expanded Reserve is that proportionately less of the provision is allocated to the departments. For example, in the financial year 1988–9, almost 2 per cent of the planned growth in real spending was unallocated. As in practice the allocation of that Reserve is not made on a proportionate basis, some programmes will grow by much larger amounts. For future years, the programme allocations are less reliable still as predictions of what will happen. The proportion of unallocated to allocated expenditure in those two forward years is much greater still. In the plans for 1990–1, nearly 4 per cent (£7 billion) of the Planning Total remained unallocated, while for the following year it was 5.5 per cent (£10.5 billion). The growth in real spending in any particular programme for those years could be very much greater than planned in the PEWP when the Reserve is eventually allocated. The growth rates for individual services in those years, which in most cases are small or negative, are virtually meaningless as indicators of what is likely to happen or what the government plans to happen to real expenditure. Moreover, as the planned distribution of expenditure is changed with the roll-forward of the Reserve, and a part of it allocated, it becomes impossible to verify *ex post* whether or not the planned distribution of expenditure between services has been achieved.

The Treasury and Civil Service Select Committee (1988*a*) has argued that less public expenditure is planned than was the case before 1984; and that as a result it has become more difficult to determine what has happened to the allocations from the Reserve. There is little in this, as all changes to expenditure are now funded from the Reserve, and allocations from it to departmental programmes were itemized in the PEWP and Autumn Statement. However, neither of these provided a 'statement of account' of the handling of the Reserve's 'credits and debits'. The figures provided by the Treasury tend to incorporate changes in allocations which result from classification changes. There is no differentiation of the cost of routine schemes, such as end-year flexibility, which are analytically distinct from other 'policy' calls on the Reserve.

It is more difficult to resist the argument that less is planned: a larger proportion of the Planning/Control Total is unallocated to programmes than was the case previously. If a sum equivalent to the pre-1984 Reserve totals is deducted from totals of £3.5 billion, £7 billion, and £10.5 billion, there remains unallocated a total of £7 billion in year three and £3.5 billion in year two. The Treasury argues that if the latter sum of £3.5 billion was allocated to programmes in year two there would still be claims on the Reserve 'in-year', and it would be necessary to ask some departments to surrender what had previously been allocated in year two to finance those claims. A high Reserve in years two and three is necessary therefore to cope with uncertainty and to avoid over-shooting the Planning/Control Total. Further, the Treasury argues that years two and three have always been provisional, and that few departments now look that far ahead, apart perhaps from the M.o.D. and Transport (Assistant Secretary, GEP). Under the new rules, the fact that a third of the Total Reserve is not allocated until year two, and then a further third in year one, has only a marginal effect on the planning of departmental programmes.

With a larger proportion of the Planning Total unallocated through the three years, it is more difficult to assess the growth pattern of intended spending, programme by programme. The Treasury is less concerned with 'planning the path', as it once used to be, and much more concerned with controlling the total. 'It is the planning total which is crucial, not whether it has been allocated,' commented a senior Treasury official in 1990. That is an understandable reaction to the experience of the early 1980s. It is difficult, however, to resist the conclusion that the redefinition of the Reserve as a control mechanism for the whole of public expenditure, and the determination with which the new rules have been enforced, have further elevated the control function at the expense of planning. Faced with a credible Reserve or a 'honeypot', the Treasury understandably opted for the former.

There is no evidence that the Conservative Government intended that a larger Reserve should constrain the growth of public expenditure. Nor has it had that effect in practice. It could happen if the Reserve were not fully allocated in year one, in circumstances when there were no additional receipts (above £5.5 billion) and no net underspending as a result of savings on some departmental programmes. The outturn would be less than the Planning/Control Total by the amount of the unused Reserve. But unless departments were denied additional discretionary and non-discretionary expenditure which normally they would expect the Treasury to allow, the effect would merely be less expenditure than expected rather than a squeeze. The most likely circumstances in which the Reserve might squeeze the Planning Total would be the need to cut expenditure quickly in-year. A part or the whole of the Reserve might be frozen. While the effect of that would be to cut the total, it would not squeeze the planned expenditure for departmental programmes agreed in the Survey negotiations.

17

The Operation and Effects of
Cash Limits

Cash limits were introduced in 1976 as an administrative device to control the annual amount of cash spent on government programmes. They were applied to some 60 per cent of total public expenditure, excluding those programmes where demand-determined expenditure was too difficult to estimate. In 1992–3 about 56 per cent of the Control Total was cash-limited, the greater part of which was Supply Expenditure. Some changes have been made to the coverage of cash limits during the last fifteen years, for example cash limits have been prescribed for expenditure on some health and community services previously excluded, but more than a third of total public expenditure remains non-cash-limited. Other changes made to the system include the assimilation of cash limits with the Estimates; the extension of cash discipline to three-year cash plans (1982–3); the introduction of a system for carrying forward some kinds of expenditure from one cash limit to that of the next year; and the separation of expenditure on pay and administration costs from other programme expenditure in 'running costs' cash limits prescribed for each central department. End-year flexibility schemes and running costs are dealt with in Chapters 18 and 19 and are discussed here only in so far as they contribute to total under- and overspending.

THE ROLE OF CASH LIMITS

The earlier concern of analysts with the use and effects of cash limits as an explicit or surrogate incomes policy for public-sector pay (see Bevan, Sisson, and Way 1981) evaporated with the Conservative Government's abandonment of pay policies for the public sector. 'Pay factors' incorporated into cash limits from 1979 were abandoned in 1986. From then until 1993–4, when a limit of 1.5 per cent was imposed, there were no formal, explicit pay norms for the public sector. The associated issue, much discussed in the early years of cash limits, of the use of cash limits to secure cuts in public spending by 'squeezing' volumes through the underfunding of the expected movement of pay and prices, has been subsumed in the wider issue of the extent to which cash limits have helped to achieve improved management in the use of resources, through greater emphasis on value-for-money, costs savings, and output enhancement. The extent to which fewer resources have induced greater efficiency, or led to a reduction in the quantity or quality of the goods and services provided in cash-limited programmes, is of course very much a live issue. The main burden of this chapter is, however, to analyse and explain the operation of the cash-limits regime to achieve financial discipline and control. It seeks to answer three questions: first, to what extent do cash limits predict the final outturn of cash-limited expenditure? Secondly, to what extent are cash limits stable throughout the year? Thirdly, do the operation and the effects of cash limits achieve the objectives of balancing strict control with effective and flexible management? To answer these questions we look at the effects of cash limits on the total outturns of cash-limited expenditure since their inception. In an analysis of the extent of over- and underspending, particular attention is given to the dominant characteristic of the operation of cash limits, the phenomenon of persistent underspending, and to its causes and effects. In the concluding section it is argued that its occurrence enabled the Treasury to operate cash limits flexibly, with little or no net cost to the Planning Total, until 1989. Thereafter, the net costs of revising cash limits in-year to accommodate the structural, cyclical, and electoral pressures for more spending added substantially to the Planning Total.

A cash limit 'represents the maximum amount of cash that the Government proposes to spend on the services covered by that limit in the financial year' (Cmnd. 6440). Cash limits are prescribed for cash blocks, each of which is allocated each year a fixed sum of money. The number of blocks and their size have been revised from time to time since 1976. There are four main types: those for central government expenditure, numerically and as a proportion of total cash-limited expenditure, account for the greater part of cash limits. There are about 120 blocks and since the assimilation of cash limits with the Supply Estimates each comprises a Vote. More than three-fifths of all Votes are cash-limited. The second type of cash block comprises non-voted expenditure controlled by central government departments. In 1990–1 there were eighteen such blocks, covering mainly credit approvals of local authorities and some other public sector bodies like the Bank of England. The third category does not, strictly speaking, comprise cash blocks, but covers the External Financing Limits (EFLs) agreed with the nationalized industries by the central government. Briefly, an EFL is the difference between net investment and sources of internal finance; between what goes out and what comes in. The difference can be covered either by borrowing, or by grant from central government, or by a reduction in the level of a nationalized industry's reserves. The EFL is a limit on the monies extraneous to those raised by the industry. The 'limit' can be negative—a nationalized industry may be obliged to contribute to General Government Expenditure from the surplus achieved after providing for the whole of its borrowing requirements from its internal revenue. The fourth type of cash limits comprises the running costs of central government departments, and was introduced in 1986–7.

The rules of the game of budgetary politics have changed over the last fifteen years. Cash limits have achieved the Treasury's aim of imposing a strict financial discipline and control on two-thirds of public spending. Breaches of cash limits are rare, and where they have occurred have tended to be small.[1] Underspending on cash-limited programmes has become the norm; it is customary and, at least in aggregate, predictable. It has replaced the norm of 'overspending' which characterized many programmes in the mid-1970s and which precipitated the introduction of cash limits. Table 17.1 sets out the trends of cash-limited expenditure, and aggregates the net outturn of each of the three main types of cash blocks. In each case outturn is compared with final cash limits, that is, after all in-year changes to original cash limits have been included. The net outturn of all cash-limited blocks has only twice registered overspend since the introduction of cash limits in 1976. In most years there has been very substantial net underspending, for example more than £2.2 billion in 1982–3 and £1.8 billion in 1987–8. Central government blocks, comprising roughly 40 per cent annually of all cash-limited expenditure, have been underspent in aggregate every year since 1976. The tight control of cash-limited expenditure has therefore contributed very substantially to restraining the growth of total public expenditure, and helping the Treasury to deliver the agreed Planning/Control Total.

Underspending on central government bodies was not concentrated in a few programmes. More than 80 per cent of all blocks were underspent each year, between a quarter and a half by more than 2 per cent of their cash limits, mostly within a range of £1–10 million. However, some of the larger cash blocks had sizeable underspends. The Ministry of Defence, whose five blocks count as one cash limit, was underspent by £551 million in 1986–7 (3.1 per cent of the cash limit),

---

[1] The analysis presented in the rest of this chapter is based upon the statistical tables and other data in Thain and Wright 1988*e*.

TABLE 17.1. *Outturn (+/– over/underspending) compared with final cash limits, 1976–1977 to 1991–1992*

	Central government expenditure		Local authority expenditure[a]		Running costs		TOTAL (£m)
	£m	%	£m	%	£m	%	
1991–2	−432,113	−0.4	−117,500	−1.0	−407,510	−2.5	−957,123
1990–1	−174,060	−0.2	−126,900	−1.2	+1,632	0	−299,328
1989–90	−581,165	−0.8	−57,700	−0.9	−46,871	−0.3	−685,736
1988–9	−911,804	−1.4	−163,800	−3.1	−73,976	−0.5	−1,149,580
1987–8	−1,169,235	−1.8	−646,000	−7.5	−39,006	−0.3	−1,854,241
1986–7	−897,457	−1.5	+183,700	+2.4	−103,086	−0.8	−816,843
1985–6	−491,955	−0.9	+900,300	+12.6			+408,345
1984–5	−501,769	−0.9	+938,200	+13.7			+436,431
1983–4	−861,686	−1.7	+366,000	+5.2			−495,686
1982–3	−1,025,269	−2.1	−1,192,500	−15.1			−2,217,769
1981–2	−794,463	−1.8	−958,000	−13.1			−1,752,463
1980–1	−446,673	−1.1	−263,200	−4.0			−709,873
1979–80	−231,470	−0.7	−115,700	−2.1			−347,170
1978–9	−453,300	−1.5	−537,400	−10.5			−990,700
1977–8	−741,200	−2.6	−514,000	−11.2			−1,255,200
1976–7	−686,400	−2.6	n/a				

[a] Non-voted local government capital expenditure and capital expenditure of certain other bodies, e.g. water authorities, new towns, housing corporations.

Source: Cash Limits Provisional Outturn and Final Outturn, Cmnd./Cm. papers, annually, 1977–93.

and £224 million in 1983–4 (1.5 per cent). Some small and medium-sized blocks underspent by as much as 30 or 40 per cent of the cash limit, although such large underspends were less frequent in the 1990s. The introduction of end-year flexibility schemes in 1984–5 enabled departments to carry forward a proportion of certain kinds of unspent expenditures, but had little effect over time on the frequency of underspending.

There was a much higher proportion of underspending on local authority than central government blocks. However, the trend was more erratic. The years of underspending which followed the introduction of cash limits were succeeded by four years of overspending, and from 1987–8 a reversion to underspending. As with central government blocks, there was a wide distribution of underspending among them. Each year some 75–80 per cent of all blocks were underspent. The aggregate outturn of the cash-limited borrowing requirements of the nationalized industries fluctuated from large underspending to large overspending. On two occasions the aggregate EFLs were exceeded by more than 100 per cent, while in 1982–3 and 1987–8 there was underspending of between 40 and 50 per cent. Under- and overspending was evenly distributed between the nationalized industries. As with central government and local authority controlled blocks, the phenomenon of persistent widespread underspending was evident. In every year from 1982–3 to 1988–9, more than a half of all nationalized industries underspent their EFL.

We now go on to explain why there have been so few breaches of cash limits; examine the effect of the persistent and consistent underspending which results from the operation of the cash-limits regime, and consider the extent to which this is encouraged by the Treasury. Finally we discuss the implications for Treasury control of the increasing flexibility with which the system is administered.

Cash limits are limits not targets

When cash limits were introduced in 1976, it was not clear whether departments were required to aim at a fixed cash target, or to keep within the limits. The former would allow the possibility of 'near misses'—over- as well as undershooting the target. It quickly became apparent that breaches of cash limits were impermissible; departments were expected to treat cash limits as limits and to keep within them. How close to each limit departments could, and would, be expected to get has never been prescribed publicly. The Treasury's aim is that departments should 'hold the cash limit', which is interpreted as getting within a few percentage points of the final cash limit. In consequence, departments have tended to underspend their limits by small margins. While the distribution varies between Votes and departments from one year to the next, the aggregate of underspending is consistent.

It is not clear whether initially the Treasury adopted a strategy of encouraging underspending. In the aftermath of the criticism directed at it in 1974–6 for its failure to control expenditure, it would have been justified in doing so. In any case the difficulty and uncertainty in introducing a new concept made it essential to demonstrate quickly that cash limits were working, i.e. were effective in preventing overspending. The size of the underspend in the years 1976–8 was partly due to the inexperience of programme managers, and the understandable caution with which they managed cash flow in the new regime. At that time, there was great emphasis upon the inviolability of prescribed cash limits. In the early days of cash limits, it was widely believed by analysts and commentators that the Treasury would turn off the tap before the end of the financial year where a cash limit was exhausted, and spending authorities would be required to lay off staff and suspend services until the next financial year. While it is true that some spending authorities (particularly health and local authorities) have experienced such conditions, the possibility of persuading the Treasury to revise fixed cash limits has provided an additional safety-valve to release expenditure pressure.

Control through cash limits would not have been possible without an improvement in the quality and regularity of financial information. The introduction of financial information systems in the Treasury and the spending departments has provided the means to monitor cash flow more quickly and accurately. In theory, better and earlier warning of potential overspend would enable corrective action to be taken to adjust cash flow. Again in the early years of the installation of such systems, there was understandably greater caution in interpreting information and preventing overspend. This also contributed to the underspending of early years. However, there is now nearly twenty years' experience, and the systems themselves and the data they generate have been improved. The narrow limits within which most cash blocks are underspent suggests an ability to fine-tune the outturn, but a preference for doing so *within* the limit. However, it is true that under/overspending on cash limits is counter-cyclical. In boom conditions, departments may find it more difficult to spend their allocations as firms with more private sector work are less interested in government contracts, and as receipts are more buoyant. Conversely, in a period of recession, bills are presented for payment more promptly, and receipts are less buoyant.

The acceptance of cash limits as limits rather than targets would not in itself ensure that limits were 'held' within a small margin. Unless spending authorities incurred some penalty or suffered serious disadvantages as a consequence of exceeding their limits, there would be an insufficient incentive to ensure that cash limits were consistently underspent. 'A serious view is taken of any overspending' (Cmnd. 8175). All breaches are reported to the Chief Secretary; the Prime Minister may be alerted. The usual corrective procedures are applied, 'including an investigation into the causes of the breach, an examination of the financial procedures of the department or industry concerned and, where appropriate, a reduction in the corresponding cash limit, running costs limit or external financing limit in the following year' (Cm. 1587). A Minister obliged to explain why and how an overspend had occurred could be acutely embarrassed. The consequences could be more serious than the deduction of the overspending from the cash limit of the following year: his bid for more resources in the next Survey round would be subject to closer scrutiny. In practice, however, there are few breaches and most are technical—the late presentation of a bill for payment, the non-arrival of forecasted receipts. The Treasury regards these as 'minor system-failures' (Assistant Secretary, GEP); nevertheless the cause of each breach is investigated. More serious or persistent breaches of cash limits by a department would be the subject of extensive scrutiny by Treasury Expenditure Controllers in the Expenditure Divisions, and raise doubts about the efficacy of that department's financial management system.

There are, of course, less direct sanctions of a more traditional kind associated with the control and accountability exercised by the Comptroller and Auditor General, the National Audit Office, the PAC, and by Parliament itself.

The effects of underspending

There are two main effects of the phenomenon of consistent underspending. First, a presumption of aggregate underspending is incorporated into the calculation of the Planning/Control Total. As a result, the amount planned and allocated for the Reserve is set at a lower level; the Planning/Control Total is thus lower than it would otherwise be. The Reserve is boosted by the amount of underspending which occurs. Secondly, the aggregated outturn of cash-limited expenditure, voted and non-voted, has had a significant effect on the total outturn of planned expenditure, cash-limited plus non-cash-limited expenditure, enabling the Treasury to deliver nearer to the Planning/

TABLE 17.2. *The effect of cash-limits underspending on the (old) Planning Total in cash terms, 1980–1990*[a]

	Planned[b] in yr 1 (£m)	Final outturn[c] (£m)	% difference	Outturn[d] without cash limits (£m)	% difference without cash limits
1989–90	167,055	167,055	0	167,740	+0.4
1988–9	156,800	153,400	−2.2	154,549	−1.4
1987–8	148,600	145,700	−2.0	147,860	−0.5
1986–7	139,100	139,300	+0.1	140,019	+0.7
1985–6	132,100	133,800	+1.3	133,266	+0.9
1984–5	126,400	129,900	+2.8	127,531	+0.9
1983–4	119,600	120,400	+0.7	121,379	+1.5
1982–3	115,200	113,600	−1.4	116,918	+1.5
1981–2	104,000	104,000	0	105,752	+1.7
1980–1	94,000	92,700	−1.4	93,409	−0.6

[a] An underspend on cash limits, if excluded from the Planning Total outturn, would have produced a higher overspend on total public spending or a smaller underspend; a cash-limits overspend would have produced the reverse.

[b] Taken from the White Paper published preceding the financial year in question.

[c] For the figures up to 1987–8 outturn data is from Cm. 621; thereafter Cm. 1021.

[d] Based on data from Table 17.1.

Control Total. Table 17.2 shows the effect of underspending on the Planning Total. In 1987–8, £1.8 billion underspend on cash-limited expenditure, together with £627 million underspend on the EFLs of the nationalized industries, contributed most of the total underspend; while the previous year's very small overspend on the Planning Total would have been very much greater without the £0.8 billion underspend on cash-limited expenditure. In 1982–3, the £3.3 billion underspend on cash-limited expenditure (including EFLs) converted a 1.5 per cent overspend on the Planning Total into a 1.4 per cent underspend.

These effects have proved expedient and undeniably helpful to the Treasury. What is much less certain are the causes of the underspending. Here the issue is the extent to which the Treasury has directly or tacitly encouraged underspending by central government departments. The Treasury admits only that it has acquiesced in that underspending. It rejects the notion of a tacit underspending norm, arguing that a cash limit is a ceiling within which departments have to live; some underspending is inevitable if that ceiling is not to be exceeded; evidence of good management is getting within two or three percentage points of the limit. Departments are now better at managing their expenditure, at 'going near the water without getting wet', as one senior Treasury official in GEP explained. This is partly the result of a greater capacity for 'fine-tuning' expenditures using improved expenditure-profiles and better techniques of monitoring cash flow. It reflects also a greater confidence than in the early days of cash limits that managers can deliver their totals nearer to the limit.

While persuasive, this argument does not dispose conclusively of the possibility that the expectation of aggregate underspending has influenced the behaviour of programme managers and departmental finance officers. As argued above, the effects of the constant underspending on central government blocks has proved advantageous in that a higher than anticipated underspend on some programmes has the effect of tightening the fiscal stance, an outcome consistent with the Government's macro-economic strategy in most years since 1979.

While there may be no underspending norm in the Treasury Expenditure Divisions, departmental PFOs may behave as though there were because it is prudent so to do. Their behaviour is influenced by the Treasury's 'anticipated reactions'. The need to 'hold the cash limit' dictates an underspending strategy at the margin. Holding it at 96–8 per cent is both acceptable and evidence of the soundness of the department's financial management system. A breach of the cash limit, other than for technical reasons, would be both unacceptable and, if serious or repeated, cause for Treasury inquiry into the effectiveness of the financial management system, and tougher negotiating in the bilaterals in the next PES round. Whether departments could 'fine-tune' their expenditure to get closer still to the limit without risk of a breach is uncertain. In the last decade, the number of blocks underspent by more than 2 per cent has remained fairly constant, averaging some 40–50 per cent each year. There may also be an element of randomness in the distribution of underspending between the 120 blocks of central government spending. There is no easy way of confirming that, as the Treasury does not publish time-series data (which it collects) on underspending by Vote and department.

CHANGES TO CASH LIMITS

From the introduction of cash limits in 1976 the Treasury has repeatedly insisted that cash limits are fixed, immutable. They 'represent the maximum which the Government propose to spend on the services in question, and departments manage their programmes so as to keep within the limits' (Cmnd. 7515: para. 8). White Papers and Treasury publications throughout the 1980s abound with stern injunctions: 'Changes in cash limits are uncommon'; 'The presumption is that cash limits—once set—will not be changed' (Cabinet Office and Treasury 1989: 47); 'Once set the limits are changed only in exceptional circumstances' (Treasury 1991*b*: 6). Such tough rhetoric is of course necessary to establish and maintain the discipline of the cash-limits regime. As one senior Treasury official in GEP put it: 'You don't have soft rhetoric because it would result in even softer practice.'

From the outset the Treasury admitted that it might be necessary, exceptionally, to change a cash limit.

Cash limits are thus not normally increased during the year unless pay or prices turn out substantially higher than envisaged when the cash limits were set, and the Government, having reviewed all the circumstances, decide that increased provision should be sought; or unless further decisions are taken to introduce new measures or to add to existing programmes. New measures, or additions to programmes, unless met by adjustments within planned programmes, represent a claim on the contingency reserve included in the Government's expenditure plans. (Cmnd. 7515: para. 9)

Treasury practice presents a different picture. Changes to cash limits are not exceptional. They are common, and characteristic of the operation of the system since its inception.

Each year the Treasury approves a large number of changes to blocks of cash-limited expenditure, both voted and non-voted. Changes to cash block Votes are announced, 'subject to Parliamentary approval of the necessary Supplementary Estimate'. Between a third and a half of the 120 cash limits set for central government blocks are changed each year, slightly more being raised than lowered. About a half of all local authority blocks are changed, with more being lowered than raised. On average between a half and two-thirds of the blocks of central departments' running costs are changed each year, most resulting in increases to the original cash limits.

Changes to blocks which occur as a result of carry-over of unspent money under the end-year flexibility scheme introduced in 1983 are limited to 5 per cent of the total cash limit. Carry-over on capital expenditure is the main type of change, reflected in the higher proportions of changed blocks in local authority than central government blocks.

While the original cash limits are changed for most blocks during the course of a financial year, the value of the net changes for the four types varies. The annual value of the changes to central government blocks has fluctuated between a total of a reduction of some £127 million to an increase of £2.8 billion. The latter is equivalent to nearly 4 per cent of the original cash limit. Changes to local authority and nationalized industries' blocks have been much larger as a proportion of the original cash limit, those for running costs very much smaller.

The Treasury has carefully avoided defining the precise circumstances and the conditions upon which it would agree to allow such changes, but has said that they are the 'result of a substantial policy decision' (Cabinet Office and Treasury 1989: 47). 'Policy' is a notoriously slippery concept. What counts as a 'change' rather than an extension of policy is contestable. However, if changes were normally allowed only if they were of a 'policy nature', we should expect that most if not all of those approved would fall within that broad category. While the published evidence does not allow a detailed analysis of why and how such changes are made, it does suggest that changes are made for reasons other than policy, however defined.

We can distinguish at least two purposes in allowing changes: first, those which result from the introduction of a new policy or the revision an existing policy. Such changes include pay awards not provided for in the original cash limit. Where Parliamentary approval follows a Treasury request, the means to finance it must be found. However, while the cash block is sometimes increased to finance such new or revised policy, equally the new cash limit may be set after transfers between it and other cash blocks. The Treasury may ask, or insist, that the department find compensating savings to cover the whole or a part of the projected increase. Transfers between blocks within the same spending authority are common. Some of the 'trade-offs' are quite complex (see the example below). Where no compensating savings can be found, or are insufficient to cover the increase in the cash limit, the Treasury may authorize a call on the Reserve which will lead to a Supplementary Estimate if the money is voted money.

The second kind of change occurs where a spending authority anticipates over- or underspending the cash limit on a cash block because of an under- or overestimate of the likely expenditure, and seeks Treasury approval for a revised limit. This may arise from unanticipated demand or take-up, or from a change in the circumstances in which expenditure occurs; from poor estimating; or lack of control. The reasons for changes of this kind are not easy to disentangle. It is difficult to establish (from the published evidence) whether the spending authority could be blamed or not.

The Cash Limits White Papers provide only general guidance. The brief statements made there, and in announcements by spending ministers to the House of Commons (having obtained the Chief Secretary's approval), to justify changes to cash limits, suggest that most revisions are made to provide for the costs of new policies or changes to existing policies. The most common example is a pay award. Changes are made much less frequently because of unanticipated demand or take-up of a service, or because of 'unavoidable increases' in costs. It is not possible to determine the causes of many of the changes; the brief explanations are open to different interpretations. For example, from time to time, the DES obtained a revised cash limit 'to enable the work of scientific bodies to be sustained'. Whether the costs of that work had been under-estimated, or poorly controlled during the year, or had increased be-cause of developments in that work during the year, is impossible to tell. Several of the reasons advanced to justify changes appear in this example from the Welsh Office, Class XV1, Vote 1, where the cash limit for 1984–5 was increased by £5.489 million. It indicates the complexity of some of the trade-offs between Votes:

Increase of £8.166 million to take account of pay awards to doctors, dentists, midwives and professions allied to medicine . . . Increase of £1.943 million to take account of pay awards to staff who are not covered by pay review bodies. Savings of £2.025 million from the roads and transport programme and to offset overspend on selective financial assistance on Class XV1, Vote 3, (non cash limited) . . . Reduction of £10.573 million to reflect decreased spending on the trunk road programme mainly on account of protracted negotiations on land acquisitions and a lower rate of spend on schemes under construction than forecast . . . Reduction of £3 million to offset an increase in the external financial limit of the Welsh Water Authority. (Cmnd. 9569)

On the basis of the (admittedly thin) published evidence, it is difficult to argue that control has been subordinated to flexibility. Or that the number and size of the changes made annually to cash limits represent a significant loss of control. The net effect of the changes varies from additional expenditure on local authority and nationalized industries' blocks to reduced expenditure on central government blocks, although the latter changes show large increases of the aggregate, between £1.3 and £2.8 billion since 1986–7. Most of the additional expenditure pro-vided through transfers or increased cash limits is to finance new or revised policy, approved by Parliament. Finally, any assessment of the balance struck between control and flexibility must include in the calcu-lation those requests for changes to cash limits, whether through trans-fers or otherwise, which are turned down by the Treasury. There is no published data about unsuccessful bids: 'neither the Treasury nor de-partments would want to keep a record of unsuccessful bids' (Assistant Secretary, GEP). It is impossible to determine the extent to which the norm of underspending the limit, and the Treasury's behaviour in its relationship with spending authorities, deters them in certain circumstances from seeking a change. In any case it is difficult to distinguish clearly between 'successful' and 'unsuccessful' requests to revise cash limits, because they are made for different reasons. A department may be deterred from making a bid because the Treasury had made it clear that such a bid would not be granted. On the other hand, the Treasury might encourage a department to make a bid. A department might make a bid not with the expectation of 'success', but to sound out the Treasury's attitude. A bid might be partly successful and partly not, as the Treasury acceded to one part but not another.

The published evidence allows us to show the extent of the flexibility with which cash limits are operated, and to offer an explanation why the Treasury is prepared to countenance it in practice. Before doing so we can dispose of the puzzle why so few breaches of cash limits occur when there are no apparent formal sanctions to deter departments. Accepting that the climate within which financial discipline and control are exercised has changed since the 1970s and contributes to the observance of cash limits, nevertheless few cash limits are breached, because if an overspend can be foreseen the Treasury can normally be persuaded to revise the cash limit to accommodate it. Improvement in financial management systems will normally provide, through the careful monitoring of cash flow, early warning of a potential overspend, where additional resources have not been provided for a new policy or a change to an existing one. Hence breaches are technical or 'minor system-failures', or occur as a result of unanticipated expenditure towards the end of the financial year, too late for corrective action to be taken.

The degree of flexibility with which cash limits are operated by the Treasury can be shown in two ways. First, by analysis of the number and incidence of in-year changes. Changes made to cash limits from 1976 onwards were widespread and common through all blocks for all three main types. The trend since the mid-1980s is for more frequent changes still. Although coincidental with the introduction of end-year flexibility, that scheme has had only a marginal effect on the number of the changes. Secondly, the significance of the flexible administration of cash limits can be shown by an analysis of the aggregate cash value of the changes made. For central government blocks, annual changes to cash limits have averaged between 1 and 2 per cent of the aggregate cost, for the period 1976–7 to 1985–6. Since that date there has been a sharp increase in the cash value of the annual changes, totalling in aggregate between £1.3 and £2.8 billion, sums equivalent to 4 per cent of the original cash limits. The cash value of changes made to local authority expenditure blocks was more varied, with both negative and positive values. In both, values were often in excess of 2 per cent of the original cash limits. In the operation of running costs cash limits, the cash value of the increases has averaged less than 1 per cent of the original cash limits, although that for 1990–1 was more than double that figure.

Why has the Treasury operated cash limits with a much greater degree of flexibility than its rhetoric suggests, and than has been apparent from the published record? Has it sacrificed a degree of control in so doing? Several different elements, whose relative weights are arguable, contribute to the explanation. First, from the outset it was accepted that cash limits could not be operated without providing for some element of flexibility to deal with exceptional circumstances. Secondly, there is evidence that, with the security of the discipline of cash limits established, the Treasury has been prepared to be more responsive to the needs of departmental programme managers in agreeing to an end-year flexibility scheme in 1984–5 and the introduction of running costs limits in 1986–7. Thirdly, there is more pressure on the Treasury in the period preceding general elections to agree more policy changes in-year.

Both end-year flexibility and running costs are discussed in detail in the following chapters. Here it should be noted that end-year flexibility schemes allowing carry-forward of unspent monies represented a long-resisted concession by the Treasury to the difficulty in managing the cash flow on certain kinds of expenditure, particularly capital expenditure programmes where the phasing of contracted work and progress-payments could be affected by conditions and circumstances beyond the control of the spending authority. While the scheme provides an additional element of flexibility in managing the cash limit between one year and the next, it is uncertain whether that represents a loss of control. The introduction of running costs limits provides both more flexibility for programme managers, and a tightening of control. Pay and administrative costs are treated as one cash block. Previously such costs were not separated out, but distributed through all cash blocks. That distribution enabled programme managers to 'raid' programmes to finance the costs of staff, both numbers and pay. With a single cash block for pay and allied staff costs, such 'raids' are no longer possible, except through specific agreement between the Treasury, the spending department, and its Next Steps Agency. Agencies are allowed more managerial freedom (discussed in Chapter 24). On the other hand, there is greater flexibility for managing the whole of staff costs. One effect of this is that the tendency of public sector pay to run ahead of the negotiated awards should disappear.

There is a further element which contributes to the greater *de facto* flexibility with which cash limits are operated. In earlier chapters we have argued that the Treasury's main aim and concern in controlling expenditure is to deliver the Planning/Control Total prescribed in the Autumn Statement/Budget. Control of cash-limited expenditure is important but secondary. Until 1989 the Treasury was able and willing to administer cash-limit controls more flexibly because it was confident that it could simultaneously maintain control of the Planning Total. We demonstrated above the persistence of the phenomenon of underspending. In every year since the introduction of cash limits the aggregate outturn for central government blocks has been less than the *final* (i.e. revised) cash limits (see Table 17.3). A similar trend is observable in the outturn for running costs (Table 17.5). This was true also for blocks for local authority expenditure, apart from the years 1983–4 to 1986–7 when final cash limits were overspent in aggregate (Table 17.4). With a predictable underspend of about 2 per cent on the aggregate of final cash limits for central government expenditure, rather more for local authority blocks, the Treasury could with reasonable confidence agree to substantial changes in individual cash-limited blocks, provided that the cost of all the changes was predicted to fall within the margin of the expected aggregate underspend. In other words, the costs of flexibility were met by the predictable underspend. This can be shown by comparing the net costs of the changes made to cash limits, that is the outturn on final cash limits less the costs of the increases to the original cash limits. The final column of Table 17.3 shows that the net effect on the Planning Total was negative for central government blocks from 1976–7 to 1986–7. The Planning Total was some £200–500 million less each year *than if the original cash limits had remained unchanged and fully spent*. Thereafter the net effect of changing cash limits for central government expenditure added substantially to the Planning Total. In the three years 1989–90 to 1991–2, the years of both the Lawson boom and the run-up to the general election, the net effect was to add between £1.8 and £2.7 billion to the Planning Total. The net effect of the costs of changing cash limits for local authority blocks has been more erratic, with both negative and positive values since 1976–7 (Table 17.4). The positive effects in the period 1984–5 to 1986–7 were due less to the size of the changes made to the original cash limits than to substantial overspend on the final cash limits. In most years the Treasury has been able to approve numerous changes to running costs cash limits with only marginal cost effects on the Planning Total (Table 17.5).

The combined effect of the net costs of changes to the cash limits of all three types of blocks on the Planning Total is shown in Table 17.6.

TABLE 17.3. *Effects of changes to central government cash-limited blocks, 1976–1977 to 1992–1973 (£m)*

	Original cash limits	Final cash limits	Changes to outturn	Final outturn	Over/underspend on final cash limit	Effects on Planning Total of net cost of changes to cash limits
1992–3	114,744	114,173	−571	113,252[a]	−921[a]	−1,492[a]
1991–2	98,171	101,388	+3,217	100,956	−432	+2,785
1990–1	88,527	90,507	+1,980	90,333	−174	+1,806
1989–90	71,419	74,236	+2,817	73,655	−581	+2,236
1988–9	66,190	67,035	+845	66,124	−912	−67
1987–8	62,915	64,309	+1,394	63,139	−1,170	+224
1986–7	58,300	59,633	+1,333	58,736	−897	+436
1985–6	55,916	55,789	−127	55,297	−491	−618
1984–5	54,106	54,083	−23	53,581	−502	−525
1983–4	51,302	51,567	+265	50,706	−861	−596
1982–3	48,294	48,757	+463	47,732	−1,025	−562
1981–2	44,163	44,741	+578	43,947	−794	−216
1980–1	40,459	40,684	+225	40,237	−447	−222
1979–80	28,234	34,318[b]	+6,084	34,086	−232	+5,852
1978–9	30,109	30,252	+143	29,799	−453	−310
1977–8	27,816	27,992	+176	27,251	−741	−565
1976–7	25,713	26,079	+366	25,392	−687	−321

[a] Provisional .
[b] Exceptionally, cash limits were revised upwards twice during the year. The size of the increase was partly due to the cost of pay awards in the system when the Conservative Government took office, and partly due to the underestimating of the costs of the departing Labour Government's expanding programmes

Source: Cash Limits White Papers, Final and Provisional Outturns, 1976–93.

TABLE 17.4. *Effects of changes to local authority cash-limited blocks, 1976–1977 to 1992–1993 (£m)*

	Original cash limits	Final cash limits	Changes to cash limits	Final outturn	Over/underspend on final cash limits	Effects on Planning Total of net cost of changes to cash limits
1992–3	12,506	13,590	+1,084	13,435[a]	−155[a]	+929[a]
1991–2	11,486	11,715	+229	11,597	−117	+112
1990–1	10,192	10,378	+186	10,251	−127	+59
1989–90	5,847	6,107	+260	6,049	−58	+202
1988–9	5,568	5,477	−91	5,313	−164	−255
1987–8	8,717	8,559	−158	7,913	−646	−804
1986–7	7,785	7,797	+12	7,981	+184	+196
1985–6	7,124	7,143	+19	8,043	+900	+919
1984–5	6,881	6,838	−43	7,776	+938	+895
1983–4	7,401	6,983	−418	7,349	+366	−52
1982–3	6,064	7,878	+1,814	6,680	−1,198	+616
1981–2	7,202	7,304	+102	6,346	−958	−856
1980–1	6,668	6,645	−23	6,382	−263	−286
1979–80	5,902	5,379	−523	5,264	−115	−638
1978–9	5,104	5,136	+32	4,599	−537	−505
1977–8	4,478	4,594	+116	4,080	−514	−398
1976–7	2,821	2,692	−129	2,239	−453	−582

[a] Provisional.

Source: Cash Limits White Papers, Final and Provisional Outturns, 1976–93.

TABLE 17.5. *Effects of changes to departmental running costs cash-limited blocks, 1986–1987 to 1992–1993 (£m)*

	Original cash limits	Final cash limits	Changes to cash limits	Final outturn	Over/underspend on final cash limit	Effects on Planning Total of net costs of changes to cash limits
1992–3	17,452	17,629[a]	+177[a]	17,351[a]	−277[a]	−100[a]
1991–2	16,322	16,626	+304	16,219	−407	−103
1990–1	14,920	15,284	+364	15,286	+2	+366
1989–90	14,151	14,260	+109	14,213	−47	+62
1988–9	13,733	13,767	+34	13,693	−74	−40
1987–8	13,073	13,197	+124	13,158	−39	+85
1986–7	12,665	13,171	+506	13,068	−103	+403

[a] Provisional.

Source: Cash Limits White Papers, Final and Provisional Outturns, 1986–93.

From 1976–7 to 1983–4, it was negative, apart from the exceptional transitional year of 1979–80. In the following three years the net effect on the Planning Total was positive, due substantially to the large overspend on the aggregate of the final cash limits for local authority blocks. While 'losses' here were substantially offset by 'gains' on the net costs of changes made to central government and running costs blocks, nevertheless there was an addition to the Planning Total in cash in two of the three years of some £300–£400 million. In a Planning Total of some £140 billion this was insignificant. In the run-up to the general election of 1987, the net cost of changes to cash limits added more than £1 billion to the Planning Total. Thereafter the more relaxed stance of the Conservative Government towards public spending, coincident with the Lawson boom, the economic recession, and the approaching general election of 1992, was reflected in much greater net costs to the Planning Total of £2.5, £2.2, and £2.8 billion. With the formal admission of a financial crisis in the summer of 1992, the imposition of tighter Treasury control seemed set to produce the more familiar negative effect on the New Control Total of the net cost of in-year changes to cash limits.

The evidence of the operation of cash limits, from their introduction until the end of the 1980s, shows that the control of the Planning Total was not seriously threatened by the Treasury's agreement to widespread and costly in-year changes to cash limits. It could control the aggregate of public expenditure *and* permit greater flexibility in the management of cash-limited programmes. More flexibility did not mean less overall control. However, towards the end of the decade the loosening up of the Conservative Government's objectives for public expenditure, together with the occurrence of a sharp economic recession, combined to put even greater pressure on prescribed cash limits in-year. The greater number of changes to central government cash-limited blocks and their rising net cost proved more difficult to balance with the margin afforded by aggregate underspending.

In such circumstances the Treasury was less confident, in agreeing to changes in cash limits, that it would be able to accommodate the aggregate costs of so doing within the predictable margin of aggregate underspending on final cash limits. Changes of the magnitude of those agreed for central government blocks from 1986–7 to 1991–2 could not be accommodated within it. The net costs of such changes added substantially to the Planning Total and made control of the outturn more difficult. To protect the New Control Total introduced in 1992–3, the Treasury is obliged to try to operate cash limits less flexibly, to agree less readily to changes in-year, and to insist more strongly on the principle of self-financing. But where such proposed changes arise from policy

TABLE 17.6. *Effect on Planning Total of net costs of changes to cash limits, 1976–1977 to 1992–1993* (£m)

	Central government	Local authority	Running costs	TOTAL
1992–3[a]	−1,492	+929	−100	−663
1991–2	+2,785	+112	−103	+2,794
1990–1	+1,806	+59	+366	+2,231
1989–90	+2,236	+202	+62	+2,500
1988–9	−67	−255	−40	−362
1987–8	+224	−804	+85	−495
1986–7	+436	+196	+403	+1,035
1985–6	−618	+909	—	+291
1984–5	−525	+895	—	+370
1983–4	−596	−52	—	−648
1982–3	−562	+621	—	+59
1981–2	−216	−856	—	−1,072
1980–1	−222	−286	—	−508
1979–80	+5,852	−638	—	+5,214
1978–9	−310	−505	—	−815
1977–8	−565	−398	—	−963
1976–7	−321	−582	—	−903

[a] Provisional.

Source: Cash Limits White Papers, Final and Provisional Outturns, 1976–93.

agreed by ministers, and offsetting savings are resisted or unobtainable, its room for manœuvre is limited.

CONCLUSION

We may now conclude by returning to the questions posed at the beginning of the chapter. First, there are few breaches of cash limits. Improvement in departmental financial management systems will normally provide financial controllers, through the careful monitoring of cash flow, with early warning of the potential overspend. If overspend can be foreseen the Treasury can normally be persuaded to revise a cash limit to accommodate it, either by agreeing to offsetting savings or by increasing the cash limit where agreed policy changes require additional resources. Hence breaches are technical or 'minor system-failures', which occur mainly as a result of unanticipated expenditure towards the end of the financial year, too late for corrective action. Secondly, the persistent and predictable underspending on cash-limited expenditure enabled the

Treasury for most of the period 1976–92 to administer the cash-limits regime flexibly without sacrificing control of the Planning/Control Total. Indeed, underspending contributed to a lower Planning/Control Total through the setting of a lower Reserve. The 'rules of the game' of budgetary politics changed with the introduction of cash limits. Underspending on cash-limited programmes became the norm; it was customary and, at least in aggregate, predictable. It replaced the norm of overspending which characterized many programmes in the mid-1970s and which precipitated the introduction of cash limits. In the narrow but important sense of 'reversing the ratchet' cash limits have been successful. The Treasury acquiesces in underspending. Whether it encourages departments to hold their limits within a few percentage points is more difficult to say. It does, however, regard that result as successful financial management, and the inference can be drawn that there is a tacit norm of about 2 per cent underspending. Thirdly, the incidence of change to prescribed and apparently 'fixed' cash limits has not impaired their credibility as a control mechanism. While Treasury rhetoric that cash limits are fixed and changes uncommon is belied by practice, there is no evidence that changes are approved without careful scrutiny, or that they contribute to looser financial discipline. Moreover, the Treasury can tighten the screws (as in 1984–6 and from 1992–3), without the need to make changes to the cash-limits regime, by insisting that any increases to cash limits (even those arising from policy changes) are wholly or mainly self-financing.

Whether it was envisaged that cash limits could be operated as flexibly as the evidence suggests, and as programme managers appear to need, is problematic. However, the phenomenon of aggregate shortfall was experienced and allowed for before the introduction of cash limits, while from the outset provision was made for change in exceptional circumstances. From the introduction of cash limits in 1976, both changes to cash limits and underspending on them have been characteristic. However, the scale and net cost of those changes increased sharply towards the end of the 1980s, making it more difficult for the Treasury to continue to 'square the circle'—to provide both for flexibility in the financial management of increasingly decentralized departmental programmes and tight central control of the Planning/Control Total.

18

Running Costs, Pay, and Manpower Controls

Containing the pay and allied costs and numbers of civil servants and other public officials has been a priority of governments from 1976 onwards. This is not surprising, since in a period of public expenditure restraint the 'administrative costs' of government are seen as an important area where the Treasury can exert pressure. Civil Service numbers have become a highly charged political issue, with all the associated rhetoric of 'bureaucracy' and 'waste'.

Separate budgets—running costs control—for central government departments' administrative expenditure, itemized in Parliamentary Supply Estimates, and the subject of cash limits, were introduced in April 1986. From April 1988 manpower targeting was fully integrated into the system. The running costs control mechanism represented a further evolution of the Treasury's cash-based public spending control regime which had begun in 1976 with the introduction of cash limits and had continued with the abolition of volume planning and its replacement with cash planning in 1982. Running costs control was also pre-eminently the most significant by-product of the FMI. The administrative and accounting changes which flowed from the introduction of market-based financial management techniques in Whitehall and the delegation of decision-making down-the-line to programme managers provided the data upon which to differentiate between administrative and programme expenditure.

This chapter focuses on how the Treasury has handled the issues raised by Civil Service pay and manpower as they impact on the administrative costs of central government. It has three themes. First, running costs control is yet a further example of the Treasury's twin-track approach to the management of public spending since 1979 which we have described in earlier chapters: the simultaneous desire to tighten central *control* of the spending of Whitehall departments in order to restrain the growth of public spending in aggregate, and the commitment to give programme managers greater *flexibility* in how they operate their budgets. Second, we argue that, although this new control mechanism is presented by the Treasury as a technical improvement aimed at controlling the costs of administration, it in fact deals with highly charged political issues to do with the internal management of departments and with the ability of departments to switch between programme expenditure and administrative expenditure. Third, running costs controls have fashioned for the Treasury new instruments to aid it in delivering value-for-money in public spending and in influencing departments' financial management systems. The new mechanism is but one of a number of examples of what could be called the increasing *monetization* of public administration (other examples being General Practitioners' Budgets in the NHS and Local Management in Schools). Running costs control therefore has implications for the accountability of public agencies, for relationships between the Treasury and departments, and relationships between the Finance Divisions of departments and agencies and their Policy Divisions, and for the politics of resource allocation.

We discuss first the antecedents to running costs control and manpower planning, and give a brief sketch of the more immediate background factors to the introduction of running costs control. We then discuss the rationale for the system. This is followed by an analysis of the details of the implementation of running costs control and the evolution of the regime up to the end of 1992. The final part of the chapter outlines some of the main effects of the implementation of the controls, focusing in particular on three issues which cause tension between the Treasury and the spending departments and agencies.

THE ANTECEDENTS OF RUNNING COSTS CONTROL AND MANPOWER PLANNING

Pay and cash limits, 1976–1986

There have been two episodes in the history of the Treasury's handling of public sector pay in the cash-limits system from 1976 to 1986. The first occurred in the early days of cash limits, between 1976 and 1978, when, under the Labour Government, the new cash-limits rules were used in order to operate a voluntary incomes policy for the public sector. The second episode began in 1982 when, after a period of some confusion in the handling of pay issues by the new Conservative Government, it introduced 'pay factors' within the cash-limits system.

Cash limits were introduced by Chancellor Healey as part of a range of anti-inflation measures which included a 'voluntary' pay agreement with the TUC leadership. This meant that in the first few years of operation cash limits could be maintained whilst containing public sector pay costs. The crucial mechanism was the estimate for inflation used in the revaluation of cash limits from year one to year two. The temptation for the Treasury was to underestimate inflation in order to influence inflationary expectations (Heald 1983). However, when a pay policy was in operation, 'the Government was well placed to estimate inflation' fairly accurately and 'impose a gentle squeeze' on expenditure volumes (Bevan 1980: 33). In such an environment cash limits did not carry the additional burden of acting as a pay policy which was to be the case later.

The new Conservative Government elected in 1979 faced the collapse of the Labour Government's 5 per cent pay policy, following the Winter of Discontent in 1978–9. The result was a 'catching-up' process which invariably follows any sustained period when public sector pay growth is restrained relative to that in the private sector (Price 1979: 70). The Labour Government had tried to ensure industrial peace by referring many of the public-sector wage demands to the Clegg Pay Comparability Commission. The Conservative Government agreed to abide by the results of the Commission's deliberations, and this added £4.6 billion in cash terms to public spending in 1980–1. During this initial period of Conservative government no definite decisions were taken about how to handle public sector pay; Treasury ministers were caught between their monetarist rhetoric—which implied that pay levels were fairly unimportant in determining inflation—and the reality of rising public sector pay costs undermining the Treasury's ability to achieve public spending cuts.

The Treasury's pay assumptions were criticized as being unrealistic (Treasury and Civil Service Committee 1980*b*). The 1980–1 cash limit contained an allowance for only a 14 per cent increase in Civil Service pay when pay was expected to rise by 25 per cent more than in 1979–80. The Treasury and Civil Service Committee not only doubted that the Government was being 'firm on public sector pay' (p. xi) but also remained to be 'convinced that cash limits are fully effective in controlling public sector pay' (p. xi). There followed a series of highly critical reports from both the Treasury Committee and the Public Accounts Committee on the Treasury's decision to stage pay awards as a ruse for coping with the difficulty of fitting large pay awards into strictly determined annual cash limits (see Treasury and Civil Service Committee 1980*a*, 1980*d*; PAC 1980*a*). The staging of awards in this way enabled larger increases in pay in the pay round than were allowed for in the year-on-year inflation allowance of the cash limits (Bevan 1980).

The consequence of these problems of controlling pay in the public sector was a series of actions taken by the Conservative Government in the period to 1982. The Civil Service pay comparability machinery had been established in 1957 after the report of the Priestley Royal Commission on the Civil Service, and was subsequently strengthened by the Civil Service Pay Research Unit in 1971. It was effectively scrapped in October 1980 when the Government decided not to implement pay research findings and thus unilaterally ended the Civil Service pay agreement (Fry 1984). In addition, the Treasury used the cash limits system to introduce an unofficial pay policy for the public sector.

In the absence of a formal pay policy any attempt by the Treasury to set an allowance for pay rises within each cash limit posed particular problems:

The inflation allowances implicit in cash limits have been frequently criticised as being consistently too low. This has been interpreted as a 'back door' method of securing expenditure reductions; no announcement has to be made when volume is squeezed by a deliberate underestimate . . . Nevertheless, the Treasury faces a dilemma when it sets cash limits. Any forecast which it adopts is likely to become a target to be exceeded in collective bargaining, a fact which encourages it to use underestimates since use of the best-estimate would in the event guarantee that this turned out to be too low. (Heald 1983: 227)

From 1981–2 the Treasury continued to estimate for inflation in this way, but went further by announcing a figure representing the allowance made within the cash-limits total for public sector pay. These 'pay factors' were to assume major importance in discussions about the control of public expenditure, and also in public-sector pay bargaining. The status of the 'pay factor' was outlined in a Treasury statement on 1 October 1982 (Treasury 1982*b*: 3). The setting of it was described as part of 'the process of reaching final decisions on the cash total for each programme'. The provision of money for wages and salaries 'is determined principally by the numbers employed and the rates of pay at which they are paid'. This decision was said to concern only 'the cash provision to be made in public expenditure', and was not to be regarded as 'a pay norm'. The statement went on to note that 'each department has its own specific budget, within which expenditure on wages and salaries must be accommodated'.

In effect, the Treasury was using the cash-limits system as a way of avoiding or devolving its responsibilities as an employer to give a lead in wage bargaining (Bevan 1980). Using cash limits in this way also seemed to remove the need for government to involve itself in the politically difficult world of collective pay bargaining; 'pay factors' removed the need to tackle complex issues of pay in the public sector, something which appealed to a government committed to free market ideas (Heald 1983). In addition, the 'pay factor' was also a useful device to enforce 'market discipline' within the public sector:

the concept is seductively straightforward. In theory, management in the public services and the nationalized industries will be given blocks of cash and it is for them to decide how to spend it. If management and trade unions agree to excessive pay rises, then they will have to raise their charges or reduce the services. (Bevan, Sisson, and Way 1981: 380)

There was also an assumption that public sector wage negotiations would be conducted against the background of possible job losses if pay demands were conceded which breached the 'pay factor'—another incentive to produce 'realism' in pay discussions. Yet manipulating the rules in pay bargaining could also be seen as bringing some flexibility to the cash-limits system, through reductions in staffing or in the staging of an award (Bevan, Sisson, and Way 1981).

The Treasury's use of cash limits to contain public sector pay began in 1981–2, when it set a 'pay factor' which allowed for a 6 per cent rise in pay and related costs within the cash limits set for that financial year. The Public Expenditure White Paper (Cmnd. 8175) noted that the cash limits contained provision for an 11 per cent rise in the prices of items other than pay, and 6 per cent for pay, with the proviso that 'the Government will decide nearer the time what can be afforded for public sector pay after July 1981' (p. 5). The Treasury and Civil Service Committee (1981*b*) was sceptical about how realistic this provision was, given that it represented an assumption that pay levels in the public sector would rise by 2.5 per cent less than the Retail Price Index (p. xi). Furthermore, errors in such assumptions would be expensive: every percentage point added to the pay bill above the pay assumption of 6 per cent would add some £300 million to public spending at current prices or would require a reduction of about 50,000 employees in the public services (p. xi).

In subsequent years, 'pay factors' were set at 4 per cent in 1982–3, 3.5 per cent in 1983–4, and at 3 per cent in both 1984–5 and 1985–6. Michael Scholar, then Under Secretary in charge of GEP, told the Treasury and Civil Service Committee that a pay factor 'was not a norm; it is designed to determine the result in the public sector pay negotiations . . . It is a measure of what the Government has decided is affordable' (Treasury and Civil Service Committee 1985*a*: qu. 158). The Committee remained unimpressed at the credibility of 'pay factors' when the actual wages and salaries bill of the public sector had exceeded plans announced in Public

TABLE 18.1. *Pay factors and outturn: 1981–1986*

	'Pay factor' (% of pay bill)	Public services pay outturn (%)	Difference (%)
1981–2	6.0	9.5	3.5
1982–3	4.0	6.5	2.5
1983–4	3.5	5.5	2.0
1984–5	3.0	5.5	2.5
1985–6	3.0	6.5	3.5
Average	3.9	6.7	2.8

Source: Based on Trinder 1987: 83.

Expenditure White Papers by £1.2 billion, £1.7 billion, and £1.1 billion in 1982–3, 1983–4, and 1984–5 respectively (p. xiii). Indeed, public services pay outturn was on average 2.8 per cent higher each year than the 'pay factors' set during the period 1981–2 to 1985–6 (Trinder 1987). Table 18.1 gives details of plans and outturns during this period. In addition, public-sector pay rises were considerably lower than in the economy as a whole, with pay rising by an average of 8.7 per cent during this period compared with 6.7 per cent a year in the public sector. Thus, although 'pay factors' had not led to pay in the public sector rising in line with Treasury plans, they had contributed to a general squeeze on pay rises in the public sector. This had 'merely stored up future problems of a major scale for industrial relations and spending in public services' (Trinder 1987: 82).

During this period, critics argued that the Treasury was stretching the fabric of the cash-limits system and threatening its credibility, as cash limits were being used not just as a mechanism aimed at ensuring that outturn matched planned expenditure but also to provide a public sector pay negotiating framework (Bevan 1980; Else and Marshall 1981). Moreover, the failure to hit prescribed pay factors further weakened the credibility of the system (Likierman 1983). What was equally clear was that the unsatisfactory operation of 'pay factors' was symptomatic of a general 'disarray in public service pay strategy, a disarray, however, which is by no means peculiar to the 1980s, but which may be becoming more serious than in earlier times' (Trinder 1987: 82).

The Treasury's willingness to return to the imposition of pay factors or pay norms in economic crisis was evidenced by the decision in the 1992 Autumn Statement to limit increases in the public sector to between 0 and 1.5 per cent from November 1992. By focusing on the impact of this in releasing £1.5 billion in cash savings in 1993–4, the

Treasury was returning to the same rationale for policy used in the early 1980s. We return to this issue later in the chapter.

Civil Service manpower targeting

Cutting the number of civil servants employed by central government departments, and the number of employees in the public sector as a whole, can be seen as part of the Thatcher Governments' 'Grand Strategy' for the Civil Service (Fry 1984; see also Dunsire and Hood 1989). One of the first acts of the Prime Minister, on entering office in May 1979, was to initiate a review of Civil Service manpower and appoint Sir Derek (now Lord) Rayner as her special adviser on efficiency. This was to lead, by progression, to the efficiency strategy, Rayner reviews, and FMI, discussed in Chapter 4.

The early cautious phase of this process resulted in a Commons statement by Paul Channon, then Minister of State at the Civil Service Department. The review, he argued, 'of the size and cost of the Civil Service' was undertaken for three reasons: cutting the role of Government was 'in the national interest'; central administration should make a contribution to the process of restraining public spending; and 'it is essential to examine any large organisation, public or private' on occasion to identify areas of activity no longer needed (Parliamentary Debates, HC, 6 Dec. 1979, col. 627). The review had identified annual savings of £212 million (at 1979 Survey prices), most of which would accrue in 1982–3 financial year, and staff reductions of approximately 39,000.

After the initial short-term manpower savings had been identified, a medium-term set of targets was announced by the Prime Minister, which committed the Government to a 14 per cent reduction in 'staff in post' in the Civil Service between May 1979 and 1 April 1984, reducing its size from 732,000 to 630,000. This initial medium-term target was followed, in the period up to April 1988, by a 'rolling' programme of annual targets based on staffing on 1 April each year for central government departments, incorporated into the Public Expenditure White Papers from 1986 onwards. The Treasury announced in February 1987 that the process of centrally monitored 'spot-date targets' for Civil Service numbers would end on 1 April 1988 when manpower targeting would be incorporated into running costs projections. Tables 18.2 and 18.3 show the record of targets and outturn during the period from May 1979 to April 1988. Civil Service manpower referred to in these tables was defined as 'staff-in-post' in the central government departments and included both 'industrial' and 'non-industrial' civil servants; the reduc-

TABLE 18.2. *Civil Service manpower: targets and outturns, 1979–1984*

Spot-dates	May 1979	1 Apr. 1980	1 Apr. 1981	1 Apr. 1982	1 Apr. 1983	1 Apr. 1984
Target	732,275	—	—	—	—	630,000
Outturn	732,275	704,903	689,602	666,362	648,953	623,972
% change on previous yr		−3.7	−2.2	−3.4	−2.6	−3.8
% change on May 1979		−3.7	−5.8	−9.0	−11.4	−14.8

Sources: We are grateful to HM Treasury for checking this data and for providing some updated figures. Also based on Public Expenditure White Papers and reports of the Treasury and Civil Service Committee.

TABLE 18.3. *Civil Service manpower: targets and outturns, 1984–1988*

Spot-dates	May 1979	1 Apr. 1984	1 Apr. 1985	1 Apr. 1986	1 Apr. 1987	1 Apr. 1988
Targets						
1984 PEWP			599,026	605,255	600,554	592,723
1986 PEWP				600,500	600,400	590,400
1987 PEWP					605,300	590,400
1988 PEWP						593,000
Outturn	732,275	623,972	599,026	594,365	597,814	579,626
% change on previous yr			−4.0	−0.8	+0.6	−3.0
% change on Apr. 1984			−4.0	−4.7	−4.2	−7.1
% change on May 1979		−14.8	−18.2	−18.8	−18.4	−20.8

Sources: We are grateful to HM Treasury for checking this data and for providing some updated figures. Also based on Public Expenditure White Papers and reports of the Treasury and Civil Service Committee.

tions were 'net', that is after an allowance for increases in staffing in some departments (Treasury and Civil Service Committee 1981c: 2).

As Table 18.2 shows, the Prime Minister's ambitious target, to reduce Civil Service manpower by 102,000 by April 1984, was in fact more than achieved. Total staff employed in the Civil Service fell by 108,000 or 14.8 per cent over the target period. While it is difficult to calculate the total savings generated over the whole period, it was estimated that the manpower reductions made in 1981–2 alone saved the Treasury the equivalent of £70.7 million in a full year (Treasury and Civil Service Committee 1981c: p. xvi). Similarly, savings made through net reductions in manpower in 1982–3 were calculated to be £144.4 million in a full year (Treasury and Civil Service Committee 1982e: 11).

Table 18.3 shows a slightly less tidy picture. Nevertheless, a story of successful targetry emerges. Overall, total numbers of 'staff-in-post' in the Civil Service were nearly 21 per cent lower in April 1988 than when the Conservative Government came to power in May 1979. When we compare the two periods—the first up to April 1984 when there was a medium-term target and the second from 1984 to April 1988 when there was a series of 'rolling targets'—it is clear that it became more difficult to cut Civil Service numbers as time went on. Total numbers of staff fell by 14 per cent in the first period and by 7.1 per cent between April 1984 and April 1988. This is a predictable pattern. Once the 'fat' had been trimmed in the early years, departmental managers increasingly found it harder to reduce staffing numbers. It also became harder to disguise cuts through transferring functions outside the numbers-count, or by converting full-time posts into part-time (the figures are full-time equivalents); or by careful timing of recruitment to avoid the 'spot dates' for calculating departmental staff.

From the discussion in this section we can conclude that the Treasury (and Civil Service Department up to 1981) was more successful in achieving its goals for reducing the size of the Civil Service than it was in implementing the 'pay factor' policy. The reduction in Civil Service manpower from 1980 to 1988 must rank as one of the clearest policy 'successes' in the field of public expenditure restraint (see Dunsire and Hood 1989 for a discussion of this). We return to the issue of 'success' in this policy area when we discuss the impact of the abolition of manpower targeting on manpower levels once the running costs control regime was fully bedded in.

THE BACKGROUND TO THE INTRODUCTION OF RUNNING COSTS CONTROL

It was clear from the Government's White Paper on Civil Service efficiency (Cmnd. 8293) that, as early as July 1981, preliminary work had been done on separating administrative running costs from other programme expenditure. The White Paper commented on a series of initiatives aimed at 'helping those responsible for the consumption of goods and services to do a better job by giving them more accountability, not least through carrying the cost of their own budget' (p. 4). These included improving management information available to departments so that Ministers and officials were able 'first to know and then question their costs'; MINIS was given as an example (see Likierman 1982). It made departments responsible for paying for services such as accommodation, and common services like messengers and telephones provided by other departments and agencies. There was also a review of the operation of agencies which delivered common services, such as the PSA.

There is some evidence that the main impetus for developing running costs further into a control mechanism, rather than just remaining a vehicle for the Treasury to undertake spot checks on departmental administrative costs, came not from the Treasury but initially from Sir Derek Rayner's efficiency scrutiny exercises and later from the Management and Personnel Office, located in the Cabinet Office (Hennessy 1989). The Treasury was initially more circumspect in its approach because a full-blown control system would endanger the manpower targets, which, as we have seen, represented a clear, very effective, though crude, approach to reducing Civil Service manpower. The manpower targets had the advantages of conveying a strong message to Whitehall about the need for reductions in staffing (especially when the original commitment to reducing the size of the Civil Service came from the Prime Minster), and produced quick political credit for the Government in delivering cuts in the 'bureaucracy'. Indeed, there was some support for the Treasury's initial misgivings when the Treasury and Civil Service Select Committee questioned whether the downgrading of manpower targets might result in less pressure on departments to control staff numbers, especially if running costs control 'discipline' was not sufficiently 'biting' (Treasury and Civil Service Committee 1987a: para. 28).

We discussed in Chapter 4 the significance of the Financial Management Initiative (FMI) in public spending control. David Butler, the first head of the Treasury's Running Costs and Management Group (RCM), in evidence to the Treasury and Civil Service Committee stressed that the control regime was introduced because 'the Government, having experience of collecting the information over the last few years, found that it was in a position where it could introduce a control from 1986–87' (Treasury and Civil Service Committee 1986a: qu. 97). FMI had produced improvements in the accounting and budgeting procedures of departments which enabled the Treasury and the departments to separate running costs from other items of expenditure and it would not have been possible to introduce the regime without FMI.

A further spur to the evolution of running costs control was the *Multi-Departmental Review of Budgeting* co-ordinated by the Treasury which reported in March 1986 (Treasury 1986*b*, 1986*c*). The aim of the review was to 'encourage the development of budgeting as an effective instrument of expenditure planning and control and as a tool which management can use to improve its resources allocation and to deliver greater economy, efficiency and effectiveness' (Treasury 1986*b*: 7). The report raised many issues which were later to generate tensions and lead to increased flexibility in the operation of controls such as the definition of capital spending and running costs, central pay assumptions, and net and gross controls. On the general issue of running costs control, the report stressed that 'on balance, the introduction of single departmental running costs limits should help the thrust of devolved budgeting' (Treasury 1986*b*: 18).

THE RATIONALE FOR RUNNING COSTS CONTROL

The introduction of running costs control was presented by the Treasury both as an efficiency measure and an innovation designed to give departments greater freedom to allocate resources according to priorities determined departmentally rather than centrally. The 'objective of this control is to exert downward pressure on administrative costs . . . while allowing departments greater freedom to allocate resources within their overall limits' (Treasury 1988*c*: para. 56). Butler stressed the mutual benefits to be derived for both the departments and the Treasury from the new regime. Control would be better exerted under the arrangements because departments had to live within a cash limit for specifically *administrative* expenditure for the first time: 'running costs control provide an envelope of cash for departments within which they have to find the expenditure on all their running cost items' (Treasury and Civil Service Committee 1986*a*: qu. 97). However, departments gained because 'the control that will be in place will, we hope, be more appropriate to the requirements of the department rather than some centrally imposed norm such as pay' (qu. 97). Programme managers would, under the running costs regime, be able to choose to reorder expenditure between the various subheadings according to specific needs. The Treasury also sought to place running costs in the context of the Government's objectives about the size and scope of the public sector. Containing departmental running costs and manpower levels was seen as indicative of a more general desire to limit the amount of resources consumed by the public sector.

In addition to the 'official' explanation, there were also two less well articulated reasons why the Treasury favoured the introduction of a more rigorous control regime. The first was that it was one way of ending a rather muddled era of pay restraint in the public sector, discussed earlier. Departmental limits on *all* departmental administrative costs, not just pay, submerged the issue of how much the Treasury was setting aside for pay in any financial year; in addition, it avoided the potential political embarrassment of headline-grabbing 'pay norms'.

A second reason was that running costs provided the Treasury with a 'window' on a significant aspect of departmental financial management. Whilst it is true to say that running costs limits do not represent a large proportion of many Whitehall departments' total expenditure, detailed monitoring of such costs does give the Treasury's expenditure controllers an opportunity to probe the effectiveness of a department's financial management system. Departments have been expected to produce management plans on how they intend to deploy staff, at what cost and with what projected efficiency improvements, and to supply appropriate value-for-money and output data for a three-year period. Taken together, the control regime and three-year plans act as a proxy for how a department more generally sets its objectives, manages resources, and delegates authority from the centre. By probing on running costs, Treasury expenditure controllers are able to find out more about the departments and the agencies that they shadow.

THE COMPONENTS AND IMPLEMENTATION OF RUNNING COSTS CONTROL

The running costs regime has evolved substantially since 1986. As with all the control innovations initiated by the Treasury, after an early period of inflexibility in the operation of the new system, once it was 'bedded in' modifications were made and flexibilities added. Many (although not all) of these in the running costs control regime have been spurred on by pressures generated on budgeting systems by the creation of Next Steps Agencies.

For most central government departments running costs control is operated on the gross administrative costs of the department and those agencies within its control (and which are consistent with the coverage of Civil Service manpower accounting). In essence, running costs are made up of five general types of expenditure: wages and salaries (including overtime payments, employers' National Insurance contributions);

personnel overheads (travel, subsistence, removals, entertainment, catering support, protective clothing, and training); accommodation costs (rates, heating, lighting, utilities, furniture and fittings, and market rental values for property); office services (postage, telecommunications, stationery, printing, binding, publication, library services, publicity and advertisements, and current expenditure on computers, office equipment, and vehicles); and other costs such as services provided by the Post Office, other agencies, and departments. From the outset, bodies which operated as trading funds within the public sector (such as the Royal Mint, HMSO, and The Crown Suppliers) were exempt from running costs control, although their staff were included in the manpower count.

From an early stage in the running costs regime some departments or parts of departments or agencies which were 'self-financing', and had a 'robust financial' framework in which 'efficiency targets and performance measures' were achieved, were able to 'apply for exemption from gross running costs control to enable them to respond flexibly to changes in levels of demand' (Treasury 1988c: para. 57). This was an incentive to encourage departments and agencies to improve their financial management. Exemption did not entail the removal of all public spending control, but rather expenditure previously included in the specific running costs system could be returned back to the larger element of programmed expenditure, thus giving departments greater flexibility in the prioritizing of spending. The Treasury regarded such exemptions as conferring its seal of good housekeeping on the department concerned.

From April 1991, the Treasury ended exemption and moved to a *net* running costs control regime, allowing some departments and their Next Steps Agencies to negotiate net rather than gross running costs 'for areas where expenditure and receipts vary in line with demand and which have suitably robust monitoring and management systems' (Cm. 1520: 43). In 1992–3 there were twenty-seven 'net controlled areas', all but five of which were Next Steps Executive Agencies.

Running costs are agreed between the Treasury and spending departments during the Public Expenditure Survey; they are published alongside the department's estimates, treated as a control limit for the year ahead, and form part of the Parliamentary Supply procedure with increases and reductions notified to Parliament through Supplementary or Revised Supply Estimates. 'Running costs limits are centrally monitored and any excess leads to an investigation into the causes, including an examination of the financial procedures for its control' (Treasury

1988*c*: para. 56); departments are 'expected to live within that total' agreed at the beginning of the financial year (Butler: Treasury and Civil Service Committee 1986*a*: qu. 97).

Departmental managers are allowed to move expenditure between the headings within their running costs limits; but they are not allowed to 'move money into their running costs provision from their programme expenditure or capital items without coming to the Treasury, gaining the approval of the Chief Secretary' (ibid.: qu. 97). This firm rule was modified in the wake of pressure for greater flexibility from Next Steps Agencies. The process began with some departmental Finance Divisions negotiating specific arrangements on behalf of their prospective agencies. In such cases the Treasury has a right of review; the agency is not given an automatic right. The Treasury cannot delegate to a department or agency the general right to vire money between Votes or subheadings because of the need to ensure that Parliament's authority over expenditure is not infringed. Such *ad hoc* arrangements were formalized across Whitehall with the announcement of the allowance of greater flexibility and virement for some Next Steps Agencies and departments in December 1989 in Cm. 914 *The Financing and Accountability of Next Steps Agencies*. Essentially the Treasury has agreed to 'define in advance the conditions in which a department and an Agency might expect Treasury support' for reallocation between Votes, virement between subheadings, and agreement to a Supplementary Estimate to increase expenditure in line with receipts (Cm. 914: 9–10). All of which has been heavily qualified and circumscribed: with, for example, no Treasury agreement to reallocate 'from programme into running costs subheads where the underlying objective of the provision as originally voted requires it to be spent outside Government departments'.

Departments discuss 'bids' with the Treasury, which include individual departmental pay assumptions. There are 'no Treasury instructions' on what assumptions should be included. 'Each department not only chose its pay assumption but other assumptions ... Those bids were examined by the Treasury and discussed with the departments and at the end of the process there was an agreement as to what the final figure should be' (Butler, in Treasury and Civil Service Committee 1986*a*: qu. 97).

Each department's running costs allocation assumes that 'there should be progressive efficiency gains equivalent to at least 1.5 per cent of running costs a year'. Departments are therefore expected to 'prepare options to meet any additional pressures from within their agreed running costs provision, either by making further efficiency savings or by re-ordering priorities' (Treasury 1988*c*: para. 59). Each department is expected to provide the Treasury with an explanation of how efficiency gains of at least 1.5 per cent (more if this can be agreed between the Treasury's Expenditure Division and the department concerned) are to be delivered and whether these are in the form of cash savings or in increased output.

A limited scheme allowing departments to carry forward some underspending on running costs into the following financial year was introduced, with effect from 1989–90. This running costs end-year flexibility scheme is not as generous as that operating on cash-limited capital spending (discussed in the next chapter), but it is intended to cover those elements of running costs which are equivalent to capital spending, such as payments to consultants working on computer installation. Departments are allowed to carry forward 0.5 per cent of eligible spending (or £50,000, whichever is greater), and the spending covered by the scheme amounts to about 2 per cent of non-pay running costs.

The Treasury agrees manpower plans with each department as part of the Survey, and a quarterly report on staff numbers continues to be given to Ministers (Treasury 1988*c*: para. 58). These 'indicative manpower plans rather than firm manpower planning targets' (Chief Secretary MacGregor, Treasury and Civil Service Committee 1987*a*: qu. 130) are then published in the annual Public Expenditure White Paper (or latterly the Statistical Annex to the Budget Statement). There is a presumption that in most departments the combination of manpower plans and running costs control will mean lower staffing or 'a different grade mix' and increased 'office automation and capital equipment rather than staffing' (Chief Secretary, Treasury and Civil Service Committee 1988*a*: qu. 160). The running costs control element in the combination of manpower plans and running costs is intended to be dominant, and the discipline exerted by running costs control results in cuts to manpower levels if, for example, 'there is a higher pay settlement in any one year than has been assumed in drawing up the departmental running costs' (Chief Secretary, Treasury and Civil Service Committee 1987*a*: qu. 130). Running costs controls are intended to remove the need for central manpower targets because departments will 'fall below manpower targets originally set because the running costs are squeezing them' (qu. 132). The efficiency assumptions also imply that departments will be able over time to perform the same or increased functions with a static or smaller staffing level.

Even allowing for the constraints imposed by running costs control, in theory departments are given greater freedom to plan the mix of expenditure *within* the running costs total, the aim of the new system being 'to give departments greater flexibility in how they utilise their running costs to get the best value from them' (Chief Secretary: Treasury and Civil Service Committee 1988*a*: qu. 160).

Having set up a running costs control mechanism which imposed real constraints on departments, the Treasury has gradually allowed a significant increase in the amount of flexibility in its operation. Departments have benefited from the consequential abandonment of manpower controls. Initially when running costs control was set up in 1986 the Treasury deferred a decision on the future of manpower targeting. The 1986 PEWP stated that 'overall manpower controls relating to the published targets will remain until at least 1 April 1988. When running costs control is working effectively the Government will review the need for separate manpower control' (Cmnd. 9702-II). The Chief Secretary later admitted that it was difficult to run manpower targets alongside running costs control, especially as 'the "belt and braces" approach runs counter to our other broad objective of extending greater responsibility for financial management and budgeting to Departments and much further down the line within Departments' (Parliamentary Debates, HC, 18 Feb. 1987, col. 933). Running costs control in theory gave programme managers the freedom to hire more staff, provided that savings were made on other costs, such as travelling. In the first two years of the running costs innovation, the existence of central manpower targets in parallel to the controls effectively removed that element of flexibility. Departments were still required to remain within staffing totals agreed for 1 April each year. The Chief Secretary, John MacGregor, indicated that consideration of such disadvantages had contributed to the decision to abandon centrally imposed manpower targets from the beginning of 1988–9 (Treasury and Civil Service Committee 1987*a*: qu. 130).

It remains difficult, however, to assess the impact of the move to 'indicative' manpower planning. This is particularly acute because there have been a number of other developments—such as Next Steps Agencies, privatization, and market-testing—which could also be responsible for changes in manpower levels. The Treasury emphasizes the greater flexibility being offered to departments by the change, but it is unclear whether the impact of the efficiency savings targets built into the system, which may enable departments to justify their staffing levels, will outweigh the presumption that staffing will suffer if other costs rise. The Treasury can still squeeze manpower levels since the running costs allocation to each department is largely based on numbers of staff employed.

However, there is some evidence that the combination of policy changes—the advent of Next Steps Agencies, the move to net running costs control in some departments and agencies, and the abolition of manpower targets—has halted the reduction in Civil Service numbers. As we noted earlier, these declined by nearly 21 per cent between 1979 and the ending of manpower targets in 1988. From April 1988 to April 1991 there was a further decline of over 4 per cent. This was followed by the first rise in the total since 1979, when numbers grew by 11,456 or 2 per cent between April 1991 and April 1992, to stand at over 565,000, the highest level since 1989. The Treasury's and departments' explanations for the rise included increased pressure on departments and agencies (asylum-seekers, unemployment levels, vehicles and houses registered); policy changes (expansion of the prison service, new responsibilities in education, extra legal responsibilities in Health and Safety); and efforts to improve efficiency (for example in Government Statistics). But it is clear that the twenty-eight oldest Executive Agencies have increased their manpower by 12 per cent between 1988 and 1992, to meet increased demands and increased activity arising from their exploitation of greater managerial freedom. At the same time extra staff have also been required to devolve responsibilities from departmental headquarters, resulting in some duplication of function (*Financial Times*, 8 Feb. 1993). It could be argued that the relaxation of Treasury control of manpower and increased flexibility granted to departments and agencies since 1986 have contributed to an expansion in the Civil Service. If that trend continued there would be pressure to reimpose raw manpower targets which proved so successful in the early 1980s in producing real cuts in the numbers of civil servants.

We discussed in Chapter 5 the extent to which Next Steps Agencies have put pressure on the Treasury to allow further modifications to the running costs regime. The two most important changes are the facility to allow limited virement between running costs and other expenditure heads (initially a cardinal principle of the regime) announced in 1989 (Cm. 914) and more generalized Treasury agreement to net rather than gross running costs control effective from April 1991 'for areas where expenditure and receipts vary in line with demand and which have suitably robust monitoring and management systems' (Cm. 1520: 43). Here we concentrate on two further examples of flexibility: revisions to running costs control limits during the financial year via the tabling of Supplementary and revised Supply Estimates; and the introduction of an end-year flexibility scheme.

If we take the revisions to running costs cash limits in the first three years of the operation of the regime from 1986–7 to 1988–9, it is apparent that there is a great deal of flexibility in the system (see Thain and Wright 1989*d* for further details). There were twenty-one changes in individual running costs totals in 1986–7, thirty-one in 1987–8, and thirty-two in 1988–9. This represented changes to more than half of the cash-limit blocks during the first three years of running costs control. Most of these revisions entailed the allocation of additional monies to running costs control figures. Some blocks were changed twice during the financial year, and there were three revisions to the running costs limits of both the D.o.E. and Office of Population (OPCS) in 1988–9. Two conclusions can be drawn from the number and frequency of such in-year changes. First, the Treasury appears to be flexible in its response to requests by departments for adjustments to their running costs limits in the course of the financial year. Secondly, this creates a degree of uncertainty in the running costs budgeting of some departments or, perhaps more accurately, there are rather too frequent policy changes for the mechanism to be capable of offering managers a clear cash-control limit.

The scheme which allows carry-forward on some running costs underspending was introduced by the Treasury with effect from the beginning of the 1989–90 financial year. It is another example of the much greater flexibility in the administration of the system than is apparent from the rhetoric. We discuss in the next chapter the operation of an equivalent scheme for underspending of cash-limited capital expenditure. The running costs scheme is less generous in scope. It is yet another case of the Treasury attaching 'strings' to its flexibility. Departments have to 'earn' end-year flexibility; decisions by Treasury officials on whether to sanction carry-forward are based on an assessment of the soundness of a department's financial system. Any expenditure approved is subject to the terms of the scheme (no more than 0.5 per cent of eligible expenditure and only on non-pay 'procurement' type spending). Once sanctioned by officials this is then referred for approval to the Chief Secretary to the Treasury, as the carry-forward into year two is financed by a call on the Reserve.

Delegating responsibility down the line

While Finance Divisions have a key role in presenting their departments' case to the Treasury for running costs, they also have a role in ensuring value-for-money in the distribution of those resources internally. Two salient issues are the use and development of delegated budgeting of running costs, and the importance of central allocation of running costs to agencies.

Most departments have now delegated responsibility to line managers for running costs, although the speed of this and the specific subheadings delegated have varied. Examples from three departments give a flavour of what happened. In one department delegated budgeting had been going for some time, and was 'part of the culture now'. All of the running costs budget was delegated to Deputy Secretary commands, and then down the line. At the start of the year the whole DRC settlement was divided between them. Finance Division maintained a minimal monitoring function. Each Deputy Secretary was responsible for sorting out potential under/overspends within his command, and reported each quarter to the Senior Management Board. In the second department, DRCs were divided into pay, accommodation, and non-pay costs. Pay assumptions and accommodation costings were dealt with centrally by the PFO, and then put to top management. In the delegated budget system 80 per cent of DRCs were allocated to over fifty budget-holders. In the much smaller, third department a delegated budgeting system had only recently been introduced after experimentation and a series of pilot studies. The delegation involved all those running costs that commands could be reasonably expected to affect: manpower, salaries, travel, and subsistence, but not accommodation costs. Budget-holders—Deputy Secretaries and the PFO and PEO—could move running costs within their commands to adjust for under/overspending. Delegation to line managers was limited to those running costs for which they had direct responsibility.

In those departments which support a significant number of Executive Agencies, or where agencies are large in relation to central departmental headquarters, problems and advantages are created by having a single running costs pot for the whole department. Usually within this single limit there were separate 'performance agreements' with each agency and in addition each had rights to end-year flexibility on its running costs. A tacit advantage for the Treasury was that the single limit gave the responsibility to the central finance department to adjust under- and overspends internally rather than come back to it. Many departmental Finance Divisions supported the single limit because it reaffirmed the unitary nature of a department in which all parts were answerable to a single Minister, and because it gave the Finance Division a 'handle on the activities and financial control of other parts of the department' in a fluid, potentially centripetal situation. It was felt that, without the 'lever' of having one running costs pot, it might be more difficult to co-ordinate activity and press agencies to provide information or improve management.

THE EFFECTS OF RUNNING COSTS CONTROL

The measurement of the effects of an administrative reform depends on who is doing the measuring and for what purpose. There are at least four perspectives through which the effects of running costs control can be assessed: that of the Treasury's Expenditure Controller; that of the Treasury's specialist Running Costs Division; that of a department's Finance Division; and that of a department's specialist Policy Divisions. There is the further perspective, beyond the scope of this chapter, of the clients of a department—the citizens who benefit from the goods and services provided by government agencies. We illustrate these perspectives by focusing on three main issues in the running costs regime which highlight the inherent tension between central Treasury control and departmental managerial autonomy: management plans, efficiency gains, and pay assumptions.

Management plans

The negotiation of the preparation, revision, and roll-forward of departmental management plans is the source of most tension between the Treasury's Expenditure Divisions and departmental Finance Divisions in the administration of the running costs regime. As part of the arrangements for 'firm-deals' on running costs, departments have to provide the Treasury with a management plan for the three-year period. It includes information on the basic assumptions upon which departmental programmes are based (such items as number of benefit claimants or pupils educated), forecast expenditure, how efficiency savings are to be made, and the cumulative impact of efficiency savings over time. The Treasury may want to 'cash in' efficiency gains which are in the form of increased output if these are in low-priority policy areas, although such gains in high-priority areas such as drug-detection may be approved. On occasion, the Treasury approves 'spend-to-save' projects, providing that value-for-money data is clearly established. A 'firm-deal' will not be struck with a department if its plan is considered poorly constructed, or if a department has not developed a robust financial management system. The Treasury's intention is to provide an additional incentive to departments to adjust to the new culture of value-for-money and financial management.

There is considerable uncertainty on both sides about the real purpose of management plans—whether the intention is to enhance the Treasury's control of the detail of running costs, or to oblige departments to plan and manage their manpower more strategically and in the broader context of policy planning and resource management. This uncertainty, coupled with doubt about their effectiveness for either purpose, is reflected in the inconsistency with which the principles are implemented by the Treasury's Expenditure Divisions. PFOs complain that the Treasury's requests for information are more concerned with the form of management plans than their content, with what the system produces by way of data and not what is actually done with it. A frequent criticism was that, of the three parts of the management plan, the Treasury showed little interest in the Executive Summary (listing the department's aims and objectives for the year ahead) or in the Group Plans, which the Treasury found too detailed and even 'impenetrable'. Its interest was confined to the section on Targets and Outcomes, fuelling suspicion that the Treasury's primary purpose was to obtain more cost savings.

Nevertheless, despite uncertainty about the Treasury's intention with regard to the purpose of obtaining such information, and concern that it would be used instrumentally to maintain pressure on running costs, departments were prepared to play the game. One tactic was to give the Expenditure Division as much information as possible in the belief that 'they won't have time to read it; we haven't'; another was to produce plans to meet the requirements of individual Expenditure Divisions, but 'tailored to remove highly confidential bits which were for internal consumption only' (Assistant Secretary, medium-sized department).

Departments' attitudes towards the concept of management plans vary, and hence they have different perceptions of the role they should or could play in the management of the department. Some departments conducted similar planning exercises long before the introduction of management plans. Here the issue may be an internal debate about how best to react to Treasury pressure to change the current practice to accord with developing Treasury principles. In such circumstances the PFO and his staff are often cross-pressured, by Policy Divisions (and some within his own Finance Division) who want to resist Treasury demands, and by broader strategies and longer-term needs to maintain good relationships with the Expenditure Division.

Even those departments who felt more positive about the value of management plans for their own planning purposes, and tried to integrate them into financial management systems, often found it difficult to reconcile the conflicting informational needs of the Expenditure Division with those of their internal system. In such circumstances there was a risk that as the Treasury made management plans 'more and more formalised and regimented they are less useful as a management tool in their proper departmental setting . . . departments would end up producing two documents: one for Treasury consumption; the other for the "real" task of management' (PFO, large department). Extreme cynicism about the purpose and value of the exercise has led some departments to produce documents merely to satisfy the formal Treasury requirements, claiming putative efficiency gains and cost savings which were impossible to measure or verify.

The three-year 'firm-deals' which form a significant part of the rationale for management plans are not immutable. The department or the Treasury may reopen discussions on the agreement at any time during the period. This may occur because the inflation assumption was underestimated or because there has been a change in the number of clients supported by a programme. The Treasury does not rule out increasing a department's budget retrospectively if the evidence on such matters is 'compelling' (Major, Treasury and Civil Service Committee 1988*d*: qu. 171). Reopening discussions involves the Treasury examining all elements in the management plan, not just those that are contentious, with the risk for the department that the Treasury may find offsetting savings elsewhere in the running costs limits. The emphasis is on both partners to the 'deal' doing their best to deliver it. In practice almost all departments reopened their deals in 1989, the first year of review.

What benefits are there for a department if it negotiates a 'firm-deal' with the Treasury? A three-year running costs allocation (or programme allocation) does offer the prospect for it to plan its budget over a medium-term period and gives programme managers a greater degree of certainty than in the past. This is true during a period of stable or even falling inflation, but in a period when inflation is rising a three-year deal made in cash in year one buys less goods and services for a department by year three than had been planned. Departments also gain from the less easily quantifiable benefits of having been given the Treasury's seal of approval. The benefits for the Treasury are clearer: it obtains agreement to fixed cash totals for the plan period, and it has by implication brought the relevant department's financial management system up to the standard the Treasury regards as acceptable.

Efficiency gains

The efficiency assumption built into the running costs regime implies a further tightening of Treasury control. Departments (and Next Steps Agencies and other NDPBs) are expected to produce 'efficiency savings' year-on-year equivalent to 1.5 per cent of their running costs. The Treasury chose this figure as a reasonable starting-point until the system became 'bedded in' and accepted as part of the Survey process.

The implication is that, in the future, higher targets may be set as the norm. Departments are also expected to build into their budgeting procedures enough flexibility to cope with such contingencies as uncertainty over inflation or the incidence of unexpected additional costs. Thus the Treasury wants departments to so order their priorities that less important priorities can be dropped if necessary to free resources for such contingencies. This is similar to the 'assumed efficiency savings' built into DHSS/D.o.H. funding of Health Authority allocations since 1983, and may produce a similar additional squeeze on expenditure volumes. It would be fair to note that many departmental Finance Divisions are broadly supportive of the need to increase efficiency, and welcomed Treasury pressure as a stimulus to keeping their own Policy Divisions and agencies alert. Yet there is considerable criticism of the way the Treasury puts the general principle into practice.

The definition of efficiency gain (cash savings or output increases) is a source of debate between the Treasury and the departments; it is a contested concept. To maintain as much room for manœuvre as possible in the running costs allocation agreed with the Treasury on the basis of management plans, Finance Divisions try to exploit the ambiguities in the term. Treasury definitions of the concept and value of efficiency gains are contested by most departments. Many departments regard the interpretation of gains as cost savings as both narrow and simplistic. As one Assistant Secretary noted, efficiency gains are not the same as efficiency savings: 'The Treasury emphasises the latter and calls it "cost-improving", and wants us to identify them. We say to them that the Survey *Guidelines* ask for details of gains not savings and we identify "output-enhancing" developments.' Greater efficiency through obtaining more service delivery without additional running costs is less acceptable to the Treasury than reductions in running costs allocations. Output increases and cost savings resulting from information technology, scrutinies, and staff inspection are often seen by Finance Divisions as a means by which the Treasury tries to obtain still further cost-cutting. Predicting and promising efficiency savings three years ahead, in management plans as required by the Treasury, is difficult for Finance Divisions who 'have plenty to say to the Treasury on the matter' (PFO, medium-sized department).

Many departments have over time become adept at playing the game. Some departments, by the nature of their work, can obtain efficiency gains more easily than others and this leads many Finance Divisions to question the robustness of the Treasury line on this. For example, ostensible efficiency gains can be achieved when you process 'things or people', simply by increasing the number of customers dealt with. Cyclical peaks and troughs in any activity mean that it is possible to phase the work-shifts of staff; or customers can be dealt with more quickly and hence increase the productivity of (fewer) staff. Most efficiency gains so far have been achieved in big areas like computerization. Such gains are not immune from Treasury probing and an Expenditure Division may press a Finance Division to confirm that its department had achieved everything promised as a result of the introduction of information technology. If Treasury pressure increases, many departments can still fall back on separating out minor efficiency gains on small programmes in order to amass the required overall gains.

Departments are also critical of what they regard as the Treasury's naïve requests for output and value-for-money measures. One department regarded the requirement to provide cost-per-staff measures, for example, as so meaningless that they resisted supplying them. This was not only because it would be providing the Treasury with ammunition but because such data was misleading and the Finance Division would rather argue with them on the basis of 'useful data'. Similarly, multifunctional departments found it difficult to measure output across a range of activities. One Principal in a large department noted that it was simplistic of the Treasury to expect the management plan to help in the process of providing overall 1.5 per cent efficiency gains. 'The process was artificial in that if one part of the department finds its efficiency gains falling below 1.5 per cent you can't suddenly ask another part of the department to increase gains above 2 per cent to compensate. This is just not practical let alone helpful for morale in the department.'

The efficiency assumption itself may have far-reaching consequences. One indication is the degree to which the running costs regime has given a spur to the Government's policy of dispersing civil servants out of the South-East region. By 1988 only 12,000 posts had been relocated because of the 'forces of inertia; that people may need to be encouraged to look at things' (Turnbull, Treasury and Civil Service Committee 1988*d*: qu. 21). The running costs innovation gave departments an extra incentive, as they needed to look for more cost-effective ways of carrying out their work and deliver efficiency savings. The inclusion of actual office rents among the items included in departmental running costs was an additional incentive to relocate outside the South-East. The Treasury was even prepared to look sympathetically at departmental requests for additional monies to cover the short-term costs incurred during relocation (qu. 13). The DSS and Benefits Agency were given support to move staff to Leeds in 1992.

The Treasury has constructed the system so that it benefits, whatever the outcome of departmental decisions on relocation. If, for example, as officials suggested to the committee, 'real' savings can be made from relocation and 'real' benefits accrue in terms of improving the effectiveness of departments, the Treasury delivers lower spending and value-for-money to the public. Departments, on the other hand, may only derive one-off benefits from savings made in this way (or the savings may be kept conceivably for up to three years in the case of 'firm-deals'). When they come back to the Treasury to renegotiate their annual (or triennial) running costs budgets, the Treasury will (*a*) assume that the department will have saved 1.5 per cent anyway and (*b*) begin bilateral discussions from the new, lower, base of *actual* departmental spending. From the departments' perspective there are other real limitations on the scope for savings from relocation. Despite the official Treasury line that it would be 'sympathetic' towards providing short-term resources to allow relocation, as this would be regarded as a spend-to-save project, in practice departments found this sympathy short-lived. In addition there are administrative constraints. One department with a network of regional offices pursued devolution of responsibilities to them from London, but such relocation had to be on a large enough scale to provide a viable career structure for its staff.

Pay assumptions

From 1986 until the fiscal crisis of 1992 the Treasury no longer provided departments with uniform, central pay factors or assumptions for the public service. It claimed also that its Pay Divisions provided no guidance to Expenditure Divisions or departmental Finance Divisions about the probable outcome of negotiations with unions and hence the likely 'going rate'. The Treasury did not always reject a department's pay assumption just because it was too high. Running costs, it argued, were settled by taking account of all the pressures facing a department, for example the amount of efficiency which could be squeezed out of a department, or how much flexibility the department had when things went wrong. 'It is a judgemental process' (Treasury, Assistant Secretary). The Treasury would consider a department's case where it had a particular mix of staffing, for example one with a high technical grade content where the pay levels for such staff were expected to rise faster than those in other general grades. The size of a department's running costs was also a factor. In the M.o.D., pay review bodies account for only 20 per cent of total spending, while in the NHS it is closer to 70 per cent.

Pay assumptions were a source of tension in the relationships between the Treasury and departments, as one which turned out to have been too low meant diverting resources away from other running costs headings; they represented a major constraint on departments' discretion. Similarly, departments were critical of the Treasury's general inflation assumptions as well. One PFO in a major department argued that 'PES inflation rarely catches up with real inflation. The Treasury thinks we are knaves and fools on this. Treasury inflation and real inflation are two parallel lines that never meet.'

On pay negotiated directly by the Treasury with the Civil Service unions, departments were brought in to discuss specific problems, such as the recruitment and retention of specialist staff. There were both formal and informal mechanisms for discussing such problems. If the Treasury agreed that a particular group of staff should be treated more favourably in a pay round, that was 'clocked up' on the department's pay assumptions, and offset against the next year's settlement. Pay review bodies are independent of the Treasury, whose influence on their decisions is limited to the submission of evidence, usually drawing attention to broader economic and financial pressures which ought to be taken into account.

Departments were expected to (and did) incorporate their own pay assumptions into their running costs bids. Unless they were 'patently absurd', either way, the Treasury did not normally interfere. If, however, the Finance Division put in a very low pay assumption—3.5 per cent when pay settlements were running at 7 per cent—the Expenditure Division would ask the department to justify it. It was in the Treasury's interest to 'weed out' low as well as high pay assumptions: too low and there was a risk that the department would come under pressure on its running costs later in the year and have to ask the Treasury for a Supplementary Estimate. If the assumption was absurdly high, and a department insisted on it, the Treasury Expenditure Division might decline to fund it, and respond with a figure for global running costs based on a much lower pay assumption.

The Treasury argued that if departments were given a precise pay assumption, there was the risk that they would come back and ask the Treasury to fund the difference if the figure proved to be too low. This occurred in the early 1980s when pay factors were provided centrally. While the Treasury did not always agree to provide additional resources, nevertheless there was always pressure for it to do so. Thereafter, the onus was on departments to decide the appropriate assumption. They were able to do that, the Treasury argued disingenuously, because they could monitor pay negotiations and settlements, and interpret the trends and the likely going rates as easily as the Treasury.

Departmental practice in handling the vexed issue of pay assumptions varied. In one department the PFO regularly contacted the Under

Secretary in the Treasury's Pay Division, who gave 'sound and frank advice about whether a pay assumption included in the running costs bid was reasonable . . . He would say "under x would be sensible or a little more than last year", you then probe a bit more until you are satisfied that you had the message. He was accurate last year and we didn't get clobbered.' In contrast, in another department the PFO was critical of the fact that the Treasury Expenditure Division did not seem to talk to its own Pay Division (or accounting people). These officials would be dealing with pay in the Civil Service and were therefore in a good position to know the likely 'going rate'. The Expenditure Division did not advise the department what pay assumption to use in its running costs bid, but it 'would say something if their assumption was on the high side of the Treasury's implicit norm; certainly *not* if it is lower'.

There is, however, the informal network of Whitehall PFOs, through which medium the issue of the 'going rate' for running costs pay assumptions was talked over, and experience of dealing with the Treasury exchanged. In recent years it has been supplemented by a regular, informal lunch group of PFOs from the major departments, mainly Deputy Secretaries and some Under Secretaries. Here information and ideas on pay and related issues of running costs are exchanged. It is claimed that mutual awareness makes it less likely that departments will be 'picked off one by one' by the Treasury. The occasion is also used for informal discussions of other common problems—the reopening of three-year firm-deals for example, and experience of Expenditure Divisions' use and handling of management plans.

The tension between the Treasury's stated aim of increasing the amount of delegation and flexibility granted to departments and agencies and its overriding objective of controlling total public spending was thrown into sharp relief by the events of the early 1990s. In July 1991 Chancellor Lamont announced the Treasury's intention of encouraging greater pay delegation in the Civil Service. This involved renegotiating pay arrangements, encouraging greater use of performance-related pay, and, in the cases of some departments and agencies, granting the right to full delegated powers over pay and grading, subject to a value-for-money test. An early example of the impact of the drive to performance-related pay was the Civil Service-wide agreement between the Treasury and unions in 1992 which allowed for discretionary pay increments to be decided at departmental and agency level after discussions between the individual management and unions in those departments and agencies. The first round of negotiations began in departments and agencies in October/November 1992, when discus-

sions were held on giving additional increments on the basis of performance to staff in Grades 5 to 7 (Assistant Secretary to Principal).

The move towards departmental autonomy in pay and staffing was
arrested by the urgent need to reimpose central control of the aggregate
of public spending in the wake of the fiscal crisis which became apparent
after the 1992 general election. Chancellor Lamont pressed the Cabinet's EDX Committee to approve for a limited period a 1.5 per cent pay
ceiling to be imposed on the public sector. In the Autumn Statement,
plans announced for the New Control Total included estimated savings
of £1.5 billion in 1993–4 on previous plans as a result of setting a limit of
between 0 and 1.5 per cent on pay settlements from November 1992.
This policy ran counter to the Treasury's stated objective of allowing
greater flexibility and was criticized on those grounds by the Treasury
and Civil Service Committee (1992: pp. xlviii) and the Civil Service
unions. The Chief Secretary (Portillo) responded by stressing that
within the limit there remained scope for 'management to differentiate
between their various employees' (qu. 357). The public sector pay policy
implied by the decision was also meant to apply only to 1993–4 and to
be reviewed in later years, although there was pressure from the other
Ministers in EDX to extend the restraint for a further year, and this was
implemented for 1994–5. This episode is a good example of the way in
which the Treasury is prepared to subordinate other policy objectives to
the paramount aim of containing public expenditure in times of acute
fiscal crisis.

CONCLUSIONS

The Treasury has gradually evolved a sophisticated control mechanism
capable of bearing down on departments' administrative costs. At the
same time running costs control and manpower planning are the means
by which the Treasury seeks simultaneously to infuse the ethos of a
changing management culture into central government, create a framework which encourages administrative efficiency, squeeze staffing in the
Civil Service, encourage relocation out of London, and submerge the
issue of public sector pay. Whether a single control mechanism can
deliver all of these equally and simultaneously is problematic. More
certainly, the Treasury's administration of running costs control is the
source of the greatest tension in the relationships between it and the
spending departments and their agencies. The issues which arise are
essentially about the balance to be struck between, on the one hand, the
need for central control of the aggregates of public spending and depart-

mental financial management systems, and the needs of managerial autonomy in a more devolved and flexible departmental structure, on the other. Partly because of pressure from departments and agencies, the Treasury has introduced greater flexibility into the operation of the running costs regime since 1986. Some of these flexibilities are less significant than others. The end-year flexibility scheme gives departments very limited scope to carry forward underspending and the scheme is less generous in scope than the equivalent capital spending scheme. Of greater import, however, have been the changes inspired by Next Steps Agencies, particularly the granting of virement and the increased scope for net rather than gross control. These changes go to the heart of the original design of the system.

Most departmental PFOs and their staff regard the negotiation and setting and operating of running costs as the single most important and contentious issue in their relationships with the Treasury. As a relatively new regime, detailed Treasury control of running costs appears to departments to run counter to the Treasury's broader aim of improving financial management in departments, and in particular, of delegating more authority to departmental line managers to determine and control their own budgets. Management plans are seen by some departments as a means by which the Treasury has sought to encroach on areas of activity which are traditionally their preserve.

Secondly, running costs are a sensitive internal issue for all departments. They need sufficient staff to enable them to achieve the objectives set by their Ministers. At the same time, staffing and related costs—pay, promotion, travel and subsistence, bonuses, accommodation—are a matter of concern to all civil servants. Thirdly, the rigid separation of running costs from programme expenditure has not only made cross-subsidization more difficult: departments complain of loss of managerial discretion and flexibility with which to obtain the best value-for-money. Providing a service or activity in-house, financed through running costs, can be more efficient and cost-effective than employing contractors paid out of programme expenditure.

It is not surprising that PFOs and their staff feel constrained by, and complain about, both the principle and operation of the Treasury's running costs regime. Such attitudes are seen by the Treasury as evidence that its aim of squeezing running costs is being achieved. But there are more serious criticisms by some departments that there is basic unfairness in the way the system is operated. Some departments do better than others. Size is often a factor. Small departments, or those where programme expenditure is declining, and hence running costs vulnerable to sharp cut-back, complain that for them 'everything is transparent': an argument with the Treasury over the costs of a half-dozen people would in a larger department or one whose programmes were increasing be lost in the 'rounding up'. Small or large, departmental PFOs know the 'score', and the position of their department in the Whitehall league-table. Informally they compare and weigh success and failure in dealing with the Treasury. Those squeezed hard may experience more than usual difficulty in the allocation of running costs settlement after the conclusion of the bilaterals. Senior Finance Division officials are involved in the tense and time-consuming task of juggling with the allocation to make it fit budget-holders' needs.

Criticism of the administration of the running costs regime is directed less at the Treasury's Expenditure Divisions than the Treasury's central divisions—Running Costs, Pay, and Financial Management. A belief shared by many PFOs and their staff is that the 'doctrines' of the regime are attributable to the 'theologians' in the central divisions. Many Expenditure Controllers, they claim, evince little enthusiasm in conveying the 'messages' about running costs and management plans, often bluntly disclaiming responsibility. Such statements, however, need to be interpreted with caution. Just as a Finance Division often uses the Treasury's Expenditure Division as a whipping-boy when arguing with its own Policy Divisions, so an Expenditure Division may find it convenient to attribute responsibility for its hard line to its own central divisions. Nevertheless, the implementation of the running costs control regime is a cause of considerable tension in the relationships between the Treasury and the spending departments and agencies. The three most contentious issues are management plans, efficiency gains, and the handling of pay issues. All of them are central to the continuing debate about the reconciliation of the need for central control of the aggregate of public spending with the pressures in a devolved financial management system for more departmental and agency discretion to determine and manage their own budgets. We return to this wider issue in Chapter 24.

19

End-Year Flexibility

As we have explained in earlier chapters, the Treasury struggled hard to reassert short-term control of public spending following the economic crises of the mid-1970s. The evolutionary move to annual cash control of public spending, with the introduction of cash limits in 1976, cash planning in 1982, and running costs control in 1986, has helped it to control spending more effectively. But spending departments have forfeited the right to extra resources in-year if prices have moved against them and, because the doctrine of *annuality* (that resources are provided for use in a particular year) has been enforced more tightly through cash limits and cash planning, they have lost managerial flexibility in planning those programmes which do not fit neatly into the one-year cycle. This chapter focuses on the tensions which have arisen as a result, and which have eventually obliged the Treasury to accede to departmental demands for some modification to the principle of firm annual cash limits.

In July 1983 the Treasury agreed to the introduction of an end-year flexibility scheme (EYF), which allowed central government departments to carry forward a limited amount of underspending on capital programmes from one financial year to the next, on both voted and non-voted cash limits. The novel concept of 'end-year flexibility' has subsequently been extended to cover other aspects of public spending, such as running costs, local authorities' expenditure, and nationalized industries finances (EFLs). In addition, special schemes have been introduced to deal with particular departmental needs, such as a scheme for M.o.D. procurement and for health spending.

How the Treasury and departments manage public spending cash flow is one of a number of key issues in Treasury–department relationships. The demand by some departments for flexibility to carry forward unused capital expenditure was but a proxy for a more fundamental disagreement with the Treasury over the reimposition of central control over public expenditure. This came through clearly in the background to the eventual introduction of EYF in a long-running, and at times acrimonious, debate between the Treasury and the M.o.D. over the interpretation of the original Cash Limits White Paper (Cmnd. 6440). EYF provides yet another example of the Janus-faced nature of

Treasury policy: strong rhetoric on the immutability of spending controls yet clear evidence of a pragmatic flexibility in the operation of
those same rules.

In the first section of the chapter we explain how attitudes to EYF
reflected deeper differences between key actors in the policy process;
differences which were themselves predicated on disparate organizational goals and conceptions of what constituted a 'rational' public-
spending control regime. Later we explain how the Treasury shifted its
ground as it became more confident about the viability of the cash limits
system, and as pressures to contain the PSBR abated in the post-
recession mid-1980s. As the EYF scheme became established, the
Treasury agreed to modifications which increased the usefulness of
carry-forward to the departments, and widened its scope by agreeing to
specific *ad hoc* arrangements. Departments in turn became more adept
at using the facilities available.

BACKGROUND TO THE INTRODUCTION OF EYF

The original 1976 Cash Limits White Paper made only one provision for
flexibility in the operation of what were otherwise to be seen as strictly
observed annual limits. For those programmes where 'the timing of the
expenditure on existing projects cannot be precisely controlled, some
arrangements are needed to allow a limited amount of flexibility between successive financial years and between current and capital expenditure' (Cmnd. 6440: para. 18). Little use was made of this provision
in the next three years. However, the Treasury had approved some
degree of limited carry-over, for example the arrangement under which
regional health authorities were allowed by the DHSS to carry forward
up to 1 per cent of their revenue allocations (PAC 1980c: p. vii). This
was cited by Treasury officials as evidence of how departments could
operate their budgets flexibly without the need of a general scheme
(PAC 1979: qu. 21).

It was the evidence of the M.o.D. to the Public Accounts Committee
in 1978 which made public what appears to have been a major disagreement with the Treasury over the interpretation of the 1976 Cash Limits
White Paper. The disagreement may have been more widespread in
Whitehall, but the M.o.D. was the only department to challenge publicly
the Treasury's imposition of cash limits. From 1977–8 the M.o.D. kept
up a sustained attack on the Treasury's operation of the regime.

Its case rested on four arguments. First, that greater flexibility was
required because defence procurement involved long time-horizons

and 'a steady stream of commitments rather than a series of compartmentalised annual blocks' (PAC 1979: pp. vi–vii). Secondly, the cash limits system encouraged departments to 'indulge in an end-of-year spending spree which could be detrimental to financial discipline' (PAC 1979: p. vii). Thirdly, that it was unreasonable to expect the large business of defence procurement to be efficiently managed without, in the words of Sir Frank Cooper (the combative Permanent Secretary of the Ministry), the equivalent of 'a deposit account, overdraft facility and no means of carrying anything from one year to another' (PAC 1980*b*: qu. 2291). And fourthly, because of the inflexibility of the system and the pressure to avoid overspending, the department's Accounting Officer's energies were disproportionately devoted to end-year control rather than to other aspects of improving efficiency.

The issue was brought to a head when the M.o.D. noted that its cash limits had been underspent in 1976–7 and 1977–8 by 1.1 and 1.6 per cent respectively, and attributed these to 'unavoidable delays and slippage in works and equipment programmes' (PAC 1979: 30). The department therefore applied to the Treasury for permission to activate the flexibility clause in the 1976 White Paper and to be allowed to carry forward part of their 1977–8 cash limit, which they calculated would be underspent, to the 1978–9 cash limit. They proposed that they 'should review their forecast outturn with the Treasury towards the end of each financial year, to agree a cut or an increase in the current year's cash limit and a corresponding increase or reduction in the limit for the following year'. This arrangement was to apply to procurement expenditure and the carry-over 'would not exceed 5 per cent of the expenditure concerned, representing a maximum less than 2 per cent of the total Defence budget' (PAC 1979: 30–1).

THE DEBATE IN WHITEHALL

The initial views of the Treasury

In 1978 the Treasury put forward three reasons why it could not agree to the M.o.D.'s proposal or introduce a Whitehall-wide scheme. First, the plan proposed by the M.o.D. would entail an increase in public spending, and hence the PSBR, in the second year of the two-year carry-over period. This would create an adverse reaction in the financial markets (PAC 1979: qus. 54–6). Second, a scheme agreed with the M.o.D. would have implications for other departments. The third, and by far the most strongly presented argument against, was that a modification to cash limits of the kind suggested would weaken the effectiveness of cash limits and slacken the pressure on programme managers to improve their control of spending.

The Treasury also suggested that the M.o.D. was amongst the least deserving of departments when it came to flexibility in the administration of cash limits (qu. 22). The M.o.D. had already been given a large degree of flexibility when the Treasury agreed, in its proposals on merging cash limits with the Supply Estimates, to reduce the number of cash-limited defence blocks from eleven to four and 'normally', within any one year, 'allow savings on one cash block against excesses on another' (PAC 1979: 30). In addition, the Treasury claimed that it was easier for the M.o.D. to plan its spending, given the size of its overall budget (£7 billion), compared with other departments and 'to get within 1 per cent, two years ago, and 1.5 per cent, last year is extremely good' (qu. 15).

The Treasury's position was not, however, entirely inflexible. Sir Anthony Rawlinson, then Second Permanent Secretary (Public Expenditure), agreed that 'there is an artificiality in the whole system of annual tranches' and that 'there are good managerial arguments for allowing some limited degree of carry over at the end of the year' (qu. 15). While the Treasury was disposed to try to reach some accommodation with those departments concerned about the lack of flexibility in the system, its initial reluctance was consistent with the thrust of other initiatives during this period, such as the abandonment of pay comparability for civil servants, and the eventual introduction of cash planning, concerned with tightening and maintaining spending controls. End-year flexibility was seen as a threat to the objective of reasserting the primacy of expenditure control.

At the heart of the disagreement between the Treasury and the M.o.D. were different conceptions of the inviolability of the cash-limits system. The M.o.D. wanted flexibility for overspending as well as underspending and wanted discretionary authority to operate end-year arrangements free of Treasury control. To allow overspending to be carried forward would breach the concept of fixed annual limits, and moreover, such flexibility would not guarantee that the overspend would be corrected in the following financial year, thus leading to consistently higher spending than that agreed in the annual spending round.

The Treasury's proposals

After consultation with the spending departments, the Treasury considered a scheme which allowed some limited carry-forward of spending. It was restricted to capital spending and limited to 5 per cent of the relevant cash limit. It was envisaged that a maximum of £500 million would be involved in the introduction of a scheme, but that in practice less would be required. Initially this would have to be found from the Contingency Reserve. No general right to carry over was envisaged in the proposal, as the Treasury retained the right to review the scheme. Ministers would have to decide at the end of a financial year whether the expenditure totals in the following year could be raised to allow carry-over. The Treasury was thus proposing only a modest deviation from annualized expenditure control, with no formally enshrined rules automatically allowing a department to carry forward under-spending.

Criticisms of the Treasury proposal

The M.o.D. was not impressed by the Treasury's proposals. It character-ized the Treasury's response as 'the PESC solution', allowing some discussion about carry-forward of underspending within the framework of the annual spending round. 'All experience suggests it would be unrealistic to rely upon any such . . . arrangement surviving the annual scrutiny of expenditure plans' (PAC 1980c: 24). Other departments were less critical. The Department of Transport's officials welcomed the scheme as a means of allowing programme managers to achieve outturn closer to the original cash limit (PAC 1980c: p. ix). Like the M.o.D., the Department of Transport stressed the difficulties posed by an annual cash grant having to support long-term capital programmes. Road con-struction was said to be 'an extreme case of a long-lead programme', with 85–90 per cent of prospective expenditure committed through contracts with builders by the middle of the financial year. But such programmes were also subject to delays throughout the cycle (PAC 1980c: 46). Thus 'in managing the construction programme within the cash limits . . . the department has to take a view about how the various random factors may combine to affect the outcome' (p. 47). The attend-ant problem was that outturn may not 'coincide with the target figure' and in some years it may be considerably at variance with it.

In the event, the problems of dealing with rising public spending during the recession of the 1980s, with the consequent pressure on the PSBR, led the Treasury to postpone the introduction of a scheme. Treasury ministers had decided that the initial estimated cost of £250 million needed to introduce it in the 1982–3 financial year could not be afforded from the Contingency Reserve. Sir Anthony Rawlinson stressed the Treasury's commitment to the scheme and confirmed that 'we shall keep it on the table, as it were, and look at it again' (PAC 1981: qu. 2675).

The winds of change blowing in favour of the demands of departments such as the M.o.D. for greater flexibility in the operation of cash limits were deflected by other factors too. Without specifically citing them as a reason for delaying the scheme, Rawlinson noted that 'the Department which has been most interested in flexibility—and still is— the Ministry of Defence, . . . their problem last year was overspending, not underspending' (PAC 1981: qu. 2695). There is more than a hint of substantial disagreement between the Treasury and M.o.D. in these and other exchanges (mentioned above) over the way in which cash limits were operated by the Treasury. And the protagonists in the debate used arguments involving 'various forms of trade-offs, with each side emphasising a different aspect of the control mechanism' (Likierman 1981: 18). One department's flexibility was another department's loss of control.

A scheme was eventually introduced by Chancellor Lawson in a statement to the House of Commons on 7 July 1983, as part of a package of measures aimed at stemming the rise in public expenditure in excess of the Planning Total agreed for 1983–4 in the previous February's White Paper. Indeed, the timing of the announcement was justified on the grounds that 'by reducing the end-year surge' the scheme would 'reduce expenditure in the current year by some £100 million' (Parliamentary Debates, HC, 7 July 1983, col. 45). The scheme was, he said, 'justified on managerial grounds' and was a response to the advocacy of departments such as the M.o.D. Its aim was 'to improve the management of capital programmes, where the timing of activity or payment is subject to uncertainty' (Treasury and Civil Service Committee 1984b: 32).

THE STRUCTURE OF THE SCHEMES

Since 1983 the concept of end-year flexibility has been implemented through six separate EYF schemes. The most significant is the general Whitehall-wide cash-limit capital expenditure scheme. In addition, a broad scheme was introduced in 1988 extending the concept to elements of underspending on running costs. Some other separate schemes have also been introduced for limited periods. All the EYF schemes have been regularly reviewed by the Treasury in consultation with departments. The Treasury has always stressed that each scheme's continuation was contingent upon it being satisfied that managerial benefits were still being produced, that the general goal of public-spending control was not being endangered, and that EYF was not proving to be too costly to the Reserve. There have been two major reviews, in 1985 and 1988, both leading to modifications in the operating rules of the capital scheme and its coverage.

The main capital spending EYF scheme

Both voted cash limits and non-voted cash limits are eligible for in-clusion in the scheme. Not all cash limit Votes are included because not every department is responsible for capital or near-capital expenditure as defined under the scheme. All spending which is defined in economic categorizations as capital is automatically eligible for inclusion. Where spending is deemed capital-like but not directly classified as such (such as major maintenance programmes over £100,000), the Treasury takes into account the amount and importance of capital spending within a cash limit, and the potential scope for improving the management of that spending, before deciding whether it should be included in the EYF scheme. In 1988–9, for example, only 21.6 per cent of voted and non-voted cash limits were eligible for carry-forward under the national scheme (£16.1 billion out of a total of £74.7 billion cash-limited Votes). The scheme covers capital items such as 'new construction, land, build-ings, and defence procurement' (Treasury 1988c: para. 51).

The Treasury and departments agree a list of 'eligible subheads' within the cash limits included in the scheme. Over time there have been changes in the coverage. Following the 1985 review of the scheme the Treasury asked departments to nominate current expenditure which could be deemed 'capital-like' (such as maintenance programmes), which, following Treasury scrutiny to check that the department con-cerned had adequate monitoring procedures, could then be included. The discussions between the Treasury and departments about which subheadings should be included in the scheme are not normally contro-versial, although when the scheme was set up there were disputes about what could be deemed eligible.

Departments are allowed to carry forward up to 5 per cent (or £2 million, whichever is the greater) of underspending on 'eligible' items into the following financial year. The £2 million figure was included in the scheme as a result of the 1985 review, and was aimed at helping departments with small amounts of eligible capital expenditure.

The departments submit returns to the Expenditure Divisions of the Treasury after bills are brought to account in May/June and when an accurate figure of underspending can be determined. Expenditure Divisions match underspending against the eligible subheadings under the EYF scheme and pass the data on to GEP2 (the General Expenditure division of the Treasury which deals with in-year control issues). Departments are guaranteed the 'entitlement' to carry forward, provided that the item falls into the subheading deemed to be eligible under the scheme, but actual take-up of this entitlement is subject to normal Treasury scrutiny: that additional expenditure is defensible to Parliament and justifiable in terms of need and realism. Thus blocks of expenditure are carried forward, rather than particular programmes or subprogrammes. The general 'right' is regarded as essential if departmental programme managers are to have confidence in EYF and avoid end-year spending sprees.

Provision of cash to meet carry-forward of expenditure under the scheme is voted by Parliament through the Supplementary Estimates procedure, but in planning terms the take-up of EYF is set against, and is a claim on, the Reserve. The EYF schemes are regarded as 'irresistible claims' on the Reserve and take precedence over other exceptional in-year claims which may be made. The Chief Secretary must formally approve the expenditure.

Running costs EYF

We discussed the operation of this scheme briefly in Chapter 18. Three further points need emphasis here. First, the scheme was introduced following a Treasury review of the EYF in November 1988 and was the result of departments persuading the Treasury during the review that they would benefit from the extension of EYF to cover running costs. This is a further example of the Treasury being more accommodating to departments' concerns than official rhetoric suggests. Secondly, following on from the special health service scheme, it was a further extension of flexibility to what were, in effect, non-capital expenditure items. About 25 per cent of gross running costs provisions were deemed to cover spending prone to similar sorts of slippage as capital spending—such as consultancy contracts on computer installation and maintenance. The decision to allow carry-forward of up to 0.5 per cent of total running costs (or £50,000, whichever was the higher) was the result of the Treasury deciding that 2 per cent of that part of running costs not spent on pay and accommodation was appropriate, and on average approximately one-quarter of running costs came into this non-pay and accommodation category. Thirdly, the Treasury's agreement comes with 'strings': only departments which have agreed three-year running costs settlements with the Treasury, and hence have approved 'management plans', are able to apply for inclusion in the scheme. Departments so eligible have also to convince the Treasury that EYF will help improve their efficiency.

Other schemes

A special scheme was introduced in December 1986 which allowed the M.o.D. to claim up to £400 million carry-forward in each of the following three years, in addition to that which could be claimed under the national scheme. It was a transitional scheme, arising from the change in the basis of dealing with contractors' bills, and was introduced to help the M.o.D. cope with the uncertainty created by the new procurement policy. In the four years of its operation, the M.o.D. was allowed to carry forward just over £1.3 billion.

The scheme introduced in 1988 to cover Department of Health spending is unusual in that it covers both *capital* and *current* spending on the Health and Community Service Vote as a whole. The department can carry forward up to 0.5 per cent of this Vote. The Treasury does, however, scrutinize requests in more detail than for the EYF for cash limits as a whole. It has to be convinced that the underspending is not due to poor estimating, and the D.o.H. must be able to say why the case could not have been handled through *brokerage*—the exchange of underspending by one health authority with overspending by another. It is designed to avoid the wastage of senior health service managers' time in trying to match outturn closely to plan. The scheme is subject to review.

Two other EYF schemes were introduced at the same time as the national cash-limits scheme. A local authority capital end-year flexibility scheme was introduced in November 1983, was suspended in 1989, and now is applied to non-voted cash limits in the same way as the general capital end-year flexibility scheme. Nationalized industries have a different form of EYF. They are allowed temporary borrowing in excess of their EFLs, up to 1 per cent of the sum of current forecast turnover and fixed asset expenditure. The amount is deducted from the following year's EFL. This scheme allows *anticipation* of borrowing provision, the opposite of the schemes for cash and running costs limits.

The impact of Next Steps Agencies

As we discussed in Chapter 5 (and return to in Chapter 24), the evolution of the financial regime applied to Next Steps Agencies has added further flexibilities to the management of public spending. This is also true of EYF. In addition to qualifying for EYF on capital expenditure and running costs, individual agencies have been given specific extra entitlements. Companies House, for example, was granted the right to carry forward up to 25 per cent of its capital expenditure from one year to the next (Cm. 914).

THE OPERATION OF THE SCHEMES

How much flexibility has been given to the departments by the Treasury through the medium of the EYF schemes as they have evolved since 1983? To answer that question we focus on four sets of issues: the schemes' coverage and procedures; the conditionality of the flexibility granted; the 'cost' to the Treasury; and the benefits to the departments.

Coverage and procedure

The national scheme's flexibility has been extended in terms of its coverage and procedure. (In addition we have already noted that some Next Steps Agencies have been able to agree with the Treasury specific extra flexibilities on a case-by-case basis.) First, following the 1985 review, the Treasury relaxed the limit on carry-forward from 5 per cent of eligible capital spending to 5 per cent or £2 million, whichever was the greater. This has had a marked impact on the degree to which small departments benefit from the scheme. A good example is provided by the Department of Transport's central administration Vote, which under the new rules was entitled to carry forward from 1986–7 £4.9 million underspending instead of the £2.9 million under the old rules (see Thain and Wright 1989c for further details). Greater flexibility was introduced also as a result of the Treasury's decision, following the 1985 review, to invite departments to nominate subheadings which included expenditure similar to capital spending for inclusion in the scheme. This was the major reason why the total number of Votes eligible under the EYF scheme increased from fifty-one in the 1986–7 Estimates to seventy-three in 1990–1. Thirdly, following the 1988 review, departments were allowed to add unused entitlement to their eligible capital provision in the calculation of the 5 per cent of cash limit ceiling. Thus, for example, the M.o.D. did not use its entitlement to carry forward underspending of £322.7 million from 1987–8 to 1988–9 and under the old rules the baseline for calculating the entitlement to carry forward in the following year, that is from 1988–9 to 1989–90, would not have included this unused figure. Under the new rules the baseline for calculating carry-forward on M.o.D. eligible capital expenditure was increased by approximately £16.1 million (5 per cent of £322.7 million). However, where unused entitlement amounts to little more than 1 per cent of that originally agreed, the new rule only marginally increases the degree of flexibility in the scheme. Finally, the concept of EYF was extended to running costs following the 1988 review.

Conditionality

In the 1988 review of the EYF scheme the Treasury exhorted departments to pass down to line managers the benefits derived from EYF, rather than maintain a central 'fund'. The Treasury believed that some departments held a 'pot of gold'. That the Treasury had to resort to urging departments to spread the benefits of EYF leads to a more general conclusion about the way the Treasury conducts its relationship with spending departments. It does not engage in detailed scrutiny once a department's entitlement to carry-forward has been established. Departments may also carry forward the same underspending from year to year, subject to a ceiling of 5 per cent of total eligible provision and carry-over of entitlement not taken up. The Treasury does not even differentiate between 'worthy' and 'unworthy' reasons for underspending. Hence a department may be using its entitlement to carry forward because it has not budgeted very well during the course of the year or because it has actually saved money through increased efficiency. This relative freedom to departments is one of the 'costs' of the scheme to the Treasury. It is only relative freedom, however, as the rules of the EYF scheme require departments to offset underspending against overspending elsewhere on their cash limit before submitting a request for carry-forward. In any event Expenditure Controllers in the Treasury probe a department's use of EYF if it is overclaiming or if a major problem has occurred in the department's financial management system. Nevertheless, such intervention is rare; EYF has become a more or less routine part of the cash-limits regime.

Other evidence suggests that the Treasury has implicitly recognized the lack of conditionality in the national cash-limits EYF scheme as it was originally framed. For example, the Treasury added 'strings' to its initiative to departments to nominate capital-like spending to be considered for status as eligible spending under the scheme. It had first to be convinced that the department concerned had a sufficiently robust financial system to derive benefits from the concession. This reflects the broader trend of greater Treasury monitoring of departments' financial management systems, apparent in the way the running costs system has been implemented as we noted in Chapter 18. The EYF scheme for running costs, announced after the 1988 review, has been constructed with far more constraints and 'strings' than the 1983 EYF scheme. Departments are only eligible for carry-forward if they have three-year running costs settlements with the Treasury. Thus flexibility is conditional upon the department 'delivering' to the Treasury a 'sound' financial management system.

Costs to the Treasury

A measure of the degree to which any modification to a control regime represents a real concession on the part of the controller to the controlled is the cost to the controller of the flexibility granted. Calculating the 'cost' of EYF is not a straightforward matter. There are two measures of the expenditure costs of the schemes. The first is the call on the Reserve. The *entitlement* to carry-forward under all the schemes totalled £3.8 billion between 1983–4 and 1991–2. This is the figure used by the Treasury in calculating the amount of money left in the Reserve for other claims, although in fact, as we have noted, not all entitlement is taken up in the form of Supplementary Estimates. The net cost to the Reserve has been nearly £700 million lower, at £3 billion. In addition, the Treasury uses 'carry-in' and 'carry-out' to measure the *real* cost to the Reserve. Thus the initial underspending delivered by the departments at the end of year one ('carry-in' and counted as a positive contribution to the Reserve) is counted before calculation of carry-forward into year two ('carry-out' when it is presented as a Supplementary Estimate). The real charge on the Reserve using this measure has been negative (that is, payments in have exceeded payments out) in all but one year.

The second way the Treasury calculates the expenditure costs of the scheme is by hypothesizing what the aggregate level of spending would have been in the absence of EYF. As we showed in Chapter 17, cash limits have delivered to the Treasury a regular amount of aggregate underspending. EYF reduces the level of underspending, in that over a two-year cycle a department can claw back some of the underspending which previously it would have surrendered in its entirety to the Treasury. To complete the picture we need to include in the calculation the likely level of end-year spending sprees which were said to occur prior to the schemes' introduction and which would have continued had EYF not been instituted. Taking these factors into account the Treasury's estimate is that spending is about £200 million higher each year than might have been the case had the scheme not been introduced. The

EYF schemes have partly addressed the criticism by departments, such as the M.o.D. expressed during the debate over EYF in the late 1970s and early 1980s, that cash limits inhibit programme managers from delivering outturn close to plan. This is a benefit to the department, but a cost to the Treasury because the Treasury relies on a certain amount of 'give' in the Planning/Control Total in order to allow for some over-spending elsewhere (from demand-led programmes, for example) and so that it can operate on a tightly budgeted Reserve. The 1988 review of EYF concluded that if EYF was improving programme managers' abil-ity to bring outturn closer to plan then the Treasury would need to bear this in mind when setting the aggregate Planning Total.

We have already touched on another 'cost' to the Treasury of EYF: that some underspending which the departments *should* have surren-dered—because of poor calculations in their Survey bids or because of weak in-year programme management—can be rescued by them through the schemes. Thus there is a weakening of the pressure on departments to improve their estimating and monitoring procedures. This had been one of the Comptroller and Auditor General's concerns when he reported on EYF for the PAC in 1980 (PAC 1980c: 3). The Treasury recognizes this as a cost of accommodating departmental pressures for greater flexibility. To some extent this is offset by other gains: less incentive for departments to indulge in end-year spend-ing sprees; the improvement of the morale of departmental Finance Officers; departmental incentives to get better value-for-money out of contractors; and, less tangibly, the removal of a grievance against what was seen as the Treasury's inflexible implementation of the cash limits regime.

Benefits to the departments

We should be clear first what benefits have *not* been delivered to the departments by the EYF schemes. Departments have not been given their own cheque books to cover over- and underspending free from Treasury control, as Sir Frank Cooper implied was needed during the earlier debate in Whitehall. The scheme has, however, gradually be-come more generous, especially to smaller departments who have less scope to reorder their spending when bills are delayed. But it has remained a scheme covering a relatively small proportion of voted and non-voted cash limits and has been confined to capital and near-capital spending, so that not every department has been eligible for inclusion. The 5 per cent ceiling on carry-forward has also meant, in practice, that only about 2.5 per cent of spending on eligible subheadings has been transferred between years. Departments had only carried forward just over £3 billion in the eight years of the schemes from 1983 to 1991, and the lion's share of this was to the benefit of the M.o.D.; in the first six years of the scheme only £714.3 million of carry-forward was given for all other Whitehall departments (or 1.7 per cent of their eligible cash limits).

The Ministry of Defence has been a major beneficiary (for the statistical detail see Thain and Wright 1990*e*). When the special M.o.D. scheme is added, it is no exaggeration to characterize public spending end-year flexibility as 'Defence EYF' (the M.o.D. took over 72 per cent of all EYF granted between 1983 and 1989). There is an element in this of the Treasury buying off one of the departments which it has traditionally found difficult to shadow. The Ministry itself is clear about the value of EYF. It emphasizes the role EYF played in helping it to manage a complex and highly sophisticated equipment procurement budget:

Carry forward is central to our drive for better value for money, as it allows our project managers to defer expenditure from one financial year to another without fear that it will be lost to the M.o.D. We anticipate that the carry forward will help to sustain the equipment programme by providing the financial buttress necessary to make payments previously expected to fall due at an earlier stage. (Defence Committee 1989: 93)

Other departments have benefited in a number of ways. Finance Officers have been able to concentrate on tasks other than trying to obtain a precise match between outturn and plan. Programme managers have been able to plan with greater confidence because they are assured of carry-forward on eligible items. In particular, large capital programmes have not been endangered because of unforeseen difficulties; the existence of the schemes has reduced the pressure on programme managers to pay bills, even though there may have been doubt about the quality of the goods or services provided; and there has been less end-year spending on low-priority items simply to use up underspending.

CONCLUSIONS

By introducing an element of carry-forward of underspending on certain categories of public spending the Treasury has responded to the criticism that it has inflexibly administered the cash limits regime. The end-year flexibility scheme introduced in 1983, and subsequently amended and widened, is a further example of how in practice the

Treasury has been more accommodating to departments than its rhetoric often suggests. The schemes do give departments a significant degree of flexibility at a 'cost' to the Treasury of underspending forgone and central control loosened. The M.o.D. is seen as the biggest beneficiary; other departments have benefited to a lesser extent in monetary terms, although programme managers have been freed from time-consuming tasks of end-year monitoring, wasteful spending sprees have been avoided, and the damage done to policy objectives by unavoidable programme slippage reduced. What began as a limited and containable response by the Treasury to sustained pressure from departments from 1978 (especially the M.o.D.) for greater flexibility has become a routinized part of the public spending control system, with the concept of EYF extended to non-capital expenditure. An important background factor here was the changed public spending climate from 1984 when public spending was declining as a proportion of GDP and the Treasury was more easily able to achieve PSBR targets and even engineer a budget surplus. In the 1980s EYF represented a genuine (if limited) concession on the part of a Treasury more confident that it had re-asserted general control of the spending aggregates. By the 1990s the concept and practice was so well integrated into the public spending planning and control system that it has survived the harsher climate created by the re-emergence of a large PSBR as the economy entered recession.

PART V

The Outputs of the System

20

Objectives and Achievements

How well or ill have Conservative Governments been served by the PES system since 1979? To answer that question we need to ask what those governments required of it. The objectives set for public expenditure are of two kinds: broad, medium-term policy objectives and annual objectives set for the Planning/Control Total. The distinction is necessary because the latter are not always consistent with the former. During the late 1980s, the Government began to give greater weight to achieving its broad macro-policy objectives 'over the whole cycle', acknowledging that the objective of reducing or stabilizing the share of GDP absorbed by public spending had to allow at certain stages in the economic cycle for short-term policy deflections which might lead to an increase in spending, for example in conditions of recession where more on social security, unemployment benefit, and training was inescapable and justified. Thus the Planning Total set in any one year might be inconsistent with the broad policy objective. A further cause of inconsistency, temporarily deflecting government from the path towards its medium-term objective, was the increase in public expenditure at particular stages in the electoral cycle, in 1986–7 for example, and again in 1990–1 and 1991–2.

In this chapter we assess the effectiveness of the system for planning and controlling public expenditure by assessing the extent to which governments have achieved their stated objectives. It is of course true that success or failure is not only or mainly determined by the efficiency of the PES system or its operation by the Treasury and the spending departments. As we explained in Chapter 2, the system is operated within a specific politico-economic context which influences the setting and changing of objectives for public spending and their achievement in both the short and medium term. We begin with an examination of the broad medium-term objectives and describe the changes made to them in the period 1976–92. We then analyse the trends of the main public expenditure aggregates and assess the extent to which those objectives were achieved. We argue that the Treasury failed to achieve either the objectives set in 1980 or those modified objectives set in the middle of the decade.

For nearly thirty years after the Second World War governments had little difficulty in reconciling their performance with their objectives: public expenditure rose in real terms year by year, and from the mid-1950s this reflected the general objective of government that it should do so. While Conservative Governments were motivated less by doctrine than pragmatism, they too embraced the aim of increasing public expenditure. The change in the 'assumptive worlds' of key policy-makers was evident in the 1976 Public Expenditure White Paper (Cmnd. 6393), which warned of the twin problems of managing spending: rising public expectations about improving levels of public services not matched by growth in output, and high cost-inflation. The Labour Government committed itself to plans which aimed 'broadly to stabilise the level of resources taken by public expenditure programmes after 1976–77'. The White Paper went on to note that 'if this is achieved public expenditure will fall as a proportion of national output from its present exceptionally high level' (pp. 1–2). Yet this was seen as a short-term modification to policy objectives: elsewhere in the document commitments were made to resuming the growth of spending once GDP growth returned and the economy was stabilized; and priority was given to spending on industry and employment support. By the following year it was clear that, at least temporarily, the Labour Government had jettisoned much of the post-war consensus on the need for ever-rising levels of spending. The 1977 Public Expenditure White Paper (Cmnd. 6721) was the most significant produced under Chancellor Healey, and was testimony to the severity of the crisis which had resulted in the IMF loan. Instead of stabilizing the level of aggregate spending, the Government committed itself to reducing the volume of spending and the ratio of public spending to GDP in 1977–8 and 1978–9. This included an explicit commitment to bring the direct expenditure on goods and services by central government as a proportion of GDP to the level prevailing in 1971–2.

This was no monetarist revolution, however, as we argued in Chapter 2. In both the 1978 and 1979 Treasury White Papers the Government committed itself to a resumption of spending growth, 'within the prospective growth rate of National Income' (Cmnd. 7049: 1). In addition, the aim of the Government was to achieve a 'greater degree of stability' than earlier plans 'so that expenditure programmes can be managed with confidence that they will not be subjected to the disruption of sudden cuts'. Nevertheless, there was no return to the orthodox Keynesian position prevailing before 1975; the 'party was over'. Plans were constrained by 'broader economic objectives' to a greater extent than in the 1960s or early 1970s; control procedures were given greater prominence than before; and the 1979 White Paper (Cmnd. 7439) was particularly scathing about the foolishness of relying on economic projections when economic relationships had become so 'fragile', 'insecure', and 'uncertain' (p. 5).

CHANGES UNDER THE CONSERVATIVES, 1979–1992

Whilst it is clear that the Labour Government responded to the economic problems of the time with unprecedented restraint on public spending, this was based more on pragmatism than a repudiation of its importance. We must look to the early years of the first Thatcher Government for signs of a significant and committed change of public spending regime. The first major statement by the new government contained a sustained attack on the post-war consensus on the need for ever-increasing levels of public spending. The November 1979 Public Expenditure White Paper (Cmnd. 7746) placed public spending 'at the heart of Britain's present economic difficulties'. The new aim of public spending policy was 'to plan for spending which is not only compatible with the necessary objectives for taxation and borrowing, but is also based on a realistic assessment of the prospects for economic growth'. The change in objectives reflected the conversion of the leadership of the Conservative Party to neo-liberal economic policies during the years of Opposition, and its doctrinal distaste for the policies of collective consumption. Notwithstanding the firm rhetoric and hint of medium-term plans, the White Paper was surprisingly cautious. The short-term objective was to 'stabilise public spending, for the time being'. Given the previous government's commitment to spending growth, this meant cuts in plans.

The 1980 White Paper (Cmnd. 7841) marked an even more significant and unprecedented change of objective. For the first time, within the context of a PESC round and without the pressure of an external crisis, a government committed itself to a sustained medium-term plan reducing the Planning Total by nearly 4 per cent in volume in the four years to 1983–4. It also committed itself to a cut in the proportion of GDP this total implied. The White Paper asserted that 'the Government is determined not merely to halt the growth of public expenditure but progressively reduce it'. Moreover, the plans were incorporated into overall economic strategy in a unique form through their inclusion in the MTFS unveiled in the March 1980 Budget, when cuts in spending were integrated with targets for the PSBR and money supply and a commitment to reduce taxation.

The achievement of the unambiguous objective of cutting the real level of spending was put immediately at risk. Substantial overspending occurred. The outturn for 1980–1 was 2 per cent higher than planned. The broad policy objectives remained unchanged, although the target reduction was scaled down to 1 per cent and deferred to the end of the plan period. By the time of the emergence of a second substantial overspend the following year, the Government had taken action to tighten Treasury control by the introduction of cash planning (discussed in Chapter 3), and to change the presentation of its plans to deflect attention from the continuing volume increases. The 1982 White Paper made no reference to the Government's policy objective of reducing expenditure.

Throughout the period 1976–93, the 'goal posts' were regularly moved as a response to the failure to achieve earlier stated objectives. Particular problems had been created for the Conservative Government in this regard. Normally, policy objectives are stated in very general terms and so modifications can be effected by more explicit interpretation, or by emphasizing a particular facet of a general policy stance, or by expressing and presenting objectives in a different form. This sort of politically rational strategy was more difficult for the Government to accomplish simply because its objectives, and the unambiguous publication of a financial framework codifying those objectives, were so clear and signals had been given to its supporters and the public that there was a change in regime.

The occurrence of a third year of overspending convinced the Treasury that, at least for the immediate future, the Government's policy objective was impossible to achieve. There then followed a gradual process over the next six years when the Government moved the public spending policy 'goal posts' and slowly brought them into line with the inexorable growth of aggregate public spending. It was not until 1984 that this change in policy objectives was recognized in spending documents, when the Green Paper on Expenditure and Taxation (Cmnd. 9189: 20) noted that the aim of the Government was to hold 'spending broadly at its present level in real terms'. M. C. Scholar, the then Treasury Under Secretary in charge of the General Expenditure Policy Group, made the change of objectives explicit in evidence to the Treasury and Civil Service Committee (1985a) in February 1985: 'I think if you go back five years, the Government's aspirations were then in terms of *cutting* public expenditure in real terms. That was not achieved. The Government's aspirations are now expressed in terms of keeping expenditure flat in real terms' (qu. 20). The 1985 White Paper (Cmnd. 9428: 6) then emphasized a second, related aim, of reducing public spending as a proportion of GDP. Its plans were said to imply a ratio at its 'lowest since 1978–79' by 1987–8. If the objective of keeping public expenditure level in real terms was achieved, then the growth of GDP would bring about the objective of reducing the share of GDP taken by public expenditure. After stagnating in the recession of the early 1980s, the economy, conveniently for public spending objective-setters, began to grow again.

The increasing confidence of the Treasury was reflected in revised presentation of the public expenditure plans in the annual White Paper. In 1986 (Cmnd. 9702) it included for the first time a section headed 'Aims and Objectives', which repeated more explicitly the intention to hold public spending broadly constant in real terms. Moreover, by redefining the public expenditure target in terms of General Government Expenditure, it was able to demonstrate a progressive reduction in the share of GDP pre-empted by the public sector from the high point of 1982–3.

However, public spending continued to rise in real terms. The 'goal posts' were moved for the second time in autumn 1986, and the aim of holding public spending broadly constant in real terms was quietly abandoned. A yet more limited objective took its place: 'to see to it that total public spending even without taking account of privatisation proceeds, continues to decline as a percentage of GDP' (Cm. 14). This was confirmed in the 1987 White Paper and MTFS plans. The reasons for this change were not given by the Government and are open to different interpretations. The one most favoured at the time by analysts and commentators was that the Conservative Government had abandoned its hostility towards public spending, and was now beginning upon an expansionary phase. An alternative interpretation is that the Treasury had acknowledged that even the more limited objective of holding spending steady could not be achieved in the immediate future, and the expansionary plans announced were a recognition of what had happened, and was happening, to public expenditure. As some said, it was making a virtue of necessity, and enabled the Government to claim the credit for willing increases in an election year. On that interpretation the Treasury was a bystander in seeing objectives brought into line with what was feasible. This is tantamount to an admission that the Government's aims and objectives and the Treasury's control could not prevent public expenditure rising in real terms.

Whatever the real motives, having decided to plan for an increase in public spending for the first time since 1979, it could not simultaneously maintain the objective of holding spending broadly steady. The 'goal posts' had been moved yet again to bring them in line with the new play.

From the previous objective of cutting expenditure in real terms, the Treasury now hoped that, although spending would rise in aggregate in real terms, it would do so at a rate less than the growth in GDP. Challenged by the Treasury and Civil Service Committee (1986*e*), Chancellor Lawson and Treasury officials argued that the reduction in the public expenditure/GDP ratio had been an underlying aim of the Government since 1979. It had appeared in the general election manifesto of that year, and was to be found earlier still in the Conservative Party's policy document, *The Right Approach to the Economy*. The committee was told 'that theme has been there continuously and it is that which accurately describes what has happened since 1982–83'. The Committee accepted that as an underlying objective, but reported that 'spending policy since 1979 had been formulated in stronger terms. Before the shift to cash planning, the operational objective was to reduce public expenditure in volume terms. Since then it has been to hold expenditure constant, or broadly constant, in real terms' (para. 30, p. x). The Chancellor argued that the changes were in the presentation of policy rather than in the objectives themselves:

I think the policy has been consistent throughout . . . in so far as there has been any change it has been an improvement. The rate of growth in real terms of public expenditure has slowed down. I think it is the presentation which has changed slightly. I would not want to make too much of it. (qu. 86)

Treasury officials were less convincing still, arguing that the Autumn Statement represented 'less a change of objective but more a change of speed at which the objective is being achieved'.

There then followed a period from 1986 to 1990 when overall spending objectives continued to be couched in terms of the 1986 objective. This was a period when the Treasury could claim considerable credit, as public spending fell as a proportion of GDP throughout the rest of the 1980s: the more limited objective had been achieved. However, rather more credit was due to the growth of the economy. Public expenditure continued to rise throughout the period 1986–90, but could be represented as under 'control' as it absorbed a declining share of expanding GDP. The circumstances in which that growth occurred were short-lived and non-recurring. Public expenditure was ratcheted up, with long-term consequences which were to become apparent in 1992. Yet even when the economy began to slow down, Chancellor Major was able to state confidently in April 1990 that 'proportionately public expenditure remains on a very shallow but nevertheless declining trend over the period of the PES round' (qu. 264).

Later in the year the goal posts were moved for a fourth time. Chancellor Lamont told the Treasury and Civil Service Committee that 'although it was the Government's policy to reduce GGE as a proportion of GDP, that would not necessarily happen every single year and that there might be periods when activity was weak and the ratio would rise' (Treasury and Civil Service Committee 1990c: qu. 227). The *Financial Statement and Budget Report* in the following March made explicit the modification to public spending objectives: 'the Government intends that public spending should continue to take a declining share of national income over time' (Treasury 1991a: 14). The official line remained that the modifications to objectives were based on success rather than the failure to deliver. Alex Allan, then Under Secretary in charge of the Treasury's General Expenditure Policy Group, told the Treasury and Civil Service Committee (1991c):

There have been changes in our formulation of our objective for the budget deficit and also for our objective on public spending. When the Government took office in 1979 its priority was to make actual cuts in spending, as you describe; after those cuts had been made and the budget brought into balance, there was scope for looking at the objectives again, and these were reformulated into its present pair of objectives, one of which is to balance the budget, the PSBR, over the economic cycle; the other is to reduce public spending as a share of GDP over-time. These are the two objectives. The public spending objective remains unchanged from last year. (qu. 5)

A balanced budget over the medium term was described as a 'clear and simple rule which ensures that a prudent fiscal policy supports monetary policy in the fight against inflation' (Treasury 1991a: 11). The existence of the economic cycle and automatic stabilizers allowed for a PSBR in the short term and, provided the deficit was the result of recession impacting on revenues and public spending, was 'consistent with a sound underlying position'.

This formulation of the objective survived the changes made to the public expenditure planning and control system in July 1992. The 'intermediate' target remained the reduction of GGE as a proportion of GDP over time, whilst ensuring greater value-for-money. However, there was a subtle change of emphasis which presaged a further relaxation of objectives. The New Control Total, as we discussed in Chapter 11, was introduced in tandem with a specific target of 2 per cent per year for the real growth of GGE. This was predicated on the assumption that the trend rate of growth of GDP was above this level, and therefore that achievement of the target would produce a declining GGE/GDP ratio. The Treasury was no longer wedded to the ratio as a symbol of policy success, a narrower, more operational and realizable, target having superseded it.

The modifications to the current (1993) central public spending objective highlight the problems with the use of the public spending/GDP ratio as a measure of government performance in achieving public-spending policy goals and in controlling the aggregate of public spending. Fluctuations in GDP from year to year make the relationship between these two variables unstable. If GDP statistics are underestimated, or if there is very rapid economic growth, public spending may decline as a proportion of GDP. For the Treasury to claim 'success' here is misleading since the factors determining the decline in the ratio are outside its direct control. It would be equally wrong to accuse the Treasury of 'failure' if GDP statistics are overestimated or if the economy is in recession and public spending rises as a proportion of GDP. The real test of 'success' or 'failure' would be how far the Treasury had kept total government spending in real terms to the targets it had set. It was a measure of the force of these criticisms, and the practical problems of targeting the ratio during the prolonged recession of the late 1980s and early 1990s, that in July 1992 there was the subtle shift in objectives discussed above.

From the initial objective of cutting spending in real terms, the Conservative Government had arrived, a decade later, first at a position where an increase in public spending was justifiable provided it was less than the growth of GDP, and subsequently at a position where a rise in the ratio was justifiable provided it was the result of the impact of that most Keynesian of concepts—the use of 'automatic stabilizers' during a recession. Paradoxically, in so doing it had returned to the broad policy objectives of the 1960s and 1970s. The changes in objectives, and the changes in the public presentation of those objectives, were part of a long and difficult learning process for the Conservative Government as it devised expedient strategies for coping with the difficulties experienced in the years after 1979. As the pressures for more public spending became manifestly uncontainable, objectives were changed pragmatically. More chastening still was the lesson of the late 1980s that public spending in aggregate could not be forced to follow the downward trend in the economic cycle. Changing the objectives was a rational coping strategy, although one not easy to present without risking the charge of having executed an anathematic U-turn. Arresting the momentum of the historic trend of rising public expenditure in the circumstances of the 1980–2 recession proved impossible. After that date, the Conservative Government had to face the contingent social expenditures of high unemployment, spending associated with the miners' strike, persistent overspending by local authorities, the effects of the longest and deepest recession since 1945, and more generally an unwillingness of individual Ministers to translate their abstract commitment to reducing aggregate spending into concrete cuts in their budgets.

We now turn to analysis of the trends in the main public expenditure aggregates to assess how successful governments were in achieving their objectives, and to explain why at certain times in the period 1976–93 it became necessary to modify them as described above.

ACHIEVEMENTS: THE ANALYSIS OF TRENDS IN PUBLIC EXPENDITURE

Changing definitions of the composition and classification of public expenditure pose formidable analytical and methodological problems for the construction of a continuous and comparable time-series data set. It is an understatement to assert that any assessment of the trends in public spending is made very difficult by the frequency with which the Treasury has changed the aggregate used to measure performance and the composition of those aggregates in the period 1976–92. Whilst the Treasury revises all previous figures in a time-series when there is a major definitional change, there remains a break in the figures which makes it difficult to measure outturns against earlier plans, as happened with the introduction of the New Planning Total in 1988. In addition, changes in the price bases have compounded those problems. Issues of the measurement of real growth, the definition of expenditure, and the determination of the price base have become inextricably linked since 1979. In the next chapter, we discuss the trends in individual programmes, and note how classification and other changes have made it difficult to measure accurately who has 'won' and 'lost'. This is far from being a minor technical issue, since 'prevailing definitions have profoundly affected both policy debates and substantive policy decisions' (Heald 1991: 75). Moreover, the dividing line between justifiable technical changes and those politically motivated to massage the presentation of 'success' has become even harder to detect. This raises further wider issues about the degree to which the Treasury (irrespective of which party is in power) has had a free hand in 'moving the goal posts' and therefore arguably obscuring the public debate about the trends in spending. This is discussed in more detail elsewhere (Thain and Wright 1990*b*). Here we relieve the reader of the burden of grappling with the technical problems of measurement and analysis (see Thain and Wright 1989*a* for greater detail). In what follows it is necessary to know only that the analysis of trends of public spending in real terms uses both the Planning Total, which emerged from the late 1970s as the Treasury's key spending definition, and General Government Expenditure (GGE), which became a favoured yardstick of measurement from 1986 onwards. GGE, excluding privatization proceeds, adjusted for general inflation using the GDP deflator, is the least distorted and therefore most consistent measure of trends in the total of public expenditure. But neither it nor the Planning Total can be used to assess trends over the whole period, because the introduction of the New Planning Total in 1988 only allows consistent analysis from 1984–5. In this section we assess aggregate spending in real terms, using both the old and new definitions of the Planning Total. This is followed by an analysis of GGE measured in real terms, as a proportion of GDP, and using trend rates of growth over time. We provide data (where available) on two specific time periods: from 1973–4, the last year of the Conservative Government of (Sir) Edward Heath; and from 1978–9, the last year of the Labour Government of (Lord) James Callaghan. This allows us to compare the record of the Labour Government with that of the Conservative Governments of Margaret Thatcher and John Major.

The 'old' and 'new' Planning Totals in real terms

Figs. 20.1 and 20.2 show the trends in spending using the old definition of the Planning Total. Over the whole period, from the end of the Heath Administration in 1974 to the last year in which this definition applied, 1989, real spending rose by 16 per cent. If only the Conservative period is highlighted, the Planning Total grew 11 per cent in real terms between 1978–9 and 1989–90.

However, these statistics hide considerable variation within each period. The largest annual rise *and* annual fall in spending occurred between 1973–4 and 1977–8. Spending grew in real terms by nearly 12.5 per cent in the first year of the Labour Government; it fell by 10.7 per cent between 1974–5 and 1977–8. This was a result of the expansion of social programmes under the 'social contract' and of rising inflation; the crisis of control in the mid-1970s; the impact of the cut-backs announced as part of the IMF-loan package and of the squeeze imposed by the introduction of cash limits. The early record of the Thatcher Governments was one of sharply rising expenditure in the wake of the recession of the early 1980s, and the growth in local authority spending: spending grew by over 10 per cent in real terms between 1978–9 and 1984–5. This was followed by a period of real decline in aggregate spending, which fell by 3 per cent between 1984–5 and 1988–9. Much of this decline was

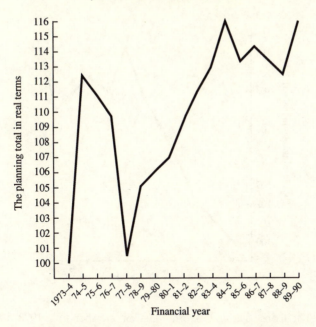

FIG. 20.1. Conservative and Labour Governments' public spending, 1973–1990

Note: 100 = 1973–4 base year. Figures for the 'old' Planning Total (prior to 1988–9) in real terms, i.e. cash figures adjusted to 1987–8 prices by excluding the effect of general inflation using a deflator of GDP at market prices.

Source: Based on Cm. 621: 73.

the result of falling social security spending due to lower unemployment, and the buoyant sales of assets such as council houses and public utilities. The end of the period saw a return to real growth, with the Planning Total growing by 3.6 per cent between 1988–9 and 1989–90.

Trends in spending using the New Planning Total show a markedly different picture (shown in Fig. 20.3). In the period between 1984–5 and 1988–9 spending fell by 7 per cent in real terms, thereafter there was a clear and accelerating trend of growth. This pattern shows the impact of finance for local authorities on spending trends both positively, when the exclusion of local authorities' own spending contributed to the decline in total spending, and negatively when the increase in central government support for local authorities as a result of the crisis over the community charge placed upward pressure on the aggregate. In addition, the sharp rise in spending (up nearly 14 per cent between 1988–9 and 1991–2) in the latter period was the result of a relaxation of tight spending policies prior to the general election of 1992, a more relaxed attitude generally to spending after 1987, and the impact of rising

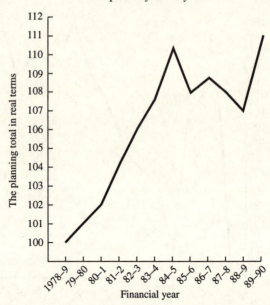

FIG. 20.2. The Conservative Governments' public spending, 1978–1990

Note: 100 = 1978–9 base year. Figures for the 'old' Planning Total (prior to 1988–9) in real terms, i.e. cash figures adjusted to 1987–8 prices by excluding the effect of general inflation using a deflator of GDP at market prices.

Source: Based on Cm. 621: 73.

demand-led pressures as the economy moved into recession. In the period from 1991–2 to 1994–5 there was a further 12.7 per cent real increase in spending planned. From these figures it is clear that, if the New Planning Total was introduced in part to show a more 'controlled' profile of spending, the presentational change did not produce the desired effect. In the event it did not prove possible for the New Planning Total to be fully insulated from the effects of local authority expenditure. This lack of success accounted for its replacement by the New Control Total in 1992.

Further evidence of the relaxation of spending policies is provided in Fig. 20.4, which shows the trend in central government's own spending, excluding local authorities and nationalized industries. This figure also shows how central government has contributed as much to the growth of spending as local authorities over the period from 1978–9: indeed, central government's own spending grew by 5 per cent more in real terms than the old Planning Total as a whole between 1978–9 and 1984–5. Central government's own expenditure grew by nearly 33 per cent between 1978–9 and 1992–3.

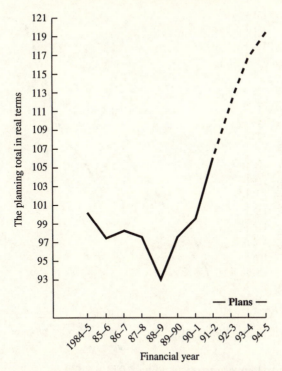

FIG. 20.3. The Conservative Governments' public spending, 1984–1995

Note: 100 = 1984–5 base year. Figures for the 'new' Planning Total (1988–9 to 1992–3) in real terms, i.e. cash figures adjusted to 1990–1 prices by excluding the effect of general inflation using a deflator of GDP at market prices.

Source: Based on Cm. 1920: 11.

General Government Expenditure in real terms

Figs. 20.5 and 20.6 measure GGE in real terms, that is spending is cash-adjusted for general inflation in the economy, as measured by the GDP deflator over the whole period from 1973–4, and also more narrowly during the period of the Thatcher and Major Governments. As we noted earlier, this is the most accurate definition and one used by the Treasury since the late 1980s as a target for the purpose of setting medium-term objectives. It is also the most comprehensive definition since it includes local authorities' own expenditure, and debt interest.

Fig. 20.5 shows that, using this definition, apart from a dip in spending in the mid-1970s and late 1980s, there has been a steady and continuous rise in real spending. Between 1973–4 and 1992–3 GGE rose by over 38 per cent. Fig. 20.6 shows that GGE grew by 20 per cent between 1978–

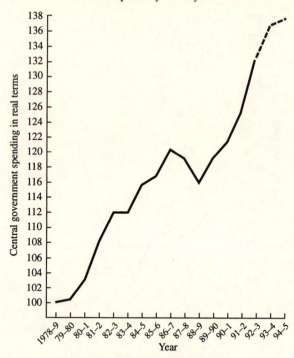

FIG. 20.4. Central government spending, 1978–1995

Note: 100 = 1978–9 base year. The spending of central government depts. and the financing requirements of public corporations, but excluding nationalized industries and support for local authorities. Figures in real terms, i.e. cash figures adjusted to 1991–2 prices by excluding the effect of general inflation using a deflator of GDP at market prices.

Source: Based on Cm. 2219: 39.

9 and 1992–3. There were three phases within this general pattern of growth. From 1978–9 to 1984–5 spending rose remorselessly to be 14 per cent higher in real terms, despite the initial commitment of the Conservative Government to cut spending in real terms. This was followed by a period when growth slowed between 1984–5 and 1987–8, and actually declined between 1986–7 and 1988–9. There was another slight dip in real spending between 1989–90 and 1990–1. Real spending growth resumed after 1990–1 and is projected in the 1992 Autumn Statement plans to rise by a further 12 per cent between 1991–2 and 1994–5.

The decline in spending in 1988 was associated with the rapid growth in the economy during the so-called Lawson boom. At that time spending on unemployment benefit and employment support fell sharply. The GGE aggregate tends to underplay the impact of these events compared

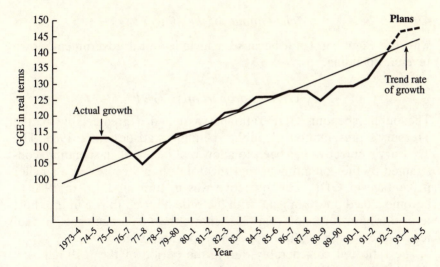

FIG. 20.5. General government expenditure in real terms, 1973–1995
Note: 100 = 1973–4 base year. Cash figures adjusted to price levels of 1991–2.
Source: Based on Cm. 2219: 15.

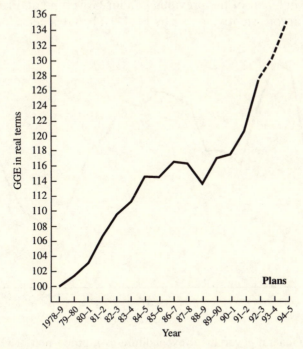

FIG. 20.6. General government expenditure under Conservative Governments,
1978–1995
Note: 100 = 1978–9 base year. Cash figures adjusted to price levels of 1991–2.
Source: Based on Cm. 2219: 15.

with the Planning Total because it includes local government's own revenue spending.

GGE as a proportion of GDP

The public spending/GDP ratio has assumed a greater role in the Treasury's presentation of public spending statistics since 1985. The Treasury's objective has been to allow real increases in spending, constrained by the commitment that this total should represent a smaller percentage of GDP. This objective was in turn modified in 1990 to become a medium-term goal, with the ratio allowed to rise in the short term during a recession. Fig. 20.7 charts the GGE aggregate in real terms (excluding privatization) as a proportion of money GDP.

The ratio fell considerably during the period of the IMF-imposed crisis measures in the 1975–7 period, only to rise slightly in the last two years of the Labour Government. During the period of the Conservative Governments the ratio rose during the recession of 1980–2 to reach a peak of 47.5 per cent of GDP in 1982–3, some 3.5 per cent higher than in the last full year of the previous Labour Government. From 1982–3 the ratio fell consistently, so that by 1988–9 it had reached a low of 39.25

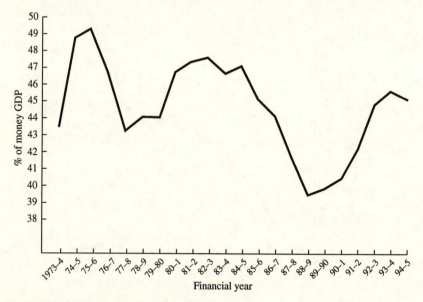

FIG. 20.7. General government expenditure as a proportion of GDP, 1973–1995

Note: GGE excluding privatization proceeds as a proportion of money GDP.

Source: Based on Cm. 2219: 15.

per cent of GDP, the lowest figure since 1966–7. As the economy slowed
in the aftermath of the credit boom of the late 1980s, the ratio levelled
off at around 40 per cent, rose sharply to 44.75 per cent by 1992–3, and
is projected to rise to over 45 per cent in 1993–4 before levelling off. The
severity of the recession and the shallowness of the recovery suggests
that this latter forecast is likely to be optimistic, thus endangering what
had since 1984 been the Treasury's most 'successful' public spending
yardstick.

The trend rate of growth in public expenditure

To what extent have Conservative Governments since 1979 succeeded
in slowing the trend rate of growth of public spending? Table 20.1
provides mixed evidence in support of the claim that since 1978–9 real
spending has grown at a slower pace than during the 1960s, 1970s, and
early 1980s. Over the period as a whole, real spending grew faster than
in the 1970s, but that calculation includes the impact of the 1990s recession. The plans for the period from 1992–3 to 1995–6 suggest an
average projected rate of growth of 2.7 per cent per year, which, if
achieved, would be higher than the period from the first oil crisis to the
last year of the previous Labour Government. This suggests that the

TABLE 20.1. *Annual growth of General Government Expenditure in real terms,*
1963–1996[a]

	Average % annual growth	Government
1963–4 to 1969–70	3.2	Labour (Wilson)
1969–70 to 1973–4	5.3	Conservative (Heath)
1973–4 to 1978–9	1.8[b]	Labour (Wilson; Callaghan)
1978–9 to 1992–3	1.9	Conservative (Thatcher; Major)
1992–3 to 1995–6	2.7	Conservative (Major)

[a] GGE is the expenditure of central and local government excluding transfers between them. The figure used here excludes the impact of privatization
receipts. Cash figures have been adjusted to 1990–1 prices by excluding the
effect of general inflation using a deflator of GDP at market prices.

[b] This period is characterized by three distinct phases: from 1973–4 to 1975–
6 GGE grew in real terms on average of 6% per annum; real GGE *declined* by
3.7% per annum on average in the period from 1975–6 to 1977–8; and GGE
grew by 5% from 1977–8 to 1978–9.

Source: Treasury 1993*b*: 15.

record from the mid- to the late 1980s owed as much to economic boom as to the sound management of public spending.

It is clear, however, that any conclusion drawn depends on which period is chosen for analysis. It is apparent that within each period there have been distinct phases of accelerating growth, followed by static or even falling real levels of expenditure. Thus, the early period of the Conservative Governments up to 1983–4 witnessed *higher* real growth, at 2.3 per cent per year, than during the previous Labour Government, when average real growth over the whole period from 1973–4 to 1978–9 had been 1.8 per cent per year. On the other hand, real growth has averaged less than 1 per cent a year during the period from 1983–4 to 1991–2.

CONCLUSIONS

Four conclusions may be drawn from this analysis about the achievement of objectives set by governments. First, governments have failed to reduce public expenditure in real terms since the mid-1970s, with the exception of the crisis year of 1976 and the economic boom in the 1987–9 period. General Government Expenditure rose on average by about 2 per cent per year between 1973 and 1993.

Secondly, there is little evidence that growth in spending decelerated in the period after 1979, compared with that of the 1970s. As we noted earlier, there is some evidence to support the view that spending growth slowed in the period from 1983–4 to 1989–90. But public spending plans for the early 1990s show a resurgence of the growth of spending comparable with the crisis years of the previous Labour Government. Thirdly, governments have succeeded in cutting public expenditure in real or volume terms only at times of major external economic crisis, or during economic boom, and then only for limited periods. Absolute reductions in real growth did occur during the major economic crisis of the mid-1970s: GGE declined in real terms by 8 per cent between 1975–6 and 1977–8; and during the economic boom in 1987–9. It is clear, however, that whatever the nature of the environmental factors behind real cuts or static spending, real reductions in spending have been a short-term phenomenon: the trend growth in spending resumed in 1978–9 under the Labour Government, and under the Conservative Government of John Major from 1991–2.

Fourthly, governments have been more successful in the period after 1979 in holding spending as a steady or a declining proportion of GDP.

There is evidence to suggest that, unusually, the acceleration of economic growth in the period from 1985 to 1988 led to a decline in the ratio. This can be seen as in part a measure of the Treasury's success in substantially modifying the PES system after 1982. But this is a short-lived phenomenon, as the demand-led pressures resulting from the recession from 1989 in conjunction with the contraction of the economy made it impossible to stop the ratio rising substantially during the early to mid-1990s. The decline in the ratio was an isolated phenomenon, more the result of an overheating economy than a changed agenda on public spending.

A comparison of the records of the last Labour Government and the Governments of Margaret Thatcher and John Major provides mixed conclusions. We have already noted in our discussion on the public expenditure/GDP ratio that the most significant annual decline occurred during the middle years of the last Labour Government. But the most significant annual increase was also presided over by a Labour Chancellor. Under the Conservative Governments it was not until 1982–3 that the ratio took a downward path; by 1986–7 it was at a lower point than that inherited from the previous Labour Government. However, if privatization receipts are excluded, it was not until 1987–8 that the GGE/GDP ratio was lower than in 1978–9. Using this rather crude measure of comparative performance, only if the later years of the Conservative Government are used can it be said that Conservatives have been more 'successful' than the last Labour Government, and this against the background of differing policy objectives: Conservative Governments were ideologically committed to reducing public expenditure; Labour only expediently and temporarily so.

When the GGE is measured in real terms from 1973–4 for Labour and from 1978–9 for Conservatives, it is clear that real GGE grew on average by about 1.8 per cent real growth per annum; and under the Conservatives GGE, excluding asset sales, grew on average by 1.9 per cent per year. These figures seem to show that, even when the sale of public corporations is excluded, the *average* growth in public spending under the Conservative Governments is higher than that under the previous Labour Government.

After fourteen years of ideological hostility towards public spending, numerous changes in the planning and control system, and frequent modifications to policy objectives and targets, public spending is set to rise in the 1990s in real terms at a level last experienced in the crisis years of the 1970s. The conclusion is irresistible: Conservative Governments were unable to achieve either the heroic objectives set in 1980 or the less ambitious ones which replaced them in the mid-1980s. In the next chapter we assess which departments and programmes 'won' and 'lost' in the implementation of those objectives, and in Chapter 22 we assess the effects and effectiveness of the PES system as the main mechanism for delivering them.

21

Departmental 'Winners' and 'Losers'

The most significant output of the PES system is the aggregate total of public expenditure planned for the coming financial year, discussed in the previous chapter. This is measured in terms of the Government's short- and long-term public spending objectives, in the context of its broader politico-economic objectives, and is attributable to the Government collectively and to the Treasury as the instrument of its policy. The intermediate outputs of the system with which we are concerned here are the departmental allocations published formerly in the November Autumn Statement, and from 1993 the Unified Budget. An assessment of the final outputs of the system, the goods provided and the services delivered when those resources are finally committed and consumed by the clients, customers, and consumers of the various spending authorities, lies outside the scope of this book.

The PES allocations cannot be read as a scorecard of who has won and lost in the process of bidding and negotiating with the Treasury and Cabinet Expenditure Committee. There are problems of definition, measurement, and interpretation. Success or failure in each departmental allocation is assessed differently by the Treasury and the spending departments. Factors which affect the latter's subjective assessment include the aims, objectives, and strategy of each department, both in the context of an individual spending round and over a period of years; the particular politico-economic context which informs the spending round (whether it is in a pre-election period or whether there is a crisis over public borrowing for example), and any changes to it as the round proceeds; and the particular tactics employed by the Treasury in relation to a department's programme. Each spending department has its own internal assessment of success or failure of its bidding and negotiating strategies, judged against its short- and long-term objectives, programme by programme, distinguishing what it hoped to obtain from what it expected the outcome to be and what, perhaps, it was obliged or agreed to settle for. Departmental assessments of such kinds are impossible to determine from outside without knowledge of 'bottom-line' margins, which in any case may be adjusted during the course of the spending round in response to changes in the politico-economic context.

Nor can success or failure be read off from the scorecard. An apparent loss of resources recorded there is not necessarily an indication of lack of success in the PES processes. Where a programme is declining historically, a slowing down of that rate of decline may represent success for a department's spending strategy. Likewise, the maintenance of an existing allocation in circumstances of general cuts and squeezes may also represent success. Conversely, a department which gains resources may nevertheless have obtained less than it deemed necessary to sustain a programme at its present level of provision, or have gained resources in nominal terms but suffered a real terms reduction.

The price basis used to measure growth or decline will affect the assessment of success or failure. As we discuss later, the Treasury's favoured measure is cash adjusted for general inflation in the economy as a whole. Arguably this distorts the trends in allocations, as seen from the perspective of the departments and their client agencies and pressure groups. Apparent 'success' using a general inflation index may actually be real failure if a Minister does not obtain a settlement which adequately covers the differential cost pressures on his or her programmes.

Even if this is allowed for, success cannot be measured solely in terms of real spending increases. If a department obtains real increases but these are not as great as those obtained by other departments, that is *relative* failure. If aggregate spending as a whole is rising, it is a fair measure to ask whether a department has shared in the general increase in allocation. We need therefore to assess whether a department's spending has grown or at least remained steady as a proportion of GDP and of total public spending. Of course, in times of public spending retrenchment, success might be measured by a static or slightly lower spending profile.

Even with these qualifications, the approach we adopt here does not adequately allow for the complexity of the programmes run by departments. How do we assess the success of a Minister in a department with a large number of demand-led or statutorily constrained programmes, which the Treasury regards as 'inescapable commitments'? On that criterion, in most years the Social Security Minister is the most successful spending minister. Other departments besides Social Security and Employment are responsible for programmes that rest on entitlements enshrined in statute or for which there is substantial political necessity (health spending and central government allocations to reduce the impact of the community charge are two obvious recent cases). We therefore need some measure of a Minister's success or failure in obtaining extra *discretionary* resources. On this basis, the Social Security Minister would be successful if Child Benefit was increased by more than inflation or if extra beneficiaries were brought into a programme as the result of negotiations with the Treasury. One obvious way is to look at the proportion of each department's spending which is demand-led (and non-cash limited) and what proportion is cash limited. Because of the frequency of definitional and classification changes and developments in cash-limit and Supply Estimates procedure such data is very unreliable over time. What is clear is that Ministers wishing to defend their programmes resist Treasury pressure to cash limit items previously non-cash limited. And a variation on this, since 1992, is that Ministers seek to have some of their programmes exempted from the New Control Total (which is subject to a 1.5 per cent growth ceiling) on the grounds that they may be cyclical and should be included in the 'wedge' of spending not subject to an artificial limit.

Frequent modifications in the data, and in definitions used for planning and control purposes, produced by the Treasury mean that it is no longer possible for the analyst to assess the trends in departmental spending on a consistent basis between 1976 and 1993 across narrow and broad definitions of spending. Classification changes have complicated the comparison of programmes, and analysis of their impact is often hampered by lack of information. Examples include the transfer of provision for housing benefit between departments. In almost every public expenditure document changes are made to the classification of particular items of expenditure, making the construction of consistent time-series data difficult or impossible. Any statistic which shows the growth or decline in resources allocated to a department or programme is potentially distorted. For example, trends in territorial spending indicate significant growth in Welsh Office spending in recent years. Yet this growth has been caused to a significant extent by the transfer of responsibility for rent rebates from the Department of Social Security to the Welsh Office. Similarly, a proportion of the growth in the spending of the DFE since 1978–9 is the result of the transfer of responsibility for Polytechnics from local authorities to central government.

There are, however, published time-series data for both GGE and central government's own spending, and taken together these two sets of figures give a proxy for the assessment of the success or failure of each spending department. Judgements of success or failure based on allocations after a single spending round would be misleading. Some investment programmes have long lead-times, and annual allocations can be 'front-' or 'end-loaded', or evenly spread through the life of a programme; a gradual but substantial shift in the relative priorities between programmes may be imperceptible in the outcomes of one or even two or three PES rounds; while the occurrence within the period of a single round of a major policy initiative, or a crisis, may distort the relativities between programmes over the period of a year or two. We must look therefore at the trends in the allocations to programmes and departments, after allowing for the effects of inflation, over the whole of the period 1976–93.

'REAL' TERMS MEASUREMENT

We measure first the trends in the real level of spending, and then calculate the proportion of GDP and of total spending taken by the most important programmes, to show the relative priority accorded to different types of spending by Conservative Governments. From these three measurements we derive an assessment of who has won and lost.

GGE in real terms

Table 21.1 shows that for the thirteen GGE programmes identified in 1992 there are three unambiguous 'winners' and two losers. The unambiguous winners are law and order, social security, and health and personal social services, all of which exhibited real growth and a larger share of GDP and total spending from 1978. The two clear 'losers', showing real decline and smaller shares of GDP and total spending, are housing, and trade, industry, and energy. The remaining eight programmes fall into a 'relative losers' category, programmes which have been allocated more resources in real terms but which have either maintained their share of GDP and total spending or have suffered reductions. If the final column is used as a yardstick (analysing a programme's absolute share of total GGE on services in 1978 and in 1993, and expressing the difference as a percentage of the 1978 level), nine out of the thirteen programmes can be said to have been *relative* losers over the period.

Within the 'winners' category, the law and order programme grew on average by nearly 7 per cent per year in real terms. But, as a relatively small programme, even though its share of total spending was nearly 50 per cent higher in 1993 than its 1978 level, this represented an increase in its share of GGE of under 2 per cent and a less than 1 per cent increase in its share of GDP over the period. By contrast the social security programme grew by just over 4.5 per cent per year on average but its share of GGE grew by nearly 7 per cent and of GDP by over 3 per cent between 1978 and 1993. Similarly, the health programme grew by just over 4 per cent per year and took a significantly higher proportion of GGE and GDP over the period.

TABLE 21.1. *'Winners', relative 'losers', and 'losers' in public spending, 1978–1993*

	Real growth (%)	Share of GDP and total spending		
		% of GDP	% of GGE	% of 1978–9 level
Programme				
Winners				
Law and order	+95.7	+0.9	+1.9	+49.6
Social Security	+65.0	+3.2	+6.9	+32.9
Health and personal social services	+58.2	+1.4	+2.3	+21.3
Relative Losers				
National Heritage	+30.0	same	same	same
Transport	+28.4	same	−0.1	−2.2
Education	+25.5	same	−0.6	−4.3
Other environment	+22.1	−0.1	−0.3	−7.7
Overseas services	+20.7	same	−0.1	−8.5
Agriculture	+14.3	same	−0.2	−12.5
Employment	+13.8	same	−0.2	−12.8
Defence	+11.2	−0.5	−1.7	−14.7
Losers				
Housing	−52.4	−1.7	−4.4	−62.9
Trade, Industry, and Energy	−55.4	−1.2	−3.1	−65.9

Source: Cm. 2219: tables 2.3 and 2.4.

As Figs. 21.1 and 21.2 show, both the law and order and the health programmes grew steadily over the period. Law and order spending only fell in real terms, year-on-year, in 1985–6; health spending grew in real terms every year, and apart from the 1985–7 period, its share of GGE and GDP grew steadily year-on-year. By contrast the social security programme's growth has been a little more uneven, reflecting the economic cycle. Having said this, it is somewhat surprising that the programme only declined in real terms year-on-year in three years (1987–8, 1988–9, and 1989–90). Of the clear losers, both the housing and the trade and industry programmes fell on average by just under 4 per cent per year and by 1993 represented a significantly smaller proportion

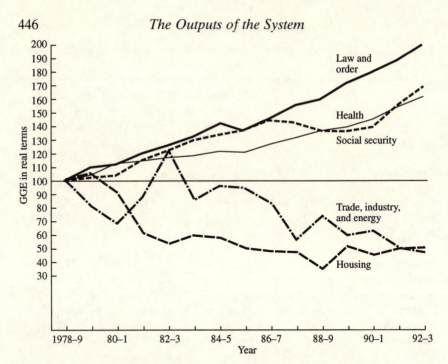

FIG. 21.1. 'Winners' and 'losers': GGE in real terms, 1978–1993

Note: 100 = 1978–9 base year. Cash figures adjusted to 1991–2 prices by excluding the effect of general inflation.

Source: Based on Cm. 2219: 18.

of GGE and GDP. Figs. 21.2 and 21.3 show that both programmes grew year-on-year in five years and fell in the other nine, but with a steady, fairly remorseless decline in their share of GGE and GDP over the period.

In the intermediate category, significant real growth in spending occurred in some of the programmes—for example by more than 2 per cent per year on average for national heritage and transport and more than 1.5 per cent a year for education and overseas services. But in each case the growth rate was not high enough to increase its share of GDP, and in seven of the eight cases led to a lower share of total spending. Indeed, defence spending share of total spending in 1993 was nearly 15 per cent lower than its 1978 level.

Central governments' own spending in real terms

One advantage of using this definition is that it avoids figures which would be distorted by the recent changes in local government finance,

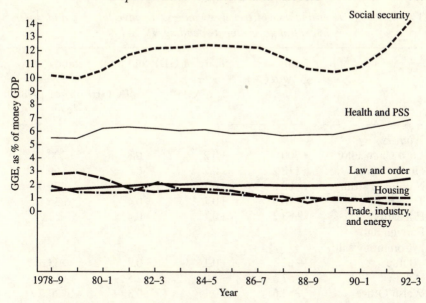

Fig. 21.2. 'Winners' and 'losers': share of GDP, 1978–1993
Source: Based on Cm. 2219: 19.

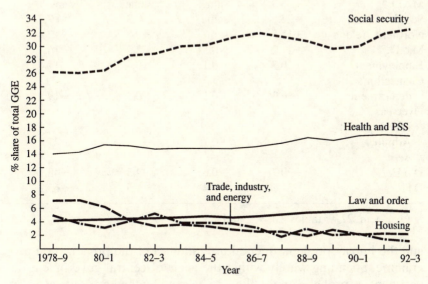

Fig. 21.3. 'Winners' and 'losers': share of total GGE, 1978–1993
Source: Based on Cm. 2219: 18.

TABLE 21.2. *Departments which were 'winners', relative 'losers', and 'losers' in central government spending, 1978–1993*

	Real growth (%)	Share of GDP and total spending		
		% of GDP	% of GGE	% of 1978–9 level
Winners				
Lord Chancellor	+300	+0.2	+0.8	+200
Home Office	+118.2	+0.2	+0.6	+66.7
National Heritage	+80.0	+0.1	+0.1	+25.0
Transport	+78.5	+0.1	+0.4	+36.4
Education	+68.2	+0.1	+0.4	+22.2
Foreign and Commonwealth Office	+62.5	+0.1	+0.2	+33.3
Health	+57.3	+1.0	+2.5	+18.1
Welsh Office	+52.6	+0.1	+0.3	+20.0
Social Security	+51.0	+1.9	+4.8	+13.6
Cabinet Office	+50.0	+0.1	+0.1	+12.5
Relative Losers				
MAFF	+35.3	same	same	same
Scottish Office	+23.5	same	−0.3	−7.3
Northern Ireland	+15.5	same	−0.6	−12.8
M.o.D.	+11.2	−0.5	−2.7	−16.4
Employment	+10.7	−0.1	−0.4	−17.4
Chancellor's departments	+6.3	−0.1	−0.5	−19.2
Overseas Development Admin.	0	−0.1	−0.5	−27.8
Losers				
D.o.E.	−29.7	−0.6	−2.5	−48.1
DTI	−51.7	−0.4	−1.5	−65.2

Source: Cm. 2219: tables 2.4, 4.2, and 4.3.

and the impact on departmental programmes of the privatization programme. Spending wholly within the aegis of central government departments is probably more likely to be used by the key political actors in the process—Ministers and their officials—in their assessment of political 'success' and 'failure'.

Sixteen out of the nineteen departmental programmes grew in real terms during the 1978–9 to 1992–3 period. Of these, ten were unambiguous 'winners' using our analysis, that is departments whose spending grew in real terms and as a proportion of GDP and of total central government spending. The most significant percentage growth was recorded by the Lord Chancellor's and Law Officer's departments, whose programmes grew by 300 per cent in real terms. The Home Office's programmes grew by more than 118 per cent. A further four programmes—National Heritage, Transport, Department for Education, and the FCO—grew by more than 60 per cent during the fourteen-year period since 1978–9. All these programmes, however, had relative gains, as measured by their increased share of GDP and of total spending, of modest amounts, whereas social security spending grew by nearly 2 per cent of GDP and by nearly 5 per cent of total spending. Similarly, the Health Department's central government spending grew by 1 per cent of GDP and 2.5 per cent of total spending.

There were seven 'relative losers', departments whose programmes grew in real terms, or in the case of Overseas Development remained stable, but which represented a static or declining share both of GDP and of total spending. Of these, MAFF's spending grew in real terms on average by 2.5 per cent a year and that of the Scottish Office by nearly 1.75 per cent per year. Yet even growth of this level was insufficient to lead to an increased share of GDP or total spending between 1978 and 1993. If share of GDP is a yardstick, six out of the nineteen programmes were 'losers'. And if share of total central government spending is used, nearly half the departments were 'relative losers'.

The Departments of the Environment and of Trade and Industry were the two clear and unambiguous losers. Both departments suffered real declines in spending and they took a smaller share of GDP and of total spending in 1993 compared to 1978. On average, DTI spending fell by 3.7 per cent per year; and D.o.E.'s by 2.1 per cent per year. The decline in the D.o.E.'s total programme spend hides even more significant reductions in the separately analysed 'other environment' spending component, which fell by 60 per cent in real terms over the period; the housing component fell by a more modest 22.7 per cent.

RELATIVE PRICE EFFECTS

What does 'winning' and 'losing' mean in terms of the real resources available to departments and hence their ability to provide a given amount of goods and a given standard of service? An answer to this is far from easy and involves delving into the contested ground of the appropriate measure of the costs of providing goods and services, and the assessment of both input and output in relation to 'need' and 'demand' for those goods and services (Webb and Wistow 1983). The underlying question here is the extent to which 'winners' have really won. 'Winning', measured by the Treasury's criterion of the GDP deflator, may mean losing when the yardstick is the actual costs of a programme measured by a specific differential rather than general price index. The significance of the question is this: to what extent does the price basis currently used in PES discussions constrain the growth of public expenditure in general, and departmental programmes in particular?

The way spending is measured and which price base is used can be a highly charged and significant aspect of public spending management. Prior to 1982, volume planning was undertaken on the basis of *constant prices* at unique *survey prices*, that is expenditure in whole or part was measured in relation to prevailing price levels, roughly at the beginning of each Survey. Comparisons of plans and outturn between one Survey and another were virtually impossible (Heald 1983: ch. 8) and the construction of time-series data a formidable statistical exercise. These difficulties contributed to the crisis of control in the mid-1970s, as measurement in 'funny money' meant neither the departments nor the Treasury knew the cash costs of planned expenditure.

Cash planning was intended to remove such difficulties from the system. However, further problems have been created. While in principle the cash cost of expenditure was now fixed, the volume of goods and services purchased was no longer estimated, nor measured in outturn. It is difficult therefore to determine whether the cash limited expenditure purchases more or less goods and services. Despite some improvement over time in the amount of information presented by the Treasury, the impact of cash plans on service delivery is not transparent. A further complicating factor is the adoption of a definition of 'real terms' which excludes allowance for how much prices in the public sector rise or fall relative to prices in the economy as a whole (RPE). Such real terms figures do not purport to be, and are not, a reliable indicator of volume changes, particularly for individual programmes. Statistics on 'real growth' or decline, cuts or increases, are a minefield and are among the 'counters' used in the bid for more resources. It is important to construct a broader measure of the growth and decline of programmes which makes allowance for differential movements in costs, in order to assess the demands and pressures on individual programmes.

The price basis used by the Conservative Government and the Treasury (and used in our tables) is 'real terms', that is, cash outlays adjusted by the GDP deflator (inflation across the economy as a whole).

(Even this measure has been subject to distortion as a result of the fall in the value of sterling as discussed by the Treasury and Civil Service Committee 1993.) The Treasury has not explicitly provided either generally for the whole of public expenditure, or for each programme differentially, for any relative price effects, positive or negative. The argument for their exclusion is that they measure the costs of inputs; the more important measurement (in the view of the Treasury) is that of outputs, which provides an incentive to greater efficiency and productivity in the use of resources. Whether or not an allowance should be made, or an attempt made to measure the effects of differential price increases in and within programmes, is contested. Our concern is to ascertain the extent to which some or all departments have 'lost' through the PES system because their costs have been underestimated and resources underprovided. If departments are not able to compensate with gains made in efficiency and productivity increases—cutting costs or enhancing output—then with fewer real resources they may be unable to produce the same amount and/or quality of service. For example, if the health service requires an increase in resources in real terms of 2 per cent per year to provide the same level of service, because of the additional pressures of demographic and technological change, then the Treasury's analysis of real growth as measured by the GDP deflator understates the 'level funding' requirement (Levitt and Joyce 1987). Using GGE data provided in Table 21.1, health and personal social services grew by 58.2 per cent, whereas in terms of differential cost pressures it grew by only 30 per cent. This still represents 'winning' but less dramatically than the Treasury's raw data suggests, with programme growth averaging just over 2 per cent per year using this adjusted basis instead of 4.2 per cent derived from Treasury figures.

The dispute over health service funding in the 1980s is only the most obvious example of a more general issue. The political debate on the funding of the public services tends to concentrate heavily on analysis of the trends in spending. Analysis of education spending, for example, points up the problem: the apparent paradox of government claims that funding was going up in real terms and the constant criticism that the education system had poorer and poorer facilities. National Account figures for the volume of education spending show that education spending by local authorities, expressed in 1985 prices, fell steadily during the early 1980s, reaching a low point in 1985. This was followed by volume increases, so that by 1988 spending had returned to 1979 levels, only to dip slightly in 1989 and 1990.

Other analysis (Johnson 1990) suggests that the Treasury's 'real term' index understates the costs of financing General Government Expenditure on goods and services by about 0.8 per cent per year in the 1980–

TABLE 21.3. *Relative price effects, 1980–1989*

Item	% change[a]
Public-service pay	+1.5
Defence	+0.4
NHS	+2.0
Education	+1.1
General government goods and services	
Final consumption	+1.1
Fixed capital	−2.2
Total public expenditure	+0.8
Personal transfers	−0.3

[a] The degree to which prices in the public sector rise faster (+) or slower (−) than prices in the economy generally. These figures are compound % averages, with the base year 1979.

Source: Based on Johnson 1990: 74.

9 period. That is to say, for the public sector as a whole, the relative price effect since 1980 has been positive. Specific measures of the relative price effect for some of the main programmes are reproduced in Table 21.3. If we adjust some of the data produced in the earlier tables for this analysis of the relative price effect the pecking order between departments alters. Thus, for example, the real growth of education spending in GGE terms over the 1978–9 to 1992–3 period is reduced from an average of 1.8 per cent a year to 0.7 per cent; and that of defence from 0.8 per cent a year on average to less than 0.5 per cent per year. In other words, for at least one of the 'winners' and two of the 'relative losers', programmes grew by less when the Treasury's data is revised to allow for the relative costs in the public sector.

The Treasury argues that some allowance for the historic movement of prices greater than that measured by the GDP deflator may be admissible, but that the relative price effect on a programme-wide basis is not (the reasons for this were explained in Chapter 12). In addition, the Treasury is critical of such statistics because they measure inputs (expenditure and costs) not outputs (the quality and volume of service provided). There is, however, no reliable and accurate method of measuring the relative outputs of the nineteen programmes analysed here; certainly the Treasury has no such method. But if we use specific RPE figures for defence, health, and education and then the average RPE figure produced by Johnson for general government spending for

TABLE 21.4. *Real growth adjusted for RPE, 1978–1993*

	Real growth			
	GDP deflator		RPE adjusted	
	TOTAL (%)	Average (%) p.a.	TOTAL (%)	Average (%) p.a.
Law and order	+95.7	+6.8	+84.5	+6.0
Social Security	+65.0	+4.6	+53.8	+3.8
Health and personal social services	+58.2	+4.2	+30.2	+2.2
National Heritage	+30.0	+2.1	+18.8	+1.3
Transport	+28.4	+2.0	+17.2	+1.2
Education	+25.5	+1.8	+10.1	+0.7
Other environment	+22.1	+1.6	+10.9	+0.8
Overseas services	+20.7	+1.5	+9.5	+0.7
Agriculture	+14.3	+1.0	+3.1	+0.2
Employment	+13.8	+1.0	+2.6	+0.2
Defence	+11.2	+0.8	+5.6	+0.4
Housing	−52.4	−3.7	−63.6	−4.5
Trade, Industry, and Energy	−55.4	−3.9	−66.6	−4.8

Source: Based on Cm. 2219: tables 2.3 and 2.4; and Johnson 1990.

all other GGE programmes, a different picture emerges of 'winning' and 'losing'. This is shown in Table 21.4. While no programme moves from being a winner in terms of real growth in spending to suffering real cuts in allocation, the 'losers' lose more heavily and all winners fare less well. When the GDP deflator is used there are five programmes which grew by more than 2 per cent per year and ten which grew by more than 1 per cent per year on average. When RPE is included there are only three programmes which grow by more than 2 per cent and only five which grow by more than 1 per cent.

Several factors potentially contribute to the explanation of the variation in departmental expenditures. However, Dunsire and Hood's analysis (1989) of the pattern of growth and decline of departmental programmes for the period 1974–85 found no unambiguous correlation with any of their four main explanatory factors, ideology, socioeconomic trends, bureaucratic behaviour, and departmental structure and organization. We take issue with their analysis and conclusion on a number of counts. First, 'bureaucratic behaviour' and 'departmental structure and organization' provide only for the 'way of working' within departments; they do not measure the interaction between the Treasury and the spending departments in the PES processes described in previous chapters. Indeed, Dunsire and Hood nowhere mention the Survey, nor explicitly allow for the possibility that the 'ways of working' in the PES processes, which determine the total and allocation of expenditure in a given year, may be a factor in explaining the pattern of expenditure. Second, their analysis is insensitive to the structural and organizational elements which help to define those relationships, such as the size, structure, and organization of the Treasury's Expenditure Divisions on the one hand and the spending departments' Finance Divisions on the other. More seriously still, their analysis does not allow for the political prioritization of different expenditure programmes. While they accept the existence of 'political clout', by which they mean the status and seniority of Cabinet and non-Cabinet Ministers, they found no positive correlation between it and obtaining a greater share of resources or ability to resist cut-back. However, Treasury and departmental officials interpret political clout as the power which derives from the collective agreement of ministers to afford a programme or a part of a programme greater priority in the PES allocations. On that interpretation and from the prima facie evidence of our analysis of 'winners and losers' we hypothesize that since 1985 there has been a stronger correlation, and perhaps causal relationship, between ideological factors (here, Conservative Governments' expenditure priorities) and the pattern of allocation. Our reasons are, first, that after 1983 the sale of public sector assets led to the run-down of some sponsor departments like Energy and DTI, and a steep decline in programmes associated with those sales; secondly, the introduction of the 'enterprise culture' in 1988 led to a retrenchment in regional and general aid for industry; and thirdly, after 1985 the change in priorities initiated through incremental adjustments to other programmes (for example, the programmes of the Home Office and Lord Chancellor's department) began to come through in the spending trends.

The extent to which 'winning and losing' is affected by the intrinsic properties of the PES system is more difficult to determine, but there is evidence that over time the cumulative results of a decade's marginal year-by-year decisions were in accord with the Conservative Government's broad political objectives. Moreover, the PES system has been the medium for the implementation of *changing* priorities and preferences over time. The patterns of expenditure on both the defence and roads programmes provide two such examples. Between 1985 and 1993

PART VI

Effects and Effectiveness

22

The Effects and Effectiveness of the PES System

The effectiveness of the system for planning and controlling public expenditure can be assessed in a number of different ways according to the criteria used. Success or failure in helping governments to achieve their broad objectives for public expenditure is one such measure, although as we saw in Chapter 20 when we compared objectives and achievements, other factors besides the system have to be taken into account when making such an assessment. The extent to which the system enables the Chief Secretary to achieve through the PES processes the Planning/Control Total targeted at the July Cabinet, and then through in-year monitoring and control to avoid overspending (or underspending) that total, provides other criteria for an assessment. We use them in the next chapter, where we discuss more generally the effectiveness of the Treasury's control as a constraint on the growth of public expenditure. In this chapter we use two other criteria: first, we assess the effectiveness of the system for making decisions about public expenditure, for regulating the interdependent relationships of the Treasury and the spending departments, described in earlier chapters. Secondly, we assess the extent to which the system provides for the participation of Ministers collectively in the processes of deciding the priorities of both the total of public expenditure and its composition. In the conclusion we directly address the issue of whose interests are best served by the system.

THE SURVEY AS A REGULATORY SYSTEM

How effective is the Survey as a system for making decisions about public expenditure? To put it another way: how effective is it as a system for regulating the relationships of those who make decisions about public expenditure? PES is a universal system for deciding about public expenditure. This is an important advantage to both Treasury and departmental officials. All decisions about public expenditure issues are taken within the Survey processes during the annual round, or by reference to it at other times of the year. When expenditure is committed by Treasury agreement 'in-year', outside the Survey round, it is done so in the context of what has already been agreed in total or by programme allocation, by claim on the Reserve for the existing year, or by reference to agreements on those categories for future years. When such commitments are made they are subject to review within the next Survey. Although Treasury agreement may have been obtained, a department has to bid afresh for that expenditure. There is no automatic right to it; the expenditure will be obliged to compete with other claims from the same department, and compete with bids from other departments. There are no off-Budget expenditures, as in the USA, or numerous special accounts, as is the case in Japan. The Survey is the focus for all expenditure decisions.

Universality underpins the effectiveness of the Survey as a system for regulating the interdependent relationships of the insiders within the Whitehall expenditure community, principally Treasury and departmental ministers and officials. It brings them together and it keeps them together. The 'insiders' identified in Chapter 9 comprise a small, permanent, stable, cohesive, and exclusive policy network focused on the Survey processes. Membership is precisely defined by the circulation list of the Survey *Guidelines*, some 200 officials (and their Ministers) from the Whitehall spending departments. The inner core of key members is equally defined by the PFOs of the nineteen principal spending departments and senior Treasury Expenditure Controllers. Relationships within the policy network are regulated by policy rules which determine the agenda of expenditure issues and how they are handled, and behavioural rules which govern the conduct of the members towards each other when they transact expenditure business. Those rules are prescribed formally and informally in the Survey processes, for example in the *Guidelines*, the rules for revaluing the baseline, the procedures for bidding, the preparation (formerly) of Agenda Letters, the conduct of the bilaterals, and so on. There is also the tacit acceptance and observance of behavioural rules which determine the kinds of information and argument to be used in support of bids, the mode of exchange, and the use made of information thus obtained; for example rules about levels and modes of communication, legitimate enquiry, prior notification, reasonable and unreasonable behaviour.

The Survey provides an efficient and effective means of regulating the expenditure business which Treasury and departmental ministers have to determine year by year. The processes of deciding are known, clear, automatic, and comprehensive in their coverage of expenditure business. Both Treasury and departments benefit, but not equally. The distribution of resources of authority, information, and expertise among them is asymmetrical and varies over time and by issue. For example, the Treasury possesses latent resources of constitutional and hierarchical authority which it draws upon infrequently, usually at moments of great economic or financial crisis, as with the introduction of cash limits in 1976, cash planning in 1983, the New Planning Total in 1988, and the New Control Total in 1992. Even then, its preferred strategy will tend to be negotiative rather than directive or impositional. Conversely, Cabinet commitment to a new policy initiative may enhance the statutory and hierarchical resources possessed by a departmental minister and his officials. Informational and technical resources are distributed asymmetrically too, and on any issue may be possessed in greater or smaller amounts by the Treasury and departments, and used up or hoarded according to preferred strategies.

Because the relationships are interdependent, all participants are concerned to maintain them in a good state of repair while simultaneously seeking to maximize their individual values on any issue. Outcomes are constrained by the need to ensure that they are mutually acceptable: the objective is win/win rather than win/lose, or at least the possibility of representing the outcome as the former rather than the latter. The Treasury and spending departments are constantly engaged in a trade-off between the values represented by certain preferred outcomes and those of maintaining good and stable relationships. On some issues, and over time, some players will win or lose more than others. But all will expect, over time, to win sufficiently to make the game worth playing according to the prescribed rules. In a policy network, disaffected losers have two options: voice and exit (Hirschman 1970). The latter is impossible for organizations which departmental ministers and officials represent, although individual ministers may threaten resignation or resign on a particular expenditure issue. Where key players perceive that their interests are disadvantaged by the current rules of the game they will use their voice to seek to change them, normally but not invariably within the network. The separation of programme expenditure from running costs in 1986, and the introduction of the New Control Total in 1992, are recent examples of changes in the rules initiated by the Treasury, which felt disadvantaged in its attempt to maximize its value of controlling the aggregate of expenditure. The introduction of the end-year flexibility scheme in 1983 is an example of a departmentally inspired change in the rules, which arose principally from the frustration of the M.o.D. and D.o.T. that they were disadvantaged by the rules governing underspending on capital projects. The campaign to provide more flexibility in the provision of carry-over was conducted and sustained publicly outside the network, when it became apparent that the Treasury would not agree to a negotiated solution within it. Had more key members brought pressure to bear on the Treasury, it is probable that a scheme would have been introduced much earlier. Most, however, believed the benefits were only marginal to their interests.

While the Treasury's core position in the network normally enables it to take the initiative in the introduction of changes or new policy rules, for example the annual revaluation factor to be used in the update of baseline expenditure, or the efficiency savings on running costs, it needs the support and approval or acquiescence of the principal participants. Thus there are behavioural rules for changing existing policy, and behavioural rules which incorporate notification, prior consultation, and discussion, even negotiation and bargaining. Major changes such as the introduction of cash limits or cash planning have to be discussed and approved by, at least, the key members of the network. Departments may be irritated by the effects of some changes, running costs and management plans being two current examples (but not cash limits controls), but their frustration and complaint are normally about conditions of uncertainty, such as in the preparation and subsequent use of management plans required by the Treasury under the new running costs controls, or the breach of unwritten rules of behaviour by some Expenditure Controllers, who allegedly act 'irrationally', or without prior warning, or who use information acquired from departments' Finance or Policy Divisions 'illegitimately'. Expenditure Controllers have similar complaints of occasional breaches of the rules of the game by their opposite numbers in departmental Finance Divisions.

The stability of the policy network and its permanent, almost unvarying membership, its control of the agenda, and its rules of the game make it a highly effective means of regulating the relationships of those Treasury and departmental ministers and officials who make and carry out expenditure decisions. Effective is not optimal. Objection can be raised to the underlying premiss that making decisions about public expenditure is about designing and operating a closed system to regulate relationships predicated upon interdependence. Alternative systems—more open, more inclusive—could be envisaged in which the role played by the central strategic co-ordinating authority was either more, or less, directive than that currently played by the Treasury. Here we confine our assessment to the purposes outlined earlier.

On its own terms the Survey disadvantages 'outsiders'. Parliament and its committees participate only at the conclusion of the Survey processes, when the Autumn Statement/Unified Budget is published in November. Their contribution to those processes in the preceding ten months is negligible; at best, they may hope to have an indirect influence through the scrutiny and examination of past expenditure plans. *Ex post facto* accountability, for example through the Select Committee on the Treasury and Civil Service, has had some influence on those processes. There the annual examination of Treasury ministers and officials provides the opportunity for discussion about a whole range of Survey issues, and in several cases has prompted important changes of both substance and procedure.

The Survey processes were neither open nor transparent throughout the years 1976–93. Neither Parliament nor the public had any direct share in the remit given to the Chief Secretary by the Cabinet in July to conduct the bilaterals which provided the context within which the size of the Planning/Control Total emerged in November. The contents of the Bidding and Agenda Letters were not divulged, nor the Treasury's reaction to them. Bilaterals were conducted in secrecy, the only clue to the issues and size of disagreement provided by occasional strategic leaks to the media employed by both sides to enhance their bargaining positions. The November Planning Total and the Autumn Statement were published as *faits accomplis*. The changes introduced in 1992 have done little to increase the openness and transparency of the PES processes. The options for the allocation of the New Control Total to programmes which the Chief Secretary brings to successive meetings of EDX and full Cabinet are not formally published. Final allocations are decided without reference to Parliament and are published as a *fait accompli* in the November/December Budget.

Public spending authorities excluded from the network are prima facie disadvantaged. Local authorities, public corporations, and Next Steps Executive Agencies deal mainly with the Treasury at second hand, indirectly through their sponsor departments. They do not bid directly, nor negotiate with the Treasury Expenditure Divisions, nor participate in ministerial bilaterals. Above all, they do not help to make and shape the rules of the game by which the business is conducted. Complaints from local authorities and their associations at their exclusion from the Survey processes are long-standing and continuous, despite, or because of, their subsidiary role in the decisions on the aggregate levels of local spending. The Consultative Councils have not met since 1980. The lack of direct representation for public corporations and Next Steps Agencies is a cause of similar expressions of frustration and frequent complaint that their case is not always adequately presented or firmly argued by their sponsoring departments. It is impossible to determine whether the lack of 'insider status' means that they are losers from the system.

SYSTEMIC EFFECTS

To what extent does the Survey system or its operation predispose particular types of outcome? More narrowly, does the Survey have in-built bias? The significance of this for our discussion of effectiveness is that, if there is bias, the distribution of any consequential benefits conferred or disadvantages experienced as a result may make it more or less effective as a planning or control system. In other words, independently of the objectives of the government and Treasury officials, the design and operation of the Survey system may predispose the results in particular ways. We limit our analysis to system-wide effects; the effects on individual programmes require a more elaborate and extended analysis of the kind conducted by Dunsire and Hood for the period 1974–85 (Dunsire and Hood 1989). We return to this issue later.

If we compare the effects of the introduction of cash limits and associated changes in Treasury and departmental financial management systems in 1976 with the pre-existing Survey system, *pace* Heclo and Wildavsky, it was easier for spending departments to win than lose. This was so for two main reasons: first, once new expenditures had been incorporated into the annual Survey through the then PESC processes, it was difficult for the Treasury to get them out. Spending departments could exploit the system to gain and maintain advantage, in addition to the political priority that any programme might be accorded in a Survey round. The rules of the game of expenditure politics before 1976 were such that there were few losers among the spending departments. A major cause of this was the second factor, the method of costing the prices of goods and services in unique Survey prices related to volume inputs. With hindsight, it is obvious enough that volume planning was inherently expansionary. Departments were able to finance an agreed planned volume almost irrespective of its money cost. The inability to distinguish increases in real terms costs from increases in volumes enabled departments to let their programmes grow. These were not the only causes of the growth of public expenditure before 1976 (see Peacock and Wiseman 1961; Heald 1983), but the in-built expansionary bias of the Survey system was a major contributory factor.

Very different systemic effects were said to be observable in the years 1976–8, following the introduction of cash limits. A common criticism at that time was that the operation of the new control regime, in conjunction with an explicit pay policy for public sector employees, had the effect of constraining the growth of public expenditure. Evidence for this new negative bias in the system was apparently provided by a decline in total public spending for 1976–7 and 1977–8 greater than that planned by the Labour Government. It was argued (see, for example, Heald 1983) that the implementation of cash limits resulted in 'back door' cuts in programme allocations. As the costs of those programmes incorporated target figures for pay and prices set below the estimated rates of inflation, those unable to achieve sufficient efficiency gains to compensate for loss of resources experienced cuts and squeezes. Added to this was greater uncertainty about the impact of the new regime on cash flow: managers were understandably cautious in controlling cash flow to avoid breaking the new limits or running out of money before the end of the financial year.

The effects of that proclaimed in-built negative bias were soon over-shadowed by the resumption of growth as the Labour Government returned to the more familiar policy objective of expanding pro-grammes in the run-up to the 1979 general election. Cuts made to placate the IMF were restored, public sector pay policies collapsed, and line managers became more experienced in delivering nearer to the cash limit.

Cash limits were introduced at a time when cuts in public expenditure were enjoined upon the Labour Government by the crisis conditions of 1975–6. Their conjunction obscured the extent to which cash limits and the tighter financial discipline implied by the concurrent changes in financial management systems introduced a negative bias into the Survey processes. If we take a longer time-horizon, beyond the years 1980–4 when the Conservative Government tried to cut the aggregate in real terms, we can better estimate the effects of cash limits, in times of intended and unintended growth as well as decline.

Since 1976 Treasury rhetoric has consistently and persistently empha-sized that cash limits are immutable, and that managers must learn to manage their programmes within them. Treasury practice has proved otherwise, as we have shown in Chapter 17. From the outset, the fears of spending departments and their sponsored agencies and organizations that prescribed cash limits could not be revised in-year proved ground-less. The need to accommodate additional expenditure pressures, and to provide for more managerial flexibility in operating programmes, belied the Treasury's own tough rhetoric. This is not to deny that cash limits imposed a tougher discipline of financial control in which line managers were expected to live within prescribed cash allocations. Nor to deny that line managers and street bureaucrats in local authorities, hospitals, and schools frequently exhausted their limits before the end of the year and often received no supplementation: tightly set cash limits have imposed real terms cuts and squeezes. But these effects of cash limits are due less to the prescription of *fixed* limits than the allocations negotiated by spending departments with the Treasury which they incorporate. Cuts and squeezes which resulted from the implementation of tightly drawn cash limits were the result of (perceived) inadequate allocations, and the failure to persuade the Treasury to agree to revise the original cash limit when line managers were in danger of exhausting their allocation before the end of the financial year. What was different was the ending of the automatic entitlement to additional expenditure (through Winter and Spring Supplementary Estimates) to finance a previously agreed volume of expenditure.

Cash limits derive directly from the programme allocations negotiated with the Treasury; they are not imposed upon departments, although it is true, until their abolition in 1986, that the pay and price revaluation factors which were incorporated within them were nonnegotiable, and in most years, deliberately or otherwise, underestimated the rate of inflation and hence imposed a squeeze. But cash limits were not primarily intended to be used as a means of cutting or squeezing the public expenditure aggregate. Their prime objective was to ensure that the Treasury could control the outturn of cash limited expenditure and deliver the total planned. The argument that cash limits also constrain public expenditure is tenable only if it can be shown that their effect is to hold down expenditure below levels fixed in the limits. That they constrain the growth of public expenditure beyond the limits fixed is true and their *raison d'être*. If prescribed cash limits remain unchanged, and line managers are obliged to live within them whatever the local (or macro-economic) pressures for additional or new spending which might arise in-year, then it could perhaps be argued that, as operated, inflexible cash limits have introduced a negative bias into the system. In practice very little such bias exists. Pressures for additional spending in-year, and the need for flexibility in the management of programmes, have obliged the Treasury, *from the outset*, to allow cash limits to be revised. As we have shown, changes are common, not exceptional; most are to accommodate increases to programmes.

In one important respect, however, the operation of cash limits controls does have a negative effect. The evidence is unambiguous: underspending on the aggregate of cash limited programmes is a persistent and consistent phenomenon. Each year between 1 and 2 per cent of total cash limited expenditure on central government programmes is underspent, equal in some years to more than £1 billion of public spending. Underspending on cash limited local expenditure (mainly capital) and the EFLs of public corporations has occurred also, but less regularly. The phenomenon of shortfall, as it was once called, is not new or peculiar to cash limits. It has been associated with the Survey from its inception. Until 1983 an estimate was included as an offsetting item in the Planning Total. The causes of underspending vary. While aggregate underspending is fairly predictable, its incidence within and between programmes is random and hence cannot be provided for in setting cash limits for individual programmes.

The phenomenon of underspending on cash limited programmes benefits Treasury ministers and officials seeking to control the aggregates of the Planning/Control Total. Underspending is added to the Reserve, which together with additional (above £5.5 billion) privatization receipts provides a bigger cushion for spending. It also provides a substantial offset for any overspending which occurs elsewhere on non-cash-limited programmes. It is, then, an important means of obtaining a better control of the aggregate Planning/Control Total. It is arguable whether Treasury encourages underspending by departments, through the operation of a tacit norm that departments should aim to deliver an underspend of about 2 or 3 per cent on each of their cash limits. Treasury officials admit only that the Treasury 'acquiesces' in the underspending. Predictable aggregate underspending also enables the Treasury to provide more flexibility in the system without the risk of loss of control. With a regular and predictable cushion of aggregate underspend (in some years more than £2 or £3 billion) it can respond to pressures for additional spending in-year by agreeing to changes in cash limits without the risk of exceeding the Planning/Control Total. Spending departments benefit from that greater flexibility; governments aiming to control the growth of total public expenditure benefit—additionally in times of economic constraint—from an unplanned reduction in the provision and consumption of collective goods and services. Some spending departments and agencies lose from this negative bias. Unspent allocations on cash limited programmes are not rolled forward, to be added to next year's allocation, except in the special circumstances provided by the capital end-year flexibility schemes introduced in 1983 and running costs end-year flexibility scheme introduced in 1988. The eligibility of expenditure items on which unspent allocations may be carried forward is strictly defined under those schemes, and the aggregate effect of the carry-forward does not substantially limit the advantage to the Treasury of the aggregate underspending noted above. Consumers lose, denied at the margin a legitimate expectation of an allocated quantum of public expenditure.

The operation of cash limits control exacerbates the phenomenon of aggregate underspending which has characterized PESC since its establishment in the 1960s. As a result, the annual outputs of some departmental programmes are less than planned, and to that extent the operation of the system of planning and controlling public expenditure has an inherent negative bias. The extent to which PES predisposes particular kinds of output, other than aggregate underspending, is more difficult to determine. Here we need to distinguish any bias in the system which exists as a result of the methodology of calculating and projecting forward the estimates of the costs of programmes, from that which inheres in the processes of making decisions about the allocation of expenditure—the characteristics of the interaction between the Treasury's Expenditure Divisions and the Finance Divisions of the spending departments. We need to determine whether the nature of the game, with its paradigm of negotiated discretion and the consequential policy and behavioural rules of the game, predisposes expansionary or contractionary outcomes, as measured by the trends of the Planning/ Control Total and the outputs of departmental programmes. We defer discussion of that broader issue, of the effectiveness of the PES system as a brake on the growth of expenditure, until the next chapter. Here we limit the discussion to the methodology of calculating costs and prices.

The most significant change in methodology after 1976 was the abandonment of volume planning and the use of RPE associated with it. Calculations in cash have made it more difficult for departments to expand their programmes by exploiting 'own cost' indices, although as we have seen in Chapter 11 the Treasury has been prepared to allow some departments to argue and receive compensation for the historic movement of prices in some programmes. Further, as we argued in the previous chapter, the use of the GDP deflator rather than RPE has had the effect of depressing all programmes. To that extent there is a negative bias in the system. The use of a general rather than programme-specific RPE is contestable, but in the Treasury's defence it can be argued that allowing fully for the movement of prices would partly reduce the incentive to seek greater efficiency through cost savings. The bias of the general GDP deflator has differential effects on programmes, according to the composition and relative weight of their inputs (pay, goods, services) and the movement of the prices and costs of each relative to the GDP deflator; the extent to which departments are able to 'make rather than take' prices and the scope for productivity gains through cost savings and output enhancement; and the extent to which, in some programmes like those for health, a given quantum of service costs more in real terms through improvements to the 'standard of service' which arise from technological developments.

Other changes in the policy rules of PES for calculating costs may also have or have had a contractionary bias. The prescription of general pay factors in the early 1980s set below the anticipated rates of retail inflation was intended to constrain pay costs, but was abandoned, partly because the general level of pay settlements exceeded those factors, as departments cross-subsidized from their programme budgets. Their replacement by running costs controls was intended to bear down more effectively on both pay and numbers, and to constrain the growth of overall departmental budgets. The general requirement of annual efficiency gains was intended to have a similar negative effect on all programmes. In addition, some programmes incorporated specific efficiency assumptions: from 1983 NHS spending allocations have included the assumption that regional health authorities would generate annual savings amounting to between 0.5 and 1 per cent of their budgets to fund part of the increase in resources spent on patient-care. The volume of any contraction resulting from these changes in the PES system is impossible to determine, because simultaneously other factors pulled in the opposite direction, contributing to the growth of some departmental programmes, and to the Planning/Control Total. It is possible that some programmes might have grown more quickly, or declined less quickly, without the constraining effects of the changes in methodology introduced in the 1980s. In the next chapter we discuss some of the causes of growth, and consider those which arise from the nature of the system before and after the changes introduced in 1992.

THE SURVEY AS EVALUATION

How effective is the Survey in ensuring that expenditure decisions provide value-for-money? To what extent is the output of a programme considered in relation to objectives, and the efficiency with which resources are used within the programme measured? To what extent are managerial cost-efficiency and cost-effectiveness factors considered in the allocation of resources among programmes?

Greater emphasis has been given to value-for-money since the early 1980s. Attempts are made to construct and use indicators of performance, but the extent to which the accumulated value-for-money data informs the decision-making process is more difficult to determine. It is not easy to separate the rhetoric of White Papers from the substance of Treasury and departmental practice. Much more data on performance and output is now collected by departments, responding to both the general emphasis given to attaining greater value-for-money in the Treasury, and the particular requests of its Expenditure Divisions. The quality of that data is variable and its use as a management tool to assess the efficiency and effectiveness of a programme problematic. Nevertheless, departments are required to justify the continuance of their baseline expenditures by some quantitative measure of output achieved and expected, and also to provide such data to support their bids for additional expenditure. Departments complain that Treasury Expenditure Divisions now ask for more and more data, whose purpose and subsequent use is not always clear to them. They suspect, and there is some evidence to support their suspicions, that Expenditure Controllers frequently reflect on to departments pressure from their own central divisions (Running Costs, Financial Management, and Pay) to obtain more quantitative information. On the evidence of one Treasury Second Permanent Secretary it was not easy at first to convince Treasury officials in the Expenditure Divisions that the government was serious about obtaining greater value-for-money, and that they should give effect to that purpose in their business with departments. There is, then, both an element of self-protection in the accumulation of value-for-money data in the Treasury Expenditure Divisions, and some reassurance in the collection and submission of that data by spending departments that they, too, are taking value-for-money seriously.

How much weight is given to information on performance, output, and achievement of objectives in the examination of departmental bids is difficult to determine, although it is much less than a reading of the Public Expenditure White Paper Departmental Reports, with their catalogue of more than 2,000 performance indicators, would suggest. We are confident that such data is not used to determine relative value-for-money between programmes, or that in a bilateral negotiation it often proves decisive.

While a department's bid is supported by value-for-money data, and Expenditure Divisions compare the returns on expenditure within a programme, there is no explicit comparison of value-for-money among programmes. Priorities are not determined, at the margin, by comparing the efficiency of resource use, or outputs achieved, across programmes. Input, intermediate output, and output data are not collected on a sufficiently uniform basis for such comparisons to be attempted.

The Cabinet decision in July 1992 to approve the Treasury's changes to the PES system, following the introduction of a New Control Total and the setting up of EDX (the Cabinet Public Expenditure Committee), offered the promise (at least in theory) of more explicit use of value-for-money and output data in discussions about how the total was to be allocated. In practice it has not done so. The Chief Secretary to the Treasury (Portillo) stressed that he did 'not want to claim that performance indicators played a great part in the Cabinet's discussion of that. It was more by way of a political discussion which I think is what one would expect' (Treasury and Civil Service Committee 1992: qu. 368). This led the Treasury Committee to press the Treasury to try and ensure that Cabinet Ministers 'have sufficient information to consider the efficiency and effectiveness, as well as the political merits, of individual programmes' (p. liii).

It is difficult to see how EDX would be able systematically to incorporate performance indicators into its discussions unless, with the support of Cabinet, Cabinet Office was encouraged to develop an analytical capacity to enable it to offer competing assessments to those of the Treasury. As before, in the bilaterals (and the Star Chamber), Ministers were free to use any information they thought best supported their case. No doubt Ministers appearing before EDX will show value-for-money and output improvements to argue their case for a larger share of the predetermined cake. The senior Ministers on the committee would not have the time, inclination, or information to contrast such *ad hoc* evidence with that provided by other colleagues. Besides, the Treasury services EDX, and the committee is chaired by the Chancellor; unless there is a sea change in the Treasury's use of such indicators it is unlikely that its briefing will move much beyond consideration of the political priority and salience of particular programmes and the broader questions of how a bid fits into other macro-economic objectives (such as the importance of capital programmes in the 1992 expenditure round). As the Treasury's Expenditure Divisions adjust to the changes, move still further away from detailed analysis of programmes, and concentrate more on the aggregates, their input into EDX discussions may include more performance-evaluation. How much of this could or would be taken into account by EDX Ministers is problematical.

THE SURVEY AS COLLECTIVE DECISION-MAKING

The effectiveness of the Survey processes may be assessed also by the extent to which they provide directly for the participation of ministers collectively in the decision-making processes, both at the time of deciding the aggregate Planning/Control Total and in the allocation between competing claims of the spending departments. This criterion was one of three which inspired the authors of the Plowden Report in 1961. We discuss first the position from 1976 up to the decision in 1992 to introduce the New Control Total and to unify the Budget, and then more briefly assess the effects of the changes made to the arrangements for collective decision-making which accompanied those decisions.

The July Cabinet which approved the recommendation of the Chancellor and Chief Secretary for the Planning Total did not normally engage in debate about the preferred size of public sector spending. This was partly because the recommended Planning Total was normally that written into the MTFS published at the time of the Budget, which was itself normally a confirmation of the total agreed at the conclusion of the last PES round and published in the Autumn Statement. It was also partly because Cabinet Ministers understood well that the final total in the following November, after the conclusion of the bilaterals, might well be greater than that recommended in July. Even at the November Cabinet, when Ministers were asked to approve the bilateral settlements and the Planning Total, there was little discussion of either.

Since July 1992, the Cabinet has been more explicitly involved in the process of determining broad public expenditure priorities, although its contribution remains marginal. Cabinet now endorses the Treasury's recommendation for the New Control Total for each of the Survey years: in 1992 that it should not grow by more than 1.5 per cent in real terms each year (equating roughly to a 2 per cent real growth rate for GGE—in line with the growth of the productive capacity of the economy as a whole). The Cabinet Committee, EDX, is then charged together with the Chief Secretary with the task of ensuring that allocations agreed for individual departmental programmes do not exceed the agreed total. And finally Cabinet has to approve the report of EDX on the allocations recommended to it. In practice, this involves a stronger commitment to the top–down totals than that agreed in the former Autumn Statement/Public Expenditure White Papers, which were supposed to be adhered to, but were invariably exceeded. Cabinet is now led more by the Treasury in the setting of broad objectives, with less room for the expansion of the total than previously, when bottom–up pressures from the departments proved almost always irresistible. EDX represents more than a further formalization of the previous role of the Star Chamber. The extensive use of Cabinet in debating and approving the report of EDX—there were extra evening sessions in November 1992 and five Cabinet meetings in all—moved PES back to the situation prevailing under the Labour Government in the late 1970s, albeit with the use of more sophisticated information. Moreover, Barnett's proposal that a small Cabinet Committee should review bids has finally been enacted.

In what sense then do Ministers collectively make expenditure decisions? To answer that we need to discuss the extent to which, both within the PES cycle and at other times of the year, Ministers collectively discuss the priorities accorded to public expenditure versus other claims on resources, and the priorities between one kind of expenditure and another.

The collective determination of priorities

At one level of explanation, it is true that the Cabinet collectively decided the relative priority of both the total of public expenditure and its composition when it approved the remit to the Chief Secretary in July and agreed to the allocation which emerged at the end of the Survey processes in November. At a deeper level, we need to determine the extent to which the Survey processes provided explicitly for a consideration of priority, and the collective discussion of it by Cabinet Ministers. Here we draw upon the material presented in Chapter 11.

Nowhere in the Survey were the bids for additional resources explicitly compared and ranked. While the Chief Secretary's expenditure strategy incorporated both a target for overall expenditure and judgements about the priority to be accorded his colleagues' bids for extra spending, consistent with Cabinet decisions about new or revised policies, Treasury officials in the Expenditure Divisions were concerned almost wholly with delivery to him of programme totals which, in aggregate, would achieve his target figure. Of course, in negotiations with individual departments, and in briefing for the ministerial bilaterals, Treasury officials were aware of the Chief Secretary's thinking about the relative priorities of his colleagues' programmes, but this fell well short of any concerted attempt to compare and weigh the relative merits of competing bids according to some economic or financial criterion. The efficacy of expenditure in terms of value-for-money measured by performance indicators was considered, if at all, programme by programme. Interprogramme comparisons were not attempted.

It is claimed that the 'Survey procedure is designed to give Ministers the fullest information on which to make their judgement within and across departments' (Treasury 1988c). The evidence suggests either that such information was not made available in a form which would enable Ministers to make comparisons; or, that that information was provided but largely disregarded. Treasury ministers and officials admitted that cross-departmental comparisons were not made systematically to determine relative priority in the Survey process or when 'in-year' changes were made. It is difficult to see how the results of a series of bilateral negotiations could provide, *faute de mieux*, the basis for Ministers collectively to make their own comparisons. At best, they would be presented with a set of *ad hominem* arguments and evidence about the merits of individual bids.

Whether or not they had the means to 'make their judgement', it could only be a partial and limited one. Not all bids were considered and compared at the same time collectively by the Cabinet and its committees. Those settled at the bilateral stage, or earlier still, were not reopened and compared with those unresolved. It is by no means certain that the priority afforded a claim settled in the bilateral, or at an earlier stage of the process, was superior to a claim unresolved in that process and taken to Cabinet or Cabinet Committee. Finally, there is little evidence that ministers had the opportunity or the political will to engage in such an exercise, even if the means to make cross-departmental comparisons were available to them. Cabinet spent little time at its July meeting on expenditure matters, while the purpose of the November Cabinet meeting and Star Chamber was more to resolve disputes than to determine priority in the way suggested.

It is difficult to resist the conclusion that the purpose of the Survey up to 1992 was less to determine priority than, in the words of a former Under Secretary in charge of the Treasury's General Expenditure Policy Division, 'to try to balance bids and savings and effectively juggle with them until it produces a new package but staying within the envelope' (Treasury and Civil Service Committee 1987c: qu. 7). It is more difficult to determine the extent to which priorities were discussed and decided continuously throughout the year, at a variety of points in the decision-making process, as Treasury ministers and officials asserted. The confidentiality of the proceedings of Cabinet Committees makes it impossible to confirm or deny such claims authoritatively. The anecdotal evidence of ministerial participants suggests that, at best, such consideration was not provided for regularly. It is true, however, that bids from spending ministers in the Survey incorporated and reflected Cabinet decisions which committed resources to new or revised policy; that commitment might have resulted from a broad review of existing policies. However, given the strength of departmental interests represented on Cabinet Committees, and in the official committees which prepared material, briefed, and advised them, it would be surprising if a decision to commit additional resources to a new or revised policy had resulted from the systematic comparison of the relative priority of both new and existing commitments.

In a formal sense, it is obviously true that the Cabinet collectively decided the relative priority of both the total and the different kinds of public expenditure. The outcome of the collective decision-making represented an order of public expenditure priority, both in total and in composition. The Cabinet indicated its preference for more or less public expenditure by its agreement or acquiescence in the Chief Secretary's proposals in July, and for more or less of particular kinds of public expenditure in its agreement to the allocation which emerged at the end of the Survey process in November. Of course, the Chief Secretary had to get it right, or else he would be unable to deliver each of his colleagues separately and get their collective approval. In that sense the allocation in the Planning Total represented an agreed order of priorities. But that prioritization was arrived at *ex post facto*. The order of priorities they then agreed to was the sum of a number of *ad hoc* decisions each determined on its merits, programme by programme, department by department, in bilateral negotiation with the Treasury.

It is, however, the nature of the criteria employed in those judgements which gave rise to concern and criticism. Here we refer to the different perspectives of the Chancellor and the Chief Secretary, the Cabinet collectively, and individual spending ministers; and the different kinds of rationality which may inform decision-making or be inferred from their behaviour. If the outcome of the bilaterals and the Star Chamber and Cabinet meetings was a Planning Total close to that which the Chancellor and Chief Secretary aimed at as part of broad macroeconomic strategy, then, however achieved, that total might be represented as 'rational' from their perspective, and defensible both politically and economically. From a different perspective, that of a spending minister whose claims for additional resources had not been wholly accepted, the total might look less economically rational. All the more if the Treasury–departmental negotiation had been followed by a less painstaking examination of comparative merits in the Star Chamber, and perhaps cruder bargaining still in Cabinet. But there is little to suggest that a departmental minister would be more satisfied with an unfavourable outcome because he felt that the process was more objective or 'rational'. Ministers would resent surrendering 'savings' on their programmes in order to finance increases of their colleagues' programmes which had been given a higher priority. Losing 'rationally' is still losing; winning, however contrived, is infinitely preferable.

A strength of the Survey system up to 1992 was that the Planning Total and its component parts represented a politically rational outcome, one that normally all Ministers were prepared to accept, however reluctantly, and which each Minister believed was defensible to his department's constituents. The extent to which the Planning Total achieved in the Autumn Statement was broadly consistent with the overall politico-economic strategy determined upon earlier by the government collectively, also represented a rational outcome. We would argue that the achievement of a politically rational outcome is a necessary but not sufficient condition of an effective system. Until 1992 it was its most important justification.

This interpretation derives from the adoption of the perspective of 'insiders' in the Whitehall expenditure community and empathy with the values inherent in their 'appreciative systems'. What are considered virtues and benefits by insiders are seen as weaknesses and disadvantages when viewed through the different perceptual lens of 'outsiders'— the line managers in local and regional spending authorities, and their clients and customers; and indeed managers in the Policy (but not Finance) Divisions and agencies of Whitehall spending departments. The determination of the Planning Total and its composition in PES and finally in Cabinet appeared to them to be too much influenced by subjective considerations, and political advantage decided by bargaining and 'horse-trading'; too little influenced by an economic, financial, or professional calculus, or by such considerations of user/consumer-rationality as the quality and reliability of service, equitable access, and fairness in distribution and delivery.

Such criticisms apply equally to the arrangements for the collective determination of priorities introduced in 1992. It is true, of course, that unlike the determination of the Planning Total, which rarely reflected what could be afforded, the New Control Total is decided after discussion of both medium- and short-term economic and financial objectives, and the available revenue to finance spending plans. But the priorities of programmes within that fixed total are still determined more by bargaining and horse-trading, albeit in the more rarefied atmosphere of Cabinet and its EDX Committee.

Cabinet is now more explicitly incorporated into the process. Rather than relying solely on the Chief Secretary to deliver an outcome for Cabinet, the new arrangements involve the Chief Secretary in acting as an intermediary between departments and EDX. The Chief Secretary continues to negotiate with colleagues to reduce 'excess' bids and to press for offsetting savings in programmes, but this has become a more politically sophisticated form of the 'ground-clearing' which preceded the bilaterals. Secondly, EDX is a permanent fixture in the PES process rather than an arbiter of last resort involved intermittently, as was the case with the Star Chamber. At the heart of the changes is a bargain: the Treasury has succeeded in gaining collective support for adherence to the overall ceiling on spending; in exchange Cabinet, initially through one of its committees, has gained a larger role in determining the allocation of the total. The Treasury is not a disinterested party. It remains involved in setting the agenda for much of the deliberations of EDX, provides the briefing for Ministers on the committee, and provides the chairman, the Chancellor. Moreover, Treasury officials remain vigilant that spending proposals with large expenditure implications for the future are not allowed to slip through. But the Treasury's involvement is more strategic and less proactive than previously. Thirdly, Cabinet Ministers are invited in the process to appeal to their senior colleagues on EDX and then to Cabinet itself, using the language of political priority and political expediency to support their spending proposals.

Does this represent a more rational way of collectively determining spending priorities? Compared with the previous approach, Cabinet is more explicitly involved. But this is more a case of moving the political horse-trading and incremental adjustments from the set-piece bilaterals between Ministers and the Chief Secretary to set-piece appearances before EDX and then later before Cabinet. It remains a political process of juggling competing demands, buying off some which have a high degree of political salience, rejecting those with lower priority. The recommendation of EDX in 1992 to impose a 1.5 per cent public-sector pay policy across the board, as a means of hitting the top–down New Control Total, shows the degree to which it became easier to obtain high-level support from influential members of the Cabinet for Treasury proposals to contain spending. To this extent EDX may represent a further dilution of Treasury hegemony over key aspects of macro-economic policy.

The political and politico-economic rationality which we have argued characterizes the system both before and after 1992 is seen by outsiders as a failure to prioritize, and an indication of the inappropriateness of the present arrangements of collective decision-making through Cabinet for deciding such issues (Dell 1985; Wass 1984; Heclo and Wildavsky 1974, 1981; Treasury and Civil Service Committee *passim*). It is argued, or assumed, that the priority determined by consideration of economic, financial, or other 'rational' criteria would be more objective and hence superior. It is by no means certain that the Cabinet would or should accept that the evidence of such calculations should outweigh or displace political judgement. That that judgement might properly be informed by other kinds of calculation and evidence which would contribute to a more informed, balanced judgement is undeniable. The difficulty lies in knowing what kinds of data are relevant and technically feasible, what weight to attach to them, and how they should be incorporated within the Survey processes. What is equally clear is that there is little evidence that the Cabinet or the Star Chamber or EDX is much influenced by either an economic or financial calculus. There is less still that Ministers have the collective will to change their preference for political bargaining. 'It is not that it is satisfactory; rather that it is the least objectionable of the possibilities to the major players in the game, for whom ambiguity means a welcome freedom of manœuvre' (Likierman 1988: 69). We return to the broader issue of improving the system in the concluding chapter.

WHO BENEFITS?

The Treasury has been the major beneficiary of the PES system since 1976. Its aim to regain the initiative and to reassert central control of public spending coincided with the changed attitudes and objectives of both Labour and Conservative Governments, which provided the opportunity, the stimulus, and the legitimacy for the restoration of those traditional values represented in its historic mission. The Treasury's overriding aim is to deliver the Planning/Control Total decided by Cabinet; it is much less concerned with the allocation of that total, although it helps the Chief Secretary ensure that political priorities are broadly reflected in the settlement agreed in the bilaterals. The primacy of this objective is reflected in the importance attached since 1982 to the cash aggregate of public spending rather than its volume or cost, and encapsulates the restatement of traditional Treasury values to control public expenditure. It is determined to avoid a recurrence of the disaster of the loss of control in the mid-1970s for which it was blamed. PES has been redesigned to give effect to the aim of delivering the Planning/Control Total and achieving financial discipline and tighter short-term control. Planning and allocating for a period ahead have become less important functions.

While the Treasury regained control in the 1980s, its operation of the PES system has not guaranteed consistent delivery of the Planning Total. As we have shown in Chapter 16, even since the use of the Reserve as a control mechanism from 1984, the Planning Total was over- and undershot. This was less the result of systemic incapacity or operational failure than the practical limitations imposed by the incompatibility of collective Cabinet government and individual ministerial autonomy. While the whole of the Planning Total was willed collectively on one occasion in July, the individual parts which comprised it were willed bilaterally on many separate occasions in the months that followed. Only at moments of rare, acute crisis did there occur a correspondence of collective and individual ministerial interests sufficient to ensure that what was planned collectively could be delivered by the exercise of political will by each minister separately. (Even then, there could be difficulties in securing the co-operation of individual ministers, as Barnett makes clear in his account of negotiations with his colleagues over cuts in the IMF crisis in 1976.) The agreement by Cabinet to the new 'top–down' control in 1992, in the circumstances of acute fiscal crisis, is one such example. Whether this will survive the inevitable 'bottom–up' pressures which occur in the run-up to a general election is open to doubt.

Conservative Governments benefited less from the PES system when a long rather than short perspective is adopted. The Thatcher and Major Governments clearly benefited from the changes made to PES to improve control after 1982. Notions of retrenchment, value-for-money, and efficiency in public spending were all within the grain of Thatcherite ideology. But there has been progressive scaling down in the ambition of overall spending objectives since 1979. Conservative Governments moved from espousing the aim of real cuts in the total, to stable real spending, to real growth but at a rate less than the growth of GDP over a medium-term period. More basically, attitudes towards public expenditure changed during the 1980s, partly because of the political imperative and other growing pressures to allocate more real resources to programmes, and partly because in two recessions the pressure for spending on income support and training programmes was irresistible. In the early 1990s the Major Government responded to pressure for increased quality of services in the NHS, education, transport, and the environment. This is a long way from the 1979 Public Expenditure White Paper, which labelled public spending as being at 'the heart of Britain's decline'.

The benefits to spending departments are less clear-cut. Their subscription to the PES system for regulating their relationships with the Treasury no longer provides a reasonable assurance that all or most will 'win', as it did in the early 1970s. In the previous chapter we argued that there have been real 'losers'. If many departments have lost 'real' resources (adjusted for both general inflation and the relative price effect) since the abolition of volume planning in 1982, then we need to explain why they have not exercised 'voice' more loudly—why there has not been more 'noise' in the system.

There are a number of alternatives, not mutually exclusive: first, the interdependent relationships are premised on a shared core-value: the orderly, annual regulation of public spending policies and processes

TABLE 22.1. *Planning Total, local authority, and central government spending*

	Planning Total[a]		Local authorities[b]		Central government	
	Cash	Real terms	Cash	Real terms[c]	Cash	Real terms
1985–6	100	100	100	100	100	100
1986–7	105.3	101.2	106.5	103.0	106.2	102.6
1987–8	110.8	101.6	113.9	110.0	111.1	101.9
1988–9	114.5	97.8	119.3	102.0	115.9	99.0
1989–90	125.2	100.6	133.9	107.5	126.9	101.9
1990–1	139.6	103.9	145.1	107.9	140.5	104.6

[a] Excluding privatization and other adjustments.

[b] Total local authority expenditure including grants from central government.

[c] Cash figures adjusted using the same deflators as for the Planning Total. No real term figures are provided in Treasury publications.

Source: Cm. 1311.

within the accepted context of collective government. The collective aim to cut back public expenditure outweighs any *ad hominem* argument about individual loss. Evidence of this accumulated in our discussions with Whitehall department officials, where it was apparent that each participant knew the 'score': the macro-economic objective of holding spending down as a proportion of GDP provided the overall context of spending discussions; and changing political priorities on certain programmes provided the specific context. Thus, given that both might change over time, and provided that Treasury officials and ministers acted 'reasonably', 'loyalty' rather than 'voice' was the appropriate response. Secondly, it might be argued that departments are able to manage their programmes to provide similar quantity and quality of service with less resources because of improved productivity or efficiency gains, and (implicitly) because they were overfunded.

The third alternative explanation is more complex: that central departments protect their own 'core budgets' (Dunleavy 1989*a*, 1989*b*) and deflect pressures to cut spending elsewhere: to local authorities; or cut back capital rather than current spending, and programme rather than administrative costs. On this argument key officials (and their ministers) in the system would have less inclination to protest. There is little evidence to support this hypothesis. Table 22.1 provides some data for the period up to 1990 on which to begin an assessment.[1] Table 22.1

[1] The frequency of classification changes since that date has made it difficult to construct reliable comparable data.

shows the growth of spending as defined by the Planning Total (which includes central government spending, support for nationalized industries, and grants to local authorities), total spending by local authorities, and central government's own expenditure. Since 1985–6, local authority spending has grown the fastest in real terms, followed by that for central government, and then the Planning Total as a whole. This does not support the view that local authorities have been used to deflect spending pressures at the centre.

As we discussed in Chapter 8, there is little support for Dunleavy's assertion that core budgets are protected. The real measure of the toughness of the running costs control regime is that it is the most controversial focal issue in Treasury–departmental relationships at the official level, although not at ministerial level. The running costs issue highlights the degree to which the interests of ministers and their officials also diverge: ministers want to press the Treasury on programme spending, even at the expense of administrative spending, whereas officials regard the running costs settlement as vital to enabling them to 'deliver' for their ministers, and necessary to maintain morale amongst staff.

Finally, it might be argued that the expectation of winning even a diminished share in real terms of a proportion of GDP is sufficient incentive to continue to play the game 'loyally'. 'Voice' is reserved for the constant argument between departments and the Treasury over the rules of the game, and the degree to which each side loses or gains flexibility (departments) or control (Treasury) as a result of their interpretation and implementation. The criticism of the running costs regime or the lack of flexibility in carrying forward underspending on capital spending (discussed in Chapter 19) are examples of spending departments exercising 'voice' at times quite loudly (if inaudibly to 'outsiders'). Within the policy network there is constant discussion, and sometimes disagreement over the rules of the game. What is at stake is the distribution of existing and additional resources of authority, information, and expertise, which affects the degree of interdependence and hence the room for manœuvre of the various participants to achieve greater satisfaction in the maximization of their values. At root this is an argument about central Treasury control and departmental managerial autonomy, and it is to that issue that we turn in the next two chapters.

23

Controlling Public Expenditure

The Treasury's historic and continuing 'mission' is to control public expenditure. Its traditions and values are those of a central strategic co-ordinator whose purpose is to provide resources to enable spending authorities to discharge efficiently and effectively their statutory obligations to provide goods and services, while protecting the interests of the taxpayer by ensuring that those resources are used economically and effectively. As the financing of the bids to provide those goods and services inevitably and invariably exceeds the resources which Chancellors believe prudent or necessary to devote to the public sector as a whole, control also means limitation and constraint. At certain times it may mean, and has meant, reductions in real terms. By tradition, belief, disposition, and habits of work, the Treasury's values are those associated with economy, the elimination of waste, and above all the protection of taxpayers' money. While this may be obvious enough, it is necessary to emphasize it here because Treasury ministers since 1979 and Treasury officials since the mid-1970s have, through the PES and 'in-year' control procedures outside the Survey, reasserted those traditional values. As argued in Chapter 3 the period of the 'high noon' of PESC, roughly 1968–74, in which uncharacteristically the Treasury presided over the rapid expansion of public expenditure, is perceived by the official Treasury to have been a disaster. While responsibility for the 'crisis of control' which followed in 1974–6 is disputed—profligate Conservative and Labour Governments of the early 1970s, with unachievable economic growth rates, and a Survey system which indexed the public sector against high rates of inflation all contributed—the Treasury was blamed for its inability to restrain growth.

The introduction and imposition of cash limits marked the end of the expansionary phase of public expenditure which the Treasury had presided over since the commitment of the Macmillan Government in the late 1950s to expand the public sector. Plowden and PESC which followed were the instruments, the means by which decisions about the growth of public expenditure were to be regulated. With hindsight they represented a radical departure from the Treasury's traditional attitudes towards public spending, and ultimately one of failure. Treasury officials have written, and continue to speak, of the failure of control in the mid-1970s, and the urgent need to re-establish and maintain it. The changes made to the PES since 1976 and its operation need to be assessed against that background.

Those changes were designed primarily to obtain a better, tighter control of expenditure. The abandonment of volume planning and the switch to cash planning in 1982, and the changes made then to the methodological rules regulating the price basis, were reinforced in 1984 by the redefinition of the Reserve and its use since then as a major tool of control. Together they provide graphic evidence of the devaluation of the planning and allocating functions in the Survey, and the predominance of the values of monitoring and control.

As we saw in Chapter 16, the changes to the Reserve were necessary because the Treasury needed to improve its control. As the estimating of non-discretionary expenditure became a more uncertain exercise in the mid-1980s, it became more difficult to predict what the outturn of total planned expenditure would be, and to ensure that that outturn more closely matched plans. The Treasury needed to provide for uncertainty in order to make public spending Planning Totals more realistic, as the Treasury Under Secretary in charge of the General Expenditure Division admitted to the Treasury and Civil Service Committee (1985*a*: qu. 147). If larger amounts of expenditure are left unallocated within a planned total, and the unallocated amounts are substantial in size, it is easier to control total outturn within a predetermined Planning Total, provided the margin is ample enough. The size of the Reserve as a proportion of the Planning Total was increased, and all 'in-year' measures, discretionary and contingent, financed from it. Thereafter, a larger proportion of the Planning Total was unallocated to programmes through all three years than was the case previously. One result of the change was that it became more difficult to assess the growth pattern of intended spending, programme by programme. Parliament and its Select Committees, and the informed public, were disadvantaged, and public discussion and debate the poorer. The Treasury appeared to be less concerned with 'planning the path', as it once was, and much more concerned with controlling the Planning/Control Total. 'It is the planning total which is crucial, not whether it has been allocated,' commented one senior Treasury official interviewed in 1990. That is an understandable reaction to the experience of the early 1980s. It is difficult, however, to resist the conclusion that the redefinition of the Reserve as a control mechanism for the whole of public expenditure, and the determination with which the new rules were enforced, further elevated the control function at the expense of planning.

Other changes to the Survey since 1982 point in the same direction of attempts to secure tighter and more effective control. The abolition of pay factors, and the separation of programme from running costs expenditure in 1986, ostensibly provided departments with more discretion and flexibility to decide (and trade off) manpower numbers and pay. But it also removed most of the discretion to switch between the two. At the same time, the Treasury continues to exercise detailed control through its scrutiny of management plans. In the rest of this chapter we assess the effectiveness of the Treasury's control in the light of these and other changes to the system. In the next, we discuss the difficulties of exercising tight control within the constitutional and practical limits imposed on the Treasury, and the tension which arises from the need to balance central control of the aggregate with discretionary authority for departmental managers in decentralized departmental financial systems to make and allocate budgets.

MEASURING THE EFFECTIVENESS OF CONTROL

How effective has Treasury control been in the period 1976–92? To answer that question we distinguish three different uses of the concept of control. First, the Treasury shares responsibility with the Finance Divisions of the spending departments for ensuring the propriety and regularity of expenditure, that money is spent only for those purposes determined by Parliament through the Votes, and in a form approved by the Treasury in accordance with prescribed accounting procedures. Together with the Accounting Officers of the spending departments and agencies, the Treasury is called to account by Parliament. The effectiveness of the Treasury's control for that purpose is not at issue. While the reports of the Comptroller and Auditor General and the PAC are sometimes critical of particular practices of the Treasury (and the spending departments), control in this narrow, technical, but important sense is largely effective.

Control is used in a second sense of the determining and delivery of the annual Planning Total, after 1992 the New Control Total. Through the Survey processes, the Treasury Expenditure Divisions collectively aim to deliver the total targeted by the Chief Secretary and the Cabinet in July. Subsequently, they aim to control the flow of cash allocated in the November Planning/Control Total through in-year monitoring and control mechanisms to avoid overspending (or underspending) that total. We examine each of these in turn.

Achieving objectives

One measure of the effectiveness of the PES processes in the achievement of the objectives set for a particular spending round is the extent to which the Chief Secretary and his officials succeed in delivering in November the Planning/Control Total targeted at the July Cabinet. The introduction in July 1992 of the New Control Total and the imposition of top–down limits was an explicit admission of the past failure of Chief Secretaries to deliver a planned total for the aggregate of public expenditure targeted in July. In theory the New Control Total agreed in July cannot be exceeded in the November Budget. Table 23.1 shows the record of all Chief Secretaries since 1979.

This measure does not indicate the intensity of the pressure on the Chief Secretary in the negotiations with his colleagues. While the tenor of the annual Survey *Guidelines* and the continuing Treasury rhetoric always emphasize the 'toughness' of the round in prospect, some years are more difficult than others. Difficulty for the Chief Secretary lies in the width of his negotiating margin, the difference between the targeted July Planning/Control Total and a November settlement consistent with the government's objective for public expenditure for the coming year. The 'envelope' within which he will negotiate with his colleagues will widen or narrow during the summer and early autumn, as revised estimates of GDP become available, inflation and employment move up or down, and the broad expenditure objective is revised to reflect changed political circumstances. The narrower the margin, the more difficult is the Chief Secretary's task. Since the introduction of top–down limits in the New Control Total, there is in theory no margin.

Pressure on him from his spending colleagues may make that task more difficult still. A measure of his effectiveness has therefore to include some element of the pressure of bids. A larger November Planning/Control Total than that targeted in July is not necessarily evidence of ineffectiveness. It may be within the envelope, and hence consistent with the government's expenditure objective. Where it falls outside, the final total may reflect the weight and pressure of his colleagues' bids, perhaps in response to demand-led expenditure increases due to changes in unemployment, or higher inflation during the progress of the Survey, rather than failure on his part.

The crucial variable over which he has no control is GDP. If GDP is estimated to increase in the coming year, then the share of public expenditure can increase without raising the GGE/GDP ratio, indeed it may fall as a result. Conversely, if GDP is expected to decline or remain

TABLE 23.1. *Planning Total: targets and outcome, 1979–1992* (cash, £bn)

	Chief Secretary (between July and Nov.)	July target	November Autumn Statement	Difference
1979	John Biffen[a]	74.5	70.5	−4.0
1980	John Biffen[b]	83.3	83.5	+0.2
1981	Leon Brittan	110.0	115.2	+5.2
1982	Leon Brittan	121.0	119.6	−1.4
1983	Peter Rees	126.4	126.4	0
1984	Peter Rees	132.0	132.1	+0.1
1985	Peter Rees/ John MacGregor	136.7	139.1	+2.4
1986	John MacGregor	143.9	148.6	+4.7
1987	John Major	154.2	156.8	+2.6
1988	John Major	167.1	167.1	0
1989	Norman Lamont[c]	179.4	179.0	−0.4
1990	Norman Lamont	192.3	200.0	+7.7
1991	David Mellor	215.0	226.6	+11.6
1992	Michael Portillo[d]	244.5	244.5	0

[a] Based on the plans of the previous Labour Government against the first Survey round of the new Conservative Government. The figures are in volume terms, converted to prices prevailing in autumn 1979 (1979 Survey Prices).

[b] The figures are in volume terms, converted to prices prevailing in autumn 1980 (1980 Survey prices). All other figures in the table are cash, following the introduction of cash planning.

[c] Figures set in terms of the New Planning Total.

[d] The New Control Total was introduced in this Survey. The figures here are those for the Planning Total, in order to provide consistency.

Source: Public Expenditure White Papers and Autumn Statements.

stable, even a constant share of public expenditure will be more difficult to attain. Chief Secretaries are fortunate if their period of office co-incides with a growing economy. With luck they can preside over growing public expenditure *and* a lower or stable GGE/GDP ratio: they can both deliver a Planning Total consistent with the broad public expenditure objective and accommodate more of their colleagues' bids. Conversely, Chief Secretaries who negotiate in times of recession have to run harder (negotiate more toughly) merely to maintain the same ratio, or to prevent public expenditure rising as a proportion of a static or declining GDP, in circumstances where the pressures to increase some kinds of (demand-led) expenditures are increasing.

Where the line is finally drawn between the totals represented by the Chief Secretary's targeted outcome and his Cabinet colleagues' 'bottom line' is also partly a function of the negotiating skills, determination, and mutual esteem and confidence of the contending parties. Tact, resolution, and the ability to deploy to the best effect the arguments and briefing material prepared by GEP and the Expenditure Divisions may make a marginal difference, especially where a Minister threatens to carry his case to Star Chamber or Cabinet. Both sides may seek, through carefully contrived leaks to the press of the progress of the bilateral, to demonstrate their toughness and inflexibility, and the intention to invoke Star Chamber procedures, or (since 1992) argue before the Cabinet's EDX Committee.

One difficulty in measuring the effectiveness of the PES processes in the period up to 1992, by comparing the November and July Planning Totals, is that the July total was explicitly stated by the Treasury (and Cabinet) as a target to aim for, or to get close to. Thus overshooting in November was not necessarily a failure, if there was no reasonable expectation in the Treasury that it could be delivered. In such circumstances the November outcome should be measured against what the Treasury aimed to try and achieve. This undisclosed calculation produced a band or envelope within which a settlement would be acceptable as broadly consistent with overall macro-economic strategy, and represented the Chief Secretary's negotiating margin. The 'bottom line' was the higher end of that band. The relative success or failure of the round thus depended upon the implementation of the Chief Secretary's strategy to deliver a Planning Total in November which fell within that band.

We cannot, however, read off success or failure from Table 23.1. The causes of over- or undershoot of the July figures are complex. As we have argued above, allowance has to be made for changes in key economic and political variables between July and November, in particular the revision of the estimate for GDP for the next financial year, which could affect judgements about what could be afforded and hence the width of the negotiating margin.

Appeal to the Star Chamber provides some circumstantial evidence for the period up to 1992. To the extent that the Treasury determined the November total without recourse to it, the negotiations were successful, as in 1983, 1984, 1988, 1989, 1990, and 1991. However, it does not necessarily mean that the Treasury achieved its real objective for the Planning Total where that announced in November was greater than that targeted in July, and appeal was not made to the Star Chamber, as in 1987, 1990, and 1991. The decision to appeal to the Star Chamber was the result of a calculation of risk, of winning and losing in conditions of greater unpredictability. Part of that calculation was an assessment of how necessary further cuts were to the achievement of the real objective. On balance the Treasury could decide to cut its losses, rather than risk losing more publicly. Hence the Planning Total achieved in November without the intervention of the Star Chamber could represent a marginal failure in the PES round to achieve the real objective.

The convening of the Star Chamber at the Treasury's behest was a symbol of failure to negotiate an acceptable settlement, but, again, was not necessarily an indication that the Treasury was looking for further reductions to achieve its objective for the Planning Total. It could indicate rather that the Treasury remained unconvinced by a department's argument in support of its bid, than that a reduction was necessary in order to achieve its objectives for the Planning Total.

Even such circumstantial evidence as this needs to be treated with caution. The institution and use of the Star Chamber was associated particularly with the style of Mrs Thatcher, and the early commitment of her governments to reducing public expenditure in real terms. The use of the Star Chamber between 1981 and 1986 and its neglect subsequently is partly to be explained by that context. There was a greater expectation that it would be used and willingness to use it, in circumstances in which public expenditure had risen rapidly. While public expenditure rose again towards the end of the decade, and sharply in the early 1990s, the Star Chamber was more of a deterrent invoked by both the Treasury and obdurate departmental ministers locked in interminable bilateral negotiations. The neglect of the Star Chamber in this period has also to be considered in the context of the loosening of the medium-term objectives for public spending, partly but not wholly in response to the recession which began in the late 1980s and which contributed to the fiscal pressure experienced in the early 1990s. Its replacement by Cabinet EDX Committees in the summer of 1992 signalled a reassertion of centralized control in an attempt to constrain the growth of spending in both the short and medium term.

Monitoring and controlling the outturn

Comparison of the outturn of aggregate public expenditure with the Planning Total set in November, to determine the effectiveness of the Treasury's in-year monitoring and control of cash flow, is bedevilled by the problems of changing definitions of public expenditure and time-series discontinuities in the data for the whole of the period 1979–93. Comparing outturn with planned expenditure is easier after the changes in the use of the Reserve from 1984 onwards because all changes to planned expenditure, whether as a result of new or revised policies in-year or unforeseen expenditures, were financed from the Reserve. Before 1984, policy changes were, in effect, counted as increases to the Planning Total. As Tables 23.2 and 23.3 show, the Treasury overshot its planned Planning/Control Total on nine occasions in the period 1980–1 to 1992–3. In percentage terms the most significant overshoots occurred in 1980–1 (as a result of spending on employment programmes and falling nationalized industry revenue, both caused by the recession) and 1984–5 (mainly as a consequence of spending which resulted from the miners' strike). In 1988–9 there was a 4.6 per cent underspend, mainly due to lower local authority capital spending (higher receipts from sale of council houses), lower grants to public corporations as a result of buoyant revenues in a booming economy, and higher privatization proceeds.

The causes of overspending on the outturn of aggregate expenditure are more difficult to distinguish, and vary from one year to the next. It may be due to a failure of the Survey processes, for example an underestimate of the costs of financing a programme where there is a non-discretionary expenditure, such as social security payments or unemployment benefits; or the occurrence in-year of unforeseen expenditures, such as the need to respond to natural disasters, war, or strike action; or general system inability to control certain kinds of expenditure, for example that of local authorities' current spending. The introduction of a New Planning Total, effective from 1989–90, was an admission that controlling that element of local authority current spending raised from local sources of finance had been impossible. The 'new' total included only that spending 'which is the responsibility of central government' (Cm. 441: 5). One immediate effect of this was that 'spending by local authorities of their own resources such as the community charge or use of receipts would not be part of the in-year control

TABLE 23.2. *Planning Total plans against outturn, 1980–1983*

	Plan (£bn)		Outturn (£bn)		Difference (£bn)		%
	Volume	Cost	Volume	Cost	Volume	Cost	
1980–1	79.25	79.95	80.6	83.0	+1.4	+3.07	+3.8
1981–2		104.48		105.2		+0.72	+0.7
1982–3		114.1		113.0		−1.1	−0.9

Source: Terry Ward's Memoranda to Treasury and Civil Service Committee.

TABLE 23.3. *Planning Total plans against outturn, 1983–1993*

	Plan (£bn)	Outturn[a] (£bn)	Difference (£bn)	%
1983–4	119.3	120.3	+0.95	+0.8
1984–5	126.5	129.8	+3.3	+2.6
1985–6	132.1	133.7	+1.6	+1.2
1986–7	139.1	139.2	+0.1	+0.07
1987–8	148.6	145.7	−2.9	−2.0
1988–9	156.9	149.6	−7.3	−4.6
1989–90[b]	161.9	162.9	+1.0	+0.6
1990–1	179.0	180.1	+1.1	+0.6
1991–2	200.3	203.5	+3.2	+1.6
1992–3[c]	226.6	226.1	−0.5	−0.2

[a] Based on plans in year one of PEWP and final outturn in PEWP two years later.

[b] Adjusted to New Planning Total figure, as are figures for 1990–3.

[c] Estimated outturn.

Source: Public Expenditure White Papers, Financial Statement and Budget Reports, and Autumn Statements.

arrangements and hence any variation from the figures in the Autumn Statement would not affect the Reserve' (p. 6). This removed one of the regular sources of overspend affecting the Planning Total. Although still counted as part of General Government Expenditure—the aggregate used for the setting of medium-term objectives—changes in local government's own spending were not part of the planning process. In practice this had no more than a presentational impact on planning and control procedures. Since GGE was then the bottom-line figure, the Treasury had cut real departmental spending to compensate for those areas not under direct central government control (Ward 1990: 57). What was once treated as an unavoidable overshoot on the Planning Total was now moved across to the non-Planning Total item in the GGE statistic. So whereas before departments were constrained by having a smaller Reserve to claim from in-year, their real programme growth was cut to compensate for higher local authority spending.

The New Control Total represented a reversal of this process. Local authorities' own expenditure was returned to the key control definition, and, therefore, in future overshoots will be a call on the Reserve. However, this adjustment has been balanced by the removal of cyclical social security expenditure, which during the recession has not only been a call on the Reserve but has been very difficult to forecast with any accuracy. The Treasury took the view that, on balance, these two changes would still lead to greater congruence between plans and outturn than under the previous system. This was an important part of the rationale for the decision to write into the NCT plans a smaller reserve for 1994–5 and 1995–6, at £7 billion and £10 billion respectively, than would have been the case if the pattern under the New Planning Total had been followed (see Portillo, Treasury and Civil Service Committee 1992: qu. 306).

Controlling the growth of public expenditure

Treasury control is also used and understood in a third sense, as limiting, constraining, or restraining the growth of public expenditure. In the remainder of the chapter we discuss why the Treasury has not been more successful in helping governments to achieve their objectives for limiting the growth of public expenditure in the medium term.

As we discussed in Chapter 20, Conservative Governments of the 1980s were more successful in controlling public expenditure, in the sense of limiting the trend rate of growth, than their predecessors in the 1960s and 1970s. The real growth of General Government Expenditure averaged 4.5 per cent per year during the 1960s, 3.2 per cent per year in the 1970s, and only 1.1 per cent during the 1980s (Cm. 2096, Autumn Statement 1992). This success is less impressive in the context of the fiscal crisis of the early 1990s. GGE is projected to grow at an annual rate of over 3 per cent in the four-year period 1990–1 to 1993–4, and only planned to slow marginally to produce an annual rate of 2.8 per cent in the period 1995–6.

Even the relative success of the 1980s was flawed. It was built on the impermanent and shifting sands of the 'Lawson boom', when GDP grew by an unsustainable annual rate of 5 and 5.5 per cent in the last half of 1987 and the first half of 1988 respectively, and continued to grow above trend rate until the last half of 1989. Moreover, public spending trends during the 1980s were not in line with the original objectives of 1979, which were that spending should fall in real terms and as a proportion of GDP. They were not even consistent with the modified objectives (officially acknowledged in 1984, but which had been effective since 1982) of holding spending steady in real terms. It was not until a further move of the goal posts in 1986 that policy became more aligned with spending trends, when the Government's objective was to see total spending (GGE), excluding privatization receipts, fall as a proportion of GDP. Even here 'success' only lasted for four years, as policy changed in 1990 and was couched in terms of expenditure taking 'a declining share of national income, while value for money is constantly improved' to allow for the fact that the recession had forced spending to rise.

What is clear is that public expenditure was not out of control, as in the mid-1970s, as a result of the exploitation of PESC by spending ministers. Since 1976, and in particular since 1982, the Treasury has employed a series of 'coping strategies' (Thain and Wright 1990*b*) aimed at keeping the lid on the inexorable pressure for spending to rise. This has included regular and sustained improvements to the PES system, making it more an instrument of control than of planning; pressing the concepts and culture of value-for-money on spending departments and agencies; and increasing the use of privatization and other forms of 'new public management' to shift the burdens for some public policies, programmes, and expenditures on to the private sector, either alone or in partnership with the public sector. However, the crisis of 1992, when the Treasury adjusted PES against the background of rising real levels of spending and a growing PSBR, is evidence that those 'coping strategies' were unable to constrain the growth of spending in line with the stated macro-economic objectives of the Conservative Governments of Thatcher and Major.

The extent to which the Treasury, rather than ministers collectively, can be held responsible for the effectiveness of control in that sense is less certain. In the past, where public spending was determined directly by the amount raised in revenue, and keeping both taxes and expenditure down was an agreed aim of government, the Treasury as the department responsible for both the raising of revenue and public expenditure was more obviously responsible for preventing the rise of public spending. As Budgets became unbalanced in the years dominated by the Keynesian consensus, when fiscal policy was used as an instrument in demand management, the responsibility of the Treasury to contain or restrain the growth of public expenditure became more ambiguous. If ministers decide collectively to increase public expenditure beyond previously agreed limits, or the consequence of their individual actions (in bidding and negotiating) has that effect, then failure to achieve prescribed expenditure objectives is more a political failure than one of system or policy process. Where the Chief Secretary and Chancellor agree or acquiesce in the higher spending urged on them by their colleagues, or decide to do so because of the cyclical effects of recession or the imminence of a general election, Treasury officials can advise and warn but not prevent. However, Treasury officials are not agnostic in the matter of more or less public spending. If their mission is now less to prevent public spending, it is certainly to act as a brake on its growth. How effective is that brake? First, we must try to distinguish the causes of the growth of public expenditure and determine those for which ministers collectively must bear responsibility.

When the Chief Secretary delivers a Planning/Control Total in November which is greater than that planned in the MTFS in the Spring it may be because the remit given to him by his Cabinet colleagues in July anticipated such an outcome; the Cabinet willed an increase in public expenditure. It may equally result from the bilateral negotiations with individual ministers; whatever the collective agreement, the actions of ministers individually results in aggregate higher spending. Again, while Treasury officials may advise and warn, they cannot prevent ministers collectively from increasing public spending. Responsibility is clearly political. It is less clear, however, whether the processes through which bids are made, argued over, and finally determined contribute to the growth of public spending, and if so by how much; in short, whether the Treasury's system of planning and control is a contributory factor. Does it predispose growth rather than restraint? Here we need to distinguish and exclude from the assessment that growth which takes place contingently as a result of changes in the politico-economic context, or from agreed changes in policy, for example to spend more in real terms on transport or hospitals.

Pressures for more spending arise from the pluralistic nature of the political system, and are mediated through budgetary processes characterized by bargaining and mutual accommodation. Wildavsky (1980) and others have argued that expenditure politics based upon such systems focused on inputs of resources tend to sustain or increase the momentum of spending. Evidence to support this hypothesis could be found in the experience of operating PESC in the 1970s, when volume planning and the methodology used by the Treasury to define, measure, and cost public spending programmes indexed them from high and rising rates of inflation. Much has changed since then, as we have shown in previous chapters, not least governmental and public attitudes towards public spending and the role of the public sector in the economy, the prescription of objectives to reduce the rate of growth in real terms, and the rules of the game of expenditure politics played out in PES.

Why public expenditure has continued to grow in real terms, despite precise policy objectives designed to reduce it, and changes to PES to control it more tightly, is a question which admits of no simple answer. The causes of growth are various, interrelated, and difficult to identify and differentiate; their particular contributions difficult to assess, witness the debate about the influence of structural and cyclical factors in accounting for the accumulating public sector Budget deficit in 1992–3 (see, for example, Treasury 1992c; OECD 1993a). Our concern here is a narrower one: not with an explanation of those causes and the appropriate weights to be assigned to them, but with an assessment of the effectiveness of the PES system; the extent to which it has helped to constrain the growth of public spending. Of course, any answer to that question is bound up with the broader causal explanations of growth; in practice, systemic and other factors are inseparable. Here we do no more than point in a general way to some of them, and assess the extent to which the PES system has played a part.

It is important to distinguish that element of growth which has occurred because of the exercise of ministerial discretion, where individually and collectively ministers have a choice between more public spending and (roughly) the continuation of existing levels in most programmes; some of course will be in decline. Discretionary expenditure is conceptually different from that growth which occurs where ministers have no such discretion, short of changing existing policies. Such a distinction allows us to ask to what extent PES makes it easier or harder for spending ministers to exercise discretion, and facilitates or constrains the growth of non-discretionary expenditure. The categories are not in practice sharply differentiated, because ministers can and do change policy assumptions within programmes of non-discretionary expenditures, by indexing benefits with price movements rather than earnings, for example, or redefining the criteria of eligibility; such changes alter the automaticity of pre-existing non-discretionary growth.

A second useful and necessary conceptual distinction can be made between the growth of expenditure which occurs as a result of 'permanent' structural changes in society and the economy, and that which arises from the 'temporary' phenomena associated with different stages of the business cycle, crudely, periods of boom and recession. By comparison with cyclically induced growth, the causes of structural growth are not self-correcting and over time may become embedded in the profile of an expenditure programme, unless directly addressed in discretionary policy changes. Here again the two categories are not as sharply differentiated in practice, and disaggregating growth using them is complex, the definitions, measurement, and calculations disputed. Nevertheless, there is recognition that some broad categories of expenditure are more affected by the stages of the business cycle than others, most obviously social security programmes which together also happened to be the largest and fastest growing component in public expenditure in the period 1976–93. However, as we discuss a little later on, even here there are significant elements of structural growth in some programmes, which remain largely unaffected by the business cycle. Nevertheless, in the changes made to PES in 1992 £15.5 billion of the total £80 billion social security spending (1993–4 figures) was removed from the New Control Total on the grounds that its growth was cyclically determined.

The extent to which the growth of discretionary expenditure is constrained or facilitated by the PES system, and the modifications made to it after 1976 designed to tighten control, can be broadly assessed by the contribution to growth of ideologically determined spending. For the period before 1979, the answer to the question 'Do Parties Make a Difference?' was broadly a negative one (Klein 1976; Rose 1984): briefly, that the trends of public expenditure growth were only marginally affected by the ideological preferences of the party in power. We have argued in Chapter 21 that, since 1979, there have been both winners and losers; measured by output, some programmes gained more or lost more than others. We have also argued that the trend rate of aggregate public expenditure was higher for the whole period of Conservative Governments since 1979 than Labour Governments in the 1974–9 period. Thus we conclude that, despite the changes to PES designed to constrain the growth of spending, ministers were able to exploit PES and exercise discretion to increase spending consistently with ideological preferences and manifesto commitments. Throughout the 1980s and early 1990s this was most obviously the case at certain stages in the electoral cycle, when governments concerned with re-election increased discretionary expenditure. In both the spending rounds of 1990–1 and 1991–2 Conservative Governments increased public spending in anticipation of the impending general election. In the 1991 Autumn Statement, the Government of John Major increased the Planning Total by £8.1 billion for 1992–3 and £13 billion for 1993–4 (excluding privatization) above the plans outlined in 1990. About half of this was not directly attributable to the costs of the recession, leaving a possible 'election effect' of up to £10 billion over the two financial years, and possibly as much as £6 billion in 1992–3 alone (based on Ward 1991; Treasury and Civil Service Committee 1991*a*).

A further element of discretionary expenditure is provided for in the Reserve, to fund not only all additional spending above that fixed in the previous year, but unforeseen expenditures and those contingent on events such as war, natural disasters, and the costs of strike action. Thus, for example, the costs incurred as a consequence of the miners' strike in 1984–5 added £3.85 billion to total expenditure (Treasury and Civil Service Committee 1985*b*). While such contingent expenditures are one-off, and non-recurrent, they may add to the total where the Reserve is inadequate to fund them, and the expansion of the Planning/Control Total which results is not necessarily self-correcting.

What was the effect of the PES system on the growth of non-discretionary expenditure? Did PES facilitate or constrain the growth of those expenditures categorized as non-discretionary? To take the most obvious case: would social security spending have grown faster or slower without the changes made to PES after 1976? Given the policy criteria enshrined in legislation, were the number of claimants and their entitlements affected by PES? Social security and associated expenditures were not subject to cash limits or rationing: the size of the programme was determined by demand, although in practice a target figure was prescribed based on estimates of unemployment and so on.

Until 1992 the effect of counting social security spending as an integral part of the public spending aggregate under PES was inherently expansionary. But the increase in social spending was partly due to structural factors and partly caused by the business cycle. Control of structural factors, changes in demographic and social structures, required the exercise of discretionary authority by ministers to change existing policies, for example by changing the criteria determining the level of benefit and eligibility, or by rationing the availability and take-up. The PES system cannot be convicted for a failure to control that growth which was attributable to ministerial unwillingness or inability to change policies. Indirectly, there was perhaps a failure to distinguish sufficiently the causes of that growth and to separate it from other kinds of expenditure growth, as happened in 1992. This might have been done earlier, for example in 1988 when the New Planning Total was introduced. But a change of this magnitude, with knock-on effects, required the conditions of crisis to elicit the political will and to secure the support for a radical change in the rules of the game. In 1988 there was no apparent fiscal crisis; public sector debt was being repaid. The problem in 1988 was controlling local government spending, and the changes in the definition of the Planning Total were designed to separate out expenditures which could be controlled by the central government in the Planning Total from those which could not. There is a nice irony in that those expenditures excluded from the 1988 New Planning Total have been reinstalled in the New Control Total.

Social spending due to cyclical factors was assumed until recently to be largely self-correcting, that is to say, while it increased in times of recession and growing unemployment, it fell in times of boom and a reduction of unemployment. However, in practice not all social spending has proved to be self-correcting. Experience has shown that the level does not return automatically to the pre-existing level at the end of a recessionary period.

It is now evident that there is a core element of long-term unemployed workers, the size of which is unaffected by the increase of demand in the business cycle. Further, the size of that core is growing relatively to that at comparable stages in previous business cycles, and has been rising from one cycle to the next. At the height of the 1980s boom 1.6 million were registered as unemployed, an estimated increase of 1.3 million over the number at the same point in the cycle twenty years previously.

The number of claimants for certain kinds of related benefits has risen due to structural as well as cyclical factors. The most often cited example of this phenomenon is the increase in the number of those claiming invalidity benefit. The causes of these structural phenomena are complex and broadly based in changes in culture and social structures, for example the dissolution of the nuclear family, the size, composition, and rate of household formation, the work ethic, employment practices, wage structures, and the increase in poverty of the poorest 10 per cent of the population since 1979. To take just one example: the number of self-contained, single-parent families increased from 2.1 per cent in 1981 to 3.8 per cent in 1991, the result of long-term profound social changes, including high and rising rates of separation and divorce, the break-up of traditional family units, the increasing number of economically active females in the labour force, and the rise in part-time employment practices. Broader cultural factors have contributed as well to the structural growth of some kinds of social security payments. Recession and the phenomenon of long-term structural unemployment have contributed to greater awareness of the availability of a whole range of income-support benefits, and a greater willingness to claim them. Take-up rates for many kinds of benefit have increased since 1979. The most quoted example of this has been the increased number of invalidity benefits, which more than doubled from 600,000 in 1978–9 to 1.5 million in 1992, with an associated increase in costs from £840 million to £6.2 billion.

The PES system of bidding and negotiating for additional resources required to fund that kind of structurally based growth reflected or rather refracted those changes. It can be argued whether it should have, or could have, alerted ministers earlier, or pointed to the longer-term consequences of continuing to fund the expansion of social spending due to structural rather than cyclical changes. Some attention was given in the late 1980s to the problems of demand-led expenditures, and attempts to cash limit some of them, such as GPs' prescriptions.

Although the growth of social spending which occurred as a result of the business cycle was not entirely self-correcting, as employment rose an element which was so attributable fell. But, until 1992, PES rules of the game did not deny to ministers the resources so released. The space created by the fall in the aggregate of social spending was filled by successful bids for additional resources by other ministers; a classic case of the operation of Parkinson's law: public spending expands to fill the space available. In other words, the total of public spending was broadly unaffected by a fall in cyclically based expenditures, because those expenditures were not separately distinguished in the then Planning Total. To that extent PES facilitated and encouraged the expansion of public spending in aggregate. In theory, since 1992 this can no longer occur. About 20 per cent of total social security spending is no longer counted as part of the New Control Total. Reductions in such cyclical spending is 'below the line'. In practice, if such reductions occur in times of boom, as tax revenues grow there will be pressure to expand the NCT, particularly if such conditions occur in the run-up to a general election.

In comparison with the PESC system of the 1970s, the changes made to PES, particularly the abandonment of volume planning and the introduction of cash limits and cash planning, have made the system less inherently expansionary. The indexing of volumes against the full effects of inflation facilitated the growth of public spending in the mid-1970s. Changes in the price basis, the use of a general GDP deflator, the separation of baseline expenditures, the introduction of running costs—all these and other changes described in previous chapters have contributed to a more effective brake on the growth of public expenditure. Nevertheless, it can be argued that the broadly based pluralist system of bidding, negotiating, and arbitrating is inherently expansionary. *Ipso facto*, bids are for more resources, not less. So strongly entrenched is the expectation of marginal increases to programmes that even in the crisis conditions of 1992–3, the Treasury was unable to prevent departments from bidding for additional resources, reflecting pressures on them internally and externally to increase their share of scarce resources.

Irrespective of their structural or cyclical origins, both discretionary and non-discretionary expenditures may cost more to finance a given quantum of benefit or service, depending upon the methodology employed to measure the costs, both of labour and the prices of goods and materials purchased; and upon the productivity of using labour and capital. Expenditures will grow in real terms, discounting the effects of structural and cyclical factors, if an allowance is made for the movement of prices and labour costs which enables departments to purchase more. Here we begin to confront systemic factors, those associated with the definition and measurement of public expenditure, and the methodology of the price basis used in the revaluation of the estimated costs of existing expenditures in baselines and bids for additional resources. In earlier chapters we have discussed the expansionary nature of volume planning prior to the introduction of cash limits, and the indexing of the rising costs of providing agreed volumes of spending. It is more difficult to determine the extent to which, since 1984, the changes in the rules of the game have reduced this element of systemic growth. The GDP deflator and the imposition of 1.5 per cent efficiency gains have squeezed costs; departments have become increasingly obliged to make rather than take prices for the goods and services they purchase; pay factors have been abolished; and running costs controls forced departments to trade off pay with jobs—all of which has made it more difficult for spending departments to expand their programmes through allowable costs than in the 1970s.

More broad systemic factors are associated with the methods of obtaining additional resources through the rules of the game regulating the processes of bidding, negotiating, and adjudicating, and of monitoring and controlling their use. Bidding above the baseline without full offsetting savings is inherently expansionary, whatever the cause and justification for requesting additional resources. The expectation of more, even an incremental adjustment to existing programmes, to say nothing of the costs of financing new policies and programmes, through nineteen spending departments, has added year by year to the growth of the aggregate. Attempts to change the bidding mentality, through Treasury injunctions to departments that nothing but baseline expenditures will be entertained, have been effective only for brief periods of crisis, as in 1976, and in any case have not applied to non-discretionary expenditures, and have been frustrated at other times by the unwillingness of individual departmental spending ministers to be denied what they claim as necessary increases, as happened in both the 1992 and 1993 rounds.

In the next chapter we explain why the Treasury has not been more effective in controlling expenditure, and argue that besides the practical difficulties there are constitutional limitations to the exercise of a tight control of the annual Planning/Control Total and the growth of spending over time.

24

Central Control and Departmental Autonomy

In the last chapter we argued that one important element in the Treasury's historic mission in controlling public spending is to act as a brake on its growth. The intermittent achievement of that purpose in the period from 1976 to 1993 was partly because in practice the Treasury is much less powerful and its administration of the planning and control system much more flexible than is apparent or commonly supposed. The appearance of tough, uncompromising Treasury control is belied by the much softer, accommodating practice. In this chapter we discuss the constitutional and practical limitations to the exercise of Treasury control, focusing on the tension between central control and departmental autonomy, with its roots in the historical continuity of the principles and practice of collective government. We argue that, while this tension is both inevitable and provides necessary flexibility in the operation of the system of planning and control, the progressive decentralization of financial management and control which has taken place since 1979 presages a profound shift in the balancing of the relationship between the Treasury and the spending departments. After a brief historical review of the constitutional limits to the Treasury's authority and discretion, we bring together the evidence of previous chapters to illustrate the flexible operation of its controls, and discuss in the concluding sections the pressures for still further flexibility which have arisen from the implementation of FMI, Next Steps, and the 'Further Steps' of market-testing, leading to the emergence of a putative 'contract state' in which formal contractual relationships between purchaser/provider pose a dilemma for public accountability.

THE LIMITS TO TREASURY CONTROL

The Treasury is the 'department of departments' at 'the heart of our whole administrative system', wrote its first Permanent Secretary in 1869 (quoted in Wright 1969: 1). With the reconcentration of responsibility for most of the traditional functions of the management of the Civil Service in the 1980s, it has resumed that role at the centre of British Government. The need for such a role, the *raison d'être* of the Treasury since the reform of the public finances in the first half of the nineteenth century, was summarized in the 1918 Haldane Report:

The interests of the tax-payer cannot be left to the spending departments; that those interests require the careful consideration of each item of expenditure in its relation to other items and to the available resources of the State, as well as the vigilant supervision of some authority not directly concerned in the expenditure itself; and that such supervision can be most naturally and effectively exercised by the Department which is responsible for raising the revenue itself.

The contemporary concern of the Treasury with economy, efficiency, and effectiveness to achieve value-for-money is entirely consistent with that prescription, evidence of the enduring nature of its historic mission. The 'watchwords' of Gladstonian finance were economy and efficiency. If there is now more emphasis on the effectiveness of public spending, with the accompaniment of objectives, priorities, targets, and outputs, and attempts to define, prescribe, and measure them quantitatively, its origins are in direct line of descent from those earlier precepts.

Allied to those traditional concerns is the Treasury's role in controlling the growth of public expenditure. As the Plowden Report stated: 'The central problem is that of how to bring the growth of public expenditure under better control and how to constrain it within such limits as the Government may think desirable' (Cmnd. 1432). It was central to the politico-economic conditions of the mid-Victorian state and its concern with limited government; to the initiation of 'big government' in the early years of the twentieth century; to the period from the 1950s onwards in which the growth of public spending was the concomitant of the expansion of welfare and social services and the consequence of Keynesian demand management; to the neo-liberal ideology of the Conservative Governments of the 1980s; and to the fiscal crisis of the early 1990s. Gladstone's prescription that money 'should be left to fructify in the pockets of the taxpayer' matches exactly the presumptions of Conservative Governments throughout the 1980s.

By the second half of the nineteenth century, the mid-Victorian Treasury had acquired the constitutional authority to control public expenditure through observance of the requirement of prior approval of all new items of expenditure and the reform of the public accounts. But the limitations of Treasury control were apparent even then and continued to echo through periodic inquiries in the next 100 years. The administrative histories of the Treasury and other major departments in both the nineteenth and twentieth centuries emphasize more the weaknesses and the limitations of the Treasury's control than the exercise of unconstrained powers (Roseveare 1969; Wright 1969, 1972). From Gladstone onwards, ministers and senior officials repeatedly affirmed publicly and privately, in official and semi-official correspondence in their departments, that the spending departments could not be controlled directly by the imposition of the Chancellor's 'power of the purse'. Asked whether the Treasury exercised a direct and effectual control over the spending departments, Gladstone replied 'We are only one department side by side with others, with very limited powers; it is more after all by moral suasion and pointing out things that our influence is exercised, than by any large power we have' (quoted in Wright 1969: 348). He denied that the Treasury had any direct power to regulate and control public expenditure. 'I am afraid that the other departments would consider that we were creating a sort of tyranny over them if we got that power; this thing is certain; that we have not got it; that the Treasury have never possessed it, and that we have gone on very well without it.' Treasury Permanent Secretaries echoed this view both in private and before numerous committees of inquiry: Playfair (1873), Ridley (1888), and the MacDonnell Commission (1912–14) all criticized the Treasury for its weakness in controlling the increase in the numbers of civil servants, and made recommendations, largely ignored, to strengthen its authority. Sir Richard Welby, Permanent Secretary to the Treasury, in evidence to the Ridley Commission emphasized the practical difficulties in exercising control. 'A powerful Cabinet Minister does not accept readily a decision of the Treasury which overrules something he proposes, and, in practice that is a considerable check upon the power of control' (quoted in Wright 1972: 198). Thirty years later another Permanent Secretary to the Treasury admitted much the same: 'Departments are to a great extent autonomous and the Treasury is certainly not in a position to dictate to them to the extent to which, I believe, public opinion generally believes' (ibid., p. 225).

Complaints of Treasury 'interference', concern with the details of spending, 'cheeseparing', and the saving of candle-ends, have persisted throughout the last 150 years, but are not necessarily symptoms of strict control in the sense of restraining the growth of public expenditure. The Gladstonian concern with rigid economy, which derived from liberal doctrines of free trade and a minimal role for the state, was reflected in the Treasury's traditional hostility to public spending. Sustained into an era of collectivism, that attitude was a source of increasing tension between the Chancellor and his spending colleagues as the nineteenth century drew to a close (see Roseveare 1969: 183–234). The turning-point came in the 1880s, since when, according to Welby, 'the wind was in the sails of the spending departments' (p. 199). The costs of military and naval expenditure, the Boer Wars, and the First World War added to the growing pressures to initiate and expand social and welfare pro-grammes to which the Liberals had responded with their 'new liberal-ism' in the governments of 1905–15.

While steps were taken to strengthen the Treasury and its control after the First World War, and the politico-economic conditions were for a time more favourable to the exercise of firm Treasury control, nevertheless 'even in peacetime individual spending departments could make overwhelming cases for expenditure on particular proposals', which the Treasury could not resist (Peden 1983: 375). When backed by the Cabinet, it could and did cut public spending. But its supremacy over the spending departments 'lasted only so long as the Cabinet was prepared to keep within the limitation of at least the goal of a balanced budget. When financial orthodoxy was abandoned, as in war, the Treas-ury's control was greatly weakened. The Treasury was strong, in fact, only so long as the Cabinet willed it' (Peden 1983: 385).

Traditional Treasury hostility towards public expenditure persisted in the inter-war period, and was for a time consistent with the temper of the times of retrenchment and financial stringency in which Geddes wielded his famous axe in the 1920s. But spending on social policy soon resumed its upwards progression with the rise in unemployment. Sir Richard Hopkins, Second (later Permanent) Secretary at the Treasury, noted in the early 1930s that the Treasury could not halt 'the onward march of the cost of Education, Widows' Pensions, Housing and other things' (quoted in Peden 1983: 381). The conversion to Keynesianism, and the expansion of welfare programmes in the 1940s produced still more pressures for public spending. As the aggregate of public expendi-ture became a tool in the management of the national economy to influence the level of demand and hence employment, traditional Treasury hostility towards its growth became obsolescent. Attention switched to the containment of that growth within the resources ex-pected to be available in conditions of anticipated economic growth. But in any case, long before the conversion to Keynesian demand management, there had been a shift from the detailed control with its roots in the Gladstonian era. Such control was not only less practicable with the growth of social and welfare programmes, as collectivism took hold towards the end of the nineteenth century: it was also inconsistent with the acceptance by ministers and officials in both the Treasury and the spending departments that controlling public expenditure was a co-operative undertaking. As the Treasury delegated increased authority to spending departments to determine expenditure within agreed limits without the need to obtain prior approval, they were expected to bear a greater responsibility for controlling their own expenditure through improved financial self-discipline.

Greenleaf (1987) has described this as a paradigm shift, away from the detailed control derived from the hostility towards public spending which characterized the liberalism of mid-Victorian governments concerned mainly with regulatory functions, towards co-operation and negotiation with departments now required to provide more goods and services in an era of collectivism. On this view the 'high ground of control was perforce formally surrendered because of the sheer weight of public expenditure and the impossibility of sustaining the traditional position' (p. 272). It is true that there was a shift in attitudes towards the control of public spending, from traditional Treasury hostility towards spending to an acceptance that government programmes would continue to grow. This was especially so from the mid-1950s onwards. But it did not represent a paradigmatic change in the nature of the Treasury's authority to control, or in the practical limitations to the exercise of that authority.

While the Treasury's historic mission has been unchanging, its constitutional authority and organizational capacity to play the role assigned to it, to control and contain public expenditure, have been much exaggerated, a myth sustained and nurtured by governments and spending departments, and by the rhetoric of the Treasury itself. Sir Warren Fisher, echoing the refrain of other Treasury Permanent Secretaries before him, said in the 1930s that:

It is not only members of the public who have been misled by the phrase 'Treasury Control'; there have been times when even officials of the Treasury have, to its solemn refrain, conjured up a picture of themselves as the single-handed champions of solvency keeping ceaseless vigil on the buccaneering proclivities of Permanent heads of Department. (Quoted in Burns 1993: 22)

The appearance of a powerful and omniscient department has, apart from brief periods of financial crisis, been belied by both the substance of its authority and the practice of its control; and demonstrably by the inexorable growth of public expenditure. Historically, it has rarely been able to contain it for more than brief periods. The exercise of its authority has depended more upon 'moral suasion', on achieving a negotiated accommodation with spending departments, and upon the deterrent effect of the threat to use its reserve powers. As public spending grew, the limitations of Treasury control have attracted more criticism (as in 1958, 1976, 1981, and 1992) than complaints that it acted with an 'autocratic caprice'.

CONTROL AND FLEXIBILITY IN THE PROCESS

In previous chapters we have shown that the control of public expenditure inheres in the relationship between the Treasury and each spending department. It is not a relationship of principal and agent, in which the former has authority to direct and impose decisions on compliant and complaisant departments. While the Treasury has authority to allocate among spending departments a total agreed to collectively by Cabinet (not imposed upon them), that allocation process is constrained in practice by the independent authority (and obligation) of each Secretary of State derived from statute to provide services, benefits, and goods. In the allocation of resources among them, the Treasury cannot be insensitive to the needs to continue to provide a service of the level and quality urged by a Secretary of State. This is most obviously the case where statute determines the level of benefit, as in social security, unemployment, training, and the Treasury is bound to agree to provide for all those deemed eligible. But it is true, too, of the provision of a standard of service, hospital care, education for the 5–16 age group, defence (international agreements), agricultural payments to the EC.

While the Treasury is held responsible for the control of public expenditure, through the 'power of the purse', in practice it is normally unable and unwilling to dictate either a predetermined total or allocations to spending departments which collectively comprise a loose federation of autonomous 'states'. It needs to operate the system of control firmly to try to ensure the maintenance of financial discipline in those departments, to help government achieve its expenditure objectives, to ensure value-for-money, and to prevent waste and inefficiency in the use of resources. But it can impose its authority only in those exceptional circumstances of economic or financial crisis when spending ministers acquiesce. Normally it is unable or unwilling to exploit its potential authority to say 'no' to a spending proposal without the opportunity for both sides to argue and attempt to achieve a negotiated settlement. 'Brute force' or 'unreasonable behaviour' can rarely be sustained, as we saw in Chapter 10.

As we explained in Chapter 9, the exercise of the Treasury's control is negotiated in a highly centralized closed and stable network, within a set of interdependent relationships in which resources of authority, money, information, and expertise are shared and exchanged. The balancing of relationships between the members of that network creates a tension between the Treasury's concern for taut control on the one hand, and pressure from the spending departments for more resources and discretion in the management of them on the other. In practice, neither the Treasury nor a spending department can achieve its objectives, nor attempt to maximize its values without the other. This is obvious enough with a spending department which needs the Treasury for money: to allocate it, and for authority to approve its use subsequently. But it is equally true of the Treasury: it needs information (most of which only the spending departments possess), and the spending departments' expertise in the assessment/analysis of the need for particular kinds of spending, for it to be able to decide how much to target for the public sector and to allocate it among competing claims.

In managing their spending relationships, the Treasury and each spending department seek to maximize opposing organizational values—crudely, control/autonomy—through strategies which exploit the potential of the resources which they each possess. In a network of interdependent relationships their discretionary authority—room to manœuvre in the policy process—is mutually constrained. Their behaviour in the network is regulated by policy and behavioural rules of the game, described in previous chapters.

To understand how and why the Treasury and spending departments conduct their business in this way, two additional dimensions to the analysis are necessary. First, an understanding of the historico-analytical context. The lineage of the structure, organization, and behavioural norms of the expenditure side of the contemporary Treasury can be traced from the department which emerged from the reorganization of 1856. In Chapter 3 we examined the recent origins of the system for planning and controlling public expenditure (PESC) with its Keynesian assumptions of growth, and described its near-collapse in the crisis of 1974–6, the result of ministerial political will for more public expenditure, and the weakness of the control system exposed by the condition of rising inflation. This precipitated changes in the rules of the game, reflected in the introduction of cash limits, and later cash planning and the use of the Reserve. The origins of the norms of behaviour of Expenditure Controllers, principally scepticism, detachment, critical enquiry, lay much further back, and are evident in the mid-Victorian Treasury. In Chapters 4 and 5 we showed how attempts have been made to change the administrative culture in which Treasury and spending departments' officials perceive public spending, and make decisions. Some of the resultant tensions are discussed below.

The second additional dimension is the politico-economic context. As we have shown, public expenditure objectives, plans, and their achievement are inextricably linked to the broader issues of political economy. At any period of time, that context provides opportunities and constraints for both the Treasury and the spending departments to attempt to maximize their different organizational values. It influences the strategies adopted by each, as they exploit resources of money, information, and authority in conducting their business. The three most significant politico-economic factors are the performance of the economy (GDP growth or decline in its European and international setting); the political policy objectives of the government and the priority given to them; and the stage of the electoral cycle.

Where the balance is struck between Treasury control and departmental autonomy on a particular spending issue—a bid for additional resources, an in-year change of cash limits, a draw on the Reserve, approval to spend, delegated authority—is determined by the resources of information, authority, money, and expertise possessed at that time by the Treasury and the spending department, and how each is prepared to use them in exchange with the other. The management by both of the interaction depends not only upon the particularity of the circumstances and the strategy adopted by each, but also by the politico-economic and cultural contexts within which the 'game' is played according to the current policy rules of the planning and control system (PESC/PES), and the prevailing norms of behaviour.

Departments will always seek more flexibility in the interpretation and application of new or revised rules of the game (to which they agree or in which they acquiesce). Changes in the politico-economic or administrative contexts provide both opportunities and constraints to exercise 'voice' within (and sometimes without) the network for concessions, exemptions, and exceptions. When the Treasury modified the control regime to tighten its control in 1976, 1982, and 1992, departments sought to exploit their resources of authority, information, organization, and expertise 'to limit the damage', searching for loopholes, seeking concessions and exemptions, negotiating additional flexibilities, in order to create more space and opportunity for discretionary room for manœuvre. Thus the Treasury conceded greater flexibility in the operation of the cash limits regime: changes in limits became common rather than exceptional as Treasury rules and rhetoric at first insisted; the carry-forward of some unused capital expenditure was allowed, and later extended to some elements of running costs as well. The Treasury continued to allow the territorial departments to manage a large part of the spending under the responsibility of each

Secretary of State as a 'block', with discretion to move resources to reflect local priorities.

While frustration with the Treasury's alleged inflexible operation of the rules sometimes erupts publicly, as with the Ministry of Defence and the carry-forward of capital expenditure, we have argued in previous chapters that there is much more flexibility in the operation of the planning and control system than the Treasury's tough rhetoric would suggest. In most years up to 1992, the Chancellor and the Chief Secretary were prepared to accommodate some of the pressures for additional spending beyond the previously agreed Planning Total. Sometimes those pressures could be accommodated within a growing GDP while maintaining broad medium-term objectives for public spending. In other years their accommodation led to a scaling down in the ambition of those objectives, or in the progress towards them. The Reserve was also used to accommodate some of those pressures and the costs of policy changes in-year. Consistent underspending on the aggregate of cash limited expenditure also provided additional flexibility to offset overspending on non-cash limited expenditure.

The Treasury's recurring dilemma is how much flexibility it can permit while still retaining sufficient control of the aggregate and, simultaneously, safeguarding financial discipline, enhancing value-for-money, and accounting to Parliament. When it responds to the pressures from spending departments for concessions and exemptions, and concedes flexibilities in the interpretation and application of the rules of the game it does so normally because it believes that there is little risk to the maintenance of effective control. Threat to the integrity and efficiency of the control system may arise from outside the expenditure policy network, and the Treasury may be obliged to make concessions and grant flexibilities which carry with them greater risk to the maintenance of effective control. Such a threat has arisen from the progressive decentralization of financial management, a process which ironically was initiated by the Treasury's own concern to change the administrative context within which departmental budgets were planned, allocated, managed, and controlled.

The incorporation of FMI into the PES processes in the late 1980s led to demands from departments for greater financial autonomy for line managers in progressively decentralized departmental budgetary systems. The implementation of FMI led inescapably and (from the perspective of departments and the Prime Minister's Efficiency Unit) logically to demands from departments for more freedom from central control, and within departments, from the control of their own Finance and Establishments Divisions. The underlying tension between central control (and accountability) and departmental autonomy now erupted publicly with the Next Steps initiative. The reconciliation of the need for firm Treasury control of the aggregate of public expenditure, and the achievement of greater efficiency and effectiveness in the use of public money, with the pressure for more delegated authority and greater flexibility in the delivery of central government services became a major issue at the heart of central government.

Next Steps and the pressure for more flexibility

The creation of Next Steps Agencies was not seen by the Treasury initially as the next logical step, witness its initial lack of enthusiasm and the carefully composed caveats which surrounded its support for the implementation of the Ibbs Report. The spending departments were quick to see Next Steps as a lever to win from the Treasury greater financial autonomy for the managers of their services. While the Treasury continued to fight hard to retain central control through the financial framework agreements negotiated with the sponsor departments of the new agencies, the principle of decentralized budgeting and more financial autonomy for line managers had been conceded. The difficulty for the Treasury was that in allowing spending departments and their agencies more flexibility in the management of their resources it would put at risk the gains in central control achieved since 1976, and make the delivery of the Planning/Control Total through the PES processes a yet more hazardous undertaking. This issue was implicit in the debate about the implementation of the Ibbs Report in the early 1990s.

By and large, the first candidates for Next Steps status did not require a substantial increase in delegated authority or increased flexibility. However, as the Next Steps initiative moved forward, pressure increased on the Treasury to grant agencies more freedom, and there has been a slow increase in the amount of flexibility granted. The Treasury's preferred strategy was to make incremental adjustments to the public expenditure control regime, dealing with each case on its merits. But as the initiative gathered pace, it came under increasing pressure to make larger and more broadly based changes.

As a result of those pressures and in order to tidy up the Parliamentary arrangements on Votes and the reporting of financial matters, the Treasury made three significant changes to its general policy of granting flexibilities to agencies. The first was an adjustment to the running costs regime to take account of the fact that many agencies were able to finance their activities through their receipts. If an agency or department was granted net running costs control, an increase in receipts allowed an increase in expenditure. Hitherto the Treasury had been against allowing a general right to net-control status because, although this would not increase public expenditure (receipts count as negative expenditure), it regarded it as akin to a right to tax. The Treasury also reiterated its decision to allow limited carry-forward on underspending of running costs.

The second change concerned virement between and within Votes. Again no general right was envisaged, but rather in some cases where efficiency would be improved the Treasury was willing to define in advance the conditions in which a department or agency might reallocate between Votes, or vire between subheadings (Cm. 914: 10). This latter flexibility was extended to include running costs which, as we discussed in Chapter 18, was a control mechanism specifically designed to preclude transfers between running costs and other expenditure. The third and most far-reaching change was the extension of trading fund status to establish agencies on a more commercial footing.

These reforms—especially net running costs control and trading fund status—were welcomed by Agency Executives but were regarded as not going nearly far enough, and the Treasury and many spending departments continued to be criticized for continuing to exercise too detailed control. These complaints were echoed in a critical report by the Efficiency Unit (the Fraser Report) in 1991 which noted that: 'there were particularly strong arguments in favour of allowing the widest measure of delegation within agreed financial limits and providing worthwhile incentives to achieve value for money' (Efficiency Unit 1991: 15). The Report also recommended that the presumption of financial matters should be reversed: within the overall disciplines of the cash limits and targets set, managers 'should be free to make their own decisions on the management of staff and resources except for specifically reserved areas' (p. 5).

The Treasury was unsympathetic to the thrust of those criticisms. When asked whether it would allow the Benefits Agency to move to a unit-based method of funding, Hayden Phillips, Treasury Deputy Secretary in charge of Pay and Management, told the Treasury and Civil Service Select Committee that the Treasury needed assurance that the accounting and management system was adequate for the purpose. It was not apparent that agencies asking for such arrangements had really thought them through, he said. And in his most telling point he suggested that, if the pay and grading system was to be changed, 'you get right to the heart of the nature of the organisation and you do not make such changes lightly' (Treasury and Civil Service Committee 1991*b*: qu.

397). The Treasury's general formula for dealing with requests for delegation of authority of pay and grading was to 'examine requests put by departments and agencies ... and see whether the flexibilities will deliver demonstrable and preferably measurable improvements in value for money' (quoted in Treasury and Civil Service Committee 1991*b*: p. xx). The committee thought this indicated that the Treasury was 'cautious in approving widespread delegation of authority'. The official response of the Government was that 'Agencies' delegations and flexibilities can be enlarged as their track record of performance is established, provided that essential controls on public expenditure are not jeopardised'. Within this limitation, the Government was committed to letting a Chief Executive have as much 'managerial authority to run his Agency as he thinks fit, unless there are good reasons to the contrary' (Cm. 1761: 5). This response put more pressure on the Treasury to allow still greater flexibility.

To place this criticism in context it should be noted that the Civil Service Order in Council of 1982 was amended on 5 February 1991 (discussed by Chapman 1991). This allowed exceptions to the rule that all Civil Service appointments should be made only on the basis of fair and open competition, such as for secondments and periods of service under five years in duration; allowed extra Civil Service grades to be added or removed and for their names to be changed; and codified the transfer of some personnel functions between the Treasury and departmental ministers, allowing the latter discretion over conditions of service, appointment, and qualification for appointment within the overall framework determined by the Treasury. As a result, the Treasury now had general powers over personnel management but departments and agencies had greatly increased their independence.

Further flexibility was granted in July 1991 when the Chancellor of the Exchequer announced the Treasury's commitment to greater pay delegation in the Civil Service. Chancellor Lamont announced the Government's decision to negotiate changes in the arrangements for determining Civil Service pay, and specifically to introduce 'a range of forms of performance-related pay'. Departments and agencies could now opt for full delegated powers for pay and grading of all or some of their staff, subject to the proviso that such arrangements produced value-for-money greater than from following the centrally determined arrangements. A department granted delegated power could thus determine its own pay system. Where such extensive discretion was not felt appropriate, the Treasury allowed departments and agencies to negotiate flexibilities of their own within the total central Civil Service pay envelope negotiated by the Treasury (*Official Report*, 24 July 1991, co. 607).

The Efficiency Unit had not only pressed the case for more financial flexibility along these lines but carried on where the Ibbs Report left off, in arguing the need for the centre to reduce its role. It suggested that the Treasury and OMCS needed to review their 'role and size', as the core spending departments had been pressed to do under the impact of Next Steps. But more significantly:

The public expenditure side of the Treasury should focus increasingly on key measures of outcome as it moves to a more strategic style of control of the public sector. The detailed management of resources to achieve those outcomes should be left to Agencies and information gathering should be limited accordingly. (Efficiency Unit 1991: 9)

The last comment struck a chord in many a departmental Finance Division. The Report was critical of the centre's (read Treasury and perhaps centres of departments) demands for 'yet more information with no clear indication of what purpose it served' (p. 21). Stripped of its code, the general recommendation represented a concerted assault on the Treasury's *raison d'être* since it reimposed control over public spending after the crisis in the mid-1970s.

The Treasury's response was along traditional lines. Its role in Next Steps was twofold: 'through the normal processes of the Public Expenditure Survey and monitoring' to ensure that the agencies were set the right targets and that these were met; and to enable departments and agencies who 'want to make a case for getting further delegated freedoms and flexibilities to manage their own affairs within the framework to do so while keeping an eye on cost control and value for money' (Treasury and Civil Service Committee 1991*b*: qu. 389, p. 57). Once again, the stress was on the overall public expenditure framework and on individual departments and agencies having to argue, case by case, for further flexibilities. While this might result in a 'variegated' pattern across Whitehall, coherence would be maintained by such factors as ministerial responsibility, and 'the need for real and tight public expenditure control, the need to sustain standards of conduct and probity' (qu. 393). The Government's official view was that the role of the central departments needed to be reviewed in the light of Next Steps and that this was being 'taken forward' (Cm. 1761: 3).

Conspicuously absent from the implementation of the Ibbs Report was any attempt to follow through its recommendations to change the way the core departments did their work (Metcalfe and Richards 1990). This omission was taken up by the Fraser Report in one of its most far-reaching recommendations. It recommended that all departments should review the internal services they provide; move to a position where these were costed on a full-cost basis; and allow budget holders to shop around for the best value-for-money. In addition, departments 'should formulate a clear statement of their evolving role and the part their agencies play in the delivery of their policy objectives' (Efficiency Unit 1991: 7). The result of the review should lead to a reduction in the functions and staffing of the core department. The Report suggested a 25 per cent reduction in the number of staff in the centre of departments, a figure accepted by Sir Angus Fraser as having been plucked from the air.

The Government's reaction to these proposals, and the principles to guide future policy, were set out by the Prime Minister in May 1991. In strengthening the relations between Ministers and agency Chief Executives, departments must give 'well-informed and authoritative support' to Ministers so that they can give clear strategic directions to agencies consistent with Government's overall objectives. This meant that officials in the centre of departments must help the Minister to 'determine the financial resources available; select and set suitably robust and meaningful targets covering quality of service, financial performance and efficiency; and call chief executives to account for the performance'. This was to be strategic advice and not day-to-day involvement and 'as a result, the number of people at the centres of departments can be reduced'. Chief Executives needed increased personal authority and responsibility if they were to be accountable for delivering improved performance. 'Agencies' delegations and flexibilities can be enlarged as their track record of performance is established, provided that essential controls on public expenditure are not jeopardised.'

This carefully worded response to the Fraser Report was taken by the Treasury as a summary of government policy and as providing the ground rules for further developments. As such it neither endorsed nor rejected many of the criticisms and recommendations made in the Fraser Report. But it is clear that the strongest recommendations urging looser control by the Treasury and the central departments had been shelved.

It is a nice irony that, just as this debate about control and autonomy began to tip the balance away from the Treasury towards spending departments and their agencies, the need to reassert central control became paramount with the public acknowledgement in 1992 of the serious deterioration of the national public finances, both revenue and expenditure. While the recession of the late 1980s and the 1992 general election were contributory factors in that deterioration, as we have argued in previous chapters the growth of public expenditure through-out the 1980s was not constrained consistently with stated objectives. The underlying causes of that growth were already apparent, masked by the favourable but temporary macro-economic conditions which obtained in 1986–8 which enabled the Chancellor to pay off some of the National Debt. The receipts of the sale of assets, counting as negative expenditure, provided a boost of £5–8 billion a year.

It is, of course, not inconsistent to impose top–down control on the aggregate of public expenditure while simultaneously delegating authority to spending authorities to determine agreed allocations. The emphasis upon limiting the future growth of the aggregate precipitated a major review, led vigorously from the centre by the Chief Secretary, of all spending programmes. In such a climate the further extension of flexibilities to spending departments and agencies was slowed. Priority was now given to measures to cut costs directly through a comprehensive review of all spending programmes in the run-up to the first Unified Budget in November 1993, and an acceleration of the programme of market-testing the provision of in-house services by Whitehall spending departments with a view to achieving greater economies in running costs. This in turn has raised issues of public accountability, and the future direction of the process of reforming the management of the Civil Service and changing the 'administrative culture' begun with FMI and carried on through Next Steps. We conclude this chapter with a brief review of the phenomenon of the emergent 'contract state'.

Towards the contract state

The initiatives begun with FMI and carried on through Next Steps were elements of the phenomenon observable more widely in the public sector throughout the 1980s concerned with the improvement of managerial performance, and the quality and accountability of services delivered to clients and customers. The political rationalization of that movement achieved prominence (and provoked scepticism) in the concept of the Citizen's Charter, a personal initiative of John Major. A key element in the implementation of the commitment to quality and service in central government was contained in *Competing for Quality* (Cm. 1730), published by the Treasury in 1991, the principles of which were derived from the experience of competitive tendering in local government and the health service. Following legislation making competitive tendering compulsory for the direct service organizations of local authorities, the NHS reforms transformed the role of the district health authorities into purchasers of services from their own and private hospitals. The purchaser/provider, client/contractor principle which underlay the new contractual relationships in both local government and the NHS was extended to central government departments. *Competing for Quality* committed the Government (read Treasury) to the extension of market-testing throughout Whitehall spending departments.

This White Paper followed logically too from the progression of the Next Steps initiative and the Fraser Report, which raised the issue of the future role and residual functions of the 'core departments', after the completion of the process of delegating authority to manage and deliver central services to Executive Agencies, and the conclusion of framework financial agreements prescribing relations between them, their sponsor departments, and the Treasury. *Competing for Quality* represented 'Further Steps' to decentralize the financial management and delivery of many of those services which remained in core departments, through a process of contracting out after competitive tendering following market-testing.

The programme of market-testing in Whitehall departments was led and co-ordinated by the Prime Minister's Efficiency Adviser, Sir Peter Levene, formerly Chief of Defence Procurement. The programme launched in November 1992 put £1.5 billion of services out to tender, involving more than 44,000 staff, and 350 areas of activity. More market-testing is planned, with the aim of exposing some 50 per cent of the Civil Service's running costs to competitive tendering. However, the attractiveness of the initiative to private contractors and in-house management teams was initially affected by uncertainty over the application to contracting-out of the EC's Acquired Rights Directive, which safeguards the jobs, pay, and conditions of service of employees when jobs are transferred from one employer to another. The ambition of the programme will take it into some of the core activities of spending departments—payroll, legal services, information technology, and a wide range of specific activities across the whole of Whitehall.

Government by contract has become a dominant element in the emerging position of public management. Work previously carried out directly by public sector organisations and controlled through organisational hierarchies is increasingly being carried out by contractors who are controlled not through hierarchy but through the terms of a contract, whether or not the contractor is part of the organisation or separate from it. (Stewart 1993: 7)

These and other changes in train in the early 1990s, such as the decentralization of authority to determine pay and grading under the Pay Agreement of 1992, and conditions of service to departments and agencies under the Civil Service (Management Functions) Act of 1992, will profoundly change the traditional relationships between spending departments and the Treasury. The 'core' of the former will become smaller, as the delivery of more services is transferred to Executive Agencies while others are contracted out to private sector organizations. The role of the spending departments will be more strategic, supervisory, and enabling. They will continue to bid and negotiate for resources to fund their agencies, their core functions, and the cost of contracted-out services. Whether, in so doing, the Treasury's control of the aggregate and the allocation is enhanced or weakened is uncertain. The logic of decentralized financial management and responsibility is a reduction in detailed Treasury control. But is the arm's length, strategic, and supervisory control of spending departments envisaged by the Treasury (Sir Terence Burns, Permanent Secretary, Treasury, in Burns 1993: 23) consistent with those Treasury norms of behaviour discussed in earlier chapters? Historically, the Treasury's control of spending has inhered in the examination by Expenditure Controllers of the details of requests for resources. Can the Treasury substitute control of financial systems for control of details? How can decisions be made about the relative priority of competing programmes, without knowledge and understanding of those programmes which comes from familiarity with the details? If agencies argue persuasively for value-for-money increases in resources, and are supported by their sponsor departments, how will the Treasury determine, and advise Cabinet, which has the better case? Thus far, experience of decentralized financial management through FMI does not suggest that the Treasury will relinquish control.

A second consequence, already observable, is the continuing pressure on the Treasury to grant more 'freedom' and 'flexibility' to managers in departments, agencies, and (it is assumed) in contracts with private-sector organizations, in the administration of its control mechanisms. The risk for the Treasury is that such pressure will prove irresistible, and make it more difficult to constrain the predicted growth of many spending programmes in other than circumstances of temporary crisis. The tension was apparent in the decision to impose a pay policy across the whole of central government in 1992–3 in order to constrain the growth of spending within the previously determined NCT. This was inconsistent with the Pay Agreement concluded with Civil Service unions and departments a few months earlier, which allowed the latter to set up their own pay systems and conduct their own pay negotiations with the former. The FDA held the Treasury's action a breach of the spirit, if not the letter of the Pay Agreement. The lesson of that episode is that the

Treasury retains and is prepared to use its hierarchical authority to impose control where the flexible operation of negotiated rules of the game would lead to a result inconsistent with broader objectives. If repeated more widely, for example in the abrogation of the spirit of the negotiated formal financial agreements with agencies, or a tightening of running costs or end-year flexibility, it would call into question the viability of decentralization. Chief Executives of agencies have already criticized both departments and Treasury for undue interference in the discharge of their managerial responsibilities (Mellon 1993).

The undermining of the premiss on which Next Steps is founded, in the circumstances of a continuing, severe fiscal crisis, is one possible consequence. Another more challenging to the whole concept might arise from reaction to the 'contract culture'. Market-testing has already attracted criticism from within as well as outside central government, in that it makes it more difficult to provide for public accountability of services provided by private sector organizations, and to establish lines of responsibility transparent to the consumer. To that criticism has been added a wider critique which challenges the compatibility of the contractual principle with the provision of public services (Harden 1992). It is argued that 'the role of contracts in the public sector cannot be judged by criteria drawn from the private sector. They have to be considered against criteria grounded in the process of government', a critique which has been made by others more widely on the transplant of private sector values, methods, and practices to public-sector organizations (Metcalfe and Richards 1990). Regulating relationships within central government departments, through formal contractual arrangements separating purchaser from provider, denies the responsibility of the department for the activities of both the client and the contractor. Is it possible for it to retain responsibility and overall accountability for the full range of activities carried out in its name? 'In contracting the delivery of the service to the private sector, different values may prevail', values which may not be easily protected through the terms of a contract (Stewart 1993: 11). While economy, rather than efficiency and effectiveness of performance, has provided the main impetus to contracting out, there are other equally important traditional public service values—justice, equity, citizenship, community, and democracy—which are not normally provided for by private sector organizations, and are difficult to specify in contractual arrangements. It is normally through the processes and institutions of public accountability that such values are secured and protected. Contracting out poses a dilemma for public accountability, which has not yet been satisfactorily resolved, and further consideration of the issues involved may lead to a reaction to the emergent 'contract culture'. Stewart (p. 11) has questioned whether the 'process of governing can or should be adequately expressed in contracting', arguing that governing is more than the provision of a series of services on a well-defined pattern. It is about collective action responding to the need for change, adapting to it, promoting it, and guiding it—action beyond the capacity of private contractors.

The Treasury's initial reservations about the threat of the Next Steps initiative implied in the Ibbs Report, concerned as it was to ensure that its authority to control departmental spending was not put at risk, were discussed earlier in this chapter. The extension of contracting out through market-testing posed no such threat: on the contrary, in the circumstances of the fiscal crisis of the early 1990s, there appeared to be the prospect of an immediate gain in cutting the costs of central government without the negotiation of rights, duties, and reserved powers inherent in the more complex financial agreements with Executive Agencies. The Treasury's enthusiasm for market-testing has been criticized on the grounds that this contracting out is not imbued with the concern to improve public sector management. It is different in both principle and practice from the decentralization of financial authority and managerial responsibility to manage which underpinned Next Steps. While redefining the role and functions of the residual core of departments after Next Steps was signalled in the Fraser Report, and the extension of market-testing reduces still further the service-functions of that core consistently with the concepts of delegation and accountable management, it is nevertheless open to doubt whether market-testing as envisaged in *Competing for Quality* and implemented by the Office of Public Service in 1992–3 is consistent with the philosophy of executive agencies. Tensions have appeared in the relationship between Chief Executives and civil servants in sponsor departments and the Treasury, with Chief Executives 'blocked and second-guessed at every turn' (Mellon 1993). This has led some to detect Treasury disillusionment with the operations of agencies, and a 'sharp change of direction', in which the initiative 'seems in danger of being de-railed by market testing' (Richards and Rodrigues 1993: 33).

On this interpretation, the relationships between the purchasers of services in the departments and the providers in the agencies have not worked as intended:

Framework agreements are not worth the paper they are written on. Civil Servants collude with each other and with Ministers and the terms of agreement are broken. Agency chief executives whose performance pay is decided by the person with whom they are in a quasi-contractual relationship have few rights they can or will enforce. (Richards and Rodrigues 1993: 37)

The logic of that criticism is, it is suggested, to enshrine the relationship between public producer and private provider in legally binding contracts. It is not necessary to accept wholeheartedly the tenor of such arguments; there is after all evidence from other Chief Executives and agencies which paints a more favourable picture (Fogden 1993; Devereau 1993). However, more emphasis and attention is undoubtedly being given to market-testing than Next Steps, and it is not coincidental that this is occurring at a time of a crisis of spending control when the short-term gains of quickly concluded contracts with private sector organizations promise more savings than the longer-term benefits of the more broadly based management-improvement of decentralization to agencies. It would not be the first time that a management initiative in the Civil Service has been accused of being driven more, or mainly, by considerations of economy than efficiency and effectiveness.

25

Controlling Public Expenditure More Effectively?

Through the 1990s pressures for more public spending will continue unabated, and governments will continue to attempt to restrain the growth of the aggregate, and to decide upon the allocation of increasingly scarce resources. Yet there are constitutional and practical limits to the exercise of tight Treasury control, as we have shown in previous chapters. In this chapter we discuss how the processes of making and carrying out expenditure policy might be changed to enhance the effectiveness of that control. We look first at the structure and organization of the Treasury, and at the techniques of budgeting which it employs. Next, we consider whether the collective responsibility of the Cabinet could be made more effective, in the light of the changes introduced in 1992. Finally, we discuss the circumstances in which a paradigm shift might occur. While changing the rules of the game from time to time has altered the balance of discretionary authority between the Treasury and the spending departments, reflecting agreement that particular circumstances warranted tighter or more relaxed Treasury control, the game itself, with its paradigm of negotiated discretion, has remained unchanged. It might change or be changed because of the occurrence of economic and financial crisis or as a result of the progressive Europeanization of economic, monetary, and fiscal policies. Here we enter for the first time the realm of conjecture and speculation, and risk that what we write in 1993 might be overtaken by unforeseen and unpredictable events. Writing a year earlier we would have had more confidence about the progress towards European Monetary Union than is now justified with the UK's withdrawal from the ERM on Black/White/Golden Wednesday in October 1992, and the *de facto* collapse of that system in July 1993.

ORGANIZATIONAL EFFECTIVENESS

How well organized and staffed is the Treasury to perform the tasks of planning and controlling public expenditure, to achieve the short- and medium-term objectives of the government of the day? We begin with an assessment of the Treasury's organizational effectiveness, and the efficacy of its establishments policy for the provision of efficient and effective Expenditure Divisions. In particular, we discuss the Treasury's beliefs that the cohesiveness and flexibility of the expenditure side is an advantage in dealing with expenditure business, that the benefits of small, flexible, non-hierarchical Expenditure Divisions outweigh the arguments for more staff, and that the port-hole principle is the most effective way of organizing the interface with Whitehall spending departments. We then look at the Treasury's policy for developing good all-rounders through the movement of staff into and out of the Expenditure Divisions.

The present distribution of spending responsibilities among the Expenditure Divisions dates from the reorganization of the Treasury in 1975, following the implementation of a large-scale management review. To understand the principles which guided those changes we have to go back to the 1962 reorganization, following the acceptance of the Plowden Report. Until that date, the organization of the department as a whole was based upon the 'port-hole principle', in which each government department was provided with a clear single point of entry to the Treasury. The adoption of a functional structure in 1962 meant the abandonment of that principle, except for the public expenditure side where departments continued to enjoy access through their port-hole. Concern about the fragmentation of policy formulation in the 1970s prompted a further attempt to provide a more effective functional integration between different parts of the department. On this occasion, the public expenditure side was not exempt. Some issues of public expenditure control—industrial policy, housing, and cash transfer between individuals—transcended organizational boundaries based on departmental responsibilities. Together with other parts of the Treasury, the public expenditure side was also criticized for its tendency to adopt a similar frame of reference and perspective to that of the departments for which it was responsible, when dealing with policy issues and problems. What was needed was for all Treasury divisions to bring a distinctive point of view to bear on the evolution and resolution of policy.

While there was questioning of the continued relevance and propriety of the 'port-hole principle' in the control of public expenditure, nevertheless the reorganization of the department in 1975 left it intact. That historic continuity was preserved, and the traditional belief endorsed that the Treasury could maintain effective control by 'marking' spending departments with Treasury Expenditure Divisions so organized. The extent to which organizational factors contributed to the loss of control

in the 1970s is arguable. One former Treasury official has argued that
the lack of a distinctive point of view, and a central analytic capacity
concerned with public expenditure as a whole, accounted partly for the
failure to predict the consequences of the rapid growth of expenditure
in the early 1970s, or to respond earlier to the inherent weaknesses in
the use of the relative price effect, which departments exploited to grow
their own programmes. Combined with the use of the unique constant
price basis in each Survey, departments were able to write their own
estimates for inflation. While the growth of public expenditure was
willed politically by both Conservative and Labour Governments in the
1970s, the outturns were consistently above those planned. The slowness with which the Treasury responded may have been due to 'an
administrative lack of will . . . to adapt to the new requirements of control' (Shapiro 1978: 6).

While the Treasury's Expenditure Divisions remain organized on the
'port-hole principle', changes to the principles and methodology of the
Survey, as well as other organizational changes made since 1975, have
helped to ensure a better co-ordinated and more responsive control of
public expenditure. General expenditure policy and analysis were
strengthened, and more effective use made of the public sector economists, Operations Research, and accountancy specialists. Cash control
and retrenchment in the public sector, expressed through cash limits,
cash planning, efficiency studies, and FMI, provided the ingredients for
the distinctive voice and approach to public expenditure control urged
in the 1975 management review. More particularly, after 1982 the energies of individual Expenditure Divisions were directed and concentrated on the objective of the annual targeted Planning Total and, since
1992, on the New Control Total.

The number of divisions (eighteen) has changed little since 1975, and
the distribution of spending departments among them has varied only
marginally. The amount of public spending has grown steadily in real
terms during this time, but not equally across all programmes. Since
1979 housing and industrial programmes have shown extensive reductions; those for health and law and order substantial increases. But
the size of spending is not a good guide to the volume or burden of
work. First, there has been a general increase in authority delegated to
spending departments. Secondly, in particular programmes, quite small
amounts of proposed or actual spending may cause more planning or
control work for an Expenditure Division. Some issues may be complex,
involve a variety of sensitive matters in which ministers take a close
interest, and take up an apparently disproportionate amount of time.
For such reasons, it is difficult to judge from the outside whether the

number and size of the Expenditure Divisions are about right. One alternative would be more divisions, some or all of which had a more limited sphere of responsibility; or fewer, larger divisions. Except at the margin, where the transfer of officials between divisions might make for a more cohesive unit, it is difficult to see any advantage in fewer divisions—unless there was evidence that co-ordination at the centre through GEP, RC, and FM would be thereby improved. Smaller divisions would raise the issue of providing for the co-ordination of a larger number of more formal structures.

There is already greater need than a decade ago for co-ordination between the Expenditure Divisions and the 'central ring', as a result of the increasing emphasis upon value-for-money and the effectiveness of performance, which has led to the creation within the Treasury of enhanced capacity in management accounting and financial management and central purchasing; while developments in the control system through the introduction of schemes of running costs, management plans, and end-year flexibility have led to the growth of additional central co-ordinating units for those purposes. In short, Expenditure Divisions have to deal with (and benefit from) a greater range of support and service divisions whose functions are closely allied to the planning and control of public expenditure. This reflects a growth in the technical sophistication and complexity of both the Survey and in-year control systems, the operation of which imposes an additional burden on the Expenditure Divisions.

Against this, the co-ordination of pay issues is less of a problem than a decade ago. Pay and management are now back in the Treasury, and theoretically easier to relate to Expenditure Division work than when with the CSD or MPO. As well, the abandonment of explicit pay policy and pay factors between 1986 and 1992, and the delegation of authority to departments to determine pay assumptions in the new running costs regime, relieved the Expenditure Divisions of some of the burden of an always contentious and highly charged issue.

The Treasury is a small department: less than a third of its central core staff are employed on expenditure work.[1] Are 124 Expenditure Control-

---

[1] The 'control quotient' devised by Greenleaf (1987: table 7) purporting to show the historic trend of the proportion of senior staff to supply expenditure is seriously flawed. (1) He includes only the first four grades (Permanent Secretary to Assistant Secretary and their equivalents), excluding Principals and Heads of branches with control responsibilities. (2) He includes all Treasury officials, whether employed on expenditure, the economy, finance, or Civil Service management sides. The number of senior staff employed on expenditure control since the 1930s is very much less than the number given. Moreover, the historical series does not reflect the addition and expansion of Treasury functions since 1940. Senior staff in the 19th cent. and the first two decades of the 20th

lers (1991–2), and their support staff, adequate for the purpose of help-ing the Chief Secretary plan, monitor, and control public expenditure of more than £250 billion per annum? Sir Peter Middleton, formerly Permanent Secretary, argued that 'the Treasury works better when it's got a small organisation which is moderately overworked' (Young and Sloman 1984: 42). The risk of overloading and overwhelming a small number of Expenditure Controllers is partly offset by arrange-ments for delegating authority to spending departments, but the de-cision to do so has to be balanced against the need for the Treasury to continue to maintain sufficiently rigorous control. The advantages claimed (by Treasury officials) for small numbers are speed of response, adaptability, ease of both formal and informal communication, and the informality of the non-hierarchical, collegial style of working in the Treasury. Small teams for *ad hoc* reviews and inquiries can be as-sembled quickly, cutting across responsibilities and hierarchies. The ability to transcend hierarchical command structures within the Treas-ury, and to establish personal networks both there and with spending departments and agencies, is believed to be a function of size. Profes-sional informality among Expenditure Controllers provides an impor-tant medium for the circulation and exchange of the assessments of the strengths and weaknesses of officials in the Finance and Policy Divisions of the spending departments, and the financial management systems they operate.

Unlike larger Whitehall Departments, Treasury officials know each other well and in the words of a former Under Secretary 'can of course communicate with each other almost in code' (Young and Sloman 1984: 23): 'There is almost an old boys' fellowship. People who have been in the Treasury will tell you that it's a very enjoyable place to work, and although there are rivals, tensions between groups, it's small enough to know everyone' (p. 27). The atmosphere of 'clubbable con-fidentiality' described by a former Treasury economist 'developed in the fifties and sixties, when the Treasury really felt it was running the world' (p. 27). The *esprit de corps* bred by the intimacy of a small organization is fostered by the 'collegiate atmosphere that you get in an institution which is constantly embattled', where the beleaguered co-horts of the Expenditure Divisions share a siege mentality as they are constantly assaulted by the much bigger battalions of the spending departments.

were employed only on expenditure control, later an increasing number worked on the new tasks of economic and financial policy-making. (3) The aggregate of supply services expenditure is given in cash rather than real terms, which exaggerates the 'control quotient' for the post-war period and the effects of inflation.

The Treasury is in constant dialogue with itself, in *ad hoc* and formal meetings, and above all on paper. More so than in other Whitehall departments, a great deal is written down, copied, and circulated widely, as part of the process of keeping everybody in touch, 'making sure that everyone who should know does know what is going on' (Burns 1993: 26). The non-hierarchical, collegial style of working encourages a tradition of internal argument and debate. 'Much of the debate on policy is the battle for the Chancellor's mind' (ibid. 26). It is reflected in a distinctive style of writing memoranda. The Treasury house-style is to discuss the arguments first before presenting the conclusions. In most other Whitehall departments, memoranda begin with a summary of the main issues, present the recommendations for actions, and then indicate the timetable. Detailed discussion of the issues, and the arguments for and against, come after.

An important part of the ethos . . . is allowing dissent, and allowing dissent to reach ministers. If you want to exercise the right to disagree you can . . . you get quite violent arguments of an intellectual kind, up and down and sideways between all the different bits of the Treasury. (Young and Sloman 1984: 25)

While this continued to be the case in the discussion of expenditure policy, dissent was less tolerated in the shaping of economic policy in the heyday of monetarism under the Thatcher Administrations; indeed, not to be 'one of us' was to risk banishment.

Outsiders brought into the Treasury on secondment from the private sector and other Whitehall departments are struck by the volume of work and the pressure. A Bank of England official was 'enormously impressed by the amount of work they get through and by the speed with which the Treasury can actually produce a recommendation or view on almost any subject that's put to them, day or night' (Young and Sloman 1984: 26), a view confirmed more recently by a Treasury Deputy Secretary brought in after long service elsewhere in Whitehall. 'Issues blow up and the Treasury has to take a view. Colleagues in Departments (and the Treasury) only get in touch when it *matters* to them and you can't say "give me two weeks"' (interview, 1992). While its small size, habits of work, and co-ordination enable the Treasury to react quickly to the normal pressure of events and issues, at times of great crisis— devaluation in 1967, Black/White Wednesday in 1992—it stands nevertheless accused of dilatoriness.

Compared with private sector organizations and Whitehall spending departments, the Treasury is less problem-oriented. An Assistant Secretary in the Social Services and Territorial Division in the mid-1980s commented on her return from secondment at a merchant bank:

In the Treasury none of the problems has a solution, they only have one least bad solution, and you can't be sure that when you've solved the problem you've got the right answer, or indeed that it was an answer at all, because the problems go on. You can never actually say, in the way you can in the City, 'we did the deal and we won'. There are occasions, discreet occasions, in the Treasury when you can say that 'we had this particular view about an expenditure proposal and we think we were right, and ministers argued it out and they came to our way of thinking.' But it doesn't mean that the problem has gone away, it's going to come back in a different form. (Young and Sloman 1984: 28)

Expenditure Controllers, especially those brought in from other parts of Whitehall, frequently contrast the ease of communication which the Treasury size and organization permits with the more formal command systems in many other departments. One example of this is the Treasury's relationship with the M.o.D. The Treasury argued in 1991 that the twenty-eight people in Defence Expenditure Divisions (DM) were able to act more quickly and far more flexibly than the complex and cumbersome, multi-hierarchical department 'across the road' (Under Secretary). There are advantages to be gained by being 'flexible to their inflexibility'. It was recognized that there was a trade-off between expanding DM's staffing and perhaps thereby giving it a wider skill-base from which to tackle the M.o.D.'s large range of 'businesses', and the loss of ease of internal communication such expansion would entail. But the Treasury claimed that it was often better informed about what was going on in parts of the M.o.D. than the M.o.D.'s own specialist Finance and Policy Divisions, because DM is less inhibited by the formal organizational lines of communication than civil servants within the Ministry; and Expenditure Controllers can use and develop specific contacts on particular issues, move in and out quickly. The prevailing view is that this is a major advantage not to be sacrificed lightly by increasing the number of staff.

There are other consequential advantages. In a small community of officials it does not take long for an Expenditure Controller to get to know his colleagues and be able to draw rapidly on information and expertise. This is particularly important, given the turnover of staff, and the secondment of officials from other Whitehall departments. It is possible to keep everybody well informed and briefed on most issues through the circulation of 'copied' letters and memoranda. Because numbers are small, Expenditure Controllers can keep up with what is happening throughout the expenditure side. Size is also a factor in the transmission of departmental norms. One Expenditure Controller, in comparing his experience of the Treasury and the CSD, noted that the Treasury was more 'hard-nosed, tightly manned and graded' and therefore more aggressive in pursuit of the constraint of pay and allowances.

Movement of staff into and out of the Expenditure Divisions, and between them, is the consequence of the policy of developing good all-rounders, discussed in Chapter 6. Two questions arise: what is the optimal length of time in a post, and how long should Principals and Assistant Secretaries spend on the expenditure side? General postings policy was stated in 1985 to be to try to ensure that an individual remained in post long enough to be able to do the job effectively, and to give the department some continuity in a given core of work. At the same time, there were other considerations: first, that an individual did not become 'stale' by doing the same job for too long; secondly, that there was sufficient movement to provide the department with a flexible workforce; thirdly, that an official was given an opportunity to make full use of the range of skills and experience; and fourthly, that he or she was given the opportunity to deepen and broaden experience in the grade to prepare for competitions in promotion to the next grade.

There is a major tension implicit in the application of that policy: between the length of time in post needed to do the job effectively and to deepen (and broaden) experience, and the time beyond that when the individual's 'value-added' might have peaked, or even declined as he or she becomes 'stale'. The need to maximize flexibility in the deployment of staff, together with the needs of emergent priority areas and recurrent issues, will push towards a shorter period of time in the post. The need to provide opportunities to develop and use skills to the full, and to deepen experience by a variety of related jobs, pulls towards a longer period. This tension has to be reconciled, or rather the benefits and disadvantages have to be traded off. The risk is that too rapid a turnover will mean less effectiveness in a post, insufficient continuity in a 'core of work', and perhaps instability in divisions. Too long in a post can lead to a feeling of staleness and a loss of enthusiasm.

In the mid-1980s, following the report of the (unpublished) internal Barratt Inquiry, the Treasury decided that 'the minimum length of completed postings in expenditure divisions should be raised to 3 years', and that four years in post should not be regarded as exceptional. The expectation was that that greater length of time would provide greater stability in the Expenditure Divisions, and at the same time give Expenditure Controllers greater depth of experience in particular areas of work. Briefly, the Barratt Inquiry had found much more rapid movement of staff, into and out of the Expenditure Divisions and within them, than was thought desirable or consistent with the aims of effectiveness or continuity. On that criterion of stability, then, the Expenditure Divisions had been implicitly less effective. We need not here go into the reasons, although the Treasury cited an increase in the workload, accompanied by a reduction in staff, the latter as a result of the Conservative Government's policy to reduce the size of the Civil Service. There was also the perennial problem of dealing with 'priority demands at short notice', which often cut across career and departmental personnel planning.

Since 1985 the evidence is that, for much the same kind of reasons, together with the increasing difficulty of recruiting and retaining Expenditure Controllers of the appropriate experience and quality in a more competitive labour market, there has been little if any improvement. The minimum time in post of three years is rarely achieved. Expenditure Controllers are in post barely long enough to get on top of the job and establish the crucial working relationships with their opposite numbers, and with the Treasury central divisions. Nor are they able to contribute as effectively and constructively—by having the time, energy, and confidence which comes with experience of the work—to identify issues and areas of the business which can be 'attacked', that is to adopt a proactive mode, rather than merely reacting to the proposals that come to them. A further disadvantage of rapid turnover is the loss of cohesiveness in the expenditure side of the department, where (as we discussed above) the informal structures are important in the development and implementation of Treasury policy.

While time in each post might be less than the desirable norm of three to four years, rapid turnover might occur mainly within the Expenditure Divisions, that is, Expenditure Controllers could be broadening their experience by a succession of expenditure postings, although their effectiveness in each post would be limited by the short duration of each. If this were the case, it could be said that the policy of providing staff with experience of a core of work was achieved. In fact the rapid turnover between posts occurs as well between the expenditure side and other parts of the Treasury, and other departments and organizations outside.

On leaving office as Second Permanent Secretary in 1966, Sir Richard Clarke admitted that 'the worst weakness, and one which was damaging our work, was the rapid turnover of staff' (1978: 135). From the evidence available for the 1980s, we conclude that the effectiveness of the Expenditure Divisions, according to the Treasury's own criteria of stability and continuity as measured by time in post, is less than it should be. Secondly, again on the Treasury's own prescription of the need to obtain experience of a 'core of work', less time is spent continuously in the Expenditure Divisions than is consistent with the achievement of that policy. It is impossible to measure the degree of ineffectiveness quantitatively. The evidence of our interviews provided negative confirmation, in that we obtained no evidence that Expenditure Controllers were complaining of 'staleness', the result of spending too long in one post, or on the expenditure side of the Treasury; if anything, the reverse was true. One consequence of rapid turnover, due to a shortage of qualified able people, is more rapid promotion, which in turn exacerbates the trend.

How well Expenditure Divisions and their controllers perform is largely a matter of self-assessment. While from time to time the Select Committee on the Treasury and the Civil Service, the PAC, and the NAO examine and report on the operation of control, the Treasury alone has no central department to which it is obliged to demonstrate value-for-money, argue the case for running costs provision, and submit its management plan. In common with other Whitehall departments, the Treasury publishes performance targets in Expenditure Departmental Reports. None of them are helpful in the measurement of performance of the Expenditure Divisions. One simple, crude indicator might be the extent to which each Expenditure Division was able to deliver the targeted total agreed with GEP and the Chief Secretary as part of the expenditure strategy of each Survey. Expenditure Controllers agree that the 'target' of trying to scale down a department's bids for additional resources provides them with a sharp discipline and clear objectives around which to build the job. But any specific failure to achieve targeted reductions might be due to factors over which the Expenditure Division has little influence or control during the course of the Survey round: the priority accorded by the Chief Secretary (and his Cabinet colleagues) to particular programmes, the bargaining in the bilaterals and in EDX. Consistent 'failure' might be due to historically difficult relationships with a spending department, or to a climate which favoured the department against the Treasury, as occurred in the early 1980s when defence expenditure was linked to a NATO commitment.

Another indicator of effectiveness might be the extent to which an Expenditure Division was able to monitor and control its department's expenditure to ensure a close match between the planned total and the final outturn. But here again, the occurrence of policy changes, and unforeseen expenditures in-year beyond the control of Expenditure Controllers, make it difficult to measure quantitatively, or to assess the effectiveness of one Expenditure Division compared with another. More difficult still would be any objective assessment of the Expenditure Division's success in ensuring that its departments obtained value-for-money in their programmes.

The effectiveness of the Expenditure Division in planning and controlling the expenditure within its sphere of responsibility is measured more or mainly in qualitative terms, by the reputation, esteem, and reliability of its Expenditure Controllers, and by the quality of their relationships with departmental Finance and Policy Divisions. Some Expenditure Controllers are perceived to be more effective than others; and that judgement is made by their peers, and by senior staff. GEP conducts a post-mortem of the Survey which includes an assessment of the success and failure of the tactics and approaches employed by Expenditure Divisions and their contribution to the success of the Chief Secretary's expenditure strategy. At the end of the Survey the Group Heads may discuss with their teams how well the Survey discussions were handled. There are also several other occasions during the Survey process when Deputy Secretaries and the Second Permanent Secretary are able to assess the quality of the Agenda Letters and briefing material prepared by Expenditure Controllers, and their success in predicting the likely response of the departments they shadow to the Treasury's negotiating moves during the heat of the Survey battle. Judgements are also made by 'opposite numbers', by PFOs and their staff in the Finance Divisions of the spending departments.

Thus far we have discussed the efficiency and effectiveness of the Expenditure Controllers to perform the tasks of planning and controlling public expenditure in terms of their traditional roles, and the qualifications, skills, and experience needed to perform them. A more fundamental question is whether more effective planning and control might be achieved if the role played by Expenditure Controllers was defined differently and their qualifications, experience, and skills changed to reflect it.

Treasury Expenditure Controllers are quintessentially 'good all-rounders'. Objections to the 'philosophy of the amateur administrator', such as those made in the Fulton Report and elsewhere, it is claimed, apply with greater force to Treasury administrators, and hence Expenditure Controllers. These and similar criticisms have been endlessly debated, resurfacing from time to time in the 1980s in the reports of Parliamentary Select Committees. The issue of generalists and specialists is well-trodden ground. Here we deal only with the specific charge that Expenditure Controllers, as 'good all-rounders', lack the specialist knowledge and training, and perhaps extramural experience as well, to deal with those who are more specialist in the spending departments. The first point to note is that Expenditure Controllers are not dealing with specialists, in the narrow sense of trained health service or transport or education specialists. They deal with a similar species of professional administrators, good all-rounders in different subject areas. Indeed, in the departmental Finance Divisions they are dealing with departmental 'all-rounders', normally with varied experience in Policy Divisions and Executive Agencies.

It is true of course that, in those areas, the administrators in Finance and Policy Divisions with whom the Expenditure Controllers deal will know, or should know, more about the substantive policy issues; more about the need, growth, and development of particular policy programmes; have access to better technical data; and be more expert in the detail of each programme. As we have seen, the Treasury does not try to match that specialist knowledge. Arguments for more specialist Expenditure Controllers tend to emphasize the difficulty of non-specialists dealing with departmental specialists. (In a wider context, the latter are of course criticized as being generalists.) The assumption is that expenditure cannot be effectively planned, monitored, and controlled unless controllers possess specialist knowledge to match that of the departments. It is not immediately obvious that the Expenditure Division dealing with (say) agriculture or defence would be more effective if its controllers had qualifications, training, and experience thought relevant and appropriate to understanding and contributing to the formation, development, and carrying out of agricultural or defence policy. Leaving aside consideration of what would be appropriate, how would such controllers be better able to perform the tasks of planning, monitoring, and controlling, as defined by the Treasury? They might know more about the detail of agriculture, but would they be better able to identify weaknesses in an expenditure argument? There would be a risk of loss of detachment, with a closer professional identity with agriculture. It is by no means obvious that the result would be better. Relationships would be different—the adversarial mode would become customary. More importantly, there would be a direct challenge to departmental competence and expertise as controllers argued as specialists versed in the technical details. Who would decide between competing professional judgements?

A further difficulty would be that specialized Expenditure Controllers would be less mobile. Movement of trained, experienced, and qualified manpower would be minimal. Controllers would spend a career in the Treasury, or related postings in other departments and public and private sector organizations, in agriculture or defence. Whether or not they would become 'stale' as a result of the continuous practice of a specialism can be argued over.

A second common criticism of the Treasury's concept of the role of the Expenditure Controller derives from the presumption that experience is more important than knowledge; broadening experience by rotation through a succession of linked jobs, it is argued, is a better training for the production of efficient and effective Expenditure Controllers. In practice, the Treasury acknowledges the need to balance the two but has a preference for the former; yet, as we have explained, the exigencies of staff management have meant that Expenditure Controllers were moved more frequently than the guiding norm. The extent and rapidity of movement between jobs is of course both a consequence and a reinforcement of prevailing norms. By definition, the need and opportunity to move specialists trained and experienced in particular policy fields such as agriculture or defence would be more circumscribed. The particular issue within that broader debate is the Treasury's guiding norm: that a minimum of three years is necessary in a division to maximize value-added. It is difficult to judge the adequacy of a three-year posting without reference to the Treasury's concept of the Expenditure Controller as a professional, non-specialist controller whose effectiveness in the job will depend partly on the knowledge and experience acquired in that and previous Treasury postings, but more crucially upon the successful deployment of that knowledge and experience in the development and maintenance of productive relationships with the Finance and Policy Divisions of the spending departments. If it is accepted, as we have argued in previous chapters, that those relationships are a critical factor, then how long is needed in post to establish, maintain, and exploit them for the purpose of efficient and effective control? The answer to that question will depend partly on the self-assessment of Expenditure Controllers, and partly on the perception of their effectiveness by their opposite numbers in the spending departments. There appears to be little disagreement among those we have interviewed that a period less than about the three-year minimum may reduce the effectiveness of some controllers. Most take the view that a year or eighteen months is needed to get on top of the work of a new desk, and that thereafter it is possible for the controller to create time and opportunity to generate ideas for achieving better value-for-money, grounded in familiarity and confidence with both the substance and the relationships through which those ideas will be transmitted. After about three or possibly four years, the belief among controllers is that the momentum of such control may be better sustained by the importation of fresh ideas, approaches, and perhaps methods of working. While staleness might be a risk, more significant is that after such a period of time a controller may have exhausted the possibilities of new approaches or ideas, or be in danger of becoming 'captured' by the department, and that a wholly different approach and style may better generate momentum and fresh thinking. It is difficult to assess the validity of that claim according to any objective criteria. The repetition of the 'rule of three' by Expenditure Controllers serves only to reinforce the norm and create and foster the expectation of movement after that length of time. Treasury controllers are well aware that mobility is the key to promotion, and are conditioned accordingly to expect and justify frequent movement between posts and different sides of the Treasury.

From the perspective of the spending department, frequent rotation between Treasury posts is thought to be a disadvantage, unless of course relations with a particular controller have been poor. If time and familiarity with the subject-matter are necessary to create the basis for a good and effective working relationship with the Treasury, then a departmental Finance Division may regret a system which moves controllers almost as soon as, or before, they have acquired experience. The department would in such cases naturally prefer to continue to deal with controllers whose reactions are predictable, and with whom a relationship has been established—when, as some PFOs say, they have 'house-trained' their Expenditure Controller. For just that reason, the Treasury would prefer to move people and restore a less predictable element to the relationship and the fresh or different approach which may accompany a change of controller. From the Treasury's perspective, what Finance Divisions may perceive as a good working relationship may have become too comfortable or cosy one, in which the 'slight edge' which should always be there has become blunted with time and familiarity. In practice, in recent years there has been very little risk of that occurring. As we have shown, controllers are moved more rapidly than the guiding norm. The risk is much greater that the Finance Divisions feel frustrated at the lack of continuity and stability in their relationships, and that they perceive the Treasury to be less effective.

A further criticism derived from the Treasury's concept of the professional, non-specialist controller moving frequently between different posts, is that controllers are as a result insufficiently positive and constructive. Factors which would tend to reinforce that complaint are the behavioural norm that Treasury officials react to spending proposals and do not initiate them; and that, through too little time in post, they are less able to react constructively, should there be time and opportunity to do so. Behaviour which emphasizes the norms of scepticism, detachment, and critical inquiry can become, or appear from the perspective of the spending department, negative and hostile.

While spending departments sometimes complain about the attitude of individual controllers, there is very little criticism of the quality of those selected or posted to the Expenditure Divisions. The Treasury continues to recruit a small number each year from among the ablest of those recruited by the Civil Service Commission, and to bring into the department at Principal, Assistant Secretary, and Under Secretary levels, on secondment from other departments, some of the most promising young officials in Whitehall. A few of these stay beyond the normal two to three years.

Other criticisms of the Treasury's control, that it is negative, hostile to public expenditure, and that calculations of relative priority are only weakly articulated in the processes of decision-making, are misconceived, if we accept the Treasury's definition of its expenditure mission. We have argued in previous chapters that the prime task of the Expenditure Divisions is to help the Chief Secretary achieve his public expenditure objective expressed in a target for the annual Planning/Control Total, and to try to deliver it to him at the end of the financial year. This means looking for, obtaining, and sustaining cuts in departmental bids for additional resources. The purpose of the interaction between the Expenditure Division and a department is not through inquisitorial means to establish an objective 'truth', but adversarially through argument, critical examination, and counter-argument to oblige departments to justify their bids. On this definition, Expenditure Controllers do not need to be specialists matching the expertise and professional competence of the departments, because the intention is not to substitute their professional judgement for that of the departments.

Arguments for dividing the Treasury, and creating separate departments responsible for economic policy-making and expenditure control derive more from criticism of the former than the latter; there is a concern that the Treasury is driven too much by its expenditure function, and that as a consequence a predominantly negative culture permeates the making of economic policy and its attitude towards industry. Expenditure control might be less rather than more effective, if separated from the Treasury's other functions. 'It would make the total and content of public spending *less* subject to macro-economic and supply side influences, and those responsible for it *more* susceptible to a negative culture' (Burns 1993: 21). Moreover, the Treasury would lose the benefits of the cross-fertilization of experience and knowledge between the economic and expenditure sides of the departments, which occurs for example in local government finance, social security, EC finance, and the Unified Budget.

Budgeting methods

In Chapter 3 we argued that the techniques of planning and control based on volume planning were inherently expansionary in conditions of high inflation in the 1970s. Or rather the ambitions of Conservative and Labour Ministers to expand their programmes were more difficult for Treasury ministers and officials to restrain through the operation of volume planning and control. The abandonment of volume planning, and the introduction of cash limits, cash planning, and the Reserve, against the background of a renewed commitment to obtaining value-for-money through cost savings and output-enhancement, have made it more difficult for spending departments to 'grow their programmes' in the 1980s than the 1970s. As we have shown, some departments lost resources in real terms.

While the methodological basis of the measurement of costs and prices in PES changed, the techniques of bidding and negotiating remained fundamentally unaltered until 1992. Decisions about increases or reductions were still made incrementally. Indeed, the separation out of baseline expenditure in the early 1980s, and its automatic revaluation, focused still more attention on the additional spending, the margin, requested by departments. Incremental budgeting is an incentive for spending departments to increase public spending. The invitation to bid for additional resources above the baseline is a presumption of growth. While spending departments were expected to look for offsetting savings, and to make efficiency gains, nevertheless they continued to bid for additional resources. Except in times of financial crisis, spending on new projects is not expected to be financed entirely from savings found elsewhere. Further, it can be argued that the consideration and discussion of each bid on its merits, and the conduct of bilateral negotiations, exacerbated the tendency towards incremental growth. While it is true that the Chief Secretary and the spending ministers with whom he negotiated were sensitive to the politico-economic context in which the spending round took place, nevertheless their discussion focused on issues of 'more or less' on items of a particular programme. We have argued in previous chapters that the effect of the changes introduced in 1992 will not fundamentally alter the processes of bidding for resources for existing and new policies. Within the New Control Total, and perhaps prescribed limits for departmental programmes, Ministers will continue to argue in bilateral negotiations with the Chief Secretary to justify maintaining their baseline expenditure and to bid for additional resources. Responding to cues from changes in the politico-economic context Ministers individually and collectively will put pressure on the Treasury's prescribed Control Totals.

The main alternative budgetary techniques to incrementalism are the Planning, Programming, and Budgeting System (PPBS), and Zero-Based Budgeting (ZBB). Neither is practised in the UK, the USA, or any other major industrialized country. Experiments with PPBS in the UK in the 1970s were soon abandoned, as the practical difficulties of incorporating complex policy analysis into annual processes of scrutiny and review became apparent. The conceptual difficulties of producing operational definitions of objectives proved formidable. PPBS introduced into the US Defense Department in 1961 and extended to the Federal Budget by President Johnson in 1965 was later abandoned, as much for the practical difficulties of assimilating prodigious amounts of information produced by legions of policy analysts. Similar conceptual and practical difficulties apply to the introduction of a full-blown ZBB system. Treasury Chief Secretaries have occasionally hinted that such analysis was undertaken periodically, but no attempt has been made to incorporate it into the budgetary process. However, *ad hoc* formal and informal policy reviews have traditionally been part of British central government. Through the prompting of Treasury Expenditure Controllers, or on the initiative of a Minister or as a result of Prime Ministerial intervention, the purpose, costs, financing, and outputs of particular programmes are subject to periodic review. In the 1980s, there have been major reviews of health, social security, education, transport, industrial assistance, defence. In the 1992–3 PES round, the Chief Secretary initiated a major review of the four largest principal spending programmes as part of the cost-cutting exercise needed to achieve the Control Totals prescribed in 1992, and set in train a medium-term review of all spending programmes.

There is considerable scepticism about the usefulness of both PPBS and ZBB. 'They have lost their allure', wrote Wildavsky, an advocate of the former in the 1970s. The ranking of objectives more rationally, if it can be done, is, he argued, less relevant to the circumstances of high and rising public expenditure and deficit financing. While he was writing with reference to the USA, that argument applies with equal force to the UK and other major industrialized countries in both the G7 and the EC: 'Now what matters is the level and distribution of spending. Size replaces efficiency as the criterion of a good budget. In a time of growing budgetary dissensus [in the US], a concern with radical changes in process replaces concern with modest alteration in techniques' (Wildavsky 1988: 420).

Incrementalization is not only a technique, it is also a characteristic of the process—or more accurately, we would argue, incremental adjustments to the allocations to programmes result from the nature of the process. We now consider the extent to which those processes contribute to the difficulty of containing the growth of public spending, and conclude with a brief discussion of ways in which 'radical changes in process' might contribute to more effective control.

'Radical changes in process'

We have argued that the Treasury's exercise of control is inherent in the regulation of the interdependent relationships which result from its responsibility for the central planning and allocating of resources and the spending departments' statutory obligations to provide goods and services. Treasury power to control is the exercise of discretionary authority constrained by the exercise of countervailing discretionary power by each autonomous spending department in the particular circumstances of an expenditure proposal. The constitutional context within which those relationships are regulated is provided by the principle of collective government, institutionalized in the Cabinet, its committees, and the Cabinet Office, and their roles and procedures in the making of policy. We have shown also how the balance between the Treasury and the spending departments is affected by the politico-economic context within which expenditure is discussed, and by the development and operation of the system of decision-making (broadly, PESC/PES) and the rules of the game. It is also affected by the prevailing 'administrative culture'—since 1979 by the inculcation of the new managerialism which, through the pursuit of greater efficiency and effectiveness, has sought to achieve better value-for-money in the use of resources. The balancing and rebalancing of the relationships between the Treasury and the spending departments which takes place as a result of contextual changes—for example, by the opportunities and constraints provided by the growth of GDP and the electoral cycle; as a result of changes to PES; or as a result of the evolution of FMI and Next Steps—occurs without fundamental disturbance to the maintenance of relationships embedded in the principle of the collective nature of central government. The principle of the collective responsibility of the Cabinet for spending (and other) policy may be difficult to reconcile with practice, for example in accountability to Parliament. Nevertheless, that principle underpins the PES system and its operation, and ensures that expenditure business is conducted co-operatively between the Treasury and spending departments, predicated on the acceptance by both of the collective nature of British central government.

Proposals to strengthen the Treasury's control of public expenditure *vis-à-vis* the spending departments have consequences for that shared core value. Above we examined critically proposals which are sometimes made to strengthen the Treasury by making Expenditure Controllers specialists in the programmes and departments they shadow. Apart from the practical difficulties of so doing, we argued that competing with the specialist knowledge and professional competence of the spending departments would mean either that the Treasury's judgement prevailed or that there would be need for arbitration between two conflicting, professional judgements. The consequence would be a fundamental shift in the nature of the interdependent relationship. In either case the exchange of crucial resources of information and expertise would be affected—departments would have less incentive to provide information. The consequential effect of so doing would be to undermine the working principle of co-operation grounded in the collective nature of government. The Treasury could not become more directive, imposing its authority on spending departments, without changing the basis of their present co-operation.

Such proposals raise fundamental issues of the collective nature of British central government: strengthening the process whereby decisions are made means either strengthening the practice of collective responsibility or abandoning the principle in favour of the undivided responsibility of the Chancellor or the Chancellor and the Prime Minister combined. How can the collective responsibility of central government be strengthened to improve expenditure decision-making? There are two main issues: first, how to strengthen the Chancellor and the Treasury *vis-à-vis* individual spending ministers and their departments, in the delivery of an annual Planning/Control Total collectively determined and agreed; secondly, how to improve the process whereby allocations are made.

It has often been suggested in the past that the collective discussion and decision-making on expenditure could be improved by referring bids early in the PES round to a senior committee of the Cabinet. The changes introduced in 1992 go some way to meeting this, but EDX is not involved until quite late in the round, in mid-July for a general 'path-finding' meeting and then in September to discuss Treasury proposals for allocation. While the Cabinet endorses the Chancellor's proposal for the aggregate of expenditure, it is less certain that the involvement of the Cabinet Committee, EDX, in the discussion of the allocation of that total has achieved a more informed and coherent determination of the relative priority of the spending programmes.

There are a number of practical difficulties which the 1992 changes have not removed. First, Cabinet Ministers in EDX are not involved collectively in the PES process of determining the allocation until quite late in the round, by which time decisions on individual programmes have been discussed bilaterally between officials and ministers, and decisions have begun to be firmed up. While it is true that those discussions, and the Chief Secretary's strategy, reflect broadly the priority which the Government attaches to particular spending programmes, explicit interprogramme comparisons are not made during the earlier stages of the Survey processes, as we have shown. If Ministers collectively in EDX are to engage in the determination of the relative priorities of all spending programmes, they would need to do so much earlier in the PES process, to guide the subsequent discussions between the Treasury and the departments. Secondly, they would have to display the political will to determine expenditure priorities thus, and be prepared to handle a mass of information, argument, and counter-argument from at least nineteen spending departments and some 200 discrete programmes. The investment of time and energy would be disproportionate to the 'political return' for an individual Minister. Thirdly, all spending ministers would have to be prepared to accept the conclusions of that process, with appeal to full Cabinet allowed only in exceptional and prescribed limited circumstances. Previous experience of such a committee, in the early years of PESC, suggested that while this could be done successfully with a small number of programmes and limited amounts of information, there are cognitive limits on the assimilation of material. Practically, Ministers show little enthusiasm for such an exercise; most prefer to deal bilaterally with the Chief Secretary. Fourthly, as we have argued, EDX is dependent upon the analysis and advice of the Treasury; it has no alternative source with which to challenge the recommendations made to it. If it or some similarly constituted Cabinet Committee is to do more than approve the recommendations of the Chancellor and the Chief Secretary and their strategy for public spending, as happens now in July with the New Control Totals proposed at the Cabinet, and at its subsequent meetings in October and November to discuss allocations, there would be a considerable additional burden on senior ministers.

Certainly the Star Chamber never performed that function in the 1980s. Its role was to arbitrate between contending parties, to resolve disputes. It was concerned to decide each case on its merits, not to compare the merits of the spending proposal brought to it with those agreed or settled at an earlier stage. EDX is unlikely to be able to do more than resolve differences between the Treasury and those spending ministries which could not be reconciled in the bilaterals. While the opportunity exists for a more thorough discussion of priorities than in the Star Chamber, unlike the latter the agenda and most of the evidence submitted is controlled by the Treasury, and EDX is chaired by the Chancellor of the Exchequer.

These practical difficulties raise the perennially debated issue of the role and strength of the core of central government, and in particular its analytic capability. Proposals to strengthen the latter have taken several forms. The enlargement of the Prime Minister's Office on the model of the Executive Office of the US President was exhaustively discussed at the time of the abolition of the CPRS and the CSD in the early 1980s and rejected; it is not, for the time being, on the agenda. Such enlargement, it is argued, would strengthen the capacity for policy analysis and provide more information to enable the Prime Minister to have a better understanding of strategy, and the priorities of public spending. But such advice would not contribute directly to collective decision-making on public spending, unless he or she (with the support of the Chancellor) attempted to impose a strategy not only for the total but also its allocation on his colleagues, in much the way that the US President does with the help of his Executive Office and the Office of Management and Budget. However, that strategy is subject to scrutiny, revision, and objection in Congress. Dell (1985) has argued that the Prime Minister should be more personally involved in public spending decisions, and with the Chancellor decide both the total and its allocation to Cabinet colleagues. Agreement on the former is easier, now that the Cabinet has accepted the principle of top–down control limits, than deciding appropriate allocations to programmes and departments. To do that effectively there would be need of an advisory capacity for both the Prime Minister and the Chancellor, provided wholly by the Treasury or competitively with an independent agency, such as the former CPRS. The changes initiated in 1992 were guided by the interests of the Treasury, and the creation of a competing analytic capacity was understandably not part of its agenda of proposed changes. The Prime Minister has no alternative source of informed analysis and advice, grounded in the detail of departmental bids, to that provided by his Chancellor and Chief Secretary, and hence no means to exercise greater authority in the processes of deciding the total and its allocation. Those who have argued and urged the need for a central analytical capacity in British government see part of its function to help ministers collectively make better, informed decisions about public spending. The provision of such capacity would, they argue, create an alternative source of analysis and advice on public spending matters to that currently provided by the Treasury collectively for the Cabinet. The Treasury does so at various times in the PES round, but most importantly at the time of recommendation on the three-year New Control Totals at the July Cabinet, when the Chancellor and Chief Secretary outline their thinking and general strategy, and subsequently when EDX discusses the allocations of the year one total and makes recommendations to Cabinet.

Strengthening the analysis and advice available to Cabinet collectively could occur either through an enlargement of the functions and staff of the Cabinet Office, or the re-creation of a think-tank, such as the former CPRS. Part of the function of such a general analytical capability would be to provide more analysis, information, and advice on the effectiveness of spending programmes and the alternative uses of resources allocated to them. This could be provided jointly with the Treasury, as sometimes happened in the early 1970s when the CPRS provided papers on overall priorities in the PES round. Or such a body could provide an alternative and possibly competing perspective on public spending. However and by whomever such analysis and advice is provided, the general aim would be to equip ministers collectively to make more informed decisions about public spending. The assumption underlying such proposals is that neither Cabinet nor its committees have adequate analysis and advice to determine the appropriate strategy for overall public spending and to consider the alternative ways in which resources could be distributed between programmes. An alternative assumption is that it has advice provided by the Treasury but has no means to challenge a monolithic perspective and appreciation.

All such proposals assume that ministers collectively would be willing to play such a role: to take a closer and more informed interest in the process whereby the total of public spending is decided, and would be prepared to discuss the cost-effectiveness of each other's programmes and hence compete *collectively* for additional resources. It is doubtful whether ministers have the time, energy, or inclination to inform themselves about a complex and time-consuming subject which does not directly affect their individual sectional interests. Moreover, even with access to improved analysis, and better information about costed alternatives, it is by no means certain that ministers would decide expenditure business other than by the political rationality to which we referred in Chapter 11. While they might accept an alternative to the Treasury's overview at the July Cabinet, in the bilaterals face-to-face with the Chief Secretary they would continue to press their departmental interest as hard as before, albeit within the context of fixed limits for a total whose previous elasticity has for the time being been eliminated.

Proposals for strengthening the Treasury *vis-à-vis* the spending departments, other than through changes to the rules of the game by which their relations are presently regulated, as in 1976 (cash limits), 1982 (cash planning), 1988 (New Planning Total), and 1992 (New Control Total), would require a paradigm shift in the principle and practice of collective government. Such a shift could occur if it were accepted that the aggregate of public expenditure should be limited each year to a fixed proportion of GDP, and hence proof against arguments to relax it under the imperative of a purely political calculus. This has been canvassed by Wildavsky and others in the USA, where it would require an amendment to the Constitution. In the UK any such legislation would not be binding on future governments, who could simply repeal it; the implications of any EC-imposed constraint are discussed a little later on. Convention would be difficult to establish and depend for its observance on success in the achievement of the fixed proportions. While 'capping' the aggregate, as with the New Control Total, helps to restrain the growth of public expenditure, it does not provide a more rational means of distributing it. Ministers individually continue as before to try to win as big a share of any predetermined total. The integration of the budgetary procedures for dealing with taxation and spending introduced in November 1993 does oblige ministers collectively to confront the implications of spending proposals more directly than they have done in the past, where individual negotiations and collective discussion of the implications of those negotiations for the Planning Total took place six to nine months before consideration of the means for financing the agreed expenditures. Bringing together expenditure and taxation will make it easier for the Treasury to register simultaneously the financial (and political) costs of additional spending, but much will depend on the interest of ministers collectively in Cabinet, and on the exercise of mutual political will to restrain the 'buccaneering proclivities' of each of them individually, as self-interested spending ministers.

A PARADIGM SHIFT: FROM NEGOTIATED DISCRETION TO CENTRAL PRESCRIPTION?

The future evolution of public spending policy objectives, and of the design of the planning and control system to implement them, depends on the interplay of a range of factors. As we have shown in earlier chapters, both have evolved pragmatically in response to the exigencies of recurrent political and economic crises, ideological shifts, pressure-group activity, demographic and technological changes, and the clash of institutional interests. Such factors will continue to exert powerful effects throughout the 1990s. Moreover, the broader context of external economic and political developments—especially the 'Europeanization' of economic policy—will be more determinate, irrespective of the particular shape of European integration.

Whether the result is a paradigm shift in the system for planning and controlling public spending depends on the intensity of the pressures experienced by governments in the 1990s. By paradigm shift we mean the permanent abandonment (not merely temporary relaxation) of the pre-existing paradigm of negotiated discretion, which has historically characterized the relationships between the Treasury and the spending departments in planning and controlling both the total and the allocation of public expenditure. The imposition of top–down limits in 1992 may mark the beginning of such a shift, but it remains to be seen whether that and other changes designed to tighten central control and strengthen the collective responsibility of the Cabinet can be sustained when (and if) the proximate cause for its occurrence, the exceptional and temporary conditions of acute financial crisis, has abated. The test will come with the resumption of economic growth and the political imperatives of an impending general election and/or the progressive erosion of a government's authority in the House of Commons. In the remainder of this chapter we discuss the economic and political conditions which might precipitate a permanent, paradigm shift, and examine the implications of three alternative hypotheses. We leave to one side changes in the electoral system or in constitutional arrangements which might occur independently of broader economic and financial events, or be precipitated by them.

We hypothesize first a 'steady state' situation, in which in the absence of acute economic or financial crisis, the PES system continues to evolve gradually and pragmatically as further experience is gained of its operation by the Treasury, the spending departments, and the Cabinet. The 'learning process' which has characterized the operation of PESC/PES by its principal participants since the early 1960s would continue, with changes in the rules of the game to reflect the still more urgent need to contain the inexorable pressures for more spending. The second hypothesis envisages a deepening domestic economic and fiscal crisis; the third, a significant increase in European integration with consequential constraints on the formation of economic policy, and further loss of independence of action in domestic monetary and fiscal policy. Both of the last two hypothetical situations would provide the conditions for a paradigm shift. An economic crisis *and* the Europeanization of policy could of course occur simultaneously.

PES in a steady state

Here the assumption is that public spending policy objectives and the PES system remain unchanged in all essentials, although subject to further adjustments and refinements, such as have characterized its development since 1976. Spending departments continue to negotiate with the Treasury for discretionary room to manœuvre, subject to the constraints of top–down limits imposed by the Treasury, and the exercise of collective responsibility by the Cabinet under the 1992 arrangements.

The macro-economic context favourable to this hypothesis is one of relative economic buoyancy. Inflation remains fairly stable, within the band of 1 to 4 per cent targeted by the Treasury in 1992. Economic growth is strong in the recovery from recession and then remains for the rest of the decade at the top end of projections made by the Treasury, its 'seven wise men', and outside forecasters, that is in excess of the trend rate of growth and at a historically high 3 per cent average rate of growth. This is fuelled by a competitive exchange rate outside the ERM, low wage and unit costs relative to the UK's European competitors, the continued influx of foreign capital, and a more interventionist, pro-manufacturing policy by the DTI, Department of Employment, and Treasury. Largely as a consequence of higher economic growth, the fiscal crisis of the early 1990s subsides. The assumption underlying this hypothesis is the successful adherence to the NCT and GGE limits of 1.5 and 2 per cent respectively, low interest rates making the servicing of an increased national debt manageable, and relatively low inflation enabling the Treasury to deliver to departments further real increases in resources. Economic growth of 3 per cent and inflation (measured by the GDP deflator) at 2.5 per cent per year in the period to 1997 would produce a PSBR of 2.75 per cent of GDP, General Government Expenditure of 42.75 per cent of GDP, and public debt at 48 per cent of GDP (Martin 1992). The Department of Social Security assumes that if GDP grew on average by 3 per cent per year and unemployment was 'about half less' in 1999/2000 than in 1993, social security spending would fall as a proportion of GDP from 12.3 per cent in 1992–3 to 11.3 per cent by the end of the millennium (DSS 1993). Combined, these very optimistic projections produce an almost golden scenario.

It implicitly assumes the continuation of Conservative Governments; and a large degree of national sovereignty in determining macro-economic policy and, in particular, monetary policy, which seems likelier as a result of the effective collapse of the ERM in 1993. At the very least, there will be delay in the progress towards European Monetary Union envisaged in the Maastricht Treaty timetable, in particular the operation of the convergence criteria by 1997 or 1999, and the additional costs of bringing the poorer EC states up to a compatible level of economic performance (OECD 1993*b*), the continued strains of the process of German unification, and the political and economic pressures created by the absorption of additional members.

This hypothesis is not incompatible with significant adjustments to the scope and scale of individual spending programmes and further reordering of priorities. Nor does it argue that there will be necessarily a slowing down of the trends noted in the previous chapter towards a more decentralized and increasingly market-led and privatized public service. The Treasury will continue to need coping strategies aimed at: (*a*) holding the aggregate NCT and GGE targets, (*b*) stemming the tide of increased pressures for more spending as a result of 'uncontrollable' elements of spending, and (*c*) making room for new political and economic priorities. But we are assuming that 'fundamental reviews' of public spending, such as that announced as a medium-term component of the July 1992 package, cannot deliver more than marginal reductions in the existing spending commitments of government, short of a deeper and longer-lasting political and economic crisis than that which occurred in 1992–3. Even under the ideological administrations of Thatcher only twenty of the 227 programmes inherited in 1979 had been terminated by 1985, while twenty-eight new programmes were started (Rose 1990). Almost all the reforms to the welfare state initiated under her leadership were compromises which left intact the commitments inherited in 1979; the Fowler social security reforms left unmoved much of the social security system; the NHS reforms, whilst radical, did not institute an insurance-based system; and education reforms have left the vast majority of schools under local authority control. What is far more likely is piecemeal reform, chipping away at the edges of state provision, particularly in those areas where pressure groups are weakest, or those least likely to alter the 'social wage' enjoyed by the majority of (middle-class) voters.

Nevertheless, there will be scope for significant but gradual and evolutionary changes, the accumulation of which might lead to an altered landscape, if not in state provision then of the institutions and processes by which that provision is delivered. Changes in the rules of the game rebalancing the tension between central Treasury control and departmental autonomy would provide tauter central control, such as: stricter cash limits; increased efficiency gains on running costs; (temporary) annual abrogation of the 1992 Pay Agreements by imposed central limits; Treasury-backed schemes of performance-related pay; more rigorous scrutiny of management plans with tighter criteria for the granting of flexibilities and concessions; more stringent conditions for delegating authority; tightening the rules for determining territorial allocations, by restricting the discretion of Secretaries of State; new criteria for deciding the block grant; further encouragement of private sector contribution to capital projects.

Redrawing the boundaries between the Treasury and the spending departments described by PES rules would be consistent with the gradual and pragmatic developments discussed in previous chapters. A more radical, perhaps paradigmatic shift, could occur simultaneously in the managerial context. As we have shown, the improvement of managerial practice in the Civil Service has hitherto equally been a process of gradual evolution, principally through FMI and Next Steps. The 'Further Steps' towards the creation of a contract state of privatized services and agencies, in which cost-controls could be legally enforced, noted in the previous chapter, has profound implications for public control and accountability throughout the Civil Service.

Domestic crisis and a paradigm shift

It requires little imagination to argue that the optimism of the first hypothesis might be misplaced. The continuation of a sluggish performance by the UK economy (or even worse of stagnation), coupled with continued high levels of unemployment and a return to an indifferent inflation performance, would transform the context of public spending planning and control in the second half of the 1990s.

If the economy grew by 2 per cent per year and General Government Expenditure by 3.5 per cent per year in the period to 1997, the PSBR would be at Italian proportions of more than 10 per cent of GDP, public debt would be at 72 per cent of GDP (both well above the fiscal policy criteria envisaged in the original Maastricht Treaty). GGE would represent 48 per cent of GDP, higher than at any time since the 1976 crisis. Assuming GDP growth of 2 per cent per year until the end of the century and unemployment at three million, the DSS projects that social security spending would grow by 3.3 per cent per year to stand nearly £20 billion higher in real terms or 13.5 per cent of GDP by 1999–2000 (DSS 1993).

Such economic performance would risk a cumulative crisis as it became harder to fund the PSBR without higher interest rates; interest payments would pre-empt a larger share of total GGE; the exchange rate would depreciate as foreign holders of sterling required a premium before giving further support; and the private sector would be crowded out in the competition with the public sector for funds. Other longer-term factors, such as the decline of manufacturing capacity and a high balance-of-payments deficit, would further limit the room for flexibility in domestic policy-making.

Leaving aside the many political, social, and institutional consequences of this economic and financial crisis, the prevailing public spending paradigm of negotiated discretion would become untenable. The PES system would change in terms of the top–down limits on spending, how spending was allocated, and would presage a fundamental review of the state provision of the whole range of welfare services.

In these circumstances the medium- to long-term policy rules for the limits on the growth of the NCT and GGE set in July 1992 could not be sustained. Not only would the economy be growing at less than trend rate but, because tax revenues would be lower, there would be pressure to cut spending growth still further. This assumes that the resistance of taxpayers to increased indirect and direct taxation would limit the scope for cutting the PSBR by those means. In addition, the pressure on GGE from increased debt payments and higher unemployment would reduce still further the scope for real increases in the spending counted as part of the NCT. Should the growth of the NCT be limited to 0.5 or 0.75 per cent growth in real terms, as would seem likely under these conditions, it is difficult to see how the Cabinet could continue with the present arrangements. The political infighting for a share of an ever-smaller cake, against the background of continued or even mounting pressure for higher spending, would overwhelm the existing basis of Treasury–department negotiations and EDX adjudication. For example, if we assume that social security spending could not be radically reduced, then the likely projected growth of non-cyclical social security spending would absorb almost all of that lower NCT growth ceiling. Other departments would then be required to reduce not only bids but *baselines* in order to make way for increases in other inescapable commitments.

The method of allocating resources would have to be fundamentally reshaped. This might take the form of significant institutional changes. It would be essential to lock the Cabinet and hence ministers collectively and individually into a system capable of delivering unpalatable outcomes in the annual expenditure and budgetary cycle. Either full Cabinet or its EDX Committee would be required to play a more central role in the formulation of expenditure policy, department by department. This would strengthen the arguments for a source of analysis and advice independent of a Treasury whose credibility was impaired by yet another loss of control. This might take the form and role of a revived Central Policy Review Staff, or an agency such as that recommended by a former Permanent Secretary of the Treasury in the 1980s (Wass 1984).

The damage to the authority of the Treasury to control on the basis of the prevailing paradigm of negotiated discretion would be substantial, providing ammunition for those external critics intent on breaking its monopoly of economic and financial power at the heart of government. In such circumstances, the centre of government might be reconstructed, with the creation of a Ministry of Economic Affairs responsible for economic and monetary policy and forecasting, and a Ministry of Finance responsible for taxation and spending. The perception of a weak, too-weak Treasury might paradoxically lead to its enhancement, with the acceptance by ministers collectively that it needed more not less authority to *impose* settlements on individual Ministries and their programmes rather than to negotiate them. With the principle of greater involvement by the rest of the Cabinet in allocating resources through EDX already conceded by the Treasury in 1992, and the need for demonstrable political backing for unpalatable decisions from a wider group of Ministers and departments, it seems unlikely that Ministers would willingly agree to strengthen the Treasury's authority and its role at the centre. At the very least, senior Ministers would demand greater involvement in a wider range of economic policy decisions than hitherto, in return for such a move; ironically, such involvement would be more feasible as a result of the Treasury's introduction of the Unified Budget from November 1993.

Whatever the institutional rearrangements, a crisis of this magnitude would require a fundamental reappraisal of the level and scope of public spending, simply because the figures would not add up. Even allowing for no new policy initiatives, the costs of public spending rise faster than the economy as a whole. We noted in Chapter 21 that RPE alone would account for about 0.8 per cent 'real increase' in GGE each year. Non-cash limited spending, that is demand-led spending, accounted for 38 per cent of Supply Expenditure in 1992–3 and this would generate commitments almost impossible to avoid. The scope for further privatization would be limited as most of the saleable pieces of the public sector were disposed of in the £50 billion sale of assets in the 1983–93 programme. To square the circle, real commitments would have to be jettisoned, a re-run of the proposals in the CPRS report shelved in 1982 which advocated options such as education vouchers, health insurance to replace part of the NHS, and the cancellation of Trident (Lawson 1992) against a background of a much less severe economic crisis than the one hypothesized here.

We noted earlier the DSS estimates of the level of the social security budget against the background of low growth and high unemployment. That budget would be the first to be targeted. Possible changes would range in degree of radicalism from the taxing of benefits (such as Child Benefit) to the ending of universal benefits, limiting eligibility to invalidity and sickness benefit, and the contracting out of state provision to the private sector. The basic retirement pensions accounted for some 34.4 per cent of the total £74 billion of social security benefits distributed in 1992–3, while Child Benefit accounted for a further 8 per cent (DSS 1993).

The eight next largest programmes within the NCT after social security are the local authority support budget of the D.o.E., the programmes of the Department of Health, followed by Defence, the Scottish Office, local authorities' self-financed spending, the housing programme of the D.o.E., Education, and Transport. Radical policies in these areas would include such politically controversial solutions as increasing fees and charges and private provision in the NHS, a further tightening of central control of local government, further reductions in defence commitments, private fees in universities, the privatization of opted-out schools, and increased use of toll roads and private funding for road building. None of these is without powerful advocates; even in 1992–3 they were beginning to assume the status of 'ideas-in-good-currency' within the Treasury and some spending departments, and to be discussed more widely outside it. If, as we argue in the first hypothesis, the 1992–3 review of spending programmes results in the slaughter of few if any of the sacred cows among the spending programmes, it may have greater significance for the conditions of acute and sustained crisis hypothesized here. Unthinkable options will have been canvassed and debated, and while no more palatable next time round than last, the agenda threshold will already have been crossed.

External constraints and a paradigm shift

A paradigm shift in the planning and control of public spending could occur without the circumstances of acute economic and financial crisis described above, as a result of EU membership and subscription to the original Maastricht Treaty obligations for the convergence of fiscal and monetary systems, which provided for limits on the size of the public sector aggregate. Consequential effects on the determination of the relative priorities of spending programmes and the allocation of resources to them—decisions within the control of member states—could lead to a more directive system of control than that inherent in negotiated discretion. On a longer time-scale, the implications of the free movement of labour, capital, and goods are a convergence of the regulations and payments in social security and income maintenance, for example sick pay, maternity and child benefits, unemployment and redundancy benefits. EC directives on some of these have already been incorporated into UK legislation.

The collapse of the ERM in 1993 has created uncertainty about the future of European Monetary Union, and indeed the scope and time-scale of European integration. At the very least, progress towards EMU will be slower than scheduled in the Maastricht Treaty. Stage two, where each member state commits itself to 'endeavour to avoid excess-ive deficits', may now be delayed, while stage three, where there is a commitment to avoid them, now appears unlikely to operate before 1999. The convergence criteria to guide member states may not survive in their present form, but have independently of the Treaty obligations become a useful rule-of-thumb by which comparisons are made about the relative government-indebtedness of EC and other countries, and are worth repeating here: public sector deficits should not exceed 3 per cent of GDP, and the government debt/GDP ratio should be no more than 60 per cent.

If those or similar criteria were incorporated into a revised prospectus and timetable for EMU, to which the UK subscribed, the Treasury would have some difficulty in meeting them on the assumption of a central economic case, between the optimism and pessimism of the first two hypotheses. If the economy grew at 2 per cent per year, inflation remained low, and GGE grew by just over the current policy rule at 2.25 per cent per year, by 1997 the PSBR would be high, at 7.5 per cent of GDP, public debt would be equivalent to 65 per cent of GDP, and GGE would remain fairly stable at 45 per cent of GDP (Martin 1992). In such circumstances the UK would have a fiscal policy problem but not a crisis on the scale hypothesized earlier. However, the UK would be in breach of key elements of the original Maastricht Treaty. If the Treaty and its obligations remained extant following the collapse of the ERM, there would be an externally imposed constraint on the size of the public-spending aggregate, and its relation to GDP and government debt. How this would be enforced is unclear (see Harden 1993 for a discussion of this). No useful purpose is served by speculating further about the putative effects of Treaty obligations which may be abandoned *de facto* if not *de jure*, for example, the efficacy of the proposed institutional arrangements for monitoring and enforcing compliance with those rules and the imposition of sanctions for their breach. Progress towards EMU appears to have been delayed, and with it the possibility of an externally imposed paradigm shift in the UK's planning and control system has receded. If such a shift occurs in the 1990s, while it may be in response to external economic and financial circumstances, it will be either because the UK Government rather than the European Commission in Brussels has willed it, or because there would exist a small core of EC members within a D-Mark zone maintaining the momentum towards some form of European economic and monetary integration (see Buiter, Corsetti, and Roubini 1993), and hence setting the 'gold standard' in terms of economic policy performance.

REFERENCES

Armstrong, Lord W. (1980), Chairman, Report of Committee of Inquiry set up by the Institute for Fiscal Studies, publ. as *Budgetary Reform in the UK* (Oxford: Oxford University Press).

Bancroft, I. (1981), 'Memorandum', in Treasury and the Civil Service Committee, *Efficiency and Effectiveness in the Civil Service*, 1981–2, Third Report, HC 236-II, Minutes of Evidence, 174–85.

Barnett, J. (1982), *Inside the Treasury* (London: André Deutsch).

Bell, P. N. (1987), 'Direct Rule in Northern Ireland', in Rose 1987.

Bevan, R. G. (1980), 'Cash Limits', *Fiscal Studies*, 1/4: 26–43.

—— Sisson, K., and Way, P. (1981), 'Cash Limits and Public Sector Pay', *Public Administration*, 59/4: 379–98.

Bosanquet, N. (1983), *After the New Right* (London: Heinemann).

Bridges, Lord E. (1964), *The Treasury* (London: Allen & Unwin).

Brittan, S. (1983), *The Role and Limits of Government: Essays in Political Economy* (London: Temple Smith).

Bruce-Gardyne, Lord J. (1986), *Ministers and Mandarins* (London: Sidgwick & Jackson).

Buiter, W. H., and Miller, M. H. (1983), *Macroeconomic Consequences of a Change in Regime: The UK under Mrs Thatcher* (Centre for Labour Economics, Discussion Paper, 179; London: London School of Economics).

—— Corsetti, G., and Roubini, N. (1993), 'Excessive Deficits: Sense and Nonsense in the Treaty of Maastricht', *Economic Policy* (Apr.), 57–100.

Bulpitt, J. (1986), 'The Discipline of the New Democracy: Mrs Thatcher's Domestic Statecraft', *Political Studies*, 34/1: 19–39.

Burch, M. (1983), 'Mrs Thatcher's Approach to Leadership in Government: 1979–June 1983', *Parliamentary Affairs*, 36/4: 399–416.

—— (1990), 'Cabinet Government', *Contemporary Record*, 4/1: 5–8.

Burk, K., and Cairncross, A. (1992), *'Goodbye Great Britain': The 1976 IMF Crisis* (London: Yale University Press).

Burns, T. (1988), 'The UK Government's Financial Strategy', in W. Eltis and P. Sinclair (eds.), *Keynes and Economic Policy: The Relevance of The General Theory after Fifty Years* (London: Macmillan).

—— (1993), 'Some Reflections on the Treasury', preliminary version of an article to be publ. in S. Holly (ed.), *Essays in Honour of Sir James Ball's Sixtieth Birthday* (Brighton: Harvester, 1994).

Butler, F. E. R., and Aldred, K. (1977), 'Financial Information Systems Project', *Management Services in Government*, 32: 77–87.

Cabinet Office (1991), *The Civil Service Yearbook 1991* (London: HMSO).

—— (1992), *Civil Service Yearbook 1992* (London: HMSO).

—— (1993), *Civil Service Yearbook 1993* (London: HMSO).

—— and Treasury (1989), *Public Expenditure Management*, i. *Public Expenditure Survey* (London: HMSO).

Cairncross, A. (1985), *Years of Recovery: British Economic Policy 1945–51* (London: Methuen).

Castle, B. (1980), *The Castle Diaries, 1974–6* (London: Weidenfeld).

Chapman, R. A. (1991), 'Editorial: New Arrangements for Recruitment in the British Civil Service: Cause for Concern', *Public Policy and Administration*, 6/3 (Winter), 1–6.

Chouraqui, J.-C., and Price, R. W. R. (1984), 'Medium-Term Financial Strategy: The Co-ordination of Fiscal and Monetary Policy', *OECD Economic Studies*, 2 (Spring), 7–50.

Clarke, R. (1971), *New Trends in Government* (London: HMSO).

—— (1978), *Public Expenditure Management and Control*, ed. Alec Cairncross (London: Macmillan).

Cm. 14 (1986), *Autumn Statement 1986*, HM Treasury (London: HMSO, Nov.).

Cm. 56 (1987), *The Government's Expenditure Plans 1987–88 to 1989–90* (in 2 vols.; London: HMSO, Jan.).

Cm. 94 (1987), *Supply Estimates 1987–88: Summary and Guide*, HM Treasury (London: HMSO, Mar.).

Cm. 288 (1988), *The Government's Expenditure Plans 1988–89 to 1990–91* (London: HMSO, Jan.).

Cm. 328 (1988), *Supply Estimates 1988–89: Summary and Guide*, HM Treasury (London: HMSO, Mar.).

Cm. 375 (1988), *Financial Reporting to Parliament*, HM Treasury (London: HMSO, May).

Cm. 441 (1988), *A New Planning Total*, HM Treasury (London: HMSO, July).

Cm. 621 (1989), *The Government's Expenditure Plans 1989–90 to 1991–92*: Chapter 21—Supplementary Analysis and index, HM Treasury (London: HMSO, Jan.).

Cm. 633 (1989), *Supply Estimates 1989–90: Summary and Guide*, HM Treasury (London: HMSO, Mar.).

Cm. 914 (1989), *The Financing and Accountability of Next Steps Agencies*, HM Treasury (London: HMSO, Dec.).

Cm. 980 (1990), *Supply Estimates 1990–91: Summary and Guide*, HM Treasury (London: HMSO, Mar.).

Cm. 1021 (1990), *The Government's Expenditure Plans 1990–91 to 1992–93*: Chapter 21—Supplementary Analysis and Index, HM Treasury (London: HMSO, Jan.).

Cm. 1311 (1990), *Autumn Statement 1990*, HM Treasury (London: HMSO, Nov.).

Cm. 1454 (1991), *Supply Estimates 1991–92: Summary and Guide*, HM Treasury (London: HMSO, Mar.).

Cm. 1515 (1991), *Serving Scotland's Needs: The Government's Expenditure Plans 1991–92 to 1992–93*, Presented to Parliament by the Secretary of State for Scotland and the Chief Secretary to the Treasury (Edinburgh:

HMSO, Feb.).

Cm. 1516 (1991), *The Government's Expenditure Plans 1991–92 to 1992–93: Departmental Report by the Welsh Office*, Presented to Parliament by the Secretary of State for Wales and the Chief Secretary to the Treasury (London: HMSO, Feb.).

Cm. 1517 (1991), *Northern Ireland Expenditure Plans and Priorities: The Government's Expenditure Plans 1991–92 to 1992–93*, Presented to Parliament by the Secretary of State for Northern Ireland and the Chief Secretary to the Treasury (London: HMSO, Feb.).

Cm. 1520 (1991), *Public Expenditure Analyses to 1993–94: Statistical Supplement to the 1990 Autumn Statement*, HM Treasury (London: HMSO, Feb.).

Cm. 1587 (1991), *Cash Limits 1990–91*, HM Treasury (London: HMSO, July).

Cm. 1729 (1991), *Autumn Statement 1991*, HM Treasury (London: HMSO, Nov.).

Cm. 1730 (1991), *Competing for Quality*, HM Treasury (London: HMSO).

Cm. 1761 (1991), *Improving Management in Government: The Next Steps Agencies Review 1991*, Prime Minister (London: HMSO, Nov.).

Cm. 1844 (1992), *Supply Estimates 1992–93: Summary and Guide*, HM Treasury (London: HMSO, Mar.).

Cm. 1867 (1992), *Budgetary Reform*, HM Treasury (London: HMSO, Mar.).

Cm. 1920 (1992), *Public Expenditure Analyses to 1994–95: Statistical Supplement to the 1991 Autumn Statement*, HM Treasury (London: HMSO, Feb.).

Cm. 2096 (1992), *Autumn Statement 1992*, HM Treasury (London: HMSO, Nov.).

Cm. 2101 (1992), *The Citizen's Charter First Report: 1992*, Prime Minister and Chancellor of the Duchy of Lancaster (London: HMSO, Nov.).

Cm. 2111 (1992), *The Next Steps Agencies: Review 1992*, Chancellor of the Duchy of Lancaster (London: HMSO, Dec.).

Cm. 2203 (1993), *The Government's Expenditure Plans 1993–94 to 1995–96: Departmental Report by the Ministry of Agriculture, Fisheries and Food and Intervention Board*, MAFF (London: HMSO, Feb.).

Cm. 2208 (1993), *The Goverment's Expenditure Plans 1993–94 to 1995–96 for the Home Office and Charity Commission*, Home Office (London: HMSO, Feb.).

Cm. 2214 (1993), *Serving Scotland's Needs: The Government's Expenditure Plans 1993–94 to 1995–96*, Scottish Office (London: HMSO, Feb.).

Cm. 2215 (1993), *The Government's Expenditure Plans 1993–94 to 1995–96: Departmental Report by the Welsh Office*, Welsh Office (London: HMSO, Feb.).

Cm. 2216 (1993), *Expenditure Plans and Priorities: Northern Ireland: The Government's Expenditure Plans 1993–94 to 1995–96*, Northern Ireland Office (London: HMSO, Feb.).

Cm. 2217 (1993), *Departmental Report of the Chancellor of the Exchequer's Departments: The Government's Expenditure Plans 1993–94 to 1995–96* (London: HMSO, Feb.).

Cm. 2219 (1993), *Public Expenditure Analyses to 1995–96: Statistical Summary to the 1992 Autumn Statement*, HM Treasury (London: HMSO, Feb.).

Cm. 2230 (1993), *Supply Estimates 1993–94: Summary and Guide*, HM Treasury (London: HMSO, Mar.).

Cmnd. 1432 (1961), *Control of Public Expenditure*, Chairman: Edwin Plowden (London: HMSO).

Cmnd. 6393 (1976), *Public Expenditure to 1979–80* (London: HMSO, Feb.).

Cmnd. 6440 (1976), *Cash Limits on Public Expenditure*, HM Treasury (London: HMSO).

Cmnd. 6452 (1976), *Supply Estimates 1976–77, for the Year Ending March 31: Memorandum by the Chief Secretary to the Treasury*, HM Treasury (London: HMSO, Mar.).

Cmnd. 6721 (1977), *The Goverment's Expenditure Plans* (London: HMSO, Jan.).

Cmnd. 6769 (1977), *Supply Estimates 1977–78, for the Year Ending 31 March: Memorandum by the Chief Secretary to the Treasury*, HM Treasury (London: HMSO, Mar.).

Cmnd. 7049 (1978), *The Government's Expenditure Plans 1979–80 to 1981–82* (London: HMSO, Jan.).

Cmnd. 7157 (1978), *Supply Estimates 1978–79, for the Year Ending 31 March: Memorandum by the Chief Secretary to the Treasury*, HM Treasury (London: HMSO, Mar.).

Cmnd. 7439 (1979), *The Government's Expenditure Plans 1979–80 to 1982–83* (London: HMSO, Jan.).

Cmnd. 7515 (1979), *Cash Limits, 1979–80*, HM Treasury (London: HMSO).

Cmnd. 7524 (1979), *Supply Estimates 1979–80, for the Year Ending 31 March: Memorandum by the Chief Secretary to the Treasury*, HM Treasury (London: HMSO, Mar.).

Cmnd. 7746 (1979), *The Government's Expenditure Plans 1980–81* (London: HMSO, Nov.).

Cmnd. 7841 (1980), *The Government's Expenditure Plans 1980–81 to 1983–84* (London: HMSO, Mar.).

Cmnd. 7869 (1980), *Supply Estimates 1980–81, for the Year Ending 31 March: Memorandum by the Chief Secretary to the Treasury*, HM Treasury (London: HMSO, Mar.).

Cmnd. 8170 (1981), *The Future of the Civil Service Department* (London: HMSO, Jan.).

Cmnd. 8175 (1981), *The Government's Expenditure Plans 1981–82 to 1983–84* (London: HMSO, Mar.).

Cmnd. 8184 (1981), *Supply Estimates 1981–82, for the Year Ending 31 March: Memorandum by the Chief Secretary to the Treasury*, HM Treasury (London: HMSO, Mar.).

Cmnd. 8293 (1981), *Efficiency in the Civil Service*, Report by the Lord President of the Council (London: HMSO, July).

Cmnd. 8494 (1982), *The Government's Expenditure Plans 1982–83 to 1984–85*

(London: HMSO, Mar.).

Cmnd. 8512 (1982), *Supply Estimates 1982–83, for the Year Ending 31 March: Memorandum by the Chief Secretary to the Treasury*, HM Treasury (London: HMSO, Mar.).

Cmnd. 8616 (1982), *Efficiency and Effectiveness in the Civil Service: Government Observations on the 3rd Report from the Treasury and Civil Service Committee, Session 1981–82* (London: HMSO, Sept.).

Cmnd. 8789 (1983), *The Government's Expenditure Plans 1983–84 to 1985–86* (London: HMSO, Feb.).

Cmnd. 8817 (1983), *Supply Estimates 1983–84: Memorandum by the Chief Secretary to the Treasury*, HM Treasury (London: HMSO, Mar.).

Cmnd. 9058 (1983), *Financial Management in Government Departments* (London: HMSO).

Cmnd. 9143 (1984), *The Government's Expenditure Plans 1984–85 to 1986–87* (London: HMSO, Feb.).

Cmnd. 9161 (1984), *Supply Estimates 1984–85: Memorandum by the Chief Secretary to the Treasury*, HM Treasury (London: HMSO, Mar.).

Cmnd. 9189 (1984), *The Next Ten Years: Public Expenditure and Taxation into the 1990s*, HM Treasury (London: HMSO, July).

Cmnd. 9297 (1984), *Progress in Financial Management in Government Departments* (London: HMSO, Sept.).

Cmnd. 9428 (1985), *The Government's Expenditure Plans 1985–86 to 1987–88* (London: HMSO, Jan.).

Cmnd. 9450 (1985), *Supply Estimates 1985–86: Summary and Guide*, HM Treasury (London: HMSO, Mar.).

Cmnd. 9569 (1985), *Cash Limits 1984–85 Provisional Outturn (and 1983–84 Outturn)*, HM Treasury (London: HMSO).

Cmnd. 9702-II (1986), *The Government's Expenditure Plans 1986–87 to 1988–89*, ii (London: HMSO, Jan.).

Cmnd. 9742 (1986), *Supply Estimates 1986–87: Summary and Guide*, HM Treasury (London: HMSO, Mar.).

Congdon, T. (1982), *Monetary Control in Britain* (London: Macmillan).

—— (1989), *Monetarism Lost and Why it Must be Regained* (Policy Study, 106; London: Centre for Policy Studies).

Connolly, M. (1990), *Politics and Policy Making in Northern Ireland* (London: Philip Allan).

CSD (1981), *Responsibilities of the Principal Establishment Officer*, Memorandum, 17 June.

Davies, A., and Willman, J. (1991), *What Next?: Agencies, Departments, and the Civil Service* (IPPR Constitution Paper, 5; London: Institute For Public Policy Research).

Defence Committee (1989), *Statement on the Defence Estimates 1989* (1988–9, Fourth Report, HC 383; London: HMSO, June).

—— (1990), *Statement on the Defence Estimates 1990* (1989–90, Eighth Report, HC 388; London: HMSO, June).

Dell, E. (1985), 'Collective Ministerial Control of Public Expenditure', in F. Terry (ed.), *Collective Decision Making in Government* (London: Public Finance Foundation).

—— (1991), *A Hard Pounding: Politics and Economic Crisis 1974–76* (Oxford: Oxford University Press).

Devereau, M. (1993), 'Costing Efficiency at the Central Office of Information (COI)', *Public Money and Management*, 13/3 (July–Sept.): 4–6.

Diamond, Lord J. (1975), *Public Expenditure in Practice* (London: Allen & Unwin).

Dilnot, A., and Robson, M. (1993), 'The UK Moves from March to December Budgets', *Fiscal Studies*, 14/1 (Feb.): 78–88.

DSS (1993), *The Growth of Social Security* (London: HMSO).

Dunleavy, P. (1989*a*), 'The Architecture of the British Central State, Part I: Framework for Analysis', *Public Administration*, 67/3: 249–75.

—— (1989*b*), 'The Architecture of the British Central State, Part II: Empirical Findings', *Public Administration*, 67/4: 391–417.

Dunsire, A., and Hood, C. (1989), *Cutback Management in Public Bureaucracies: Popular Theories and Observed Outcomes in Whitehall* (Cambridge: Cambridge University Press).

Efficiency Unit (1988), *Improving Management in Government: The Next Steps*, Report to the Prime Minister (London: HMSO).

—— (1991), *Making the Most of Next Steps: The Management of Ministers' Departments and Their Executive Agencies*, Report to the Prime Minister (London: HMSO, May).

Else, P. K., and Marshall, G. P. (1981), 'The Unplanning of Public Expenditure: Recent Problems in Expenditure Planning and the Consequences of Cash Limits', *Public Expenditure*, 59/3: 253–78.

FCO (1992), *Survey of Current Affairs*, 22/4–6 (London: HMSO, Apr.–June).

Fforde, J. S. (1983), 'Setting Monetary Objectives', *Bank of England Quarterly Bulletin*, 23/2: 200–8.

Flynn, A., Gray, A., and Jenkins, W. I. (1990), 'Taking the Next Steps: The Changing Management of Government', *Parliamentary Affairs*, 43/2: 159–78.

FMU (1985*a*), *Top Management Systems* (London: Treasury).

—— (1985*b*), *Policy Work and the FMI: Report to the Cabinet Office (MPO)/ Treasury Financial Management Unit* (London: Treasury).

—— (1985*c*), *Resource Allocation in Departments: Role of PFO* (London: Treasury).

Fogden, M. E. G. (1993), 'Managing Change in the Employment Service', *Public Money and Management*, 13/2 (Apr.–June), 9–16.

Friedman, M. (1980), 'Response to Questionnaire on Monetary Policy', in Treasury and Civil Service Committee, *Memoranda on Monetary Policy* (1979–80, HC 720; London: HMSO, July).

Fry, G. K. (1984), 'The Development of the Thatcher Government's "Grand Strategy" for the Civil Service: A Public Policy Perspective', *Public Administration*, 62/3: 322–35.

Fry, G. K. (1988), 'The Thatcher Government, the Financial Management Initiative and the "New Civil Service"', *Public Administration*, 66/1: 1–20.

Godley, W. (1975), 'Evidence', in Select Committee on Expenditure 1975: 213–23.

Goldman, S. (1973), *The Developing System of Public Expenditure Management and Control* (Civil Service College Studies, 2; London: HMSO).

Goldsworthy, D. (1991), *Setting up Next Steps: A Short Account of the Origins, Launch and Implementation of the Next Steps Project in the British Civil Service* (London: HMSO, May).

Goodhart, C. A. E. (1989), *Money, Information and Uncertainty*, 5th edn. (London: Macmillan).

Gray, A., and Jenkins, W., with Flynn, A., and Rutherford, B. (1991), 'The Management of Change in Whitehall: The Experience of the FMI', *Public Administration*, 69/1: 41–59.

Greenleaf, W. H. (1987), *The British Political Tradition*, iii. *A Much Governed Nation* (London: Methuen).

Haldane, R. B. (1918), *Ministry of Reconstruction* (Report of the Machinery of Government Committee, Cd. 9230; London: HMSO).

Hall, P. (1986), *Governing the Economy: The Politics of State Intervention in Britain and France* (Oxford: Polity Press).

Harden, I. (1992), *The Contracting State* (Buckingham: Open University Press).

—— (1993), 'Budgets: Objectives, Norms and Procedures', in E. Zapico Goni (ed.), *Can Norms and Rules Enable EC Member States to Secure Sustainable Convergence?* (Maastricht: European Institute of Public Administration and Martinus Nijhoff).

Heald, D. (1980a), *Territorial Equity and Public Finance: Concepts and Confusion* (Studies in Public Policy, 75; Glasgow: Centre for the Study of Public Policy).

—— (1980b), 'Scotland's Public Expenditure "Needs"', in H. M. Drucker and N. L. Drucker (eds.), *The Scottish Government Yearbook 1981* (Edinburgh: Paul Harris Publishing).

—— (1983), *Public Expenditure: Its Defence and Reform* (Oxford: Martin Robertson).

—— (1991), 'The Political Implications of Redefining Public Expenditure in the United Kingdom', *Political Studies*, 39/2: 75–99.

—— (1992), *Formula-based Territorial Public Expenditure in the United Kingdom* (Aberdeen: Aberdeen Papers in Accountancy Finance and Management, W7).

Healey, D. (1981), 'Managing the Economy', City-Association Lecture, given to the Certified Accountants Educational Trust and City of London Polytechnic (transcript from Certified Accountants Educational Trust).

—— (1989), *Time of My Life* (London: Michael Joseph).

Heclo, H., and Wildavsky, A. (1974), *The Private Government of Public Money* (London: Macmillan).

———— (1981), *The Private Government of Public Money*, 2nd edn.

(London: Macmillan).

Hennessy, P. (1989), *Whitehall* (London: Secker & Warburg).

Hirschman, A. O. (1970), *Exit, Voice and Loyalty: A Response to Decline in Firms, Organisations and States* (Cambridge, Mass.: Harvard University Press).

Hood, C. (1991), 'A Public Management for All Seasons', *Public Administration*, 69/1: 3–19.

—— and Wright, M. (eds.) (1981), *Big Government in Hard Times* (Oxford: Martin Robertson).

Jenkins, S. (1985), 'The "Star Chamber", PESC and the Cabinet', *Political Quarterly*, 56/2: 113–21.

Johnson, C. (1990), 'Public Spending Plans', Memorandum to the Treasury and Civil Service Committee 1990c: 67–78.

—— (1991), *The Economy under Mrs Thatcher 1979–1990* (London: Penguin).

Joubert, C. (1981), 'Note by the DoE: Control of Departmental Running Costs', in Treasury and Civil Service Committee 1982a.

Keating, M., and Midwinter, A. (1983), *The Government of Scotland* (Edinburgh: Mainstream Publishing).

Keegan, W. (1984), *Mrs Thatcher's Economic Experiment* (London: Allen Lane).

—— (1989), *Mr Lawson's Gamble* (London: Hodder & Stoughton).

Klein, R. (1976), 'The Politics of Public Expenditure: American Theory and British Practice', *British Journal of Political Science*, 6/4: 401–32.

Krasner, S. (1988), 'Sovereignty: An Institutional Perspective', *Comparative Political Studies*, 21: 66–94.

Lawson, N. (1984), 'The Chancellor's Lecture: The British Experiment—The Fifth Mais Lecture', London: HM Treasury, Press Release.

—— (1990), 'Stamp Memorial Lecture: Rules Versus Discretion in the Conduct of Economic Policy', lecture given on 26 Nov. at the London School of Economics, Press Release.

—— (1992), *The View From No. 11: Memoirs of a Tory Radical* (London, Bantam Press).

Levitt, M. S. (ed.) (1987), *New Priorities in Public Spending* (London: Gower).

—— and Joyce, M. A. S. (1987), *The Growth and Efficiency of Public Spending* (Cambridge: Cambridge University Press).

Likierman, A. (1981), *Cash Limits and External Financing Limits* (Civil Service College Handbook, 22; London: HMSO).

—— (1982), 'Management Information for Ministers: MINIS in the Department of the Environment', *Public Administration*, 60/2: 127–42.

—— (1983), 'Maintaining the Credibility of Cash Limits', *Fiscal Studies*, 4/1: 29–43.

—— (1986), 'Squaring the Circle: Reconciling Predictive Uncertainty with the Control of Public Expenditure in the UK', *Policy and Politics*, 14/2: 285–307.

—— (1988), *Public Expenditure: The Public Spending Process* (London: Penguin).

MacGregor, J. (1986), 'Speech to the Public Finance Foundation', London: HM Treasury, Press Release, 7 July.

Major, J. (1988), 'Speech on Public Expenditure to the National Association of Conservative Graduates', London: HM Treasury, Press Release.

March, J., and Olsen, J. (1984), 'The New Institutionalism: Organisational factors in Political Life', *American Political Science Review*, 78: 734–49.

Marsh, D. (1991), 'Privatisation under Mrs Thatcher: A Review of the Literature', *Public Administration*, 69/4: 459–80.

Martin, B. (1992), 'The 1992 Autumn Statement', in Treasury and Civil Service Committee 1992: 106–28.

Mellon, E. (1993), 'Executive Agencies: Leading Change from the Outside-in', *Public Money and Management*, 13/2 (Apr.–June): 25–31.

Metcalfe, L., and Richards, S. (1984), 'The Impact of the Efficiency Strategy: Political Clout or Cultural Change?', *Public Administration*, 62/4: 439–54.

—— (1987), *Improving Public Management* (London: Sage).

—— (1990), *Improving Public Management*, 2nd edn. (London: Sage).

Middleton, P. (1985), 'Managing Public Expenditure', Speech to CIPFA/PFF Conference, 20 June, London: HM Treasury, Press Release.

—— (1989), 'Economic Policy Formulation in the Treasury in the Post-War Period', NIESR Jubilee Lecture, 28 Nov. 1988, repr. in *National Institute Economic Review*, 127 (Feb.), 46–51.

Mountfield, P. (1983), 'Recent Developments in the Control of Public Expenditure in the UK', *Public Budgeting and Finance* (USA, autumn).

NAO (1986), *The Financial Management Initiative*, Report from the Comptroller and Auditor General/National Audit Office (1985–6, HC 588; London: HMSO).

—— (1989), *Manpower Planning in the Civil Service*, Report from the Comptroller and Auditor General/National Audit Office (1988–9, HC 398; London: HMSO, May).

OECD (1979), *Monetary Targets and Inflation Control* (OECD Monetary Studies Series; Paris: OECD).

—— (1987), *The Medium-Term Macroeconomic Strategy Revisited* (Dept. of Economics and Statistics Working Paper, 48; Paris: OECD).

—— (1990), *The Public Sector: Issues for the 1990s* (Dept. of Economics and Statistics Working Paper, 90; Paris: OECD).

—— (1993a), *OECD Economic Outlook*, 53 (Paris: OECD, June).

—— (1993b), 'Adjustment under Fixed Exchange Rates: Application to the European Monetary Union', *OECD Economic Studies*, 20 (Paris: OECD, spring), 7–40.

Olsen, J. P. (1988), 'Political Science and Organization Theory', Paper to Conference on Political Institutions and Interest Intermediation, Konstanz, 20–1 Apr.

OMCS (1988), 'Memorandum by the Office of the Minister for Civil Service', in Treasury and Civil Service Committee, Eighth Report, *Civil Service Management Reform: The Next Steps*, ii (1987–8, Eighth Report, HC 494-II; London:

HMSO, July), 1–5.

Osborne, D., and Gaebler, T. (1992), *Reinventing Government* (New York: Addison-Wesley).

PAC (1979), *Parliamentary Control of Expenditure* (1978–9, Third Report, HC 232; London: HMSO).

—— (1980*a*), *Provision for Civil Service Pay Increases in the 1980–81 Estimates* (1979–80, Fourth Report; London: HMSO).

—— (1980*b*), *Matters Relating to the Ministry of Defence* (1979–80, Sixteenth Report, HC 648; London: HMSO).

—— (1980*c*), *Carry-Over of Cash Limits at the End of the Financial Year* (1979–80, Twenty-Seventh Report, HC 766; London: HMSO).

—— (1981), *HM Treasury: Carry-Over of Cash Limits at the End of the Financial Year* (1980–1, Fourteenth Report, HC 376; London: HMSO).

—— (1988), *The Financial Management Initiative* (1987–8, Thirteenth Report, HC 61; London: HMSO).

Parry, R. (1987), 'The Centralization of the Scottish Office', in Rose 1987.

Peacock, A. T., and Wiseman, J. (1961), *The Growth of Public Expenditure in the United Kingdom* (London: Oxford University Press).

Peden, G. C. (1983), 'The Treasury as the Central Department of Government 1919–1939', *Public Administration*, 61/4: 371–85.

Pliatzky, L. (1982), *Getting and Spending: Public Expenditure, Employment and Inflation* (Oxford: Blackwell).

—— (1983), 'Have Volumes Gone Underground?', *Public Administration*, 61/3: 323–30.

—— (1989), *The Treasury under Mrs Thatcher* (Oxford: Blackwell).

Pollitt, C. (1977), 'The Public Expenditure Survey 1961–72', *Public Administration*, 57/2: 127–42.

—— (1984), *Manipulating the Machine: Changing Patterns of Ministerial Departments, 1960–83* (London: Allen & Unwin).

Price, R. W. R. (1979), 'Public Expenditure: Policy and Control', *National Institute Economic Review*, 90 (Nov.), 68–91.

Pym, F. (1984), *The Politics of Consent* (London: Hamish Hamilton).

Rayner, Lord D. (1984), 'The Unfinished Agenda', Stamp Memorial Lecture, University of London, 6 Nov.

Rees, P. (1984), Parliamentary Debates, HC, 6 Dec., col. 588.

Rhodes, R. A. W. (1988), *Beyond Westminster and Whitehall: The Sub-Central Governments of Britain* (London: Unwin Hyman).

Richards, S., and Rodrigues, J. (1993), 'Strategies for Management in the Civil Service: Change of Direction', *Public Money and Management*, 13/2 (Apr.–June): 33–8.

Ridley, N. (1991), *My Style of Government: The Thatcher Years* (London: Hutchinson).

RIPA (1991), *The Civil Service Reformed: The Next Steps Initiative* (London: Royal Institute of Public Administration).

Rose, R. (ed.) (1969), *Policy-Making in Britain* (London: Macmillan).

Rose, R. (1982), *Understanding the United Kingdom: The Territorial Dimension in Government* (London: Longman).

—— (1984), *Do Parties Make a Difference?*, 2nd edn. (London: Macmillan).

—— (1987), *Ministers and Ministries: A Functional Analysis* (Oxford: Clarendon Press).

—— (1990), 'Inheritance Before Choice in Public Policy', *Journal of Theoretical Politics*, 2/3: 263–91.

Roseveare, H. (1969), *The Treasury: The Evolution of a British Institution* (London: Allen Lane).

Russell, A. W. (1984), 'The Financial Management Unit of the Cabinet Office (MPO) and Treasury', *Management in Government*, 39/2: 146–52.

Scott, W. (1987), 'The Adolescence of Institutional Theory', *Administrative Science Quarterly*, 32: 493–511.

Select Committee on Estimates (1958), *Treasury Control of Expenditure* (1957–8, Sixth Report, HC 254; London: HMSO).

Select Committee on Expenditure (1971), *Command Papers on Public Expenditure* (Third Report, HC 549; London: HMSO).

—— (1975), *The Financing of Public Expenditure* (1975–6, First Report, HC 69-II; London: HMSO).

Shapiro, D. (1978), 'The Policy Implications of Treasury Organisation', paper presented to the Annual Conference of the Public Administration Committee, University of York, Sept.

Smith, D. (1987), *The Rise and Fall of Monetarism: The Theory and Politics of an Economic Experiment* (Harmondsworth: Penguin).

Stewart, J. (1993), 'The Limitations of Government by Contract', *Public Money and Management*, 13/3 (July–Sept.), 7–12.

Tebbit, N. (1988), *Upwardly Mobile: An Autobiography* (London: Weidenfeld & Nicolson).

Thain, C. (1984), 'The Treasury and Britain's Decline', *Political Studies*, 32/4: 581–95.

—— (1985), 'The Education of the Treasury: The Medium-Term Financial Strategy 1980–84', *Public Administration*, 63/3: 261–85.

—— (1987), 'Implementing Economic Policy: An Analytical Framework', *Policy and Politics*, 15/2: 67–75.

—— (1992), 'Government and the Economy', ch. 14 in B. Jones and L. Robins (eds.), *Two Decades in British Politics* (Manchester: Manchester University Press).

—— and Wright, M. (1987), *Public Spending Planning and Control, 1976–88: A Research Agenda and a Framework for Analysis* (The Treasury and Whitehall Working Paper Series, 1; Exeter).

—— —— (1988*a*), 'Public Expenditure in the UK since 1976: Still the "Private Government of Public Money"?', *Public Policy and Administration*, 3/1 (Spring): 1–18.

—— —— (1988*b*), *Public Spending Planning and Control: A Classified Bibliography, 1976–88* (The Treasury and Whitehall Working Paper Series, 2;

Exeter).

—— —— (1988c), *Cash Planning* (The Treasury and Whitehall Working Paper Series, 3; Exeter).

—— —— (1988d), *Coping with Difficulty: The Treasury and Public Expenditure, 1976–88* (The Treasury and Whitehall Working Paper Series, 5; Exeter).

—— —— (1988e), *The Operation and Effects of Cash Limits, 1976–88* (The Treasury and Whitehall Working Paper Series, 6; Exeter).

—— —— (1988f), *The Public Expenditure Reserve* (The Treasury and Whitehall Working Paper Series, 7; Exeter).

—— —— (1989a), *Trends in Public Spending, 1976–89* (The Treasury and Whitehall Working Paper Series, 4; Exeter).

—— —— (1989b), 'The Advent of Cash Planning', *Financial Accountability and Management*, 5/3 (Autumn): 149–62.

—— —— (1989c), *The Cash Limits End-Year Flexibility Scheme* (The Treasury and Whitehall Working Paper Series, 8; Exeter).

—— —— (1989d), *Running Costs and Manpower Planning* (The Treasury and Whitehall Working Paper Series, 9; Exeter).

—— —— (1989e), *Running Costs Control in Central Government: A New Agenda in Public Spending Control?* (The Treasury and Whitehall Working Paper Series, 12; Exeter).

—— —— (1989f), *The Cabinet's Public Spending 'Star Chamber'* (The Treasury and Whitehall Working Paper Series, 13; Exeter).

—— —— (1990a), *The Role and Work of the Treasury's Expenditure Divisions* (The Treasury and Whitehall Working Paper Series, 14; Exeter).

—— —— (1990b), 'Coping with Difficulty: The Treasury and Public Spending, 1976–89', *Policy and Politics*, 18/1 (Jan.): 1–15.

—— —— (1990c), *The Public Expenditure Survey* (The Treasury and Whitehall Working Paper Series, 10; Exeter).

—— —— (1990d), *The Determination of Public Expenditure Priorities* (The Treasury and Whitehall Working Paper Series, 11; Exeter).

—— —— (1990e), 'Conceding Flexibility in Fiscal Management: The Case of Public Spending End-Year Flexibility', *Fiscal Studies*, 11/4: 63–83.

—— —— (1990f), 'Running Costs Control in UK Central Government', *Financial Accountability and Management*, 6/2 (Summer): 115–31.

—— —— (1990g), 'Haggling in Mr Clarke's Turkish Bazaar: The 1990 Public Spending Round', *Public Money and Management*, 10/4 (Winter): 51–5.

—— —— (1991a), 'Public Expenditure', ch. 2 in Francis Terry and Helen Roberts (eds.), *Public Domain 1991* (London: Public Finance Foundation), 23–40.

—— —— (1991b), *Departmental-Treasury Relationships* (The Treasury and Whitehall Working Paper Series, 15; Exeter).

—— —— (1991c), *The Role and Work of the Treasury's Second Permanent Secretary (Public Expenditure)* (The Treasury and Whitehall Working Paper Series, 16; Exeter).

—— —— (1991d), *The PES Process in the Departments* (The Treasury and

Whitehall Working Paper Series, 17; Exeter).

Thain, C., and Wright, M. (1991*e*), *The Role and Work of the Chief Secretary to the Treasury* (The Treasury and Whitehall Working Paper Series, 18; Exeter).

—— —— (1992*a*), 'Planning and Controlling Public Expenditure in the UK, Part I: The Treasury's Public Expenditure Survey', *Public Administration*, 70/1 (Spring), 3–24.

—— —— (1992*b*), 'Planning and Controlling Public Expenditure in the UK, Part II: The Effects and Effectiveness of the Survey', *Public Administration*, 70/2 (Summer), 193–224.

—— —— (1992*c*), *The Politico-Economic Context of Planning and Controlling Public Expenditure* (The Treasury and Whitehall Working Paper Series, 19; Exeter).

—— —— (1992*d*), *The Origins and Development of PESC* (The Treasury and Whitehall Working Paper Series, 20; Exeter).

—— —— (1992*e*), *The Structure and Organisation of Whitehall Spending Departments* (The Treasury and Whitehall Working Paper Series, 21; Exeter).

—— —— (1992*f*), *The Territorial Dimension in the Planning and Control of Public Spending* (The Treasury and Whitehall Working Paper Series, 22; Exeter).

—— —— (1992*g*), *The Public Expenditure Survey: Effects and Effectiveness* (The Treasury and Whitehall Working Paper Series, 23; Exeter).

—— —— (1992*h*), *The Treasury and FMI* (The Treasury and Whitehall Working Paper Series, 24; Exeter).

—— —— (1992*i*), *The Treasury and Next Steps* (The Treasury and Whitehall Working Paper Series, 25; Exeter).

Thomas, I. C. (1987), 'Giving Direction to the Welsh Office', in Rose 1987.

Treasury (1976), *Financial Statement and Budget Report 1976–77* (HC 306; London: HMSO, Apr.).

—— (1977), *Financial Statement and Budget Report 1977–78* (HC 271; London: HMSO, Mar.).

—— (1978), *Financial Statement and Budget Report 1978–79* (HC 310; London: HMSO, Apr.).

—— (1979*a*), *Needs Assessment—Report*, Report of an interdepartmental study co-ordinated by HM Treasury on the Relative Public Expenditure Needs in England, Scotland, Wales and, Northern Ireland (London: HMSO).

—— (1979*b*), *Financial Statement and Budget Report 1979–80* (HC 98; London: HMSO, June).

—— (1980), *Financial Statement and Budget Report 1980–81* (HC 500; London: HMSO, Mar.).

—— (1981*a*), 'Memorandum', in Treasury and Civil Service Committee 1981*a*: 86–95.

—— (1981*b*), 'Background to the Government's Economic Policy', in Treasury and Civil Service Committee 1981*a*: 68–93.

—— (1981*c*), *Financial Statement and Budget Report 1981–82* (HC 197; London: HMSO, Mar.).

—— (1981*d*), *Responsibilities of a Principal Finance Officer*, Memorandum (London: HM Treasury, June).

—— (1982*a*), *Financial Statement and Budget Report 1982–83* (HC 237; London: HMSO, Mar.).

—— (1982*b*), *Economic Progress Report*, 150 (London: HMSO, Oct.).

—— (1982*c*), *Autumn Statement 1982* (HC 10; London: HMSO, Nov.).

—— (1983*a*), *Financial Statement and Budget Report 1983–84* (HC 216; London: HMSO, Mar.).

—— (1983*b*), *Autumn Statement 1983* (HC 112; London: HMSO, Nov.).

—— (1984*a*), *Financial Statement and Budget Report 1984–85* (HC 304; London: HMSO, Mar.).

—— (1984*b*), *Autumn Statement 1984* (HC 12; London: HMSO, Nov.).

—— (1985*a*), 'Memorandum by HM Treasury: The Government's Economic Policy: 1984 Autumn Statement—Government Observations on the First Report from the Committee in Session 1984–85 (HC 44)', in Treasury and Civil Service Committee 1984*b*: 42–4.

—— (1985*b*), *Financial Statement and Budget Report 1985–86* (HC 265; London: HMSO, Mar.).

—— (1985*c*), *Working in the Treasury: A Guide to Personnel Policies* (London: HM Treasury, Mar.).

—— (1985*d*), *Autumn Statement 1985* (HC 22; London: HMSO, Nov.).

—— (1986*a*), *Financial Statement and Budget Report 1986–87* (HC 273; London: HMSO, Mar.).

—— (1986*b*), *The Multi-Departmental Review of Budgeting: Executive Summary* (London: HM Treasury, Mar.).

—— (1986*c*), *The Multi-Departmental Review of Budgeting: Final Central Report* (London: HM Treasury, Mar.).

—— (1986*d*), *The Management of Public Expenditure*, General Expenditure Policy Group (London: HM Treasury, May).

—— (1987*a*), *Financial Statement and Budget Report 1987–88* (HC 195; London: HMSO, Mar.).

—— (1987*b*), *Working Patterns*, A Study Document (London: HM Treasury).

—— (1987*c*), *Autumn Statement 1987* (HC 110; London: HMSO, Nov.).

—— (1988*a*), *Her Majesty's Treasury* (London: HM Treasury).

—— (1988*b*), *Financial Statement and Budget Report 1988–89* (HC 361; London: HMSO, Mar.).

—— (1988*c*), *The Management of Public Expenditure*, 2nd edn., General Expenditure Policy Group (London: HM Treasury, May).

—— (1988*d*), 'Memorandum', in Treasury and Civil Service Committee 1988*c*: 68–73.

—— (1989*a*), *Financial Statement and Budget Report 1989–90* (HC 235; London: HMSO, Mar.).

—— (1989*b*), *Government Accounting: A Guide on Accounting and Financial Procedures for the Use of Government Departments* (London: HMSO, Dec.; subsequently amended five times, Apr. 1990, Jan. 1991, June 1991, Apr. 1992, and Oct. 1992).

Treasury (1990), *Financial Statement and Budget Report 1990–91* (HC 286; London: HMSO, Mar.).

—— (1991*a*), *Financial Statement and Budget Report 1991–92* (HC 300; London: HMSO, Mar.).

—— (1991*b*), *Economic Briefing*, 2 (London: HMSO, May).

—— (1991*c*), *Staff in Post* (London: HM Treasury, Dec.).

—— (1992*a*), *Financial Statement and Budget Report 1992–93* (HC 319; London: HMSO, Mar.).

—— (1992*b*), 'Trends in Public Sector Capital Spending', *Treasury Bulletin*, 3/1 (Winter 1991–2): 55–74.

—— (1992*c*), 'Recent Developments in UK Economic Policy', *Treasury Bulletin*, 3/3 (Autumn): 1–10.

—— (1992*d*), 'A New Approach to Controlling Public Expenditure', *Treasury Bulletin*, 3/3 (Autumn): 11–18.

—— (1993*a*), *The Panel of Independent Forecasters: February 1993 Report* (London: HM Treasury).

—— (1993*b*), *Financial Statement and Budget Report 1993–94* (HC 547; London: HMSO, Mar.).

—— (1993*c*), *The Panel of Independent Forecasters: July 1993 Report* (London: HM Treasury).

Treasury and Civil Service Committee (1980*a*), *Provision for Civil Service Pay Increases in the 1980–81 Estimates* (1979–80, First Report, HC 371; London: HMSO, Jan.).

—— (1980*b*), *The Budget and the Government's Expenditure Plans 1980–81 to 1983–84* (1979–80, Second Report, HC 584; London: HMSO, Apr.).

—— (1980*c*), *Civil Service Manpower Reductions* (1979–80, Fourth Report, HC 71; London: HMSO, July).

—— (1980*d*), *Provision for Civil Service Pay Increases in the 1980–81 Estimates* (1979–80, Fifth Report, HC 730; London: HMSO, July).

—— (1980*e*), *The Future of the Civil Service Department* (1980–1, First Report, HC 54; London: HMSO, Dec.).

—— (1980*f*), *The Government's Economic Policy: Autumn Review* (1980–1, Second Report, HC 79; London: HMSO, Dec.).

—— (1981*a*), *Monetary Policy*, in 3 vols. (1980–1, Third Report, HC 163; London: HMSO, Feb.).

—— (1981*b*), *The 1981 Budget and the Government's Expenditure Plans 1981–82 to 1983–84* (1980–1, Fifth Report, HC 232; London: HMSO, Apr.).

—— (1981*c*), *Civil Service Manpower Reductions* (1980–1, Seventh Report, HC 325; London: HMSO, July).

—— (1981*d*), *The Government's Economic Policy: Autumn Review* (1981–2, First Report, HC 28; London: HMSO, Dec.).

—— (1982*a*), *Efficiency and Effectiveness in the Civil Service*, in 3 vols. (1981–2, Third Report, HC 236; London: HMSO, Mar.).

—— (1982*b*), *The 1982 Budget* (1981–2, Fourth Report, HC 270; London:

HMSO, Mar.).

—— (1982c), *The Government's Expenditure Plans 1982–83 to 1984–85* (1981–2, Fifth Report, HC 316; London: HMSO, Apr.).

—— (1982d), *Budgetary Reform* (1981–2, Sixth Report, HC 137; London: HMSO, May).

—— (1982e), *Civil Service Manpower Reductions* (1982–3, First Special Report, HC 46; London: HMSO, Nov.).

—— (1982f), *The Government's Economic Policy: Autumn Statement* (1982–3, First Report, HC 49; London: HMSO, Dec.).

—— (1983a), *The Government's Expenditure Plans 1982–83 to 1985–86* (1982–3, Third Report, HC 204; London: HMSO, Feb.).

—— (1983b), *The 1983 Budget* (1982–3, Fourth Report, HC 286; London: HMSO, Apr.).

—— (1984a), *The Government's Economic Policy: Autumn Statement* (1983–4, First Report, HC 170; London: HMSO, Feb.).

—— (1984b), *The Government's Expenditure Plans 1984–85 to 1986–87* (1983–4, Third Report, HC 284; London: HMSO, Mar.).

—— (1984c), *The Government's Expenditure Plans 1984–85 to 1986–87: Government Observations on the Third Report from the Committee in Session 1983–84* (Third Special Report from the Treasury and Civil Service Committee, 1983–4, HC 410; London: HMSO, Apr.).

—— (1984d), *The 1984 Budget* (1983–4, Fourth Report, HC 341; London: HMSO, Apr.).

—— (1984e), *The Government's Economic Policy: Autumn Statement* (1984–5, First Report, HC 44; London: HMSO, Dec.).

—— (1985a), *The Government's Expenditure Plans 1985–86 to 1987–88* (1984–5, Sixth Report, HC 213; London: HMSO, Feb.).

—— (1985b), *The 1985 Budget* (1984–5, Eighth Report, HC 306; London: HMSO, Apr.).

—— (1985c), *The Government's Economic Policy: Autumn Statement* (1985–6, Second Report, HC 57; London: HMSO, Dec.).

—— (1986a), *The Government's Expenditure Plans 1986–87 to 1988–89 (Cmnd. 9702)* (1985–6, Third Report, HC 192; London: HMSO, Feb.).

—— (1986b), *The 1986 Budget* (1985–6, Fourth Report, HC 313; London: HMSO, Apr.).

—— (1986c), *Civil Servants and Ministers: Duties and Responsibilities*, in 2 vols. (1985–6, Seventh Report, HC 92; London: HMSO, May).

—— (1986d), *Ministers and Civil Servants* (1986–7, First Report, HC 62; London: HMSO, Dec.).

—— (1986e), *The Government's Economic Policy: Autumn Statement* (1986–7, Second Report, HC 27; London: HMSO, Dec.).

—— (1987a), *The Government's Expenditure Plans 1987–88 to 1989–90 (Cm. 56)* (1986–7, Third Report, HC 153; London: HMSO, Feb.).

—— (1987b), *The 1987 Budget* (1986–7, Sixth Report, HC 293; London: HMSO, Apr.).

Treasury and Civil Service Committee (1987*c*), *The Government's Economic Policy: Autumn Statement* (1987–8, First Report, HC 197; London: HMSO, Dec.).

—— (1988*a*), *The Government's Expenditure Plans 1988–89 to 1990–91 (Cm. 288)* (1987–8, Second Report, HC 292; London: HMSO, Feb.).

—— (1988*b*), *The 1988 Budget* (1987–8, Fourth Report, HC 400; London: HMSO, Apr.).

—— (1988*c*), *Civil Service Management Reform: The Next Steps*, ii (1987–8, Eighth Report, HC 494-II; London: HMSO, July).

—— (1988*d*), *Autumn Statement 1988* (1988–9, First Report, HC 89; London: HMSO, Dec.).

—— (1989*a*), *The 1989 Budget* (1988–9, Second Report, HC 288; London: HMSO, Apr.).

—— (1989*b*), *Developments in The Next Steps Programme* (1988–9, Fifth Report, HC 348; London: HMSO, July).

—— (1989*c*), *The 1989 Autumn Statement* (1989–90, First Report, HC 20; London: HMSO, Dec.).

—— (1990*a*), *The 1990 Budget* (1989–90, Fourth Report, HC 314; London: HMSO, Apr.).

—— (1990*b*), *Progress in the Next Steps Initiative* (1989–90, Eighth Report, HC 481; London: HMSO, July).

—— (1990*c*), *The 1990 Autumn Statement* (1990–1, First Report, HC 41; London: HMSO, Dec.).

—— (1991*a*), *The 1991 Budget* (1990–1, Second Report, HC 289; London: HMSO, Apr.).

—— (1991*b*), *The Next Steps Initiative* (1990–1, Seventh Report, HC 496; London: HMSO, July).

—— (1991*c*), *The 1991 Autumn Statement* (1991–2, First Report, HC 58; London: HMSO, Dec.).

—— (1992), *The 1992 Autumn Statement and the Conduct of Economic Policy* (1992–3, First Report, HC 201; London: HMSO, Dec.).

—— (1993*a*), *Prospects for Monetary Union* (1992–3, Third Report, HC 438; London: HMSO, Apr.).

—— (1993*b*), *The March 1993 Budget* (1992–3, Fourth Report, HC 578; London: HMSO, Apr.).

—— (1993*c*), *The Government's Proposals for Budgetary Reform* (1992–3, Fifth Report, HC 583; London: HMSO, May).

—— (1993*d*), *The Role of the Civil Service: Interim Report*, 2 vols. (1992–3, Sixth Report, HC 390; London: HMSO, July).

Treasury and CSD (1981), *Control of Expenditure: Departmental Responsibilities*, Memorandum (London: HM Treasury and Civil Service Dept., 28 May).

Treasury and MPO (1982), *Financial Management* (London: HM Treasury, May; reproduced in Cmnd. 8616 (1982), app. 3).

Trinder, C. (1987), 'Public Service Pay', in M. S. Levitt (ed.), *New Priorities in*

Public Spending (Aldershot: Gower).

Trollope, Anthony (1949), *Phineas Finn*, i (Oxford: Oxford University Press).

Vickers, G. (1965), *The Art of Judgement* (London: Chapman & Hall).

Vintner, P. (1979), 'The Executive Control of Public Expenditure', ch. 3 in C. Sandford (ed.), *Control of Public Expenditure* (Occasional Paper, 14; Centre for Fiscal Studies, University of Bath).

Walker, P. (1991), *Staying Power: Peter Walker—An Autobiography* (London: Bloomsbury).

Walshe, G. (1987), *Planning Public Spending in the UK* (Basingstoke: Macmillan).

Walters, A. (1986), *Britain's Economic Renaissance: Margaret Thatcher's Reforms 1979–1984* (New York: Oxford University Press).

—— (1990), *Sterling in Danger: The Economic Consequences of Pegged Exchange Rates* (London: Fontana).

Ward, T. (1983), 'Cash Planning', *Public Administration*, 61/1: 85–90.

—— (1990), 'Notes on the 1990 Public Expenditure Plans', in Treasury and Civil Service Committee 1990*c*: 56–9.

—— (1991), 'The 1991 Autumn Statement Public Expenditure Plans', in Treasury and Civil Service Committee 1991*c*: 63–6.

Wass, D. (1978), 'The Changing Problems of Economic Management', Lecture to the Johnian Society in Cambridge on 15 Feb., repr. in CSO, *Economic Trends*, 293: 97–104.

—— (1984), *Government and the Governed* (London: Allen & Unwin).

Webb, A., and Wistow, G. (1983), 'Public Expenditure and Policy Implementation: The Case of Community Care', *Public Administration*, 61/1: 21–44.

Webber, C., and Wildavsky, A. (1986), *A History of Taxation and Expenditure in the Western World* (New York: Simon & Schuster).

Wildavsky, A. (1975), *Budgeting: A Comparative Theory of Budgetary Processes* (Boston, Mass.: Little, Brown and Co.).

—— (1980), *How to Limit Government Spending* (Los Angeles, Calif.: University of California Press).

—— (1988), *The New Politics of the Budgetary Process* (New York: Harper Collins).

Wilding, R. (1982), *Management Information and Control: The Role of the Centre* (London: Royal Institute of Public Administration).

Wilks, S. (1987), 'Administrative Culture and Policy Making in the Department of the Environment', *Public Policy and Administration*, 2/1: 25–41.

—— and Wright, M. (eds.) (1987), *Comparative Government–Industry Relations: Western Europe, the United States and Japan* (Oxford: Oxford University Press).

—— —— (eds.) (1991), *The Promotion and Regulation of Industry in Japan* (London: Macmillan).

Wilson, H. (1976), *The Governance of Britain* (London: Weidenfeld & Nicolson and Michael Joseph).

Wright, M. (1969), *Treasury Control of the Civil Service 1854–1874* (Oxford: Clarendon).

—— (1972), 'Treasury Control, 1854–1914', in G. Sutherland (ed.), *Studies in the Growth of Nineteenth Century Government* (London: Routledge & Kegan Paul).

—— (1988*a*), 'Policy Community, Policy Network and Comparative Industrial Policies', *Political Studies*, 36/2: 593–612.

—— (1988*b*), 'City Rules OK? Policy Community, Policy Network and Take-over Bids', *Public Administration*, 66/4: 389–410.

—— (1991), 'The Comparative Analysis of Industrial Policies: Policy Networks and Sectoral Governance Structures in Britain and France', *Staatswissenschaften und Staatspraxis*, 4: 503–33.

Young, H. (1989), *One of Us: A Biography of Margaret Thatcher* (London: Macmillan).

—— and Sloman, A. (1984), *But Chancellor: An Inquiry into the Treasury* (London: BBC).

INDEX

N.B. Page references to figures and tables are in italic.